D1564684

Mary Ward

Henriette Peters

translated by Helen Butterworth

Mary Ward

A World in Contemplation

Henriette Peters

translated by Helen Butterworth

Gracewing.

First published in German in 1991 by Tyrolia Verlog, Innsbrück Wien

This Edition First Published in 1994
Gracewing
Fowler Wright Books
Southern Avenue, Leominster
Herefordshire HR6 0QF

Gracewing Books are distributed

In New Zealand by:
Catholic Supplies Ltd
80 Adelaide Rd
Wellington
New Zealand

In Australia by:
Charles Paine Pty
8 Ferris Street
North Parramatta
NSW 2151 Australia

In U.S.A. by:
Morehouse Publishing
P.O. Box 1321
Harrisburg
PA 17105
U.S.A.

In Canada by:
Meakin and Associates
Unit 17, 81 Auriga Drive
Nepean, Ontario, KZE 7Y5
Canada

© Text Henriette Peters 1991
© Translation Helen Butterworth 1994

© Cover Photograph and all reproductions taken from the painted life, Studio Tanner, D-8964 Nesselwang

© Cover design by Gill Onions

ISBN 0 85244 268 8

Typesetting by Action Typesetting Limited, Gloucester
Printed by The Cromwell Press,
Broughton Gifford, Melksham, Wiltshire SN12 8PH

CONTENTS

List of Illustrations for Mary Ward

FOREWORD

I took some time considering Reverend Mother General Immolata Wetter's suggestion to write a biography of Mary Ward, as a great number of books and articles have already been written about her, and it did not seem that another was necessary. It was only when I was working in the Belgian State Archives in Liège that it occurred to me that the events of Mary Ward's life could well be presented from a fresh angle.

The Liège sources offer a new insight, although they by no means form a complete unity. They have many gaps, which means that they need to be supplemented by the other sources in order to be understood.

For this present biography I had at my disposal all the sources in the Generalate of the Institute of the Blessed Virgin Mary in Rome, collected during the course of some decades. All these documents and deeds were collected from the archives of ten countries, as part of the preparation towards the canonization process of the foundress of the Institute of the Blessed Virgin Mary, Mary Ward, and were accompanied by explanatory notes. These documents are currently being prepared for publication; without this invaluable resource, the present biography could not have been written. The resources of the Holy Office in the Vatican Archives were not, however, available to me for research. It was Mother Theodolinde Winkler who first collaborated with Fr Joseph Grisar, SJ to whom the supervision of the research was entrusted. After her death, it was continued by Mother Edelburga Eibl and Mother Immolata Wetter. They worked for years with exhaustive and meticulous precision over the hundreds of relevant documents which they had located. In this connection too, mention should be made of the help given by Sister Pauline Parker and Sister Helen Butterworth of the English Province.

There are three reasons why the documents are difficult to understand and interpret: their baroque style, sometimes inclined to overstatement; the reticence of the members of the Institute – in their then politically dangerous situation – to mention names of people or places, added to which was their use of aliases; finally, the fact that the letters and papers are in six different languages.

As well as outside sources – existence of which can only be mentioned here – there are the writings of Mary Ward herself. Her confessor, Father Roger Lee SJ, ordered her to write her autobiography. But Mary Ward was no writer, and there remain only a few statements from the eight autobiographical fragments of various stages of her life. As a mature woman she looked back on the events of her youth up to 1609, when she left England to become a religious in St Omer. From a historical point of view these statements offer little, but it is in these that Mary Ward's spiritual development is revealed. From these it is clearly evident that her relationship with God was the centre of her life. Deep insight into her life of prayer is given by remarks found principally in her retreat notes.These form the 'Various Papers', written between 1614 and 1624. A larger collection of sayings, exhortations and addresses is mentioned by Marcus Fridl in his two-volume work 'Englische Tugend-schul Mariae'. He took these from a 'Libellus allocutionum' and 'Libellus colloquiorum', now lost. Three addresses to the first members of her Institute still survive, at least in an abridged version, in the so-called 'Liber ruber'; in these Mary Ward explains the great difficulties facing her Institute. A great number of letters, from her certainly more extensive correspondence from 1608 until shortly before her death, have been preserved for posterity. It need not be emphasized that these are of inestimable value towards an understanding both of Mary Ward's personality and her Institute. The two oldest biographies, the English Life – in all probability written by Mary Poyntz, one of the first members, – and the considerably shorter Italian Vita, compiled by Mary Ward's friend and confidante in the Institute, Winefrid Wigmore, form a link between the documents and the earliest biographies written by those outside the Institute. Although these two first biographies are of prime importance as sources for an understanding of Mary Ward, they need occasional correction. To give just two examples – they simply fail to give any definite statement about the shaping of the English women's congregation as an Ignatian Institute, and completely omit the matter of the debts accumulated by them in Liège, facts which were of far-reaching consequence for the Institute's future history. The authors had no intention of publishing falsehoods or of concealing the truth. But, in evaluating these two sources, it must be borne in mind that at the time of writing – some twenty years after Mary Ward's death – such matters could not be aired. The Institute was suppressed, and Mary Ward had been condemned as a heretic. Although Pope Urban VIII tacitly tolerated the Institute for some years before Mary Ward's final departure from Rome, the harsh judgement passed by the Holy Office was never rescinded. One can easily understand that Mary Ward's contemporaries had little occasion to state the real facts of the matter. The earliest writings, of which only part has been published, are derived mainly from these two biographies. Pagetti, Bissel and Lohner had the benefit of the memories of the first members, of course, but it is sometimes difficult to disentangle fact from fiction. In the first chapter of the present work statements from these early works will be placed alongside those from other sources, and thus enable critical comparisons to be made.

Mary Elizabeth Chambers too, whose 'Life of Mary Ward' appeared in London in 1885, drew largely from these two lives, though she also worked on documentary material in the Institute Archives in Munich/Nymphenburg as well as other manuscripts; she did not have access to the rich resources of the Vatican Archives nor the Archives of the Society of Jesus in Rome.

Most of the later biographies and articles about Mary Ward refer to Mary Elizabeth Chambers.

It is entirely due to Father Joseph Grisar and Mother Immolata Wetter, with their work — written and spoken — on the wealth of the source material amassed, that it has been possible to move beyond the limits of these two biographies and their subsequent literature, and throw a new light on the matter.

The fact that the present work is entitled 'Mary Ward: her personality and her Institute', shows that the scope has been restricted. It has been assumed that many lesser incidents in the life of this outstanding Englishwoman have been described already. Emphasis has been laid, on the one hand, on her background and youth in England as the basis of her maturing personality; on the other, I have tried to demonstrate her utterly loyal consistency in carrying out the commission which God had entrusted to her: to found a congregation for women on the model of the Society of Jesus. It was only in the terrible struggle for this Institute, reviled by her opponents as either ridiculous or totally unsuitable, that the shy young girl from Yorkshire developed into a great woman who bears comparison with the saints.

I hope that my efforts may contribute to make her greatness better known — it was a greatness that was anchored in an unshakeable love of God.

I would like to thank: Reverend Mother General Immolata Wetter and her successor Reverend Mother General Michaeli Pelli, the two Provincials of the Austrian Province, Dr Maria Glasauer and her successor Mother Marianne Stockinger, who set me free for this work. I also thank my two sisters, Frau Madeleine Pustjens and Frau Bertha Bastiaens, with whom I lived while I undertook researches in Liège, Brussels and St Omer, and my nephew, who was my personal chauffeur in Belgium and France. I would like to thank the archivists and librarians for all their help and advice.

My very special thanks go to Father Johann Wrba, SJ, for his critical assessment of the material, Frau Anna Kitajew and Sister Johanna Pickl, who undertook the correction of the manuscript with such care. Sister Johanna Pickl, moreover, as Provincial Secretary, gave every free moment of her time to make a fair copy of the manuscript. I thank her most sincerely.

Vienna, January, 1991   Henrietta Peters

Translator's Note:
This book is already very long but I feel that I must add a little to acknowledge all the help I have received.

First and foremost, both in Austria and in England, my thanks go to Sr Dr Henrietta Peters and Sr Dr Maria Glasauer. Without the author's agreement and encouragement, and unfailing interest, I would never have dared to undertake the translation. Without Sr Maria Glasauer's help and forbearance, I would not have got very far: she spent hours going over the translation word by word. I would also like to thank Gesa Thiessen, a friend from Dublin days, who gave very much time and advice during her reading of the final draft from the German. Sr Gemma Brennan, IBVM, whom I cajoled into reading the English typescript, was responsible for many helpful comments and corrections. She was a generous and challenging reader. Sr Elizabeth Aldworth in my community undertook the daunting task of checking all the notes with me, taking whatever language appeared in her stride, with cheerful insouciance. I would like to thank my Provincial, Sr Pia Buxton, and my community in Cambridge, for their interest and encouragement during the sixteen months it has taken me to do the translation.

During this time, Mary Ward's personality has become clearer, and my respect and love for her have deepened. With the author, I hope this translation will help to make her better known and understood.

Finally, I would like to offer this work in gratitude to the members of the Austrian province of the Institute for so many kindnesses received over more years than I would like to tell.

Cambridge, December 1992   Helen Butterworth

I

ROOTS

The turning point

*Henry VIII – the deaths of John Fisher and Thomas More –
the King's divorce and England's break with Rome – Edward
VI – Catholic Mary and Elizabeth I – England's rise to
power – the situation of Catholics*

Exactly fifty years after Henry VII had acquired the crown of
England (1485) as its first Tudor king, his son and successor Henry
VIII effectively ruptured its history. He ordered the beheading of the
Bishop of Rochester, John Fisher, and his former Lord Chancellor,
Thomas More, both prominent men of fine character who died for a
matter of principle. It was not the first act of violence of this gifted
and, initially, popular monarch. The list of martyrs was to increase
during his reign, grow longer during those of Elizabeth I and James
I, and continue into that of Charles I. Henry VIII acquired an
unhappy memorial to himself by his six marriages – 'divorced,
beheaded, died; divorced, beheaded, survived.' After the king's
high-handed divorce proceedings in 1533, the Pope threatened him
with canonical censure but the Act of Supremacy (1534) was readily
passed by Parliament. In it, government officials and clergy were
constrained to declare on oath their assent to England's break with
Rome and to the sovereignty of the king over the English Church.
Next followed the suppression of the monasteries, first of all with
the lesser monasteries in 1535 and then, in 1539 with the larger, more
richly endowed foundations from which the bankrupt king was able
to fill his empty pockets. When Henry died in 1547, the Catholic
Church, once flourishing throughout the length and breadth of the
land – at least outwardly – was reduced to a minority. A militant
minority, however.

One might well ask how such a reversal was possible. Was it really
the result of the arbitrary decrees of a despot in a country which had
the oldest parliament in Europe? Hardly. From the late Middle Ages
the Church in England had been dependent on the monarch in many
respects. The tithes and taxes paid to an ever-wealthier Church had
become increasingly unpopular; the privileged position of the clergy
who sometimes led a life that was the reverse of edifying was an

1

irritant and, above all, there was a native mistrust of the papacy, whose influence was seen as that of a foreign power. Yet it cannot be said that there was an anti-clerical movement in England. There had always been small pockets of anti-clericalism, and some of these existed into the sixteenth century under the strong influence of the famous humanist Erasmus of Rotterdam, who spent a considerable time in England and was a friend of the Chancellor Thomas More. In England the Reformation was imposed from above, introduced as it was by Henry VIII and completed by Elizabeth I. The figures of the two martyrs, the Bishop and the Chancellor, are macabre symbols of the many arbitrary and cruel events of that time.

Under the brief reign of Henry VIII's son, Edward VI (1547–1553), who came to the throne at the age of ten, the Anglican Church was further developed. This was mainly the work of his advisers, Edward Seymour, Duke of Somerset and Thomas Cranmer, Archbishop of Canterbury. Much protestant doctrine was added to the Anglican Church; this is evident from Cranmer's Book of Sermons, the Catechism with its Lutheran model and the Book of Common Prayer, from all of which the Church of England emerged with its particular balance between the Roman Catholic and Lutheran Churches.

Henry's daughter Mary reigned only five years (1553–1558); she had been brought up a catholic and married Philip II of Spain. Sceptre and sword were now directed against the Anglican Church. The nobles, and the crown too, for that matter, held the expropriated goods of the suppressed monasteries, but that did not prevent catholicism from being re-established in a savage manner. Only after the death of 'Bloody Mary' did the time come for England's drive to power.

In spite of the less attractive aspects of her character, and her unscrupulous policies, the title 'Great' cannot be denied Elizabeth I (1558–1603). Like her father, she intervened in the concerns on the Continent only when it was to England's advantage; it was in her reign that the country attained a previously unknown prosperity in trade, industry and navigation. Courageous explorers and calculating entrepreneurs were laying the foundations of the future empire, and national culture sprang to its height with the name of William Shakespeare.

The first years of her reign, however, were bitter ones for Elizabeth. Many Catholics regarded her as a bastard, which she was. Many looked hopefully to Mary Stuart, Queen of Scotland and Queen of France, with a rightful claim to the throne of England. But in 1560, when her young husband Francis II died, his equally young widow returned to her Scottish homeland. With that, England's danger of being caught in a pincer-like grasp between France and Scotland receded, and foreign policy could again be freely cultivated. But Mary Stuart's challenge remained. On the death of catholic Queen Mary, Mary Stuart adopted the title and coat of arms of a queen of England, to herald her claim. Her fascinating beauty could have posed a more powerful threat, had she also been gifted with the political acumen of her rival Elizabeth.

Among the shadows of Henry's reign there was much that was pleasant. In the long reign of Elizabeth one has to seek out the shadows, but they were certainly there. Religion as such may not have been of particular interest to Elizabeth, and for the first ten years of her reign she did not mobilise much opposition against catholics. True, Henry's innovations were buttressed, and extravagant fines demanded of those who refused to attend Anglican Church services or take the Oath of Supremacy but, generally speaking, it was not government policy to forge martyrs for the Roman Catholic Church.

This situation changed in 1568 when Mary Stuart was confined in an English prison. The ever-turbulent North, especially Northumberland and Yorkshire, started up in protest against both the Church of England and the imprisonment of the Scottish Queen. The rising was put down in 1569. A year later Pope Pius V unchurched Elizabeth with his Bull of Excommunication. The official position of Rome was thus made plain but it forced many loyal English people into a crisis of conscience. The reaction of Elizabeth's government matched the Bull. From 1570 on there began a crushing persecution of catholics. A brutal death was prepared for those imprisoned: hanging to the point of suffocation, followed by quartering and disembowelling; their hearts were burnt. The road from Holborn to Tyburn became more than ever London's Via Dolorosa, bespattered with the blood of those dragged on hurdles to the place of execution. Volumes could be written too of those others compelled to pay high fines which stripped them to penury while their possessions disappeared into the unappeasable maw of the court faction; still more about the agonies of conscience of those who broke under torture.

It is an acknowledged fact that atrocities were common practice during the wars of religion. Torture was run-of-the-mill whether in London, catholic Madrid, Vienna or Rome. But one fact must not be overlooked: in England the struggle did not originate from religious conviction but from the undisciplined sensuality of a king. This highlights an important difference without justifying the harassing course of the law.

It was only after Mary Stuart's execution on 8th February, 1587, that Philip II of Spain reacted by sending a huge fleet, 'the invincible Armada', northwards. It was put to rout in the Channel by the smaller and therefore tactically more agile English ships. Those escaping were shattered on Scottish rocks. In this event the English saw the hand of God, and from then on, though naturally also from other causes, the power of Catholic Spain diminished. Two dangerous adversaries of this Catholic supremacy had developed in western Europe: England and the northern Netherlands. Both were sea-going powers, both Protestant. The already precarious situation of Catholics had been further imperilled by these two events: the excommunication of the queen by the Pope, and the King of Spain's sending of the Armada, both actions of foreign powers. As a result, the bulk of the population inclined towards the Government. Simple and uneducated citizens might not have grasped the meaning of learned disputations but they were well enough aware of the dangers presented to England by two catholic powers: the Papacy and Spain. To be a papist was synonymous with being a traitor.

The successful government of a woman will always arouse special interest as a rarity in a patriarchal society. Inevitably, her successor will be overshadowed. When Elizabeth died at long last on 3rd April, 1603, she was succeeded by Mary Stuart's son, James VI of Scotland, in England James I. The dead queen had been unable to bar the House of Stuart from the throne of England. But there was no repetition of what occurred when Catholic Mary came to the throne, for James I had been brought up as a Calvinist, and joined the Anglican Church.

The Ward Family

Descent — property in Yorkshire — Wards of Givendale —
Sir Roger senior — Sir Roger junior — Sir Christopher —
John Ward of Skelton — Alison Withes married to Ward —
the family in the earliest recorded sources

The north of England, the restless border facing Scotland, has always shown individuality. 'On those roadless fells,' writes Trevelyan, 'society consisted of mounted clans of farmer-warriors.'[1] They often feuded among themselves or were at war with the Scots. Trevelyan styles the men warriors and most of the women heroines. These people prized their personal freedom highly and followed their leaders into war, even against the house of Tudor. The feudal system still prevailed here and most of the expansion of England into a modern state such as had been initiated under Elizabeth I was unknown to those people of the border. In religious matters northerners were critical, even towards their own clergy, though they remained loyal to catholicism when Henry VIII turned from the Roman Church

In 1536 they resisted the King's writ but their uprising, 'The pilgrimage of Grace' in defence of the suppressed monasteries, was put down. Again, after the imprisonment of Mary Stuart (1568), they protested with the rebellion of the North (1569) and this too was harshly suppressed. Leaders such as Percy, Earl of Northumberland and Neville, Earl of Westmoreland, were forced to abandon their resistance, but resentment against a government that opposed the most deeply-held convictions of the mass of the people and treated their religious adherence as an offence, grew steadily until it exploded on one of the darkest days of England's cloudy history.

To this rugged bastion of resistance belonged one of the oldest families in Yorkshire: the Wards. Their genealogy can be traced back to the eleventh century with connections by inter-marriage with northern families of some consequence. Exact identification of all the Wards is not possible, as there are too many gaps in the sources and, in addition, the name has spread too widely.

About the first half of the seventeenth century there was a considerable number of families of this name in London[2] without any traceable connection with one another or with the county. Not even in Yorkshire itself, by no means so densely populated then or now, would it be possible or even likely that one could establish a genealogy of all the Wards mentioned. The older Wards were feudatories of the knightly class, whose task was mainly one of military service though they were also occasionally concerned with the administration of specific areas. Their coat of arms was a cross patonce or, on an azure field.

Their status was that of gentry, at the level of well-to-do-property owners between nobility and burgher, which sometimes was elevated into the nobility or entered it by marriage.

The Wards had already settled in the neighbourhood of Ripon by the twelfth century. They owned stretches of feudal properties in Givendale, Newby, Skelton and, as far as one can make out, held their tenure from the Archbishop of York and the Collegiate Church in Ripon. They were also possessed of property in Ripon.[3] These remarks indicate only a part, and probably a limited part of the family possessions. There can be no doubt that certain important documents are no longer in existence, so that the derivation and inheritance of the once extensive lands cannot be established.

The older line of the Ward family was named from their original large property: Ward of Givendale. For generations the head of the family had been knighted and used the titular prefix 'Sir'. Their burial place was in the Priory of Cistercian nuns at Esholt, of which they were founding benefactors. The church and all monuments were destroyed in Henry VIII's time.

From the wills of individual members of the family it emerges that the fifteenth century Wards were not only very wealthy, but culturally far above the average of the then simple country people. In Joan Ward's will of 1472[4] there is this legacy: her fur-trimmed overmantel with three-cornered kerchief and a girdle of white, gold-worked material adorned with gold, was to be sold, and the benefit thereof given to the Cistercian nunnery at Esholt. Her nephew, Christopher Ward, was to receive a girdle of yellow, gold-embroidered silk, adorned with gold; her sister Margaret a green silk girdle embroidered with gold; Elisabeth Wontworth, to receive another valuable overmantel with a gold-decorated girdle of black silk. Joan Ward had a rosary string of beads of coral,[5] adorned with chalcedony. These were to be sold to pay for a picture of the madonna to be given to Esholt Priory.

A similarly named Joan Ward [6] offered a gold brooch set with precious stones to be sold for the purchase of a chalice to be fashioned for a priest. One of her relations, Christopher Ward, was to receive a silver beaker with a cover, certainly a valuable object.

It is evident from these gifts that these were not only wealthy but cultured people.

Sir Christopher Ward was the grandson of a Sir Roger Ward, senior, and son of a Sir Roger Ward junior. With him we come to somewhat firmer ground, and to dates. Doubtless he was the child (unnamed) of Sir Roger Ward junior who was baptised in 1453 by Prior Thomas Swynton of the Benedictine Abbey of Fountains near Ripon.[7] Exactly twenty one years later, 1474, a Christopher Ward of Givendale took his oath of fealty to the Chapter of the Collegiate church of SS.Peter and Wilfrid in Ripon for properties in Givendale and Newby, a sign that in this year he had attained his majority.[8]

Of his brothers and sisters we know little more than their names: Simon, Robert, Margaret, who married Sir John Norton, Elizabeth, Joan – presumably the Prioress of Esholt from 1480–497, – Eleanor and John. The latter will concern us again later. Whether these siblings are named in the right order is also questionable, or even if the list of them is complete.

Sir Christopher married a Margaret Gascoigne. Her parents, Sir William Gascoigne of Gawthorpe, Knight, and Joan Neville, belonged to one of the powerful families of the county and were richly propertied. When Sir Christopher died, on 31st December, 1521, he had reached the good age, for those times, of sixty eight years. It is perhaps because of his age or his state of health that he handed over his large manor to certain trustees on 20th March, 1519. The inventory of the possessions had already been completed on 7th March, 1519. The 'Inquisitio post mortem' (4.2.1523)[9] or inventory of goods of the deceased, gives us a glimpse into the state of Sir Christopher Ward's affairs.

Only the manors with their lands are named: Givendale, with a gross total of 80 Marks, Newby with 20 Marks, Guiseley with 40 Marks, Esholt with 20 Marks. East-Keswick yielded a gross total of 20 Marks, Adwalton of 10 pounds, Drighlington of 8 pounds, Green Hammerton's return was unknown to the officials of the commission at the time of the inventory. Finally, Great Ouseburn brought in an annual income of 20 pounds. From his manors alone

GENEALOGY OF THE WARD FAMILY – simplified

GIVENDALE

Sir Rogert snr, Kt.
b. 1383 d. 1453 10.VIII
buried at Esholt
m. Joan Markenfield
d. 1472/75 before 29.III.
buried Esholt

Sir Roger jnr. Kt.
b. 1430? d. 28, XI.1472
m. Joan Tunstall
d. 1507/8 23.III
buried at Wighill

William   Nicholas

Joan
d. 1474/5
before 29.III.
buried Esholt

Margaret

Sir Christopher Kt.
b. 1453
d. 31.XIII 1521
buried Esholt
m. Margaret Gascoigne

SKELTON

John
1472, 1502, 1507/08
1518/9, 1523, 1531?

Anne
m.l.John
Wandesford Esq.
2. Ralph
Neville Esq.

Joan
b. 1487?
m. Sir Edward
Musgrave Kt.

Margaret
d. 1521
m. John
Lawrance

Roger (illegit)

N.N. Ward (of Skelton?)
m. Alison Withes d. 1558 before 30.X.
buried in Ripon

MULWITH
Walter, Gent.
d. 1555 before 26.V.
buried in Ripon
m. Anne N.N.

Edward

Christopher
m. Elizabeth NN

Marmaduke, Gent.
b.c. 1552
d.?
m. Ursula Wright, widow
of John Constable (d. 1581)

Barbara   William   Thomas   Roger

Marmaduke
of Newby, Yeom.
d.9.V.1606?
m. Elizabeth Simpson 1.
Susan N.N. 2.

Elizabeth

Anne
m.
N.N. Earle

Anne   Ellyn   Thomas
b./d. 1598

MARY
b. 23.1.1585
in Mulwith
d. 30. Jan.
1645, at
Heworth.

David
c. 1587
died
before
1615

Frances
1590
Carmelite
1610
d. 11.4.1649
buried in
Antwerp

Elizabeth
b. 30.4.1591.
IBVM
before 1616

Barbara
21.11.1592.
IBVM
d. 25.1.1623
buried in
Rome

George
b. 18.5.1595
Jesuit
d. 21.6.1654
London

Sir Christopher had some 180 Marks and 38 pounds gross income. These possessions lay south of Ripon, in the old West Riding of the county of York, now North Yorkshire. Other members of the many-branched Ward family had possessions in this part of the country.[10] Sir Christopher, it seems, did not administer this property alone, for his brother John and others were interested participants.[11] Expressly separate from the above were those properties which his brother John had inherited as his own. These were possessions in Great Ouseburn, Collingham, Heathfield, Guiseley, Skelton and Bridge Hewick, and lay, geographically speaking, on the perimeter of Christopher's lands.

It may be asked why John did not assume possession of his brother's property. It can be inferred that he was not the next heir, and it is doubtful if he had the necessary capital. He owed his mother a considerable sum of money in 1507/8.[12] He would also have had to buy out their father's inheritance from his brother Christopher's children. Moreover, Sir Christopher aimed at appointing both his surviving daughters and their families as his heirs.[13] The result of this arrangement was the break-up of the Ward of Givendale property. The family would never again own it in its entirety. Sir Christopher owned other properties, the extent of which cannot be established, nor can it be ascertained that his daughters inherited these.

After 1521 there enters John of Skelton, historically a far more shadowy figure and considerably less blessed with material goods. With him a new line of the family comes to light: Skelton.

As already mentioned, John Ward's property was excluded from that of Sir Christopher. Possibly John owned the greater part of his land outside church tenure, so that only a fraction of it can be shown as his with certainty. In the will of his aunt Joan[14] John Ward is shown as having property in Skelton. There is no doubt that this was an ancient possession of the family. In 1502 John took possession of a farm with appurtenances in Great Ouseburn and at the same time fifteen properties with appurtenances in Great Ouseburn, Brampton and Haytfield, as well as one third of the mill in Brampton and of a manor, also in Great Ouseburn.[15]

On 4th February, 1523, John Ward was among those sworn in for the process of the Informatio post mortem of his brother Christopher; on 25th April, 1525 it was probably the same John Ward who paid dues to the Chapter of the Collegiate Church of Ripon for lands in Bridge Hewick[16] and it would seem to be the same John Ward who, on the 19th October, 1531,[17] acted as executor of the will of John Withes, and whose children received a legacy. This attendance as executor is important in several respects for links within the Ward family, and deserves further mention.

The Withes lived in Westwick, near Bishop Monkton and Wilsthorpe, some distance from Long Marston. It is not clear from his will whether John Withes was particularly wealthy. It is simply and briefly compiled: for his burial place he gives a fattened cow to the church of St Wilfrid (St Wilfrid before the Roode). To the main altar of this church he donates three shillings and four pence for forgotten tithes. Both the chapels at Roecliffe near Boroughbridge and the Roode house in Ripon received three shillings and four pence. Then followed the legacies for his family. Forty shillings each were received by his daughter Emott with her son John, the children of William Withes, of Margaret Knarisburghe, and of John Ward respectively. It should be emphasized that the daughter Emott received, together with her son, the same sum as the unnamed children of the remaining relations, who however were not included as heirs. These children would appear to be the descendants of the brothers and sisters of John Withes; there is an absence of closer relatives.

Then followed legacies in kind; the best mare from the stable went to Alice Ward his daughter; his servant Agnes Smythe received a young cow, and his sister with the same name, Agnes Smythe, one of the best cows. What is remarkable about this order of names is that the last-named women were apparently childless; added to which, these three women received bequests in kind, and not in money.

But to confine ourselves to people with the name of Ward – the question of paramount importance is: what was their exact relationship?

John Ward was referred to as Mister. That points to an elevated social status.

Moreover, this John Ward must have stood in a particular relationship to the dead John Withes, for not only did his children receive a legacy of equal value to that of his daughter Emott with her son, but he himself was also an executor, together with John Wilson and Miles Withes, the son of the deceased.

But first and foremost comes the question: is this John Ward to be identified as the brother of Sir Christopher? The attempt to compile the family tree of the Ward family from some years after the death of Sir Christopher – about 1530–40 – is extremely difficult and must, strictly speaking, remain hypothetical, based on a series of only partially convincing assumptions.

It has already been mentioned that Joan Ward, the sister of Sir Roger Ward, junior, remembered a John Ward in her will. She bound her brother Nicholas in her will to surrender, after his death 'quoddam tenementum in villa de Skeltone'[18] to John Ward, brother of Sir Christopher. It is not known if this was done. It is also unknown when this John Ward was born; he was in debt to his mother for corn and cattle in 1507/8[19], so by that time he was already independent. By then, too, he had an illegitimate son. His date of birth must be prior to 1472, for at that time his father Sir

Roger Ward junior, was dead.[20] By 1531 John Ward must have been in his sixties or over if he really was the brother of Sir Christopher Ward. From this, it is possible that this John Ward may be considered as the father-in-law of Alice Ward, nèe Withes; he could hardly have been her husband. The same holds good were John to have belonged to another branch of the Ward family. It will be seen that, as well as her son Walter Ward, Alison Ward had close connections with Skelton, whose inhabitants she remembered individually in her will. What is certain is that Alison was married to a Ward from Skelton, but one whose christian name is unknown.

In 1541 one John Ward died. Six shillings and eight pence were paid for his burial place[21] and the church of St Wilfrid received a bequest of 20 pence.[22] It can be assumed that the division of the properties occurred at about this time. In 1546/7 a John Ward, William Smyth, Thomas Stele and Thomas Talyour paid 40 shillings for 'Free rents' in Skelton.[23] Alison Ward and her son Walter paid, in the same year, eight pounds for 'one tenement with certen landes in Mulwath'.[24] Already, by 1535, the annual duty had increased to this large amount of money.[25] In 1555,[26] Walter Ward provided in his will for the gift of a sack of malt to John Ward of Skelton, and Alison his mother in her will dated 1557,[27] gave to John Ward of Skelton a French crown, to his wife a sack of malt, to his son John – her godchild – three shillings and four pence and to both his daughters, Jane and Dorothy, a sheep and a lamb each. Alison's husband remains nameless, but it may be supposed that he was the son of that John Ward who had inherited a freehold in Skelton years before.

Alison's date of birth is unknown, and similarly the date of her marriage. We only know that she was married to a Ward in 1531 but at that time had no children. In 1546/7 she was already a widow[28] and the mother of three children, Walter, Edward and Christopher. She died before 30th September, 1558,[29] probably on 18th August of that year[30] and was buried in the Collegiate church of SS Wilfrid and Peter in Ripon by the side of her husband. She outlived her eldest son Walter by more than three years, but it is better to study the details of her will before that of her son.

Alison Ward drafted her will on 14th November, 1557. It reveals a deep sense of family and a close connection with the inhabitants of Skelton and, not least, a comfortable life-style. In setting out her will she did not begin with properties, as her father had done, but according to membership of the family. It brings us a step nearer to drawing up a Ward family tree.

First come instructions about her burial: the full church choir is to be present, and all the secular clergy belonging to the church of SS Wilfrid and Peter. On the day of her burial the considerable sum of thirteen pounds and six shillings and eight pence was to be dispensed among the poor. She gave ten shillings for the main altar of the church in settlement of forgotten dues; for the maintenance of God's house she gave three shillings and four pence. Monetary bequests were received also by the curates of the collegiate church and the poor women of both the hospitals of S.Mary Magdalen and S.Anne. Then followed the legacies to her children and relations: her son Edward received a bedcover and a large accounts' table,[31] her son Christopher three 'oxgangs' of land[32] in Skelton. Here Alison was disposing of freehold, or she would not have had lands at her disposal. Both sons, Edward and Christopher, received in addition all her leasehold claims and rents in Wilsthorpe, as well as her unpaid debts. These cannot have amounted to very much. Edward must have been unmarried or a childless widower; he was mentioned in this will only.

Next came Christopher's wife, Elizabeth. She received a cow and an old gold coin. Afterwards came bequests to Christopher's children: his son Marmaduke of Newby (not to be confused with the son of her deceased son Walter, with the same name) received a young steer, a second steer, a silver spoon and twenty shillings. Elizabeth, Christopher's daughter, received six pounds thirteen shillings and four pence in ready money, and her younger sisters Anne and Joan each had a young cow and twenty shillings. Moreover, Christopher's three daughters and Walter's daughter Barbara had all the household effects that remained.

Walter's widow received a legacy equal to that of Christopher's wife: a cow and a gold coin. His oldest son Marmaduke – later the father of Mary Ward – received a steer, a basin with a jug, a fermenting vat, a large roasting spit, a large copper cauldron, a silver spoon and a copper mortar. Both the younger sons were remembered with a young steer, a silver spoon and twenty shillings. The youngest son Roger also had a young steer and twenty shillings but no silver spoon. The daughter Barbara was richly endowed: she had ten pounds in ready money, a cow and a feather bed, and she too, like Christopher's daughters, had her share in the household goods.

Then came the turn of a Randall Ward, with forty shillings, and his wife with a coin and each of his children with two shillings. A Catherine Bell received a coin, and each of her children two shillings. Presumably this Catherine was born Ward, as she was also remembered in Walter Ward's will.

Finally there comes a John Ward of Skelton. He receives a coin and a sack of malt, and his wife a sack of malt, his son – Alison's godchild – three shillings and four pence and both his daughters Jane and Dorothy a sheep and a lamb each. So much for the legacies to the Ward family. What is striking is the strict even-handed disposal of the possessions.

It was otherwise in the case of distant relatives, who received considerably less. But they had their turn and it would be quite possible that Randall as well as Catherine Bell and John Ward of Skelton were brothers and sisters of the husband of Alison Ward, deceased. They were, after all, mentioned before her own sister's children. And the godchild John, son of John of Skelton, could point in this direction, though this assumption must remain merely a suggestion.

Of the remaining legatees only Alison's sister Emott is named, whose children — by 1531 she had one child only — each received three shillings and four pence. The Wright family is represented here with three members: the unnamed son of Jenet received a young mare and five shillings. Jenet's sister Margaret, a saddle and her son, five shillings.

The needy, or perhaps the poorer families in Skelton were not forgotten. Each house, that is, every family, received four pence and every house that did not cultivate its own corn, a quarter-bushel of rye. The poor of Boroughbridge, Aldborough, Langthorpe, and Kirbymoorside likewise received larger sums.[33]

The executors of Alison's prosperous will were her sons Edward and Christopher and Walter's eldest, though very young son, Marmaduke. Miles Withes, Alison's brother and his son John, were supervisors. The many small legacies have been omitted, as their inclusion would be superfluous. Moreover, they are less valuable for establishing family connections. At best they underline the considerable wealth of this woman, who gave generously to relieve the needs of those who had less; a beautiful trait that must surely have been recognised during her life-time. So much for the documents of the Ward family.

How did the early writings handle this lineage? Documents tend to have a sobering effect on one's train of thought. The earliest biographies, however, overflow with a prodigality of imaginative invention. The English life, compiled about fifty years after Mary Ward's death, barely mentions the Ward line of descent. But the Italian biography gives prominence to the age and nobility of the family. It begins with the fateful year 1066, when William the Conqueror came from Normandy, landed in England, and won the Battle of Hastings. In the Ward family of those days were seven brothers, all 'equites aurati' or Golden Knights. Such knights had special privileges, among others that of wearing golden spurs, hence their name. They held lands in fee from the king but had to pay him dues at their own expense with forty days knights' service.[34] An expensive matter. This dignity, says the authoress of the biography, was then more greatly esteemed than the position of a Markgraf or Count in her own day. The oldest of these brothers was the King's governor in Yorkshire.[35] It is worth noting that the English Life emphasizes the size of the property, whereas the Italian Vita stresses the nobility and antiquity of the family.

And the family? How do the writings show this? Vincenzo Pagetti's short account, 'Breve Racconto della Vita di Donna Maria della Guardia' comes next. Pagetti was secretary of Prince Borghese in Rome and had a living in the Borghese chapel in the church of Santa Maria Maggiore. He died in Rome on 5th July, 1674.[36] Pagetti composed his record out of respect for Mary Ward, who had heard his request for a cure from an eye affliction. It is not known why he dedicated this short account to Electress Adelheid of Bavaria. Perhaps he was encouraged by the members of the Institute then still in Rome, perhaps by Catherine Dawson the superior, who herself wrote about Mary Ward. It cannot be stated with certainty that Pagetti knew the Italian Life, but he too wrote that Mary Ward had a distinguished ancestry and came from one of the noblest familes of England.[37]

Twelve years later, in 1674, one of the Canons of Augsburg, Dominicus Bissel, wrote his 'Vita Venerabilis Virginis ac Matris Mariae Warth Anglae, fundatricis Societatis Virginum Anglicarum dictarum'.[38] Bissel, who died in Augsburg on 19th December 1710,[39] certainly knew the two first lives, Mary Ward's auto-biographical sketches, and Pagetti's biography. He could also have obtained information from those who had known Mary Ward: Mary Poyntz, Isabella Laiton, and Catherine Hamilton. It does not, however, seem likely that they would have given him this task; it was probably not intended for the members, as Bissel wrote it in Latin. Here we are given a very different picture of the Ward family. The Italian Life had been taken as its basis, certainly, but it had been remembered with embellish-ments: the Wards belonged to the aristocracy; they were closely connected to the Earl of Northumberland and other members of the nobility. The antiquity of the family and the 'Golden Knights' was adopted wholesale.[40] In 1689 the Jesuit Tobias Lohner dedi-cated his 'Gottseeliges Leben und fuertreffliche Tugendten, Donna Maria della Guardia, Hochlöblichen Stiffterin der Engeländischen Gesellschaft'.[41] Tobias Lohner, SJ., held various positions in the upper German province of his order, which he had entered in 1637.[42] He wrote his biography for pastoral reasons, not least as spiritual encouragement for the Englishwomen. He too described Mary Ward as a member of the high aristocracy. Here the seven Golden Knights have turned into Marmaduke's brothers, and they have become 'Knights of the Golden Fleece'.[43] But the Order of the Golden Fleece was founded in 1430 by Duke Philip the Good of Burgundy and, after the extinction of the house of Burgundy, was continued by the House of Austria. It is still today bestowed by the head of the House of Habsburg on princes and aristocrats.

In 1717 there appeared the first impression of the 'Relatio de origine et propagatione Instituti Mariae nuncupati Virginum Anglarum seu Anglicanarum atque adversus infensum earum scriptorem justa defensione' of the Benedictine Corbinian Khamm[44] who, as the verbose title conveys, was more concerned with the defence of the Institute than with the biography of Mary Ward. He too pronounces the family briefly but conclusively as of antiquity, and noble.[45]

1732 saw the publication of the two-volume 'Englische Tugendschul Mariae unter denen von Ihro Päbstlichen Heiligkeit Clemente XI gutgeheissnen und bestättigten Reglen dess von der Hochgebohrnen Frauen, Frauen Maria Ward, als Stiffterin aufgerichteten Edlen Instituts Mariae, insgemein unter dem Namen der Englischen Fräulein.'[46] Its author was the parish priest of Morenweiss in Bavaria, Marcus Fridl. In this work which was much read in his day, he writes, 'among other ancestral lines of the county, the old and noble line of the lords Ward was very famous and distinguished for its properties, the high respect in which they were held, and for their distinguished connections.'[47] And, as though that were not enough, Mary Ward's birthplace becomes the demesne and castle of Mulwith,[48] the brothers were knights of the 'golden spurs'[49] and the coat of arms is described as 'a golden cross on a black field with white fleur de lys in the quarters, with a white helmet lined with red, surmounted by a black bear's head, adorned with black and yellow plumage, which surround the black shield together with the cross.' [50] Thus Fridl. He quoted Bissel and handed on the substance to posterity unquestioningly. The description of the coat of arms he acquired from 'The Baronetage of England', Part II, page I.

And once again, in 1735, someone picked up the quill – this time the secular priest Johannes von Unterberg, who wrote his 'Kurtzen Begriff dess wunderbarlichen Lebens der Ehrwuerdigen und Hoch-Gebohrnen Frauen Frauen Maria von Ward, Stiffterin dess mehr als vor hundert Jahren angefangenen und unter denen von Papst Clemente XI gutgeheissenen und bestaetigten Regeln aufgerichteten edlen Instituts Mariae, ins gemein unter dem Namen der Englischen Fraeulein genannt.'[51] Here the highly-noble Mary von Ward was a descendant of the noble, very ancient catholic family of Ward. Mary Chambers was more cautious in her 'Life of Mary Ward' in the German text printed in Regensburg in 1888.[52] Although she too quoted Bissel, she made some valuable references, though unfortunately, without naming her sources.

This survey has attempted to show the trend of past interpretations in order to give some idea of the free play given to extremely doubtful, and very exaggerated, assertions. The reliable statements of documents and records keep to dispassionate, historical truth. Certainly the early writers were upright people who did not intend to mislead. It was rather their baroque style which inclined them to florid and discursive expressions. We must assume that they received it in that form from those who provided them with the information, either in writing or by word of mouth. All of these people were of their time. We must, however, distance ourselves from them as sources, or at least weigh them very carefully, unless they are confirmed elsewhere.

The Grandparents

Walter Ward of Mulwith — his wife Anne — their property - Walter's Will — the Wright family — lineage — property — Robert and Ursula Wright

Of Mary's grandparents on the paternal side, little is known; at best there are dates to prove their existence. Of her grandmother Anne we have her first name only, not her maiden name; the inter-relationship is shown by two legacies that give definite indications: from her mother-in-law Alison, a gold coin and a cow[53] and, after her husband's death, all his estates, with the proviso that only after their son Marmaduke had reached the age of twenty-four, was she to share these properties with him. The last mention of Anne Ward comes in 1567/8: Simon Musgrove, Anne Ward and her son Marmaduke, who were witnesses to the transfer of pasture land in Givendale to Richard Thornton and William Mason.[54]

By 1572 Marmaduke Ward was acting on his own behalf.[55] It is not certain if his mother was still alive, but certainly by then Marmaduke had attained his majority.

Matters are not much better when it comes to Mary Ward's grandfather, Walter Ward. It is thought that Alison Ward probably did not yet have any children by 1531,[56] though in 1546/7 she and her son Walter paid for a property with appurtenances in Mulwith.[57] We do not have her husband's will and therefore do not know if it contained a clause concerning the management of his property, as was the case when Walter came later to make his will. In 1546/7 Walter must still have been a minor, otherwise he would have acted alone. The same probably holds good about an agreement of 22nd July, 1551.[58] A certain Oswald Wyllestrop, knight, transferred to Ralf Dicconson of Widdington, Roger Withes of Westwick and Walter Ward of Mulwith, a property in the manor of Wilsthorpe. It could be that Roger Withes was acting here as Walter Ward's guardian, for this was a matter of a landed estate and not of a farm with appurtenances. Next in chronology comes Walter's will. It was drafted on 1st March, 1555 and proved on 26th May in the same year. Walter died between those two dates, very probably on 5th April, for in 1557 on that date there was an offering for the repose of his soul.[59]

From this it emerges that Walter was fatherless very young, and therefore had to take charge of the property. That may be the reason for his stipulation concerning his own son and heir, Marmaduke.

The shortness of the time between the drafting and the proving of the will points to the fact that Walter cannot have been ill long. His will is relatively brief,[60] considerably shorter than that of his mother some years later, with its detailed legacies.

Walter wished to be buried in the Collegiate Church of SS Wilfrid and Peter, close to his ancestors. To each of the six curates of Ripon he left a fattened wether, his sole legacy to the Church. Next come his leaseholds; these were to remain in the possession of his widow until his son Marmaduke had attained his twenty-fourth year. This clause could be an indication of the heavy burden placed on him in his own youth. Only when he was a mature young man of twenty four was Marmaduke to share with his mother the half of the leaseholds, unless she were to marry again. Excluded were those properties that Walter's mother Alison had previously owned, as also his claim to the property in Wilsthorpe.[61] Walter Ward could not dispose of his lands, as they lay within the competence of the law. Unfortunately that particular inquisitio post mortem no longer exists, so the measure of his estate cannot be established.

Walter left five young children: Marmaduke, later to be Mary Ward's father, Barbara, William, Thomas and Roger. His eldest daughter Barbara received as her dowry twenty-six shillings and eight pence every year for ten years from the house known as Watson's house. This totalled more than thirteen pounds. Together with her grandmother Alison's legacy of something in the region of ten pounds, young Barbara was certainly not ill-provided.

His three sons William, Thomas and Roger were the sole remaining heirs. Walter gave few other bequests. Catherine Bell, who was to be remembered a few years later by Alison Ward, received forty shillings for her daughter; John Ward of Skelton, a sack of malt; the children of Jenet and Margaret Wright, also legatees of Alison Wright, received five shillings each. Some smaller legacies do not need to be mentioned. Walter also gave a quarter of a bushel of rye to every household in Skelton that possessed an 'oxgang' of land.

We are somewhat better informed about Mary Ward's maternal grandparents, Robert and Ursula Wright. The Wrights came originally from the county of Kent,[62] where a John Wright had been steward to Henry VIII. It is not known when he moved to Yorkshire, but it must have been before the suppression of the monasteries. He inherited extensive properties in the south-eastern part of Yorkshire, today's Humberside, and through his wife Alice (nee Ryther),[63] he acquired Ploughland Hall, (a property once belonging to Bolton Priory), where Mary Ward spent some years of her childhood.

John Wright died on 25th May, 1540, survived by his wife. His inquisitio post mortem of 2nd July, 1541[64] is extant and consequently the size of his estate can be known. Without going into a tedious list of place-names, it is enough to say that John Wright owned thirteen farmsteads, seven houses, a windmill, two barns and a broad stretch of arable land, meadows, pastures, woods and heathland. Possibly he had as large an income from all this as Sir Christopher Ward had enjoyed twenty years before from his property, but the difference between the two estates was marked: the Wards owned what was predominantly arable land, while the Wrights had farmland with cattle.

The son and heir of John Wright, Sir Robert Wright, Esq., was born in 1520 and buried in Welwick on 18th July, 1574.[65]

He was first married to Anna Grimston, who came from a recusant family and died young.[66] From his second marriage with Ursula Rudston,[67] Robert Wright had five children, who all played a role in Mary Ward's life: first, Ursula her mother; then her uncles John and Christopher, who were conspirators in the Gunpowder Plot of 1605; her aunt Alice, who had a clandestine betrothal in 1593 with William Readshaw in Marmaduke Ward's house, and finally, her aunt Martha who was married to Thomas Percy, another conspirator in the Gunpowder Plot. The family was evidently politically active.

As a small child, Mary Ward probably did not have much to do with her grandfather Robert Wright during her stay in Ploughland, although it was only in the middle of 1595 that he died.[68] In those days the relationship between a very young person with the head of the family was very different from that of today. Her upbringing was mainly in the hands of his wife Ursula.

It is only in her autobiographical fragments,[69] written ten years later that Mary Ward gives a description of her grandmother; she limited this to certain moral aspects of her character; anything else seemed superfluous. She wrote that her grandmother was well-known and respected for her uprightness, that she had suffered fourteen years' imprisonment when she was younger, and had often defended her catholic faith before magistrates. Once she was locked up among criminals because of her outspoken manner of giving her opinion – so not as a political prisoner – but she was soon removed by the intervention of some relatives, and transferred to prison in the Castle keep.

Ursula Wright led an intensive prayer life; when Mary Ward fell asleep at night and woke in the morning, she found her at prayer. She was generous, especially to those in prison, for she had experienced the life, or rather the living conditions, of the disgusting dungeons of her day. The date of her death is not known, nor her burial place, though probably that, too, was in Welwick.

The Parents

Marmaduke Ward of Mulwith — character — his qualities — his wife Ursula Wright — her first marriage with John Constable — Ursula Constable as widow — her second marriage to Marmaduke Ward

Such narrative sources as there are about Mary Ward's parents are unsatisfactory and inadequate, and often need modification, which lessens their value. Documentary sources are less colourful but safer. First of all, there is information from Mary Ward herself, from the short extract she wrote in 1617 as a young woman of twenty-three. Her first sentence runs almost like a maxim of her childhood memories — 'Both my parents were virtuous and suffered much for the Catholic cause.'[70] In a few words, two people's lives are sketched and framed against the dark background of their time. Mary, it seems, was closer to her father. She certainly describes him in more detail; she hardly mentions her mother. The reason is not immediately obvious. Perhaps Marmaduke Ward was more deeply religious and therefore had a better rapport in this respect with his responsive and spiritually-minded daughter. It is also conceivable that, during the impressionable years spent with her grandmother, she found in the latter a substitute for her absent mother, while her grandfather did not replace Marmaduke in at all the same way. Possibly it was a psychological factor which drew father and daughter together, something that cannot and need not be explained.

Mary Ward named two qualities as quintessential to her father's character: his great love of the poor, and his concern for the morals and faith of his children. She writes: 'his love for the poor and his kindness to all in need were such that I have never seen in any secular person.' Marmaduke Ward was loyal to Catholicism, a faith much disparaged and hated in England at that time. He longed to educate and encourage his children in it, and Mary illustrated this with two examples: before the children met their Anglican relatives, he always briefed them on the value of catholic beliefs and their necessity for salvation, and confided to them his desire that they should all live and die members of the church.

Once Mary as a four year old was playing with another small girl in her father's room, where he was busy writing. During the game the other child suddenly burst out with 'By Christ's holy wounds...!', an expression she had evidently picked up somewhere. Mary repeated it, several times, partly — as she later wrote — to scold her friend, and partly, by showing her disapproval, to gain approval from her father for herself. But Marmaduke was so absorbed in his work that all he heard was his daughter, saying 'By Christ's holy wounds...' Ignorant of the scenario, he rose and punished her with his own hand. Then he listened. Mary Ward added that this was the first and last time that he punished his children in the heat of the moment. But the experience of his indignation must have left an impression on his daughter. In this account, unconsciously and unintentionally, Mary reveals two of her own inherent qualities — love of the poor and constancy in her defence of the catholic faith. About thirty years after she had written these words, certain other loving but unskilled hands chiselled on her tombstone: 'To love the poore ...'

The first biographies are more generous with their information about the foundress's background. The English Life[71] has Marmaduke Ward as 'of Givendale', owning a Manor in Mulwith and Newby, and still acknowledged, at the time when the biography was written, as a man of good appearance, a courageous and steadfast catholic and admirable in his concern for the poor. When times were hard and prices rose, no needy person was ever turned from his door. Commonly sixty to eighty, even a hundred people received something daily. In friendship, Marmaduke was loyal.

We can see here that, while the substance of this is true, the facts are unreal. Marmaduke did not live in Givendale but in Mulwith, where his father Walter Ward had an estate. It is true that the Wards of Mulwith had properties in Givendale close by, but that does not justify the title 'of Givendale'. It has already been shown that the male line of the Wards of Givendale had expired with the death of Sir Christopher Ward in 1521. Marmaduke inherited a manor in Mulwith in 1588; it was burnt down in 1595 and probably never rebuilt. At all events, there was no further mention of Marmaduke Ward of Mulwith. This matter will be referred to later.

The Italian Life[72] gives the Illustrissimo Signore Marmaduca della Guardia di Gindal and the Signora Orsola Wright di Pluland as of noble lineage in England. Marmaduke is closely related to the Duke(!) of Northumberland and of all the most ancient aristocrats of the region. He is still renowned as an outstanding catholic and benefactor to the poor, not only in elevated circles but among the people. Nothing is said concerning his status, probably he was regarded as a gentleman at arms. He was handsome and well-built, with good features and perfect deportment, intelligent and adorned with all suitable and necessary virtues.

At this point, certain facts must be stated. The Ward family certainly belonged to one of the oldest in the county, and was related to those of Percy, Neville, Strickland, Constable, Mallory, Markenfeld, Musgrave and Gascoigne, but they themselves did not belong to the nobility, but were armigerous landed gentry. On the Continent, such a family might be reckoned minor nobility, but not in England. To give a typical instance: many years later, on 6th November, 1621,[73] Father Muzio Vitelleschi, General of the Society of Jesus, addressed a letter to Mary Ward, entitled 'Perillustri ac pietissimae Dominae'. Immediately some English Jesuits reacted with the warning that such a form of address was not her due, as she was not noble. The General defended himself to the Provincial, Richard Blount, answering that on this occasion he had followed Italian custom.[74] The Englishwomen were known without exception on the Continent as 'virgines nobiles'. Mary Ward signed herself as 'Maria della Guardia' and she was also addressed with 'von.' Other English people did the same, for one, Thomas Sackville, who will shortly enter the scene. He entitled himself 'Graf' or Count Sackville, although he was not the eldest son and heir of his father.

It would be interesting to know, in this context, if Marmaduke Ward bore a coat of arms. Up to now there has been no satisfactory statement, as his coat of arms has not been given us. It was mentioned earlier that the Ward family originally bore a cross patonce Or on an Azure field on their shield. But did this descend, after the male line had died out with the death of Sir Christopher, to the collateral line in Skelton and Mulwith, or was the entire family entitled to this escutcheon? It remains a mystery that Marmaduke's coat of arms is not displayed in the Heraldic Visitation carried out in Yorkshire in 1585.[75]

Chambers' assertion[76] that this was from fear of persecution or from indifference to the value of ancient lineage, does not hold water, for in that case why did Marmaduke Ward certify the coat of arms of his wife and her first husband, John Constable? There could of course be other reasons for exclusion from the Visitation, but they must have been substantial. One would not lightly fail to confirm the right to bear a coat of arms. For in this matter, one must not forget, Marmaduke could not act for personal reasons, however solid and acceptable, but was answerable for the social significance it carried for his family.

On the other hand, Marmaduke Ward was always referred to as 'Gentleman', and that would have been impossible for a man who was not armigerous. Howevever that may be, when Mary Ward later sealed important letters, this sign of authentication was as similar as possible to the seal of the Society of Jesus. She never used a personal seal that would have shown a family coat of arms.

The 17th and 18th century writings overreach themselves in idealisation or exaggeration. Pagetti alone remains simple: Mary Ward's parents were firm members of the Catholic Church, which explains why the family could produce a child as blessed as Mary.[77]

Bissel gives Marmaduke Ward of Givendale as Lord of Mulwith and Newby, and her mother Ursula Wright of Ploughland (both of them of noblest birth), closely related to the Duke of Northumberland and other nobility.[78] The sources from which Bissel took his material is evident.

Lohner stands by these statements, adds somewhat to them,[79] and ends saying that Marmaduke would have stood firm during time of persecution 'as his house seems to have been more like a well-ordered monastery than a worldly palace.' Ursula Wright's mother, too, was born of the 'ancient stock of Rudstons.'

Fridl flies higher into princely terminology when he writes: 'Her noble Father was Marmaduke Ward, at that time the first born son of the house and demesne of the Lord of Ghindal, Old and New Mulwith and Newby.'[80] Ursula's mother was 'born of the ancient lineage of Rudston'.[81]

Unterberg, again, makes Marmaduke 'von' Givendale, a 'Lord of the New Molvvoth and Naemby (sic)', a friend of the Dukes of Normandia (sic) and Northumberland, who, as an ancient 'Cavalier', could trace his family tree back to 1066, for more than six hundred years.[82]

Marmaduke had done nothing of the kind.

If we turn to the documents, we find quite a different picture. We do not know the exact date of Marmaduke's birth, though we can come close to the year of it. At his father's death he was not yet twenty four. We know about the clause in Walter Ward's will. This does not help us much further in determining his date of birth, for in this respect, twenty four years is a longish span. In 1567/8 Marmaduke seems still to have been a minor, for his mother and Simon Musgrave made over pastureland in Givendale to a Richard Thornton and a William Mason.[83] But, on 25th June, 1572, Marmaduke alone entered into a process against widow Margaret Birnand, who denied him access to his land in Roecliff.[84] Moreover, this document[85] leads us a little closer to his date of birth, as the difficulties with Widow Birnand had begun 'about six yeres last past.' At that time Marmaduke would have been about 14 years old 'being but aboute fourtene yeres'. If he, then, six years earlier, in 1566, had been about 14 years old, it follows that he was born in 1552. It may be that his mother Anne was already dead by 1572, for if he had been born in 1552, then he was twenty one years old in 1572 and so of age by English law, but as he was not yet twenty four he was debarred by the clause in his father's will from taking over half of his property. After his mother's death this clause was eo ipso null and void. At this time Marmaduke Ward must have been the young and active owner of a large estate, who saw to his rights and was prepared, when needful, to fight for his property for, and this should be stressed, the wealth of this property was part of the realm of England. Only relatively late, in 1582/3, did Marmaduke Ward marry Ursula Wright. If he was a widower at that time, who had lost his wife early and remained childless, this is not supported by any indication in the sources.

One can also work out Mary Ward's mother's date of birth, approximately, from the documents. Her oldest brother John was baptised on 16th January, 1568 in Welwick.[86] Her youngest brother

Christopher was born in 1570, for at his death in the skirmish at Holbeach he was about thirty-five years old.[87] It is accepted that Ursula was born before both her brothers. Had she been born after her brother Christopher, and had glimpsed her first light after 1570, say in 1571, then she would have been ten years old at the death of her first husband, John Constable.

It is true that child marriage was then no rarity, but a ten year old widow would have been bitterly young even in the sixteenth century, especially since her first husband, John Constable, was twenty six or twenty seven in 1581 when he died.[88] In addition, there is this: on 23rd January, 1585, Ursula gave birth to Mary, the eldest child of her second marriage to Marmaduke Ward. The date of the conception of this daughter can therefore be set in the second half of April, 1584. Now, even though biologically possible, to be a mother at the age of thirteen or fourteen is very young. And at that time Marmaduke was over thirty. But if Ursula was born before her brother John, in 1565 or 1566 at the latest, she would have been fifteen or sixteen when her first husband died and so nineteen or twenty at the birth of her daughter Mary.

John Constable must have died in the middle of 1581, for on 18th July of that year[89] the management of his inherited property was conveyed to his wife. One year later, on 17th July, 1582,[90] Henry Dalkins of Brandesburton undertook to pay an annual inheritance of thirty pounds from his estates in Brandesburton, Ulrome and Catfoss to the benefit of William Ingleby and William Wright during the lifetime of Ursula Constable, widow of John Constable of Great Hatfield. For the first time, in this long-winded document, the name of Marmaduke Ward appears together with that of Ursula, a widowed Constable. It is a sign that he had contacts with the families of Constable and Wright, or at least that he had been asked to be witness to this legally binding document. It also means that Marmaduke and Ursula were not yet married by 17th July, 1582. So their wedding must have taken place between this date and April 1584, when Ursula was expecting their first child. The marriage was probably harmonious, perhaps even happy, as it was blessed with six children in ten years. To be sure, that was no absolute guarantee of happiness, given the status of women in those days. Her father concerned himself with the morals of the household, Mary writes.[91] 'He would never permit to be read or kept such books as treated of sensual or worldly love; and I remember that he caused my mother to turn away such servants, who were otherwise very profitable, for some such little signs of lightness'. As though in exoneration she added, between brackets, that her mother was just as careful of modest behaviour in her own demeanour as well as that 'she kept over the men and maids of the household.'

What did these two young people have in common, in their youth? Hardly reminiscences from their early childhood. They had lived too far apart for that, and the age difference was too marked. Perhaps it would be better to ask: what great events happened during their youth? In 1568, Mary Stuart was imprisoned. Marmaduke was then about sixteen years old, and would undoubtedly have shared the outrage of his fellow catholics, who saw in the Scottish Queen a possible catholic successor to the English throne. Ursula Wright was far too young at that time to be capable of any such sentiments. Certain leaders of the Rebellion of the North in 1569 were either related to or known by the Wards: Thomas Percy, Earl of Northumberland, who emerged with a fine, John Neville, Earl of Westmoreland, who had to flee to Flanders, Francis Norton and others. It is more than possible that Marmaduke must have seen their cavalry and infantry when they reached Boroughbridge on 18th November and two days later were in Ripon Cathedral, attending Mass celebrated with all due solemnity in the catholic tradition. And surely he shared the triumphant rejoicing of the population, or their fear of reprisals.

He may well have seen some of those insurgents who had been hanged in the villages after the harsh oppression of the uprising and have felt deep compassion and wonder, when he saw their heads bowed over the halter, their faces blue and convulsed in death.

During these years, in Ploughland where things were more peaceful, Ursula's two brothers, John and Christopher, were born. A little while later, Marmaduke, a young landowner, was bringing his lawsuit against Widow Margaret Birnand in defence of his property. Barely ten years later came the first undercover and courageous missionaries until, in 1580, the Society of Jesus sent Jesuits trained specifically in the English College in Rome for the English mission. There were constant upheavals in the country, especially in the North, which had never been easy to govern. Edmund Grindal had been Archbishop of York since 1571; in 1572 Henry Hastings, Earl of Huntingdon, had been named the President of the Commission of the North. Both were Puritans, and extremely hostile towards catholicism. The strict laws against English papists were their chief weapons. Prisons were filled. Hull prison, already notorious, contained sixteen prisoners who were there for their religious convictions, among them some aged priests.[92] The gaols were emptied again: on 22nd August, 1582, Richard Kirkman and William Lacy were martyred in York, on 28th November of the same year James Thompson, on 15th March 1583, William Hart and on 29th May, Richard Thirkhill.[93]

The Wards must have demonstrated their catholicism during these years, for in 1578 a Robert Constable received lands (assigned him by the Queen) which had once belonged to Alison and Walter Ward.[94] It is during these years that Ursula Wright's mother probably spent part of her long time in imprisonment. It was in the very same year in which John Constable died that the Queen promulgated new laws against catholics. The not inconsiderable fines were magnified to an exorbitant sum, far beyond the means of the people. The penalty for absence on a Sunday from Anglican Church service for an Englishman increased from one shilling to 20 pounds. A priest who was discovered celebrating a catholic mass was fined 200 marks and received a prison sentence of one year. Whoever was absent from the Anglican church for longer than one year paid the same penalty of 20 pounds as before, but in addition he had to arrange for two citizens to pledge 200 for this Anglican commitment — which he did not have.

It was this sort of oppression that was particularly repugnant, for who could make his catholic faith dependent on someone else's money? To admit one's catholicism was the equivalent of admitting to high treason.[95]

It was during this time that Ursula Wright became John Constable's widow. We do not know where she and Marmaduke were married, probably clandestinely, just as Mary received the sacraments. One thing, however, is certain, that Marmaduke Ward and Ursula Wright spent their youth in a time of threat and fear. But it was, too, a time of heroes and heroines.

Notes:

1. G.M. Trevelyan, English Social History. A Survey of Six Centuries. Chaucer to Queen Victoria, London (4) 1947, p. 19.
2. T.C. Dale, The Inhabitants of London in 1638. Edit. from Ms. 272 in the Lambeth Palace Library, London 1931.
3. W. Paley Baildon, Baildon and the Baildons, I, P. 1. 1912, p. 222–223.
4. UYBI, York, Prob. Reg. 4, f. 7rv.
5. The present form of the rosary is far more recent. In those days it consisted of a string of eleven beads, (1 Pater Noster, 10 Ave Marias). One large bead, often decorated, or a cross, marked the beginning.
6. UYBI York, Prob. Reg. 4, f. 7v.
7. Walbran, Memorials II/I = Surt. soc. 67/1876/II(1878), p. 104-106.
8. Fowler, Acts = Surt. Soc. 64/1874/II/1875, p. 246.
9. PRO London, Inquisitio post mortem. Chancery Series 2, vol. 39, Nr. 68.
10. Members of the Ward family lived in Bishop Monkton, Markington and Bishop Thornton.
11. As above, note 9.
12. In her Will dated 24.2.1507/8, Joan Ward, widow of Sir Roger Ward, jnr., and later wife of Sir William Stapleton, provided 10 marks which John Ward owed her for corn and cattle, for his illegitimate son, Richard. Raine, Test. Ebor. IV = Surt. Soc. 53/II/1868 (1869), p. 273–274 Nr. CLVIII.
13. Anne was married to Ralph Neville, Esq., and Joan to Edward Musgrave Esq. The third daughter, Margaret, died before her father. Anne was the only one to have heirs, three daughters, of whom Catherine was married to Walter Strickland, Esq; Joan to John Constable, Esq., and Clare to Sir Thomas Neville.
14. As above, note 4.
15. In 1505. Feet of Fines of the Tudor Period, Pt. I, YATA RS II, 1887, p. 19.
16. Fowler, Memorials III = Surt. Soc. 81/1886/I(1888), p. 277.

17. Sheepscar Library Archives Leeds, Archdeaconry of Richmond, Register of Wills 1503–1546, RP 4, f. 149v.
18. As above, note 4.
19. As above, note 12.
20. As above, note 4.
21. As above, note 16 p.193.
22. ibid.
23. Ibid. p. 11.
24. ibid p. 29.
25. ibid p. 8.
26. UYBI York, York Wills, vol. 15/I, f.35rv.
27. ibid. vol. 15/III, f.55rv.
28. With her son Walter she paid the fine for a farm in Mulwith.
29. The date her will was read.
30. On 18th August, 1558, an offering was made for the repose of her soul.
31. "on great counter". Counter has various meanings: a table marked for coins, a serving front in a shop, a money chest and shapes for counting, all of which denote business activities.
32. An ancient measure, varying from 10–18 acres of arable land; an area which could be ploughed by an ox in one year.
33. "Peck", old measure of capacity, about 9 litres.
34. Chambers I E p. 102, appendix II; I D p. 400 appendix II according to Robson's British Herald I, p. 75.
35. Vita I. p. 1.
36. The manuscript is in the Institute Archives, Munich. On the first page of the manuscript is a remark in another handwriting: Pageti, secretario del Cardinal Burghesio. But Pagetti is not named among Cardinal Borghese's secretaries in the Vatican Archives' list. He may have been the secretary of Prince Borghese.
37. Pagetti p. 2.
38. Staatsbibl. Munich, Clm 1971.
39. He made his profession in the Augsburg Chorherrenstift of Holy Cross in Babenhausen, Swabia. F. A. Veith, Bibliotheca Augustana, complectens notitias varias de vita et scriptis eruditorum quos Augusta Vindelica orbi litterato vel dedit vel aluit II, Augsburg 1786, p. 27–29.
40. Bissel, pp. 5–6.
41. Five manuscripts are still extant. Two copies are in the Institute Archives in Altoetting, and one copy is in each of the Institute archives in Rome, Munich and Ascot. The Rome copy was used here.
42. Fr Lohner, SJ was close to the Englishwomen in Munich, and their confessor. He esteemed Mary Ward greatly. B. Duhr, Gesch. d. Jesuiten in den Ländern deutscher Zunge III, p. 546–550.
43. Lohner, p. 13.
44. Printed in 1717 by Lucas Straub in Munich.
45. Khamm, p. 3.
46. This two-volume work was issued in 1732 by Martin Happach's descendants and wife in Augsburg.
47. Fridl, vol. I, p. 3.
48. ibid, p. 2.
49. ibid. p. 3. The legendary Order of the Golden Spurs was allegedly founded by Pope Sylvester I. However, it may have come into existence in the 16th century only, as a military decoration in the Papal States. It was renewed in 1841 by Gregory XVI as the Order of Sylvester, but separated from this again in 1905 by Pius X. LthK. IX, Sp. 738.
50. Fridl, vol. I. P. 3.
51. Printed in 1735 in Augsburg by Frantz Joseph Klugheimer.

52. English version: The Life of Mary Ward (1585–1645) by Mary Catharine Elizabeth Chambers of the Institute of the Blessed Virgin Mary. Edit. by Henry James Coleridge of the Society of Jesus, vol. I, London 1882, vol. II. London 1885.
53. See p. 11.
54. Feet of Fines of the Tudor Period, Part I, YATA RS II, 1887, p. 350.
55. PRO London, Chancery Rolls, Duchy Lancaster I/96 W 21, f.50, W 21 a f.50 and W 21 b f. 51.
56. See p. 9, 10.
57. See p. 10, note 28.
58. C.T. Clay, Yorkshire Deeds VII = YATA RS 83/1932, p. 181 Nr. 525.
59. Fowler, Memorials III = Surt. Soc. 81/1886/I (1888) p. 316.
60. UYBI York, York Wills vol. 15/I, f. 35 rv.
61. 1551 Walter had inherited estates there. The Withes had possessions in Wilthorpe.
62. George Poulson, The History and Antiquities of the Seigniory of Holderness in the East Riding of the County of York II, Hull 1841, p. 516.
63. Chambers I E, p. 7 and I D, p. 7–8 as well as the writings mentioned there.
64. University Library, Hull, DHO 8/37.
65. On 19th July, 1594, the day after his burial, rights of administration of his property were granted to his widow Ursula and his oldest son John. UYBI York, Act Book, Holderness 1588–1596, f. 73v.
66. Pedigree: The Genealogist, London 1912, p. 94–100.
67. Pedigree: The Genealogist, NS London 1905, p. 264–265.
68. Vita E.f.lv. gives him erroneously as William Wright. Vita I, p. 2 adopts this mistake while praising his zeal for the Catholic church. Chambers, based on both lives, likewise calls him William.
69. AB/A pp. 8–10, Inst. Arch. Munich.
70. AB/A Inst. Arch. Munich. These notes concern years 1585–1595.
71. Vita E, f.l.r.
72. Vita I, pp. 1–2.
73. ARSI Rom, Germ. 113, pp. 46–47.
74. On 5th March 1622, ARSI Rom. Angl. 1/I f. 153v.
75. Chambers I E p. 5, notes 9 and 210 and I D p. 6, notes 10 and 11.
76. Chambers I E p. 4, I D p. 6.
77. Pagetti, pp. 2–3.
78. Bissel, p. 5.
79. Lohner, p. 14 and p. 18.
80. Fridl I, p. 4.
81. ibid. p. 5.
82. Unterberg, p. 2.
83. Feet of fines of the Tudor Period I YATA RS II, 1887, p. 350.
84. PRO London, Chancery Rolls Duchy Lancaster I/96 W 21 f.50, 21a f.50 and W 21b f. 51.
85. ibid. W 21 f. 50.
86. Genealogical table: George Poulson, The History and Antiquities of the Seigniory of Holderness in the East Riding of the county of York, II. Hull 1841, p. 516.
87. ibid.
88. Genealogical table: J. Foster, Visitation of Yorkshire, London 1875, p. 506.
89. UYBI York, Act Book Holderness 1575 to 1582 s.f.
90. SLAL, Ingleby Records Nr. 364.
91. AB/A p. 7. Inst. Arch. Munich.

92. Dodd's Church History of England from the Commencement of the Six-teenth Century to the Revolution in 1688, III, p. 161. John Cumberford was 80 years old. John Almond 70. Both were priests.
93. ibid. p. 161–162.
94. PRO, London. Patent Rolls 4th pars, 20 Elizabeth (1578) Membrane 31, C 66/1167.
95. 23 Eliz. c. 1. Statutes of the Realm IV, p. 657.

II

MARY – THE DAUGHTER
Mulwith (1585–1590)

Birth – baptismal name – first words – childhood memories – birth of her brother David – her father as bailiff of the Earl of Northumberland's property in Spofforth Park – her uncle Christopher Ward of Newby, recusant – the manor of Mulwith – her father's lease to secure their properties – birth of her sisters Frances and Elizabeth.

In 1585, the year in which war began on the high seas between England and Spain, while the Jesuits were pursuing their hidden and successful missions up and down the country and people were being sent into exile[1], Ursula Ward gave birth to her first child on 23rd January,[2]. It was a girl, and according to the first two biographies she received the baptismal name of Johanna.[3]

The Italian Life gives for good measure the name of the saints honoured on that day: St Emerentiana, St John the Almoner, and St Ildefonsus. The holy martyr Emerentiana, according to the author, blessed the newly-born child with a steadfast desire for martyrdom, while St John endowed her with her love for the poor and St Ildefonsus, her devotion to Mary. Both biographies – and this one too – give the baptismal name of the small girl as Johanna, with the name of Mary added by her at confirmation. This may be correct, but certain difficulties arise – where was Mary Ward baptised? Ripon parish registers are incomplete. It is possible, of course, that Mary Ward was baptised secretly, though neither of the two sources hint that. One might also ask, where was Mary Ward confirmed? The last catholic Archbishop of York, Nicholas Heath, had already been removed from his see by 1559. The sacrament of confirmation should, by rights, be administered by a bishop, and we have no information that in those days soon after the Council of Trent (1563) any exception had been made in this respect, either through delegation of the faculty to one or more deans, of which there were still several, or to a member of one of the religious orders.

Could Mary have been confirmed in England at all? It is possible that she received this sacrament in Flanders. We know that the

Bishop of St Omer confirmed certain young girls in the English-women's chapel in the town of St Omer, some years later.[4] There are indications that it was shortly after her arrival in St Omer that Mary Ward entered the convent of the Walloon Poor Clares. There would have been ample time to prepare for and receive the sacrament; it is hard to believe that she would have been accepted and permission given for her to be professed without having been confirmed. In which case the change of her baptismal name would only have been for a short time, as the Poor Clares adopt a religious name. It was at just that time that some young English sisters of the convent took an additional name – 'of St John'. Elisabeth Darrel was given the name of Lucy of St John, Margaret Fowler, Clare of St John, Anne Brook, Anne of St John; a young Belgian too was called Antoinette of St John. Two sisters had the name of St Stephen: the novice mistress Mary Goudge was called Mary of St Stephen, and Ellen Burton, Clare of St Stephen. Two other sisters were given or kept the name of St Francis; Frances Courtes was called, after her profession, Frances of St Thomas and Anne Tholward, Anne of St Francis.[5] These were sisters who entered at the same time as Mary Ward, either in St Omer or in Gravelines. Certainly, Mary Ward could have considered taking the name of the Mother of God as a religious name, or it could have been chosen for her, say Mary of St John. No one could have known at that time that she would not be taking her vows as a Poor Clare. However, all that is supposition and without proof. It is rather strange, though, that Mary Ward herself does not say a word about it, although her confirmation and the change of one's name in religious life were certainly worth mentioning. Facts about her religious formation rank high in her writings. However it came about, the oldest daughter of Marmaduke Ward was called Mary in every one of the sources.[6]

We know hardly anything of the first years of her life. A child of tender years does not make history, at least, not of its own accord. The English Life describes the small child as destined for heaven from birth.[7] That is to say, in the opinion of the authoress, she had none of the defects normal to children of her age, but was endowed with all that was agreeable and pleasant. [8] In general this view would appear to correspond to the truth. Her later life gives sufficient proof of her distinguished and yet friendly manner, but she would not have been a lively child if she had not been up to something now and again.

Both the Lives tell us the following episode from the earliest days of her life.[9] The small child could not yet speak and was barely able to walk when she was one day in danger of having an accident. Horrified, her mother exclaimed, 'Jesus, bless my child!' Upon which the child turned and repeated the word 'Jesus' clearly. It was her first, and for several months, her only word. The Painted Life begins its series of fifty pictures with a portrayal of the story.[10]

It is a reminder of the scene in her father's room, when Mary was playing with a small friend and repeated the oath 'By Christ's wounds', to gain her father's attention. Something similar happened during her stay in Ploughland. When her grandmother ordered some chickens to be prepared for prisoners, Mary declared that she too would like to send the hen that she had been given as a present a short time before. Later she was to write frankly and without excuse, 'This seemed to please her much, but I said it only to gain her esteem'.[11] Fridl alone[12] mentions the scene when she swore, and Marmaduke's outraged reaction, though he does not translate it correctly; the other writings are silent about both these happenings. How should one judge them? One is inclined to look upon her as a child who is looking for attention and love, sometimes even at the expense of others, until one reflects. In her writings, Mary Ward exposes the weaknesses in her character, and even exaggerates them, in order to give all the honour to God for his providence and support. She most certainly saw it in that way, in retrospect, and did not intentionally discredit herself. Her extremely sensitive conscience, refined by prayer, self-examination and striving after virtue for years, looked on her faults and the few good features she had, as though seen through a prism, and magnified.

In all fairness too it must not be forgotten that Mary Ward was extremely shy. Later, she blushed easily and was inclined to draw back diffidently. But in these instances the shy child is trying to attract the attention, or rather, the love of those whom she loves. Reserved people are always lonely. Ought not this 'failing' rather be seen as an attempt to break the barriers of introversion, by seeking contact with those close to her? It is significant that Mary Ward took decisions in this matter which cannot have been easy for her.

Saintliness is not endowed at birth, but achieved with difficulty. Her first years were probably filled with minor details, with circumstances which may have been important to her. Certainly the birth of her brother David was one, when he was born before 16th November, 1588.[13] The importance of this event, the beginning of the life of a new human being, she would certainly not have grasped at three years old, and yet it was of significance in her world. Health and sickness, joys and sorrows, would have come in turn; a young life, monotonous and yet full of excitements, enjoyed and suffered in a rich, enclosed world.

In this smaller circle of her family something happened to cause quite a stir. On 8th September, 1585, the very year of her birth, Sir Henry Percy, 9th Earl of Northumberland, deputed Marmaduke Ward as Bailiff for life of his properties in Spofforth, northwest of Wetherby, and as Keeper of Spofforth Park.[14] It was an honourable and lucrative post. The estates, buildings, farming, servants and employees and, not least, the defence of the whole property, came under the supervision of the Bailiff. He had to make regular reports to the Earl about his affairs, and Marmaduke did that most conscientiously.[15] Specialized knowledge of a variety of fields was presupposed for such a position, as well as a good reputation, and the ability to establish friendly contacts.

Who was this Henry Percy, Earl of Northumberland? Members of the Norman family of Percy, in England since 1066, were among the Tudors' most dangerous enemies. Thomas Percy, brother of the 6th Earl, Henry, had been hanged in 1536 because he was catholic. His son Thomas succeeded as 7th Earl and was also hanged in 1572. The 8th Earl, Henry Percy, encountered the same fate. He had twice been imprisoned in the Tower and died there because he had taken part in the attempt to free Mary Stuart and been implicated in the Throckmorton Plot. After his death in 1585, his son Henry succeeded him. This Henry Percy was born in 1564. He was very young, about 21 years old, when he came into his vast inheritance. At first he was regarded with a certain mistrust by the government in London. Percy spent his youth in the south of England and was frequently there later, on one or other of his estates. In 1585–88, he did military service and became Governor of Tynemouth, one of the most important ports in the county of Northumberland. His marriage to an Anglican made him appear more trustworthy in the eyes of those in power. In 1599 he was made General over the northern counties and Justice of the Peace.[16] Yet, he remained an enigma. He played a double role, as he was later involved in the Gunpowder Plot, which he financed in large measure out of his enormous means. He was imprisoned in the Tower for sixteen years, until 1621.

It was to this man that Marmaduke Ward owed his important office. It would be interesting to know if Marmaduke had applied for it himself, or if a recommendation had been made by someone else, say by Thomas Percy, a cousin of the Earl, who had been appointed his agent in the north. Thomas may even at that time have had connections with the Wright family, for some years later, on 21st November, 1591, he married Martha Wright, Ursula Wright's sister and Mary Ward's aunt. In 1605 Thomas Percy was one of the arch-plotters and seems even to have been the organiser of the Gunpowder Plot. He died on 9th November, 1605, at the plotter's hide-out at Holbeach.

It would be equally interesting to know why Marmaduke accepted the post. It was an honourable position, but there were probably other reasons. There was, after all, sufficient work for him on his own estates. Of one thing we can be certain, Marmaduke Ward, his employer Henry Percy and his agent, Thomas Percy would not have conversed merely about things agricultural. The difficult position of catholics has already been emphasized. Mary Ward had hardly begun to take her first steps when her great-uncle, Christopher Ward of Newby, suffered a setback. On 6th August, 1586, a summons was issued to Ninian Buck of Thornton, Henry Withes of Bridge Hewick – certainly a relation of Alison Ward nee Withes – and his wife, and also Christopher Ward of Newby, to appear before the justices.[17] They were under suspicion of not having communicated during the past year in the Anglican church. Notice of such offence would be brought usually through the Anglican clergy or the churchwarden, or sometimes naturally enough from personal enemies. Then followed one or more warnings, and finally the summons. It can therefore be assumed that Christopher Ward had been under observation for some time, for there is reference to the past year.The suspect would be ordered to receive communion in the Anglican church upon which, on the following 16th September, a certificate would be produced. From this it is evident that the State Church was forced to take drastic measures. Christopher Ward had not put in an appearance, which meant that he had taken no notice of the final order. He was henceforth declared a recusant (et Dominus Ward pronunciatus contumax). This resulted in house-searches, higher fines, and limitations of his freedom of movement to a radius of five miles.

In 1588 Marmaduke Ward was able to increase his property considerably. On 19th February,[18] for reasons unknown, he took possession of the manor of Oulston from Thomas Posthumus Hoby of Hackness, until the majority of the youthful owner, William Redshaw.[19] Towards the end of the year, on 16th November[20] Marmaduke purchased for himself, his wife Ursula and his son David all the feudal tenures and the Manor with appurtenances of Mulwith by Givendale from the Hospital of St Mary Magdalen in Ripon. Only after this did Marmaduke become 'Lord' of Mulwith, although he had previously been working the property. It has been mentioned earlier that in 1546/7 his grandmother Alison and his father Walter Ward had paid eight pounds for a tenement in Mulwith. The contract concluded by Marmaduke for himself, his wife and his son, was to hold until the death of the last survivor.

Three weeks after taking possession of Oulston, on 5th December,[21] Marmaduke concluded an agreement with a Christopher Daye from North Lees. It may be that the contract was common at that time, but it strikes one as curious. In it, Marmaduke leased premises with appurtenances in Horsefayr Street in Ripon, previously possessed by one Richard Thornton, as well as four acres of arable land by Bishopton, which Christopher Daye had owned, for the price of six pounds, thirteen shillings and four pence and a yearly tax of twenty-four shillings and two shillings to a Lord Parr. Christopher Daye took possession of the building in Ripon, Marmaduke took responsibility for the necessary repairs. So far, so good. Now comes the final clause: should the possession be withdrawn from Christopher Daye by law, and possession be given to another, it would return to Marmaduke Ward with corresponding compensation by Christopher Daye. The contract had already come into force on 29th September, 1588. It was so defined lest creditors – in the event of Christopher Daye's possible insolvency – could lay hands also on the Ward properties, of course without the agreed tax. By this clause, Marmaduke had from the outset taken his property thus pledged out of any possible future distraint on Christopher Daye's estate. Were Christopher Daye to be brought to trial on religious grounds, the authorities could deprive him of his property. Marmaduke Ward would, of course, remain the landlord, but his tenant could possibly be an enemy. Were Marmaduke Ward accused and his goods confiscated, this lease would be valid for ten years at least and would remain in the assuredly safe hands of Christopher Daye.

More of such manoeuvres will be met, for they were the means by which catholics sought to protect their property against the insatiable appetite of their enemies. As has been said, on 8th September, 1588, Marmaduke Ward became the Earl of North-umberland's bailiff in Spofforth Park. Now, barely five years later, on 8th April, 1590,[22] the Earl leased to his bailiff and four other landowners the whole of the pasture-land, rights of pasture and buildings in the enclosure of Spofforth Park. The right of forestry, coal-mining and quarrying he reserved to himself. The agreement was valid for twenty-one years, until 1611, and the rent amounted to the colossal sum of £100 a year, payable at two appointed times. This involved a rent of twenty pounds a year for each lessee. The agreement seems baffling, for here was Marmaduke Ward leasing lands that he was to administer for the Earl, moreover it was a very extensive property and the annual rent amounted to two and a half times the tax that he had to pay for the Mulwith estate.

What did it mean? The answer probably lies in the equally baffling contract which Marmaduke concluded a short two months later, on 1st June, 1590,[23] with a distant relative, Sir William Ingleby of Ripley Castle. In this agreement, Marmaduke trans-ferred the Manor of Oulston for the time stated, the Manor of Mulwith for fifty years and his position in Spofforth for the time of his life. One is inclined to ask – who owned what? Precisely. It is very uncertain that there was any actual transfer of the prop-erties mentioned. Marmaduke's entire acquisitions and all of his income from his occupation hardly point to ruined finances, rather the contrary. But in 1586 his uncle Christopher Ward had been listed as a recusant; Marmaduke and his wife Ursula were too, just three months after the transfer of their property on 12th August, 1590.[24] Several warnings preceded this legal declaration, which carried severe financial consequences for those concerned. This can be assumed in Marmaduke Ward's case also, though there is no proof for it. The agreement with William Ingleby is doubtless to be taken as a safeguard for Marmaduke's properties. Ostensibly, these have been leased for nine years, but theoretically only. The final clause of the contract reveals that. Theoretically, the properties belonged to William Ingleby but only in the eventuality of Marmaduke not meeting the large sum of £50 annually.

If Marmaduke were convicted, the property could not be requisitioned; he possessed the benefits (usufructs) merely, and William the title, again, only if Marmaduke failed in his obligations.[25] Before the blow fell, Marmaduke protected himself as far as possible: with four others, he owned rights of pasture for his cattle in Spofforth Park and knew that his property was in the hands of a relative.

It is not clear whether that extremely high tax had to be paid, but as far as other things went, there was little change. When Mulwith burnt on 2nd February, 1595,[26] Marmaduke and his family were living there, and on 24th May[27] of the same year Sir Henry Percy handed over to Sampson Ingleby, the brother of William Ingleby, Marmaduke Ward's position in Spofforth Park.

During this difficult time, Ursula Ward bore her fourth child. On 30th April, 1591,[28] a year after her sister Frances, Elizabeth Ward was born. Before this, Marmaduke had sent his oldest little daughter to his parents-in-law.

Ploughland

(1590 – 94/5)

The Wright family in Ploughland – Mary Ward, her grand-mother and her aunt Alice Redshaw – her spiritual life

The Wright's large estate Ploughland, near Welwick in Holderness, no longer exists. In the sixteenth century, judging by Mary Ward's description, there must have been a considerable dwelling place there. Robert Wright and his second wife Ursula lived there in 1590 and the youngest daughters were then very likely still at home. Nothing has come down to us about the children from the first marriage to Anne Grimston. From this second marriage, the eldest son John was twenty-one at this time, and his brother Christopher eighteen. Both were interested in politics and involved in them; both were imprisoned in the White Lion in London in 1600 for taking part in the Essex Plot, with John being put into solitary confinement.[29] It was obviously a tendency they had inherited. Their mother had spent long years in prison before she took Mary into her house in 1590, and her two daughters must have been much younger than their brothers. Martha Wright was married soon after Mary Ward's arrival, in November 1591, to Thomas Percy, already mentioned as agent to Henry Percy, Earl of Northumberland; two years

later, in December 1593, there took place the clandestine marriage of
Alice Wright to William Redshaw[30] in Marmaduke Ward's house.

Why did Marmaduke Ward send his young daughter, to whom
he was devoted, to his parents-in-law, in remote Ploughland? It is
a question that cannot be answered with certainty. Not even Mary
Ward knew the reason.[31] If we try to recapture the situation of the
family in Mulwith, we find Marmaduke and his wife under threat of
conviction of recusancy. Such a threat had already become a reality
long before in Ploughland, and Ursula Ward would have remembered what it meant to have a mother in prison. The child Mary
herself, in her five-year-old simplicity could have chatted away and
let something slip — say, about Mass in the house, or of a priest
in hiding, which would have called down greater reprisals than
among the long-recognised recusant Wright family. Again, it was
customary in those days to send children to relatives or friends,
though this as a social practice would have been strange for the
Wards to have followed in their ambiguous situation. A solution
that makes good sense could lie in the fact that Ursula Ward was
awaiting her third child; her second daughter, Frances, was born in
this year.[32] Three small children in circumstances which could entail
any sudden removal to prison would aggravate the dangers of their
position. A year later Elizabeth was born[33] and again a year later,
Barbara.[34] It is perfectly possible that what had been planned as a
short stay developed into one lasting five years, particularly if Mary
had settled down happily in Ploughland. It is not known what was
arranged for the other children; they too may have been accommodated elsewhere temporarily.

The narrative sources are silent about Mary's stay with her grandparents. If it were not for her own account[35] we would simply find,
in Lohner[36] and Unterberg[37] the fact that she spent five years with
her grandparents. Neither of them adds where this was, far from
giving any details. Fridl[38] is somewhat fuller, but vague. Chambers[39]
keeps to the text of the autobiographical fragments, but hardly adds
what can be termed a commentary. And yet Mary Ward's own
information gives important signals for the understanding of her
personality. In the first place, she describes her grandmother as a
woman of rare and noble qualities: righteous, catholic in belief and
unshakeable in her adherence to it. When Mary Ward was brought
to Ploughland, Ursula Wright had been released from prison only
two years before. She was obviously extremely vigilant in her care of
the child entrusted to her. She hardly ever let her out of her sight, in
case she should fall into idle or bad company. The grandmother had
good reason for such caution. Ploughland was not entirely a haven
of irreproachable behaviour; immorality was present there too.

Mary Ward does not name the person, but she had a relative
in the house who led a frivolous life under the influence of her
maid. One suspects that this was Alice Wright.[40] If a man or maid

servant had shown any such tendencies, they would have been dismissed on the spot, which is why we may turn in all justice to Alice, Ursula Wright's daughter. As Mary Ward relates, Alice had taken into her service a young girl who seemed outwardly respectable but in actual fact led a loose life and had a harmful influence on her young mistress.

It must be remarked here that it is unthinkable that Ursula Wright did not keep an eye on her own daughter. But there is no guarantee that Alice had not become lax during the long years of her mother's imprisonment and now, as a young married woman who possessed a certain amount of independence, had engaged this girl as a lady's maid.

At all events, Mary Ward noticed her relative acting in ways that were not correct, although they could not be judged dishonourable. Once, certainly, she saw a man in her room 'where her mother never allowed a man admission'. There was something going on of which Ursula Wright had no knowledge. But was it all so dubious? We know that Mary Ward set an extremely high standard when judging her own failings. She names some of these: she asked for her fortune to be told, and believed the nonsense. Fortune-telling and astrology were held in esteem in England in those days, especially among women. She had probably been forecast a happy future, because she rejoiced at what it disclosed. Also, on one occasion, she planned to fast on St Agnes' Eve. On 20th January, the night before St Agnes' feast, marriageable maidens fasted in the hope of seeing their future husbands in a dream. Her relative, who went in for this fast, persuaded her to do the same. Then once, Mary continues, she caused the forbidden 'sieve and scissors' to be used.[41] She tried this kind of flummery because she wanted to find a trifle that she had mislaid. All in all, they were not serious failings. What was more dangerous was the likelihood of her coming under the influence of this attractive girl with a zest for life, who fostered an inclination to mischief. Both were drawn to one another. Whenever it was possible to leave her grandmother, Mary went to Alice. There she was initiated into plans and projects and treated as an equal. It could have done her great harm, she reflects in her notes, if God had not protected her.[42]

When she was writing her memoirs later, she was of the more mature opinion that she should have reported what was going on, but Alice had sworn her to secrecy. Mary Ward writes 'as far as I can judge, I felt myself inclined by nature to say nothing about it.' This silence, she believed, had been the cause of the later downfall of this relative. If, in the beginning, all this had been brought to the attention of someone in authority, then her later life would have been different and not the cause of such scandal.

Two qualities of character are shown here: the ability to keep confidences, and awareness of responsibility. Mary Ward was a shy but sharply observant child; she knew how to keep silence, and she was true to her word. Loyalty and chivalry − even for a woman − were underlying principles with her. Later, as will be seen, she was extremely careful in her remarks about others. She must have had a keen insight into good and evil, even as a young girl. Evil frightened her. For, at the end she writes, 'I am morally certain that in the carrying out of these last three (fortune-telling, fasting and 'sieve and scissors'), I experienced some fear, and an understanding that they could be sinful.'

The perception of evil, and fear of it, are closely related. For those striving for holiness they are inextricably bound together; in the deepest awareness of their being, they experience evil in all its fearfulness as the one real tragedy of life.

Her spiritual life in these years was uneventful. Mary saw her own character during her stay in Ploughland as insignificant compared to the personality of her heroic grandmother. She writes: 'I did not practise any virtue. When my grandmother commanded me to pray, I sat in the place but spent my time in sports. Yet I did not lack quickness in order to seek cunningly to have my own will often from others, and to excuse it, sometimes openly or otherwise.' Even God needs time.

Mulwith

(1585 − 1598)

Settling into Mulwith − her parents as recusants − Mulwith in ashes − Mary and prayer to Our Lady − her fall and its consequences

The summer of 1594 brought the death of Robert Wright and at the turn of the year 1594/5 Marmaduke Ward fetched his little daughter home to Mulwith.[43] Things had changed here in ways that ten-year-old Mary could not have failed to notice. Her father's estate had become smaller and so, consequently, had his income as provider for the family. The reason was not far to seek. Marmaduke and his wife had to pay enormous sums in fines as recusants. They were not the only ones to do so. Among the hundreds upon hundreds of entries on the parchment rolls, the 'Recusant Rolls'[44] in the Record Office in London, are the names of the following, and the amount of the fines:

Jana Wise (= Jane Withes), wife of Simon Wise of Clint	40 pounds;
Ursula Ward, wife of Marmaduke Ward of Newby,	40 pounds;
NN Ward, wife of Marmaduke Ward of Mulwith	40 pounds;
NN Ward, wife of Robert Ward, formerly of Mulwith	240 pounds;

Jane Withes, wife of Simon Withes, formerly of Clint   120 pounds;
Henry Ward from the parish of Mickleton,   20 pounds.

It is worth noting that in certain cases these amounts represent the remaining amounts of a much higher sum that had been imposed as a fine. Like Jane Withes, Mary Ward's mother was apparently fined twice over. Her husband is indeed given once as from Mulwith and another time as from Newby, but that is easily explained. Recusants frequently changed their place of residence, in order to evade the constant shadowing of spies, neighbours, or Anglican clergy. It did not always succeed, for recusants were fair game.

Of the few years spent in her parents' house, Mary Ward describes only one, very unhappy, event – the destruction of her father's manor by fire. On 2nd February, 1595, the feast of Our Lady, Candlemas, a fire broke out. Mary Ward was at home and was aware of the danger. Her statement could lead one to believe that she had been outside the house and from there had seen the fire beginning. That this was not the case is made clear by the second narrative. Three of Marmaduke's five children were on a high storey of the house, and they were alone. At first it seems, it did not appear to be dangerous; it was only when she heard the noise made by the people who had gathered outside that Mary realised their real danger. Immediately she took her two sisters, Elizabeth and Barbara, and went into a lower room, one nearer the ground floor. A chest stood there, filled with linen which Mary's mother had put aside for her trousseau. The children pushed this chest to the fireplace, sat on it, and began to pray. They could easily have been burnt to death, Mary continues in her narrative. As the house was in flames and there was no possibility of saving it, her father called his children to him. Temporarily, in the excitement, the three girls had been overlooked. When he realised that they were missing, he immediately rushed back into the burning house and saved them. On closer examination, the children's behaviour is rather extraordinary, Mary's above all, because Elizabeth was only four years old and Barbara two and a half. Granted, at first they probably did not know what was happening, but after that most ten-year-olds would have tried to get out, or at least shouted for help. We are confronted with this baffling behaviour of Mary's. We have heard of her as a timorous child. At the beginning of her account she writes that already in 'younger years' she had a great confidence in the power and help of our Lady. One can take it for granted that the Ward family had celebrated the feast of the Purification of Our Lady's Candlemas in some form or other on this 2nd February. To be sure, there were not many opportunities for recusants to celebrate, but Mary's enormous trust in Our Lady must have been aroused and fostered in the family circle. This confidence was the child's first reaction when she perceived the danger '. . . then

I called on our Blessed Lady, beseeching her to extinguish the fire; often repeated, with great confidence that were it not her feast, I should fear the worst'... Then she continues, that as 'this day was dedicated to her, I had no doubt but that she would help.' Even in those days children's prayers pierced the clouds. If we compare this confident prayer with her statement that in Ploughland she had no particular inclination for prayer, it is remarkable what rapid progress this young girl had made in the spiritual life, even if we know that extreme need is prayer's best tutor.[45]

It would be interesting to know what caused the fire. Was it a fire in a fireplace which, had it been discovered in time, could have been put out? It was in the middle of winter, and the children would certainly have been kept in a heated room. Was it from an open fire too close to the house? Mary Ward implored our Lady to 'put out the fire'. Or was it arson? In view of what was to happen in the next few years, one wonders.

The family probably remained only a short time longer in Mulwith. The manor may have been in ruins, but Marmaduke possessed other farms there. His grandmother Alison and his father Walter had acquired property in Mulwith. At the end of the Easter term of the legal year in 1597, Marmaduke had made over two properties in Mulwith and Newby to Henry Topham[46] with authority against an eventual claim on the part of his son and heir, David. This was a transfer in actual fact. Shortly afterwards Marmaduke and his family left Mulwith for, a year later, on 8th February, 1598[47] he is signing himself as Marmaduke Ward of Topcliffe Great Park. He was once again in one of the properties of the Earl of Northumberland, not very far away on the north side of Boroughbridge. Together with William Redshaw of Oulston, John Wright of Oulston and Richard Milner of London, Marmaduke Ward signed a pledge for the extremely high sum of 500 pounds. The creditor was Anthony Wade, probably from the family of Wades settled in Yorkshire from which came Armigal Wade, who was called the English Columbus on account of his expeditions. His son Sir William Wade was Lord Lieutenant of the Tower of London in 1605. A great number of the prisoners, among them survivors of the Gunpowder Plot, were left to his cruelly inventive methods of torture. Concerning those who also signed the pledge for 500 pounds: William Redshaw, who married Alice Wright, has already been mentioned. He will be referred to again in other sources in connection with Richard Milner. On 21st January, 1598 he was warned of this Milner, who was threatening his marriage.[48] John Wright of Oulston is undoubtedly John Wright of Ploughland, who had at this time a house in Twigmore, Lincolnshire and in 1605 also had a house in Lapworth, Worcestershire.

The pledge was duly drawn up in Westminster before the Court of Common Pleas, as a Staple Statute. This was a legal procedure according to a statue of 1531. By this means the creditor had good legal means for the quickest and surest recovery of his money. The debtor had to answer with his entire possessions. If he did not keep to the agreement, he was under obligation for the sum in question to the Crown, whose authorities had their own methods for obtaining the money.[49]

The date of repayment was set as 25th March. That was little more than six weeks. Those who signed it therefore borrowed a large sum of capital for a very short time. In Marmaduke Ward's case, and perhaps that of the others, it can be suspected that as recusants they could not pay their way without endangering what possessions they still owned.

With the exception of Pagetti and Lohner, all the biographies describe an incident that happened at this time.[50] Mary Ward herself says nothing about it. One evening, probably after a somewhat excited game, and before the children were taken to bed, Mary wanted to be carried on the shoulder of one of the maids. This she did. Perhaps in her excitement the child made an unexpected movement; at all events, she fell on the ground and hit her head hard on the flagstones. She could not speak, and was quickly carried to her bed by the horrified woman. The devil, so it was said, was seeking the child's life. But Mary was fully conscious and thought that if she could just speak the name of Jesus once, then she would be ready for death. When she finally managed to say His name, she felt an unspeakable inner joy, and was perfectly well. The event is undoubtedly genuine, but the child may have had a shock which can result in exhaustion of bodily power without loss of consciousness. It is also possible that it was a momentary contraction of the diaphragm, as can happen with nervous and delicate children after a violent blow. It is clear that the child, during those anxious and frightening moments, wanted to say the name of Jesus. Did Mary want to die? Probably the child thought that she was about to die, and wanted to say the name of Jesus once more. She then recovered.

It is not certain if the whole of the Ward family, which now included six children, could be accommodated in Topcliffe Great Park. But Mary had to leave the family, which was now considerably poorer. What happened to the rest of the children, to David, who was about two years younger than Mary, or to Frances, who was already seven years old, we do not know. The younger children probably remained with their parents.[51]

Harewell

(1598 – 1600)

Move to Harewell – Mrs Catherine Ardington – requests for Mary's hand according to the narrative sources – Marmaduke's message – first communion

Not far from Ripon and south-west from Ripley Castle in rolling hill country lies an old, sixteenth-century house. It stands at some height and offers a good view of the surroundings, an absolute necessity for recusants, who had to be prepared day and night for raids and house-searches. This applied to anyone suspected of harbouring a priest. Even today the house stands almost alone. Low, drystone walls, typical of Yorkshire, enclose the fields. The countless flocks of sheep constitute the farmer's wealth.

This was the home of Mrs Catherine Ardington, daughter of Sir William Ingleby of Ripley Castle, and a distant connection of Mary Ward. In 1586/7 and 1594 she had been taken from her home here in Nidderdale and put into the ill-famed city prison in York,[52] but she remained steadfast in her catholicism. The house had a hiding-hole, reached by a secret passage where priests took refuge from the pursuivants. Mrs Ardington offered help to other recusants, and Marmaduke Ward found her ready to accept his daughter into her household.

We have nothing in Mary Ward's own writings of these two or three years of her life. The short entry about the perplexity caused her by a messenger would seem to have occurred during the time of her stay with Lady Babthorpe.

The oldest biographies of the seventeenth and eighteenth centuries, however, do include an extraordinary event. To understand it, a brief interruption must be made in the chronological course of her life's history, so that the time between years 1595 – 1606 can be considered from a particular angle.

One may picture the girl Mary Ward grown tall, slim, fair-haired and with blue eyes. She was finely featured, and held herself well – this she was to do all her life, despite a wearing illness. It was inevitable that this glowing young creature attracted the interest of young men, although she was very reserved and withdrawn, and not at all encouraging in this respect. As far as suitors for her hand were concerned, that was all there was to it. The oldest biographies are here not consistent in their statements. If we follow the chronological order of the early biographies, the English Life comes first. Her own record of this is extremely spare.

Because Mary Ward was the eldest daughter and, – so it says – beautiful and the cause of great expectations by her parents, they were seeking out a suitable husband for her from her tenth year. An eligible one was indeed found, and one recommended by a relative, the Earl of Northumberland.[53] The child liked the young man, who had to travel to London on business and died there some months later.[54] The ten year old soon forgot him. The second advance was made in Harewell. That is, her father informed her in writing of an offer he had received from a Talbot of Grafton.[55] A third suitor appeared when Mary was thirteen, therefore in 1598. The English Life[56] mentions no name, but this must have taken place in Harewell, as Mary remained there until 1600. And once more, seven years later, she received an offer from an unnamed man who later became a priest.[57]

The Italian Life likewise names four suitors, giving the last as Neville of Westmoreland.[58]

In his biography Pagetti accepts the youthfulness of the intended bride, and also that Mary had been sought after by the Earl of Northumberland himself as his wife.[59] This cannot be correct, as the extremely rich Earl, Henry Percy, married Lady Dorothy Devereux in 1595, an Anglican and sister of Robert Devereux, 2nd Earl of Essex. Henry Percy was, up to then, a claimant to the throne in the eyes of catholics, who wished to see him married to Lady Arabella Stuart. It is not likely that a man with such high aspirations would have sought the hand of Mary Ward, however old and wealthy her family. Pagetti does not name any other suitors.

Bissel[60] knows of four suitors, and names them. In the first place he adopts the information of the English and Italian Lives, then names the first suitor as Redshaw, identified by Pagetti as the Earl of Northumberland. It is not clear who is meant. As is known, a William Redshaw had been married to Alice Wright, from the end of 1593. Bissel is informed of a second suitor when Mary Ward was twelve years old and probably still in Mulwith, a Shafto from Northumberland.[61] As the third, Bissel names the Earl of Shrewsbury, (Talbot) who sought her hand during her stay in Harewell.[62] And finally a Rudolf Eldrington,[63] knight of the golden spurs, tried his luck. All were rejected.

The Painted Life, too, shows four suitors for Mary's hand.[64] The same number is given by Lohner[65] though his sequence is different : Redshaw – Shafto – Eldrington – Neville, the last being claimant to the title of Earl of Westmoreland.

Khamm[66] takes all the names together and so counts five candidates in the series: Redshaw – Shafto – Talbot of Grafton – Eldrington – Neville of Westmoreland. This number stands in Fridl's account [67] and that of Unterberg.[68]
Chambers follows Lohner and the Painted Life.[69]

If we have spent so much time over what was relatively unimportant in Mary Ward's life, it is to show that the writings of the seventeenth and eighteenth centuries must be treated with caution. The further in time from the event, the more imaginative is the presentation.

And Mary Ward? What does she say? She mentions three suitors without giving their names. As we have already noticed in Ploughland, she was discreet. Her references, which naturally carry most credibility, relate to the time when she was staying with the Babthorpe family in 1600, when she was fifteen. It is worth giving the words of her text. She writes[70] that her parents hoped 'that I would be sooner drawn into marriage living abroad, than I had been at home. (Though I refused not those they offered me because of any desire to be a religious, nor for any other reason than that I could not like them).This latter, as I have since thought, was the chief cause they (her parents) sent me from them, though I remember the first (the climate) was particularly alleged, and both might well be true, for they loved me dearly.'

This text is retained in the Italian Life.[71] In another fragment,[72] she writes, 'My parents, who were very pious, in no way wanted to give their permission (to enter a convent) because I was the oldest and they loved me much, especially my father. So I had to wait six years and several months in England. At that time, there were several offers which in the world would be seen as happy.' Those were the facts of the matter.

We have doubts about the statement that Marmaduke Ward wanted to find a husband for his 'tenderly loved' daughter when she was ten years old, although we recognise that marriage between children was not rare in those days. Marmaduke Ward probably tried later, when Mary Ward wanted to enter. But to return to Harewell, where the thirteen year old had been sent. The narrative sources give a good deal of space to an event which is supposed to have taken place there.

One day, towards evening, a man on horseback came and asked to speak to Mary Ward. He was in great haste and showed her a letter from her father, which he was allowed to read to her but not to hand over. In it Marmaduke ordered her to stop the preparations for her first communion, as he had a prospective match for her, with a Talbot of Grafton. Having said this, the rider left. Mary was in great uncertainty. Should she disobey her father? She shunned the chapel, until God reproached her ingratitude, upon which she received communion at the next opportunity. Thus the English Life.[73]

The Painted Life shows the event in one of the most beautiful of its panels (No 6). To the right of the picture is a grand castle with red-washed walls and defensive towers, and an entrance flanked with columns and surmounted by a balcony. The building is enclosed by a simple farm fence. Roundabout, in the French style, there is a park in which two ladies are walking. In the middle of the picture is Mary Ward in a brocade dress with a rich ruff, upright

and graceful; behind her, at a fitting distance, a maid. Mary's hand
is outstretched, but beyond the fence is the rider, in red hose and
wearing a breastplate, a brown cape thrown carelessly over one
shoulder as he busily reads out the letter which he holds in his
right hand. Above, the clouds are banked up, restless and threatening. The mood of the picture catches the mystery, the lurking evil
that is concentrated in the objectionable features of the rider. Even
the horse looks on wickedly.

We have no wish to make an issue of the matter in the realm
of fables. Indeed, it is useless to speculate on the reasons for
Marmaduke's incomprehensible behaviour. They are, quite simply,
not known. The early writings break out into romantic embellish-
ments which are omitted here as they would be too much of
a digression. The later account of the event, by Unterberg, is
enough:

> the messenger was Marmaduke's valet by name Francis Carle,
> who gave Mary the information that her father had betrothed her
> to Earl Talbot of Grafton; that she should postpone communion
> till a suitable time. She later found that her father had never sent
> a message to Harewell; that it was mostly likely the hellish fiend
> himself who, assuming the appearance of a valet, wished to stop
> her from receiving communion.

If all this is unacceptable, we can be certain of one thing. It was
to become clear to Marmaduke Ward that, in the matter of her
spiritual life, Mary Ward would go her own way. It was to be a
precipitous one.

Osgodby

(1600–1606)

*The Babthorpe family – Margaret Garret's stories – call
to religious life – first asceticism, first temptations – new
suitors*

Mary Ward gives two reasons for her stay in Osgodby with the
Babthorpes: her parent's move to Northumberland where the
climate was too harsh for her delicate health, and their proposal to place her among more people than had been possible at
Harewell, in order to have better opportunity of finding a suitable
partner.[74]

It was almost certainly for reasons of security that the Wards
withdrew into Northumberland. Recusants were constantly driven
to find new hiding places or refuges. In this case, in addition,

Mary would have reached the age of sixteen on 23rd January, 1601. According to England law, on that day she would come of age in religious matters, which means that she was obliged to live as an Anglican, attend church services and receive the sacraments in the Anglican rite. If she did not comply with these State regulations, she would come under the relentless legal system of fines for recusants. Marmaduke and Ursula Ward already had a heavy charge imposed upon them. Could the parents afford to pay for their eldest daughter's loyalty to her faith in the near future? Were she to be away from home, however, especially in a position of service, she would be exempt.[75] That explains the remark in Mary Ward's account, that she was to act as companion to the lady of the house (on whom I was to attend). Nowadays one would say that she was an au pair in the Babthorpe household, with food and lodging for her duties. In this way both families benefited.

South of York, between the rivers Ouse and Derwent near Hemingborough, lies the once rich property of the Babthorpes. The family − landed gentry − was not only very wealthy but very old. Sir Ralph was the owner of the estates in 1600 and the eighteenth in line in his family.[76] He had married Lady Grace, daughter and heiress of William Birnand of Brimham. She gave him seven children; two sons, Ralph and Thomas, entered the Society of Jesus and another, Robert, became a Benedictine. Her oldest son, William, later sold the Manor of Osgodby as well as the estate in Babthorpe, and entered the service of the King of Spain. In 1635 he was killed at Ardres in France. Of the three daughters Catherine married a George Palmes from Naburn and Elisabeth a John Constable of Carenthorpe. Barbara later entered Mary Ward's Institute. Even today the old and extensive building in Babthorpe and the remains of Osgodby[77] bear witness to the great wealth of the family.

Sir Ralph and his wife were harassed mercilessly because of their catholicism. A great part of their estate was confiscated and their own lives pushed to the limit with imprisonment. For a short time Sir Ralph bent under such pressures and attended Anglican services, but through his wife's influence he later returned to the catholic church. Lady Grace was imprisoned in 1592 under that formidable president of the North, Lord Huntingdon, for two years in Sheriff Hutton Castle near York.

She spent a total of five years of her life in prison. When the family went into exile in Flanders in 1617, they were ruined financially and lived in very modest circumstances. Sir Ralph died in 1617 in Louvain; some years later Lady Grace entered St Monica's Benedictine Convent in Louvain and died there in 1635. When Mary Ward reached Osgodby in 1600 she found hospitality with this threatened but staunchly loyal family, to whom she was related on her mother's side.[78] Certainly the younger children, Ralph, Thomas and Barbara were still living at home with their parents. It is

possible that the eldest son William and his wife, and Catherine with
her husband George Palmes were also there.[79]

Mary was now fifteen years old, an age when most young people
have begun to think about themselves and their future. We have
already heard from her how she had refused suitors for the
simple reason that she did not particularly like them. So, with
an uncommitted heart, she now came under the influence of the
Babthorpe household's strictly religious regime. Its daily programme
is known.[80]

On Sundays the doors were bolted and all the inhabitants of the
house attended Mass, for the entire household was catholic. On
Sundays and feastdays a sermon was heard and religious instruction
given. During the week there was usually an opportunity to attend
Mass twice during the day, once at 6 a.m. and one at 8 a.m. Vespers
were said at 4 p.m. in the afternoon and, later in the evening, Matins.
Several of the household made one or more meditations and used
meditative forms of prayer. At least once a fortnight there was confession and reception of holy communion. At nine o'clock, after the
evening meal, they prayed a litany and went to bed. From time to
time two or three priests were lodged there. The house was like a
monastery. One has to ask oneself if Marmaduke Ward could really
have intended to send his daughter here to find a husband, especially
as she had shown so little inclination towards marriage.

It was the example of Lady Babthorpe, and the ordered life of
prayer that most of all appealed to Mary Ward; it was as if she was
drawn into its rhythm. Among this group of spiritual people she
began to seek out those who would talk with her about God. She
found what she wanted in an old, simple, but very devout maid who
looked after the chapel and probably did light work. One day Mary
and this maid Margaret Garret[81] were busy with sewing. They were
talking in this way when Margaret told a story that took place in the
days when there were still monasteries and nunneries in England. A
nun had become involved with a man and sinned seriously against her
vows. The consequences followed. After the birth of the child she was
re-admitted to the community but, among other punishments, she
was given a crushing and long humiliation for several years: whenever
the sisters went into the choir, she had to lie before the chapel or choir
door, so that the other nuns would step over her as they entered.

We have Mary's reaction to this story in two forms from her own
hand.[82] On the whole both are the same. It was neither repugnance at
the offence nor acquiescence with the harsh penalty, nor compassion
with the offender that prevailed in her, but simply and solely a high
regard for religious life in an Order which imposed such challenging
demands and saw to it that they were upheld. She soon began her
first steps in the spiritual life; she practised forms of asceticism, read
spiritual books and, above all, prayed a great deal. It was particularly the quietness of prayer that corresponded to her preference for

retirement, and she experienced the first joys of a life focussed on God. Now and again she fasted slightly but also undertook stricter forms of penance by interior and exterior mortification. For example, as an exercise in humility she tried to be taken by strangers as a maid in the house.[83] In those days of the gulf between social classes that was no small thing. The first Lives add the following incident:[84] one day when one of the maids had the itch (scabies) and had to stay in bed, Mary got into bed with her in order to overcome her great partiality for cleanliness. She became infected, and even prayed not to be healed, but found no hearing and soon recovered.

She was now avidly reading books about convent life.[85] From the 'Christian Rule of Life', which is unobtainable today,[86] she learnt to divide up the days of the week for practising various virtues, and to dedicate the different rooms of the house to different saints, in order to keep more constantly in the presence of God. On visiting the place in later years, she remembered these first practices of hers, and the house seemed like a paradise to her.[87] She still suffered from her great shyness. It took a year before she could bring herself to speak to her confessor about her vocation. And she dared not take the vow of chastity for fear of great temptation in the choice of a way of life; she even had difficulties in making a good confession. The following incident probably happened at this time. Mary Ward does not, in fact, give either names or dates, but they can be reconstructed, at least as to the time. For some years she lived, she says, in a house where another person, who loved her in an unauthorised way, also lived. She kept silent about it, but did not leave the house. One day her confessor, who directed her in spiritual matters, asked her whether the man really had shown her such behaviour. Although it was a fact, she answered the question negatively for her own sake and for that of another woman in the house. Again, as years before in Ploughland, she concealed 'what perhaps ought to have been told'. The cause of her behaviour this time did not lie in lack of appreciation of the difficulty of the situation, or in playing it down, but in a 'hidden fear that if I told the truth I should commit the sin of slander, a mortal sin.' Also, she continues, she could unconsciously have shown self-love, as her confessor had informed her that he would leave the house if the person referred to were indeed like that. In which case she would have lost her confessor, who was also her spiritual director. Two conclusions can be drawn from these vague accounts. Chronologically, it must have happened after Mary had spoken with her confessor about her plans for entering, so at the earliest, two years after her arrival at Osgodby. She also writes that the other lady who was importuned went away very soon.[88]

It is idle and not worth the trouble inquiring who this man may have been, though it could not have been any harmless youth. Mary Ward and the other woman would have reacted more boldly and the priest would not have threatened to leave. It is far more important for us to know why Mary Ward was silent. Once again, it was fear — how often we are to meet this word — fear of harming someone else and thus committing a grave sin herself. Her fresh start in life included a desire to be finished with the past and she wanted to make a general confession. But it was just then that her confessor was away for a longer time and the Jesuit who was staying in Osgodby thought she was inclined to be scrupulous. Instead of hearing her general confession, he gave her an excellent spiritual book, which was to be her tutor for long years to come. It was the 'Spiritual Combat', written by the Theatine father, Lorenzo Scupoli.[89]

From other sources we know of three priests who stayed with the Babthorpes at that time: Fr James Sharp, S.J. alias Pollard, between 1604 and 1607/8; undoubtedly Fr Richard Holtby, S.J. alias North who worked in the north of England from 1593–1605/6 and was to play a decisive part in Mary Ward's life and the secular priest John Mush. The latter took himself off to Rome at the beginning of 1602 in order to direct operations in the deplorable dissension between the secular and regular clergy in England. The Father who hesitated to hear her general confession could have been Fr Holtby; Mary Ward names him as a Jesuit. Her confessor was John Mush, who returned from Rome in November 1602 and gave her permission to make it. He knew his penitent better.

She prepared most carefully for this confession from December 1602 to Holy Saturday, 1603.[90] Still, after decades, her misdemeanours of those days were clearly remembered: lack of restraint at table — as though she could have controlled the appetite of a healthy, growing girl[91] — excessive enjoyment of food at mealtimes, even on fast days,[92] conversations at a time when she should have been in bed, and moreover those with a man she had reason to distrust,[93] and a certain inclination to self-love.[94] These slight failings are imprinted on the soul of the mature Mary Ward with the utmost clarity. It is irrelevant here to reason from contemporary standards. Mary Ward lived the piety of her time and she had the responsibility of a child of her time. In her life we will hear of an accumulation of prayers and devotions. She was not alone in such practices. It was not and is not the amount that was important; these can, according to custom and need, be altered radically. What is important is the love with which they were offered. Up to that time all her spiritual practices had brought her joy. But the person seeking God does not find an integrated world, and cannot create it, even interiorly. The first crisis struck.[95] She knew of the innumerable ways, the infinite possibilities of practising virtue. This depressed her and filled her with fear of being unable to perform them. She became confused. It was only the perception that these possibilities were simply possibilities, and not obligations, that eventually helped her. In the freedom of generous love that does not inquire after amount or measure, she found peace again. It was a step towards complete dedication to God, whatever the consequences, even if this were to demand martyrdom.[96]

It was obvious to all around her, relatives and friends, what direction Mary was taking. Her confessor noted that her eyes would fill with tears when people spoke of the life of nuns in Catholic countries. Opposition was unanimous. Her delicate health was argued as the main reason. This was the only one that carried weight with Mary, for she was anything but robust.[97] Marmaduke Ward came to talk to his daughter, probably having been informed of her intention to leave England, and absolutely forbade her to do so. She did not argue with him, for she loved her father deeply, but she stood firm by her intention of crossing over to the Continent.[98] God, however, did not allow that to happen. Her father's refusal would have been reinforced by the suit of Edward or Edmund Neville. He was no longer young, but could lay legitimate claim to the title of Earl of Westmoreland and therefore to the extensive estates that went with it.[99] He would have been an ideal partner, although he was not rich. Even her confessor approved of the union − 'his motives were upright, prudent and directed to the service of God and the general good', writes Mary herself.[100] From which it may be deduced that her spiritual father, probably Fr Holtby, suggested that she should marry and give England a catholic family. The English Life adds that the confessor thought she should marry Neville and that, as he was such an excellent man, even if she had already been a novice in a convent, it would have been her duty to leave it.[101] Strong words, coming from one who was himself a religious. Mary Ward did not accept the offer.

In her quandary she prayed a great deal, and tried to be indifferent and to leave herself entirely to God's will.[102] She was to find frequent opportunity to exercise this attitude in her life. And while Mary survived this attack on her vocation, England entered some of the darkest days of its history. On 24th March, 1603 according to the English calendar, Queen Elizabeth died in the 70th year of her life and the 45th year of her reign. James VI of Scotland succeeded her as James lst of England. At first he had given catholics some hope of relief from their burdens; instead, he increased them. Retribution was not slow.

Notes:
1. 27 Eliz. c. 2. Statutes of the Realm IV, p. 706.
2. Mary Ward gives this date in the second introduction to her autobiographical notes A, AB/A p. 4, Inst. Arch. Munich.
3. Vita E, f.lv; Vita I, p. 2.
4. On 16th June, 1619. Recueil Historique de Jean Hendricq, Bourgeois de Saint-Omer III. 1615−1623, p. 115. AM Saint-Omer Ms. 808; Ch. F. Deneuville, Annales de la Ville de Saint-Omer sous les Evêques de Saint Omer II.1553−1726, p. 154. ibid. Ms. 1358.

5. W.M. Hunnybun and J. Gillow, Registers of the English Poor Clares at Gravelines including those who founded filiations at Aire, Dunkirk and Rouen. 1608–1837 = CRS XIV, Misc. IX, London 1914, p. 31–32.
6. It is interesting to see how the early writings dealt with her name. Pagetti, pp. 3–4, knew considerably more: "She was given the name Johanna at Baptism, this was afterwards changed at Confirmation at her own request to Maria in honour of the Blessed Virgin, on account of the veneration which she already cherished for her as a child, so that she never mentioned the name 'Maria' without adding 'Blessed'." Bissel wrote on similar lines, p. 9–10. Lohner, p. 19, wrote " ... had the name Joanna in Baptism, but afterwards when she received the sacrament of confirmation, changed it to the glorious name of Maria so that she gave a clear sign then what a fervent lover and servant of the most glorious Queen of Heaven she would become ..." This assertion continued into the 18th century. Khamm, p. 3; Unterberg, p. 4; and Fridl, I p. 8. Chambers, I.E. p. 8 and I.D. p. 9 makes a connection between Mary Ward's birthday and the Church feast of the Nuptials of Mary, introduced later. She draws even more on tradition when she adds: "She was already dedicated to the holy virgin from her cradle and before she could even speak clearly had already learnt, as has been related, the Litanies of Loreto, the Angelus, the Salve Regina and the Rosary and said these prayers out loud and openly." An extraordinary achievement.
7. Vita E, f.lv.
8. ibid. f.lv. – 2r.
9. Vita E, f.l.v; Vita I, pp. 2–3; Pagetti p. 3; Bissel p. 10; Lohner p. 20; Khamm p. 3; Unterberg p. 4; Fridl I, p. 9. Fridl pinpoints the place: by a window or a stair. Chambers I E p. 9, I D. p. 9 adopts this.
10. The Painted Life in the Augsburg house of the Institute.
11. AB/A p. 10, Inst. Arch. Munich.
12. Fridl I, p. 15.
13. When Marmaduke Ward took possession of the manors of Oulston and Mulwith and entered on his duties in Spofforth Park on 1st June, 1590, the inheritance of Mulwith was mentioned under the date 16th November 1588, and his son David was named in connection with this. SLAL Leeds, Ingleby Records Nr. 994.
14. ibid.
15. Marmaduke Ward was Bailiff in Spofforth until 24th May, 1595, but was often represented by his brother Thomas. G.R. Batho, The Household Papers of Henry Percy, 9th Earl of Northumberland, 1564–1632, London 1962 and Syon House, Alnwick. Mss. from 1584–1595, X, II. 6 Boxes 7, 8, 11, 12, and 14.
16. DNB XV, Sp. 856–858; G.R. Batho, The Percies of Petworth, 1574–1632 = Sussex Arch. Coll. 95, p. 58; ditto The Wizard Earl in the Tower, 1605–1621, History Today VI, 1956, p. 344–351; Cl. Cross, The Puritan Earl, The Life of Henry Hastings, third Earl of Huntingdon, 1536–1595, London 1966, p. 167.
17. UYBI York, York Diocesan Records, Archiepiscopal Visitation Book 1586/CB f. 97r. 100r.
18. SLAL Leeds, Ingleby Records Nr. 994, Thomas Posthumus Hoby was the youngest son of Sir Thomas Hoby and Elizabeth, nee Cooke. In 1596 Thomas jnr. married Margaret Dakins and with her settled in Hackness. He was an Anglican and was later raised to the nobility. DNB IX, Sp. 949; Cl. Cross, The Puritan Earl, passim; M. Hartley and J. Ingilby, The Wonders of Yorkshire, London 1959, p. 230.
19. This was the son of Christopher Redshaw of Oulston and Coxwold (d. 1588). After the death of his uncle William (1587) the young William Redshaw had already inherited the manors of Oulston and Newton Wallis, and extensive

estates as well. In 1593 he married Alice, sister of Ursula Wright, and was therefore Mary Ward's uncle.

20. SLAL Leeds, Ingleby Records Nr. 994.
21. ibid. Nr. 1078.
22. Syon House, Alnwick, Mss. X. II. 6, Box 14.
23. as above, note 20.
24. UYBI York, Diocesan Registry York, Archiepiscopal Visitation Book 1590–1591/CB 1, f. 56r, 64r.
25. The text of this condition runs: "Provided allwais and upon condicion that yf the said Marmaduke Warde, his heyres, executors, administrators or assignes, do yearely during the tearme of nyne yeares next ensuing the date herof, content and pay or cause to be contented and paid unto the said William Ingleby, his executors, administrators or assignes, the some of fyftye pounds of lawfull English money at the feasts of Penticost and St Martin the byshop in winter ... by eaven and equall porcions ..."
26. AB/H, p. 1, Inst. Arch. Munich.
27. Syon House, Alnwick, Mss X. II.; 6, Box II.
28. Parish Archives Ripon, Parish Register I, p. 9.
29. The British Library, London, add. Ms. 5847 f. 329. Also imprisoned was John Grant, who had taken part in the Gunpowder Plot in 1605.
30. Marmaduke Ward possessed the Manor of Oulston from 1588–1590. He handed the estate over to William Ingleby on 1st June, 1590.
31. AB/A p. 8, Inst. Arch. Munich.
32. Her exact date of birth is unknown.
33. Elizabeth Ward was entered into the baptismal register of SS Peter and Wilfred in Ripon on 30th April, 1591. Parish archives of SS Peter and Wilfrid Ripon, Parish Register I, p. 9.
34. Barbara Ward was entered on 21st November, 1592 in the baptismal register of SS Peter and Wilfrid, Ripon . ibid. p. 11.
35. AB/A pp. 8–16, Inst. Arch. Munich.
36. Lohner, pp. 25–28.
37. Unterberg, p. 5.
38. Fridl I, p. 16–17.
39. Chambers E I, p. 12–22; D I, p. 12–21.
40. It is not known when Alice Wright was born, but Mary Ward wrote that her relative was not much older than herself. On 10th December, 1593, Alice married William Redshaw. She must have been at least thirteen at that time. Mary was then aged eight.
41. One had to try to hold both the sieve and the shears high up in equal balance, while uttering a special formula and the name of the person suspected or desired. If the sieve moved during this operation, the person named was held as the guilty one, or the person sought.
42. AB/A pp. 14–15,. Inst. Arch. Munich.
43. AB/A p. 17, and AB/H p.1, Inst. Arch. Munich.
44. M.M. Calthrop, Recusant Roll Nr. 1. Michaelmas 1592–1593, Exchequer Lord Treasurer's Remembrancer Pipe Officer Series.=CRS 18/1916, p. 61, 65, 98, 103, 108, 125.
45. AB/H p. 1. Inst. Arch. Munich; PL, T.4.
46. Feet of Fines of the Tudor Period IV, YATA, RS VIII, 1890, p. 72.
47. SLAL, Leeds, Newton Wallis Deeds (Bland) DB 35/27.
48. UYBI York, High Commission Act book 1599–1603, pp. 264–265.
49. Jowitt, The Dictionary of English Law II, London, 1959, p. 1485, 1671; P.G. Osborn, A Concise Law Dictionary, London 1964, p. 300–301.
50. Vita E, f. 3rv; Vita I, p. 5. Bissel, p. 19; Khamm, p. 3; Fridl I, p. 18; Unterberg, p. 5. Chambers I E, p. 23–24; I D, p. 21–22, following the English Vita.

51. The youngest child, the son George, was born on 18th May, 1595. Parish Archives Ripon, Parish Register I, p. 16.
52. S.P. Ryan, Diocesan Returns of Recusants for England and Wales 1577 = CRS 22, Misc. 12/1921, p. 13; J.I. Cartwright, Chapters of the History of Yorkshire, Wakefield 1872, p. 155–156; E. Peacock, A List of Roman Catholics in the County of York in 1604, London 1872, p. 52; Morris, Troubles, Ser. III, p. 164, 327–328. It can be seen from the Recusant List that they stayed in their house in Harewell in 1597.
53. Vita E, f. 2rv; Vita I, p. 3–4.
54. Italian Vita, p. 4, writes: some years later.
55. Vita E, f. 4r.
56. ibid. f. 5r.
57. ibid. f. 8r.
58. Vita I, p. 11.
59. Pagetti, p. 3.
60. Bissel, pp. 14, 20, 22 and 26.
61. The Shafto family had many branches in Northumberland. Ch. B. Norcliffe, Visitation of Yorkshire 1563–1564 = Publ. of the Harleian Soc. 16/1881, p. 284; J. Foster, Pedigrees recorded at the visitation of ... Durham in 1575, 1615, 1666, London 1887, p. 285. It is not clear who is referred to here.
62. Perhaps Sir George Talbot of Grafton (1564–1630), 9th Earl of Shrewsbury. It is not certain if he was ordained priest before 1618 and became Earl of Shrewsbury in the same year. Doyle, Baronage III, p. 322; DNB 19, p. 318.
63. Nothing more is heard of this suitor.
64. PL T.2, 5, 6, 8.
65. Lohner, pp. 28–45.
66. Khamm, p. 4–5.
67. Fridl, I, p. 21–26, 36, 59.
68. Unterberg, p. 6–7.
69. Chambers I E, p. 29–30, 35–36, 67–68, 96–97; I D, p. 26–27, 31, 62–63, 82–83 with three suitors: Redshaw, Talbot and Neville.
70. AB/C p. 1, Inst. Archiv. Munich.
71. Ab/F p. 1, Inst. Archiv. Munich.
72. AB/G p. 1. Inst. Archiv. Munich.
73. Vita E, ff. 3v–4v.
74. AB/C p. 1. Inst. Archiv. Munich.
75. A law passed in 1593 forbade recusants to travel further than a five mile radius from where they lived. Exempt were those whose business lay further afield. Mary Ward writes (AB/C p. 1) "Being about 15 years owld .. my parence had occation to remove to a much coulder clement .. and I being very sickely, they ... sent me to a kinswoemen of my mother's ..." A note to the words 'my parence had occation": Marmaduke and Ursula Ward were recusants. The sick were named as those exempt from this law ("or by suche sicknes or infirmitye of bodye as they shall not be able to travell without ymmynent danger of lief ..." 35 Eliz. c. 2. Statutes of the Realm IV, p. 843–846.
76. Mary Ward gives no names but later sources reveal that she went to the Babthorpe family in 1600. For this family see Morris, Troubles, III, series: Father Pollard's Recollections of the Yorkshire Mission, p. 467–470; the Responsa Scholarum of the English College, Rome I. 1598–1621 = CRS 54/1962; Foley, Records III, p. 192–203 with the genealogy on p. 192 and pp. 245–246, and p. 288–289.
77. The original house no longer exists. A fine new house stands in a well-tended garden.
78. The table referred to: Sir William Mallory, Studley

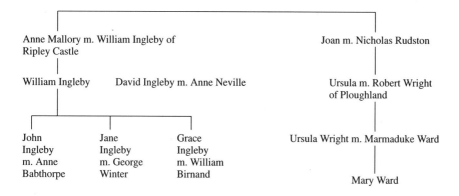

79. Foley, Records III, p. 202 note 13.
80. Father Pollard describes this in detail. Morris, Troubles, p. 468, note 1.
81. AB/C p. 3–4, Inst. Arch. Munich, Bissel first, p. 29 and PL, T.9. give these names.
82. AB/C p. 4–5, Inst. Arch. Munich; AB/D I. p. 2, ibid.
83. AB/G p. 1, Inst. Arch. Munich; Vita E.f. 6v; Vita I, p. 10.
84. Vita E.f. 7r; Vita I, p. 10.
85. AB/C p. 6; AB/G p. 1, Instit. Arch. Munich.
86. Those which might be considered: 1) Thomas a Kempis "The following of Christ", a translation from the Latin by R. Whitford, Rouen, 1585. This contains "The golden epistle of St Bernarde", also translated by Whitford, and "Rules of a Christian Lyfe" by Joh. Picus the Elder, Count of Mirandula. This Rule comprises six sides of the little work. 2) Gaspare Loarte, "The Exercise of a Christian Life" from the Italian, translated by J(ames) S(ancher), Paris 1579, Rouen 1584.
87. AB/G p. 2, Inst. Arch. Munich.
88. AB/B pp. 1–3, Inst. Arch. Munich.
89. Lorenzo Scupoli died in 1610. Fr John Gerard (alias Tomson) translated the little book into English. The first edition appeared in London in 1598 (place of printing: Antwerp!), the second in 1599 in Douai.
90. AB/C p. 6; AB/G p. 3, Inst. Arch. Munich.
91. AB/C p. 7, Inst. Arch Munich.
92. ibid. p. 7/8.
93. ibid p. 8.
94. ibid. p. 9.
95. AB/G p. 4, Inst. Arch. Munich.
96. ibid p. 5; The PL T.10 again shows graphically the desire for martyrdom.
97 AB/G/p.6, Inst. Arch. Munich.
98. ibid. p. 5. Inst. Arch. Munich.
99. Edmund or Edward Neville was born in 1563 and was therefore about forty years old when he sought Mary Ward's hand. He was a schismatic until he was 28, attending Anglican services, although without inner conviction. He became a convert. He had legitimate claim to the title Earl of Westmoreland, but after the Gunpowder Plot (1605) he could not count on the King's leniency. He had sworn, should Mary Ward refuse him, to seek no other wife. His claim to the title and possessions fell into Anglican hands. In 1606 he entered the English College in Rome (alias Eliseus Nelson) and became a

Jesuit. Neville died in 1648 on the English mission. The PL T.13 refers to Neville's suit. W. Kelly, Annales Collegii I = CRS 37/1940, p. 145, Nr. 438; A. Kobler, Die Martyrer und Bekenner der Gesellschaft Jesu in England 1580–1681, Innsbruck 1886, p. 488–493; Foley, I, p. 220–223, 669–670.
100. AB/G p. 6, Inst. Arch. Munich.
101. Vita E, f. 8r.
102. ibid.

III

THE GUNPOWDER PLOT

James I and the Catholics — the conspirators

To follow in the footsteps of a ruler like Queen Elizabeth demanded a measure of greatness. James I did not have the stature. It was Robert Cecil, Lord Salisbury, who did. He was an astute politician, already established under Elizabeth as Secretary of State, and he retained his position in the new regime.

Politically, England, Scotland and Ireland were united; England had obtained Scotland by acceptance of the royal house of Stuart and kept Ireland by force of arms. Religious matters were of interest to the King, but so had they been to Henry VIII. English catholics anticipated an improvement in their state of affairs from this son of the beheaded Scottish Queen, whom they revered as a martyr. Before his arrival the new sovereign had indeed promised some sort of amelioration but, instead, matters became worse.

James had made limp protests against his mother's execution in Scotland in 1587, and could probably have done little else in England in 1604 than keep to the path trodden by his Tudor predecessor. Be that as it may, by this discrepancy between word and deed the king inevitably betrayed a considerable number of his people. Catholic frustration at this was underpinned by continuous hostility, injustice and aggression. There developed in catholic ranks an embryonic plot, in this land of plots. It was daring but amateurish in execution: to blow up the Houses of Parliament while in session together with the King, and seize power. Desperation could not have been expressed more clearly.

Every year on November 5th, England celebrates the prevention of the plot in 1605 and scores of books have been written about it, so it is taken here as well-known. Nonetheless, it remains one of the more obscure events in English history and leaves many questions unanswered.

Some description of the main participants may be permitted. It is assumed that Robert Catesby was the leader of the conspirators. He had taken part in the Essex Plot against Elizabeth, together with the Wright brothers, and had like them been imprisoned in the White Lion. Catesby was extremely wealthy; he had large estates, among them Lapworth in Leicestershire of which more

55

later. The organiser of the plot was Thomas Percy, nephew of Henry Percy, Earl of Northumberland, who backed the conspiracy financially; both have already been mentioned in connection with Marmaduke Ward and the Wright family. Thomas Winter, too, had taken part in Essex' rebellion. He entered into closer dealings with Catesby in February, 1604. His older brother Robert Winter owned Huddington, a place that was to play a decisive role in Marmaduke's destiny. During a diplomatic mission to the Netherlands, Robert Winter met Guy Fawkes, the man who was to put the fuse to the powder kegs piled up in the cellars below Parliament. Little is known about Keyes, or Bates, Catesby's servant. In August 1605, John Grant of Northbrook Manor and Ambrose Rookwood joined the conspirators. Everard Digby − a very rich man − and Francis Tresham were also drawn into it. Finally, John and Christopher Wright are named, Mary Ward's uncles. The coup was unsuccessful. About two o'clock on the morning of 5th November, Guy Fawkes was caught on his way to the powder kegs and arrested.

The conspirators did what they should have avoided doing at all costs. They fled. They did not dare believe that Guy Fawkes could hold out against inhuman torture for five days before giving the names of his fellow conspirators, whom he then supposed to be in safety. The conspirators fled, galloping wildly from London for the time being to Ashby St Legers and Dunchurch, where they met at six o'clock in the evening. From there they moved off during the night and continued to ride west. Late in the evening they reached Warwick, where they had a longer rest. There they divided into two groups: those in charge of the ammunition rode first, then came the chief conspirators with their servants. From Warwick they continued through Norbrook, an estate of John Grant's, to Huddington, belonging to Robert Winter. About two o'clock in the afternoon of 6th November, they reached the road to Huddington. This was their last halting place before the climax.

Lapworth-Alcester-Huddington-London

Marmaduke Ward in Lapworth − his ride to Huddington − arrest and statement − transfer to London − Mrs Wright's statement

Government agents followed the fleeing conspirators and their dependants with a terrible persistence. At the same time, they made comprehensive swoops; houses were searched systematically, suspects or even strangers on their way through a township were taken prisoner without ceremony. Among these was Marmaduke Ward.

To turn northwards first of all. South-east of Birmingham is an unremarkable and not particularly attractive place, Lapworth. One of the houses still situated in the centre of it is called Catesby House, taking its name from its former owner. At the time of the Gunpowder Plot it belonged to John Wright, who had bought it from Robert Catesby. The house shows no signs of its original style, only the stables, perhaps, may have belonged to that earlier date. Catesby House was a staging post for some of the more or less chance participants in the plot. From the events of those days we are directed to few but important references concerning our subject. Marmaduke Ward's statement of 6th November before the magistrate in Beauchamp's Court,[1] that of Mrs Wright on 21st November before the Sheriff of London,[2] which contradicted his, and certain others.[3] It may seem surprising that after almost seven years without a mention, Marmaduke Ward[4] should suddenly reappear in documents and that very far from his own part of the country, in a place where the Wards had never possessed property: Warwickshire.

Meanwhile, research has revealed who had been staying in Catesby House in Lapworth on this fateful autumn day. Recorded are John Wright and his wife Dorothy;[5] Christopher Wright and his wife Margaret,[6] a certain Wayrde (perhaps another Ward — the name was often spelt like that); Martha Percy nee Wright, wife of Thomas Percy, Marmaduke Ward and the servant Mark Brittain.

On 4th November, on the way from London to Lapworth were two people: a servant William Kyddall and a William Ward.[7] Even a superficial reading shows that members of the Ward and Wright families were gathered together, and that at the actual time of 5th November. A few days later John and Christopher were dead, and the other members of the house prisoners of the Privy Council in London. The connecting links are precise, and indisputable. First, it must be explained that a prisoner in England in those times had no kind of legal assistance; he was denied a lawyer. He had to answer the questions put to him or his silence was taken for guilt. He was denied the right to call witnesses. The prisoner, for the most part unversed in law, was thus completely defenceless before his legally trained judge, and he could not know if his answers spelt deliverance or a rope around his neck.

Those taken in Alcester were led to Beauchamp's Court and questioned by Sir Fulke Greville,[8] a high official and owner of the old manor house, and Bartholomew Hales,[9] Justice of the Peace for Warwickshire. For the present they merely questioned Marmaduke about the date of his arrival in Warwickshire and what he was doing there. The answer summarized in the report is worth giving in full: the accused answered the question when he had come into the district: fourteen days ago, since when he had stayed with Mr John Wright in Lapworth. Mr Wright, however, had been absent the previous week. His sister-in-law, Mrs Wright, had asked him to take a horse to Mr

Winter at Huddington, accompanied by her servant Mark Brittain. As they came past Alcester, about an hour after the conspirators had ridden through it, Marmaduke had been arrested but the servant Brittain, who had a better horse, escaped. Furthermore, Marmaduke said he had known nothing about the riders who had also taken this road.[10]

The astounding simplicity of this answer makes it clear that Marmaduke had actually known nothing of the monstrous plan in which his wife's closest relatives were implicated. He had probably not even heard the news correctly in Alcester, at least, not the names of the conspirators. Otherwise, how could he have drawn his sister-in-law into the affair? Marmaduke knew enough about government methods to know that every word was put on the scales and measured and, if possible, used as counter-evidence. The interrogation at Beauchamp's Court presents a first glimpse of the prisoners. In other places there were similar proceedings. The real suspects were taken to London where they were to undergo more thorough interrogations.

One thing Marmaduke, apparently, was not asked, which it would be important to know: the time he left Lapworth. We can deduce from the other statements that he was in Alcester on 6th November, an hour after the group of riders had gone past.[11] Equally important is the fact that Marmaduke was on his way to Huddington with a horse. It is stated unequivocally: 'to goe to Mr Winter with a horse to Huddenton'. Others were making their way with horses towards the conspirators on the same day: John Story, Thomas Percy's servant, William Johnson, Robert Keye's servant, and James Garvey, the servant of Everard Digby. Let us look at the answers of those prisoners who were taken at the same time as Marmaduke, in the neighbourhood of Alcester and who were also interrogated by Sir Fulke Greville and Bartholomew Hales in Beauchamp's Court.[12] Richard Westburg from Norbrook was temporarily employed by John Grant, who owned the Norbrook estate. His answer was annihilating for the conspirators:

At one o'clock in the night of 6th November, Lewis Grant and his servant had come to Norbrook to change horses. Half an hour later John Grant, Ambrose Rookwood, Robert Catesby arrived with nine or ten companions, John Wright of Lapworth and his brother Christopher, Robert and John Winter and Harry Morgan, who was staying in Lapworth at the time. Thirty-two people arrived that night. Immediately afterwards fresh horses were brought from Warwick. Before it was day they had all ridden off towards Wales.

The next prisoner, Richard York, stated that on Sunday, 3rd November, he had been with Robert Winter at Mr Talbot's of

Grafton. On Monday, 4th November, he and Mr Winter had ridden to Coventry, where they spent the night. On Tuesday 5th, they went through Dunchurch and on 6th November, Wednesday, he and William Snowe, a servant of Robert Winter's, had been arrested near Alcester, because they were following a group of gentlemen from Norbrook, but they knew nothing about any plot.

The third interrogated was William Snowe, named by Richard York. He had spent the Sunday in Huddington. On Monday he rode with his master and a few others to Coventry, on Tuesday 5th to Robert Catesby at Ashby St Legers, where they found Everard Digby and other gentlemen. He and Richard York had ridden away alone.

The prisoner Robert Askew from Lapworth had been in the service of Robert Catesby for fourteen days, but had stayed at his house in the Strand. Between 4th and 6th November he was on his way to his father's. Notice that he had been arrested behind the group of conspirators, in the opposite direction to his avowed destination!

Thomas Rookwood was also on the move at the time. He wanted to do business with an Ingram of Worcester, but lost his way in Alcester as the place was in a state of alarm.

Robert Townsend of Brighton was questioned on 7th November. He said that it had been his pleasure to travel with Mr Rookwood to Clapton, where he had remained six weeks. He had followed the group that rode through Alcester but when he found the town in an uproar he had fled in the other direction, and been taken.

William Johnson, a servant of Mr Rookwood's, said in his turn that he had wanted to visit a relative. He too, on account of the disturbance in the town, had fled with Mr Rookwood and Mr Townsend in the opposite direction.

Robert Keyes from Dreighton explained that he had wanted to visit his relative Mrs Rookwood, in Clapton. When he heard there that Thomas Rookwood and others had been arrested, he had gone to Bedford, where he was taken.

Francis Pryor had been unemployed for more than a week in Alcester. Then he had been summoned by John Winter. He had also had contact with some of the other conspirators.

Richard Day, Everard Digby's servant, waited for his master on 5th November about eight o'clock in the evening and then rode with the other conspirators to Warwick, where they made a halt. They obtained fresh horses from the Castle and rode by Norbrook in the direction of Huddington. Here he and the cook, William Udall, separated from the group because they had noticed that the gentlemen had some evil purpose in mind. He had come forward on his own account, and William Udall supported this statement.

In most of these interrogations, purposely included in some detail, the servant/master relationship is stressed: 'I was sent', 'commanded', 'accompanied'. Sometimes horses and the transport of ammunition is referred to. But except for the conspirators, who were under oath to one another, no one actually knew of the plan to blow up Parliament. Northcote Parkinson[13] points out correctly that many innocent people were involved in events which they would never have even imagined. Their connection with the plotters, even if a matter of servant/master relationship, would be imputed to them as that of shared guilt.

We do not know how the interrogation in Beauchamp's Court was conducted. Everything seems to have been carried out very quickly, because Marmaduke Ward was questioned on the day of his arrest, and the same was the case with many others.

A list with the names of thirty-seven men and nine women, probably all taken in and around Alcester, identifies all the prisoners who were interrogated with Marmaduke Ward on November 6th or the next day. Marmaduke was counted among those suspected of being a priest, and connected with Winter, Grant and Rookwood.[14] The list reveals a certain division, though this is not consistently maintained, between the servants of the various gentlemen like Everard Digby, Robert Catesby, Ambrose Rookwood and others, who were placed together and the gentlemen, who on the other hand, were by themselves.

There is a far longer, undated list of prisoners from the counties of Warwickshire and Worcestershire, who were taken to London.[15] It contains the names and closer descriptions of fifty men and nine women. In addition to the plotters − even those who died in the skirmish at Holbeach − there appear the names of the Warwickshire prisoners and, on the other hand, those interrogated on 6th and 7th November in Beauchamp's Court.

Marmaduke Ward comes between Richard York and Robert Keyes, both of whom later confessed. This time there is simply their name, with the addition: 'Suspects, who are usually in touch with Mr Winter, Mr Grant and Mr Rookwood.' Among the women were Martha Percy, Dorothy and Margaret Wright.

The journey to London set off in three groups. Eight prisoners were in the charge of Edward Reade; these were Richard Dale, William Udall, Richard York, Thomas Rookwood, Robert Askew, Marmaduke Ward, Robert Keyes, and Robert Townsend.

The second group was led by Peter Burgoigne. To this belonged John Clifton, William Snowe, William Willmoore, Francis Pryor, Francis Grant, Robert Conyers, Thomas Pearce, and Thomas Maunder.

The third group was in the care of Edward Gybbes and contained the prisoners Pearson Delves, George Bartlett, Matthew Batty, Thomas Richardson, Miles Raynard, Thomas Anderton, Mark Brittain, William Thornbury and Christopher Ather.

Mr Wright's servant, Mark Brittain, who had fled on Marmaduke Ward's arrest, had therefore been caught. Whether Richard

Westburg, who had made his statement with such willingness in Beauchamp, had been freed, there is no information.

William Johnson, who appeared on the list of those arrested, is missing here. On 16th November or shortly after, they were conveyed to London. On this date Sheriff Richard Verney wrote to the Privy Council that he hoped that those prisoners named on the enclosed list could be led before the councillors; the three who had accompanied them had declared themselves answerable for the prisoners. Two people had been sent out in advance as quartermasters.[16] Most probably the prisoners were conveyed to London in carts, bound together to prevent flight or any attempts to free them. Each person in charge had eight prisoners entrusted to him, except for the third, who had nine.

The journey will have taken some days. Horses with a loaded cart could not have travelled more than fifty kilometres a day, especially in bad wintry weather. An escort of riders would have kept watch over them and quartermasters had been sent out. What sort of state would the prisoners have been in, on this journey? It was the middle of November. At this time of year in England it is mostly damp and foggy. They would not have been given much food at the halting-places and there was probably no thought of sleep. Above all, they would have been exposed to the mockery and hatred of the people and felt the agonising uncertainty of their future. The prisoners now knew the reason for their arrest. The charge in London would be that of high treason. That meant questioning, repeated, merciless, paralysing questioning. Would the painful process of the law be applied? They would be brought before the Privy Council, who had the sole right to order torture. The journey must have been crucifying.

At last they reached London. We do not know where the prisoners were taken first. Documentary material about the Gunpowder Plot is extremely fragmentary. That applies too to the list of fees to be paid by the prisoners, for candles to light their cells, and for the most primitive objects for their bodily needs. The lists contain only the names of those prisoners who were solvent. Whitehall suffered damage in 1612 from fire, and in 1666 the Great Fire practically ruined the entire City of London. Invaluable documentary evidence was lost. Of the notorious London prisons – the Clink, Gatehouse, Marshalsea, White Lion, King's Bench, Newgate, Poultry Counter and finally the Tower, all of which were overflowing in those days, few of the names of the inmates are known.

The list of prisoners in the Tower has a gap from 1605 (before the Gunpowder Plot) to 1678! The Gatehouse alone provides some names and dates, for example a William Udall was imprisoned there in 1601 from Spring to Christmas 1603, and a Thomas Ward from March 1605 to 21st March, 1616.[17] Both had been confined at the command of the Secretary of State, Cecil, and are therefore to be numbered among political prisoners.

After the discovery of the Plot the following were held in the Gatehouse:

Matthew Batty, servant of Lord Mounteagle (12 weeks)
Thomas Bates, servant of Thomas Percy, (4 weeks)
William Kendall (Kyddall), servant of Christopher Wright (8 weeks)
William Handy, whose status is not given (10 weeks)
Thomas Maunder, servant of Robert Winter (9 weeks).[18]

A Francis Priery (Pryor?) was held for 8 weeks. Evidently, only those suspected among the conspirator's servants were taken, and that for a few weeks. None of these had been Marmaduke Ward's fellow prisoners. It may seem surprising that the prison term, the interrogation, or the condemnation of Marmaduke Ward are not known. This has given rise to the supposition that he may not have been imprisoned, and that, through the intervention of his brother Thomas Ward, secretary of Lord Mounteagle, he was released.[19]

To counterbalance that, it must be remembered that among the conspirators who died in Holbeach were John and Christopher Wright, Thomas Percy and Robert Catesby. All the rest were taken prisoner and put in the Tower on 20th November. The interrogation lasted some weeks. It was only on 13th January, 1606, that Everard Digby, Robert Winter, John Grant and Thomas Bates were hanged in St Paul's Churchyard; on 31st January, Thomas Winter, Ambrose Rookwood, Robert Keyes and Guy Fawkes were hanged in Westminster, in Old Palace Yard. Of the plotters' servants, only a few were imprisoned in the Gatehouse. But where were the others, that large number of people who had also been brought to London?

And what of the 'gentlemen' who were not involved in the Plot? The loss of important sources is not acceptable as proof that prisoners who were suspected of treason could have been set free.

Another consideration: would the influence of a lesser official such as Thomas Ward, (was he really from Yorkshire where there were so many Wards?) have been great enough to have liberated a man who was on two lists of prisoners, between such heavily implicated men as Richard York and Robert Keyes — 'suspected persons, usually resorting to Mr Winter, Mr Grant and Mr Rookwood'? Not even Henry Percy, Earl of Northumberland, could obtain his own freedom, though his life was spared. It must be accepted that Marmaduke was imprisoned for a time; this will be referred to again. The wives of some of the plotters and suspects who had been arrested in Warwickshire and Worcestershire were taken to London, presumably at the same time.

On 12th November, the Justices of the Peace wrote from Warwickshire to the Secretary of State, Cecil, that Mrs Grant, Mrs Percy and the wives of the other traitors had been taken into custody.[20]

The next day, on 13th November, both they and Sheriff Verney wrote that the women would be taken to London guarded by Bartholomew Hales.[21] They would there be taken to a house of a city councillor, and entrusted to the vigilance of the Sheriff of London. It was probably in this house that Sheriff William Romeny, shortly before 21st November, heard Mrs Wright in the presence of a witness. This presumably means Dorothy, the wife of John Wright, for there is mention of a horse from the stable in Lapworth. The following very significant but confusing statement was written by the Sheriff on November 21st to his taskmaster, Cecil.[22]

At Cecil's command, so Romeny begins his letter, he has informed Mrs Wright of the Secretary of State's joy over the precious Arab horse owned by her husband. Cecil's cynical pleasure was intended for the horse, now in the possession of the Privy Council, which Marmaduke was to have taken to Huddington at Mrs Wright's request – Marmaduke's statement in Beauchamp's Court will have been made known to Cecil. We can certainly assume that this unexpected information did not fail to have an effect on the prisoner. But Mrs Wright was very careful, and in her answer she mentioned her memory, which could let her down if necessary! This horse, she said, according to her knowledge 'whiche was not whyt but dapple full of whyt spotts', which on the Tuesday morning ('the tuesday mornenge) early, about six or seven, was fetched by Marmaduke from the stable, as he wanted to ride it to his family in Newby, Yorkshire.

Let us stop for a moment at this important point. The statement was made in the second half of November, therefore long after the criminal intention of the conspirators had been forestalled, and the monstrous process was in full swing. We remember that Marmaduke had not been asked in Beauchamp's Court when he had left Lapworth. It was then said that it was apparently only necessary to know when this man from Yorkshire had come south to the county of Warwickshire and how long he had been there, and what he was doing. Here the exact date of his departure from Lapworth is given – 'the tuesday' could only be the 5th November, between six and seven early in the morning. And Mrs Wright added that on the same morning two servants had ridden off with three or four good horses, but that she did not know where.[23] It is remarkable that she says nothing about her request to Marmaduke Ward, asking him to ride to Huddington with a horse. It is clear that the statements differed widely, which was not to escape the Sheriff's notice, still less that of the Secretary of State. Was Mrs Wright trying to deceive the government? It looks like it. She can hardly have seen Marmaduke Ward after his arrest in Alcester and could certainly not have spoken with him, so she had no detailed knowledge of the circumstances, and knew nothing of his statement in Beauchamp's Court. In all of this, one is justified in asking why Marmaduke was anywhere near the conspirators John and Christopher Wright, and the Winter brothers precisely at this time of the Gunpowder Plot.

Any involvement of his in the Plot itself or even any knowledge of it must clearly be ruled out.

The plan to blow up Parliament would have been kept a strict secret between the conspirators. Marmaduke would most certainly not have let himself been made party to such an undertaking. Added to which, we have not the slightest indication that he took part in any political activities.But he did come from a long-established catholic family, he had been steward to the Earl of Northumberland for several years who, as has already been mentioned, financed the Plot. Thomas Percy was married to Marmaduke's sister-in-law, Martha Wright. And then his brothers-in-law, John and Christopher Wright, had both been tempestuously active in politics. His mother-in-law had spent long years in prison, the High Commission had brought several members of the Ward family to court and imposed heavy fines. And, finally, Marmaduke Ward and his wife had themselves been mulcted of a considerable amount. It is, therefore, quite comprehensible that, religious convictions apart, from a purely personal point of view, he ranged himself on the side of the dissatisfied. A good deal of righteous anger could have built up within a man who had suffered such wrongs.

However, it can be taken that he had journeyed South to be ready for the good that was to come. Hundreds of English catholics did so. In this context it can be seen from other plots – during the French Revolution there were certainly many people who favoured the monarchy but few who knew of the royal family's flight to Varennes (20.6.1791). In Nazi Germany there were underground movements organized by those who wanted to end the dictatorship, but only very few of them knew of the plan to murder Hitler by Graf Claus Schenk von Stauffenberg. (20.7.44.)

To return to the Gunpowder Plot; according to both statements the fact remains – unexplained – that Marmaduke was arrested in the early hours of the morning of 6th November, just as the conspirators and their retinue arrived in the neighbourhood of Huddington. He still had the horse which he should have taken to Mr Winter, for it was now in the hands of the government. So he had not yet been to Huddington, to fulfil his sister-in-law's request. But if he had ridden from Lapworth in the early morning of 5th November, (it would still have been dark) where had he been in the meantime? Lapworth is about 20 kilometers from Alcester, and he could easily have covered the ground with a good horse in a couple of hours. There is also something odd about the direction. Newby lies in Yorkshire, far to the north, and Alcester lies south of Lapworth.

From the material given it is only possible to make conjectures, and point to two statements made by James Garvey, the servant of conspirator Everard Digby. On 8th November he stated in Warwick[24] that he was arrested as he was looking for his master. Mrs Digby had told him to do so. Digby had horses at Coughton. More than a month later, on 11th December, Garvey was interrogated in London.[25] He then stated that he had accompanied Mrs Digby on 6th November to Mr Thomas Throckmorton in Coughton. She sent him with the horses to Mr Robert Winter, so to Huddington. Garvey abandoned the plotters only at Holbeach House. With some probability we may presume that Marmaduke indeed intended to return home to Newby, but only after he had gathered news of both his brothers-in-law, John and Christopher Wright. Perhaps he too was at Coughton Court; it lay a few miles away from Alcester. He did not carry out his sister-in-law's wish. If, as seems obvious, servants of the conspirators spent weeks imprisoned in the Gatehouse, how much more likely is it that a 'gentleman' from the north, an active recusant, would also have had to pay that penalty.

Baldwin Gardens

Mary Ward and her confessor Fr Richard Holtby, S.J. – conversation in London – Mass in Baldwin Gardens

We do not know when Mary Ward had her last conversation with her father. It is generally taken that it was before Marmaduke left for Lapworth, so before mid-October, 1605. After the discovery of the Gunpowder Plot, a betrothal between Mary and a catholic noble – which had been her father's intention – would not have been much to the purpose. For the Government retaliated with far stricter laws after thwarting this plot, which had effectively cancelled out any accepted participation of catholics in English social life for years to come.

This conversation, which caused Mary Ward such sorrow, in all likelihood took place in Yorkshire.[26] But the situation was very different by January 1606. It has been argued that Marmaduke Ward was still held prisoner in the capital on 21st November, 1605. It is hardly likely that a prisoner under suspicion of conspiring with the chief plotters would have been set free before their respective executions on 13th or 31st January. The government was still searching for anyone who had been implicated.

What would Marmaduke Ward's condition have been, when he left his London prison? Apart from his physical state – the care of prisoners was never adequate – he would have suffered mentally. Interrogations were so devised that the prisoner became exhausted and confused. Every word, every answer, could bring about his own condemnation. Over and above that, Marmaduke had suffered the deaths of both his brothers-in-law, of Thomas Percy, both Winters, Rookwood, of Grant who was blind, and the rest of the conspirators. Sir Henry Percy, once his lord and protector, was in the Tower and hardly likely to be set free. The question which above all would have tortured Marmaduke was of the future − 'Do I still have a future? What will happen to my wife and children, to the estates? How can I look the people of Newby in the face?' Until then he had indeed been known as a recusant, but also as a respected citizen. Would he ever be able to throw off the taint of belonging to those who wanted to overthrow and destroy England and the royal family? In those difficult days, it can be assumed that Mary Ward was with her father.[27] She would hardly have travelled the long journey from Yorkshire to London alone; it was not customary for a woman in those days. Marmaduke Ward, the released prisoner, must have faced his daughter and finally accepted that her way was not the one he had planned for her. It had taken a Gunpowder Plot to convince him.

Someone else was having second thoughts: Father Holtby.[28] During 1602−3 Mary Ward's confessor Fr Richard Holtby was in Helbourne, near Newcastle, and in 1605-6 on the Halton estate, both in Northumberland, in the north of England. It was only after the arrest of the martyr Fr Henry Garnett, SJ., (end of January, 1606) that Fr Holtby moved to London as Fr Garnett's successor, to be Superior of the Jesuits in England.

In her autobiographical notes Mary Ward says nothing at all about the following occurrence. It is only in 1624 that she mentions it as a sign of God's grace, without closer reference to time or place.[29] The English Life names the place: Baldwin Gardens, in London and, in fact, even more explicitly 'in lodgings in Bauldwin's Garden', therefore in a rented house.[30] The Italian Life simply says 'nella capella'[31] and Bissel 'in sacello domestico Londini'.[32] Which house-chapel was that? The imprisoned Lord Percy could have had no house chapel, and the Ward family had no property in London. 'Lodgings in Bauldwin's Garden' is more than likely to have been a house where Jesuits stayed. Fr Garnett had rented several houses in London, where the fathers could possibly find concealment. This is where Fr Holtby celebrated Mass during those dangerous times.

The text of Panel 14 of the Painted Life, which depicts the scene, runs: 'As Maria's confessor said Mass in London in 1616; by divine permission he overturned the chalice, which brought about such a change in him that, after the Mass was finished and she handed him a towel to dry his hands, he said to her with flowing tears, 'May it be far from me to hinder your religious project any further. Rather, I will endeavour to further it.'

Father Holtby had needed a sign, the hardest that there can be for a priest. Two other far-reaching and decisive factors must not be overlooked: that the Babthorpe family also experienced difficulties through the increased severity of the laws against catholics. After the Gunpowder Plot, the Statute of Queen Elizabeth against recusants

1606

was altered to include every English person who engaged a catholic servant or gave a catholic stranger hospitality; he had to pay £10 per month per person.[33] Marmaduke's eldest daughter was liable to this law too, because her move to Osgodby had been as that of an assistant in the Babthorpe household — and she was a catholic. So the loophole which had been opened for her in 1600 was now firmly closed. It was a matter of, either join the established church, or pay until you are penniless.

Between the dates of the two executions, 13th and 31st January, on 23rd January Mary Ward had her twenty-first birthday and so, in the eyes of English law, she had come of age.

Notes

1. PRO London, SP 14/216, GPB I, Nr. 47, 4.
2. Hatfield House, Cecil Papers 113/26.
3. These only in the context. To be indicated when they occur.
4. The last time Marmaduke Ward was mentioned was on 8th February, 1598 over the matter of a promissory note. See p. 39.
5. This emerges from Marmaduke's statement of 6th November.
6. Christopher Wright was in London, as was his brother John, on the day the Plot was discovered but his wife remained in Lapworth; Margaret was taken to London with the other residents of Lapworth.
7. PRO London, SP 14/216, GPB I Nr. 52.
8. Sir Fulke Greville (1554–1628), 1st Baron Brooke, was Secretary for Wales under Queen Elizabeth. James I confirmed him in his office for life. He lived at Beauchamps Court, Alcester Manor. DNB VIII, Sp. 602.
9. Bartholomew Hales, Justice for the Peace for Warwickshire, PRO London, SP 14/216, GPB I, Nr. 75.
10. "This examinant, beeinge demaunded when he came into this countreye, saith, a fort night since, and hath since continued at Mr John Writes at Lapworth, where Mr Write discontynuinge the space of on week past, his sister in lawe, Mrs Write, intreated him (beinge accompanied with on Marke Brittaine her man), to goe to Mr Winter with a horse to Huddenton, where as they past by Alcester about an hower after the troope past, this examinant was apprehended, but the saide Brittaine beeinge well horst, escaped. Hee further saith, hee knewe not of the companies passinge that way untill they came to Alcester, nor of theire purpose anythinge at all." Marmaduke Ward is named here as "from Newby". The family may have returned from the North at this time. It certainly does not imply a reference to his cousin, Marmaduke Ward of Newby; the latter was not related to the Wrights.
11. Cf. for example, the statements of Richard Westburg of Norbrook and Richard Day of Tylton, and writings such as: Hugh Ross Williamson, The Gunpowder Plot, London 1948/50 and Paul Durst, Intended Treason, London 1970.
12. PRO London, Sp 14/216, GPB I, Nr. 47.
13. C. Northcote Parkinson, Gunpowder, Treason and Plot, London 1976, p. 77.
14. PRO London, SP 14/216, GPB II, Nr. 134: A calendar of the names of the persons apprehended within the said countie knowne and suspected for the late conspiration and insurrence. At the end of this list: Thomas Rookewoodd of Clopton in the county of Warrick, gent(leman), Roberte Townsend of St Edmondsbury, gent(leman), Richard York of Netherdale in the countie of Yorkshire, gent(leman), Marmaduke Warde of Newbye in the county of Yorke, Pearson Deltes, gent(leman), lyinge commonly about

London." After the bracket, "suspected to be priests and usually resorting to Mr Winters, Mr Grants and Mr Rookwoode."

15. The British Library, add. Ms. 5847, pp. 322–323: "List of such as were apprehended for the Gun Powder Plot. The names of such as were taken in Warwicke and Worcestershire and then brought to London." Among them: Richard Yorke, Marmaduke Ward, Robert Key. After the bracket: "Suspected persons usually resorting to Mr Winter, Mr Grant and Mr Rookwoods."

16. HMC 17/1938, p. 529. The date is shown by the number 16, undoubtedly standing for 16th November, 1605. Likewise for the Sheriff's letter to the Secretary of State, p. 493.

17. Tower Bills 1595–1681 with Gatehouse certificates 1592–1603, contributed by Rev. J.H. Pollen SJ, p. 235–238, CRS IV/1907, respectively CRS 53/1960, p. 259–264, 269–270.

18. ibid p. 272–275.

19. Thus Henry Hawkes Spink, The Gunpowder Plot and Lord Monteagle's letter, London 1902.

20. PRO London SP 14/216, GPB I, Nr. 75.

21. ibid. Nr. 90 and 91.

22. Hatfield House, Cecil Papers 113/26.

23. "Her husband had/t/hree or fower other horses at that tyme allso in his stable of good accompte but employed that mornenge some by one man some by another but what is become of them she knowethe not."

24. PRO London, SP 14/216. GPB I, Nr. 51: "He was sent by his mistress (Mrs Digby, note) in search of his master, when he was apprehended. Sir Everard (Digby, note) had horses at Coughton, at Thomas Throckmorton's house."

25. PRO London, SP 14/216, GPB II Nr. 153: "Attended his lady (Mrs Digby, note) to mrs Throgmorton's on November 6. She sent him to Robert Winter's with horses; he left the conspirators at Holbeach House."

26. Vita E, f 8r; Vita I, p. 12.

27. See note 28.
Chambers' statement (I E, p. 86; I D, p. 74) that Marmaduke had taken his daughter with him to London, is not correct. Marmaduke travelled in a different direction, towards Lapworth. It is improbable that he should first have travelled to London, and left his daughter alone there in those unsettled times. There is no witness to Mary Ward's presence in Lapworth, nor is this likely. She would otherwise have been taken prison like all the others living in Catesby's house.

28. Chambers I E, p. 91–92; I D, p. 78–79.

29. VP/H 1: The spillinge of the challish, Inst. Arch. Munich.

30. Vita E, f. 8v.

31. Vita I, p. 12.

32. Bissel, p. 41. There is no further information in the other writings on Mary Ward's life.

33. " ... that everie person and persons which ... shall willingly mayntaine retaine releeve keepe or harboure in his or theire House any Servant Sojourner or Strainger who shall not go to or repaire to some Church or Chappell or usual Place of Common Prayer to heare Divine Service, but shall forebeare the same by the space of one moneth togeather, not having a reasonable excuse, contrary to the Lawes and Statues of this Realme, shall forfeite tenne poundes for every Monethe that he shee or they shall soe relieve mainetaine retaine keepe or harbour any such Servant Sojourner or Estraunger in his or their Howse soe forbearing as aforesaide ... " 3 Jac. I, C. 4. Statutes of the Realme IV, p. 1076.

IV

OVERSEAS

The other island

Crossing – historical development of north and south Neth-erlands – Infanta Isabella Clara Eugenia and Archduke Albrecht – situation of the Church in the southern Neth-erlands

'The Whitsuntide following that Christmas I was twenty one, I hap-pily began my long-desired journey from England towards Flanders, there to become a religious woman.'[1] Mary Ward wrote these words eighteen years after her arrival in St Omer in southern Flanders. Humanly speaking, they were not happy years, and yet this sentence echoes her surge of happiness at this, her first and hard-won crossing to Flanders. This lift of spirit was directed towards a land that was very foreign to Mary Ward, and totally different in its development from that of her own country.

The marriage of Duchess Maria of Burgundy in Ghent in 1477 had formed the beginning of an empire, for when the Duchess died early in 1482, her rich inheritance fell to her husband's house, Maximilian I of Austria, whose homeland was in the heart of Europe. Their son Philip the Fair married Johanna, heiress of Aragon and Castille. Not only Spain came from this connection with the House of Austria but soon too, a new world, because on the discovery of America (1492) the heir Charles V came into an inheritance on which in actual fact the sun never set. In 1521/22, for administrative reasons, the Habsburgs divided their lands. Henceforth the Burgundian inheritance was sub-ordinate to the Spanish branch of the Casa de Austria.

The Habsburg's vast political vision and potential for the future of Europe could not dislodge the memory of their great Burgundian past from the minds of the people of the Netherlands. Philip the Fair and Charles V were born in the Netherlands and they remained Burgundians to their people, in spite of their far-flung obligations elsewhere. It was different for Philip II, Charles V's son. He had been born in Spain and spoke only Spanish. Differences in state con-stitutions, religious opinions and certainly, also, the brutal impact of the Spanish army of occupation, led to the eighty years' war. (1568–1648)

The seven northern provinces (the majority of present-day Netherlands) had adopted Calvinism almost without exception, together with a republican form of government. The southern Netherlands (most of today's Belgium) remained Catholic and Spanish. Austrian Archduchesses ruled it for sixty years,[2] but this connection with the dynasty was broken abruptly when Philip II sent the Duke of Alba into the rebellious lands in 1567. Government of the country and command of the army was to be in one hand in the future. What three women had managed to hold in check for sixty years, was to gallop rapidly apace under five generals[3] in twenty-eight: the Secession of the Northern Netherlands. Far too late, Philip II appointed Albrecht VII as Governor of the southern Netherlands in 1598.

Archduke Albrecht of Austria was born on 13th November, 1559 son of Emperor Maximilian II and Maria, daughter of Emperor Charles V. He was educated with care, destined for the Church. At eighteen he received the Cardinal's hat, in 1594 he became the Archbishop of Toledo. From 1584–95 he was Regent of Portugal. Philip II esteemed him to such an extent that he chose him to be the husband of his favourite daughter, Infanta Isabella Clara Eugenia. Albrecht renounced his religious dignities − he had never been ordained − and the marriage was happy but childless.

The Infanta Isabella Clara Eugenia was born on 12th August, 1566 as the daughter of Philip II and Elizabeth of France. She, too, had a good education in the strict Spanish court. Her father gave her the Netherlands as a wedding gift, on condition that if she were to die without children the country reverted to Spain. After the Archduke's death (13th July, 1621), the Archduchess governed alone until her own death, (lst December, 1633). The 'Erzherzoge' as they were called by their people, led exemplary lives and were deeply revered. The country had, once again, a 'Prince naturel', as in the time of Charles V, but no one knew that the couple were closely tied by their secret pact with the King of Spain.

Wedged between the Dutch Calvinists in the north, the influence of the French Hugenots in the south, and the powerful centres of the Reformed churches of the Rhineland to the East, the Spanish Netherlands remained Catholic. True, the Church had to re-conquer ground here too, but the problems differed from those of the neighbouring countries.

It was not only in constitutional matters that the Dutch possessed and jealously safeguarded their hard-won privileges, but in Church affairs too the country and the people had acquired a character of their own. It is not to be assumed that the privileges of the secular and regular clergy, or of the secular authorities who were occupied with the church stewardship of the centralising Reformed Church were acceptable to Rome. Indeed, contemporary reports from the Nunciature reveal an abundance of complaints, not only from the papal nuncio in Brussels but also from higher curial officials.

Up to 1559 the united seventeen provinces of the Netherlands had had five Dioceses:

Arras (in Flemish: Atrecht); Cambrai (Flemish: Kamerijk); Thérouanne (Flemish: Terwaan); Tournai (Flemish: Doornik) in the south, and Utrecht in the north. Liège at that time had its own Prince-Bishop and was outside the jurisdiction of the Spanish Habsburgs.

In the north, Utrecht was suffragan to the Archbishopric of Cologne; in the south, Arras, Cambrai, Thérouanne and Tournai were suffragans of the Archbishopric of Rheims. Not a single Dutch bishopric, consequently, was under the supervision of an indigenous church province, but the invisible frontiers of foreign influences cut right across this ecclesiastically structured division.

The Burgundian princes Philip the Good and Charles the Bold had already proposed new diocesan boundaries; however, the main thrust of their political thinking was occupied with settling spheres of power and belligerent attitudes. Before Charles V left the Netherlands, he advised his son Philip II to make new and appropriate ecclesiastical boundaries. Quite apart from the political import of this, penetration by Lutheran and, even more, by Calvinist teaching made this change long overdue. Even if Philip II engages little sympathy as ruler of the Netherlands, his partition of the dioceses proved excellent. In the north Utrecht was raised to an archbishopric;[4] in the Flemish part of southern Netherlands, Malines[5] became the seat of an Archbishop, as also Cambrai in the Walloon area.[6] Not only the formation of the dioceses but also the appointment of the bishops lay in the hands of the king.

In 1559 Philip II and his successors were granted the right to nominate the Bishops and other high-ranking clerics in their lands. The main intention of the catholic Kings of Spain was to defend the Old Faith and the Roman church; induction of suitable bishops into their sees was one of the pre-requisites.

In the midst of this maelstrom, in the thirty-eighth year of the war, and after a sea journey[7] of four or five hours, Mary Ward first set foot on the soil of Flanders. She had travelled with Mrs Bentley, on whose pass she was entered as a daughter. Eventually war-weariness and exhaustion resulted[8] in a twelve-year truce in this fratricidal struggle, but for the time being fighting and terror dominated. On that spring day in 1606, Mary Ward did indeed step onto a land that was free for Catholics, but it was no happy land.

St Omer

The diocese — the bishops — Bishop Jacques Blaes — the convents — the arrival of Mary Ward — her conversation with Fr George Keynes SJ — the Poor Clare Convent

The diocese of St Omer was carved out of the old diocese of Thérouanne, named after the town of the same name; its cathedral had been destroyed in 1559 during the war. The inauguration of the new see followed legally with Pius IV's Bull 'De statu ecclesiarum' of 11th March, 1561. It had a relatively short existence, as it was suppressed in the secularisation of 1801. The town of St Omer contained at that time six parishes: St Martin, St John Baptist, St Margaret, St Aldegonde, the Holy Sepulchre and St Denis.

The first bishop was Gerard d'Haméricourt.[9] His term of office was benevolent, in spite of the difficult political situation. He founded Sunday schools with catechism classes, and the College of St Bertin for poor boys. In 1567 this was taken over by the Walloon Jesuits.In the time of his successor, Jean Stix (1581-1586) the Poor Clares travelled from Veere (northern Netherlands), via Antwerp to St Omer. Bishop Jean de Vernois (1591-1599) procured for them a whole building belonging to the Town Watch (Archers), where they lodged, uncomfortably. The top limit for the convent was set at thirty nuns.[10] It was here that Mary Ward entered as a lay sister in 1606.

In 1592 the English Jesuits had been able to settle in St Omer, by an arrangement between the King of Spain and the Town Magistrate with the help of the Bishop. For a time the see was vacant, and then Jacques Blaes was appointed Bishop (17th March, 1601 — 21st March, 1618). He is one of the most striking personalities in the short line of bishops of St Omer. Even his coat of arms emphasises his vision: URGET AETERNUM — eternity impels us.

He was born in Bruges in 1540 and therefore was Flemish; he entered the Franciscan Order when still young and gained a doctorate in theology. Later, he was Provincial of his order in Belgium. In 1597 he became Bishop of Namur and in 1601 transferred to St Omer.

The new bishop began to transform his diocese. In 1606 he published a new Ritual in French and Dutch; in 1608 he re-arranged the parishes. At that time there were eleven held by the archpriests, six of which were in the town of St Omer itself.These parishes had three patrons: the Bishop, the Chapter, and the Monastery of St Bertin. That fact alone shows that the Bishop could not always have found it easy to mark out the different areas of responsibility. He was concerned above all with education. As a good friend of the Society of Jesus, he supported the Sunday schools, which were excellently directed by Fathers Malard and Siméon. The seminary for the diocesan priests was in Douai, but many students, especially the wealthier ones, went to Paris or Louvain, so in 1604 the Bishop enlarged the Douai seminary and encouraged his students to have a closer connection with their own diocese.

He also furthered the education of girls, which had begun modestly in Flanders some time before. When Marie Aubrun, daughter of Councillor Antoine Aubrun, began to instruct poor girls in her own house, Bishop Blaes had a house built for her, begun in 1609 and finished by 1615.

In those times of persecution for English Catholics, St Omer became a centre for refugees who had left their home for religious reasons. The coastal situation of the town, and its catholicism, made it a favourable place for the English to settle. The Bishop too was involved in bettering their plight. He gave the English Jesuits a house in Watten which they maintained until 1763. He supported the veneration of Our Lady of Montaigue or Sichem (Flemish: Scherpenheuvel) practised in the house of the Walloon Jesuits, for which a confraternity soon developed. In 1611 the church of the Walloon Jesuits was consecrated, and a few years later, on 7th June, 1614, the bishop consecrated the new church of the Poor Clares.

Bishop Blaes re-organised the diocese of St Omer and re-motivated his clergy. Bled, in his account of the Bishop, comments with particular aptness: 'He was a man of great character; a man of principle, learned in many disciplines and experienced in ecclesiastical matters.'[11]

St Omer was rich in monasteries and convents. In 1606, when Mary Ward arrived in Flanders, there were several Orders and Institutes for women within its walls: the Grey sisters (Soeur Grises); the Black sisters (Soeurs Noires); the so-called 'Sun' sisters (du Soleil); the Poor Clares and the Rich Clares (Urbanists − who did not beg for a living). All of these followed the Rule of St Francis. Those following the Rule of St Dominic were the sisters of St Catherine, the Sisters of Sion, the Sisters of St Margaret. The community of the Daughters of St Agnes, who were spread all over Belgium, had a house here. At that time they were a modern foundation, 'Devotes', a pious association. Since 1609 they had been installed in what is today the rue Gambetta, near the Walloon Jesuit College. Their rule was Augustinian, like that of the Ursulines in Paris, and they devoted themselves to the education of girls of all classes.

In 1626 they received episcopal approval. In the older writings about the town and the bishopric of St Omer,they were often confused with the Englishwomen.[12] Another congregation that devoted itself to the education of girls was that of the Daughters of Our Lady of the Angels, who had a house in Valenciennes. As well as these, there were the penitential sisters, and the newly founded 'Our Lady of the Garden' of Marie Aubrun, engaged in the education of girls.

Of the men's orders, the Benedictines of St Bertin and the Jesuits were the more familiar. The Abbey of St Bertin had been founded in the seventh century; only a few ruins remain of this beautiful, extensive building. The Society of Jesus was represented by two nationalities in St Omer;from 1567 by the Walloon College at the corner of what was then the rue de la Luresse/Vieil Brusle (now rue Gambetta); from 1592 by the English Seminary in the rue St Bertin. The Town Magistrate had serious misgivings (as is often the case when new religious houses are founded) about the size of the buildings, which immediately became a centre for English catholic refugees. But the Jesuits found support with the Bishop of St Omer and the King of Spain, who gave them generous donations and an annual allowance.[13]

The founder and first Rector of the English Seminary was Fr William Flake,[14] (1592-97) who, like his successor Fr Giles Schoondonck[15] (1600–17) played an important part in Mary Ward's life. After him Fr William Baldwin,[16] an Englishman, was Rector (1622-32). He had been under considerable strain politically and had spent eight years imprisoned in the Tower. The English Seminary was soon deep in debt[17] but it had an enormous influence on the spiritual and religious development of the young Englishmen who studied with the Jesuits and most of all, the English refugees who wanted to stay in St Omer. In 1610 the Seminary had fifteen fathers and ninety-two students[18]; it is still possible to read the inscription over the main doorway of the original English building, which is now used for other purposes.

In 1629, almost 25 years after Mary Ward entered the poor Clares there, St Omer had about 3–4,000 houses and about 20,000 souls, though this may be an over-estimate.[19] The town is about 30 kilometers inland from Calais, so Mary Ward and Mrs Bentley should not have taken too long over the journey. Mary Ward's emotional state is reflected by the speed of her actions. Without wasting time in changing from her riding clothes [20] she writes, she went straight to the Seminary of the English Jesuits with Fr Holtby's letter of recommendation to Fr Flake, who had recently returned to St Omer from Ghent.

All her life Mary Ward was to act quickly when she saw her way open to God, as though any loss of time were a burden. So a reverse, caused by delay or a disappointment, hit her all the harder. Life was to provide her with many such experiences, fired as she was with enthusiasm for God.

The letters from England were addressed to Fr Flake, but it was not he who came into the hall to meet her but Fr George Keynes, Professor of Moral Theology in the English Seminary.[21] Mary Ward reports the ensuing conversation in unusual detail. We have it in two versions, in the two autobiographical sketches, E (English) and G (Italian).[22] They do not show much variation, but sometimes a shift of emphasis. The Jesuits had undoubtedly been informed of her desire to enter and of the approximate time of her arrival in St Omer. This explains why Fr Keynes dealt with her request even before Fr Flake appeared.

First of all, Fr Keynes said that Mary Ward had long been expected in the Convent of the Poor Clares in St Omer. Some young English-women had already been living there for some years. The spirit of the community, and above all of these Englishwomen, was excellent. However, she could not be admitted as a choir sister, as the convent was more than full. The nuns had decided not to accept any more Englishwomen as choir sisters but one of Lord Lumley's nieces, Anne Campian, who had recently been refused for the choir, lived there happily as a lay sister. The Abbess had even postponed Anne's clothing until Mary Ward's admission.

Let us pause here briefly.

There is nothing left of the poor Clare Convent today. As already mentioned, the sisters came from their motherhouse in Veere, a place on the island of Walcheren in the Dutch province of Zeeland. During the war they had to leave their house 'Nazareth' on 24th April 1572 and by 11th May it had been reduced to ashes by the Calvinists as they moved in. At first the sisters went to Antwerp but had to leave again (20th July, 1581) and with the influence of the English Jesuits found a temporary home for themselves in the house of the Town Guard (Archers) in St Omer which offered little opportunity for leading a peaceful life of contemplation. At last in 1594, the militia withdrew, the entire house was put at their disposal and they were allowed to stay there permanently in the short street still called 'Archers'.

The Poor Clares lived exclusively from alms and must not be con-fused with the 'Rich' Clares or Urbanists, who had settled in St Omer in 1477 and lived according to a mitigated Rule. The number of Poor Clares was limited to thirty in a house. The original sisters from Veere were Dutch, and they spoke Dutch, but twenty-five years had passed; girls from St Omer and the neighbourhood had entered the convent and these spoke French. St Omer at that time belonged to the Dutch province of Flanders but the inhabitants were French-speaking Wal-loons; their area of settlement still, today, stretches from the Pas de Calais across Hennegau to Namur and Liège. So the convent was already bi-lingual when the great flood of English arrived, presenting suitable young women for admission to the Poor Clares. The convent thereupon became tri-lingual, a difficult situation, even if one takes into consideration the silence of a contemplative life. Their caution in accepting foreigners must surely be viewed as the perfectly justifiable behaviour of convent superiors, nuns of the locality, who already had language difficulties, acting to protect themselves against an influx of English women. However pious or nobly-born these might be, they had not a word of Dutch or French between them, and could not follow convent instructions, common prayers — as far as these were not in Latin — or take part in recreation on the already limited topics of conversation. Other convents had the same national tensions and difficulties.

The English women of the Augustinian choir sisters of St Ursula in Louvain formed a splinter group and founded the Convent of St Monica in the same town. The English Benedictines had their own foundation in Brussels, the house of the Assumption.

To continue. In her autobiographical notes, Fragment E, Mary Ward writes that Fr Keynes informed her that the sisters had a place for her outside the enclosure: 'those without added an act of charity in maintaining the others by their religious labours, and an act of humility in begging for the rest'. Fragment G is shorter here. In E the text says 'the priest added that those within the enclosure and those without were one and the same order and rule, only that to those without were added an act of charity in maintaining the others.' Whether or not Fr Keyne's information was due to a misunderstanding, his statement that the out-sisters had the same life style and Rule as the choir sisters was completely untrue. What is more, it never could have been. The lay sisters followed the Third Order of St Francis. They were Tertiaries. The choir sisters had the strict Rule of St Clare. The decision of Mrs Anne Campian to lead the form of life of a Tertiary seems to imply some sort of encouragement for Mary Ward. Be that as it may,this person mentioned by Fr Keynes as a 'satisfied' religious later entered the Gravelines convent founded by Mary Ward at the end of 1608.

Fr Keynes' description may not have corresponded exactly with the facts — Mary Ward wrote that he had these from hearsay[23] — but even his line of argument was totally inadmissible. In her autobiographical notes G, Mary Ward continues 'In conclusion, he expressed his admiration for the Providence of God in the circumstances, coinciding with the great desire of the nuns to accept me so quickly, never having seen me, affirming that it certainly was the will of God and my true vocation.' With hindsight we can say that she should have recognised her instinctive impulse to refuse as a warning. But, convinced that the Rule of the Order was the same for both, that the out-sisters had more opportunity to practice humility, and that her repugnance was the reaction of pride, she ignored the danger signals given by her very sound instinct. One must not forget, either, that Mary Ward was talking to a religious thirty years older than herself, whom she regarded as a person of mature judgement. At the moment of decision, she was struck by the words 'the Will of God'. Once again 'fear' comes to the surface — 'fear of my pride and the word of the father'. It was fear of the evil within her, a warning for someone with a deep love of God. The account causes astonishment; at the very least, it raises questions.

It has to be assumed that Fr Keynes knew the Poor Clares well, as he praised the sisters, especially the English among them, for their good religious spirit. But was this spirit really so excellent? The events of the year to come make his pronouncement extremely dubious. Yet it must also be assumed that Fr Keynes did not intentionally mislead Mary Ward. The man had a good reputation both as a priest and a Jesuit.

On the one hand, we have a young English woman who wished to enter a 'strict' Order without specifying which, and without much choice, as most of the convents were completely full. On the other, here in St Omer was one which had kept a place free for an English-woman. But her hesitation, and her inner disinclination to enter as an out-sister should have acted as a warning to Fr Keynes to proceed with caution. It was only Fr Flake, a later arrival on the scene to join in her conversation with Fr Keynes, who had presumably seen the dis-appointment in the young girl's features. Fr Keynes may have left by then, or it escaped his notice. Mary Ward concludes this extract of her report with: 'Then I honestly told my confessor and the superiors of the convent how much I was suffering interiorly and how difficult it would be for me to be an out-sister. I left myself to God's providence, I had decided to do his holy will, according to what my confessor and the superiors told me.'

With this, Mary Ward left the final decision in the hands of those who were to be in charge of her spiritual direction. One cannot deny that the final decision ought to be taken by the person concerned and not by others, but here it was the matter of an open conver-sation concerning doubts about her vocation.

The superiors of the Poor Clares, who urgently needed an outsister, cannot be wholly freed from all suspicion of acting with self-interest towards an inexperienced young person on the point of making a difficult decision in her life. Morally speaking, that is more than questionable.

Notes

1. AB/E PB p.147, Inst.Arch.Munich.
2. 1506 Emperor Maximilian I appointed his daughter Margaret as Governor. After her death, 1530, Charles V installed his sister Maria, and when she died, Philip II entrusted his half-sister Margareta, Duchess of Parma, with this office.
3. Fernando Alvarez de Toledo, Duke of Alba (1567–1573), Don Luis de Requesens (1573–1576), Don Juan d'Austria (1576–1578), Alexander Farnese of Parma (1578–1592) and Archduke Ernst (1592–1595).
4. It received Groningen, Leewarden, Deventer, Haarlem and Middelburg as Suffragan bishoprics. This division in the northern Netherlands lost its signifi-cance partly during the war of independence and completely after peace was concluded in 1648; much later it formed the basis of a new arrangement.
5. Subject to this were the bishoprics of Antwerp, Bruges, Ghent, Ypres, Roermond and 's Hertogenbosch. The two last are still part of the Netherlands.
6. With the Suffragan bishoprics of Arras, Tournai, Namur and Saint-Omer.
7. AB/E,PB p.148. Inst.Arch.Munich.

8. The 'Twaalfjarig Bestand', 1609–1621. During this brief time of peace, Mary Ward's Institute in Belgium was able to develop.
9. Bled, Les Evêques, p.67 ff.
10. ibid.p.273–274.
11. Hier.Cath.IV, p. 122, 252; Bled, Les Evêques, p.333–4124; A.de Schrevel, Jacques Blaese ou Blaseus = Annales de la Société d'émulation de Bruges 1933, p.40 – 56; L.Jadin, Relations de Pays-Bas, de Liège et de Franche-Comté avec le Saint-Siège (1566–1779) = Bibl.de l'Inst.hist.Belge de Rome IV/1952, p. 55–56.
12. Bled, Les Evêques, p.391. Hendrique, in his Recueil Historique, pp. 308–309, was not able to make a clear distinction; AM Saint-Omer, Ms.808.
13. Bled, Les Evêques, p.280; ibid.Les Jésuites Anglais a Saint-Omer, Saint-Omer 1890, p.3.
14. Fr William Flake SJ was born in Suffolk in 1561. He studied at first in England, then entered the English College in Rome in 1584 and was received into the Society of Jesus in the following year. He was ordained in 1591. From 1592–4593 he assisted Fr Persons in founding the English seminary in Saint-Omer, where he held various posts until 1625. He was Rector in Ghent for three years after which he returned to Saint-Omer, where he died on 13th December 1637. He was procurator of the house for some time. Foley, Records VI, p.167 and VII/I, p.261–262.
15. Fr/Giles Schoondonck SJ was born in Bruges and entered the Society of Jesus in 1576. He was Rector of the English seminary in Saint-Omer form 1600 to his death there on 22nd January, 1617. ibid.VII/II p. 691 and p.1247–1257.
16. Fr William Baldwin SJ was born in 1563 in Cornwall. He first studied in England, then in Douai and Rheims. He was accepted into the English College in Rome in 1583 and was ordained in 1588. In 1590 he entered the Society of Jesus in Belgium and worked as professor of theology in Louvain but lived for eleven years in Brussels. During a stay in Germany in 1610 he was arrested, deported to England and kept in the Tower until 1618. He was then banished. In 1621 he was Rector in Louvain, in 1622 in Saint-Omer. He died there on 28th September, 1632. ibid, III, p.510 – 520, and VII/I, p.42.
17. Bled, Les Jésuites Anglais a Saint-Omer. p.14 gives the sum of £80,000.
18. ibid. p.3.ff.
19. L.Jadin, Procès d'information pour la nomination des evêques et abbés des Pays-Bas, de Liège et de Franche-Comte d'après les archives de la Congregation Consistoriale = Bull. de l'Instit.histor.Belge de Rome VIII/1928, p.199.ff.
20. AB/E,PB p.148: riding safeguard.
21. Fr George Keynes SJ, born 1553 in Somerset, he entered the Society of Jesus in 1593. From 1595 he was professor of moral theology in the English seminary in Saint-Omer where he had studied. He died there in 1611. Foley, Records V, p.297 and VII/I, p. 416.
22. AB/E, PB pp. 149–153, and AB/G, pp. 79, Inst.Arch.Munich. These two outlines vary a little in their statements, according to their point of view. Vita E and Vita I report the facts, but without details. The author could not give these for reasons of discretion towards the English Jesuits.
23. AB/G, p.8, Inst.Arch.Munich.

V

THE POOR CLARES

The Outsister

Mary Ward's admission to the Poor Clares — daily begging in the town — difficulties with her vocation — the Novice Mistress

The day after her arrival, Mary Ward received an invitation to stay with the nuns. She remained with them about a month, and then she was clothed.[1] Her postulancy was therefore very short, and it is doubtful if the prospective laysister had been made more than passingly familiar with the spirit of the Order.

It was the Franciscan Provincial who raised objections to her admission to the novitiate. He may have noticed that she was neither physically nor spiritually suited to the life of an outsister, but the superiors of the convent were in a driving hurry for this clothing ceremony. Afterwards, everyday life began. As an outsister, Mary Ward had to care for the needs of the kitchen with the other laysisters. This involved a daily begging routine through the streets of the town and its marshy neighbourhood; it involved facing the impoverished and often rough inhabitants; it doubtless also involved some danger from the Spanish soldiery. Most of all, it involved constant distraction, quite the reverse of a contemplative life. Immediately, involuntary though this was, she attracted attention. Town ladies asked the Abbess why such a gentle and delicate young girl had been given this sort of work. They were told that Mary Ward had herself applied for it, out of humility. It would have been nearer the truth to say that Mary Ward had accepted it, out of humility.

One is inclined to ask whether they could not have given her something else to do, either in the house or garden. Perhaps with a more meditative task, the bitterness of her disappointment would have been less. The reason why she had been appointed to this occupation of carrying heavy burdens was because some of the outsisters had committed serious faults against honesty. As a result, one of the choir sisters had been taken from the enclosure, in order to supervise them. This was to last only until a suitable sister could be found to replace her. It was now hoped that Mary Ward would be the person to take on this office. It was somewhat premature. Mary Ward adds a sentence at this point which is important for our understanding of her personality. She writes: 'If I had known before what it was that they intended, I would certainly not have entered, for even then I had, as I remembered, a different idea of the qualities which are necessary for a person in charge.' The English and Italian lives mention an illness at this time. Mary Ward was unaccustomed to carrying heavy loads or walking far every day whatever the weather. Her acts of self-denial in the Babthorpe household were child's play in comparison with what she experienced as an outsister; her reserved nature must have been tormented by it. She developed an abscess on the knee, which kept her in bed for a time.[2]

Worse than any physical pain and life out on the streets, was her inner loneliness, the feeling that she had been cheated of the sublime. For it was not because of her vocation, or her interior disposition that she had been admitted, but simply because of the immediate needs of the community. This must have been an extremely painful realisation.

Two months after her admission, in August 1606, Fr Keynes – who had said only a short time before that the role of lay sister was God's will for her – told her that the life of a lay sister was not her true vocation. At the same time, Mary Ward noticed a great difference between the Rule and life style of the choir sisters and that of the lay sisters. Even the behaviour of the nuns changed towards her. Mary Ward writes discreetly that their behaviour did not correspond with her own directness. The nuns must have noticed the inner struggle of the young sister. Disappointment was probably keen on both sides. Soon afterwards she was given a Walloon confessor; because of the language differences, she can hardly have had much opportunity of conferring; there is no mention why this particular hardship was added. Perhaps it was a consequence of Fr Keynes' change of opinion about her.

Just at this time the novice mistress and director of the lay sisters, Sister Mary Stephen Goudge, fell ill. Mary Ward had a deep affection for this capable but strict nun, an attachment that was never returned. For convalescence she returned to the enclosure; the lay sisters were probably left to themselves. The circle of human isolation round Mary Ward was complete.

St Gregory's Day, 1607

Mary Ward's spiritual distress – conversation with the Visitor and his advice – divine commission to found a convent for the English Poor Clares – departure from the convent

In her spiritually troubled state, Mary Ward's inevitable home-sickness would have been doubly painful. To a daughter of Marmaduke Ward and Ursula Wright, the very soil of her country was precious. The events of 5th November, 1605 and their consequences would have still been fresh in her memory; these were her last impressions of home. The exiles on the Continent prayed daily and made sacrifices for the conversion of England, especially those in religious orders, so it was no chance occurrence that brought about the following circumstance on St Gregory's feast day.[3]

Pope Gregory the Great, whose feast used to be celebrated by the Church on 12th March, sent an abbot and 40 monks to the pagan Anglo-Saxons in 596, and had personal oversight of their mission. Mary Ward had chosen this holy pope as her special advocate, and while she was working in silence with the other sisters on 12th March, she prayed to St Gregory. As he had helped her country so much during his life she asked him now, from heaven, to help an Englishwoman – namely herself, – so that in her distress she could make a decision in accordance with God's will. Suddenly the bell was rung. The Order's Visitor, Fr Andreas de Soto,[4] had arrived in the house, and all the sisters were summoned by the bell to receive his blessing.

The English Life [5] says that Mary Ward was the only English-woman in the house. This cannot be the case. At that time it is certain that Margaret Fowler, Elizabeth Darrell, Anne Campian, Ellen Burton, Frances Courtes and the Novice Mistress of the lay sisters, Mary Stephen Goudge, were all living there then, for the following year they transferred to the English Poor Clare convent in Gravelines, and in 1610 they were followed by Anne Brooke and Anne Tholward. There were at least eight Englishwomen in the community in addition to Mary Ward. The text probably meant that Mary Ward was the only one kept behind to talk to the Visitor. Fr de Soto told her bluntly that she was not suited to the life, and that she should consider the matter thoroughly before making her profession. Although Mary Ward was surprised at this, it was not particularly unexpected that he should ask to speak with her, or even that he knew of her problems. He could have heard of these from the Abbess or the Novice Mistress. Just as she had been silent when Fr Keynes had spoken to her on her arrival in St Omer, Mary Ward was silent now. She took her leave respectfully and gratefully, and returned to her work and her prayers to St Gregory. It was then that something remarkable happened, which is best left to her to describe:

'I was suddenly enkindled with a vehement desire to procure a monastery for the English of this Order, but not being able to moderate this vehemence and make myself indifferent before speaking or doing anything towards this, I retired alone, and earnestly intreated our Lord God that nothing that I might do in this business should have any success other than that which He willed.'[6]

It should be noted in the first place that she felt a strong inclination towards this specific task. That points to more than first thoughts about this particular possibility. Her sole reaction was a petition that she might fulfil God's will.

After that, her latent organising abilities took over. She went back quickly to the Visitor, to present her suggestion of merging two convents and giving the emptied building to the English women. He was no longer there.

The English Life[7] gives a slightly different version of the event. According to this, Mary Ward eventually met the priest again, and made her suggestion regarding the separation of the two nationalities; he is said to have answered that this was not possible.

There must have been something slightly amiss with the excellent religious spirit of the Order, especially that of the Englishwomen described by Fr Keynes, for it must be assumed that the impulse, the vehement longing for an English foundation, did not originate from Mary Ward alone but from a good few of the Englishwomen who were unhappy or at least had serious problems in the Walloon house of the Poor Clares. The future was to show that these women had been chosen as the seedbed of a thriving community. It is significant that Mary Ward had been appointed to initiate this. Consider: she was twenty-two years old, a novice and a stranger, so her position in the Order can in no way be regarded as established, although her spiritual qualities had been recognised. In addition, she was a lay sister and not a choir sister following the strict rule. Despite all this, it was precisely she who made a suggestion which could have turned the household upside down.

After Mary Ward had absorbed the Visitor's words silently, she must have thought seriously for the first time about leaving. She had a strong interior certainty − 'frequent and clear lights' − that she was not to be a lay sister, and that she might leave the convent without any scruple. God left her free to make her own decision. Mary Ward still had little experience of mystical prayer accompanied by illumination, so she remained cautious and wary. She wrote this occurrence down, intending to show it to her Novice Mistress as soon as there was an opportunity.

When Sr Mary Stephen Goudge could take up her work again, Mary handed her these notes with the request to tell her honestly whether she should be professed or not. Sr Mary Stephen handed them back, giving her opinion that Mary Ward was not called to a life outside the enclosure, that is, to live as a Tertiary of St Francis, but to the life of an enclosed nun, according to the first rule of St Clare. The inevitable happened: a few days later Mary Ward left the Walloon Convent.

Between the two Convents

The time after Mary Ward's departure – spiritual dryness –
lack of spiritual direction from her confessor Fr Keynes –
material help from Fr Roger Lee

We know very little about Mary Ward during the time between her
departure from the Walloon convent of the Poor Clares and her
admission to her own English foundation in Gravelines, that is,
from April/May 1607 to November 1609. The English and Italian
lives pass lightly over this period and Mary Ward herself has left
only a few extremely meagre sentences, in which the success of the
foundation is humbly ascribed to the goodness of God's mercy.[8]
The written sources of the Poor Clares in Gravelines are more
detailed but – and that holds good particularly for the Annals –
they are subjective, unreliable and sometimes barbed. According to
the Annals[9] Mary Ward first arrived on the Continent in 1607. On
Mrs Bentley's pass she was not entered as her daughter but as her
serving girl. Although her father loved his daughter tenderly, she
had left England secretly. As she did not possess sufficient dowry
to enter as a Choir sister, she was accepted as a lay sister. While
she was still in the Walloon convent she had heard of a gentleman
who was dying, who wished to make a foundation in Gravelines on
a piece of land there. Not a word of this is correct, as can be shown
from other reliable sources.

It was probably mainly in St Omer that Mary Ward spent the
time before admission to her own foundation. She laments the
extraordinary spiritual dryness that she had to endure for two
years. Many beginners ascribe such trials to their own imperfection.[10] Moreover, the direction she had from Fr Keynes[11] to
whom she went to confession again after she had left the convent,
was conducive to fear rather than encouragement. He suggested, for
example, that she should arouse feelings of self-hatred, and fear of
God's judgement and horror of hell. When one considers that Mary
was in any case inclined to scrupulousness and fear of sin, this would
appear to have been imprudent, however good his intentions. On 17th
September, (1608) she came to know Fr Roger Lee, SJ better[12] so
it seems likely that she changed confessors shortly after leaving the
convent.

In what sort of circumstances did Mary Ward spend this time? She
says that she was wearing ordinary clothes. Nothing else would have
been possible. But had she brought sufficient with her from England,
when she knew she was going to enter? Where did she find somewhere
suitable to live in St Omer? What did people think, when they learnt
of her leaving? Many people knew her as an out-sister of the Poor
Clare Convent. True, some women had expressed their misgivings
to the Abbess at seeing such a young girl appointed to the heavy and

dangerous work of an outsister. But did these women stay of the same mind? In addition to that, before Mary Ward left, certain laysisters had left because they had sinned against chastity. Did she now suffer the same taint? And what of all the news from the convent? Did the sisters always defend her before their visitors from the town? These are questions that must remain unanswered. There is a letter from those days, sent by Fr Richard Holtby in England to Fr Roger Lee in St Omer[13] which, although heavily coded, gives us a glimpse into her circumstances, which were certainly not comfortable. From the text it appears that Fr Roger Lee had been asking for money for Mary Ward. This petition reached its goal, but the original has not survived. On the back of the answer, which does, another handwriting has mistakenly given the date of the year as 1600. The writer, Fr Holtby, in his own writing has given the incomplete date on the text as 17th September. The year 1600 does not make sense. Mary Ward was with the Babthorpes at that time. Immediately on her arrival in St Omer, on 11th May, 1606, she entered the convent of the Poor Clares and remained there until April/May 1607. So on 17th September, 1606, Fr Lee had no reason to be asking for money for her. She undoubtedly took her dowry with her, for she wrote that she could have found acceptance in other convents.[14] In those days that would not have been possible without a dowry.

Even 1607 hardly comes into the question. Her money would have been sufficient for a simple life-style for six months. It is therefore assumed that Fr Holtby wrote his letter on 17th September,1608. By that time Mary Ward would have been living about fifteen months outside the community and was occupied with the new English foundation. She may have asked Fr Lee to negotiate for a contribution from England, both for herself and the new project. The letter was written in code. With some certainty one can make out:[15] '...but the money asked for (money = stuff, material) was already determined by Robinson (an alias) for another Order (party, company). Write if you want more. I know that she is not suffering want (she = Mary Ward) although since her leaving (progress, journey) her means (stoare, supply) has been consumed.' Mary Ward was therefore to be helped at a later date. Fr Lee never received the letter. It is lying in the Record Office in London, a sign that it had been intercepted before it could reach its destination.

Esquelbecq

Recommendations to the sovereigns for the foundation of an English Poor Clare convent − the foundation of the Governor of Gravelines in Esquelbecq − objections of Bishop Charles Maes of Ypres, against this foundation − its transfer to Gravelines

Suddenly, after a year of obscurity about Mary Ward, Bishop Jacques Blaes of St Omer breaks the silence of the sources. On 3rd April, 1608[16] he wrote a letter of recommendation to the sovereign of the Spanish Netherlands, Archduke Albrecht, for certain Englishwomen who had received a house from the Governor of of the town of Gravelines[17] in Esquelbecq, in order to found a Poor Clare Convent. Financially, the foundation would be secure through the dowries of the petitioners. This piece of information was important for gaining the Archduke's approval. The town as well as the government was protecting itself against the mendicant orders, which were a financial burden on the citizens.

The petition took the customary path through the Chancellery, and Councillor d'Asseliers was directed to inform the Archduke on 24th April.[18] But Mary Ward and certain other Englishwomen had also sent a petition.[19] On 22nd April this was presented in Brussels and pressed home on 5th May. This is more detailed than the Bishop's and, as the reason for their request, the petitioners give the fact that the convents in Flanders were filled to overflowing, which was true. The country was, in a manner of speaking, saturated with religious houses. Chambers,[20] wrote that the foundation was probably paid for to a large extent out of Mary Ward's own means. That is not correct. The sources show that the new foundation came into being as a result of an endowment of the Governor of Gravelines.[21] It consisted of a house and a piece of land. In order not to become a burden to the people, the English women wanted to dispense with begging. Mary Ward, who had suffered greatly on her own begging excursions, will hardly have raised any objections against this mitigation of the original rule; she would otherwise have imposed on the sisters of her own community a burden she had disapproved of in her own case. In addition, the Governor and his wife [22] gave the sisters an annual allowance of £25, with back payment for ten years, from 1598. The dowries were to be arranged with the Bishop of Ypres, in whose diocese the new foundation lay. Until the arrival of the dowries, the Governor and his wife gave the sisters a further loan of 1000 guilders. The return of this was later to be a cause of contention. According to the Annals of the English Poor Clares in Gravelines,[23] the sisters received larger and smaller sums from English friends. The beginning, therefore, was well in hand.

Who were these Englishwomen, these 'demoiselles d'Angleterre, refugiées pardela'? They cannot have been any of the Englishwomen from the convent of the Poor Clares. These were strictly bound by enclosure and it will be seen later, when the building was already completed, all manner of difficulties arose when they were transferred. The Annals of the English Poor Clares[24] mentions Mary Ward's sister Frances, and two lay sisters not mentioned by name.

The small village of Esquelbecq (in Flemish Eckelsbeke) now lies in the French Department Nord. In the 17th century it belonged to the province of Flanders and to the diocese of Ypres. The place was not fortified and was exposed to danger because of its geographical position during those times of war. However, the petition to the Archduke had been composed by the Bishop of St Omer. That is where Mary Ward lived, and where her English friends lived, and the Jesuits. The foundation itself, however, lay in the diocese of Ypres. What did the bishop of that diocese say? This question had to be clarified first of all. Logically enough, the Archduke Albrecht and the Infanta Isabella Clara Eugenia asked Bishop Charles Maes for an opinion, as Esquelbecq lay within his competence.[25] He posed conditions.[26] First, the foundation should not be in Esquelbecq but in a fortified town; secondly, if there were any difficulties about the amount of the nuns' dowries, these should be arranged by the Archduke and the Bishop of the place. Finally, was the convent to be subject to the local bishop? He thought that the Governor of Gravelines could have no objections against the transfer of his foundation to a fortified town.

In the meantime[27] the English envoy in Brussels, Sir Thomas Edmondes, reported to London that this foundation was the work of the Jesuits, which was not totally without substance. Three weeks later the Bishop of Ypres [28] wrote to the influential Secretary of State, Philipp Prats, that these Englishwomen were not satisfied with the conditions. On this the Bishop admitted that, with regard to the location of the new foundation, he had had in mind the decisions of the Council of Trent, but this Council had not made it obligatory for a new foundation to be in a fortified town, but had merely suggested it as good advice, which was a fact.

The future English Poor Clares accepted the Bishop of Ypres' conditions. But now the Governor of Gravelines would not hear of his foundation being transferred.[29] He did indeed possess property in both places, but had no suitable house to offer. Hence his opposition; hence the original opposition to the Englishwomen. Bishop Maes negotiated with the Archduke.[30]

When matters seemed to be going totally awry, the Bishop left them in the hands of the sovereign.[31] One is left with the impression that despite the Bishop's protests, he was not too happy about the plan to have a convent of English Poor Clares in his diocese, and somewhere in the background unknown and unnamed forces were playing games for and against.

Finally, the Governor yielded.[32] The new convent was to be built in the fortified town of Gravelines, within the diocese of St Omer. Bishop Blaes accepted the legal position of the convent as coming under his jurisdiction; he also accepted the sisters' dispensation from begging. These conditions could be ratified only after the patent for the foundation had been received from the Sovereign.

The Journey to Brussels

Mary Ward's stay in Brussels according to the sources — a wait of six months — helpers — success

Chambers[33] goes into considerable detail when describing Mary Ward's journey to Brussels, made in order to present the plans for her foundation personally. She mentions a period of waiting, spent 'at Court', but gives no source. Mary Ward herself does not make any such mention.[34] At all events, not in her letter to Nuntius Albergati[35] or to Cardinal Borghese.[36] Her sister Barbara Ward wrote at the beginning of 1619 that the new foundation had been a difficult undertaking, but she is silent about the journey to Brussels, though for that matter Barbara Ward[37] was inclined to be terse. The English Vita [38] does mention Brussels as Mary Ward's place of residence, but then passes on to the difficulties she encountered there. The length of stay is not specified but it was certainly until she obtained permission to make a foundation. Verbatim: 'she achieved her aim to the admiration of opponents as well as of her patrons, and that within the space of six months.' The Italian Vita corroborates this, [39] but there are some other assertions.

In their Annals the English Jesuits in St Omer insist on their assistance in the matter.[40] Hendricq,[41] who was well-informed on the whole, writes in his Chronicle of St Omer that the Princes were the builders of the convent, which is manifestly not the case. The English Poor Clares in Gravelines gave a different version. As said before, the annalist Sr Cicely was not sympathetic towards Mary Ward; she writes that Mary Ward had dressed in secular clothes and taken herself off to Brussels in order to obtain approval for her plan for a foundation. This somewhat later Chronicle did not know of the Governor of Guernoval's foundation in Esquelbecq, nor of the difficulties with the Bishop of Ypres, nor even of those with the Governor himself: 'When she had achieved her plan she returned to St Omer, after half a yeare spent in prosecuting this affair.'[42] One can sense disapproval in the words, yet it is precisely this source that establishes the length of Mary Ward's stay in Brussels.[43] What do the relevant documents offer? Correspondence about the new convent began, as already mentioned, on 3rd April, 1608 with Bishop Blaes of St Omer's petition to the Rulers.[44] Written negotiations ended on 7th October, 1608 [45] with the granting of the sovereigns' permission of a licence, and that is only six months, a surprisingly short time. But was Mary Ward in Brussels for the whole of that time? It was not the Government nor the Princes who created any difficulties, these came from the Bishop of Ypres, the English women themselves, and the Governor of Gravelines. The correspondence does not lead one to suppose that Archduke Albrecht or Infanta Isabella Clara Eugenia had been substantially involved in smoothing any differences.

It was Bishop Blaes who wrote to Brussels concerning the kindly co-operation of the Governor. Mary Ward must, of course, have had an audience with the Sovereigns, and probably more than one, but there is no indication that she or her companions spent the whole six months in Brussels, especially not in pursuing a campaign behind the scenes. All her life Mary Ward and the first companions too, for that matter, were able to make good contacts. The difficulties here did not originate with the Sovereigns. These kept up a regular correspondence with representatives of the Church at high level. In any case, it is hardly credible that Mary Ward should have lived 'to a certain extent' at Court. The Habsburgs. whether in Madrid, Vienna or Brussels, followed the stiff ceremonial of the Spanish Court, which preserved a degree of august condescension between subject and sovereign. Isabella Clara Eugenia and Archduke Albrecht may have been much loved by their people, but they were never at home in the southern Netherlands.

Nor must it be overlooked that it was on 8th August, 1608, Bishop Maes of Ypres wrote to the Secretary of State, Prats, and on 9th August to Archduke Albrecht,[46] about the Englishwomen's unsuccessful negotiations with the Governor of Gravelines. Who would have dealt with these matters, while Mary Ward was in Brussels? Those Englishwomen who wanted to enter? They did not have the right connections, nor the necessary language skills. It could have been the Jesuits in St Omer. That is certainly possible, but it must be remembered that they have not been mentioned as partners in the negotiations.

Chambers' suggestion[47] that Mary Ward could have stayed with the Benedictine Nuns during this time in Brussels, as she was related to the Abbess, Lady Mary Percy, has no documentary support and should therefore be treated with caution.

Interim in St Omer

Delay of the foundation because of change of location – building a house in Gravelines – temporary residence of English candidates in rented accommodation – transfer of some sisters from the old Poor Clare Convent to rented lodgings – the Abbess and Bishop Blaes – the first Abbess and the first clothings – order of the day in the Poor Clare Convent

Because of the difficulties with the Bishop of Ypres and the Governor of Gravelines, the new foundation had run into considerable delay, which was to have unpleasant consequences. After permission to make a foundation had been received, the house had then to be built. It was in the middle of 1609, almost two years after Mary Ward had left the Walloon Convent, before the building was finished, though the place was still too damp to be lived in.

Meanwhile, some English candidates had arrived in St Omer. It must have been difficult to find them accommodation that was both suitable and within their pocket. In addition, none of the Poor Clares wanted to wait any longer before beginning their religious life.

A house was rented in St Omer at the beginning of November, 1609.[48] It belonged to the Cathedral Chapter and lay close to the English Jesuit College, now rue Gambetta. Sr Cicely wrote in her Chronicle that Mary Ward, her sister Frances, and two lay sisters lived there for three months until Mary Ward could obtain permission from the Bishop for five nuns to transfer to it from the Walloon convent. These dates from the Chronicle cannot be taken seriously. A community would hardly have been founded before the granting of the patent (7th October, 1608). The Walloon nuns entered the temporary house on 7th November, 1608, so Mary Ward and the newcomers lived in it for a month at most. Five nuns came from the Walloon convent: Mary Stephen Goudge as the future Abbess, Margaret Fowler (St Clare of St John); Elizabeth Darrell (Sr Lucy of St John); two lay-sisters, St Antoinette of St John, a Walloon, and Anne Campian.[49] So from the 7th November, 1608, three choir sisters, two lay sisters and four candidates lived in this house. They were the first English Poor Clares of the new Gravelines foundation.

How did the motherhouse, and the Abbess in particular, react to this English filial-foundation which had moved into rented lodgings in the same town, not even wishing to wait for the completion of the Gravelines house? What of the reactions of the nuns concerned?

The Annual Letters of the English Jesuits in St Omer make vague insinuations as to 'problems'.[50] Hendricq was informed, apparently, about the resistance of five nuns who refused to leave their enclosure.[51] Otherwise there are merely partisan and hostile sources, in so far as there are any known details. The Register of the English Poor Clares in Gravelines simply states that the English nuns of the Walloon house moved as ordered, and under holy Obedience.[52] The English Chronicle of the Poor Clare's gives a more dramatic, somewhat disquieting slant to the move.

It was only after three months, writes Sr Cicely, that the Englishwomen were able to persuade the Bishop of St Omer to allow the transfer of five nuns from the old convent, so that these could be founder-members of the new convent in Gravelines. It was the Abbess who refused to comply in the first place. Mary Ward had thereupon turned once more to the Bishop, who promptly threatened the Abbess with excommunication. Only then did she agree. Fr Andreas Couvreur (alias de Texto), Franciscan Guardian in St Omer together with his most senior confrères, took the five nuns on the evening of the 7th November in a closed carriage to their new home, where Mary Ward had prepared all that was needful for their life of absolute poverty.[53] That is to say, straw sacks. Let us pause again.

The Abbess certainly had good reason to quibble at her nuns' departure, for to leave the enclosure voluntarily would have been a serious fault for those concerned. One of the decisions of the Council of Trent had been to enjoin strict vigilance over women's enclosure. One might object that this was no frivolous excursion over a threshold but a move to found a house of the same Order. Had it not been done in other towns? And was it not a sign of genuine religious spirit to ask other religious of the same nationality, experienced in the life, to hand on the charism of the Order? Ought it not rather to have been an occasion of joy, to have one's own English convent? It must not be forgotten that the nuns were not moving immediately into the new house in Gravelines but into a temporary one which could not, perhaps, offer the guarantee of strict enclosure – into something, in fact, which hardly amounted to enclosure at all. One can imagine the sort of thing.

On the other hand, Mary Stephen Goudge as Novice Mistress of the laysisters had lived outside the enclosure and so, probably, had Antoinette of St John and Ann Campian, the two lay-sisters. We do not know what their tasks had been in the convent.

To us, centuries later, it seems strange that no simpler modus vivendi or at least a more amicable arrangement could have been found for the Englishwomen who, through unforeseen circumstances, could find no other place to stay for months to come. Of course, and this must not be forgotten either, the Abbess lost a fifth of her community (including Mary Ward) within a short time, assuming that there really were thirty. That was an appreciable loss. And the nuns themselves? The sources report unanimously that they left their house under holy obedience. Is this 'holy obedience' to be identified as compulsion from the Abbess under vow?

That may be true in the case of Mary Stephen Goudge, who cherished no particular love of Mary Ward, but was it true of the others as well? For the Walloon Sister Antoinette of St John? She could not give nationality as a compelling reason. And how should one interpret the fact that on 4th April, 1610,[54] long after Mary Ward had left her foundation and the convent was not suffering from any lack of vocations, that two more nuns, Anne Brooke (Sr Anne of St John) and Anne Tholward (Sr Anne of St Francis) left their convent in St Omer, similarly under 'holy obedience' to transfer to the English convent in Gravelines? Is it not rather to be assumed that they were sent 'under holy obedience'?

Only rarely do the sources mention the most important approval for the foundation, namely the Pope's. It is referred to in the Chronicle of the English Poor Clares[55] and also in Hendricq's Town Chronicle,[56] and in Bishop Blaes' letter of 19th March, 1615.[57] So it cannot be assumed that this foundation neglected the rulings of Canon Law, although written proof of the documents themselves has not survived.

After the nuns from the Walloon convent had joined the tiny community, the English Jesuits and other English people came to welcome them. Sr Cicely adds expressly that they could speak with these as the grill had not yet been erected, but that when they spoke with externs they kept their veils over their faces. Their conversation was brief and always in the presence of two other members of the community.[58]

The grill was soon put up and a choir, which divided them from the world outside. In November 1608, Fr Roger Lee S.J. from the English College in St Omer gave the Thirty Days' exercises of St Ignatius, first of all to the nuns from the Walloon house and then to the candidates, among whom was Mary Ward. The Chronicle reports that the candidates had to make their meditations in the attic for lack of room. These remarks are in strange contrast to Mary Ward's statement, that the house was large and comfortable.

After the Exercises, on 28th December, 1608, Sr Mary Stephen Goudge, the former novice mistress of the lay sisters in the Walloon convent, was appointed Abbess. Here too the sources diverge widely. Mary Ward says nothing about it. The English Vita [59] says that the Bishop's permission had arrived. The Register of the English Poor Clares says on the one hand[60] that Mary Stephen Goudge was publicly elected Abbess. The Chronicle[61] reports that the Bishop came to the house at Christmas and appointed this sister as Abbess, and left written testimony of the fact for the house. Bishop Blaes himself writes that, with permission from the Nuntius, he had conducted certain nuns out of their house on 22nd July, 1609,[62] and installed one of them as Abbess. With the Poor Clares it is customary for the Abbess to be elected by the sisters. But who, one is justified in asking, could have voted for her? Neither Mary Ward, her sister Frances, nor the two other new candidates had even received the habit, and we do not know if any of the five nuns who came from the Walloon convent, except for Sister Mary Stephen Goudge herself, were entitled to vote.

However that may be, Bishop Blaes chose the first Abbess of the house and, as well he might, he mentioned the permission of the Nuntius in the matter, for Nuntius Bentivoglio allowed the Bishop a faculty which was not his according to Canon Law.

The question, how much influence Mary Ward had on the appointment of the Abbess, is difficult to make out from these contradictory sources. After her experience in the Walloon convent, it is unlikely that she would personally have put forward the name of her former novice mistress. But it is equally likely that she would have set aside her own feelings in the matter, so that a fit person might be appointed to head the new foundation. It is totally unacceptable that such an open and straightforward woman as Mary Ward would have exerted her influence with the Bishop to gain what she wanted; she was far too upright. The Chronicle of the English Poor Clares is somewhat categoric.

On the same 28th December, two lay sisters were clothed: Ellen Burton (Sr Clare of St Stephen) and Frances Courtes (Sr Frances of St Thomas). In few words Sr Cicely describes the simple ritual in the little chapel. Their hair was cut short,and the habit given with all the solemnity permitted by the lack of space. Thus two postulants were admitted to the community.

On 5th February, 1609, seven candidates received their habits, though this was merely a provisional clothing. The solemnity was to take place in the new church in Gravelines, and that happened in November, 1609. Clothed were Mary Ward and her sister Frances, Timothy Walleston (Sr Frances of St John), Elizabeth Tildesley (Sr Clare Mary Anne), Mary Bramfield, Dorothy Knightley and a candidate whose name is unknown and who was later discharged. They all longed for the completion of the new Gravelines convent. What of their daily routine?

The day began at midnight with Office in common. Afterwards the sisters meditated for an hour and then went to bed. That meant a break of about two hours in their night's rest before the early morning Mass. They slept on straw sacks. The food was not exactly nourishing; they never ate meat, not even when they were ill, except at Christmas. They spent almost the whole of the day on their knees and in silence. Any necessary conversation was conducted briefly, in a low voice and only with permission from the superior. Half an hour a day was at their free disposal. Mary Ward used this to pray for the Church, for the saints of the Order, and for the increase of new foundations (a broadness of vision from behind the grill, and within the confines of solitude). They wore a woollen habit; they did not wear linen, such as they had at home, but rough cloth. Mary Ward adds to her report that she seldom slept more than two hours because she was so hungry.[63] She will not have been the only one, because all of them were young, some still approaching adulthood.

As the day of the provisional clothing approached, Bishop Blaes asked that Mary Ward should also make her Profession. Her confessor Father Lee and other English Jesuits in the seminary[64] were of the same opinion. The Abbess refused. Later, when she wrote notes for her autobiography, Mary Ward considered that this refusal had been an act of God. It is true, had she been professed, there would have been no going back. It would, moreover, have been a profession without any proper preparation as a choir sister. Her noviceship as a tertiary in the Walloon convent could hardly be judged adequate. What is more, she had not completed this noviceship but had left it.

Mary Ward saw perfection in the strictness and seclusion. It suited her nature. She followed the convent duties with loving eagerness. She was so punctual that she was sometimes ashamed of being quicker than the others when the bell sounded, as this could seem to make them negligent to some extent.

In this quiet life of prayer, of solitary relationship with God, Mary Ward was happy. The English Vita[65] says that later she spoke of having experienced 'glimpses and hoverings'. The strongest vocation is never free from doubts and temptations, and we can regard these phenomena as normal in Mary Ward's case too. She herself probably did not pay them too much attention.

St Athanasius' Day 1609

God's direction to Mary Ward to leave the Poor Clares – her suffering, and the disapproval of her confessor Fr Roger Lee SJ – her departure – her stay in St Omer

On 2nd May, 1609, at about 10 o'clock in the morning, Mary Ward and the other nuns were making Franciscan girdles, those knotted white cords which bind the heavy Poor Clare habit around the waist. At the same time she was praying the Litany of Loreto, that whoever should wear this girdle should never commit any serious fault. So, like her sisters she was occupied in prayer and not concerned with her own matters. It was precisely at that point that God broke into her peace. It is probably best to let her own words speak:[66]

'The happening seemed to me to come from God and seized me with such force, that it annihilated me completely. My strength went, and I felt in myself no other power to do anything except that which God did. All that remained to me was only this, spiritually to see what had happened and what was to be performed in me, whether I wanted it or not. I suffered greatly, for the force was far beyond my powers; my greatest consolation was that I could see that God, in his divine benevolence, desired that I should serve him. It was also shown me that I should not stay in the holy Order of St Clare; I was to do something different, but what and in what manner I did not see, and neither could I guess. I only understood that it was something good, and was the will of God.'

If, for a moment, we take a retrospective look at the course of events concerned with the vision of St Gregory's Day in 1607, we see that her intense prayer to St Gregory was interrupted by a bell which summoned the sisters to the Visitor of the Order. The word 'interrupted' is used intentionally, for after her conversation with Fr de Soto, who recommended her leaving, she returned to her devotions to her patron saint. Only then did that vehement, inexplicable longing to found a house of their own for Englishwomen seize her. This desire was at the same time the answer to her prayer. Here, however, on St

Athanasius' Day, though the outer framework seemed the same, this time Mary Ward's prayer was not interrupted, but broken off. Only the 'view of that which had happened and what was to be performed in me' remained with her. That obviously meant her entry into the Poor Clare Order and now, the command from God to leave it; she later wrote that it had been shown her that she should not remain in the Order of St Clare but should do something different.

Is it possible to imagine a greater challenge to her constancy, after all that Mary Ward had done for the Poor Clares in such a short time? And again, as before on St Gregory's Day, the bell rang. This time, not to receive the blessing of the Superior of the Order but – significantly – to make an examination of conscience. She had no energy left, no plans, and no joy. She was thankful to be able to be alone for a short time, to compose herself.[67] Many would have been confused by what seems to be the Lord's tortuous manner of proceeding. Not Mary Ward. It is not possible to understand this wonderful life without understanding her faith, her absolute trust in God, which was rooted in her love for Him.

Already the next day – one can see her disponibility – she asked her confessor's permission to talk to him about her interior revelation under the seal of the confession. Fr Lee would not consent to this, however. In her notes,[68] Mary Ward thinks that he probably wanted to leave himself free to talk to his superiors about it. That was precisely what she feared. There, she thought – (today we might say there, with the English Jesuits) – where she had been loved and esteemed till now, she would shortly not have a single friend but on the contrary would be judged and condemned, and Fr Lee would have to suffer under it all. The thought that her confessor would be drawn into the affair weighed on her. On one side there was scepticism, on the other a shunning of exposure. Fr Lee persisted in his attitude, and the conversation took place on the same day, outside the confidentiality of the confessional.

Her confessor disapproved wholeheartedly of it all, and exhorted her to follow the Rule of the Order most exactly. That is understandable, as the spiritual development of his penitent could no longer be taken as normal. Mary Ward justifies him by saying that Fr Lee took this position perhaps to test her more. That may be so, but had she not already been extremely exact in her observance of the Rule and the order of the day? It was also a fact that she had found much joy in it. Probably, with all his experience, Fr Lee thought at first that the novice was going through a time of temptation. She followed his advice, but did not find inner peace. Only one thing remained certain: she must leave the Order of the Poor Clares and with it her beloved foundation and companions, among whom was her own sister, Frances.

In the autumn of 1609 she left, after taking a vow of chastity before Fr Lee. This time it was not only the house but the Order which she was leaving. The English and Italian Lives make reference to the behaviour of the Abbess, Mary Stephen Goudge, but that will be returned to later.

Once again, Mary Ward was alone, in a humiliating situation.

She thought that Fr Lee probably concurred with the opinion of his superiors. One of her enemies prophesied that she would have a solitary death on the streets; others thought she was besotted with her own success. In our secular age with its levelling of standards, it is difficult to imagine just exactly what was involved in leaving a convent – twice – and that from the same Order, and in the same town. It was later rumoured that Mary Ward had not had the health for the austere life of the Poor Clares, but who would have believed that rather thin claim?

Far worse, for Mary Ward, was the inner uncertainty, the question of what God wanted from her now. One can feel both compassion and envy at her remark: 'My suffering was great, but bearable, for He who imposed it, bore the burden too.'[69]

One particular aspect of God's disconcerting demand, so difficult to understand, will not have occured either to Mary Ward or to her friends. The vision relating to the foundation of a Poor Clare convent for Englishwomen fell on the feast of St Gregory, that great promoter of the mission to England. This time her vision was received on the feast of St Athanasius, the fourth century bishop and doctor of the church, who defended the Council of Nicaea's decree against the Arians, when they rejected the consubstantiality of the Father and the Son.[70] Her immediate future was to lie in her own country, which was torn by religious dissension and, as her life's story will reveal, God made use of her strengths to combat religious controversies in England.

The part played by the Jesuits

The English Jesuits in St Omer and the plan to found a religious house for English women – intermediaries – the Society and its influence on Mary Ward – strange structure of the new English Poor Clares – spiritual direction of the English Poor Clares in St Omer by the Jesuits

Long before Mary Ward could carry out her commission, the English Jesuits in St Omer had already had the idea of founding a convent for English women. They had not settled on a particular Order, but had simply noticed that the Belgian convents were filled to overflowing and that there were few places for English girls who wished to enter. In many instances these young emigrants had no real concept of convent life or of the difference between the Orders, as none had existed in their own country since 1535. Mary Ward herself had simply wanted to enter a 'strict' Order, without specifying any one in particular.

The St Omer English Jesuits' plan was regarded as ridiculous by some of their brother Jesuits and their friends; therefore it remained just that, a plan.[71] But then Mary Ward left the Walloon Poor Clare convent in the spring of 1607, in order to found a convent for English women. How much contact she then had with the Jesuits is not known, though the Fathers must have heard of the event of St Gregory's Day. Fr Keynes was her spiritual director for some time after she left.

It has already been mentioned that the English Ambassador in Brussels reported to London on 1st June, 1608 that the Jesuits had proposed Mary Ward's name when asking the government for a foundation of Poor Clares close to Gravelines.[72] The Annual Report of the English Jesuits in St Omer also stressed the close co-operation of the members of their Order: that Mary Ward was indeed outstandingly gifted, pious and courageous, but completely dependent on the Jesuits, and she had acted solely on their advice.[73] This statement needs to be qualified.

There is no doubt that the Jesuits had entertained a rather hazy plan but they had not been able to bring this to fulfilment. Mary Ward had proceeded under a God-given impulse.

Sr Cicely, in the Chronicle of the English Poor Clares in Gravelines, goes much further:[74] It is true, that Mary Ward had gone straight to the English Jesuits on her arrival in St Omer; they received her with great goodwill, but she had been sent away from there. It is equally true that the English Jesuits were the means by which this devout and intellectually-gifted English girl entered the Walloon Poor Clares. But we have already seen how matters had gone both on her entry and her departure from the convent.

The English Jesuits, writes Sr Cicely, had turned successfully to the Bishop of St Omer and the Abbot of St Bertin, as well as several of their friends. English people had given generously towards the building of the convent; English people and the English Jesuits had welcomed the nuns on their arrival into their temporary base in St Omer. From this, not incorrect but rather heavily slanted statement, it is evident that Sr Cicely was trying to present the English Jesuits as the real founders of the house, and Mary Ward as their docile instrument. Nothing is further from the truth. The heart of the matter has been left out of these narrative sources — her divine commission.

One question remains open: why did Mary Ward not turn to the Franciscans? Mary Ward had been formed by the Jesuits from her youth, as far as one can talk of religious formation at that time of scant direction of Catholics. And Mary Ward had lived on that, even in St Omer, even in the Poor Clare convent, though she was not conscious of it. This was the cause of her difficulties, which have deliberately been set aside until now: disagreements with the

Provincial of the Franciscan Order in Brussels. It was the Visitor of the Order who, in 1607, had advised Mary Ward to consider matters thoroughly before making her profession. It was with great benevolence (con dimostration d'affetto grande) that Pater de Soto met Mary Ward. The English Vita[75] adds that he had offered his help, 'I will serve you in what soever I can'. But it was quite another matter a short time later in Brussels. We do not know if Pater de Soto was in Brussels then, or if his successor, P. Johannes Neyen[76] was already there. But why should the Franciscan superiors oppose a new foundation, and with it the growth of the Poor Clares, when, so to speak, it dropped into their lap? It may be, though there is no evidence for the supposition, that the Franciscans disliked the Jesuit influence and the part they played in the matter.

The new foundation was, to put it mildly, unusual. The nuns followed the Rule of St Clare, which prescribed a mendicant life; these were not allowed to beg. They were to live in the most abject poverty; these had the security of a considerable endowment. Poor Clare convents were subject to Franciscans, yet this house was under the local Bishop. It is true that these had been the conditions laid down by the Bishop of Ypres, but they still held good when the foundation was eventually realised in the fortified town of Gravelines. Bishop Blaes had helped them greatly, but at the same time as a Franciscan he violated the constitutions of their Order when he appointed Mary Stephen Goudge as Abbess, even though he had the permission of the Nuntius to do so. The division became even more marked during the brief period when Mary Ward was making decisions, that is, after the transfer of the future nuns into the temporary house in St Omer, from October 1608 until the installation of the first Abbess on 28th December of the same year.

Mary Ward writes[77] that she had asked Fr Baldwin SJ, Vice-Prefect of the English Mission, to decide on a suitable priest as a help to the sisters at the beginning of their spiritual life. The Thirty Days' retreat of St Ignatius was among those aids. Fr Baldwin sent Fr Lee. The Jesuits were in demand as confessors and givers of retreats, even in women's orders, all of which were enclosed in those days. But one cannot help noticing that Mary Ward turned to the Jesuits and not the Franciscans. It is possible that there was no Englishman among the Franciscans, or that there was no one who spoke English sufficiently well to give sermons. But the Jesuit influence went even further. Fr Lee became the confessor to the nuns, which means that he took on their spiritual direction.

Did all the Jesuits agree with this turn of events? Not at all. Several of the Fathers showed a good deal of interest in the foundation. And the national aspect must not be forgotten, either. There is a uniting factor in a shared disaster.

There were, seemingly, other points of view. Already by 27th December, 1608,[78] the day before the installation of the Abbess, the

Jesuit General Fr Claudio Aquaviva wrote from Rome to Fr Provincial of the Gallo-Belgic province, Fr Francois Fléron, that he had received reports from England and from Belgium informing him that some English Jesuits had supported English women in the foundation of a Poor Clare convent in Gravelines, and that the Fathers were attempting to withdraw the convent from the jurisdiction of the Franciscans, while suggesting a secular priest as confessor for the nuns; that a Jesuit had given the nuns the Long retreat. The Jesuit constitutions forbade a Jesuit to direct or to intermeddle in the affairs of women's orders. In addition, in this case there was also the danger of causing discontent. The Fathers should distance themselves from this work, praiseworthy enough in itself. On the same day,[79] the General wrote a similar letter to the Vice-Prefect of the English Mission, Fr Baldwin, who lived in Brussels. Probably the protests of the Jesuits accused had reached Fr General in Rome, for on 30th May, 1609[80] – Mary Stephen Goudge had been in office for six months by now – he allowed the Jesuits of the Belgian Province limited spiritual care of the English Poor Clares, but they were to adhere strictly to the Jesuit constitutions, which allowed them to offer nuns the same spiritual help as that given to other women who attended their churches. The nuns could not go to the Jesuit church, as they were bound by strict enclosure and, moreover, were soon to be living in Gravelines. This town was at that time one day's travelling distance away.

Despite the General's strict warning, the entry in the Annals of the English Jesuits in St Omer for 1609 states that the convent of the English Poor Clares had been founded with much help from the Jesuits.

The clothing of some of the nuns had taken place, and the enclosure had been erected. In the years 1609 and 1610, the profession of the first nuns in Gravelines would be regarded as the result of what the Jesuits had done for the Order.[81] Father General's three letters appear like sheet lightning. It would be interesting to know if it was Jesuits alone who had complained to Rome, or whether Franciscans had also made their voices heard.

Mary Ward and Mary Stephen Goudge

1606 – 1609

Mary Stephen Goudge as Novice Mistress – as Abbess – her relationship with Mary Ward

It is hardly to be expected that there would be rich findings in historical archives about a Poor Clare nun who had lived a contemplative life behind a grill. This is true of Mary Stephen Goudge as far as documents are concerned, but the narrative sources tell us a good deal more, so that it is possible to draw a fairly approximate outline of her character, and to assess her relationship with Mary Ward.

Mary Stephen Goudge was born in 1577 and was therefore about eight years older than Mary Ward. She was the daughter of Thomas Goudge, Esq., whose second wife was Margaret Lloyd. Both parents came from the county of Shrewsbury. She entered the Poor Clares in St Omer in 1596 and took her vows at the age of nineteen. It is not known when she was appointed novice mistress for the lay sisters.[82]

As a religious she must have shown good qualities or the Abbess would not have placed her in such a responsible position. When Mary Ward entered in the spring of 1606, Sr Mary Stephen Goudge was about thirty years old. Mary Ward writes[83] that she had been about one month with the Poor Clares before she received the habit. So the novice mistress had only a brief opportunity of observing the young candidate and forming a judgement about her.

Mary Ward loved this Sister Mary Stephen Goudge as an example of a good religious who had been assigned her 'through obedience' as a help.[84] In mentioning her relationship with this sister, Mary Ward, who showed cautious reserve all her life, reveals something which had hurt her extremely, which she would never forget. She writes: 'I, to have given pleasure to that holy mother according to my natural feeling, would willingly have lived all my life as a slave; and she, at all times and on every occasion, appeared to have the least possible regard to me in particular.'[85] An icy coldness emanates from these words, and shows more than anywhere the utter loneliness of the young novice.

It is true that novices sometimes have an over-enthusiastic attachment to their novice mistress. Mostly they are young girls who have decided to give themselves whole-heartedly to God but have not yet found the exclusive and sometimes lonely path for their devotion. The life of a religious is one of patience, renunciation and grace. Over and above this, from childhood Mary Ward had always shown a tendency to place those whom she loved in a good light. One only has to think of the little episodes with her father at Mulwith and her grandmother at Ploughland. Of course, one must take into consideration the fact that she was writing after a gap of fifteen to eighteen years, the last seven years of which had been spent in religious life, in prayer and asceticism and examination of conscience — not to mention the chief means of progress in the spiritual life: God's grace. So a question mark remains, did Mary Stephen Goudge have the right attitude towards this young woman, who day in and day out bore the heavy burden of having to provide for the Choir sisters? Or was it a case of two strong characters in confrontation?

Mary Ward was a mature woman of about forty when she wrote: 'I treated with her in all sincerity and submitted myself to her judgement, and she, having to determine a matter that so greatly concerned both my soul and my life, suggested as if for my welfare alone, that which she sought (and indeed lawfully) for the consolation of others. At entering she told me that inside and outside the Rule was the same, and now she explained how much difference there was between the one and the other. Then, if an angel from heaven should tell me that my vocation was not with those outside, I ought not to believe him and now, such could by no means be, but my vocation was inside.'[86] And a little later she says that while she listened in silence she felt 'like a person deprived of the help and counsel necessary on such an occasion.'

Here, in those few moments, a world of respect and trust must have collapsed for Mary Ward. It was not for nothing that she mentioned the sincerity of her intentions in this long passage about Mary Stephen Goudge. One can see from her words that the relationship between novice and novice mistress had been utterly destroyed; no real rapport could have existed there, let alone sisterly love.

It is to be doubted that Mary Ward either requested or furthered the appointment of her former novice mistress as Abbess in the temporary convent in St Omer. She writes, simply, that Mary Stephen Goudge had been chosen as Abbess on account of her great merits and spirituality.[87] It has been mentioned earlier that the new foundation came under Jesuit influence because of steps taken by Mary Ward. In the Walloon convent the Abbess, her two assistants and the two lay sisters had followed the original Rule of St Clare, a mendicant life, under the spiritual guidance of the Franciscans, though for language reasons perhaps some of them had confessed to the Jesuits. It has been suggested that they had not left their convent of their own free will, and now found themselves in charge of the new convent at the Bishop's behest, or rather, of having to form it from its very foundations. Complications between the foundress and the abbess seem inevitable, for in the final analysis two Orders were involved here: the Jesuits through Mary Ward and the Franciscans through Mary Stephen Goudge.

Even during this last short span of her stay in the convent which she had founded, Mary Ward received little help from her Abbess.

Two examples may be cited in evidence. When Mary Ward informed the Abbess of her spiritual experience on St Athanasius' Day, Mary Stephen Goudge considered it a temptation or an illusion, and said that as often as it recurred, Mary Ward should take the discipline. Mary Ward followed her commands with the utmost exactitude though bodily chastisement was hardly a remedy. But after Fr Roger Lee had completely withdrawn his support for Mary Ward, the latter's serenity seems to have impressed the Abbess. She even laid her hand on her head, saying 'Is this the manner of your friends (naming the Order), to leave their penitents in temptation and greatest need?'[88] Not very consoling, all things considered.

Sister Mary Stephen Goudge was undoubtedly a good religious who lived according to the strict Rule of St Clare. Many competent people had formed a good opinion of her, like Fr Roger Lee, who said at the end of the Exercises he gave to the nuns and candidates that he liked the conduct of all the sisters but especially that of the Abbess; that her knowledge of the spiritual life had not been acquired from talks or sermons but through the influence of the Holy Spirit.[89]

Sr Cicely chronicled the fact that the Abbess was always to be found on her knees, or sitting on the floor, and was concerned about maintaining discipline. These statements are without doubt correct, but they do not present a full portrait of the woman who was Mary Stephen Goudge. Kindliness and amiability do not appear to radiate from the picture we have of her. Nevertheless, there is a final question to be asked, unmentioned so far. Mary Stephen Goudge must have known Mary Ward far better than anyone else, as novice mistress. After all, it was she who discerned that Mary Ward had a vocation to be a Poor Clare Choir sister. Could she still stand by this as Abbess? She must have had serious reservations if, in spite of the influence of Bishop Blaes and the Jesuits of the English College, she refused to let this novice make her profession early.

Mary Ward confirms the Abbess' caution when she writes: 'Here may be seen anew the greatness of my obligation to God, who willed to make use of every occasion for my greater good. If the designs of this holy Bishop had taken effect, the happiness which I now unworthily possess would have been prevented.'

The strategically fortified town of Gravelines (in Flemish Gravelingen or Grevelingen) on the coast between Calais and Dunkirk (Flemish Duinkerken) now lies in the French department Nord. At that time it belonged to Flanders. Among its finest buildings is that of the church of St Willibrord dating from the late sixteenth century. Its dedication to this Anglo-Saxon saint from Yorkshire must have afforded Mary Ward pleasure.[90] Close to the church runs the now unappealing rue des Clarisses, a memorial to the Convent of the English Poor Clares. The community moved from the rented building in St Omer on 15th September, 1609 to this then new convent,[91] the building of which is said to have cost 10,000 guilders.[92] Unfortunately, it no longer exists.

Soon after Mary Ward had left the Order, the nuns began to withdraw their house from the Bishop's jurisdiction. This information comes from a report which, though undated, is thought to be around 1628,[93] in which the foundation is attributed to the Franciscans. It would be beyond the scope of this work to discuss this confusing and inaccurate statement in detail. The house was returned to the Franciscan Order, and the Jesuit influence disappeared totally. The Abbess, Mary Stephen Goudge, was head of the community until 1613, and therefore certainly involved in this change, understandable from the viewpoint of the Poor Clare Order.

The convent survived until the French Revolution, when the nuns withdrew as once before their sisters from Veere had done; they settled in a free country in the late 18th century, their homeland, England. After she had founded her own Institute and the waves had subsided, Mary Ward had friendly relations with those in her first foundation.[94]

Notes

1. AB/G, p. 9. Inst. Arch. Munich. It is only this autobiographical sketch that gives information about Mary Ward's stay in the Poor Clare Convent. The others do not extend as far. Cf. Vita E, f. 9r. ff. and Vita I, p. 13 ff. The early writings adopt these statements, with greater or lesser embellishments.
2. Vita E, f.9v; Vita I, p. 13.
3. For these incidents, AB/G, p. 13 ff., Inst. Arch. Munich.
4. Mary Ward errs when speaking about the visit of Father General. The Visitor of the Order, Fr Andreas de Soto, was in Saint-Omer. The two Lives adopt the error. Fr de Soto lived in the Spanish Netherlands for about twenty years. He was confessor to the Infanta Isabella Clara Eugenia during that time. He also wrote several spiritual works. He died on 5th April, 1625. BNB 23, Sp. 236–242.
5. Vita E, f. 10v; Vita I, p. 14 ignores this erroneous detail.
6. AB/G, p. 14. Inst.Arch. Munich.
7. Vita E, p. 11r.
8. AB/G, p. 18, Inst. Arch. Munich.
9. Gravelines Chronicles, p. 11 ff., St Clare's Abbey, Darlington, England; Ms. 1.
10. AB/G, p. 18, Inst. Arch. Munich.
11. Mary Ward refers to this name, remarking that it was this Father who had advised her to enter the Poor Clares. AB/G, p. 19. Inst. Arch. Munich.
12. Cf. below, note 13.
13. PRO London, SP. Dom. Jas. I. vol. 188, Nr. 24.
14. AB/G, p. 8, inst. Arch. Munich.
15. The text runs: "I will not be unmindefull of any thinge that concerneth my daughter Wardes good. Mistres Good commendeth her to you, but the stuff you require was provided by an other partie before by Robinsons appointment. If you nede any more, send woord. And I knowe she will not be wanting, thoughe since her progresse she is growen out of stoare ..."
16. AGR Brussels, PEA 1944 (2).
17. The governor and captain of Gravelines at that time was Philippe le Vasseur de Guernoval et d'Eckelsbeke, General de l'Artillerie. Herckenrode, Nobiliaire II, p. 1961–1962, and Jouglas de Morenas, Grand Armorial de France VI, p. 410.
18. Marginal note about the manuscript mentioned in note 16. It is not clear which Councillor d'Asseliers was meant here. Several members of the family were councillors in the Council of Brabant or working in the Privy Council in the country's administration.
19. AGR Brussels, PEA 1944. (2)
20. Chambers, I. E, p. 154, I.D. p. 127. Pagetti had already recorded this error, p. 5.
21. Bishop Blaes to Archduke Albrecht, 3 April, 1608; Mary Ward and some Englishwomen to the sovereigns, before 22nd April, 1608; Bishop Maes of Ypres to Archduke Albrecht, 9th August, 1608, all AGR Brussels, PEA 1944 (2); Bishop Blaes to Secretary of State Philipp Prats, 26th August 1608, and the patent from the sovereigns for the foundation of the convent in Gravelines, 7th October 1608, both AGR Brussels, PEA 1946. (3).

22. De Guernoval was married to Lievine van Nieuwenhuysen, whose name would seem to show her as Flemish. Herckenrode and Jouglas de Morenas, as above, note 17.
23. Gravelines Chronicles (Chron EPC1), pp. 11 ff. St Clare's Abbey, Darlington, England. Ms. 1.
24. ibid.
25. On 6th May, 1608. AGR Brussels, PEA 1944 (2). Charles Maes (1559–1612) became Bishop of Ypres in 1607 and transferred to Ghent in 1610, where he died on 21st May, 1612. Hier Cath. IV, p. 193 and 374, BNB XIII, p. 130–131.
26. On 20th May 1608, ditto.
27. On 1st June, 1608. PRO London, SP 77/9 ff. 74r–76r. Sir Thomas Edmondes (1563?–1639) was already in the diplomatic service under Edward VI and Secretary for French affairs under Queen Elizabeth. 1604–1609 he was ambassador in Brussels, but was active in diplomatic affairs still longer. DNB VI, Sp. 391–393.
28. On 17th June, 1608. AGR Brussels, PEA 1944 (2). Philipp Prats of old Spanish aristocracy, became secretary to the Privy Council in 1585 and was Secretary of State in Brussels from 1599–1617. He died in 1635 in Brussels. BNB 18, Sp. 199–203.
29. Bishop Maes to Archduke Albrecht, 9th August 1608. AGR Brussels, PEA 1944 (2).
30. ibid to Secretary of State Prats, 8th August 1608. ibid.
31. ibid to Secretary of State Prats, 24th August 1608. ibid.
32. Bishop Blaes to Secretary of State Prats, 26th. September 1608, AGR Brussels, PEA 1946. (3)
33. Chambers I E, p. 155–166; I D, p. 128–137.
34. "Mi vestivo di secolare e, senza mora, m'applicai a procurare luogo et ogni cosa per fare uno monasterio di S. Chiara per l'Inglesi." AB/G, p. 18, Inst. Arch. Munich.
35. StA. Munich, Kl. 432/1, 16–19.
36. On 29th February, 1625, Letter Nr. 28, Inst. Arch. Munich.
37. Out of the 1st paper, Inst. Arch. Munich.
38. Vita E, f. 11v.
39. Vita I, p. 15.
40. Litterae Annuae of the English seminary in Saint-Omer, s.f. (1608) AGR Brussels, Arch. Jésuitiques, Prov. Gallo-Belg. Carton 31.
41. Recueil Historique de Jean Hendricque, Bourgeouis de Saint-Omer II (1605–1615), pp. 107–108.
42. " … she returned to Saint Omer after half a year spent in the prosecuting this affaire". Chron. EPC1, p. 11 ff.
43. Fridl alone of the earliest printed writings gives the time of waiting for the sovereigns' approval of the foundation as six months. Fridl I, p. 95. He follows the English Vita.
44. AGR Brussels, PEA 1944 (2).
45. AGR Brussels, PEA 1946 (3).
46. Both: AGR Brussels, PEA 1944 (2).
47. Chambers I E p. 155; I D, p. 128.
48. AB/G p. 20, Inst. Arch. Munich; Vita E, f. 12r; Vita I, p. 16, Chron. EPC1, p. 11 ff.; Hendricq II, p. 108.
49. Registers of the English Poor Clares at Gravelines (Reg EPC1) including those who founded filiations at Aire, Dunkirck and Rouen, 1608–1837, ed. W.M. Hunnybun and J. Gillow = CRS XIV, Misc. IV, London 1914, p. 31–32.
50. "Eductis non sine summa difficultate, …" Litt. Annuae s.f. (1608) AGR Brussels, Arch. Jésuit. Prov. Gallo-Belg. Carton 31.

51. "Les 3 recluses et les deux converses, lesquelles pourtant firent des grandes difficultées allegans leur voeu leur deffendre ne sortir." Recueil Historique II, pp. 107–108.
52. as above, note 49.
53. Chron. EPCL, p. 11 ff.
54. as above, note 49.
55. as above, note 53.
56. as above, note 51.
57. ARSI, Rome, Hist. Angl. 31/II, pp. 659–664.
58. as above, note 53.
59. Vita e, f. 11v.
60. as above, note 49.
61. That is considerably later than the exodus of the nuns from their convent, which took place on 8th November 1608, but verbal permission for this was doubtless given.
62 as above, note 57.
63. AB/G p. 25, Inst. Arch. Munich.
64. ibid. p. 21
65. Vita E, f. 12v.
66. AB/G, p. 23, Inst. Arch. Munich.
67. ibid.
68. ibid.
69. "La pena fu grande, ma molto supportabile, perchè chi caricava, portava anco il peso ..." ibid. p. 25.
70. LThK I, sp. 756–763.
71. Litterae Annuae of the English seminary in Saint-Omer, s.f. (1608), AGR Brussels, Arch. Jésuitiques, Prov. Gallo-Belg. Carton 31.
72. Thomas Edmondes to Robert Cecil 1st June, 1608, PRO London, Sp 77/9, ff. 74r–76r.
73. " ... a nostris tota pendens, sine quorum directione nihil facere voluit." as above, note 71.
74. Chron EPC1 p. 11 ff.
75. Vita E, f. 11r.
76. P. Johannes Neyen OFM 1607–1613, Commissar of the Flemish Province of the Order, Analecta Franciscana III, p. 113.
77. AB/G, p. 20, Inst. Arch. Munich.
78. ARSI Rome, Flandro-Belg. 1/II, p. 1107.
79. ibid.
80. ibid. p. 1124.
81. as above, note 71 for years 1609–1610.
82. She died on 23rd November, 1613 aged 36. Annals of the English Poor Clares of Gravelines and of their Foundations in Ireland and at Aire, Dunkirck and Rouen, pp. 11–12. St Clare's Abbey, Darlington.
83. AB/G, p. 9. Inst. Arch. Munich.
84. ibid. p. 17.
85. ibid.
86. ibid. pp. 17–18.
87. ibid p. 14.
88. Vita E, ff. 13v–14r.
89. Chron. EPCL p. 11ff.
90. St Willibrord was entrusted in his youth, 658, to St Wilgils as an oblate of the Irish monks in Ripon near York, and therefore lived for some time close to Mary Ward's home. He became a Benedictine, travelled to Ireland and subsequently to the continent, where he became the first bishop of Utrecht (Netherlands). He is known as the apostle of Friesland (LThK X Sp. 919–920.

91. Reg EPCL, p. 31–32.
92. Litterae Annuae of the English seminary in Saint-Omer, s.f. (1608) AGR Brussels, Arch. Jésuitiques, Prov. Gallo-Belg. Carton 31.
93. AGR, PEA 2062 s.f. (p.1 of the paper).
94. Mary Ward, quoted by Fridl I p. 106, Nr. 85. in a document now lost: "She requested a blessing from me, and I requested the same from her ..." A baroque custom.

VI

GLORIA

England 1609

Mary Ward in England once more – her uncertainty – the difficult position of Catholics – Luisa de Carvajal and her community – Mary Ward's activities

Uncertainty and diffidence about her decisions marked Mary Ward's next stage. She sought stability by taking vows, wanting to be subject to her confessor Fr Lee by obedience, prepared to become a religious by entering the Carmelite Order if that was what he commanded, or to spend some months in England working for God in the pastoral care of souls.[1] It is important to remember in this particular context that entry into a contemplative order pointed in a totally opposite direction to that of the active apostolate in pastoral work. Mary Ward had always set a limit to her stay in England, which was intended to give her time to gain a clear perspective; her anguish lay in the uncertainty between these two extremes – a contemplative life, or one dedicated to God in the world.

We do not know Father Lee's exact reaction; it is more than likely that he was considerably perplexed by his penitent. His words to her before she left the convent sound dismissive – she could be saved, whether she left or whether she stayed. Mary Ward wrote drily in her letter to Nuntius Albergati that this was all the encouragement and help she received from anyone. We do not know where Mary Ward stayed while waiting to cross over to England – whether it was in the temporary house of the Poor Clares or some rented lodging. We do not even know how or with what help she crossed the Channel.

Life had not become easier for Catholics in England in the four years since the Gunpowder Plot. The government at last had evidence and therefore political justification for taking severe measures. The papists, accomplices of the King of Spain, were enemies of the state; their elimination was therefore necessary for the state's welfare. A wave of punitive laws followed. One example of this can be shown by Luisa de Carvajal's story.[2] Born into the Spanish nobility, poetically gifted, and fired by Edmund Campion's martyrdom, she decided to take up apostolic work in England. She arrived in London in 1605 and soon won helpers for her dangerous work. She planned a Marian institute, 'Compania de la soberana Virgen Maria nuestra Senora', and drew up constitutions which, as well as the three vows, included a vow of obedience to the Pope. She did not plan a centralised government, nor enclosure, for her institute. Given the circumstances, this would have been neither appropriate nor possible in England at that time.

In spite of their caution, the activities of the small group were discovered and Luisa was arrested. Gondomar, the Spanish Ambassador, bestirred himself on her behalf and she was released. In 1608 she moved from the Barbican to Spitalfields outside the walls, but in October 1613 she was again taken prisoner, and once again freed at the intervention of the Spanish Ambassador. Her death on lst February, 1614 forestalled her deportation from the country. Mary Ward had envisaged a similar apostolate – today it would be called the active apostolate – (nel cercare di fare bene d'altri): supporting priests by preparing catholics for the sacraments, making arrangements for celebrating Mass, probably also harbouring priests and visiting prisons.

It is highly probable that Mary Ward met the courageous Spanish woman during this time and was perhaps inspired by her before she herself was enlightened by the 'Gloria Vision'.

We are even less informed about her stay in her homeland than we were about her vows. It is not known where she stayed, although it can be assumed that she spent most of the time in London.[3] The scant information in her autobiographical notes merely remarks that she did not misspend her time in England, as far as she could judge: she had not neglected to do her utmost in pursuit of her purpose in coming to England; her humble efforts had not been in vain, for several persons who now lived holy lives in different convents had said that acquaintanceship with her had helped them to decide to leave the world and enter an Order.[4]

Of all her various activities, Mary Ward chooses to emphasise this one only, that of helping others to become members of a religious order. A sign that for her the highest ideal lay in dedicated contemplation.

The 'Gloria Vision'

1609

Mary Ward's account of the vision – the experience as given in the sources – the vision as commission for a new way of life

It is not really important to know what sort of dress Mary Ward wore, or whether she did in fact live in the aristocratic quarter of

London, the Strand, as the earliest lives inform us. It is far more important that there, in the thick of this underground adult pastoral work, an absolutely unmistakable light was granted her.

Contrary to her custom, Mary Ward gave Nuntius Albergati a detailed account of that great spiritual experience which was to be decisive for her way of life. In the 'Gloria Vision' she denies any outward or sensory perceptions, just as she would in 1615, when describing the vision of the 'Just Soul' to Father Lee. Her account gains in consequence.

She writes that 'Being there (in England,) and thus employed (in the apostolate) I had a second infused light in manner as before, but much more distinct: that the work to be done was not a monastery of Teresians, but a thing much more grateful to God and so great an augmentation of his glory as I cannot declare, but not any particulars what, how and in what manner such a work should be.'[5]

Her autobiographical notes add a few important details. We learn that Mary Ward had meditated 'coldly'. By way of resolution she had decided to give financial help to someone who could otherwise not afford to enter a convent. Only then did she dress 'in the fashion of the country and the circumstances' and did her hair before a mirror.[6] She was totally lifted out of herself by this revelation, and the realisation that she was not to be a Carmelite but to undertake some new and as yet unknown unfamiliar work for the greater glory of God. For a good while the words 'Glory, Glory, Glory' sounded in her ears. Later, she thought that this had lasted almost two hours.

The English Vita[7] places the scene powerfully before us. The Italian Vita[8] is considerably more moderate in expression. The Painted Life[9] and the oldest printed material depend mainly on these two biographies.

The setting in London was completely different from those of St Gregory's or St Athanasius' Day. Here was no enclosed nun quietly occupied with handwork, but a woman active for God in his church in the world. Her thoughts were not taken up with her own problems, nor with the holiness of her sisters, but with a very practical matter – the possibility of arranging for a dowry, to enable a young woman to enter a convent. That was something concrete, requiring contacts and action. Yet it was precisely in the middle of such mundane concerns that this spiritual illumination came, clearly and unmistakably. It was even clearer than that of 2nd May, 1609, when she was directed to leave the Poor Clare Order. The physical effects, too, were noticeably more profound, more comprehensive.

It threw light on her uncertainty. She was not to enter the Carmelite Order, but to do something quite different, for God's greater glory.

The revelations given her had, one after another, become increasingly focussed:

– *to found a house in Flanders of English Poor Clares;*

— to leave that Order, and therefore her own foundation;
— to abandon the idea of becoming a Carmelite, and therefore
the idea of a contemplative life.

We can imagine the psychological and spiritual turmoil caused by
all these alternations of desolation and consolation. On St Gregory's
Day: joy in her work, and prayer that it correspond with God's will;
on St Athanasius' Day, sadness at having to leave the Order, but consolation in the conviction that God wanted to use her in his service.
And now, in England, on this very ordinary day, a burning desire
towards an as yet unspecified task seized her imagination and her
heart. The desolation that accompanied it was not self-motivated
but caused by ignorance of what action she should take. Step by
step God was drawing Mary Ward to him until he demanded the
final step — courage to undertake a completely new and unheard
of way of life for religious women, one that was to be rejected as
an absurd challenge to the social order of her day.

Mary Ward had thought of entering or founding a convent. In her
day there was no meeting point between the monastic ascetic ideal
of perfection — at least for women — and life in the world. How,
then, could women lead an active life in union with God? Added
to that there was Mary Ward's inner disquiet at the incompatibility
between her vow to obey her spiritual director, who advised entry to
the Carmelites, and this absolute conviction that she should follow
some other way for the greater glory of God. She prayed and put
on a hair shirt.

Significantly she says 'I could not resist what had been effected
in me.'[10]

These words are essential for an understanding of her life.

As far as there is light

1609 – 1611

The group of the first English women in England — their apos-
tolate — crossing to St Omer 1609/10 — apostolate among
English exiles — work with Jesuits — founding a school for
English girls in St Omer — audience with Nuntius Bentivoglio

The 'Gloria Vision' may not have given her much light about the
manner in which she was to further God's greater glory, but the
realisation that she was not to be a Carmelite was very definite. An
unknown task was involved. During her stay in England, Mary Ward
had come to know several like-minded young women, though we do
not know how or when. One may suppose that, apart from connections she had already formed, or relations, such contacts came from

her work with the sick or imprisoned, or at some festivity. These encounters probably happened soon after her arrival in England, where Mary Ward stayed a comparatively short time.

In England, apostolic work could be carried on only under the most dangerous conditions; the imprisonment of Luisa de Carvajal in 1609 is proof of that. It is possible that several of these women had already considered emigrating, and now put their plan into action under Mary Ward's guidance towards the end of 1609, or the beginning of 1610. Apart from her spiritual calibre, she had considerable talent in organisation, as the foundation in Gravelines has shown, and moreover she already knew the town of St Omer, the centre of English catholic refugees on the Continent. She would certainly have been able to count on certain friends and acquaintances, although her reputation may have suffered from having twice left a religious order.

The impetus towards forming a community at the end of 1609 may have originated from the first people who worked with her in England, and not from Mary Ward herself. She was later to write to Nuntius Albergati: 'My purposed time of stay in England expired, I retired to St Omer. Diverse followed with the intention to be religious where I should be, living together there.'[11] Looked at more closely, 'diverse' means that various people, some, but not all of those she had worked with in England, wanted to become religious sisters. According to tradition, Mary Poyntz, Winefrid Wigmore, Johanna Browne, Susan Rookwood, Catherine Smith, Barbara Babthorpe and her sister Barbara Ward, travelled with her, though it cannot be stated with certainty. Some of them had friends who had suffered much persecution and imprisonment.[12] Some of them came from Catholic families whose entire possessions had been confiscated because they remained loyal to their faith. Marmaduke Ward was one such. We do not know the exact date of their departure for St Omer or whether they travelled together or individually. It was certainly soon after the 'Gloria Vision'. Mary Ward never wasted time when it was a matter of carrying out God's will.

On 30th January, 1610,[13] the English Ambassador in Brussels, William Trumbull, wrote to Cecil, the Secretary of State, that the English Jesuits were negotiating with Archduke Albrecht to obtain permission for a new foundation of nuns in St Omer. This undoubtedly refers to Mary Ward and her first companions; there was no community of English women in St Omer at that time who were supported by the Jesuits. Trumbull, an Anglican, would probably not have recognized the difference between a convent and an association of devout women.

Where these Englishwomen disembarked at the beginning of 1610 is not known, but those begging excursions as a Poor Clare outsister will have stood Mary Ward in good stead. She knew the town inside out, and her small community could have acquired a house in what was then called Rue Grosse.[14]

They began their work of pastoral care among adults, among the English emigrants. The Annals of the English Jesuits for 1610 say: 'In the town there are living certain young Englishwomen of high birth and excellent education. They intend to devote themselves to the spiritual life and are waiting for a suitable moment to fulfil their wishes. With general consent they left their house, and they will be helped by some of ours (the English Jesuits), because their motives are excellent'.[15] The Jesuits could still, at that time, write openly in their Annals that certain young English women in St Omer were doing pastoral work among adults and that this was earning them praise from all sides. These reports were open for all members of the Order to read, above all by the General in Rome. No one took exception. Not yet. But they will soon have noticed that the daughters of the emigrants and of those who had to remain in England were exposed to danger in that they could not be given catholic religious education. Some of them, too, would have been more suitable for the teaching and education of girls than others. How keenly the first English Ladies – as they were soon called – aimed at the conversion of their country emerges clearly from a conversation with Guido Bentivoglio, Nuntius in Flanders, to whom they were introduced when he visited St Omer in September 1611. The Nuntius reported to the papal Secretary of State[16] that they were considering constitutions, which would serve not only their own religious progress but make possible the religious and secular education of English girls, so that they could either enter a convent on the Continent or return to their country and marry there. The English women, continued the Nuntius, believed in the need for their kind of work in England. They had explained to him that after a few years of sound education, some of their pupils could later perform their teachers' task, namely the education of their countrywomen in St Omer or the support of catholics and the conversion of heretics in England. The Nuntius ended his representation with 'In that country women can do something of the sort.'

From this it is evident that the young community, who were struggling for their existence and whose leader was 'dotata di molta prudenza... et di vita grandemente essemplare' had seen their house in St Omer not simply as a school and place of education for English children, but also as a future recruiting ground for their own members, with the simple task of educating and instructing English girls in St Omer, and free pastoral work in England.

By September, 1611 the English women therefore, had still not decided on a Rule, and we must assume that Mary Ward was granted her illumination about it in the late autumn or winter of 1611. That does not imply that they had no rules or order of the day. In her letter headed with the wrong date, 29th February 1625,[17] which was used as padding for another letter dated 25th March 1629,[18] Mary Ward wrote that the English women had lived in St Omer according to a Rule since 1609, and had led a conventual life-style.[19] Yet this must not be seen as a properly established rule, like that of an Order. The uncertainty at this time about the definitive type of structure for the congregation caused Mary Ward to say later that they had been the most difficult years of her life.[20] At that time they ate once a day only, slept on straw sacks, and undertook other penances.[21]

Jean Hendricq describes their still unnamed community in his Town Chronicle[22] as young Englishwomen who lived together in a house with such a strict manner of life that they might be nuns.

Notes

1. AB/G pp. 25 – 26, Inst.Arch.Munich. In her letter to Nuntius Albergati she names a third vow: to spend some months in England. Vita E ff.14v – 15r and Vita I, p18, name the view of obedience only, and the stay in England. PL T.16.refers to the vows.
2. G.Fullerton. The Life of Luisa de Carvajal, London 1881; C.M.Abad SJ, Una Misionera esponalo en la Inglaterra del siglo XVII Dona Luisa de Carvajal y Mendoza, 1566–1614, Comillas 1966.
3. It is very doubtful if there was any happy reunion of the Ward family, as Chambers surimises, I.E, p.211; I D,p.169. We do not even know if her parents were still alive. It is possible that Marmaduke would have been strenghtened in his earlier views, which his daughter opposed.
4. AB/G p.26, Inst.Arch.Munich.
5. 'Being there, and thus imploied, I had a 2nd infused light in manner as before but much more distinct: that the worke to be done was not a monastery of Teresians, but a thing much more gratfull to God and soe great an augmentation of his glory as I cannot declare, but not any perticulers what, how and in what manner such a work should be.' Mary Ward to Nuntius Albergati, (Liège, May-June, 1621), StA Munich, Kl.432/I. 16–19.
6. AB/G pp.26–27, Inst.Arch.Munich.
7. Vita E ff. 18v- 19r.
8. Vita I, p.19.
9. PL T.21. The picture shows Mary Ward in a red, gold-embroidered dress, with white blouse and ruff, sitting before a mirror, combing her hair. There is a light-coloured garment, possibly a shawl, on her lap; on the floor, a fringed stole. A warm light suffuses the scene. An open door gives a glimpse into a gallery or porch. In the upper right corner of the picture, Mary Ward kneels on a cushion before a small altar with a cross. A bedstead is in the background.
10. AB/G p.27, Inst.Arch.Munich.
11. StA Munich,Kl.432/I,16–19.
12. Barbara Ward, Out of the 1st paper, p.1, Inst. Arch.Munich; Vita E f.15r; Vita I, p.19; PL T.22.
13. Trumbull to Cecil, 30th January, 1610, PRO London, SP 77/10/1 ff.13r – 14v.
14. Now rue Carnot, corner of rue des Bleuets.
15. Litterae Annuae (1610), AGR Brussels, Arch.Jésuit.Prov.Gallo-Belg.Carton 31; Vita E fl.15v confirms this report on the whole.
16. R.Belvederi, Guido Bentivoglio.Diplomatico; II, Part II, Rovigo 1947, p. 222–223 from 5.October, 1611.
17. Letter Nr.28, Inst.Arch.Munich.

18.   AV Rome, Misc.Arm.III 37, ff.213r–215r.
19.   as above, note 18.
20.   Vita E f.16v.
21.   Vita E f.15r.
22.   Hendricq II, pp.308–309.

VII

IN THE MATTER AND THE MANNER OF THE SOCIETY OF JESUS

Take the Same of the Society — 1611

Mary Ward's report of her vision — the event in other sources — The 'Institute' of the Society of Jesus for the English women — sphere of work and freedom from enclosure — high expectations of members of the Institute — the place of women in society and in the Church in the seventeenth century

And then came enlightenment.

Twice, and each time with greater emphasis, Mary Ward described the great spiritual revelation of 1611. The text is of such consequence for her Institute and its history that it has been handed down to us verbatim. In 1619, against a background of disunity that was very dangerous for the community, she wrote to the Jesuit Rector of the English novitiate in Liège, Fr John Tomson[1]... 'What I had from God touching this was as follows, (understood as it is written, without adding or altering one syllable): 'Take the Same of the Society. Father General will never permit it. Go to him.' These are the words whose worth cannot be valued, nor the good they contain too dearly bought; these gave sight when there was none, made known what God would have done, gave strength to suffer what since hath happened, assurance of what is wished for in time to come, and if I should ever be worthy to do anything further for the Institute, then I must proceed from them. I could say much more about these words, but never enough.' We learn the facts from a letter she wrote to Nuntius Albergati [2] in 1612. Mary Ward had been very ill, and was on the way to recovery when she was granted this experience. She was alone and 'in some extraordinary repose of mind.' Intellectually, 'not by sound of voice but intellectually', she heard 'distinctly' the words 'Take the Same of the Society of Jesus, so understood as that we were to take the same both in matter and manner, that only excepted which God by diversity of sex hath prohibited.' She continues, 'These few words gave so great measure of light on that particular Institute, comfort and strength, and changed so the whole soul, as that it was impossible for me to doubt but that they came from Him, whose words are works.' One would like to know why, in a letter of such importance for the Institute, Mary Ward did not reproduce exactly for the Nuntius in 1621 what she had written for Fr Tomson in 1619: the text of the words understood by her. She made no mention to the Nuntius of the predicted reaction of the General of the Society of Jesus. On the other hand, one must remember that the letter to Nuntius Albergati is in the nature of a summary. The vision of the 'Just Soul' is not mentioned, although this, too − as will be shown − had great importance for the Institute. In any case, greater significance must be attached to the first part of the divine command.

The early writings of course knew of the vision of 1611, but they did not publicize it. That should not cause surprise. At the time when the English and Italian Lives[3] were compiled, any mention of the Institute as an Ignatian congregation was strictly forbidden. The same is true of the Painted Life. In the text for Panel 24, Mary Ward's sickness and cure, and her revelation are recorded, but we are not told the subject-matter of the revelation.

Two facts in particular characterise this vision − the precision of the command 'Take the Same of the Society of Jesus', and the clarity of the words, about which there can be no argument. And yet, what is the significance of the words 'Take the Same of the Society' for people of later centuries?

'The Same' has often been equated with the Constitutions of the Society of Jesus. Chambers[4] takes it to mean the Rule of the Jesuits. But, if we keep to the sequence of words in the letter to Albergati, which is more detailed in this respect, we have: 'Take the Same of the Society, both in matter and manner.' A few words later she says that the illumination gave much light over 'that particular Institute'. This gives the end result: 'Take the Same Institute of the Society of Jesus'.

But again, what does 'Institute of the Society of Jesus' mean? The word 'Institute' comprises on the one hand the organisation and form, and on the other, the way of life and activity of the Order (propria vivendi atque operandi ratio). The 'Institute' is recorded in the General Examen in the Constitutions and the Rule of the Order and summarized in the Formula Instituti, the oldest constitutional document of the Society.[5] Which document was meant here? We know that, with the following exposé, we are diverging widely from the customary views held until now in writings about Mary Ward,[6] and are presenting new ways of thought. But we believe it can be proved from the sources.

After this vision the English women − there were still only about ten of them[7] − promptly adopted the Formula of the Institute of the Jesuits. In an open letter dated 19th March, 1615, Bishop Blaes of St Omer wrote that the Englishwomen devoted themselves entirely to the instruction and education of girls sent to them from England, all the

more so as, having read the Rule (Regulas Societatis) of the Society
of Jesus, they had decided to follow this as far as their sex allowed.
This Rule was published and had been translated into English.[8] Later
on, the letter states that they had made a written summary of their
way of life and of the Formula of their Institute (vivendi modum et
Instituti sui Formulam) and laid it before the Bishop.

Let us limit ourselves first to the information given by the Bishop.
His remarkable letter will need more detailed examination later.

It is not immediately evident what the Bishop meant by the 'Rule'
of the Society of Jesus. In England at that time 'The Rules of the
Society of Jesus' were being circulated in a translation made by the
martyr Fr Henry Garnett,SJ, who had been accused of assisting in the
Gunpowder Plot and executed after torture on 3rd May at Tyburn.
This contains the Rules of the co-adjutors, the Summary of the Constitutions, the Regulae Communes, the letter on Obedience, the list
of prayers and the formula of the Vows. Circulated at first among
the Jesuits in handwritten form, this collection was printed in 1670
in St Omer by Carlier.[9]

It could hardly be this Rule that was intended here, as it only
appeared in print much later. Also, Bishop Blaes spoke in his letter
of the English Ladies' way of life and the 'Formula' of their Institute,
which they had placed before him in the English language. The term
'Instituti sui Formulam' can only mean one thing, in my opinion.
The Franciscan Bishop Blaes would hardly have conjured up the
expression out of his own vocabulary.

The Bishop of St Omer's letter is not the only source that proves
the adoption of the Formula Instituti as the basis of Mary Ward's
Institute. This is also reinforced by the vision of the 'Just Soul', as
will be seen. Again in this context, we draw attention to the Petition
which the English women presented to the Pope at their audience
on 28th December, 1621.[10] By way of introduction, it says that
under divine direction they had adopted the same holy Institute
and the same way of life as that of the Society of Jesus (idem
sanctum Institutum et ordinem vivendi), which had been approved
by various Popes, namely Paul III, Julius III, and Gregory XIII,
and which they had followed for twelve years.

The text of the Formula Instituti is preserved in the Bull 'Regimini
militantis Ecclesiae' of 27th September, 1540, (Paul III) and in an
expanded form in the Bull 'Exposcit debitum' of 21st July, 1550
(Julius III). Pope Gregory XIII approved the Society of Jesus once
more with the Bull 'Ascendente Domino' of 25th May, 1584. The
Formula Instituti was accessible to all. The English women took
their Petition with them from Liège to Rome at the end of 1621.

The manuscript is undated, but the travellers could not have
counted on obtaining an audience immediately on their arrival,
before the end of the year. It is therefore wise to place the Petition
in 1622. For, when they talk of having followed the Formula of the

Institute for twelve years, this takes us back to 1611, reckoning the beginnings and ends of years as they were then observed. That was the year of the vision.

The Formula Instituti of the Society of Jesus – for women – in the 17th century!

That involved, for each individual English woman

– loving commitment to God under the banner of the Cross in a community which should be subject to the Pope alone, not to any other Order, or Bishop;

– the defence and propagation of the catholic faith under the three solemn vows of Poverty, Chastity and Obedience;

– intellectual confrontation with the heresies of their times and with the lack of christian morality which was widespread;

– a pastoral apostolate by means of catechesis; promoting reception of the sacraments; the hearing and understanding of public sermons, leading to priestly activities in distant places which had long been neglected; care for fallen women, for prisoners, the sick and dying, even the conversion of Muslims and heathens. To all these tasks were joined the instruction and bringing up of girls to be good mothers of families, or nuns in day and boarding schools, with special regard for possible future members.

All of these activities were to be performed without remuneration, each individual should rather endeavour 'to have before their eyes first God, then the matter and manner of their Institute, which is a way towards Him.'

What perspectives this opened out for Mary Ward on fire with zeal, guided gradually by God's loving providence from her natural diffidence to face a challenge unheard of in her century! Such a strongly vibrant rhythm of life demanded the same tight organisation that Ignatius had prescribed for his Society: the placement and sphere of work of each individual within the congregation; the authority of the General Superior to compose rules after consultation with members, with majority vote in case of doubt; alteration of the rules or dissolution of houses by the General Superior and a major part of the professed community (a General Congregation); the legal independence of the Order of every sort of hierarchical power such as the superior of a male Order or a Bishop, with instead every member bound in Obedience to the Pope by a Fourth vow, and not only in that sort of obedience to which all catholics are obliged as to the head of the Church but with the additional sense of mission.

That sort of organisation required mature and, not least, educated women, who wanted to submit with the whole of their being to this disciplined regime for the kingdom of God.

This revelation was to have painful consequences for Mary Ward. She had indeed received clear instructions about the type of spiritual foundation which the Institute was to adopt. She now knew that though this was not to be Carmel, with the full purity of the contemplative life, it did not preclude contemplation. Not only that. Her community must of necessity renounce any form of enclosure. By the end of 1611, she and her companions had already led a life free of enclosure for some years but now their manner of life was to be established officially and must, to this end, be submitted to the Church authorities at some time in the future. An almost unthinkable undertaking. Over and above all this, there was her relationship with her Confessor. Because of the vow of obedience she had taken to him, she now had even more cause for concern than after the 'Gloria Vision' in England, as Fr Lee was a Jesuit. Mary Ward knew only too well that the Society of Jesus would never suffer an Institute of women based on Ignatian structures alongside their own. Jesuits were strictly forbidden by the Constitutions of their Order to undertake the direction of female Orders and Congregations. That had already been made clear in the history of the Gravelines' Poor Clares. But how could a small group of women with little or no theology take on the spirituality of the Society of Jesus, other than by intensive education from those very Jesuits?

Finally, the divine direction, 'Go to Father General. He will never permit it', contained a contradiction in itself. Moses too, received a similar charge when God sent him to Pharaoh. This was followed by the words: 'But I know that the King of Egypt will not let you go if he is not forced to do so.'[11] The Egyptians experienced this force when the waters of the Nile broke over their heads. Perhaps Mary Ward had this incident from the Old Testament in mind for her own case, when she wrote to Nuntius Albergati that God's words are deeds.

The main difficulty lay ultimately in women's place in society and also, unfortunately, in the Church at that time. Man was master and woman was his tool. She had hardly any rights, only duties; it was either marriage or the cloister. In most cases her husband was chosen for her by her parents or relations, and once betrothed, she was subject to him for better or worse; she was ranked as one of her husband's possessions. Her duty was to care for the children — several, for the most part — and the household. At higher levels of society there were greater possibilities of education and even of influence in social and cultural life, but it was precisely in certain princely marriages that an almost merciless patriarchal social structure was evident. Such was women's position in law, or rather in the absence of law. There were, of course, good marriages, whose union and mutual love smoothed hardships, or prevented them from arising. Sometimes, too differences of character and personal abilities were determining factors in the situation of women.

Things were no different in the ecclesiastical world. St Paul's words: 'Mulier taceat in ecclesia' held good. Women not only had to keep silent, but were refused a share in co-operating in the life of the Church. And the cloister? Almost all of these were enclosed; there were few exceptions, to name one here – the Oblates of Tor de' Specchi, founded by St Francesca Romana in 15th century. Probably some Orders were occupied in educating girls but were successful only to a limited extent. Children were accepted for education within the enclosure, which had to be equally strictly observed by them too.

In the period after the Council of Trent which ended in 1563, directions about enclosure were re-issued and reinforced most stringently, and any relaxation was sharply censured by the Church. An unenclosed Order for women was utterly inconceivable at that time. Mary Ward probably knew that she would sow the seed and watch it germinate, but never see the harvest. And yet what magnificent freedom, disponibility lies in her words: 'All is as done with me; it only remains that I be faithful'[12]. Such an attitude of soul must be anchored in the unassailable belief that God can never be his own enemy. When, towards the end of 1611, she knew the tool she was to use for her Institute, her absolute loyalty would brook no delay. Like St Ignatius, Mary Ward was 'loving and active' when it was a matter of the greater glory of God.

Notes:

1. PB, Inst. Arch. Munich, pp. 41–42.
2. StA Munich, Kl. 432/ I 16–19.
3. Vita E f. 17v; Vita I, pp. 19–20, gives this text in similar words, as also the earliest manuscript and printed writings.
4. Chambers I E, p. 283, I D, p. 266: "Take the Same of the Society/ of Jesus/" in the sense, that we should adopt the same Rule as well as the character and the form.
5. Ludwig Koch SJ, Jesuiten-Lexicon. Die Gesellschaft Jesu einst und jetzt. Paderborn, 1934, under "Institut", Sp. 881–882.
6. Finally: Grisar, Institut, p. 14 ff.
7. Nuntius Bentivoglio gives this total on 5th October, 1611, R. Belvederi, Guido Bentivoglio, Diplomatico II, parte II, Rovigo 1947, p. 222–223.
8. " ... totas se virginum ac puellarum quae ex Anglia a parentibus mitterentur, instructioni et educationi impendere statuerunt eoque magis, dum regulas Societatis publice iam prostantes et in Anglicum conversas nactae, desiderii ac propositi sui perfectissimum exemplar legerent, hoc vita genus, quatenus suo sexui conveniret sequi deinceps decernentes." Letter patent from Bishop Jacques Blaes of Saint-Omer, 19th March 1615 as a collated copy of 3rd April, 1617. ARSI Rome, Hist. Anglia 31/II, pp. 659–664. fully printed in Grisar, Die ersten Anklagen in Rom gegen das Institut Maria Wards. (1622) Misc. Hist. Pont. XXII, Rom 1959, p. 223–233.
9. Sommervogel, Bibliothèque de la Compagnie de Jésu III, sp. 1892; V Sp. 1226.
10. BV Rome, Fondo Capponi 47, ff. 50v–51v.
11. Exod. 3 Gen. 10, 19, 4, 19.
12. "So her usuall expression hereof was 'all is as done with me, it onely remains that I be faithfull'." Vita E F.17v. Vita I does not record these words.

VIII

UNLIKE THE SOCIETY OF JESUS

The Plan of the Institute: 'Schola Beatae Virginis' (1612)

The Jesuits' opinion of the Ignatian model for the English-women's Institute — proposal of plans for their community — these declined by the Englishwomen — the plan 'Schola Beatae Virginis'

The Englishwomen's attempts to form their Institute on the same basis as that of the Society of Jesus aroused a negative response from most English Jesuits. Yet it can be taken that, initially, most of them were well-disposed towards the Institute. They had seen the results of the women's achievements in the teaching and education of many of their young countrywomen and in this saw signs of hope, and believed in the future of the congregation. Not only that. The Englishwomen attended services in Jesuit churches, listened to their sermons and confessed to them. The fathers therefore had first hand knowledge of the deep devotion and seriousness of these admirable young women, and knew of their total readiness to serve. It is not surprising that some Jesuits, having learnt of the first members' intentions after Mary Ward's vision of 1611, tried to establish some firm foundation for the young congregation, a foundation that would correspond to a certain extent with the Society of Jesus, but which would never actually become a Society of Jesus for women.

To be as objective as possible about the plans of the Institute that have come down to us, it must be remembered that these were not prepared by Mary Ward or her first members, but by friends of the Institute.

Thus the 'Scholae Beatae Virginis' was produced by some Jesuits; the 'Scholae Beatae Mariae' was probably put together by Fr Roger Lee; the 'Relatio' is ascribed to the Bishop of St Omer and, finally, the 'Ratio Instituti' was drawn up by Jesuits, likewise unknown. To which we have Mary Ward's words to Nuntius Albergati (1621): 'My confessor opposed, all the Society (of Jesus) resisted. Divers Institutes were drawn up by several persons, some of which were approved and greatly recommended to us by the late Bishop Blaes of St Omer, our great friend, and some other divines. These were offered us, and as they would have been imposed upon us, there was no remedy but to refuse them, which caused us infinite troubles.'[1]

It was not the Englishwomen who were taking issue with the Society of Jesus but the other way round — the Society with the Englishwomen. The historical interest of these plans is not in the gradual overcoming of the mountains of difficulties which accumulated after Mary Ward's 1611 vision, but in their establishing the possibility of approximating a Society of Jesus for women, without actually achieving it. If Mary Ward herself had outlined these plans or commissioned them, her visions — and especially that of 1611 — would have lost credibility, and her statement that this mystical experience had given so much light and transformed her soul, would have been a falsehood.

During this time several Jesuits had made attempts to set up a plan for a community of English women who devoted themselves to the teaching and education of English girls on the Continent. On 24th May, 1612, the well-known Belgian theologian, Fr Leonhard Lessius, SJ, wrote to the Rector of the English College in St Omer, Fr Giles Schoondonck,[2] that he had read and examined the 'Schola Beatae Virginis', which certain devout men had considered for the benefit of England; that he much approved of such schools, and added certain reasons why they were worth promoting. Fr Rivers,[3] too, Socius of the Superior of the English Mission, from whose collection of letters to Fr Persons in Rome this passage was taken, encouraged the setting up of such schools.

This Plan, which unfortunately has not survived, was certainly written for the Englishwomen, as a marginal note in Fr Rivers' correspondence shows: '1612, maii 24. Pater Lessius laudat Institutum virginum, quae imitari volebant Societatem Jesu.' This could only have been a reference to the Englishwomen's Institute. There were no other English women who taught children and whose aim was to have a Society of Jesus for women. The Jesuits in St Omer, and especially the English among them, were divided in their opinion about this Plan. The more radical, who rejected any government by Jesuits of female congregations, let alone any co-operation in the setting up of such a congregation, followed proceedings with eagle eyes. It is worth noting that this was solely a matter of schools, of the teaching of English children by English women. There was no mention of the active apostolate by some members of that Institute in England. Such work for women had not even been considered then, although in the end this was to give the final tip to the scales.

On 25th August, 1612,[4] almost exactly three months after Father Lessius had passed judgement on the Englishwomen's teaching ability, Fr General Aquaviva wrote to Jean Heren, Provincial of the Gallo-Belgian province of the Order, that a secular priest should take over the administration of the Englishwomen who taught girls.

Here too it can only be members of the Institute who were intended, for once again: there were no other English women in Belgium who had undertaken this task and been directed by a Jesuit.

Barely three weeks later, on 12th September [5], Fr General wrote to Fr Busleyden in Munich, that the English women (Virgines illae Anglae religiosae) in Belgium were not religious sisters. They merely attended the Jesuit church, as did other women. Moreover he, the General, had expressly forbidden the Fathers to take on the direction of their community. A month later, on 13th October [6], there followed a renewed prohibition from the General to Fr Provincial Jean Heren for the Jesuits of his province, that they should not direct the community of women who wished to live like the Jesuits.

These decrees from the highest authority of the Order sound the first echo of the vision of 1611 — 'Father General will never allow it'. It was not only the General in Rome who took up this position. In St Omer, the English Jesuits had been the first to oppose the establishment of a female Ignatian Institute. They took the only way open to them: constant complaints to the General of their Order in a correspondence that was extremely disparaging to the English women's Institute. It is not known, and never can be known, when and how the 'Schola Beatae Mariae' was presented to the Englishwomen, though one can certainly assume that it was drawn up for the Institute. It was probably in the first half of 1612. The question as to whether they accepted this earliest Plan of the Institute can be answered with a decisive negative. Proof lies in Mary Ward's remarks in her letter to Nuntius Albergati, and also in the existence of later Plans, which would not have been written if the members had been satisfied with the 'Schola Beatae Mariae'. On 13th October, 1612, Fr General Aquaviva still referred to Englishwomen who wanted to live like Jesuits. When one considers that these women had the Formula of the Institute of the Society before their eyes, it is obvious that they would have that as their target for their Institute. However, one should be very cautious about use of the egoistical word 'want'. Mary Ward did not 'want' to be a Jesuit. She had received a divine command to become one.

Father Roger Lee SJ and the Englishwomen's Institute

1611–1615

Fr Roger Lee — Mary Ward's confessor and spiritual director — her high regard for him — Fr Lee between Mary Ward and his brethren in the Society

Fr Roger Lee[7] was born in 1568. He entered the Society in 1600, aged thirty-two, and was ordained in 1604. He did not do higher studies[8] but worked in the English College in St Omer from 1605–1614 and occupied various offices there. At the end of 1614 he was moved, due to the prompting of Mary Ward's opponents.[9] His considerable devotion to the Englishwomen's community was doubtless the cause. He died at Dunkirk in 1615 on his way to England, while waiting for a boat to take him home.

Fr Lee probably came to know Mary Ward soon after his arrival in St Omer, without having much to do with her. In 1606 he had been in the town only a short time. Their closer association may have begun during the Thirty Days' retreat, which he gave in November, 1608 to the future English Poor Clares in their temporary house in St Omer. It is true that he adopted the same dismissive attitude as his fellow Jesuits in the English College after she left the Poor Clares, but at the same time, as her spiritual director, he accepted her vow of obedience. He did not abandon her. He gave his approval to her stay in England, and did not advise her to become a Carmelite as other Fathers probably did and as Mary Ward feared that he might, after the 'Gloria Vision'. The English Vita[10] devotes a long passage to Mary Ward's director. Fr Lee, it says, continued to hear her confessions. He saw that God had bestowed special graces on her and was leading her in a unique way. But, adds the biographer, a great privilege is sometimes accompanied by great suffering. That was certainly true.

We know from Mary Ward herself how highly she regarded Fr Lee, both for himself and as a priest. That comes across most clearly in her letter of 27th November, 1615.[11] Some years after his death[12] in a talk given to the members of the Institute in St Omer, she mentioned this good priest who had done so much for her and for the Institute. And, as late as 1624,[13] she added to the notes she wrote in Rome, her conviction that Fr Lee had been given her by the Lord as a guide and help. All the same, it is wise to differentiate between the value and personal esteem that Mary Ward had for him with regard to her own spiritual life, and her concern about his influence on her Institute.

The relationship between the two changed after Mary Ward's vision of 1611, when the Englishwomen adopted the Jesuit model, taking on the structure and aims of the Society of Jesus. Mary Ward wrote to Nuntius Albergati 'my confessor resisted.' Fr Lee certainly believed in Mary Ward and her life of mystical prayer, and her enlightenment about the Institute. Otherwise he would have declined to direct her, and no longer exposed himself to the opposition and accusations of his confrères. But Fr Lee stood between his brethren and the almost incomprehensible task which God had given Mary Ward. The Fathers were not simply against the Englishwomen's adoption of the form of the Society of Jesus. They were far more concerned that these wanted to take the very name 'Society of Jesus', for a women's congregation. They pressed Fr Lee to join them in rejecting this. Later, as Mary Ward was to add in her report to Nuntius Albergati, she understood that Fr Lee was acting against his own convictions when he gave in to his brethren. Once, when they were pressing him very strongly on this matter of the name, he answered that they would not dare to demand a change, if they were in his place ('if their case was his'). There can be no doubt that this good Jesuit did a great deal for the Institute, which is why he has often been called its founder.[14]

In the Plan of the Institute 'Schola Beatae Mariae', most probably written by Fr Lee, the Englishwomen were exhorted to pray for the founder of their congregation. One can hardly think that this meant St Ignatius, who had already been canonised. But it is certainly not correct to regard Fr Lee as the founder of the Englishwomens' Institute, for that would be to identify the divine commission given to Mary Ward with the Plan 'Schola Beatae Mariae'. That would indeed be a great mistake.

The Plan of the Institute: 'Schola Beatae Mariae'

(1612–1614)

Fr Lee as the presumed author of the plan of the Institute – arrangement and assessment of the Plan according to the sources – Fr Lee and the Rules of the Englishwomen's Institute

How far Fr Lee modelled his own plan for the Englishwomen on that of the 'Schola Beatae Mariae' of 1612 cannot be verified, as the first plan has not survived and cannot be produced for comparison. The only manuscript of the 'Schola Beatae Mariae', clearly an original in the ornate script of an experienced writer, lies in the archives of the Generalate of the Society of Jesus in Rome.[15] However, the marginal entry, and subsequently added title 'Schola Beatae Mariae' (respectively 'Discipulae Beatae Virginis'), and the concluding 'Gloria Jesu ac Beatae Virgini Mariae', were written in the same hand as the copy of Bishop Blaes' letter of 19th March, 1615, which was made on 3rd April, 1617. The Bishop's 'Relatio', which can be ascribed to 1616, is also in the same handwriting. It is a powerful, masculine hand, upright and regular, but in no official style. The plan of the Institute has 'De Instituto Discipularum Scholae Beatae Mariae seu Virginum Anglarum in Belgio', in an unsteady hand on the reverse. 'B(eatae) Mariae' was perhaps added afterwards by the same writer. Close to this, in another hand: Institutum Scola Discipularum B(eatae) M(ariae) V(irginis).

A closer look at this plan of the Institute shows that it is divided into 57 paragraphs, and these have been once more divided into bundles with marginal headings.

A. The Ratio Instituti.

The reason for founding the Institute lies in the unhappy state of England, and the opinion that not only men but women too should co-operate in the conversion of this country, but in a way that differs from that of other convents. § 1-2

Then follows the manner of life in general and the name of the Institute. The intention was to have a 'vita mixta', such as the Lord had taught the Apostles and as His Mother and St Mary Magdalen, Martha, Praxedis, Pudentiana, Cecilia, Lucia etc., had lived. § 3.

The Institute was to be called 'Schola Beatae Mariae'; the members (virgins and widows): 'Pupils or disciples of the Blessed Virgin.' § 4.

The aim of the Institute consists in the salvation of its own members and the education of girls both in England and beyond (sive extra Angliam sive in ipsa Anglia). § 5.

B. Degrees.

After a noviceship of 2 years, they will make a spiritual retreat and general confession, and take the three vows. They will be called 'sorores', sisters. § 6.

The same will apply to lay sisters who are occupied with work in the house and will be called 'admissae' – co-adjutors. § 7.

Seven years at the earliest after entering, and after they have reached the age of twenty-five, the sisters will take the three solemn vows, with the approval of the Superior, in the hands of the Bishop of the place, and pledge themselves by a fourth vow to the education of girls. § 8.

The house sisters too will take their three vows in the hands of the Bishop. § 9.

C. Offices.

The Mothers (teachers) and sisters (but not the lay sisters), will elect a superior for three years; her term of office may first of all be extended to a further three years and finally, by a vote with three-quarters majority, for an unspecified time. § 10

The sister with the nearest number of votes will be nominated Vicaress, Mater Substituta, and will represent the superior. Together with the teachers, the Superior elects four consultors and a monitor. (Monitrix) § 11.

With her representative and four consultors, the Superior selects the remaining holders of offices: the procurator, novice mistress, school prefect, teachers, sacristan, portress, infirmarian, sewing mistress, gardner, etc. § 12.

Appointment to an office and removal from it should be accepted with indifference. § 13.

D. Rules of Enclosure.

Because of the political situation in England, conventual enclosure cannot be practised, but at home these rules will be strictly observed. Externs are to have admission to the chapel and school only, and then with good reason and the Bishop's permission. Those conversations allowed with externs are to be in a parlour, in the presence of another sister. § 14.

The Rector of the chapel appointed by the Bishop may have admission to the house solely to give the Sacraments, and that only in the presence of the superior or her representative and two professed. The same holds good for workmen doing necessary repairs and other work. § 15.

The members of the Institute may not visit any externs. A church will be appointed them for Mass and sermons, and reception of the Sacraments. § 16.

E. Obedience.

The most prompt obedience should be observed by subjects; modesty and humility by those in office. § 17.

The same obtains for the interior disposition of all. § 18.

Next follow many directives and rules of behaviour. The consultors should convey their suggestions with great modesty; the superior should not bring any influence to bear on their suggestions, but it is she who is to make the final decision of what, in her opinion, is for the greater glory of God. In matters of great importance she should not, however, act without consulting the spiritual director, as far as he can judge in the matter. § 19.

The superior may admit someone into the noviceship only after consultation with her representative and the consultors. She cannot admit anyone to profession without the consent of her representative, the novice mistress and two or three of the consultors. Should a novice be found unsuitable, she should be sent away with consideration and when the time is right. § 20.

The novices should be examined closely as to their suitability for the Institute and their bent for teaching. § 21.

No one should interfere in the work of others, but take care of their own. When rebuked by a superior 'they should believe that they had been reproved by the Holy Virgin.' They should maintain their interior peace and draw benefit from the admonition. § 22.

The monitor should fulfil her office responsibly and with humility, after having considered her words in prayer. § 23.

Should the superior die in office, the Mothers are to vote for a successor in secret vote. § 24.

The person newly elected should make her statement of faith, and take an oath 'not to change anything in the Institute concerning the education of girls, but to take care that the Rule be followed to the greater glory of God'. § 25.

If several were to enter with the desire to educate English girls, the community (in St Omer) was to be divided. The superior should give the new community exact instructions. She and the Mothers were to elect the new superior, to be called the Principal, and be approved by the Bishop. Once a year the Superior will visit the new house and arrange communication with the motherhouse. § 26.

F. Poverty

Poverty should be practised as Christ and his mother practised this virture. § 27.

They should not talk much about the worldly goods which they have left behind them, but rejoice when the least things in the house are given them. § 28.

All will receive the same food, clean household effects and 'a black, serious, and modest dress', which they would one day like to have confirmed. The boarders will wear secular, modest clothing. § 29.

A secular bailiff is to take care of their possessions. The individual members will bring a sufficient dowry with them, but will not have it at their disposal. § 30.

The acceptance of gifts, letters or messages without the permission of the superior is forbidden. Each one has a bed in the bedroom for her need. § 31.

G.Chastity

As brides of Christ they should live chastely. 'The hair must be modest and always under a veil, without being shown.' § 32.

They will speak little and eat with moderation. They keep the laws of church abstinence and fasting for the conversion of England and such times as:

> Advent (28th November – 25th December); Eve of Rogation Days (before the Ascension) to Pentecost (about 14 days, according to the church's year); from the beginning of August to the Feast of the Assumption (1st – 15th August).

On Friday and Saturday they will practise abstinence. Once in the week they will take the discipline. With permission of the superior they will wear a hair shirt and undertake other penances. § 33.

During illness, they will be dispensed from penances by the Superior so that they may continue to devote the work they have undertaken to the greater glory of God. § 34.

If they should have a recurring illness, they must follow the advice of the infirmarian and the prescriptions of the doctor. § 35.

There will be reading at meals (from a spiritual book). Silence will be observed in the refectory, the kitchen, places of work, in the bedroom and obviously too in the chapel. § 36.

Recreation takes place after meals. § 37.

H. Order of the Day.

In summer and winter they will rise at 4 o'clock and devote the morning to prayer and meditation. They will recite the great Canonical or the Marian book of hours, according to inclination. Lay sisters will say the rosary. They will make an examination of conscience twice a day. § 38.

On week days they will have spiritual exercises and catechism lessons in their own groups. Every day they will read spiritual books. Once a week and on feasts of the church they will go to confession and communion. § 39.

Prayer

Their life of prayer was mainly directed to the conversion of England.

The celebration of Mass was the basis of the stiff, impersonal litury of those days. The intentions were, to a certain extent, prescribed in a sort of rota:

SUNDAY:	Mass of the Holy Trinity for Pope Paul V, for the Cardinals and other clergy.
MONDAY:	Mass for the Dead.
TUESDAY:	Mass of the Holy Angels for the Nuntius and the Bishop.
WEDNESDAY:	Mass of the Holy Spirit for the Princes of the country.
THURSDAY:	Mass of the Blessed Sacrament for the conversion of England and for the Royal Family; for this they also undertook corporal penances.
FRIDAY:	Mass of the sufferings of Christ for the Orders.
SATURDAY:	Mass of Mary, the Mother of God, for all friends of England. § 40/41.

Sometimes, on the previous day, the prayer intentions and the names of benefactors of the Institutes would be made known. The members were to remember particularly in their prayers: the clergy, the Princes and councillors of the country who had been helpful to their congregation, and the founder of the Society (peculiariter...potissimum fundatoris quem Deus ad id excitaverit cuius quotidie praeter addicenda ei sacra habebitur memoria). § 42.

Three times a year they were to renew their vows after a period of three days' recollection and a general confession. § 43.

They should often ask the superior for a penance for their failings against the Rule. § 44.

Every month the Rules should be read publicly in the refectory; individuals should read the rules of their offices once a week in private; they should reverence the Rules of the Institute as written by the hand of God and follow them exactly. § 45.

K. Virtues

The following – § 46 – offers an inventory of virtues:

> Piety, striving after perfection, zeal for souls, discernment (of spirits), strength of soul, etc. 'Perfecta caritas', unfortunately, lies in the last place but one...

Paragraphs 47–56 show clearly that this Plan of the Institute was not intended for the Pope but for their negotiators with the Society of Jesus. According to these paragraphs, the members of the Institute esteem the Order of the Society of Jesus above all other Orders. Although the Jesuits cannot take on the direction of the (Institute), they go just as other christians do, to the churches of their Order, to confession and to hear their sermons. § 47–48.

For language reasons, the English women go to the church of the English Jesuits. § 49.

They confess to them, because as religious they can help them more easily than secular priests. For daily Mass in their chapel they have a secular priest. They endeavour to obtain instruction and interior enlightenment from the Jesuits. § 50.

The work of the Institute, namely that of teaching and educating the young, will awaken a vocation in many girls. § 51.

Or make good wives of them in the world. § 52.

The curriculum given under paragraph § 53 will be dealt with in another part, as also the list of virtues for the pupils. § 54.

Occasionally girls who have fallen into error will be admitted as boarders. § 55.

Just as the pupils were to be educated with gentleness, so too should superiors deal with members of the Institute. § 56.

A summary of the Plan of the Institute: to save one's own soul and to educate girls in order to help England. § 57.

Such was the Jesuit's suggestion for Mary Ward's Institute.

The 'Schola Beatae Mariae' is unsatisfactory. It is simply a series of regulations for setting up a Marian Institute, which could at best send some teachers back to the home country, England. Would this undertaking have offered any hope of success? The founding of a catholic school in England during a time of persecution for catholics would have been out of the question, and individual tuition would have been a tremendous drain on personnel.

As well as that, the members in England could not possibly have lived the sort of life drawn up for the sisters in St Omer, programmed as it was in every detail. Had they tried to do so for any length of time, disunity would surely have been the result. Those in St Omer were almost totally cut off from the outside world by strict regulations. This can be seen even more clearly in Bishop Blaes' 'Relatio' to the Nuntius in Brussels.[16] The weakest point of this Plan, not in itself badly conceived, is glaringly obvious: the function of the Bishop.

He received the vows of the members (paragraphs 8–9); confirmed the superior (paras. 10, 24, 26), and the rector of the house chapel (para. 15), and gave his approval to any necessary exception to the rules of enclosure. (para. 14) One is justified in asking if the Institute should in fact be subject to a Bishop? The straight answer is 'no'. The Institute was even to be independent of any male Order (para. 47) This can only have been a reference to the Society of Jesus, preferred by the Englishwomen. However, as far as practice went, it was virtually an episcopal right.

As to organisational structures, the 'Schola Beatae Maria' had taken some of these from the Society of Jesus: the two-year novitiate, which was not then common for women's orders; the division of the members into two degrees; the length of the superior's term of office, etc. Several things had been copied from the arrangements in the house, and the penitential practices of the Jesuits.

But how much is not mentioned! The Jesuit's fourth vow of obedience to the Pope (connected with the sending of an individual on a mission), is here twisted into a fourth vow by teachers to teach, and this to be made into the hands of the local ordinary. Even more important and decisive, neither the name nor 'the matter and the manner of the Society' are to be found in this Jesuit-flavoured plan of the Institute.

But there could be no modification of 'The same of the Society.'

To return to the beginning of this chapter: a good deal of Fr Lee's idea of the Institute is revealed in the talks which he gave them at various times. In the small 'Liber ruber' in the Munich Institute Archives with its invaluable handwritten contents copied by the first members of the Institute – perhaps several of them – there remains material that Fr Lee gave his listeners as matter for meditation. The little book contains food for ascetical thought which, although baroque, still has much to offer today. Leaving this aside though, and concentrating on the formation of the Institute and its structure, it puts the 'Schola Beatae Mariae' squarely before us. Fr Lee was plainly speaking to teachers in a Marian Institute who 'seek the honour of the Mother of God, particularly in the education of the children, whom they teach to see how much good has come to us through Mary' and that she is the mediatrix who helps us to happiness.[17] There is no mention of the open pastoral apostolate, unless perhaps in the reference to the beauty of nature, to be seen as God's presence for those who go out and are surrounded by distractions. This, maybe, was to be taken as touching on the English women in the open apostolate.

That Fr Lee looked on the Institute as Marian can also be seen from a talk he gave on New Year's Day. At that time the Church celebrated the feast of the Name of Jesus on the first of January, a big feast for the Society of Jesus, and Fr Lee was talking to the theme. Referring to the first pain which the Lord suffered on the day of his circumcision in accordance with the Law, Fr Lee said that for those people who really wanted to to be the Lord's disciples, only those could bear the name of Jesus if they likewise endured pain.[18] Chambers[19] takes this statement as referring to members of the Institute who were suffering because their congregation had not yet been approved. One cannot really presume that, as quite apart from the fact that the Jesuits opposed the Englishwomen's adoption of the name 'Society of Jesus', the community was only just five years old, and not yet clearly defined. The statement should rather be taken as referring to the Fathers of the Society and Fr Lee himself, for when he spoke these words he was on the point of leaving St Omer, which may not have been easy for him.

Later, in the same talk, Fr Lee said 'We see that Our Lady became the mother of God because of her humility. Those who wish to reach perfection should have this same humility and especially those whose vocation it is to imitate the Virgin Mary; they should take every opportunity to humble themselves and to seek humiliations, for His sake'.[20] Words certainly intended for the Englishwomen.

In one of his last talks to the them shortly before his departure from St Omer, given in the presence of his successor (unnamed), Fr Lee explained the Rules of the Institute.[21] Thirty-two points were dealt with, and it is worth looking at a brief summary of them:

1. The Englishwomen should perform their work for the greater glory of God.
2. They are particularly to seek to honour the Blessed Virgin Mary in their education of girls.
3. Obedience is the best remedy for egoism.
4. The education and teaching of girls will consist primarily in religion lessons, though other subjects may be included which are useful to them.
5. Virtue will not be achieved by flight from opportunities to do good, nor by the removal of difficulties. They should rather use every opportunity and always take refuge with God in prayer.
6. Although one virtue is more important for their manner of life than another, they should however practise all virtues according to time and opportunity.
7. Upon entering, they should begin at once with mortification of self, for love of self is the greatest obstacle on the way to perfection. We desire what we cannot have, or we have a bigger burden laid upon us than we wish to carry. It is salutary for inner peace to respect everything that we use, for we deserve the worst.
8. Obedience is the best means to perfection. Tasks should be accepted as coming from God. Reference to St Ignatius. The superior's commands are a means of attaining perfection.
9. The superior should care for each one and exclude none.

10. They should confess their sins to their confessor, and talk over their difficulties with their superior and take her advice.
11. They shall not talk of difficulties among themselves, as they are unable to help one another and will cause harm.
12. Their characteristic tendencies are to be confided to their superior. The director, as an outsider, cannot know everything. Before practising forms of penance they should ask the superior.
13. Not discussed.
14. The superior likewise should know their progress, so that she may make better use of them. In conversation with seculars they should take care, in case they disappoint them.
15. Control of the tongue in conversation.
16. They should endeavour to live in the presence of God.
17. Public penance (self-accusation).
18. Concerning their behaviour in the company of those who tell jokes with a double meaning or other such conversation.
19. Concerning behaviour in sickness – obedience to the doctor's orders.
20. and 21. not mentioned.
22. Daily meditation before Mass.
23. Each is to eat what is put before her.
24. Attention to the needs of others.
25. Even during recreation their behaviour should be reserved (rules of touch).
26. They should not complain to others.
27. Their manner of speech to others should be as though they spoke to a superior, and such that could be uttered anywhere. They should inform the superior of any severe temptations, but confess sins to the confessor.
28. They should not reprimand one another. The person in charge of different duties has her responsibilities which she should either use or in certain cases leave to the superior.
29. It is good to report failings to the superior, but that should be done openly and not from malice. Rebukes should be accepted well.
30. Censorship of letters.
31. Consultations between the confessor (director) and the superior concerning members of the Institute.
32. Observance of the Rules. Each one should have a copy and read them often.

It is obvious that Fr Lee directed the Englishwomen on the lines presented above, for in his talks he often referred to one or other of the virtues named here and, as can be seen, some of the instructions to Jesuits were worked into these points. However, it was not the Institute of the Society of Jesus which had made them available.

The Conflict between her vow and her vision

(1609 – 1615)

Rapid growth of the English women's congregation – purchase of three houses in St Omer – Mary Ward's journey to England, 1614 – her resolve concerning Fr Lee – extracts from her talks to members of the Institute

Relatively little is known about Mary Ward during these first years of the Institute, from 1609 – 1615. We know of her endeavours to found the Institute, that she purchased a house in St Omer and that her name was known to the English Ambassador, William Trumbull in Brussels and to George Abbot, the Archbishop of Canterbury, who was a great opponent of catholicism. But how did she stand with regard to her Institute, which was developing before her very eyes in a form that was not according to the command given her, which had 'transformed her soul and had brought her so much enlightenment?'

One should first of all consider the position of the community.

In St Omer the number of Institute members and boarders had grown rapidly. Teaching and education make great demands on space. The house bought in 1611 had become too small for this steadily growing enterprise. In the second half of 1612 a petition was presented to the Infanta Isabella Clara Eugenia in the names of Barbara Babthorpe, Anne Gage and Mary Ward. They were asking for support for their request to the Bishop and town Magistrate that they 'y permitan vivir quietamente y sin molestacion'.[22] The sender of the letter, it emerges from subsequent correspondence, was the Jesuit, Fr Antonio Colasso, who had spent several years at the court of the Spanish King as procurator of his Order for Portugal.[23] During his time in Belgium he had great influence at the Brussels' court.[24] As a result, on 8th September 1612 a request was sent from the Rulers of the country to the town of St Omer and the Bishop.[25] From this we learn that the Englishwomen were extending their work, for they already had daughters entrusted to them from families like those of George Talbot, Earl of Shrewsbury and the Earl of Southampton. Later, some of the daughters of these families entered the Institute. George Talbot in particular was a great friend and benefactor of the Jesuits.

It can be seen from this that Jesuits – not least Father Colasso – helped Mary Ward in her undertakings in St Omer. Bishop Blaes would have raised no objections. All the same, it seems curious that the Englishwomen had to ask the Rulers to request the Bishop's co-operation.

The town hesitated.[26] At the beginning of October, 1612, one of its officials made reference to the Rulers' letter on behalf of the Englishwomen,[27] saying that their recommendation should be discussed in Council and the town's difficulties put before the Bishop and the Governor. Archduke Albrecht should be acquainted with the fact that the town was suffering from an influx of such communities.

On 2nd May, 1613,[28] the Infanta promised once more to help the Englishwomen in their successful work. As a town, St Omer was certainly not hostile to convents, for it was one of the most devout in Flanders and had parried the advance of Calvinism. But it also defended the rights of its citizens, like other towns in other countries. For, with the foundation of a religious community, part of their land inevitably, sometimes to a large extent, passed into mortmain and therefore, according to ancient legal usage, was free from tax. And, as has already been said, St Omer was a town abundantly supplied with convents and monasteries. However their deliberations were fruitless, for on 2nd October 1612 the Englishwomen were able to buy a second house, this time from a Jacques Ricquart.[29] On 20th January, 1614,[30] came the purchase of a third house, formerly the possession of the Cistercian Abbey of Ravensberg near Watten. It was 1616 before the town could be prompted to confirm these purchases legally.[31]

It seems remarkable that Mary Ward stayed so long in England at this time. Perhaps she was in London on that 18th October,1613, when the Spanish missionary, Luisa de Carvajal, was taken prisoner for the second time in shameful circumstances. She describes this event in such detail and so dramatically that one could imagine she had been a witness.[32] We know for certain that she was there from the middle of April, 1614 until presumably the middle of July, and again in the Advent of the same year until at least March, 1615. For these journeys, assuredly taken for good reasons, she needed the approval of her director, to whom she had taken a vow of obedience.

In the same year Mary Ward wrote 'resolutions', and this at a time when Fr Lee was absent from St Omer. She shows this in entry 19 given below. According to our calculations, this could have been at the end of 1614, after Fr Lee had already left St Omer and she was still there. Or, perhaps, in the spring of 1615, when she had returned from her second journey to England.

Let us look closely at these resolutions,[33] lifting out only those which refer to her confessor and director. These are thirteen out of a total of   thirty-five entries − almost a third.

1.[7]   I will endeavour to make a general confession twice a year with great honesty and openness and to the priest to whom, according to God's will, I shall entrust my soul completely and whom I request for God's sake not to abandon me, until he has led me to heaven. I will also renew my vows and make a complete manifestation of conscience, which consists of what is both good and bad.

2.[10] I will never contravene my director in desire, work or deed.

3.[11] I will accept all his words and commands with full assent of my will and judgement and carry out with complete exactness and reverence whatever he orders or desires.

4.[12] I will endeavour daily to become perfect in obedience. I will kiss the five wounds of our saviour, that in this virtue I may act as he would have me act.

5.[13] As to what concerns the Institute and this course of life, I will do only what the confessor holds for the best.

6.[14] When I experience repugnance or feel tempted inwardly on occasions connected with obedience, I will not confess these, if I have not concurred with them. I will always endeavour to proceed in a manner such as I have undertaken.

7.[15] If I have insights or some such impulses concerning the Institute, I will always place myself in the holy wounds of Christ and make acts of submission.

8.[19] Those things that I wish to discuss with my absent director, I will converse with in prayer to God, who is ever present.

9.[22] I will always, in all things, let myself be guided by my director and accommodate myself to his will and judgement.

10.[24] I will pray for grace for myself and all others, especially for those of our Company and the Society.

11.[26] I will endeavour to be of one mind with my spiritual father, for it is through him that God leads me and gives me grace. He tells me what is God's will. If I follow his guidance, I shall certainly receive grace sufficient to enable me to do God's will.

12.[27] I will not permit myself the slightest resistance against the commands of obedience, nor hold any contrary opinion. My will on all occasions will submit in obedience, whether it is a question of great or small matters, something agreeable or disagreeable, easy or difficult.

13.[35] I will pay particular attention to the exact attention of the order of the day and the Rules, both by myself and others. I will always love this holy Institute, esteem it and give it preference, if I may be permitted. For myself and my dealings, I will earnestly strive to gain those virtues that are peculiar to this Institute, and I will practise these with faithfulness and firmness and as perfectly as possible. Finally, I will take it as a model, according to which I shall direct my life and actions, as far as obedience allows it. We must arm ourselves with a great desire for suffering.

Although this text, these words wrung from her, give sufficient witness of her bitter interior conflict, it would be good to make a few comments here.

Apart from the difficulty between her determination to obey, which was at one and the same time faithfulness to her vow of obedience and to the clear vision that remained indelibly printed on her soul, three points in particular show her position with regard to the Institute.

In entry 5,[13] Mary Ward submits herself to Fr Lee's Institute. She even sets aside further visions and impulses (entry 7,[15] From these two resolutions, it must not be concluded that Mary Ward had doubts about the illumination God had granted her. They are rather a sign of her conviction that God could not act against himself. The English *Vita* has already indicated this belief of Mary Ward's.[34] It is the final entry that poses the difficulty.13,[35] When she writes, 'I will always love this holy Institute, esteem it and give it preference', one is justified in asking 'Which Institute is Mary Ward talking about?' Was it the one which she received in her vision, 'Take the manner and matter of the Society'? 'At first it seems so, but this is hardly possible. Her heart was already directed towards God, and did not need to be spurred on to love and esteem the 'manner and the matter' by any resolution. It would be disturbing to imply that a qualification was added: 'if I am allowed this'. One must keep to reality. Fr Lee knew that any deviation from her vision, alterations such as those envisaged in his 'Schola Beatae Mariae' Plan, must cause her great interior suffering. He believed that her vision of the Institute was of divine origin, although he was prevented by the Constitutions of his Order to help in promoting it. It must be assumed that he allowed Mary Ward considerable inner freedom. This is the direction in which her qualification points, surely, if she said that she would have accepted this Institute as a model for her life. Here, too, it is followed by 'as far as obedience permits me'.

A great inner struggle, great tension lies behind those words, produced as though in travail and concentrated here into resolutions, or basic propositions. Far worse than the martyrdom of gall-stones which was just beginning for her, or the difficulties of a new foundation from a human and practical point of view, was this constantly nagging discrepancy between her vision and her vow which, with hindsight, was only a prelude to the difficulties that were to come. At some later date the word 'Institute' which appears twice in entry 13,[35] was struck out. At first this seems strange, as it occurs here only. Certainly, in the entries given above, 5,[13] 7[15] and 10,[24] the subject at issue was Fr Lee's Institute, her vision, and her prayer. But in this final entry what is referred to is her inner conviction, her deep engagement to an Institute which, in its 'manner and matter' differed only a little from that which had been conveyed to her in her vision. We believe it is possible to interpret Mary Ward's erasure of both those entries as her rejection of Fr Lee's Marian educational Institute, after his death.

But it was not only Fr Lee who had an influence on the members. He was confessor and gave them occasional talks, and offered them a framework for the Institute that was practicable at that time. The regular instruction of the members would certainly have been given by Mary Ward, or in her absence by her representative.

For his book 'Englische Tugend-Schule', Marcus Fridl drew on a lost collection of talks given by Mary Ward which he refers to as 'Allocutiones' when talking of her addressess. These scattered and summarized sayings consist of about thirty statements. Whether the topics imply an equal number of conferences, and whether all were given by Mary Ward must remain unanswered. Fridl may have grafted several points, or taken just lines of thought from one conference. It is certain, however, that these talks stem from the first years of the Institute. That can be established from internal proofs, even though these may sometimes be weak.[35] Only those remarks that refer in some way to the Institute will be dealt with here, eight points, almost a quarter of the Allocutiones which have survived.

The first point[36] treats of observance of the Rules. These, of course, are the Rules that Fr Lee has prescribed, and which Mary Ward has observed, under obedience. It states that it cannot be expected that all will possess the virtues mentioned in them, but that they should, however, endeavour to do so. As to the superiors of the Institute – they are not obliged to direct members towards perfection with severity, as with other Orders, for no penitential practices are prescribed in the Institute. If a penance were to be imposed on a novice, it was to be understood as helping towards her own progress, and not as punitive.

In part three, dated 21st July, 1613[37], Mary Ward gave addresses on the renewal of vows, but sadly these were not written down. It is interesting to note that already, in those early days, the sisters were renewing their vows. It is assumed that immediately after their arrival in St Omer at the beginning of 1610, the first members of the Institute spent some time in prayer and penance and that after Mary Ward's vision towards the end of 1611 or the beginning of 1612, they took vows for the first time. The vows are dealt with again, probably on the occasion of a first profession.[38] It is not clear if it was Mary Ward who gave the address; possibly this time it was Fr Lee who spoke to the members. It is slightly strange that the terms 'your Institute' and 'your Rule' are used: that even if the English-women take vows they are free to leave 'their Institute', but later, when 'their' Rule has been approved or confirmed, they will not be able to do so.

As members of an Institute which had not yet been approved, the Englishwomen, in accordance with Canon Law, took private vows and, at first, for a limited time. They were not, therefore, obliged to remain in the congregation. However, after taking perpetual vows and after the approval of the Institute, the situation would be quite different.

A later conference would also seem to have been given by Fr Lee. 'It is necessary for 'your' Institute that you are kindly and amiable to all. For whoever does not have these virtues, however many others she may have will neither be able to honour God truly nor be of use to him'.[39] And, with felicitous brevity, 'Those are most fit to go out who are satisfied with staying at home,'[40] and later, 'We never wish to go out without asking God that he may direct our words and works to a good end, and we should take good care that we do all we can for the salvation of our neighbour. If we do not, it were better if we had stayed at home.' [41] Finally, 'Each one who goes out should desire as much as she can, to act so as to give good example, otherwise it were better not to go out'.[42] We can see from these words how often and expressly Mary Ward pointed to contact with the world outside, and equally, how determined she was to preserve the inner enclosure of someone totally given to God.

There are four mentions of St Ignatius in these statements,[43] a sign of Mary Ward's deep solidarity with the founder of the Society of Jesus. Once[44] she spoke reverently of St Gregory, the patron of England. The talk was on the eve of his feast, therefore on 11th March. Most members, she said, wanted to obtain an indulgence on this feast. Mary Ward called on them to offer their actions on this day for England and to think particularly of the Institute. Fridl's German translation runs: This blessed saint has a great desire to help us, and as I take for certain, he wants to be asked by us. You have great cause to be thankful to St Gregory, and to set great trust in him, for he has borne our concern for many years and knows well how far it will go, and he loves it.' She must certainly have been thinking of that St Gregory's Day, when she was first given the commission to work for England.

More Enlightenment

(End of 1614)

Difficulties for the Institute after Fr Lee's move to England — his farewell speech — Bishop Blaes of St Omer as the Institute's protector — discord among the members of the community

By the end of 1614, the situation in the Institute was tense. Fr Lee was on the point of leaving for Louvain, Mary Ward had been in England since Advent and uncertainty, if not downright depression, held sway in the community. During this time Fr Lee gave a talk which should perhaps be better described as an admission.[45]

He began by saying that although he loved the whole community, he knew little of the spiritual progress of some of them. That was why he thought it right to give them a fuller explanation, ('a little more') and information about their situation, as well as the reason for his departure. His move had not been determined by obedience solely, but was also the result of the comments and attitudes taken by certain people (probably his confrères). He was telling them this, as there might be some people (probably Jesuits again) who would want to test the religious spirit of the English women in order to find out if they were really sound.

As to their Superior, they knew her worth as did the Englishwomen themselves ('for your Superior they knowe what she was and all of you'); that was why such people had not interfered, as they knew how she would react ('they knew what your superior would doe'). He, Fr Lee, had always dealt with his highest superiors, with the most important fathers of the Society of Jesus, and with the Bishop. These had certainly taken note of what he was doing, in case he undertook something which could not be brought to a satisfactory conclusion. As for other people (Jesuits), it was not necessary that they should know about matters concerning the situation of the English women; that would be indiscreet and would make the members of the Institute dependent to some extent on their opinion (of the Jesuits). With these few words Fr Lee sketched the extremely delicate position of the Institute with regard to the Jesuits in St Omer, and perhaps those in Louvain also.

The members may not have realised the difficulties fully. The reason for his being moved – sensitively touched on by his reference to the obedience of a Jesuit – would probably have been taken by most members of the Institute with dismay. The remark about the superior deserves close attention. It is in the imperfect tense, 'what she was'. Mary Ward was just then – 1614 – in England for the second time. The information that Fr Lee always dealt with his highest superiors is interesting, for this probably implies the General, though there is no proof of this for such an exchange of correspondence would be entered in Fr General Aquaviva's catalogue. Most probably he was in touch with Fr Thomas Owen, one of the most important fathers of the Society of Jesus. Since 1610, Fr Thomas Owen had been Rector of the English College and Prefect of the English Mission in Rome.[46]

Fr Lee next turned to the immediate situation. Fr Owen, he continued, had written to him that the Bishop's authority could contribute much to the confirmation of their Institute, and that this could be soon. The Bishop was well-disposed towards the Institute. Fr Lee had been granted an audience by the Bishop before his departure and had spoken about the Institute on that occasion. He had recommended Mary Ward to the Bishop and mentioned the popularity of the Institute in connection with the increasing number of members of the congregation. He also mentioned what Fr Owen had said to him about episcopal authority. Fr Lee had recommended the Institute to the Bishop's protection, as he had always been kindly disposed towards them. Bishop Blaes had answered: 'Father, whatever I can do for them (the English Ladies), they will always find me ready, but let me know if you should need help. I will do what I can to promote them, as that will be for the salvation of their country.'

It is remarkable that Fr Lee conducted negotiations with an influential member of the Society of Jesus and with the Bishop about the standing of the Institute. Apparently, Mary Ward did not seem to be part of these consultations. One is led to suppose that she had been passed over because she had not been present. Bishop Blaes offered his help for the Institute to Fr Lee, although he knew he was on the point of leaving St Omer.

It is true that influential people were protecting the Institute, and Fr Lee encouraged the Englishwomen to be constant. He said, too, that there were many enemies who were forecasting that they would show no spiritual progress after his departure. But they had proved their worth once before, when he had been absent, although then their superior had been with them. Humility, prudence, and trust in God would help them to overcome such testing circumstances. Fr Lee concluded his talk with the confidence that Mary Ward would return soon ('come again ere it be longe'), but however that might be, their enterprise would continue, even if she did not come back ('your business shall be sett forwards, although she should never com.') This final sentence gives food for thought. The enterprise meant here was undoubtedly the attempt to obtain approval of the Institute, and that it would continue, even if Mary Ward did not return to St Omer! One's thoughts involuntarily turn to her first journey to England in 1614. Then, as she said herself, she had to do something in her own country which only she could do. It is possible to infer from this that she wanted to make the 'Schola Beatae Mariae' known to those members who had remained in England. This would have limited activity in England to the teaching and education of girls and would, moreover, bind the members to this by vow.

At the end of 1614, Mary Ward went to England again. In doing so, did she want to distance herself from an Institute which the English Jesuits were transforming into their idea of a Marian educational congregation? She harboured thoughts similar to these some years later, when the community ran into a difficult situation after the new foundation in Liège. She was to write then: 'I felt a disinclination to leave this company before it was approved.'

Once before, after leaving the Poor Clare Order in 1609, Mary Ward had travelled to England to obtain a clearer perspective. If one looks at it from this angle, the words just quoted give special weight to her spiritual need.

But what exactly had Fr Lee disclosed? What was the information contained in 'a little more light and knowledge of your state?'

To recapitulate: Fr Lee spoke of the reason for his move; about the probable behaviour of the enemies of the Institute after his departure; about his negotiations in the interest of the congregation with regard to its approval and, finally, about his conversation with the Bishop who had agreed to help the community. All of which was interlaced with words of encouragement for the Englishwomen. Humility, prudence, and trust in God would continue to help them promote their enterprise, even without Mary Ward. Did this satisfy the English women? Were they now clear about their Institute, which was going to continue no matter what? Hardly. How did the members react? Disunity flared up among them, for they were subjected to conflicting influences, within and without the confessional, which carried with it spiritual direction.

It must be presumed that there were discussions between the first members of the Institute and the episcopal curia, perhaps even with the Bishop himself, and with the English Jesuits.

Not long after Fr Lee left St Omer, Bishop Blaes published an open letter, the clarity of which leaves nothing to be desired. This will be dealt with in a later chapter.

Soon after, on 2nd May 1615,[47] Fr Lee wrote a letter to the novices in St Omer from which only a few essential points are taken here. He calls them – as though he were a devoted mother – his beloved children. A mother weeps with her children and suffers with them. It is with great travail that she has brought them into the world and she rejoices when they are prompt and obedient. It is for these reasons that he, Fr Lee, calls them his children. They have been steadfast in virtue, and generous, but the following of Christ must involve suffering. He would not wish to dwell on their enemies: the world, their own sensuality, the devil. He would rather encourage them by indicating the benefits they have received from God. They should follow their vocation freely, and for the love of God alone, without letting others persuade them to the contrary. As God had called them to the Institute, departure from the Institute would not bring them happiness. No human ridicule should drive them to take such a step, as it came from those who had their own designs. The Institute offered them the means of holiness. Women in religious communities are in God's presence, even if the title religious is refused them. It would cause him much pain if any one of them suffered shipwreck and left the Institute.

It is clear from these words that either parents or relatives wanted to persuade some of the novices to leave. Perthaps several of them had become uncertain. They could not be blamed if they had, for who could these young people turn to?

Some weeks later, on 24th June,[48] Fr Lee wrote a letter which must be taken as a serious warning to the whole community.

Although he was bound by obedience,[49] began Fr Lee, he would like to try to help them. Even if they were attacked from outside, they should examine what the present times required. He might not be well-informed as to what difficulties the last storm had caused, but it seemed that disunity had broken out among them. As their way (your course) was not yet entirely known by the world, he had always tried to hold them together in unity of spirit so that later, in the case of his no longer being with them, they might proceed with one mind.

Probably the women, in their uncertainty, had sought consolation and information from their confessors, as Fr Lee warned them about long confessions and encouraged them to be independent in talking of their difficulties — so long as these were not sins — with their superior. A splinter group would make no progress in the spiritual life. Murmuring against superiors came from the devil.

It is not known who prompted Fr Lee to write either of these letters. Perhaps some of his colleagues in St Omer may have drawn his attention to the difficulties within the community — perhaps the young superior, Barbara Babthorpe, had asked him to intercede.

One thing, however, is quite certain. Someone had thrown a spanner in the works.

Notes

1. "My confessor resisted, all the Society opposed; diverse Institutes were drawne by severall persons, some of which were approved and greatly commended by the last bishopp Blasius of Saint-Omers, our soe great friend and some other divines. These were offered us and as it were pressed upon us, there was noe remedy but refuse them, which caused infinitt troubles." StA Munich, Kl. 432/I, 16–19.

2. ARSI Rome, Anglia 37, f 117e.

3. Fr Antony Rivers SJ, Socius of Fr Henry Garnett, Superior of the English Mission in London. He probably fled after Fr Garnett's execution and met Fr Persons in Rome. He died before 1620/21 in all probability, as he is not mentioned in the oldest lists of the province. Neither does he appear in the 1610 list of Jesuits active in England, Foley, Records VII, p. 653.

4. ARSI, Rome, Gall-Belg. 1/I, p. 12.

5. It emerges from the letter that Father Busleyden had written to Father General about the foundation of a community of women along Jesuit lines in Munich. This should be prevented and Duke Wilhelm of Bavaria informed accordingly. ARSI Rome, Germ. Sup. 4. f. 316r (34r).

6. ARSI, Rome, Gallo-Belg. 1/I, p. 20. A similar letter on the same date to Fr Rector Jean van Crombeeck. ibid. p. 21.

7. Foley I, p. 456–466; VI, p. 446–447.

8. The Secretary of Propaganda Fide, Francesco Ingoli, numbers him among the "Jesuitae casistae", among the few educated Jesuits. Ingoli to Cardinal Millini, 23rd July, 1624, APF Rome, Vol. 205, f. 442 r.

9. This comes from one of his last addresses to the Englishwomen. LR pp. 94–95. The historian of the English Jesuit province, Fr Henry More SJ, protects his confrere by giving ill-health as grounds for his move from Saint-Omer. The necrology covers for this deserving man with effusive language. AGR Brussels, Arch-Jésuit. Prov. Gallo-Belg., Carton 31 (1615–1616).

10. Vita E ff. 16v.–17r.

11. Letter Nr. 2. Inst. Arch. Munich.

12. LR p. 233. Inst. Arch. Munich.

13. VP/H 1, Inst. Arch. Munich.

14. Fr Robert Sherwood OSB in his report to Pope Gregory XV, before the end of May, 1622, BV Rome, Fondo Capp. 47, ff. 64r–65v; Matthew Kellison in his report to Nuntius Francesco Guidi di Bagno of 26th October, 1622. WA London, Vol. 16, p. 645 ff. and Secretary Ingoli in his dorsal comment on the petition of the English Agent Rant to Pope Urban VIII, before 23rd July, 1624, APF Rome, vol. 205, f 435rv.

15. ARSI Rome, Fondo Gesuitico 1435, Fasz. 1, Nr. 3.
16. see below, p. 183.
17. LR. p. 109, Inst. Arch. Munich.
18. ibid. pp. 161–162.
19. Chambers I E, p. 323; I D, p. 259.
20. LR pp. 163–164, Inst. Arch. Munich.
21. ibid. pp. 108–133.
22. On 8th September, 1612; AGR Brussels, PEA 1894. (2)
23. Pater Colasso to Secretary of State Prats, before 2nd October 1612; Prats to the Bishop of Saint-Omer and Governor Charles de Souastre, 1st October, 1612, both AGR Brussels, PEA 1944(3) as also to the Mayor of Saint-Omer, AM Saint-Omer, CCXXXIX 17–18, Filles Anglaises, f. 39.
24. Fr Antonio Colasso SJ (1568–1647) from Portugal, entered the Society of Jesus in 1586. He was a writer, and died in Madrid in 1647. Sommervogel II, Sp. 1292–93.
25. AM St Omer, CCXXXIX 16, Filles Anglaises, ff. 1–2 and f. 15.
26. On 1st October 1612; Secret. of State Prats to Bishop Blaes, AGR Brussels, PEA 1944 (3).
27. After 2nd October 1612, AM Saint-Omer, CCXXXIX 17–18, Filles Anglaises, f. 20.
28. Infanta Isabella Clara Eugenia to Mary Ward, AGR Brussels, PEA 1947 (1).
29. see below, note 31.
30. ibid.
31. On 18th May, 1616. AM Saint-Omer, CCXXXIX 17–18, Filles Anglaises, p. 37.
32. Fridl I, p. 150, Nr. 121, from a lost Libellus Colloquiorum.
33. VP/A 1, Inst. Arch. Munich.
34. Vita E, f. 17r.
35. Fridl II, p. 522, Nr. 771, from Allocutiones f. 29. Perhaps, too, Fridl I, p. 106, Nr. 85, from Allocutiones f. 81. This concerns Mary Ward's relationship with the English Poor Clares in Gravelines; Mary Ward visited them. This will have been soon after the founding of her own Institute. Mary Ward left Saint-Omer at the end of 1616 and from then on returned there only sporadically.
36. Fridl II, p. 481, Nr. 749, from Allocutiones f. 1.
37. ibid. p. 522, Nr. 771, from Allocutiones f. 29.
38. ibid. p. 524, Nr. 772, from Allocutiones f. 53.
39. ibid. pp. 554–555, Nr. 789, from Allocutiones f. 66.
40. ibid p. 572, Nr. 801, from Allocutiones f. 66.
41. ibid. p. 572, Nr. 801, from Allocutiones f. 126.
42. ibid. p. 572, Nr. 801, from Allocutiones f. 127.
43. ibid. pp. 91–92, Nr. 482, from Allocutiones f. 86, pp. 226–227, Nr. 582, from Allocutiones f. 88; p. 92 Nr. 482, from Allocutiones f. 112 and p. 91, Nr. 482, from Allocutiones f. 86. In this quotation the foliation of the Allocutiones have been given precedence.
44. ibid. p. 89–90, Nr. 481, from Allocutiones f. 121.
45. LR pp. 94–108, Inst. Arch. Munich.
46. Fr Thomas Owen SJ (1556–1618) was born in Hampshire. He entered the Society of Jesus in 1579 in Lyons. He was Rector of the English College and Prefect of the English Mission in Rome from 1610 to his death. he died aged 62 on 6th December, 1618 in Rome. Foley, Records VII, p. 562 and p. 1444; Sommervogel, Bibliothèque VI, p. 50.
47. LR pp. 24–52, Inst. Arch. Munich.
48. ibid. pp. 1–23.
49. " ... my poore endevours allwais limeted with the bounds of obedience ... "

IX

THE 'PIUM INSTITUTUM'

The Institute as judged by Fr Leonhard Lessius,SJ
End of 1614, beginning of 1615

Questions put to the moral theologian Fr Lessius concerning the Englishwomen − their presumed author and his reasons for them − Lessius' opinion: as a 'Pium Institutum' depending on the Bishop, the Englishwomen could carry on their programme of teaching and educating English girls without enclosure; the three vows as determinative factors

The controversy concerning the Institute's right to exist, and its status, was brought to a head within the Society of Jesus.[1] This fact must never be forgotten.

The first Plan of the Institute, the 'Schola Beatae Virginis', drafted by Jesuits who favoured the Englishwomen, together with the 'Schola Beatae Mariae' version probably altered by them, seems to have run into opposition from most of the English Jesuits in Belgium, for soon afterwards certain questions involving the matter of the Institute were laid before the noted moral theologian, Leonhard Lessius.

This celebrated scholar[2] was born in 1554 and entered the Society in 1572. He studied in the Roman College under the renowned canonist, Francis Suarez. From 1585 he was Professor of Theology in the University of Louvain and was also a writer. He died on 15th January, 1623. His scholarship was drawn on several times in matters concerning the Institute. As a Fleming, Lessius had a considerably more open approach to the authorization of those women's congregations which had come into being outside the usual control of the Church hierarchy or that of a male Order. His approach was a good deal more liberal than that of many of his colleagues in the Society from the south of Europe. In his own Flanders there were many congregations without conventual enclosure whose members were engaged in girls' education, as well as nursing. Other communities, too, led a devout form of life without being concerned with any specific work. One only has to think of the Beguines, who have made a great contribution in the Netherlands towards the development of social work, despite their difficulties and temporary suppressions.

144

The questions put to Lessius about the Englishwomen's Institute were doubtless drawn up by those hostile to the Plan 'Schola Beatae Mariae', which had at least approved of the members teaching girls in England. That does not imply that they were out-and-out enemies of the women. They would not have turned to Fr Lessius had they been that. It is not clear when this paper was drafted, but it could have been shortly after the emergence of the 'Schola Beatae Mariae', and must have been before 19th March, 1615, for that was the date of Bishop Blaes' writing, and he based his recommendation on Lessius' opinion. The request for the latter's judgement presupposes a rapidly growing community. The time and energy of a busy scholar would hardly have been interrupted for the ten Ladies of 1611. The contemporary dorsal comment: 'Lessius: De Statu Vitae' guarantees the authenticity of the report. This important document has been copied several times and lies in various archives.[3]

From the questions placed before him, it emerges that it was the canonical position of the Institute that came under special fire. Lessius knew his colleagues' original plan of the Institute, 'Schola Beatae Mariae', which had been given him in 1612. At that time the attacks had been mainly focussed on the educational work of the Englishwomen in St Omer, which differed totally in method from that practised within the walls of the enclosed Orders of the day.

Meantime, infuriated letters had flown to the General of the Society in Rome. In addition to that, Bishop Blaes had received a letter from an anonymous Englishman[4] in 1612, attacking the Institute. It is not known what accusations were advanced, but most likely these would have been connected with the activities of the women in England. The Bishop sent a written reply.

What questions were now being set before Lessius? First of all, the way the Institute was represented did not, strictly speaking, correspond to the facts. It is shown here as a community of Englishwomen who have left their country for religious reasons and come together gradually as a congregation. They follow a certain rule of life (certam vivendi Formulam), devote themselves to the salvation of their own and their neighbour's souls, especially (potissimum) by the teaching and education of English girls entrusted to their care. They elect a superior, and after trial period of two years, they take the three simple vows for the whole of their life. To which the following questions were set:

1 Is this Institute allowed and pious?
2 Can the Bishop approve it and authorize it?
3 Can the Institute be considered a reliable state for its members?

Lessius was a moral theologian, and it was as such that he accepted this task, drawing almost exclusively on the works of the great moral theologians in his commentary. What position did he take, and what were his answers?

1. Is the Institute permitted and pious?

Yes, said Lessius. Not only are its aims good – the salvation of one's own soul and that of one's neighbour – but also its means – vows, teaching and education of girls, following a rule.

True, the founding of new Orders had been forbidden by the Councils but this prohibition did not apply to a 'Pium Institutum', a religious community which was not an Order in the canonical sense, whose members wore no habit, were not looked on as nuns and did not wish to become members of an Order. There were similar communities in Italy and Belgium: the Oratory, the Beguines, Fratenser, and the Hospitallers. The Church had never forbidden such groups. The Englishwomen did not wish to enter one of the approved Orders. Their work was to teach and educate English girls who were sent from England, and this occasioned the need to journey to England, 'so that they might seek out the prospective fruit of their labours'. Enclosure would not be compatible with this. Entry into an enclosed Order is not always the most meritorious of actions. The interior relationship with God by living according to the three vows of Poverty, Chastity and Obedience is what is determinative.

In this, Lessius side-steps fact. The members' journeys for 'business' was not the primary reason for their non-acceptance of enclosure. This was intrinsic to the 'matter and manner' of the Institute, and related to their two important spheres of work: pastoral care of souls and the teaching and education of youth.

As for the third question – **can the Institute be considered a reliable state for its members** – to this also Lessius gave an affirmative answer. For, he said, in particular the vow of chastity taken for God was no less a life-long promise than that of the marriage vow between two people. A life contract (conditio) is, however, a status. Dissolution of this vow could be performed licitly by the Pope alone, and that for serious reasons only. Morally however, the vow of chastity, which has been taken for life, is indissoluble. The members of this Institute also take a perpetual vow of obedience and poverty and follow a particular rule of life. The vows ensure them the merits of religious without their actually canonically belonging to this state.

Embedded between these two basic questions was a problem that was to be of great significance in the everyday life of the Institute.

2. Can the Bishop approve and confirm this Institute?

There is a difference in degree between canonical approval (approbatio) and confirmation (confirmatio). Confirmation presupposes approval, but the converse does not. Again, Lessius assents. The Bishop can indeed, in his diocese, approve and confirm such an institute, for this faculty has never been withdrawn from him. It is the approval and confirmation of actual Orders only which is reserved to the Pope. But in this instance, the question of an Order does not arise, for the community would not qualify as such.

Here too a radical divergence is clearly visible: the English women did indeed wish to become a religious women's order, and be recognized as such in the future. Of course they knew that this would not be possible without papal approval, but they must have desired it, for they were striving after 'the matter and manner' of the Order of the Society of Jesus.

According to Lessius, the existence of this 'Pium Institutum' did not rest on confirmation by the Pope but on the inner commitment of its members to God by simple, perpetual vows. His defence, however, showed one important weakness – freedom from enclosure – which offered a favourable point of attack. This was to be seized on. Lessius based non-acceptance of enclosure on the Englishwomen's field of work, the education and teaching of English girls on the continent, and their travel resulting from it. This was only partially true. Eye witnesses had a different story. The Institute's pastoral work for souls in England was dealt with so discreetly in this paper that it was passed over in total silence. But this broad sphere of work existed, and had full and equal justification in the Institute entrusted to Mary Ward as her special task. Friends and foes of the Institute were alive to this discrepancy between statement and fact.

The letter of the Bishop of St Omer

19th March, 1615

The letter as defence – the place of the sources – the reason for the English women's foundation – nature of the Institute – its aim – statement about the attacks against the Institute – Fr Lessius' letter and report

Fr Lee must have left St Omer in 1614. This caused a problem: who would represent the Institute when it was threatened from outside? More, who would defend it? Up till now, he had rebutted the attacks against the Englishwomen, which had come chiefly from his fellow Jesuits. On his departure he had visited the Bishop, who had most generously offered assistance. But this carried with it the right to control the congregation. However, in practice the Bishop's relationship towards the Society of Jesus was totally different from that towards the Englishwomen's Institute.

In the first months of 1615, during the absence of Mary Ward and Fr Lee, tension had apparently increased to such an extent that the Bishop felt obliged to make a statement. It is hardly likely that the incentive came from the women themselves; they would have reacted differently. Rather one should think that the English Jesuits, who were opponents of the Institute's Plan 'Schola Beatae Mariae', requested this testimonial, as they had done in the case of Fr Lessius. Until recently, among the Mary Ward papers, this letter has been taken as one defending the Institute.[5] This is not wholly acceptable, for which Institute could be defended by a Bishop? Having read Lessius' opinion, let us now consider the letter; first, the form in which it has come down to us: this letter patent is known solely from an authenticated copy dated 3rd April, 1617 in the Archives of the Generalate of the Society of Jesus in Rome [6]. The writing is in the same hand as that on the marginal entry in 'Schola Beatae Mariae'. The original, and a copy dated 28th March, 1615 have been lost. The original had an imposing title and seal and was supplied with eight enclosures, but none of these extremely important documents have survived either. The paper is in the nature of a testimonial, as well as of a defence.

After the imposing heading comes the reason for its publication, the introduction and the basis of the paper: certain noble and pious Englishwomen have left their country because of the heresy prevailing there. They are now living in St Omer and are dedicated to the salvation of their own souls and to the education of young girls, sent to them from England for this purpose. As, in ignorance of the truth, rumours have been spread about the Institute, the Bishop hereby gives testimony in this paper that, since the very beginning of this way of life (vitae cursum), he has been informed of everything to do with it. This manner of life has been the cause of certain accusations.

Three sections are specified in this letter, which is rich in addenda:

1. The reason for the Institute.
2. The nature of the Institute.
3. Accusations against the Institute.

I. The reason for the Institute. (Occasio huius Instituti)

In this the Bishop gives a short version only of the story of Mary Ward's vocation: the foundation of the English Poor Clare convent up to her leaving it, in fact, only two years, 1608 and 1609. The

Bishop did not forget the part played by the Jesuits in this foundation! Mary Ward became aware that she would no longer be allowed any spiritual help from the Jesuits in her Poor Clare Convent, as the Abbess (M.Stephen Goudge) wished to observe the Franciscan charism of the Order. As this meant that she, Mary, would also be spiritually dependent on the Franciscans, she left. Mary Ward, continued the Bishop, was for some time undecided, although the Jesuits advised her to enter the Convent of the English Benedictines in Brussels. Fr Rector Schoondonck, in his turn, suggested the Rule of the Carmelites in Louvain. Neither of these won her approval.

Let us pause.

Granted that Bishop Blaes had no intention of writing a biography of Mary Ward, it nonetheless strikes one as curious that he did not mention her stay in the Walloon convent of the Poor Clares, and said nothing about the vision of St Gregory's Day, which was the reason why she had founded a convent for the English Poor Clares. Of his own co-operation in the founding of this convent, he only mentioned the transfer of the English Poor Clares from the motherhouse to their temporary quarters in St Omer. Likewise, he apparently knew nothing of the vision of St Athanasius' Day, which gave Mary Ward the agonising conviction that she was not to stay in the Poor Clare Order. Only the attitude of the Jesuits in St Omer was mentioned here. Even more significantly, he completely overlooked her return to England, her pastoral care for souls there, her 'Gloria' vision, and the coming together of the first members of the Institute in England.

The origin of the Institute, therefore, is not regarded as happening in England but in Flanders. The active apostolate in her own country is not mentioned, and this would have been an important fact in the information of the Bishop for his understanding of her Institute and her personality. But it was the same in Fr Lessius' report.

II. The nature of the Institute (Ratio Instituti)

Abruptly, the Bishop passes on to the existing Englishwomen's Institute in St Omer. Mary Ward and her companions (friends, actually, sodales) wanted to help the catholics of their country in a way that could not be done by convents on the Continent.These prayed together in choir, and were strictly confined to their houses by enclosure. The Englishwomen, however, could move more freely. They were educating young girls, and were totally committed to this task, all the more so as they had decided to adopt the Rule of the Society of Jesus as far as this was possible for women. This rule was available to them in an English translation.

Again − a place to pause.

At the beginning of this passage, Bishop Blaes mentioned the companions, friends of Mary Ward. Where had she been able to make their acquaintance? Not on her begging excursions in the streets of the town, nor in the English foundation. According to Bishop Blaes, the English women had made their own decision to adopt the Jesuit Rule. He totally ignored the vision of 1611,with its charge: 'Take the Same/Institute/ of the Society of Jesus,' which was determinative for the formation of their Institute.

And again, suddenly, and actually without any profound significance, the Bishop interrupts his letter to mention the purchase of a house in St Omer. The Rulers, the Nuntius, and of course the Bishop himself, had all helped in this. He then skips over the period 1612–1614, – the important years of growth – and takes up the thread again only when the Institute begins to develop.

After their community had increased in numbers, the English women composed their rule of life (vivendi modum sui Formulam) and presented it to the Bishop.

He had examined the completed Latin translation (quae nos deinde in latinum conversa), approved of it, and praised it, but advised them to make certain modifications as a result of their daily experience.[7]

A comment or two here; the Bishop wrote that the women had read an English translation of the Rule of the Society (regulas Societatis publice iam prostantes et in Anglicum conversas nactae) and had decided on that. Why did Bishop Blaes have a Latin translation made from this? The original of the Rule, the Constitutions of the Society of Jesus, were published in Latin, after all. Could he not have obtained these from one of the two colleges in St Omer? Why did it have to be re-translated into Latin?

Only when the Institute had grown to a fair number, says Bishop Blaes, did the Englishwomen compose the Rule for their Institute. In 1611, the community totalled ten members.[8] The English Spy's list, (March,1614) names a total of about twenty-six members,[9] and Fr Lee spoke of forty to fifty English women when he was with the Bishop on his final visit.[10] The Institute had therefore developed rapidly, and members came chiefly from England, perhaps from their own school, although the Englishwomen had been active for a short time only and some of their pupils were certainly far too young to enter the Institute.

The presentation of their Rule to the Bishop would therefore have taken place at the latest in 1614. But is it really acceptable that they presented Bishop Blaes with the Rule of the Society of Jesus which, as the Bishop had informed us a short time before, they wanted to adopt?

Or is it perhaps better to phrase the question slightly differently: can one really believe that Fr Lee would have allowed Mary Ward to present the Bishop with the Rules of the Society of Jesus altered for women, when he actually opposed their adoption by the women and, as a Jesuit, was obliged to do so? Again, can one believe that the Bishop would have accepted and praised this Rule? There was no doubt that he knew of the Jesuits' opposition, and of the instructions they had received on the matter. But it must be remembered that in 1612 a plan of the Institute 'Schola Beatae Virginis' had been drawn up for the Englishwomen, and then altered in 1611/14, and subsequently re-named 'Schola Beatae Mariae'. On taking leave of Fr Lee, the Bishop − and Fr Lee himself − had been happy at the imminent confirmation of the Institute. Fr Lee must have received favourable signs from Jesuit circles in Rome in those days. Here, however, in this letter, while conceding that the Rule submitted was most praiseworthy, the Bishop found something to criticise in the day-to-day arrangements. What sort of alterations of day-to-day matters could these have possibly been? It could hardly have concerned the spiritual life, as one would not refer to this as 'day-to-day'; possibly matters which concerned the daily work of the Institute.

These alterations, continues the Bishop, had been taken in hand in general (in genere) by the superior of the community, Mary Ward, a woman enlightened by God. It is only now that she is mentioned. She did not wish to enter upon any undertaking without it being previously approved by the Bishop (nihil tamen evulgando, quod non prius a nobis probaretur), so that when the time was ripe, everything could be laid before the Pope for his confirmation.

This piece of information is not without its problems. In 1614, soon after 11th April, Mary Ward left for England. Fridl[11] thought she was travelling for family reasons, and Chambers[12] accepted this reading. But was it really so? There is nothing about it in the sources. We do not even know if Mary Ward's parents were alive in 1614, and she stayed in her own country for months. Before Advent 1614, (30th November), she was back in England again and stayed there until the spring of 1615, perhaps even longer, as the Bishop's letter was written in her absence. Fr Lee was still in St Omer until the end of 1614. As he said himself,[13] he had stayed on account of his fellow Jesuits' attitude towards the Institute.

So who had really made the change?

The Bishop continued to further the aims of the Institute: with great self-denial, the members took the three simple vows for the whole of their lives and thus adopted a particular form of life without being troubled by the fact that their Institute had no name. Fr Lessius was of the same mind in his report. Their task was to educate and teach English girls. The Bishop did not say where. So − here again there was no word about the work of the English women in their own country; no word about opportunities for their boarders to take on tasks as teachers, or in boarding schools, or in the active apostolate. [14]

What is being presented here in the Bishop's document, as in that of Lessius, is an unnamed educational institute for English girls run by English women in St Omer. Not a community formed on the model of the Society of Jesus.

It is only now, in the third passage of the letter, that the Bishop takes a stand concerning opposition to it.

III. Objections to the Institute (Objectiones)

Bishop Blaes lists three objections to the Institute, and dismisses them with the evidence he enclosed.

a) They call themselves religious sisters.
Once again, the Bishop says that he has been kept informed and never, he insists, have the members claimed to be religious either by wearing a habit, or conventual enclosure, or by their actions, their own Rule, or by taking on the name of a women's Order.

They know that the title 'Religious' can be granted them by the Holy See alone. The Bishop also knows that before their superior left for England, she had warned the members of the Institute not to let themselves be taken for women religious. If indeed anyone were to consider them to be such because of their devout and nunlike behaviour, that was surely no matter for reproach.

b) They were founding missionary stations in England.
As with the questions put to Lessius for his opinion, so here too, carefully tucked in between two less important objections was the chief and most dangerous objection of all: that they were founding missions in England. But Bishop Blaes said 'Missiones apostolica non instituunt'. The verb is in the present tense, please note. Whatever had been set up before in England, which the Bishop undoubtedly knew about, there was a break here, and it was represented as no longer in existence. Here too Lessius' point was carried and even exceeded, for it is not merely business journeys that are now permissible. The English women travel to England solely for personal reasons. Further details of this objection will be dealt with in a later passage.

c) They are depriving other convents of members.
The Bishop categorically denied this charge. Since 1610, when the English women settled in St Omer, forty-nine candidates had entered other Orders from among their own boarders. The Bishop added a list, with a breakdown of the numbers. That was an average of ten candidates a year between 1610 and 1614, without mentioning their own candidates, who came to a respectable number too. In the middle of this argument, the Bishop sketched in the Jesuit's relationship to this new Institute. Usually the English women confessed to Fr Roger Lee, a true Jesuit, who acted in their regard only as his superior permitted, and whose move from St Omer was to be regretted (non sine jactura). The English women did not make any demands on the Jesuits' services other than those they gave to other christians; they

asked for sermons, the sacraments and spiritual direction. A secular priest gave them Extreme Unction and, together with a layman, had charge of their property. All of which was already in the 'Schola Beatae Mariae'. To return to the matter in hand, at first they could send fewer candidates to other Orders, as they themselves needed young people in order to build up their community. (One is inclined to add here: and quite right too). Moreover, it was not the English-women who decided on the vocation of their candidates; that was and is a matter for God alone.

Their form of life was no novelty in the Church, continued the Bishop. There had been such communities in the early church, and the Filles de Sainte Agnes, about whom nobody was complaining, lived the same sort of life. Neither was there any trouble with the Jesuits on account of this Institute. The superiors of the Order, and learned Jesuits from Italy, France, Germany, England and Belgium were high in their praises of the Institute. So too were the inhab-itants of St Omer, and their Bishop, too.

Finally, it must be asked – which Institute is Bishop Blaes defending here? The answer comes from the remaining sources: the same Institute on which Fr Lessius had commented. A 'Pium Institutum' which, in its structure and aim, did not differ much from the Belgian community of the Filles de Sainte Agnes, which did not appear as a novelty in the Church, and which was approved by the Jesuits everywhere.

This letter was certainly defending an Institute; not that Institute with which Mary Ward had been entrusted in 1611, but one such as the Jesuits wanted on the Continent for the education of English girls, one without too much similarity to the Society of Jesus. But it must not be overlooked that soon after its beginning, Bishop Blaes had stated his reservations towards Mary Ward's Institute. That was probably after an Englishman had complained to him in 1612. Moreover, finer shades of meaning must not be ignored, either; the Bishop had promised his help to the English women, and not to Mary Ward, who had merely been recommended to him.

The Bishop was, after all, acting in his pastoral capacity. He had responsibility for the Institute and its members in his own diocese alone, not for those who were active in England and did not come under his jurisdiction. Also, the Jesuits were outstandingly active in pastoral work in his country, and the English women were running an excellent educational establishment for young Englishwomen in the episcopal town of St Omer. Given certain circumstances, its existence might be threatened.

So the letter of 19th March, 1615 should be taken as a Magna Carta of the Bishop of St Omer for the 'Pium Institutum' of the English-women in his town. Two questions remain unanswered. Who was responsible for this letter? To whom was it addressed? This letter patent was not directed at anyone in particular, but can be valued as a testimonial. For outsiders, friends or foes of the Institute, the Bishop of St Omer had taken the part of an Institute which he could confirm for his diocese in accordance with the approval of the famous theologian, Leonhard Lessius. This concept of the Institute originated from Fr Lee and was to have portentous consequences for the future.

The Institute in Fr Francisco Suarez' report: 3rd June, 1615

The probable instigators of the report − the canonist Fr Suarez SJ − his judgement of the Englishwomen's Institute as against that of Fr Lessius − canonical reasons for this

After their spiritual director Fr Lee had been moved, the Bishop exerted himself on behalf of the Institute, ensuring the right to work as a Pium Institutum for the education of English girls. Those Jesuits who formed the extreme opposition must have looked on with no little apprehension. The Bishop had defended an Institute acceptable to the Jesuits and, in a particularly comprehensive paragraph, had denied any pastoral activity of its members in England. This Institute, if with very limited Ignatian charism, could continue to exist in St Omer until it obtained papal confirmation. Meanwhile, the community could continue to grow under the Bishop's protection. To be sure, there did indeed remain the possibility − perhaps in the very distant future − that the women would return to the 'manner and matter of the Society' before Roman confirmation could be sought. Who could tell? That threat remained. The opposition was well-informed about the reality of the Ignatian Institute. Could these adversaries have the Bishop's promise officially branded as dubious? Was it possible to block him in any way? Probably not, but the basis on which he had built his argument, the canonical status of the Institute, could be shown to be shaky.

For this, a man with a different outlook from that of the Flemish moral theologian Leonhard Lessius was required; a man of the calibre of the strict school of the South, the canonist Francesco Suarez. It is not known who commissioned this report to be made, any more than that of Lessius, but it must be stressed yet again that the controversy about the Englishwomen's Institute was carried on within the Society of Jesus. One thing is certain, however, the enemies of the Institute had wasted no time. Perhaps they could be found among the professors of Louvain University, where difficult theological and canonical questions were submitted and judged.

Fr Suarez was born in 1548 in Granada and entered the Society of Jesus in 1564. From 1597 he had been working in the University of

Coimbra. His name as a writer in the field of canon law was held in esteem in the whole of the West.[15] Suarez appeared on the scenes to judge the Institute from a totally different angle. Added to which, the social position of women in his native Spain differed essentially from that of the Northern countries, being far more restricted. Almost incomprehensible for us today.

Enclosure was quite simply the norm for religious sisters in the South. In countries like the Netherlands which were overrun by wars of religion, enclosure had been relaxed and was even unknown in many religious communities. One only has to think of the Canonesses, the Beguines and other new congregations who devoted themselves to education, and the teaching of young people, or care of the sick. They had never been subjected to enclosure as prescribed by the Council of Trent and earlier by Pope Paul V. The decisions of councils like of Trent, or papal decrees, were often not promulgated. In many respects, life was lived both religiously and politically according to chartered and unchartered privileges.

The same questions that had been put to Lessius were now sent to Suarez, undoubtedly accompanied by an explanatory letter and Lessius' report and, possibly, the Bishop's letter of 19th March, 1615. Suarez dated his report 3rd June, 1615, so a good two and a half months after Bishop Blaes had put signature and seal to his letter. Suarez' report certainly played its part in the proceedings against Mary Ward later. It is a remarkable fact that neither Lessius' approval, nor Burton's long defence – completed some years later and holding the same opinion as Lessius – can be found in the Archives of the Congregation of the Propaganda Fide or in the Fondo Capponi in the Vatican Library. The condemnatory judgement of the Spanish canonist is preserved there.[16]

Suarez writes with dismissive severity. The basic statements of Lessius, the moral theologian, were declared to be wrong. Suarez answered the questions from a purely juridical standpoint, citing the great canonical works. To take one of his comments, briefly:

1. Is the Institute allowed and pious?
Suarez lays the greatest emphasis on this question and gives it a good deal of consideration. He has to acknowledge that the aim and means of the Institute as presented to him are good. And yet, as he says, the Institute is not authorized canonically, for the founding of new communities has been forbidden by the Councils and the Popes.

And then he produces his objections:

> It may be stated that the Institute is not an Order; its members do not wear a habit, they take private vows and do not claim to be treated as religious (thus Lessius). Suarez does not recognize the validity of such arguments. Religious life does not consist in a habit, he says, but in the three vows and in the following of a Rule

for a common pious purpose. The members of the Institute are no different in this respect from religious, and they will be regarded as such even if the outward symbol of the habit is lacking. There is no point, Suarez continues to argue, in stating that it is not a new Order that is being founded, and in believing one is exempt from papal approval, for to all intents and purposes a new Order has indeed been founded.

As has already been seen, Lessius considered the three simple vows as binding and could not in all conscience see that they could be retracted. That is why he saw a reliable permanence in the Institute. This too Suarez rejects with a sharp reference to papal approval. As this was lacking, no new members could be accepted, nor could the profession of the English women be regarded as binding. A valid but more possible objection would be: the aim of the Institute is good and pious, for it concerns women, living according to the evangelical counsels, engaged in teaching and educating young girls. Yes, says Suarez, it is not because its aims and means are good that the Church forbids such an Institute but because it began at its own discretion and without papal permission. In the first place, certain features of this Institute should be examined, as for example its freedom from enclosure, the hazardous journeys of its members to England and their work in the active apostolate. It is true that Suarez does not mention the last activity specifically, but he quotes St Paul, 1 Cor.14,v.33/4, especially those much-abused words: 'As in all assemblies of the saints the women should remain silent; for it is ordained to them not to speak, but they should submit themselves, as the law says.'

Suarez must have had more information about the activity of the English Ladies in England than Lessius could lay claim to.

2. Can the Bishop approve and confirm the Institute?

The answer to this is easy, says Suarez. As Canon Law forbids new communities without papal approval, this approval is eo ipso reserved to the Pope. Lessius' argument that the Bishop could approve and confirm a Pius Institute for his diocese, as it was not an Order in the strict sense, is rejected by Suarez with the remark that in this instance it is not a Pius Institute but a community corresponding in all essentials to that of a real Order, and which therefore requires papal approval.

3. Can the Institute be regarded as a reliable state for its members?

In no way, says Suarez, and that because the simple, perpetual vows are insufficient — here he agrees with Lessius — but again, because the Institute has no papal permission and therefore no valid vows can be taken. Without valid vows it has no permanent status.

With such counter-arguments, Lessius' advocacy and with it the Pius Institute of the Englishwomen were destroyed at the roots.

Suarez' letter was not written to be filed away in a cabinet but to be wielded as a weapon by those who, having foreseen the outcome, did not hesitate to use it.

Notes

1. Jos. Grisar SJ. Das Urteil des Lessius', Suarez' und anderer über den Ordenstyp der Mary Ward, Gregorianum 38/1957, p. 658–712.
2. Sommervogel IV, Sp.1726 – 1751; XI Sp. 1784–1785.
3. ARSI, Anglia 31/II, ff.687 – 691; BCasR, Codex 2426 (Acta in causa Virginum Anglicanarum, f.209; Institute archives, Rome; Institute archives, Munich; Archbp.Archives, Munich, A258. In German translation: StB Munich, Codex 5393, pp. 9–12; Cgm 5399, pp 1–20.
4. Episcopal patent letter 19th March, 1615, item 13.
5. Jos.Grisar SJ, Das Urteil des Lessius', Suarez, und anderer über den Ordenstyp der Mary Ward, Gregorianum 38/1957. Grisar comes to positive conclusions when judging the episcopal letter with which we cannot concur.
6. ARSI Rome, Hist.Anglia 31/II, pp. 659–664.
7. '... insuper hortantes, ut usu et quotidiana experientia doctae adderent, demerent, mutarent, prout spiritus Dei illis suggereret.'
8. Nuntius Guido Bentivoglio to the papal Secretary of State, 5th October, 1611.R.Belvederi, Guido Bentivoglio, Diplomatico II, Parte II, Rovigo 1947, p. 222–223.
9. 'about 26 persons...' PRO London, SP 77/II, Part I, Foreign Flanders ff. 25r. – 26v.
10. LR p.98, Inst.Arch.Munich.
11. Fridl I, p.149, Nr.119.
12. Chambers, I.E., p.304, translated back; I D p.224.
13. LR p 96. Inst.Arch.Munich.
14. see the Englishwomen's information to Nuntius Bentivoglio, note 8. above.
15. Suarez died on 25th September 1617 in Lisbon. For his life and work see Sommervogel VII, p. 1661–1687.
16. Copies of the testimonial: ARSI Rome, Epp.NN.136, ff.31–36; APF Rome, Lettere di Germania, Ungaria, Boemia, Palatinato etc. vol.72, f.197,pp.9–2; WA London, vol.16 (1621), Nr.89,pp.372 ff.

X

THE ENGLISH WOMEN AND THEIR INSTITUTE

The Apostolate among adults in England

After 1609: The Englishwomen in England — Luisa de Carvajal as neighbour in Spittalfield (London) in 1611 — 1612: an enemy's complaints — Mary Ward's talk and her two journeys to England in 1614 — other members as travellers to England in 1615. 1615: complaints of an enemy — 1621: reports of witnesses

The apostolic work undertaken by the Englishwomen is not placed first here because it was their primary work, but because the Institute came into existence as a result of it.

Mary Ward's brief activity in England in 1609 can hardly have left such a lasting impression that members immediately poured in. True, the first members were young women of good standing with a large sphere of influence who had probably been apostolically active in their own country for a long time. But these had left England with Mary Ward. Who took care of future members, or arrangements for the boarders' travelling? Jesuits? Perhaps some of them, those in favour of the Institute. But it was precisely among the Jesuits that the Englishwomen had their greatest opponents in England. The Englishwomen themselves? They were mostly fully occupied with their work in school and with the boarders in St Omer. Even if individuals had made the journey to England for personal reasons and brought children and candidates over to St Omer, which is not excluded here, the English women cannot be regarded as having been a sort of transport service for people and goods.

It is more likely that some members stayed behind after Mary Ward and her first companions had left England in 1609, perhaps at first for family reasons, or because they had not yet decided on entering a convent or even perhaps because they preferred their work in the active apostolate. After all, in 1609, Mary Ward was moving towards an uncertain future; the 'Gloria Vision' had not shown her how she was to carry out God's command. For the first years we are dependent on few and sparse statements, though these provide incontrovertible evidence. In one of her talks in 1614[1] about work on the mission in England, Mary Ward spoke about the fate of Luisa de Carvajal who, as already mentioned, had been compelled to move her home in June 1611 to Spittalfields, then outside the walls of London. Mary Ward added 'and she came to our neighbourhood', which means that the Englishwomen had either a house or accommodation in Spittalfields.

At the end of 1611[2] the Englishwomen told Nuntius Bentivoglio, when he visited St Omer, that the aim of their school and educational work was for English girls entering convents or preparing them for their lives in their families. Understandably enough, they did not forget their own members. As for their work in the Institute, they mentioned their Belgian apostolate of education and teaching, and their pastoral work for souls in England.

This unusual work in their own country had already met with hostility from English catholics. Bishop Blaes mentioned the letter of an Englishman in 1612, to whom he had sent a written answer. This cannot have been about the English women in St Omer, who were living under the Bishop's eye, and were teaching English children.

Something else was said by Mary Ward in her 1614 talk: 'People have been taken prisoner, only on suspicion that they belong to the Institute, and live with the English women.'

On 13th October, 1613[3] Luisa de Carvajal was arrested in Spittalfields for the second time. The graphic description of this tragic event by Mary Ward could only have come from an eyewitness, or personal experience.

In the spring of 1614, Mary Ward went to England. In a talk on 11th April [4] of the same year, she told the members of the Institute in St Omer that 'she had a task which only she could do; she would be away two or three months.' She was back in St Omer about July, 1614 – it may be possible to give a more exact date. On 16th July of this year, Mrs Catherine Bentley, wife of Edward Bentley, received permission to travel, to visit her husband[5] in the Netherlands. Travelling with her were 'her fowre daughters, Mary, Katherine, Margarett and Anne and one man and one mayd.' These four daughters of the forty-nine year old Mrs Bentley (born 1565) need not have been very young, and it is tempting to see some Institute members among these, as also in her woman servant, in the company of a priest. Mary Ward had travelled once before with Mrs Bentley. With these baptismal names was it Catherine Smith, Margaret Horde and Anne Turner who were meant? It cannot have been Mrs Bentley's daughter Catherine, for she had entered the English Poor Clare's in St Omer before the transfer to Gravelines.[6]

Once again, in Advent, 1614,[7] between 30th November and 25th December, Mary Ward travelled to England and stayed for a longer time. It is only on 24th October, 1615[8] that she is mentioned as again in St Omer, which does not mean that she returned in the autumn.

To return to something deliberately omitted from consideration in the Bishop's letter of 19th March, 1615: the Bishop wrote that Mary Ward had gone to England for reasons of health, even producing medical evidence. He also mentioned five English women who had gone home with his permission: Mary Ward for health reasons as already said, Jane Browne to her father who was ill, and two others (so were there only four?) – for reasons of inheritance. The Bishop had evidently acted here for the passes in his official capacity. If an alias were given for a journey, whether outgoing or returning, as in Mary Ward's case in 1606, Institute members and other travellers also certainly made use of any acceptable pretext as cover, to obtain a pass. A classic example of this is the journey to England made by Jane and Frances Browne, barely one year later. On 20th May, 1616[9] a certain Edward Lomer received permission to travel to Flanders and back for himself and two distinguished ladies, Jane and Frances, daughters of Sir George Browne, who had recently died; they had been left by their father in Flanders. Two women servants and one manservant accompanied them. That may have been a fact and no subterfuge. At the end of 1614, Jane Browne went to see her father who was ill, although she – according to tradition – had been a member of the Institute since 1609. A considerable time since her father had left her behind on the Continent! It was the same with Mary Ward. The illness was genuine enough, the medical certificate too, but was London Mary Ward's home? And would this city contribute so much to her convalescence, when the authorities were on the watch for her?

Political refugees of every century would recognize this adventurous but extremely dangerous game of outwitting authority. And it was more than a matter of politics here. Barbara, Mary Ward's sister, remarked in a note[10] about the latter's journey to England in 1617, 'she went to England under the pretext of health, but the real reason was her zeal and the desire to gain souls.' For this, Mary Ward needed a point of contact in her own country from the very beginning of her Institute – a house, and like-minded helpers.

In January/February 1615,[11] an anonymous author wrote a sharp attack on the Institute in England, in which six members were mentioned whose activities were judged unsuitable for women, and who were encouraged by Jesuits. It is more than probable that Mary Ward was among these six missionaries of her Institute, as she was in England at the time.

Bishop Blaes also adverted to a letter from an Englishman in his letter of 19th March, 1615; a letter dated the beginning of March, 1615, from London. It told him how warmly the English women had been welcomed in England, and found acceptance and recognition on account of their virtue, education and nobility of birth. Do these words of the anonymous Englishman refer to Mary Ward's arrival at the end of 1614?

On 9th June, 1615,[12] hardly three months after Bishop Blaes had denied any apostolic work carried out by members of the Institute in England, Fr Richard Blount SJ, from London, informed Fr Thomas Owen in Rome that Mary Ward and her sisters (i.e. co-workers) were hunted after as though they were all priests and dangerous persons. Many women had been arrested on their account and were still in prison. On 5th October, 1615 [13] Anne Gage travelled to London to take up her post as superior. She was certainly there at the end of 1616, and probably until 1618. [14]

The number of members in England during these first years remained small. Courage, and certainly a special vocation, were needed for this sort of work. Mary Ward was committed to it. We have many reports about her work in the active apostolate but not a single one about her involvement as a teacher.

The small number of members on the English mission may be attributed to the fact that the Institute was still very young. Most members were not so well grounded that they could be exposed to the dangers accompanying this sort of activity, such as a lowering of spiritual ideals, or even the loss of vocation.

Mary Ward set high standards for those on the English mission. In the passage already quoted from her talk in 1614, she said, 'And certainly, as long as I live, no one will cross over who has not been well tested in virtue, without the least shortcoming or imperfection, as this would afterwards be a great disadvantage to the whole Institute. So, too, no one shall be accepted in England without their being tested both as to suitability to live the spiritual exercises and for having a loyal spirit towards our state. They may indeed be able to go for themselves, but will not be sent to Ours, if they are not of a particular virtue of which they have given good proof.'[15]

It is from this that we learn that members were accepted in England. After their first probation in England, they would be 'sent to Ours', that is, to the noviceship in St Omer. Less suitable girls could go 'for themselves', as 'sympathizers' of the Institute.

As well as the few documents, the English biography and the Painted Life give information concerning the activities of the members in their own country. Unfortunately, the English biography is sometimes unreliable chronologically, and some of its facts are scarcely credible. But the incidents reported before the end of 1621 certainly took place. Mary Ward went to Rome and stayed in Italy and the middle of Europe, until her final return to England in 1637.

After the foundation of a house in Liège, records the English Vita,[16] Mary Ward went back to England, where she acquired a house in which two priests had a permanent residence.[17] It is not known where this was. It has already been stated that there had been members present in England from the very beginning, and that there had even been a house in Spittalfield. Mary Ward herself, continues the English Vita, was there, sometimes dressed as a simple woman, active particularly among the poor, who could receive the services of a priest only with the greatest danger. The English members prepared them to receive the sacraments and helped the few hard-driven and overworked priests. It was because of some words from Mary Ward that a lapsed catholic woman was helped to return to the church.[18] The Painted Life captures this on Panel No 17. She also helped in the conversion of another woman. Several young women were assisted, by having their admission to a convent made easier for them. With Panels 18 and 19, the Painted Life records the conversion of a Mistress Gray, a relative of Mary Ward's.

She did not lack persecution. The Archbishop of Canterbury remarked that she was more dangerous than six Jesuits.[19] It was solely to found a noviceship in Liège, says the Englisha Vita, that Mary Ward returned to the Continent for a short time. Consequently, the year must have been 1618, for the house in the rue Pierreuse was the only foundation in Liège, as will be seen.

Probably the crossing to England was that shown in the charming Panel 26 of the Painted Life. This shows a tiny boat, barely seaworthy, in full sail. Mary Ward is seated to the very left on board wearing a black dress with a rich ruff and without any headdress but with a richly decorated travelling rug over her knees. There are four other women in the ship. Another in a dark dress is certainly a member of the Institute. A woman in a red dress is talking with raised hand to Mary Ward. Two other women, one in red and one in blue, look on anxiously, for the crew members have taken up belligerent attitudes towards one another. The text runs: 'Mary was at sea on the feast of St James, 1618 when she invoked this holy Apostle as her particular patron in order to quell a dangerous mutiny that had broken out on the ship. To the amazement of all, calm was restored and Mary afterwards declared that she had never sought any favour from God through the intercession of this great prince of heaven without it being granted to her.' One day[20] Mary was needing some relaxation. As she was just then near Lambeth Palace on the banks of the Thames, she thought she might visit the Archbishop, who had said that he would like to see her. When she could not meet him, she wrote her name on one of the Palace windows with a ring she was wearing.

This piece of bravado is almost always included in any of Mary Ward's biographies but it is really difficult to give it credence. For what would have happened, if the Archbishop had been at home? The Archbishop was one of the most committed anti-catholics of his day, and Mary Ward could not have known that he was absent.

She was certainly a courageous woman when it was a matter concerning the glory of God and his kingdom but she equally certainly observed the fifth commandment, which carries with it the obligation of one's self-protection. The English Vita reports that Mary Ward had been taken prisoner twice on those sea crossings.[21] She managed to escape, although very strictly guarded, because the radiance of her personality seemed to demand liberation. Once a servant woman gave her some things in a sack for safe-keeping.[22] When the guard demanded to see what was in it, she showed him a beautiful reliquary of rock crystal – which he returned with great reverence.

The English women had rented[23] a garden house from a protestant acquaintance. Several people gathered there, probably to celebrate Mass. They were betrayed and the house surrounded, one Saturday. Someone told Mary Ward that it would be possible to escape unseen. She refused, because God's service required her presence. Having done what she intended, she left the house on the following Monday by the main door and entered a coach. Half an hour later the authorities broke into the house and searched it.

At this time too there was the conversion of a priest, who was no longer carrying out his duties faithfully. When returning to England from the Continent, in the company of Mary Ward, he fell into the hands of the authorities. Mary Ward was arrested too, but showed no fear; instead she prayed the Litany of Loreto aloud as she was taken by coach from the court to prison. Once there, she publicly kissed the threshold, which did not anger the guards but seemed to mollify them.[24]

Not much was said about the activities of the members of the Institute in England. It was not only that it would have been dangerous. It has been possible to arrange some of our sources in chronological order, so as to establish a continual line for the presence of the first members of the Institute in England during the years 1609–1621. In the next few years their numbers grew rapidly, but thereby hangs a tale.

I would like to end this account with the statement of an anonymous Jesuit[25] who, in a very contemporary description, says that it was not only the English government who posed a threat to the English Ladies. He writes: 'As Mrs A(nne) G(age) was on the point of crossing the channel, and I was saying my morning prayers at home, it seemed to me that she was kneeling before me with her hands clasped as if asking me something. I looked at her attentively and noticed that she was dressed as though in deepest mourning. I immediately thought that she had been arrested before her departure or was in danger of drowning during the crossing. I recommended her interiorly to almighty God, particularly during Mass. Even before I had finished the holy sacrifice, I was filled with such an extraordinary joy that I was certain that she had been saved, wherever she might be. In the afternoon I shared this with another (a fellow Jesuit) whom I thought to be a friend (of the Institute). But he ascribed my interior experience to a bad impulse. So I said to him, 'Well, we will soon know whether she has been taken prisoner or escaped while crossing over.' Fourteen days later I received two letters from her from St

Omer in her own writing, in which she told me about the danger she had escaped from drowning during the crossing. I showed him (the fellow Jesuit) her two letters and made him read that she had indeed written in her own handwriting what she had informed me of before.'

If we consider how often Mary Ward had herself been exposed to similar dangers, we can begin to have some idea of the courage and intensity with which she was dedicated to the conversion of her country.

Teaching and Education in St Omer

School for English girls – good reputation – subjects taught – educational aims – request from the government for the acceptance of Belgian children – way of life of the members – their dress

Everyday life in St Omer appears to have run fairly smoothly, initially. The community and the number of boarding pupils grew so rapidly that it was possible to buy a third house on 20th January, 1614. Its whereabouts are not known. Hendricq[26] refers to rue Grosse and the early writings[27] supply the information that it was a house on the corner of rue Carnot (previously rue Grosse) and rue des Bleuets, but does not enlighten us as to which corner. It is not certain, either, if the two recently acquired houses were close to the first. At all events, in the Spring of 1615 these houses offered accommodation for some sixty people: thirty members of the Institute and thirty boarders.

The school soon gained a good reputation. It was not the first nor the only teaching establishment for girls in St Omer. A school had been opened for Walloon girls in 1611.[28] In 1612, the Daughters of Sainte Agnes were called a community 'whose members taught girls reading, writing and sewing – free.'[29]

Bishop Blaes seized on Marie Aubrun's idea in this same year, and built a house for the education of poor girls – 'Notre Dame du Jardin'.[30] In the beginning, the members of the Institute taught English children only, and it can be assumed that among the boarders from England there were also daughters of those English people living in St Omer and its neighbourhood.

There remains little information about the teaching methods of the Institute in its first years. The 'Schola Beatae Mariae' in paragraph 53 gives a summary of the subjects offered, but there is no concrete evidence that in fact these were all taught. For closer detail:

Teaching occupied between 8.00.a.m. until 10.30.a.m., and from 2.00 to 4.30.p.m.

As well as thorough religious instruction, there was teaching in ethics (moral), reading and writing in the language of the country,

Latin, housewifery, artistic skills such as singing or playing an instrument (organ, too), painting, sewing, spinning and tapestry weaving.

Pupils were also instructed in subjects which could be of use to them in everyday life, to name only a few: nursing, knowledge of medicinal herbs and simples.

Particular emphasis was laid on behaviour, though this was to be a reflection of their interior disposition. The qualities named were: serenity, self-control, reticence, reverence for God, the saints and one's neighbour, loyalty, truthfulness and integrity, prudence in speech, quietness, reading good books, and calmness under good and bad fortune. Morals and character-building were basic requirements for all these. A number of pupils and boarders were members of families who stressed deportment and bearing.

Older girls were also taught by the members, who in turn were thus able to enter more deeply into the individual subjects. This was especially the case with religious lessons, to which most emphasis was given. In the later years of the Institute in St Omer, between 1618 – 1621, classes (escoilles) for the girls of the neighbourhood were held for three years, free of charge.[31] It is not certain if English children were still in the majority at that time.

Towards the end of 1616, the Institute focussed its activity mainly on Liège. The government and the Bishop may have put pressure on the then much-reduced community to open their schools to local children. Understandably, the Infanta had often expressed this wish in her letters of recommendation, as the Belgian government had spared no pains in granting the Institute entry into Flanders.

Some comment on the dress of the members of the Institute on the Continent could be relevant here.

Their way of life was very strict; they had many and good reasons for this. Mary Ward remained an ascetic all her life, and she would have expected the same behaviour from members of her Institute. We are relatively well-informed about the dress, but must differentiate between the beginnings of the Institute and the time after Fr Lee had left St Omer.

The English Life[32] writes that after their arrival in St Omer, the first Englishwomen had worn 'grave and retyred' clothing which was suitable, or 'conformable', but not a habit ('not of the monasticall'). With this was worn a straw hat, such as was then worn in England, a 'Galerus'.[33] This may have been the same dress as that prescribed in the 'Schola Beatae Mariae', for there, in paragraph 29, a black, sober and modest dress (vestitu nigro, gravi ac modesto) is described, with a veil (paragraph 32) which was to cover the hair completely (capitis velo modeste anterius adducto semper intentur nulla capillatura apparente). The dress may not have appeared to differ very much from the habit worn by an Order. But the 'Schola Beatae Mariae' was and remained a Plan.

After 1615, things changed. The Englishwomen openly proclaimed their Ignatian charism by their dress. In 1619 a Belgian traveller, Pierre Bergeron, passing through the Ardennes[34] saw some members of the Institute in Spa. These wore a 'habit noir, tout simple, comme les Jésuites'. Here 'habit' is to be understood as clothing, and not the term for religious dress. It was simple, like the dress of the Jesuits. In those days Jesuits were wearing the gown customarily worn by the catholic priest, with a band around the waist and a biretta as head-dress. Bergeron makes no mention of any veil worn by the women.

A letter previously mentioned is informative on this point – one which Fr Provincial Heren wrote to Fr General Vitelleschi on 10th June, 1619.[35] He gives the news that the Englishwomen have exchanged their original headgear, the English Galerus, for a broad-brimmed hat, similar to a Jesuit biretta, and made of the same material. In 1620, Fr Jacques Bonfrère, SJ from Dinant in Belgium, wrote to Fr General that the Englishwomen were imitating the Jesuits even in their attire.[36]

At the Visition in Vienna in 1629, the Superior Margaret Genison spoke about the Institute's own dress, which was blessed, and could be changed by the General Superior.[37]

If one examines the Painted Life closely, it may be noticed that the headdress was not always the same. The portrait of Mary Ward, which may be a contemporary original in the Augsburg house of the Institute proves this, for Mary Ward is shown with a little white cap, surrounded by a delicate white veil.

When Pierre Paunet, Bishop of St Omer in the last days of May, 1630, finally received the command from the Congregatio de Propaganda Fide and went to suppress all that remained of the once-flourishing community of the Institute in his episcopal town, he forbade them to wear the veil they had on their little caps (quel velo ò taffettano che portavano in resta attorn'alla scuffia).[38] Even the slightest trace of anything associated with a religious Order was forbidden.

Mary Ward, personally, was simple in her dress. One of her resolutions in her retreat notes of 1619 runs: 'Dress: I will take care for simplicity and decency so as to give no cause for scandal, and in everything that I wear I will seek God's honour.'[39] And there it seems best to let the matter rest, with these few references from the sources, although there are more.

By way of summary:

The Englishwomen did not wear a habit in the ecclesial sense. They wished to be recognized as Jesuits, so they wore a simple black dress of unobtrusive cut, without ornament or decoration, similar to the Jesuit gown. They all wore it, which is why it took on the appearance of a religious habit which, however, they had neither claimed nor sought. It is not surprising, therefore, that in later plans of the Institute which were not drawn up by Mary Ward or the English

Ladies, it is emphasized that the members of the Institute did not wear religious dress. It has been seen that Bishop Blaes, in his much-quoted letter of 19th March, 1615, remarked on this. These Plans were, without question, drawn up by Jesuits. The Englishwomen's form of dress like a priest's robe, which caught the attention of Pope Gregory XV, and appeared ridiculous to their adversaries in Rome, was a thorn in a Jesuits' eye. Mary Ward and several members were frequently and for a long time in England, where the wearing of a habit would have resulted in death or imprisonment. In those days people did not think in terms of a change from 'religious' to 'secular' dress.

Notes

1. Fridl, p. 150, Nr. 121, and partly II, p. 571, Nr. 801, from the lost Libellus Colloquiorum ff. 26 and 29.
2. R. Belvederi, Guido Bentivoglio II, Parte II, p. 222–223.
3. G. Fullerton, The Life of Luisa de Carvajal, London 1881, and C.M. Abad SJ. Una misionera española en la Inglaterra del siglo XVII Dona Luisa de Carvajal y Mendoza. 1566–1614, Comillas 1966.
4. Fridl, p. 149, Nr. 119, from Libellus Colloquiorum, f. 9.
5. Acts of the Privy Council of England, May 1613–December 1614, procured by Mr Baker, London 1921, p. 499.
6. Annals, EPCL, p. 6.
7. Bishop Blaes in his letter of 19th March 1615.
8. Mary Ward made a retreat at that time with Fr Lee in St Omer.
9. Acts of the Privy Council of England 1615–1616, procured by Mr Baker, London 1925, p. 538.
10. From the 2nd paper, Inst. Arch. Munich.
11. AGR Brussels, Arch. Jesuit Prov. Flandro-Belg. Nr. 1079 à 1112, Res Missionis Anglicanae, 1085–1096, pp. 8–19.
12. Arch. Stonyhurst College, F. Chr. Grene SJ, Collectanea M.p. 95b.
13. Fridl I, p. 149, Nr. 120, from Libellus Colloquiorum, f. 46.
14. Anne Gage to Thomas More, Bentley, 7th October 1616, WA London, A XV 1616, p. 411, Nr. 155. Cf. the "Relatio ex Anglia" of an unknown Jesuit from 1616. AGR Brussels, Arch. Jesuit. Prov. Gallo-Belg. Carton 31.
15. Fridl I, p. 152, Nr. 120 and partly II, p. 571, Nr. 801.
16. Vita E f. 19r.
17. Vita E f. 19v; Vita I, p. 21.
18. Vita E.f. 20rv; Vita I, p. 22.
19. Vita E.f. 21r.
20. ibid. ff. 21v–22r.
21. ibid f. 22r.
22. ibid. f. 22rv.
23. ibid ff. 22v–23r.
24. ibid f. 23rv.
25. as above, note 14, "Relatio ex Anglia".
26. Hendricq, Recueil Historique II (1605–1615) pp. 350–351: " ... et ont pour leur demeur en cette ville qu'ils ont acceptées la maison du Sieur de Licques dans la Grosse Rue ..."/1612/; do. III (1615–1623) p. 85: " ... devant la maison des Filles Angloises jadis apartenante à Mr de Liques ..."/11.–12. May, 1618/. This was about the Englishwomen taking part in a procession.
27. J. Dernheims, Histoire civile ... de la Ville de Saint-Omer, Saint-Omer, 1843, p. 596; Bled, Evêques, p. 391–392; J. de Pas, Vieilles Rues, Vieilles

Enseignes = Mem. d.l. Soc. des Antiquaires d.l. Morinie 0/1911, p. 473; do. Table de concordance entre les noms des rues actuels et les anciens noms = Mem. d.l. Soc. des. Antiquaires d.l. Morinie 31/1913, p. 333; do. A Travers le vieux Saint-Omer, Saint-Omer 1914, p. 138–158.

28. Litterae Annuae, ARSI Rome, Flandro-Belg. 51, 1611–1619, f. 21, Collegium Audomarense.

29. Hendricq, Recueil Historique II, p. 350.

30. Bled, Evêques, p. 407.

31. In a letter of complaint to the town of Saint-Omer in 1621, before September 11th, the Englishwomen referred to "trois escoilles pour enseigner la jeunesse de la ville 3 annes de longe iusques asjoir et pour la amour de Dieu ..." AM Saint-Omer, CCXXXIX, Nr. 16, Filles Anglaises, ff. 12–14.

32. Vita E f. 15rv; Vita I, p. 19, called simply "un habito positivo", a particular dress.

33. Fr Prov. Jean Heren to Fr Gen. Vitelleschi on 10th June, 1619. ARSI Rome, Gallo-Belg. 40, ff. 26r–27v.

34. H. Michelant, Voyage de Pierre Bergeron es Ardennes, Liège et Pays-Bas en 1619 = Publ. de la Soc. des Bibliophiles liégeois 1875, p. 103.

35. see above, note 33.

36. On 14th April, 1620 " ... Societatum nostram emulentur in habitu aqui salva sexus differentia quam proximo ad nostrum accedit ..." ARSI Rome, Anglia 32/I, ff. 1r.–2v.

37. DA Vienna, suppressed convents, Jesuitesses.

38. Bishop Pierre Paunet of Saint-Omer to Nuntius Fabio de Lagonissa in Brussels, 15th May, 1630. APF Rom, SOCG Lettere de Francia etc. 1630, vol. 132, ff. 187r, 192v.

39. VP/E 25, Inst. Arch. Munich.

XI

RIGHTEOUSNESS

St Omer, October 1615

Fr Lee's last stay in St Omer – Mary Ward's retreat, October, 1615

It is not known if the disunity among the Englishwomen was settled during the course of the year, or even the exact date on which Fr Lee arrived in St Omer on his way from Louvain to Dunkirk. He was there at the end of October, for about eight days BEFORE All Saints', Mary Ward asked if she could make the Exercises. There is a problem here. An entry in her notes[1] runs:- 'About eight days before All Saints in 1615, I wrote to my confessor, for he was then ill... my desire to be allowed to make the eight days' exercises... and that at a time approved, I might make my six monthly confession to him if his health permitted. He agreed to both.'

Was Fr Lee really able to give her points for meditation? It is remarkable that the contact between Mary Ward and her director during these days was carried on in writing. On 24th October she wrote to him, asking to be allowed to make the Exercises. Hardly a week later, on 31st October, she wrote again. This letter has not survived.[2] Then, on November lst, there followed a letter about the understanding of the 'Just Soul'[3] which she had experienced. Finally, she wrote again on 27th November,[4] a letter containing, among other things, a complaint about his silence, and from which we learn that Fr Flake directed Mary Ward in Fr Lee's stead.

Was Fr Lee really so ill that he could not receive Mary Ward at the end of November? If so, how could he travel to Dunkirk in December, only thirty kilometers from St Omer, to wait for a crossing to England? It is true that he died before reaching his destination. But had his superiors really allowed such a sick man to make this strenuous journey, and to a land that could offer little help until he met with his fellow Jesuits, even if he did not travel alone?

However that may be, Mary Ward began her retreat on 24th October. Her health was very bad at that time, and she had great trouble (care) on account of writing the Plan of the Institute, which was soon to be sent to Rome.[5] Until now her Plan, the one altered

169

'in general', had been simply a Plan. After it had been submitted to Rome, however, it would bear the stamp of officialdom.

She could now rise with relief early in the morning, pray for four hours and seek union with God, who seemed to invite her by removing obstacles and giving her the interior means to do so. He alone knew, thought this great woman of prayer, how remiss she had been in the first four or five days. Then she made her confession — whether this was to Fr Lee is not certain — and resolved to spend the remaining two days more zealously and with more recollection. Her notes break off in the middle of a sentence.[6]

It is possible to draw a line from St Gregory's Day, 1607, when she joyfully undertook the charge to found a Poor Clare convent for Englishwomen, over to St Athanasius' Day, 1609, which brought her the pain of departure, then to the 1609 Vision in England, which filled her heart with a divine disquiet, and to the revelation at the end of 1611 with its unshakable certainty, right down to these later days of 1615 when she was given a final illumination. This brought concern about that other Institute, which could never completely realise the commission she had received. It also brought a longing to be near Him who in those dark days had granted a radiant vision of His and her Institute.

The 'Vision of the Just Soul'

31st October, 1615

Description of the vision in the letter dated 1st November, 1615 to Fr Lee — attempt to find its significance

A mystical experience is supernatural, barely comprehensible in words, and still more difficult to voice. Consequently, the text of Mary Ward's letter to Fr Lee about her vision makes demands on our understanding; without including the accompanying events, one cannot begin to interpret it. Her explanations, moreover, presuppose a letter to Fr Lee which is now missing, dated 31st October, the very day of the vision. This revelation, which has come down in the writings about her life as 'the vision of the Just Soul', is preserved for us as Mary Ward's oldest manuscript.[7]

In her letter to Nuntius Albergati,[8] she does not mention this vision expressly, but the words 'the constant light, that God gives in all things, great and small, as to what concerns the true practise of this Institute, cannot be easily explained', also embraces the 'Vision of the Just Soul'. In a careful unfolding of what was imparted, a clear distinction must be kept between what Mary Ward experienced in the Vision and how she pondered on this interiorly in her meditations and reflections.

'It seems a certain clear and perfect state which one should have in this life, and which is utterly indispensable for one who is to fulfil the duties of this Institute well.' She had never read anything, she writes, to which she could compare it. It was not the state of the saints, whose holiness consisted above all in that union with God which lifted them out of themselves; it was different in kind.

She continues: 'I perceived a clear difference and yet felt myself drawn to love this state and to long for it more than every other gift of grace.' And this was written by a woman favoured with mystical graces, who indeed knew what was meant by union with God which 'lifted' people 'out of themselves'.

And, further on, she says that happiness, as far as it can be expressed in words, consisted 'in a singular freedom of all dependence on earthly things, united with complete readiness and an apt disposition for all good works.'

She perceived that 'something happened also discovering' this freedom which was necessary in order to be able to refer everything to God — but this awareness may have come to her on another occasion. Mary Ward recorded, as she wrote at the beginning, what had occurred in the last two days. There is an inevitable matching of this Vision with the Foundation in the Ignatian exercises.

Intellectually, 'in my understanding', she grasped the inexpressible beauty of a soul so created, far more beautiful than she could describe.

At that time it had seemed to her, and seemed so still at the time of writing, that people in Paradise had been in this state before original sin. It seemed to her then — and she hoped this still — that God had shown her this because he wanted to invite her along that way, and give her grace at the proper time to reach this state, in some measure at least.

Let us pause, and study the beginning of this letter more closely. By way of introduction, Mary Ward wrote that she felt she loved what had been revealed to her but was distressed because she could not choose it, or trust herself to accept it as really good until it had been accepted by him, Fr Lee. Later, she says Fr Lee was to know and judge everything, although interiorly she felt 'a strong reluctance and fear' of informing him about what had taken place. Why? The answer comes: Fr Lee could, as she thought, 'look on it as futile, and be distressed by it.' These would actually be two different reactions. Both of Mary Ward's lines of thought — initially her fear, and later her anxiety — are connected with Fr Lee and his opinion; they form the framework of her attempt to describe her vision.

It has already been noted how the 'matter and manner' of the Society of Jesus of the 1611 Vision, had been hacked and hedged. Is one now to believe that the 'freedom and disponibility for God', so especially characteristic of the Jesuits, just shown her with such illuminating force in this 'Vision of the Just Soul', was a reference to the 'Schola Beatae Mariae'? It is not possible. Here, surely, she was shown in all its beauty what had been entrusted to her in 1611: the Institute of the Society of Jesus, as far as it could be realised in her congregation. Mary Ward had certainly never doubted the authenticity of her vision, but she was made hesitant by her confessor, who was bound to reject an Ignatian institute for women. And she was bound to obey him by vow.

Almost involuntarily, words of hope break into the middle of her letter:

> I have moreover thought concerning this occurrence, that this course of ours will perhaps last until the end of the world, because it came to that (namely, to this manner of life,) in which we first began'.[9]

In an undated speech,[10] Fr Lee addressed similar words to the Englishwomen and yet, with a world of difference. He said that he hoped that their state (from Latin status), would 'last until the day of judgement, and that many thousands will benefit from them'. Fr Lee was thinking of future benefits to come from the Institute but Mary Ward, of their point of departure.

One must be careful, when following Mary Ward's sometimes difficult train of thought, not to equate her comparison of a 'Just Soul' with the first people in Paradise before original sin. That is not tenable. First, it must be said that the comparison does not belong to the Vision itself, but was part of Mary Ward's reflections. It was certainly not easy to convey, with inadequate language, what she had been shown. Added to which comes the important assertion that even for the 'upright', sinfulness is a reality. Its consequences remain until death. Even the development of a social structure does not change anything, 'because it came to that'. Towards the end of the letter Mary Ward comes back again to the 'first estate', the original position. The longing for original justice stays with her, as it does to everyone striving for holiness. But that is another matter.

In Liège, in April 1619, when she was meditating on the fall of the two first humans, she wrote the following: 'O my God, is it not possible to live here on earth in this state? (of original justice). As far as anyone can have this granted them, give this, my Jesus to one whom you have made in this way and who has to carry out such things. I know that darkness of reason and sinful inclinations will remain, but these are sufferings and no sin, even though they are faults which are often the result of ignorance or rashness.'[11]

If we look back to the text of the letter, interrupted for the sake of establishing its context, we find specific virtues named, which Mary

Ward considered especially indispensable for the Institute:

> Righteousness, righteous people, works of justice and 'that we (the members) are such as we show ourselves to be, and show ourselves such as we are.' That is sincerity. There is a weakening of this in the German translation from Chambers:[12] 'that we should be as we show ourselves and should show ourselves as we are.' The text says clearly 'that we be such as we appear and appear such as we are.' There is a marked difference.

But why is it that expressions such as 'state of justice' and 'virtue of sincerity' ring in her memory after the vision? The question once came to mind, she continues, as to why righteousness and sincerity should seem to be the essential foundation for all the other virtues that ought to be practised by the members of this Institute. ('Sincerity' is often translated as a nuance of 'truthfulness', which signifies, rather, 'veracity', in English, author's note).

It seemed to her, she explained, that the Fathers of the Society of Jesus, clever and learned men, could achieve the aim of their Order by their natural abilities, without being dependent upon a particular act of God's grace, although constant vigilance and care in the practice of the virtues mentioned were necessary.

The English women, however, who lacked the learning, critical faculties or other qualifications of a man – though these are inherent with them, too – receive true wisdom and ability as a gift of grace from God's hand, in order to actualize what he has demanded for the full development of their Institute.

Mary Ward wrote these words in the seventeenth century. In her day a man's education – still more that of a Jesuit – differed enormously from that of a woman.

Righteousness, simply 'to be good for God', and sincerity of heart cherished in particular, had to replace theological formation. With fine psychological distinction, Mary Ward here explains to the Society of Jesus, the differences between men and women of her day, which the vision of 1611 had unveiled as an entity before her. Even if the 'matter and the manner' remain the same, these will be actualised variously by men or women, as determined by the difference of their sex. Mary Ward saw the psychologically-determined differentiation between men and women in the spheres of work of the Society of Jesus extremely clearly. She and her companions were soon to be heavily censured for practising a 'priestly' ministry.

Such a unity should never be seen in terms of dependence by the Institute on the Society of Jesus. Several sources attest to the self-sufficiency of the Institute, and the courage of this independence.

Towards the end of the letter, Mary Ward writes that it seemed that she understood the individual details, 'particulars' better than before, as during her meditations she thought more deeply about the 'state' of the Institute.

These particulars led each one of them individually, 'severally', to that first state as to a source, and the best disposition for a person who wished to do all things well. From there she could, with no trouble, return again to the particular virtues of the Institute, and with greater clarity and a completely tranquil understanding, judge between what was excellent and what was merely adequate.

The sense of the 'first estate' cannot be understood here as the state of the first people in Paradise for, one might ask, can the form of a congregation ever lead one back towards original innocence? Here too, according to our way of thinking, by 'what we first begun' is meant the 'matter and manner' of the Society of Jesus. Three visions helped Mary Ward as foundress of an Order on her path 'of infinite troubles':

> The 'Gloria Vision of 1609 – confirmation of her personal activity in England.
> The Vision of 1611 – the spiritual foundation for her community.
> The Vision of the Just Soul in 1615 – confirmation of her congregation as the Society of Jesus, as far as it is possible for women to operate in their sphere of work.

On these three Visions rested an entirely new concept for women's Orders, which was to transform women's congregations in the centuries to come.

The Letter of 27th November, 1615

Mary Ward without guidance from her confessor – fear of her burden of responsibility – self-accusation – three requests

Mary Ward's last letter to Fr Lee[13] expressed her fear and anxiety clearly. It was with good reason that her first passage drew on spiritual experiences which, though imprecisely articulated, concerned the Institute and its identity. In those weeks of tension and conflict, nothing could have been more important. She postponed a discussion on it to a later date, when there might be an opportunity for talk.

She expressed her fear that Fr Lee was now inclined to wipe all thoughts of the English women from his mind and not want to hear anything more of them. That certainly indicates there had not been any sort of contact between the former director of the Institute and its members during the past month of November, and that Fr Lee had neither given a talk nor written a letter to them during his last stay in St Omer. As well as this, there was the fear of the possibility of her ailing confessor's death. In this letter, Mary Ward referred to the great help she had received from him over the years, although she could not agree with him about the form of the Institute with which she had been entrusted.

Here for the first time she spoke about 'the greatness of my charge', about the weight of her burden,[14] yet she submitted to the obedience which she had solemnly promised her confessor. She accused herself of not having practised obedience adequately, and asked forgiveness. This interior disinclination, she found, was the most serious basis for her fear that she might not have been as God-centred in this as in other things about which Fr Lee had given her good guidance. She sometimes thinks, she continues, particularly since her last time of recollection,[15] that if she now had even a fraction of the means and assistance which she had received earlier (probably from Fr Lee), she would have made better use of them than before.

One can see from these words that Mary Ward felt the responsibility for her Institute as a heavy charge in this difficult situation. She never was the 'Amazon' figure so inappropriately described by the English Vita[16] when she was trying to found the house for the Poor Clares.

The end of the letter consists almost entirely of three requests, the third of which only is important for the Institute's problems.

1. If she had ever given Fr Lee cause for disgust, would he let her know the reason for it, so that she could improve.
2. That he might not give up his guidance of her spiritual life. Probably these requests refer to Fr Lee's silence to the other members and herself, otherwise they would not make much sense.

Here too we are given a glimpse into the difficulties between them both, and can see that Mary Ward must have been tortured by the almost insupportable tension between God's charge to her and her vow of obedience.

3. The third point concerns the Institute.

If Fr Lee should die during her absence (in England), and the members' way of life (course) were to continue along the lines which Fr Flake declared were those personally planned by Fr Lee, then she would a) not go to England under any circumstances before the matter was settled in Rome, however long that might be.

b) She would be prepared to see Fr Lee during his stay in England only rarely, and actually receive written guidance only from him for her spiritual life, if that were allowed.

It should be pointed out here it is only Mary Ward's personal relationship that is under discussion, and not the work of members of the Institute in England. Presumably this was not dealt with any further.

From these two instructions, which are of great significance for us, it is evident that Fr Lee was very strictly controlled in his contacts with Mary Ward, and had to conform to the Society of Jesus' repudiation of the Institute which the 1611 Vision had required of her.

If she were to send Fr Lee something wrapped in white paper, she continues, or a letter written with very fine handwriting, would he deal with the message himself.

Mary Ward's extreme caution is already evident at this stage; it was to come to perfection in the so-called 'Lemon-juice' letters from prison in the Anger convent in Munich in 1631. Such precautions were in no way directed against the authority of her former confessor's superiors — these had the right to censor letters — but against the vigilance of those acting from personal motives, or who smelt danger for the Society of Jesus at the least sign of co-operation. These would promptly have carried their suspicions to the curia of the Order in Rome.

But what must have gone on in Mary Ward's mind, when, soon afterwards, St Omer received the news of the death of her spiritual director? Obviously, in the first place, genuine human sorrow at the loss of a good friend. There was also the loss of words of consolation and encouragement; the loss of common points of understanding between two people united to God, whose whole energies were directed to God.

But possibly Fr Lee's death, coming as it did immediately after the Vision of the Just Soul, was also a sign — an extremely drastic sign, that it was not his Plan for the Institute, the Schola Beatae Mariae, which was to have a great future but that other one, conveyed by the categorical pronouncement: 'Take the same/Institute/ as of the Society of Jesus.'

It must have occurred to Mary Ward, even in all her grief and apprehension, that this death released her from her vow of obedience. Equally, she must have felt overwhelmed by the responsibility of breaking new ground in the old structures of the Roman Church.

For the task which God — 'he whose words are deeds' — had given her now lay on her shoulders alone.

Notes

1. VP/B 2, Inst. Arch. Munich.
2. Information in a letter of 1st November, 1615.
3. Letter Nr. 1 Inst. Arch. Munich.
4. Letter Nr. 2. Inst. Arch. Munich.
5. as above, note 1.
6. ibid.
7. Letter Nr. 1. Inst. Arch. Munich., GL T.25.
8. May – June 1621, StA Munich, Kl 432/I, 16–19.
9. Chambers D I, p. 280: "Überdies dachte ich mir bei dieser Gelegenheit, vielleicht dauert diese unsere Lebenswiese bis zum Ende der Welt fort, auf dass sie jene Stufe erreiche, auf der wir ursprünglich begannen."
10. Therfore, Children, have confidence in God, for I hope, your state will continue till the day of iudgment and that manie thousands will profitt by you". LR pp. 159–160, Inst. Arch. Munich.

11. VP/E 3, Inst. Arch. Munich.
12. Chambers DI, p. 280.
13. On 27th November 1615, Letter Nr. 2, Inst. Arch. Munich.
14. "Charge" can also mean task, commission.
15. She began this period of recollection at the end of October, 1615.
16. "Who can heare expresse the courage with which this holy Amazon undertook this second encounter?" Vita E, f. 11rv; Vita I p. 18, "la nostra Amazona," at any rate only before her departure, 1609.

XII

BISHOP JACQUES BLAES of ST OMER
and the
ENGLISHWOMEN'S INSTITUTE

The Petition — 1616

Sources — the Institute in the first Italian draft — in the altered Latin draft — comparison of both texts — cool attitude of the Pope

Briefly, conclusively and casually, Fr Suarez dealt with the question of whether the Bishop had the authority to approve and confirm the Englishwomen's Institute. The founding of new congregations, he said, was canonically forbidden unless there were papal approval.

Before him, Fr Lessius had been of the opinion that the Bishop could allow a 'Pium Institutum' within his diocese, but Suarez stated — with justice — that this was no Pium Institutum under proposal, but a congregation of women which showed all the requirements of a true Order and therefore was dependent on papal authorization. This approval, he thought, the Institute would never receive, as its members did not observe enclosure. If the pre-requisites were lacking for approval by the Pope, then approval could not be given by a Bishop.

This was on 3rd June, 1615, a few months after the Bishop of St Omer had released his open letter of 19th March. In this he had relegated to a remote future any submission to the Pope of Mary Ward's altered Plan for the Institute. By the middle of 1615, Fr Suarez' report could have arrived in Belgium. His final pronouncement, that the Bishop could not confirm if the pre-requisites for papal approval were lacking, cut the ground from below the Bishop of St Omer's feet.

Willy nilly, he had to take the path which he had dismissed in March until an unspecified date which he had named as 'the right time'. So, prematurely, he had to present the petition for confirmation of the Institute to those in authority over him.

It may be remembered how the Englishwomen had reacted after the Bishop had published his letter: with disunity, turning in different directions, hesitating between leaving the Institute and entering a contemplative Order. We know, too, that when she was preparing a fair copy of the Institute's Plan 'altered by her', Mary Ward, in the Vision of the Just Soul, had received confirmation that this Plan was wrong and that only the beauty of the 'first estate' would be considered suitable for her Institute.

Soon afterwards Thomas Sackville, son of England's Lord Treasurer and a great friend of the Jesuits in Belgium, was on the way to Rome with documents concerning the confirmation of the Institute. He must have reached the Holy City at the beginning of 1616, for on 3rd June he is entered in the Pilgrim Book of the English Hospice in Rome.

Bishop Blaes is also credited with playing a part in presenting the Petition to the Pope for the approval (Approbatio) of the Institute. It is no longer possible to ascertain who was approached in all this. It was certainly not the General of the Society of Jesus personally, otherwise his answer to the Bishop would have been in his draft-notes, a most carefully kept record. But there is no such entry. This was not the case with Fr Lee's correspondence. It can be assumed as most likely that once again Fr Thomas Owen, who had received a letter in June, 1615[1] from Fr Richard Blount SJ,- not a particularly friendly one — about the activities of the members of the Institute, had been drawn into the matter.

The petition was submitted in duplicate. Of the first, which was presented to the Pope, there remain two fair copies (A and B) in the same handwriting and prepared in Italian. The Pope's decision was attached[2] in another handwriting on copy B.

Copy A has no remarks. That indicates negotiations with the Pope. The Petition was undoubtedly written in Rome. Language and duplication prove that. Whether it was identical with the text of the Petition of the Bishop of St Omer, which was probably available, remains an open question.

The second draft was far less carefully written and in Latin. The marginal and dorsal annotations contain the Pope's final decision, and that of the Session of the Congregation of the Council of 23rd March, 1616.[3] It is the later draft, therefore. Both papers lie in the archives of the Congregation of the Council and among the Positios, documents for the attention of the Congregation.[4] They are undated, but must have been prepared soon after Sackville's arrival in Rome in January 1616.

But why were two copies of the Petition presented?

First, an exact comparison of the two texts shows an important variant in the definition which at first is barely perceptible.

To take the first draft: In this the members are shown as Englishwomen who devote themselves both in England and outside it (dentro il regno quanto fuori di esso) to their own salvation (alla perfettione christiana da per se). Originally they lived independently or with their parents and only later came together as a community in

St Omer. They take the three vows and help towards the conversion of England by their way of life, by their prayers and by the education of English children to whom they teach the usual basic subjects and, in particular, the christian way of life.

For this task they wish, for the time of their life in the community, to take a special – therefore a fourth vow, which would commit them to teaching and education. None of these four vows would be taken for life; they can be dissolved by the person concerned or by the community. Their work is of extreme importance for England, and has been approved by the Bishop of St Omer, to whom they have been subject since the beginnings of their community, and they are recognized as competent. For their greater consolation and to receive heaven's blessing, they petition the Pope to grant approbation to their way of life as a Pium Institutum by means of a papal brief, in order to recommend their congregation to Prelates and high-placed personages, and as well a full indulgence on entry into their community and in the hour of their death.

Extraordinary! In comparison with the 'Schola Beatae Mariae', which knew the Englishwomen's educational and teaching capabilities in England and abroad, there appear some Englishwomen who, originally living in England and elsewhere, and devoted to their own salvation, came together as a community only later in order to educate young English girls, and teach them.

Bishop Blaes said the same in his much-quoted letter. The Fourth Vow, which was extended to all the Englishwomen in the 'Schola Beatae Mariae', applies here only to those members who live in St Omer, in the Institute recognized by the Bishop.

For this episcopal Institute, which had already been approved by the Bishop of St Omer, the Englishwomen are now requesting papal confirmation of their way of life as a Pium Institutum (maniere de vivere tamquam Pium Institutum). This title is lacking in the plan of the Institute 'Schola Beatae Mariae'.

Attention should also be drawn to something else: was the greater consolation of the members of the Institute, together with richer heavenly blessings, of sufficient importance to justify a petition to the Pope for approval of their community? However, not even this sort of approach could win approval.

In the second draft of the Petition there was more mention of the noble ladies from England who had indeed come together as a community, but whose exemplary lives were no longer only for England but for the conversion of many (multos ... convertendi) and who were now educating various girls (varias puellas). No more about their greater consolation and the blessing of heaven being the reason for their petition, but the expansion of the spiritual needs of the country (aptum ad fructus spirituales in illis partibus) and the restoration of church discipline (disciplinam ecclesiasticam restituendam).

Still more striking is the difference in the Petition itself:

In the first draft the members of the Institute ask for the approval of their way of life as a Pius Institute and a recommendation to prelates and people of standing.In the second draft, on the other hand, they request nothing more than approval for their way of life (hoc vitae genus) and for a recommendation to the bishops; nothing more is said about people of standing.

The shift is clear: in referring to work in the Lord's vineyard (Schola Beatae Mariae para.l), in England and abroad (Schola Beatae Mariae, para.5) working as teachers and educators, the first draft is about Englishwomen who in and beyond England have formed a community in St Omer; the second draft, simply, of Englishwomen who have built up a community in St Omer and are now active in Belgium, for Belgians only.

The annotations also speak clearly. The first draft grants the Englishwomen an indulgence but not, as requested, on entry to the Institute and on their deathbed. The hour of death stands, but the day of entry has been changed to the Feast of our Lady's Assumption, to be received only in the Chapel. Perhaps this feast was the dedication of their church. Moreover this draft was directed by the Pope to the Congregation of the Council, with the appended question as to whether it would be wise to approve a congregation without enclosure. Nor was that all. The second draft revealed that several decisions had been taken by the Congregation of the Council.

Confirmation had been refused: (De confirmatione nihil). Recommendations to the Nuntius and Prelates were granted, likewise the indulgence, but not on day of entry. The loaded question was put once again: did they wish to teach English children or others (solum virgines Angliae vel alias etiam?).

No vestige remained of the matter and manner of the Society of Jesus; even the Institute's aims for England had been eroded step by step.

And all this happened in a matter of months after Mary Ward had been granted her vision of the Just Soul.

The Laudatio

10th April, 1616

The Institute in the 'Laudatio' – a community of English-women who teach and educate English girls are placed under the protection of the Bishop of St Omer

The referral of the Petition to the Congregation of the Council is significant for the legal process of the Curia, the pointer to the Institute's freedom from enclosure being, so to speak, the warrant

for it. Negotiations with the Congregation must have been difficult;
a second draft is otherwise hard to explain, especially this rather
carefully prepared one, from which whole phrases had been omitted
which could have caused offence.

The decision of the Cardinals came on 23rd March, 1616. It was
then that the comments were put on the reverse of the second draft
of the Petition. It took at least three weeks for the Congregation to
give their answer to the Bishop of St Omer on 10th April.[5] That
was normal official procedure. Private individuals rarely received
an answer from the papal Curia.

Certain Englishwomen, began the 'Laudatio', driven from their
country by persecution, and united as a community by their zeal
for the catholic faith, had shown the Holy Father that they devoted
themselves to their neighbour by pious works and an exemplary
way of life, and taught English girls. In order to be true to
their vocation and to serve God better they asked, among other
things (inter caetera) for the pope's recommendation to the church
authorities. Commissioned by the Pope with this task, the Cardinals
of the Congregation took the decision of entrusting the Bishop of
St Omer with the special concern and protection (praecipuam curam
ac protectionem) of the Englishwomen, so that he could, when
necessary, grant them support and, if this were possible, direct
them more and more towards the status of an Order,[6] that the
fruit of their labours might be daily enriched.If that should be the
case − as the Cardinals confidently hoped − confirmation of this
Institute by the Holy See would be considered (a Sede Apostolica
confirmando deliberabitur).

One could hardly say less in a grandiloquent reply of one hundred
and eighty-five words.   .

The good works, the exemplary way of life, and the educational
work for English girls were not enumerated very convincingly.
However, the real matter of consequence, the petition for approval
or confirmation of the Institute was touched on only superficially.
The sole request granted them was that of a recommendation to the
bishops.[7]

It is all too easy to cavil. What exactly did the author of the
Petition hope to achieve? Papal approval for a community which
was hardly five years old and which (altered 'in genere') would slot
very well into the framework of Belgian women's congregations? Or
episcopal recommendation?

To be exact, the Petition has a three-fold construction:

the request for approval, then for the recommendation to the
Bishops and, finally, for the granting of indulgences.

The most important request, as though surrounded by the other Petitions, was in the middle. This had been the case with the questions put
to Fr Lessius and Fr Suarez, and, also, in the Bishop of St Omer's

refutation of the objections against the Institute in his open letter.

The petition's second request was granted, and not only in general, but personally, by name. Still more. The Institute, or rather that nameless community of Englishwomen, was placed under the protection and care of the Bishop of St Omer. He could even support them. Given that situation,this decision was a reversal of Fr Suarez' judgement and the rehabilitation of that of Bishop Blaes. Moreover, and this must not be lost sight of – it was for an Institute that had neither any additional field of work in England, nor any connection with the Society of Jesus. Even if this was a mere hair's-breadth hold on actuality, at least the community of the Englishwomen had not been forbidden.

The apparently unenthusiastic response of the Congregation of the Council was of great importance for all those involved. The enemies of the Institute could see in it Rome's refusal of an Ignatian institute for women; its well-disposed friends regarded it as a real basis for its continuation as a Pius Institute in St Omer, and the Bishop now had an excellent boarding school – at present for English girls only – subject to him. Only those who did not wish for an episcopal Pius Institute went away empty.

The main participants, Mary Ward and those members in England and in St Omer, must not be forgotten. They had little voice in the proceedings, which were mostly conducted over their heads.

The 'Relatio of the Bishop of St Omer

May – June, 1616

The sources, the 'Relatio' as a new plan of the Institute – separation of those members on the active apostolate – connection with the community in St Omer only through the person of the Chief Superior – the members in St Omer – work of teaching and education of English girls according to the plan of the 'Schola Beatae Mariae'.

The decision of the Congregation of the Council – of 10th April to Bishop Blaes and 20th April to Nuntius Gesualdo – could only have reached their respective destinations, St Omer and Brussels, in the first half of May at the earliest. Their arrival would certainly have entailed discussions with the members of the Institute. How far the Nuntius was involved in this is not certain. It is also an open question as to whether he had been sent a copy of Bishop Blaes' 'Relatio', or had received it as the basis for the discussions, for this has survived only as a copy and left no trace of any kind in correspondence. Yet the document is of great importance for an understanding of the Institute's position at that time.

The MS is now in the Fondo Capponi of the Vatican Library.[8] Perhaps it was first sent to a Jesuit in Rome and later came to the Vatican. It is not dated, nor is the author known, but certain interior criteria will help us here.

First, as regards date: the 'Relatio' was compiled after Rome's decision had been learnt, for the Bishop quotes the Pope and the Congregation of the Council which made him the Englishwomen's protector, until the confirmation of the Institute. In the summer of 1616 Mary Ward went to Spa to take the waters for gall stone. It will be seen that she began to make connections near Liège with the intention of making a foundation there.

The manuscript could therefore have been written at the earliest in May or June, 1616, but before her journey to Liège, for it is hard to accept that negotiations with the Nuntius were conducted without her. After the death of Fr Lee there was no one in St Omer who could have spoken with such authority. Keeping the Plan of the Institute 'Schola Beatae Mariae', and the open letter of Bishop Blaes well in mind, the contents of the 'Relatio' strike the reader as utterly incredible, for they effectively constitute a new Plan for the Institute, including its controversial sphere of apostolic work, very different from the older plan, and in flat contradiction to the Bishop's letter of 1615. In this 'Relatio' we meet the same writing as in the marginal headings and notes added to the 'Schola Beatae Mariae' of the earliest plan of the Institute and Bishop Blaes' letter, mentioned recently.

The author of the writing is not known by name, but doubtless is to be found among the English Jesuits. Apart from his thorough knowledge of catholics in England, which one can hardly credit the Bishop of St Omer as possessing in spite of his contact with English refugees, the Englishwomen in St Omer were named as dwelling overseas (in partes transmarinas). It is unlikely that the Bishop of St Omer, in whose name the 'Relatio' was compiled, would have described his diocesan town on the European mainland as 'overseas'; this could, however, have come from an English pen. Then, again, the remark on the back, 'copie/of the B/ishop/of St Omero to the Nuntio', which was struck through and replaced by the Latin 'Relatio Episcopi Blasensis Apostolico Nuntio Bruxellensi', indicates an English original.

To turn to the contents of the MS: in a time turbulent with religious controversy, begins the 'Relatio', certain Englishwomen, fired with zeal for the glory of God, their own salvation and the catholic faith, particularly in England (in Anglia praesertim), have come together in a community. With the saints of the early church as their model, they work in their own country. Their community has two parts, some of the members live in England while others have crossed the seas. In England, where their numbers are growing steadily, they have elected one of their number as superior and obey her in everything. They visit priests in prison, offer gifts from their own means or from alms to those suffering need of financial support, and give priests valuable help in the conversion of heretics and schismatics. By their services eight noble ladies have returned to the Roman Church. They are a shining example to relatives; they attend to the worldly goods of those members of the Institute who live on the Continent (quae in partibus transmarinis vivunt), and make it possible for English girls to be educated. As far as the perilous conditions of everyday life permit, they live according to their Rule and follow the Order of the day. These members may be called away from England by the chief superioress (per Superiorem Primariam) for the good of their spiritual life.

These words astonish us, when we recall that the Plan of the Institute 'Schola Beatae Mariae' (1612) limited the Englishwomen in their work in England to the teaching and education of girls; that Fr Lessius' report (1614/5) confined their presence in England to 'necessary journeys' and that, above all, the letter written on 19th March, 1615, by the Bishop of St Omer (who claimed to be well-informed), stated that the Englishwomen had no 'missiones' in England. Now, six months after Fr Lee's death, the Bishop writes commending the richly-blessed work of conversion by the Englishwomen in their own country. This praise is directed at no less a personage than the papal nuntius in Brussels, Pope Paul V's representative, in whose Congregation every single mention of the women's work in England had been carefully erased, in order to draft an acceptable petition for approval of their Institute.

To summarize the text: Those Englishwomen who have withdrawn to other regions (in alias regiones) – St Omer is meant here – live in community, and are subject in obedience to a superior. For them the Plan 'Schola Beatae Mariae' is valid. Their noviceship lasts two years. They take three vows but can be sent away or leave the Institute at their own pleasure. Their daily programme, teaching and education as well as the practice of virtues, are taken almost completely from the 'Schola Beatae Mariae' but shortened considerably.

The 'Relatio' tails off in a broadly based 'apologia' of the English women, with a detailed review of the religious state of England, culminating in the Bishop's request, as one holding a mandate from the Pope to promote this Institute. Would Nuntius Gesualdo take the Englishwomen's Institute under his protection and commend it, as was being done by the Bishop of St Omer?

We may certainly assume, as will be confirmed in her letter to Nuntius Albergati, that after Fr Lee's death and her experience of the Vision of the Just Soul, Mary Ward had rejected the Plan 'Schola Beatae Mariae' for the Institute. The Bishop's 'Relatio' implied a 'manner', a way for the Institute that was inspired and written by Jesuits who supported the Englishwomen, in order to ensure their continued existence, even in England. That they should be approved, perhaps even promoted by the Nuntius, was a suggestion that must have been made by Bishop Blaes, for one cannot imagine that his name would be suggested without his knowledge.

But what did this offer mean for the Englishwomen? It was a far-reaching concession. The work in England could continue, which was one of Mary Ward's chief concerns. But the members there would, in a manner of speaking, belong to a completely different Institute, connected with the St Omer foundation only through the person of the Chief Superior. These members elected their own superior, whom they were pledged to obey. The Chief Superior alone had the right to call them to St Omer, perhaps, so that they might make their noviceship there. But St Omer was the core of the Institute. It was there that one found the members who lived like the communities of St Philip Neri, St Francesca Romana, and many Beguines; they would certainly be subordinate to the Bishop in matters of consequence. This was not expressly stated in the 'Relatio', but it was self-evident. Bishop Blaes was, after all, their protector. These members devoted themselves to the teaching and education of English girls and, what is more, they had the noviceship.

Naturally enough the Bishop could not accept responsibility for the English members in England, and presumably he did not want to, otherwise his letter of 19th March, 1625 is difficult to understand. In a hierarchical sense, England was a No Man's Land for the Roman Catholic Church; the competence of the Bishop of St Omer did not extend thus far.

One must suppose that the members knew of the draft plan for this Institute. But they would have declined it. Mary Ward speaks to Nuntius Albergati of Plans which have had to be declined.

It was not simply for reasons of health that Mary Ward went to Spa in the summer of 1616, but to hold discussions about a new foundation.[9] This decision, which will not have been taken lightly, can be seen as the outcome of the insurmountable difficulties in St Omer. By the summer of 1616, the limit had been reached.

According to our way of thinking, Mary Ward left St Omer in the interests of an undivided Institute with two equally important spheres of work, active apostolic work among adults, and the teaching and education of English girls; in the interests of an Institute which would be extra-diocesan, independent of bishops, and modelled on the Society of Jesus.

Almost imperceptibly at first, a division came into existence between the first foundation in Flanders and the second in Liège. St Omer, with its three town houses, had been legally established in 1616 by the Town magistrate,[10] but the future Institute, the noviceship, was withdrawn from this. On 24th November 1616, fifteen Englishwomen moved to Liège, ostensibly to take the waters in Spa. This not only transferred the main weight of the Institute from the diocese of St Omer and out of the Flanders' nunciature, but also from the Archduke's sphere of power. Liège was then an independent prince-bishopric, which belonged to the nunciature of Cologne in church matters and was a member of the German states, the Trier group. The first foundation in St Omer, barely seven years old, soon lost standing. Its members were still under the jurisdiction of Bishop Blaes, (died on 21st March, 1618). But they were bound by an unbreakable bond of loyalty to their General Superior.[11]

Mary Ward now stood alone against all her enemies, both within and without the Society of Jesus.

Notes

1. Letter of 9th June, 1615, Arch. Stonyhurst College F. Chr. Grene SJ Collectanea M p. 95b.
2. On the back of both copies is the address: Alla Santita di Nostro Signore per alcune nobili vergini Inglese nella città di Saint Omer in Fiandra. On copy B dorsal in another hand: Anglican(ae). Alla Congregazione dei Concilio, che veda se è bene d'approvarla senza clausura. Marginally, in a third hand: La Sua Santità ha concessa indulgenza plenaria nell'hora della morte et una volta l'anno, cioè per il giorno dell'Assontione indulgenza plenaria per la loro capella.
3. Marginal: De confirmatione nihil. Scrivendum de commendatione Nuntio et Prelatis. Et de indulgentia plenaria non in die ingressus. Nuntio pro infirmatione. An velint docere solum virgines Angliae vel alias etiam? Dorsal: Die 23 Martii, 1616. Santissimus annuit quod dentur litterae commendatitiae, animadvertit tamen, quod non impetrent neque enim carint confirmationem, sed quod concipiantur in modum ut dicatur, quod si Institutum hoc in dies erit laudabile, cogitabitur postea de confirmation. Et de indulgentia plenaria in una ex festivitatibus beatae Virginis et in mortis articulo pro descendentibus in hac congregatione, quod erit significandum.
4. AV Rome, S. Cong. Concilii Positiones (Sess) 223 I A f. 363rv, IB f. 364 rv. II f. 362 rv.
5. Revised draft AV Rome, S. Congr. Concilii, Positiones (Sess) 223, f. 361 rv; Registration entry: Arch. del Clero Rome, Liber X Literarum f. 196 rv. The original has not survived. Nuntius Ascano Gesualdo received an identical letter in Brussels. Registration entry: Arch. del Clero, Rome, Liber X, Literarum f. 199rv. According to the list which Marcus Fridl made in 1733 concerning the archives used by him, there was still available then a duplicate of the letter of the Congregation of the Council to Bishop Blaes, authenticated by the seal of Cardinal Horatio Lancelotti. The list of archives is in Inst. Arch. Munich. The original to the Nuntius has been lost.
6. Chambers, D I, append. IV, p. 420. translates the phrase "quod magis ad religionem accendantur" as "to which she, filled with so much the greater love of religion", which would not make much sense here.
7. On 20th April 1616 an identical letter was sent to Nuntius Ascano Gesualdo in Brussels. see note 5 above.
8. BV Fondo Capponi 47, ff 76r–77v. The heading originally ran: Copia relationis a Episcopi ad Nuntium, and was corrected in another hand to: Copia relationis a Reverendissimo Episcopo Blasio ad Nuntium apostolicum.
9. VP/C Inst. Arch. Munich. Her writings concerning her confession were written on Saturday, 9th July, 1616, in Spa.
10. Negotiations about recognition of ownership of the Englishwomen's house in Saint-Omer went on between 2nd–18th May, 1616. It concerned the house of Francois Marcotte, Sieur of Lannoy, which was bought on

19th July, 1611; a second house, bought on 2nd October, 1612, from Jacques Ricquart, and a third, bought on 20th January, 1614, from the Cistercian monastery in Ravensburg. AM Saint-Omer, CCXXXIX 17–18, Filles Anglaises, pp. 36–37.

11.   The "Civil Contract", see p. 203ff.

XIII

LIÈGE

The country

*Geographical situation – Prince bishop – bishops from the
Wittelsbach dynasty – Ferdinand of Wittelsbach, Elector of
Cologne and Bishop of Liège*

In Mary Ward's time the prince-bishopric of Liège[1] was bordered
on the west by the southern Netherlands (today's Belgium), to the
north by the northern Netherlands (today's Holland), in the east by
Germany in its dismembered state, and the south by Luxemburg.
Its geographical situation was therefore anything but assured. The
populace of this area was mostly French-speaking Walloon, which
still stretches from the French Department Nord, Calais, Aisne,
Ardennes, across the archduchy of Luxemburg into Belgium over
Brabant, Namur and Liège.

The diocese of Liège (Leodium) goes back to Roman times and was
raised in the 11th century to a Prince-bishopric. In the Middle Ages it
had eight deaneries, which were on Dutch, German and Luxemburg
territory. Apparently it was in the 5th century that the residence of
the bishop of Liège shifted to the more northern Maastricht, and
only at the beginning of the 8th century did it return to Liège under
saintly Bishop Hubert.

When King Philip II created a new diocesan division in 1559,
the diocese of Liège lost a fair amount of its religious territory to
the newly erected Archbishopric of Malines and to the dioceses of
Namur, Antwerp, 's Hertogenbosch and Roermond. The two last-
named now belong to Holland.

For about a century and a half, from 1581–1723, the Wittelsbach
princes of Bavaria possessed the prince-bishopric of Liège. They
usually held the dioceses of Munster, Paderborn and Hildesheim
and, as Archbishops of Cologne, were also Electors.[2] The accumulation of mitres on one head was one of the greatest abuses
in the church at that time. A stop was put to the prince-bishopric
during the French Revolution. In 1792, Bishop Antoine de Méan
was expelled by revolutionary troops; three years later, in 1795,
Liège was united to the southern Netherlands (Belgium) and by the
Concordat of 1802 the diocesan boundaries were re-arranged and

189

made subordinate to Malines. In the 17th century, as a member of the Holy Roman Empire, Liège still belonged to the Nunciature in Cologne, whose Nuncios often resided in Liège.

The Bavarian bishops were rarely resident there. They remained strangers to their people, for as Electors of Cologne they were absorbed in politics. They were politically prudent, in that they remained impartial during the eighty years of the devastating civil war between the southern and northern Netherlands. They preserved their neutrality but carried on a lucrative trade in arms with both the warring powers. At the end of the 16th century, the country went through a phase of great economic progress. The heavy industries (coal and iron) contributed most to this. When the northern Netherlands closed the mouth of the Scheldt to shipping and thus cut off the once flourishing harbour city of Antwerp in favour of its own harbour Rotterdam, the industrial products of Liège found a ready market in the Flemish west. This was favourable to early capitalism in the Liège diocese. The population was and remained francophile by inclination, and catholic in religion.

Protestantism had penetrated here, too, however. Bishop Ernst von Wittelsbach tolerated this, but forbade any propaganda on its behalf. Protestants were excluded from public office and civil rights. They were probably not as sharply persecuted as in other catholic countries but possibly had to reckon with a monetary fine or banishment from the country; it was the flourishing trade with the Calvinistic northern Netherlands that secured them tolerance. The decrees of the Council of Trent (1545-1563) were only made known in 1585. That, in itself, speaks volumes.

Since 1612, Ferdinand of Wittelsbach,[3] brother of the Elector Maximilian I of Bavaria was Prince Bishop of Liège. He was born on 7th October, 1577 in Munich the third son of Duke William V of Bavaria. Already, as a youth, he was provided with ample benefices and studied at the Jesuit university of Ingolstadt and in Rome. He was made Provost of Berchtesgaden in 1595 and so − at eighteen years old − became Coadjutor to his uncle, the Archbishop of Cologne. In 1599 he held the Abbey of Stablo-Malmédy, and after the death of the Bishop of Liège, his diocese and other dignities. Bishop Ferdinand too remained aloof from his subjects in Liège. As Bishop of Munster, Hildesheim and Paderborn, and above all as Archbishop of Cologne and Elector, his political centre lay on the Rhine. Bishop Ferdinand was the focus of the catholic restoration, and a political prop to his brother Maximilian, who protected Bavaria from heresy and was among the few princes who could be relied on to help the catholic church on the German-speaking scene. Ferdinand von Wittelsbach never received major orders; he was not unique in that.

In Liège, government business was carried on by the Privy Council. A Vicar General represented the Bishop. In 1617, when the members of the Institute first lived in Liège, Pierre Stevart took on this office. His successor, Jean de Chokier, was General Vicar from 1624 – 1656. It was during his term of office that the there occurred the sorry downfall of the Institute's foundation on Mont St Martin.

The ecclesiastical court was under the Bishop's Counsel. In 1616 Conrad Blisia held this office, in 1617, Nicholas Plenevaulx.[4] The Court was the only legal authority for the clergy, but the Counsel also had jurisdiction over individual legal cases of the laity, such as wills, marriage contracts, the selling of the property of minors, and care of young citizens. Two fiscal judges were subordinate to the Counsel. Church and State affairs often, quite understandably, overlapped in this network of authorities.

The Town

Situation – administration – the Nuntius

In the northern part of what was then the diocese of Liège, between the last foothills of the Ardennes and near the frontier of the Netherlands, lay the capital, likewise called Liège. (French Liège, Flemish Luik). Statements vary markedly as to its number of inhabitants. In 1630, the papal legate Aloysius Carafa[5] gave an estimate of 100,000 inhabitants. Pierre Bergeron,[6] who travelled through the Ardennes in 1619, went up to 150,000. Both numbers seem very exaggerated. In 1650 the number of inhabitants was about 50,000.[7] For the beginning of the century we can reckon that there were about 40,000 to 45,000.

The town was under the supervision of a Lord Mayor and his deputy. In 1616, when the English women moved into Liège, Guillaume de Beeckman and Guillaume van der Heyden a Blisia had replaced Mathieu de Trouillet,[8] who had left for foreign service. In 1617 Jean de Merlemont and Jean de Liverloo were in charge.

Fourteen lay assessors were subordinate to the two Mayors. Socially, the rich citizens (Giroux) were in opposition to the hardworking artisans (Girondins), and this led to bloody skirmishes.

Typical of Liège were the thirty-two 'metiers' or guilds.[9] Those belonging to one of these groups were granted full possession of political rights (hantise) as well as permission to practise a craft (usance). It was possible to inherit political rights and permission for a craft from one another, independently. From the beginning of the 16th century, inhabitants of the town of Liège could take the shortest of short cuts to become citizens by entering a guild. Later, particular crafts were no longer connected with particular guilds. For example, in the spring of 1620 the Englishwomen entered the guild of the blacksmiths (métier de fèvres) certainly not with any intention of practising the craft connected with it, but because the guild was the most important, and by membership in it they immediately attained the status of citizens. The English Jesuits, likewise, had been accepted into the goldsmiths' guild.[10]

As well as the then Cathedral, the town of Liège had seven collegiate churches. St Lambert was the patron of the Cathedral. This church was consecrated in 1015 and destroyed during the French Revolution in 1794. Of the collegiate churches, St Paul was founded in 969 and by the Concordat of 1802 was raised to the status of cathedral instead of St Lambert. The collegiate church of St Peter was also destroyed during the French Revolution. St Martin au Mont, near which the Englishwomen lived, will be mentioned in greater detail later. The remaining collegiate churches were St Denis, St John the Evangelist, Holy Cross and St Bartholomew.

Of the six remaining collegiate churches which had survived, five lost their rank during the decisions of the 1802 Concordat and became parish churches in the hierarchical structure of the town. These very beautiful churches from the high Middle Ages still show something of the former beauty of Liège, now unfortunately almost entirely lost.

Like St Omer, Liège was rich in religious houses. Only the most important of the women's houses and communities are given here:[11] The Carmelites, Poor Clares, Celestines, Capuchins, Recollects, Ursulines, Walloon and later, too, English Sepulchrines, the Soeurs Grises, the community of Notre Dame de la Paix, Notre Dame des Anges, and the Beguines. At a rough estimate, this meant that out of a population of about 40,000, there was a women's convent for every 3,500 of the inhabitants.

If one considers men's orders too, and the canons of the collegiate churches, it is not surprising that there was little space and less enthusiasm for a new foundation.

Relations between clergy and Bishop and, above all, the Roman Curia, were vague. The first Visitation by a Nuntius took place in 1585/6. Nuntius Albergati of Cologne conducted one such[12] in 1613, some years before the members of the Institute settled in Liège. Albergati's mission was somewhat delicate. It dealt, primarily, with the reform of the clergy. These, however, were protected by many ancient privileges. So immediately after his arrival the Chapter of St Lambert demanded to be shown the Nuntius' faculties as Visitor – and succeeded. The collegiate churches of Liège, which also enjoyed privileges, had never been visited before.[13] But there was no question of rescinding their privileges.

Not even Nuntius Pierluigi Carafa managed that, when he visited the diocese in 1629. The Nunciature's reports of his brother-in-office in Brussels are full of complaints of ancient privileges and customs, which restricted if they did not actually prevent the renewal of the clergy and the monasteries according to the mind of the Council of Trent.

Saint-Martin en Mont

The collegiate church – its chapter – its enclosure – the parish church of St Remacle

Liège owned two churches dedicated to St Martin: St Martin on the Island in the town centre and St Martin on Publemont hill. Today the picture of the old town is still dominated by this last-named church.

It was built in 965 by Bishop St Eraclus of Liège. The tower was burnt during an uprising in 1312 and merely patched up afterwards. In 1468 it suffered the same fate for a second time and was restored at the beginning of the sixteenth century in the form it still preserves today.[14]

The Chapter of St Martin consisted of thirty canons. They were almost exclusively from the nobility or rich citizens. Jean Bertho had been Dean since 1605 and Jean de Frentz, Provost of the Chapter since 1603.[15]

The Church had an enclosure for its canons stretching from the Porte St Martin towards the rue des Fossés, over the Mont St Martin to what was the court of the Beguines; the boundary was marked by a stone. Two wells supplied the water for hundreds of years for those who lived in the district.

Originally, the houses within the enclosure were dwelling places for the canons only. Later, other dependants lived there, and finally they were rented out, even to foreign lay people. The character of this enclosed area has, naturally, now been lost. The houses and their large gardens reached from the rue St Séverin near the Church to the houses of Basse Sauvenière at the foot of the hill. Most were spacious and solidly built. Opposite the Church of St Martin and sideways on to the little Church of St Remacle lay the steps 'Degrés des Bégards', which still lead down into the Boulevard de la Sauvenière. In those days this broad street was an arm of the Maas, which flowed through the town.

Near the Degrés des Bégards lay the house of a Canon Thénis, who had died in 1610.[16] At the beginning of December, 1616, when the Englishwomen arrived, it was owned by Canon Michel de Merica. The English women's parish Church, St Remacle en Mont,[17] was a small church, likewise within the enclosure, standing opposite the collegiate church. St Remacle was a foundation of the 11th and 12th centuries. Its parish area was very small and sparsely populated. On 21st November, 1803, the Church was closed and six years later, in

1809, it was demolished. The parish was then taken over by St Martin en Mont.

The tiny church was surrounded by a cemetery. Members of the Institute are buried here, those who died during those first years of the plague, dysentery and, probably, hunger too.[18] At the end of the 17th century the cemetery was closed and turned into a garden. Today Mont St Martin has far more buildings but it nonetheless remains a picturesque part of the old Liège.

Not much is known about the canons of St Martin. Research into the incumbents of this church, whose canons frequently took part in political life and were authorised to go on princely missions, would certainly be a rewarding occupation.

The English Jesuits in Liège

Building a Jesuit noviceship – situation – burden of debts up to 1617

In 1615 the English Jesuits began to build a novitiate house between the rue des Anglais, rue Montague Ste Walburge, rue Pierreuse, rue Volière and the rue Fond-St-Servais, on one of the many hills of Liège.There had been Walloon Jesuits in the town since 1595, with a well-attended College, but the English Jesuits had conceived the idea of moving their novitiate from Louvain to Liège, ostensibly to be better protected from the watchful eyes of English spies in the Infanta's lands. It was a rather thin reason, for these could equally well have been in Liège, as the neighbouring resort of Spa was frequented by English people.

First, on 30th September, 1614,[19] a William Stanley bought a garden in Fauchamps (occupying 'three days' work') from the Liège apothecary Jean Gershoven between the rue des Anglais (then called En Royal), and the rue Pierreuse. There was no publicity about this, as Stanley had changed sides during the war from Queen Elizabeth's army into the Spanish service and was Colonel in the Infanta's army and a member of her council of war. Stanley was related to the rector of the new foundation, Fr John Tomson, as was another benefactor of the English Jesuits in Liège, George Talbot of Grafton, later the Earl of Shrewsbury.

On 29th April, 1606, Gershoven had bought the property from a Guillaume Libert for an annual payment of 11 malt of wheat, and 400 Brabant guilders to the widow of Nicolas Nollet in Vivegnis.

Five weeks later, on 7th November 1614,[20] Stanley acquired a house with appurtenances from Charles Hellin, named Donchel, for a yearly payment of 142 Brabant guilders and from the advocate Laurent Pétri a house with appurtenances with an annual interest of 200 Brabant guilders. The plots of land and houses, therefore, had a total value of 400 guilders annually and an annual interest of 342 guilders. At that time interest was set at least at 6 per cent. That gave, in this case, a capital value of about 12,400 guilders. In addition there was the price of the 11½ malt wheat annually, which was not stated. Stanley probably left this property to the English Jesuits for nothing, for on 20th December, 1621[21] and 21 January, 1622, respectively, a William Stanley gave the English Jesuits a house by the wall of the Capuchin monastery as a gift. The priest Edward Stanley and a 'Sieur Guillaume Ward' were named as witnesses.

That was only the beginning. There were, of course, well-to-do friends and benefactors, but mortgages had to be taken, for the new house had yet to be built.

In 1615 Fr Tomson does not seem to have needed much capital for, according to the English Fathers' Register, a simple sort of bookkeeping for the money raised, (kept later, probably by the procurator, Fr Rodney), Fr Tomson paid Gabriel Windelen on 17th December[22] 20 guilders' payment for a capital of about 350 guilders.

In Spring, 1615, [23] the English Jesuits received official approval from the Bishop to build a house and the work was begun that August. One year later, in August 1616, the church was partly finished; on 3rd May, 1617, it was consecrated. The Jesuits continue with their project, wrote the English Ambassador in The Hague to London,[24] forty workers are constantly employed but sometimes their number totals a hundred and, he added angrily, for the most part this is paid for in good English money.

On 20th February, 1616[25] Fr Tomson raised the amount of 3,650 guilders, again from apothecary Gershoven. On 7th March he was able to pay back 650.66 guilders, so that the mortgage consisted of only 3,000 guilders.
On 16th November, 1616,[26] he raised the amount of 6,000 guilders from the widow of Pierre Gal, with an interest of 400 guilders per year.

When the members of the Institute came to Liège in 1616, the English Jesuits had, as shown, raised the mortgage to the total of 9,000 guilders at an annual rate of interest of 570 guilders.

And this was still by no means the end. Step by step further mortgages followed in 1617.[27] In the second half of the same year, Fr Tomson had raised 34,600 guilders at an annual interest of 2,220 guilders. This sum equalled a year's salary for ten average officials. But even with this sum, the end was not yet in sight.

Admittedly, up to a hundred workers had to be paid; as well, there were building materials, transport, and gardens, already much admired. But when one considers that everything was yet to be completed, that the finances of the English Jesuits came for the most part from gifts of wealthy friends, and that the economical situation of the Flemish and Walloon houses of the Society was not too rosy, these debts of 34,600 guilders give one food for thought. It is essential to know the facts about this debt if one is to understand the tragedy of the brief history of the Institute in Liège.

Members of the Institute on the Mont St Martin

1616–1617

The foundation in the narrative sources and deeds – help from Fr John Tomson and Fr Henry More

Various reasons are given in the sources for the expansion of the Institute. None of Mary Ward's autobiographical fragments extend to this year, so that apart from a brief note from her sister Barbara about her life, and a letter from the members of a later date, we are dependent on outside information.

Barbara Ward[28] wrote that after the number of members of the Institute had grown to between fifty and sixty, Mary Ward had gone to Spa for reasons of health but also with the intention of founding a house in nearby Liège. With this in mind she had drawn on the assistance of certain wealthy lady citizens with whom she had connections.[29]

The English Vita[30] manages to enhance the matter somewhat, departing from reality by stating that Mary Ward travelled from St Omer to Brussels and had an audience with the Infanta. From there she went on to Liège, where the town and clergy were under obligation to her. The novitiate was moved there.

The Italian Vita ignores the Liège foundation completely. Hendricq, in his town chronicle of St Omer,[31] speculates that Emperior Mathias is said to have allowed the Englishwomen to build a house in Liège, but that this might be only a rumour. He was certainly right about that, for the Englishwomen never had any contact with Emperor Mathias, who was briefly active as Archduke in the Netherlands from 1578–1581. The same holds good, continues Hendricq, for the opinion that they would find it easier there to receive the dowries of those entering, as Liège was neutral territory.

Deneuville[32] also mentions a foundation by Emperor Mathias, but his chronicle depends heavily on Hendricq's work.

We know of the great difficulties that Mary Ward had to contend with in St Omer; developments which, in the first half of 1616, showed themselves as unacceptable for the future of the Institute. But the question remains – and no one gives a clear answer to it – why was the town of Liège chosen by the Institute? Under the mild regime of the Infanta Isabella Clara Eugenia there were so many towns in Flanders, near the coast and within easy reach if one wanted to travel to or from England. Moreover, that is where most of the English refugees lived; there were few in Liège. It should also be pointed out that Liège was subject to another prince, to another bishop, and to another nuntius, so that from a secular and a religious point of view it was almost another country.

One great advantage that the town of Liège could offer the members, and lead them to found a house within its walls, was the presence of two English Jesuits who were supportive and who could help them: Fr John Tomson, Rector of the novitiate house under construction and Fr Henry More, his procurator, once confessor to the Englishwomen in St Omer. Perhaps it was these two fathers who, in August 1616, had been the advocates for a house of the Institute in Liège to the Elector of Cologne.[33]

The help expected from and probably offered by the Jesuits should on no account be regarded as presumption on Mary Ward's part. She knew that the fathers were forbidden to involve themselves in the formation and structuring of women's Orders. By character, too, she was anything but demanding. She carried out the task that God had given her, without by-passing the obstacles that it caused, but in great awe of her responsibility as General Superior of the community. The Jesuits had been appointed to her for the deepening of the members' vocation: by talks, by catechesis, and above all, in the confessional. In the light of documentary material, the Liège foundation, which has such a confused and tragic history, can be described from a completely fresh angle. It will be seen that it was precisely here that Mary Ward developed from shy diffidence to the maturity that her task required. This was brought about by her life of prayer with its strongest 'virtue', if one dare so express it, of her union with God.

As the Englishwomen had left St Omer on 24th November, 1616, they probably arrived in Liège about the beginning of December. This should not be regarded as a foundation, but as a temporary stay until the completion of the house they had been promised. Things turned out differently.

Both the university and town library in Liège possess a respectable number of town chronicles from the seventeenth and eighteenth centuries; these are manuscripts which are only rarely original, at least as to what concerns their references to the members of the Institute. For the most part they are copies of compilations of older sources.[34]

The Benedictine Giles Gryte[35] who was well-informed, was active in the Abbey St Jaques in Liège and composed an exhaustive town chronicle. As a contemporary, he knew the women's house – they were called Jesuitesses in Liège – on the Mont St Martin, and named it, precisely, as that belonging to Canon Thénis, deceased, of St Martin. Correctly, he puts the founding of the house in the rue

Pierreuse some years later as the first house. Gryte errs only when he states that the Englishwomen had bought a house on the Mont St Martin. They always lived as tenants.

The pre-history of the foundation is to be found in the ever well-informed but naturally biassed account of Dudley Carleton, the English ambassador in The Hague, who was staying in Spa at this time.[36]

On 12th August, 1616 [37] he was sufficiently well-informed to write to Ralph Winwood, Secretary of State in London,[38] that two Jesuits from Liège had been presented to the Elector in Cologne, to discuss the house which they had begun to build a short time previously. They had also talked of the foundation of certain Englishwomen. Contemptuously, Carleton refers to these as 'Votaries', hangers-on, reverencers of the Jesuits. They were, he continues, 'called Expectatives' which meant they were probably awaiting confirmation of their Institute by the Pope. Carleton thought it likely that they would have no opposition or great difficulty from the Elector of the country, if they had gained the town's approval so easily. That was certainly a sensitive reservation.

In the recommendatory letter from the Bishop of St Omer to the Bishop of Liège there is also a reference to the Englishwomen who are moving to Liège for health reasons.[39] Nowadays one would call onself a tourist or a visitor in a foreign country, so that once accepted, it would be possible to lengthen the time of one's stay.

Already by lst December,[40] Carleton reported that the Englishwomen whom he had seen in Spa had bought a house in Liège for the pretty sum of 11,000 guilders. The Ambassador could not have known the real state of affairs.

Mary Ward and some of the members were now on religious territory, for their Bishop was also their secular overlord. That was true of Liège and, some years later, of Cologne and Trier; it was the case in Rome, too. But the Englishwomen had grown up in a country without any ecclesiastical hierarchy, and certainly without any prince bishops. They probably did not grasp − it sounds ironic − the dangers that this implied for their community.

The Plan of the Institute 'Ratio Instituti'

1616−1617

Sources − expansion of the 'Schola Beatae Mariae' Plan − teaching and education of girls and 'other works which are needed by the church' − alteration of structures of the Institute in comparison with earlier Plans

It has already been shown that the confirmation of the Institute on the basis of the Schola Beatae Mariae was not permitted by the Congregation of the Council, and that the Bishop of St Omer's 'Relatio' had no success.

Once again a new structure was sought for the Institute. Neither the author nor the time and place of compilation of 'Ratio Instituti' are known. The manuscript has survived in copied form. It reveals a gap in the text which has been corrected though only partially. This Plan too has found its way into the archives of the General of the Society of Jesus in Rome.[41]

First, the contents:-

> The beginning was taken word for word from the 'Schola Beatae Mariae', and offers the usual reasons for founding the Institute: women too should help in the conversion of England. English women in convents on the Continent of course prayed for this, but they intended a 'mixed form of life' like that of the women in the early Church. They devoted themselves to the salvation of their own souls and to the christian teaching and education of children, and other works needed by the Church. Here there is already a deviation from the 'Schola Beatae Mariae' and more of a trend towards the Bishop of St Omer's 'Relatio'.

Then follows an appreciable change from the 'Schola Beatae Mariae': after Profession these Englishwomen take an additional vow, placing their Institute solely under the Pope. They would have no enclosure, wear no habit, and have no prescribed form of penance. They educated girls to lead a christian life by their good example and religious practices and prepared them for life in an Order or a devout life in the world.

Unsuitable members, or such as caused unrest, could be sent away even after Profession. Then followed the division of the community into four degrees:

1. The novices (novitiae) who, after two years' probation, were to take the three simple vows.
2. The lay sisters (adiutrices).
3. The teachers (magistrae). From members of this degree the chief superior would choose the holders of higher office.
4. The professed (professae). After further probation, these would take solemn and public vows with the addition of private vows. For example, never to change anything in the Institute, to allow no dependence on anyone for the Institute except the Pope, and to devote themselves to the education of girls.
    After Profession, all members are religious (religiosae) and are subject by obedience to the Chief Superior. She can dismiss members or determine on their different degrees and offices.

After which follows the statement about vows in the Institute, and the request for confirmation of the way of life they follow, for the consolation of those who have accepted this way, and for the greater encouragement of those who have devoted their life to work in England. Almost as an appendage, as it were, comes the controversial activity of the members in England. The apparently unsolicited request for confirmation inserted into the text at this point was to lead into the subject:

> In England, women have joined the way of life of these English women (quae nobis in hoc vitae cursu sese adiungent) − thus thinks the author − in order to help catholics. There are some (alias nonullas) partly members of the Institute (partim ex nostris), partly externs, (partim externis), who have bound themselves by vow and work with members of the Institute. They provide children to be educated by the community in St Omer; they prepare girls for life in religious Orders and try to protect others from the danger of heresy. 'Good God!' exclaims the author, 'what useful instruments for gaining souls!'

Only then, after this almost embarrassed exposé of their effectiveness in England, does a petition for confirmation of the Institute by the Pope come sidling in. Here the author hesitates. May the congregation be adorned with the laurel wreath of a religious Order (religiosae vitae laureolo), or at least be crowned with the name of a Pius Institute (saltem Pii Instituti nomine coronetur)? However, should the Pope doubt the permanency of the congregation, might he at least approve the members and allow them to be regarded as women religious at the hour of their death? Note the gradual diminution of favours requested. In conclusion there is a request for an unspecified indulgence which may extend to those who work as members of the Institute but do not belong to the congregation (iis quae cum laboribus nostris et ipse laborantes concurrunt, etiam si corporis nostri membra non sint). Those were helpers in England. The Plan 'Schola Beatae Mariae' was known to the unnamed author of the 'Ratio Instituti'. After the wholesale adoption of its first three passages, the 'Ratio Instituti' departs clearly from the earlier Plan, and in certain points comes closer to the 'Formula Instituti' of the Society of Jesus. It deals with three central points, especially:

1. The government of the Institute.
2. The activity of the members in England.
3. The status of the Institute.

1. The government of the Institute.
The 'Schola Beatae Mariae' envisaged an episcopal Pius Institute. The Bishop approved the rule, the members made their vows into his hands and the choice of superior was dependent upon his approval. In the 'Relatio', the Bishop of St Omer had been commissioned as intermediary between the growing Institute and the Pope. In this

draft, he is not concerned, admittedly, with interior matters of the community but he was their protector and defender. Only the Rule was to be approved by him. In the 'Ratio Instituti' on the other hand, the powers of the Chief Superior were precisely outlined, she admitted members to profession, to the different degrees; she appointed superiors and others in office, and could dismiss unsuitable members. Hers was the highest authority, and she was subordinate to the Pope.

2. *Activity in England.*

The 'Schola Beatae Mariae' allowed the members of the Institute to educate girls both in England and abroad, but combined this with a fourth vow binding them to this work. The 'Relatio' reported in detail the active apostolate among adults in England, but hardly recognized a connection between the members in England and the Institute in St Omer; they even elected their own superior. True, the Chief Superior could summon members to St Omer, but there was no mention of new members from St Omer for the English mission.

The 'Ratio Instituti' is appreciably more cautious. Alongside the teaching and educational work there is also mention of such activities as will be found good, if opportune, for the greater glory of God and the expansion of the Roman Catholic Church. Later in the text, the 'Ratio Instituti' recognizes the active apostolate in England but connects this vaquely to the Institute in St Omer. It is precisely for these that the same indulgences and approval of the Pope are requested.

3. *The status of the Institute.*

The 'Schola Beatae Mariae' does not name the status of the Institute expressly, but one may conclude that a Pius Institute was intended. It has been seen that the first draft of the Petition expressly requested confirmation as a Pius Institute; in the second draft, only the confirmation of the members' way of life. It was also remarked that even this particular request was ignored in the answer of the Congregation of the Council. Even in the Bishop of St Omer's 'Relatio', the name of the Institute was passed over.

The 'Ratio Instituti' expresses itself cautiously, even awkwardly. The Institute would like to be confirmed as an Order or as a Pius Institute, or at least that its members be accounted as women religious on their deathbed.

A world of uncertainty lies in these three different concepts.

This Plan for the Institute must have been unsuccessful too. At all events, it was given no mention in the sources that have come down to us. It was probably not even shown to Bishop Blaes, for in 1617 he made a distinct polarization between the English women in St Omer, whom he had taken under his wing as a fledgling Order, and those members who had left his diocese. This is legally correct, but it must be remembered that Bishop Blaes made no mention of the Englishwomen in England. Most Jesuits must have rejected the 'Ratio Instituti' just as they had disapproved of the 'Schola Beatae Mariae'.

And the members themselves? For the first time their collaboration is shown in this Plan. At least, the 'Ratio Instituti' and the solemn promise belonging to it are written in the same hand, doubtless by a member of the Institute.

But Mary Ward, and with her, those members who had whole-heartedly followed the 'first estate' of the Ignatian Institute, declined this Plan also; her letter to Fr Tomson in 1619[42] is incomprehensible otherwise.

The 'Ratio Instituti' did indeed concede to the members their apostolate in England, and it emphasized the independence of the Institute, which was to be divided into four degrees – three broad concessions – but priority was given to activity in school and education. That both spheres of work were of equal value for the entire Institute, as was written into the Formula Instituti of the Society of Jesus, would never be conceded to the Englishwomen. Admittedly, the 'Ratio Instituti' was more inclined to the 'Formula Instituti', but that did not imply the 'matter and the manner' of the Society of Jesus and it did not even grant the Institute a name. It may have been during this time that Mary Ward said the following words to the community, which are given here in Fridl's eighteenth century translation: 'No one can do me greater pleasure than by being especially devout on the holy feast days of Jesus and the holy father St Ignatius; on other particular feast days I know well that you will be devout.'[43]

As with the other Plans, we can assume that it was an English Jesuit who was the author. Who else would have known the Formula Instituti of the Jesuits so well that he could go into details without revealing the whole text? Who else had the text of the 'Schola Beatae Mariae' at his disposal? Again, in the 'Ratio Instituti' there was, for the first time, a mention of constitutions for the Institute. Whether this Plan was written in St Omer or in Liège can no longer be established. It cannot be ruled out that the author should be sought in Louvain. Many facts point in that direction. There will be opportunity to clarify this in the next years of the Institute's history.

The date of compilation for the 'Ratio Instituti' can be fixed as 1616–17. It states that the members had already been active for seven years. Reckoning the beginning and end of the year by this number, we come to 1610. It must not be forgotten that all those who occupied themselves in drafting Plans for the Institute ignored its English origins, and counted only the St Omer foundation as valid. It is not difficult to guess where it was written − St Omer − but that is not surprising. Members of the Institute had probably been in Liège since December, 1616, but one can hardly consider their stay in Mont St Martin as a foundation. They undertook no activity, or at least nothing worthy of the name. They had neither episcopal nor civil approval to do so. For the time being they were simply guests in the city of Liège.

The Civil Contract

1616−1617

The contract: stronger binding of the members to the General Superior by means of an additional promise − its aim: solidarity of the congregation

Fear of the dissolution of the Institute is clearly evident in certain decisions of the 'Ratio Instituti'. It is not by chance that a clause about dismissal of insubordinate members was inserted, nor the promise to bind the members to the Institute and to the General Superior.

This most recent plan of the Institute reveals the gradually growing unrest among the members, which Fr Lee had warned them might happen and which, increased by financial pressures, was to come to a head in Liège a few years later. To guard against such a possibility, a 'Civil Contract' was drawn up. This has come down to us in two drafts from a later date.

The short, Italian version[44] was probably written in 1622, the longer English form probably before 1625.[45] It was certainly introduced before this.

The years 1615 and 1616 were particularly critical for the Institute. Attacks were made against the members and their manner of life; their Institute was censured. Attempts by the English Jesuits and the Bishop of St Omer to change the Institute into a Pium Institutum and to limit its sphere of action to the education and teaching of English girls cannot have escaped the notice of many of its members. It is more than understandable, therefore, that the members tried to find some means of anchoring themselves more tightly to the structure of the Institute.

Whether the idea of such a contract came from Mary Ward herself or was proposed by friends within the Society of Jesus it is no longer possible to judge. Certainly consultation must have taken place between the head of the Institute and men who were theologically trained. Other congregations had similar contracts, like the Filles de Notre Dame des Anges in Valenciennes[46] or the Ursulines in Dijon.[47]

Mary Ward certainly did not think of establishing a civil contract constitutionally; it was to be binding only until the confirmation of the Institute. That can be seen from the text. That is probably why other sources have remained silent about it. According to Canon Law, such a contract had no validity except in foro interno, in conscience. For reasons of civil rights, as for example the inheritance of a property or the right of the Institute to dismiss a member, it would probably not have been determinative, because of the insecure situation of the Institute.

Solemnly formulated, the contract contains the promise of each individual to be true to her vocation in that way of life of the Institute (course), to which she had dedicated herself to God. Union with God and gratitude to Superiors and the company for accepting her, and for her formation in the noviceship, as well as the spirit and practice of the company, are a duty for her. For these reasons, and from a desire that this work of God should be brought to maturity and perfection in her through confirmation by the Apostolic See, she makes this contract with the Chief Superior and the whole company, and promises to desire to remain in it, despite any opposition and difficulties that may occur. In obedience, she will endeavour to serve the company in unity and subordination and never seek to be freed from this agreement, until God should grant confirmation of this Institute, and she could renew her vows. Any attempt to influence other members to leave, or encourage them to harm the company, she would regard as a great evil, as the hope of confirmation would thus be damaged. The contract was valid for the time of her stay in the Company, and, in the event of her dismissal would be annulled.

It is doubtful if all the members of the Institute made this civil contract. Such a decision could have led to the healthy elimination of demoralising forces. But perhaps it was taken by the professed only who, as foreseen in the 'Ratio Instituti', may have been allowed to take other vows after solemn professsion, according to their choice. That could be a plausible explanation of the clashes in 1619 in Liège, which did indeed turn into a disturbance, the central figure of which was the lay Sister Praxedis. Judging from documentary material, during those years of great tension a concerted stand was taken by both the houses, in St Omer and Liège.

Even if the Civil Contract had been a private agreement and carried no obligations as far as Canon Law was concerned, one must remember that for the most part, it was young Englishwomen who made this contract with the Institute and its Superior; they were people whose forefathers and followers had made their pledge of fealty to their King as the head of their country, and had a very clear perception of the concept of loyalty. We have already seen how Mary Ward had valued her vow of obedience to Fr Lee, even when, after her 1611 vision, he could not face the opposition of his fellow Jesuits. There were difficulties ahead for these women when the Curia in Rome suppressed their houses − not the Institute at first − and declared their vows null and void. To anticipate, the Englishwomen then answered that they were bound to the Institute and to their Superior by a promise.

Recollection Days

1616

Some of Mary Ward's notes on prayer

Among this mass of documentation, almost swamped between grave decisions and happenings which piled up one after another, there are some notes in Mary Ward's clear, uncomplicated writing. They consist of two double pages.[48] Some thoughts are headed 'Cloasing days,1616', but it is not certain if she recorded them in St Omer or Liège.

In the summer of 1616 Mary Ward was in Spa, so undoubtedly close to Liège. She probably returned to St Omer and travelled back to Liège at the end of November. According to the English Vita,[49] she made a detour by Brussels where she had an audience with the Infanta. In these notes she talks of her confessor and her difficulty in reaching him, which would seem to point to Liège, where the house on Mont St Martin and the Jesuit novitiate that was being built were at some little distance from one another, which did not apply to St Omer. However, that is unimportant for her train of thought.

The second double page is headed 'When one has offended Him very much' and dated Saturday, 9th July, 1616 the date of a confession day.

As much as possible, this woman graced with a life of mystical prayer, withdrew again and again interiorly in order to pray and turn to God in stillness. Without this source of strength her strivings towards holiness would have been impossible and the burden of her task unbearable.

She once said to the community in St Omer, 'Then I shall desire to unite myself to God more and more, and you will give me leave to live secretly in another house'.[50] By this she must have meant one of the houses of the scattered members living in England, for in this early time of the Institute there was no other house on the continent except St Omer, and absolutely none where she could have lived secretly. The notes sound curiously like a monologue, as though she were communing with herself. Often in the day, she continues, she is within a hair's-breadth of falling into the danger of sin, but by God's goodness and providence is held back.[51] This certainly leaves an awe of grave sin in her soul - there it is again, fear − but humility and trust as well. And these in turn lead to a 'clear dependence on

God (a more evident dependencie upon God) without which no one could exist a moment.'

Trust in her own power has gone. When she hears of the grave faults of others, she feels impelled to turn to God. She knows that she would have done the same without his helping grace. This conviction of her own weakness was always present. She was not surprised at the sinfulness of others, but indeed about God's goodness to her own poverty of spirit. And then comes a particularly characteristic sentence: 'I am so cowardly that I think I would not for anything have past times and occasions again.'[52] But the past certainly held beauty too, and value and grace and fulfilment. All this vanishes from her memory when faced with the danger of sin.

She mentions cowardice, which is probably not the right word. All the same, every hour and every moment holds within itself the possibility of the same dangers. One could perhaps insert the words 'horror of evil', the evil that was seen and experienced as a reality and which had remained with her, clinging to her.

We need only recall her meeting with Alice Wright and immediately the cry of jubilation breaks out: 'O my Lord, how liberal you are and how rich are they to whom you vouchsafe to be a friend.'[53] In those days of stock-taking, she confessed daily. How should an observer today regard the relentless clarity with which God balanced the weight of her faults and omissions on the scales of her refined conscience?

Slowness in rejecting evil and negligence left her with an after-taste of deep sinfulness. Lack of trust in God, feeling of loneliness and indecisiveness and several other weaknesses of character oppressed her soul. After absolution came peace. Anticipated difficulties did not trouble her any more, she had clear insight over the present and the future. Everything had slipped back into its proper place. Release meant freedom. Desires remained desires, bound up with an inner efficacy and a readiness to fulfil them, but without anxiety. Adversities were still dreaded but without fear; in equanimity of soul and in surrender to everything that might happen, and in peaceful trust that God's will might really come to reality, in that she reposed, free and satisfied.

Only one thing was missing, she thought. Those who love God have no assurance that they do love him. Probably by this she meant the certainty of loving God enough, and there was always a desire and longing within her to do whatever would please him. The more she did, the greater her uncertainty that she was really living in accordance with his will.[54]

This attitude gave her no new insights as to what or how things should be done. It simply showed her the reality of the present situation and her complete abandonment to God, her readiness to do everything, dependent on nothing else, desiring nothing else but to love him.

The sole anguish that remained was the uncertainty of not loving him enough.

She no longer had any inclination or desire for vain renown. Conscious of her sinfulness, she recognised her inability to imagine the state of those who were called saints.

From these words it becomes evident that her whole life, her prayer, her plans, her many arduous journeys and certainly her bodily frailty, were 'acts gracefull to Him'. We shall see again and again how 'quickly' Mary Ward lived. But none of her negotiations and none of her thoughts were empty activity. She had, on the contrary, the uncertainty of those who love and who carry with them always as an insatiable longing the awareness of the inadequacy of their measure of love.

Notes

1. The literature about Liège is extensive. A good summary of its history including the most important texts is given by Jean Lejeune, La Principauté de Liège, Liège 1949. Especially pp. 135–161: le temps des prince de Bavière (1581–1723).

2. Bishops Ernst (1581–1612), Ferdinand (1612–1560), Maximilian Heinrich (1650–1688) and Joseph Klemens (1694–1723).

3. E. Podlach, Gesch. d. Erzdiözese Koln, Mainz 1879, S. 418–431; K. Schafmeister, Herzog Ferdinand von Bayern, Erzbischof von Köln als Kurfürst von Münster, Diss. Münster, Haselünne 1912; R. Schwarz, Personal-und Amtsdaten der Kölner Erzbischofe 1500–1800, Diss. Königsberg, Köln 1913, S.16–19; P. Weiler, Die kirchl. Reform im Erzbistum Köln (1583–1615) = Reformationsgeschichtliche Studien und Texte 56–57, Münster/W 1931, S. 150–154; A. Franzen, Der Widerraufbau des kirchl. Lebens im Erzbistum Köln unter Ferdinand von Bayern, Erzbischof von Köln = Ebzend., Heft I, Münster/W 1941. ABD. Bd. 6, S. 691–697, and Hier Cath. Bd. IV, S. 156, 203, 219, 246 und 270. For information about Belgian writings, see Lejeune, under note 1.

4. For Conrad Blisia and Nicolas Plenevaulx, C. de Borman, Les Avocats de la Court Spirituelle de Liège de 1604–1794 = Bull. de l'Inst. archéolog. Liégeois XXI/1888, p. 159–236.

5. Etienne Hélin, La demographie de Liège aux XVII et XVIIIe.siècles-Académie Royale de Belgique, classe des lettres et des sciences morales et politiques Mémoires LVI, Fasc. 4, Brussels 1963, p. 131.

6. ibid. p. 304.

7. ibid. p. 62.

8. Théodore Gobert, Liège á travers les âges II, Brussels 1975, Chronologie des Bourgmestres de Liège, p. 585–601.

9. Edouard Poncelet, Les bons métiers de la cité de Liège = Bull. der l'Inst. Archéolol. Liégois 28/1899, p. 1–219, especially p. 79–80 and p. 216; George Hansotte, Règlements et privilèges des XXXII métiers de la cité de Liège, Fasc. I, Les Fèvres, Liège, 1950, p. 14–16.

10. Joseph Brassine, Les Jésuites anglais de Liège et leur orphèverie = Bull. de la Soc. d'Art et d'Hist. du Diocèse de Liège XXXIII/1947, p. 19–91.

11. The Liège convents are on Blaeu's plan of the town, engraved in 1627.

12. Henri Dessart, la Visite du Diocèse de Liège par le Nonce Antoine Albergati (1613–1614) = Bull. de la Commission Royale d'Histoire 114/1949, p. 1–135; Wolfgang Reinhard, Nuntius Antonio Albergati = Nuntiature's reports from Germany V/I, ?. Half-volume. In his reports of 22nd

January, 1612 and 7th June 1613, both addressed to Cardinal Borghese, the Nuntius writes about the scandalous state of convents of women. See Nr. 587, p. 558–562, and Nr. 824, p. 804–805.

13. Dessart, loc. cit., p. 13.
14. Théodore Gobert, Liège à travers les âges, vol. VIII, Les rues de Liège. Vol. II, Brussels, 1977, p. 209 ff. and René Bragard, Vues anciennes d'églises Liégeoises d'après un manuscrit de 1584–1586 = Bull. et chronique de la Société Royale. Le Vieux Liège, VII (1971–1975), Liège 1976, p. 209–213.
15. Dean Jean Bertho was probably related to Widow Jeanne Gal, nee Bertho, the main creditor of the Englishwoman who fell heavily into debt some years after they had settled in Liège. Lists of the elders of the Chapter of Saint-Martin in Liège = Leodium, chronique mensuelle de la société d'Art et d'Histoire du diocèse de Liège 1907, p. 25–31, and Liste des Prévôts de la collégiale de Saint-Martin à Liège, ibid. p. 32–35. At the Visitation of 1613 the Nuntius objected to the – probably costly – dress of the Canons of Saint-Martin, however these appealed to their privileges. Dessart, La visite du Diocèse de Liège par le nonce Antoine Albergati (1613–1614) = Bull. de la Comm. Royale d'Histoire 114/1949, p. 133.ff.
16. Thénis was an alias for Johannes Rillas. The extract of his will was recorded in Clausulae extractae ex libro testamentorum B concernentes legata pia facta ecclesiae collegiatae sancti Leodiensis ab anno 1510 usque ad annum 1594, ff. 25v.–26r. AE Liège Collegiale de Saint-Martin Nr. 84. As is evident, extracts of more recent date were in this handwriting. Thénis gave the church of Saint-Martin two paintings for the high altar and 22 Brabant guilders for an anniversary.
17. Gobert, loc. cit. p. 43–46.
18. On 22nd June, 1629 The Englishwomen were granted a burial place in the church by the Chapter of the Collegiate Church of Saint-Martin. It is to be queried if they ever made use of it. No sign or memorial plaque or inscription is to be found. AE Liège, Collégiale Saint-Martin 60, f. 52v.
19. AE Liège, Jésuites Anglais 1, Registre concernant les Pères Jésuites Anglais Nr. 1. pp. 1–8.
20. ibid. Nr. 12. pp. 41–48 and Nr. 13, pp. 49–56.
21. ibid. Nr. 15, pp. 57–59 and Nr. 16, pp. 60–63.
22. ibid. Nr. 24, pp. 91–92.
23. Ambassador Dudley Carleton to Secretary of State Ralph Winwood, 2nd August 1616, Albin Body Extraits des lettres du chevalier Dudley Carleton = Bull. de l'Inst. Archéolog. Liégeois XXVII/1898, p. 7–9.
24. Jos. Brassine. Les Jésuites Anglais et leur orphèverie = Bull. de la Soc. d'Art et d'Hist. du Diocèse de Liège XXXIII/1947, p. 30ff; Body loc. cit. p. 12.
25. Registre Nr. 11, pp. 38–39.
26. ibid. Nr. 33, pp. 131–136.
27. d.s. fl. 6,400 -fl 400 Interest, Jesuit Coll., Lille Register, pp. 233–234.
    3. April fl.3.000 -fl 200 Interest, Catherine de Gré. (Widow Lancenotte), ibid. p. 225 (20th April).
    21. April fl.2,800 -f 200 Interest, Jean Woet, ibid, pp. 155–8, Nr. 37.
    7. August fl.3,000 -f 200 Interest, Nicolas Rave, ibid. pp. 102–7, Nr. 29.
    16. August fl.6,400 -f 400 Interest, Jesuit College, Maubeuge, ibid, pp. 234–5.
    31. August fl.4.000 -fl 250 Interest, Jesuit College, Namur ibid pp. 237–9.
    fl.25,600-fl 1,650 Interest
    + fl.9000-fl 750 Interest, already borrowed.
    Altogether fl 34.600–fl 12.220 Interest.

28. Barbara Ward. out of the 2nd paper, Instit. Arch. Munich.
29. On 29th(!) February 1625, the Englishwomen also wrote to Cardinal Scipione Borghese about their foundations in Liège, Cologne and Trier mentioning their growing numbers and the invitation from the citizens of the town. Letter Nr. 28, Inst. Arch. Munich. The same text was used in the paper of 25th March, 1629. AV Rome, Miscell. Arm. III.37. ff. 213r–215r.
30. Vita E, f. 19r.
31. Recueil Historique III, p. 40, AM Saint-Omer, Ms. 808.
32. Annales de la Ville de Saint-Omer II, pp. 143–143, AM Saint-Omer, Ms. 1358.
33. Thus the English Ambassador in The Hague, Dudley Carleton, to Secretary of State Ralph Winwood on 12th August, 1616, HMC thirteenth Report, Appendix Part II, the Mss. of his Grace the Duke of Portland preserved at Welbeck Abbey, II, London, 1893, p. 23.
34. Of the 59 chronicles used, 35 manuscripts describe the arrival of the Englishwomen, or their stay in Liège, even if briefly and inexactly.
35. Giles Gryte, OSB was professed in 1614 and nine years later was Prior of the Abbey of Saint-Jacques in Liège. He was engaged in the early history of his monastery and in 1660 planned a chronicle of the bishops of Tongres and Liège, of which he was able to make only a sketch up to 1380. Dom Ursmer Berlière, Monasticon Belge II, Province de Liège, Liège 1928, p. 28, note 5. and Silv. Balau, La Bibliothèque de l'Abbaye de Saint-Jacques à Liège = Compte-rendu des séances de la Commission Royale d'Histoire ou Recueil de ses Bulletins 71/1902, p. 36.
36. Sir Dudley Carleton (1573–1632) was, as secretary to the Earl of Northumberland, cognisant of the circumstances of catholics abroad. He was arrested at the time of the Gunpowder Plot on suspicion of having taken part in it, but later released. He was subsequently accepted into the diplomatic service. He was first ambassador in Venice and then 1616–1625, in The Hague. DNB, III, 996–999.
37. as above, note 33.
38. Sir Ralph Winwood (1563?–1617), Ambassador in The Hague 1614–1617, Secretary of State. His hatred of catholics resulted in acts of political imprudence. DNB 21, p. 704–707.
39. On 2nd February, 1617, BV Rome, Fondo Capponi 47, f. 74rv.
40. as above, note 33, p. 15.
41. ARSI Rome, Anglia 21/II pp. 675–685.
42. PB pp. 39–45, Inst. Arch. Munich.
43. Fridl II, p. 91. Nr. 482, from Allocutiones f.140.
44. BV Rome, Fondo Capponi 47, f. 40rv.
45. WA London, vol. 19, 1625, 1625, to May, Nr. 52, p. 155. The dating emerges from the comments: marginal, above: A coppey of the Inglishe Jesuitisses vowe to Mistriss Marye Ward, who they call Mother Cheefe Superior. marginal, left: I had this on condition to showe yt to none but to my Lord of Chalcedon and to one other. So I praye, showe yt none but use it for publishe occation! The "Lord of Chalcedon" was probably Richard Smith, who had been consecrated as titular bishop of Chalcedon in 1624.
    Marginal, below: Cardinal Melino had charge of this busines, and commandment to bidd them quite dissolve their Companye and not to live togeather, none to weare anye particular habitt, nor to teache anye more schooles. This last pointe onlye is observed, the other not yet. Hee have oft toulde mee yt was an ill councelor that advised that women to come out of Englande, and that hee never liked this Institute. The Jesuitesses have one Mr Lee a prieste, Mr Lanier, Father Robert Kempe ther commendaters. On 12 November 1625 the Congregation of Bishops and Regulars published the decree evicting the Englishwomen from their house. AV Rome, Sacra Congr.

Episc. et Regul. Lettere G-O, Anno 1625.

46. Bibl. Publique de la Ville Valenciennes ms 75/171, ff. 9r – 10v.

47. J. Morey, Anne de Xainctonge I, Paris/Besancon 1892, p. 245.

48. VP/C 1 and 2 Inst. Arch. Munich.

49. Vita E, f. 19r.

50. "I shall then desire to unit me self to God more/and/more and you will give me leave to live secretly in an other house." Fridl Tugenschul II, p. 262, Nr. 607, from Libellus Colloquiorum, f. 13. Fridl repeats the word "more". Perhaps the original had "more and more", which makes better sense.

51. "Fivety tims a day com as yt wear within a hear briethe of failing both into great and lesser sinnes, yet God's mear goodness and providence brought backe as yt wear to my formere stat without hurt." VP/c 1, Inst. Arch. Munich.

52. "I am so cowardly that I me thinkes I would not for anie thinge have the time and occationes past now to come."

53. "O my Lord how liberall ar you and how rich are they to whom you will voutsafe to be a frind."

54. "Onely in this they feel a want, that they canot be certayn that they love Him; and so they endevor and desires to do some acts grateful to Him, and the more they do, the greater ther uncertaynty whether in His sight they do in deed love Him."

XIV

THE BENEFACTORS

The Bishop of St Omer's Recommendations
2nd and 10th February, 1617

Recommendation to the Bishop of Liège for the members who had moved – reasons for this – open letter on notification of Rome's decision – Laudatio for the Englishwomen in St Omer

At the beginning of 1617 the Institute appeared to consist of three parts, judging by externals. First, the members in England. Anne Gage had been made superior there by Mary Ward, who frequently travelled across and stayed for some time. Second, the foundation in St Omer, soon to experience its decline. Third, the small group which had been living in Liège since the end of 1616, for the time being with verbal permission only from the Prince Bishop, and no similar indication from the town. These fifteen women were under Mary Ward's personal direction. On 2nd February, 1617, Bishop Blaes of St Omer wrote a letter of recommendation to the Bishop of Liège about those of the Institute who had moved into his area.[1] The letter is in the warmest of terms, but requires closer examination.

The Englishwomen in St Omer, begins the Bishop, had asked him to recommend those members of their community who had travelled to Liège for reasons of health. It was not because Emperor Mathias had given them permission to have a house there, nor because they were awaiting dowries for members who had entered, as was rumoured in St Omer,[2] but for reasons of health, as the baths at Spa were in the neighbourhood. We can hardly imagine, however, that all fifteen or sixteen members of the Institute needed to take the waters, especially as most of them were young. All the same, the reason given did correspond to the truth for some of the Englishwomen. The English Ambassador in 1616[3] and the traveller Bergeron in 1619[4] had seen several of them in Spa. The decisive factor was, as has been seen, the founding of a new house. But could the Bishop of St Omer announce that to one who was a brother in office in a letter which was to be pre-filtered by subordinates in

Liège before reaching its destination, his desk? The Englishwomen were a congregation similar to an Order, and foreigners, to boot. Bishop Blaes had been Bishop of Namur before being transferred to St Omer and had a fair understanding of the Prince Bishop's diocese, and knew that the women would not immediately receive permission to stay. The town was full of convents. It would take years before they were accepted by the citizens. The Bishop's letter is therefore to be taken as a hasty note, for those members who had been recommended the previous autumn by the Archbishop of Cologne[5] were actually in Liège already.

There were three reasons for the Bishop of St Omer's letter to Liège. First, the exemplary life-style of the Englishwomen in his town, who enjoyed the esteem of the inhabitants; secondly, the Pope's injunction, which had entrusted the congregation to him a short time before; thirdly, the conviction that by writing this letter he would be doing a service to the Bishop of Liège. The English-women, he continued, were thoroughly deserving of the Prince's protection and favour, as they led praiseworthy lives and devoted themselves to teaching English girls. It was precisely this work that Bishop Ferdinand might wish to promote, thought Bishop Blaes, so that the noble daughters of Liège, too, might have the benefit of a good education from these capable foreigners. If the Prince Bishop were in his town of Liège, continued Bishop Blaes, he could assure himself personally of the virtues and the excellence of the manner of life of these women, especially that of their superior, Mary Ward.

These words should be sufficient to prove the Bishop of St Omer's connection with the Bishop of Liège.

The opening of the letter leaves one with a slightly uneasy impression. The Englishwomen in St Omer have asked their Bishop for a recommendation for those who have left. So he was not writing on his own initiative, otherwise he would have given them his recommendation to take with them, which evidently he had not. One consoling feature of this is the solidarity existing between the communities in St Omer and Liège. A week later, on 10th February [6] the Bishop once more picked up his quill, this time for the Englishwomen in his own town. This letter is of a quite different character. He again chose the solemn form of an official, open letter with his own seal but his secretary's signature, for it was this letter that gave the information of Rome's decision. This too is worth a second glance. The decision of the Congregation of the Council may be recapitulated here briefly for the sake of the context: some Englishwomen, driven from their country by persecution and gathered together as a community out of zeal for the catholic faith had, a short time before, submitted a request to the Pope, asking him to recommend them to the Church authorities. The Cardinals of the Congregation of the Council had discharged themselves of the papal task of making a judgement in the matter by entrusting him, the Bishop of St Omer, with the care and protection of the Englishwomen. He wished to direct them more and more towards the status of a religious Order, so that their work could bear greater fruit and could thereby have the confirmation of their Institute considered by the Pope.

How did the Bishop now announce the Cardinals' somewhat cautious answer?

The Form of life of the Englishwomen in St Omer had pleased the Pope and the Cardinals to such an extent (adeo placuerit) it says here, as they perform their service of their neighbour in such a praiseworthy fashion (cum laude faciunt), that they wished to promote it. For this reason they had not only wished to recommend the Englishwomen (non solum commendatissimas esse voluerint), but above all (sed praecipuam) had placed them under the Bishop's protection so that in case of need, help could be offered them and there would be even more fruitful service from such a laudable Institute (tam laudabili Instituto). To this end, indulgences flowed to them from the Church's treasury.

In this letter, the Bishop was not simply taking them under his protection as he had done before, but in obedience to the Pope and the Cardinals. He was prepared, he went on, to help the ladies' every request. He was informing them and all other readers of this letter that while the Holy See was considering confirmation of their Institute, they could enjoy all the graces, privileges and protection of the Holy See such as religious communities (ordines religiosi) possessed before confirmation, and that those who wished to join in the works of this extremely useful Institute (utilissimo Instituto), would perform a work most pleasing to the Congregation and the Pope (rem gratissimam) and receive their reward from the Lord.

Had the Cardinals of the Congregation, or Pope Paul V for that matter, anticipated such emphasis, when they entrusted the Bishop of St Omer with the protection of the congregation, whose existence they barely acknowledged? However that may be, their empty phrases of one hundred and eighty-five words had turned into a genuine 'Laudatio', somewhat effusive maybe but as firm as a rock, because it was supported by a rescript from Rome which, if considerably simpler in form, could not be ignored out of existence. In the shadow of this 'Laudatio' lay the Bishop's recommendation for the Englishwomen in Liège, which had perhaps already reached the city on the Maas while the 'Laudatio' was being composed in St Omer. Nowhere would the dissimilarities between the Bishop's Pius Institute and the Ignatian Institute be more clearly marked than in these two letters from the Bishop of St Omer.

It is not known what attitude the members in St Omer took towards all this. We only know that in later years too they kept their eyes firmly on their foundress. It is strange that they, certainly not blessed with material possessions, were not to receive anything when the Bishop's will was opened after his death, (21.3.1618) although many other Orders and congregations were richly remembered.

The Institute in Fr Edward Burton SJ's opinion
Liège — first half of 1617

Fr Burton — his relationship with Mary Ward's Ignatian Institute and Sr Praxedis — his report — the sources — assessment

Not much is known about the second Procurator of the novitiate of the English Jesuits in Liège.

Edward Catcher, alias Burton, came from an Anglican family. He was born in London in 1584, so was almost the same age as Mary Ward. In 1606, he became a convert to the Catholic church and turned to the study of theology, which led him to Rome and Valladolid. Four years later he entered the Society of Jesus in Liège. He is said to have studied there and in Douai.[7] It is not certain if he had spent any time in St Omer, or had already been moved to Liège at the time of his appointment as procurator of the new novitiate. Fr Henry More, confessor of the English women in St Omer, can certainly be proved to have been procurator and minister of the house in Liège,[8] and on 4th August, 1617, Fr Burton took over Fr More's office.[9] He was still there up to spring, 1621. On 14th April of that year, for the first time, Fr Edward Rodney paid back some of the interest that was outstanding.[10] Fr Burton must have left Liège soon afterwards, working later on the English mission. He died on 13th March, 1623 or 1624 in London. It is most likely that Fr Burton came to know the Institute in Louvain. Fr Lessius worked there, and Fr Lee was there until the end of 1615. It can also be taken as certain that Fr Burton, then in his thirties and esteemed for his scholarship, heard the discussions that took place in Louvain regarding this new, independent Institute. He would certainly have given his opinion in such a circle. Fr Burton had been entrusted with setting up an English Pius Institute which, after the example of several Belgian congregations, was to have a school for girls from England. Certainly he, like his companions, rejected an Institute with an Ignatian emphasis.

The Englishwomen had long been in touch with this gifted Jesuit. A short note in the 'Liber Ruber' runs: 'The best way of hearing Mass is Fr Burton's'.[11]. He had probably written a treatise on the celebration of the Mass, or had given them sermons about it. The fact remains, his way was known and loved by the members in St Omer. So it is not by chance that this man replaced Fr More as procurator in August, 1617, after Mary Ward and some others of the Institute had moved to Liège. He had been their confessor in St Omer, too.

On his arrival in Liège, Fr Burton found Fr John Tomson a self-willed but extremely helpful Rector, whose heart was bigger than his purse. But the new procurator also found an empty cash box and burdensome debts. On another hill of the city, on Mont St Martin, about half an hour's walk away from the novitiate building, lived a group of English women who were preparing themselves for the religious life, encouraged by Fr Tomson.

Whether Fr Burton found their 'Supérieure' there too is not certain. Mary Ward, esteemed in some Jesuit circles and under fire from others, was in England between 21st July and 21st October, 1617. Fr Burton became the Englishwomen's confessor and came to value them. The relationship between the two communities was still untroubled, at least outwardly. But poverty overtook the Institute, and it is a treacherous companion. Parallel to the approaching difficulties, and perhaps hastened by them, disagreements developed within the community about the nature of their Institute. Fr Burton took the part of those members who wished to withdraw their congregation from full commitment to the Ignatian charism.

In 1619, just as the difficulties reached their climax and Mary Ward wrote to Fr Tomson[12] about the directions given her by God, she names Fr Burton as a supporter of Sister Praxedis. Shortly afterwards the procurator compiled the Plan, which recorded the alleged visions in a biography of this sister, but Fr General stopped its publication.[13] And this was the man whom the Provincial, Fr Heren had, in all good conscience sent to Liège, although he had given no evidence of expertise as a procurator.

Like his two far more gifted brother Jesuits, the famous university professors Lessius and Suarez, Fr Burton too picked up his pen and wrote a report, or rather a defence of the Institute about which there was such debate. Whether he was asked to do so, or if members actually shared in composing it, we do not know.

There is a transcript of his paper, written in a female hand, in the Collectio Prayana of the University Library in Budapest,[14] with no clue as to how it came there, or its date. It may possibly have been in the archives of the short-lived Institute in Pressburg. A second copy, in an unknown handwriting, is in the Westminster Archives in London,[15] which points to its use by the agents of the secular clergy in Rome. Some of the documents about Mary Ward and her Institute have a real Odyssey, and their position in a particular archive cannot be explained. Fr Burton was incontestably the author of the report.[16] It is more difficult to date it exactly. Fr Burton believed that the Institute was shortly to be confirmed by the Pope. He did not seriously think that this recognition would be for Mary Ward's Ignatian Institute, but for the Institute under

Bishop Blaes' protection. This seems to point to a time of composition shortly after Bishop Blaes' two recommendatory letters of 1617.

The contents of this well-constructed but rambling report can be dismissed briefly: it has been dealt with three times by one more competent to do so.[17] Fr Burton actually answered the same questions as Fr Lessius and Fr Suarez, and Grisar[18] rightly says that Fr Burton could never have approached the depth and coherence of the two preceding works, although his work could offer advantages. Fr Burton was faced with an Institute that was more starkly exposed to danger than that which Lessius and Suarez had known. Instead of several 'doubts' and 'objections', its opponents presented a united front of rejection. Fr Burton was fully competent to confront these.

For our reflections, it is not so much a question of Canon Law as this other question: which Institute did Fr Burton defend? How did he stand with regard to Mary Ward's Ignatian Institute? As with Lessius, Suarez and Bishop Blaes, we look in vain for a name for the congregation, or for a clear statement about their rule. Here too the Institute remains a 'Pium Institutum' which has a legal position with the approval of the Bishop of St Omer, and which is awaiting confirmation as an Order. As to its work, Fr Burton described this, as had been done so often before, as the education of girls. He recognised the pastoral work of the members of the Institute as a worthwhile task although, true to his times, he imposed greater restrictions. The Englishwomen should do this work humbly, with the help of prudent priests. In this, Fr Burton went beyond Lessius and the Bishop of St Omer, but he did not yet have the Institute of the 1611 Vision before his eyes, though he mentions its divine origin.

Much is reminiscent here of the 'Ratio Instituti', drafted shortly before. Fr Burton also referred to those helping in the demanding pastoral work for souls in England, who were not bound to the Institute by vows. Fr Burton dedicated the last passage to the ecclesiastical examination of his report. Fr Lessius could have put his signature to it with a clear conscience.

As with the 'Ratio Instituti', it must be stated here: the procurator's treatise conceded a good deal to the Institute, but in no way did it allow the Englishwomen a 'Society of Jesus'.

The Bishop of Liège's letter of protection

27th May, 1617

The Englishwomen and the town of Liège − Mary Ward's plea for protection for her novices from a housebreaker − safeguard for the ladies by the Bishop's council

It is not known how the Bishop of Liège, in Cologne, received the Bishop of St Omer's recommendation for the Englishwomen. In fact, it may never have reached him, but remained jammed in the filter of the bishop's chancellery in Liège. It is quite possible that it was taken as supplementary documentation to a meeting in Liège, perhaps by a Jesuit or some influential person. As far as we know there was no response from the Elector, nor any indication of his reaction; in any case it is most unlikely that one would have been given in writing. It is only towards the middle of the year, 27th May, 1617,[19] that there is any sign of contact.

This came about for a particular reason. Mary Ward had turned to the Bishop's Privy Council with a request. The members were peaceful inhabitants of the town, devoting themselves to God's service and desiring to perform good works for the furtherance of the church in England, if God wished to recall them there.[20] For this, seclusion was required, and assurance of protection against disturbers of the peace. However, the Master Cellarer, Giles David, infected with the plague from Ste.Marguerite,[21] had stolen into the Englishwomen's house. As can be imagined, this had shaken them greatly. In 1617 in Liège [22] the plague had claimed many victims. House-servants had removed the unfortunate man, who had at first defended himself with fisticuffs. No one knew exactly what it was he wanted from the Englishwomen.

The Bishop of Liège, or rather his Privy Council, as the letter was written in Liège, took the Englishwomen under his protection upon receiving this plea from the 'Supérieure', Mary Ward.[23]

The letter is headed 'Sauvegarde', and is to be understood as a promise of protection in the narrow sense. It is also a sign that the diocesan authorities in Liège accepted the presence of the Englishwomen, although official approval for their stay was not yet forthcoming.

Apart from the fact that the 'Sauvegarde' is proof of Mary Ward's presence in Liège,[24] it also gives two valuable indications as to the Institute's role in this town. If Mary Ward, who was extremely busy, totally occupied in the work of her Institute, requested protection for the seclusion and security of those living in the house on Mont St Martin, it undoubtedly meant that she wanted to ensure peace and quiet for a novitiate house.

The Englishwomen could not undertake work in the shape of a school or a house for boarders, as the building necessary for that was not yet available, but there would have been a suitable setting for a noviceship in the spacious house on Mont St Martin.

Something else is rather remarkable. These novices, these young Englishwomen, were educated for the pressing needs of their country, either for teaching and educating young English girls, or for the active apostolate on the English mission, 'quand il plairait au Seigneur Dieu de les rappeler.' There is a world of difference between this, and the contents of the Bishop of St Omer's recommendation, which had introduced the Englishwomen as teachers of children of the Belgian nobility.

Apparently it was left at that: good intentions, for not a single source gives information about the actual relationship of the Englishwomen with church or civil life in Liège. Language differences and perhaps also the customs of the country and, most of all, the exclusive orientation towards England were in many respects a brake on activities in Liège itself. There was, too, increasing poverty.

On 13th November, 1617[25] – hardly six months after they had moved into Liège – the Englishwomen had sent a request to the Chapter of the Collegiate Church of St Martin for financial help. They were looking for a guarantee of part of the Chapter's income as security for the rent payable to the owner of the house, Canon Michel de Merica. The Chapter did not show much enthusiasm in possibly becoming involved in future litigations, which could put their property at risk, and so refused help. It is not likely that this threatening omen would have come to the ears of the Bishop of Liège, but it was brought to the attention of the Bishop of St Omer. Four months before, on 21st July,[26] the English Ambassador in Brussels had been able to report to the Secretary of State in London that the English Jesuits in St Omer had run into debt, and were considering moving the college to another town. That the Englishwomen were also in debt and Mary Ward had even been legally prosecuted, but the affair had been settled by the Mayor of St Omer with the utmost secrecy. If this report is correct – the Ambassador had obtained it from a Flemish acquaintance – the debts of the members in St Omer could only be connected with the difficult situation of the Institute in Liège. There was no possible reason why the congregation in St Omer, which had been flourishing a short time before, should suddenly have become financially unstable. Not even possible outstanding payments for board or dowries could have reached such a total that they brought Mary Ward into danger of being taken to court. It will shortly be seen that the debts of the two houses, of St Omer and Liège, went in tandem. It was a clear if painful sign of their solidarity.

Fr John Tomson SJ and the Institute

1616–1621

Fr Tomson, builder of the English Jesuit novitiate house in Liège – his position in the Society – Fr Tomson and Mary Ward

His name was really John Gerard, but he had many an alias. In

Belgium he was known as John Tomson; he also received letters from the General of his Order in this name. He was the second son of Sir Thomas Gerard of Bryn in Lancashire and his wife Elizabeth, daughter of Sir John Port of Etwall, Derbyshire. His parents remained Catholic and consequently had to suffer under the government's laws.

John Tomson was born on 4th October, 1564 in Derbyshire. He was about twenty years older than Mary Ward. He began his studies in Oxford when he was eleven, but remained there only briefly, as he would have had to receive communion at Easter in an Anglican church. On 15th August, hardly twenty-two years old, he was accepted into the English College in Rome, received lower Orders there, and entered the Society in 1588. He was ordained in July, 1588 together with Fr Edward Oldcorne, later a martyr, and they returned to England together. Fr Tomson worked on the mission there in many dangerous situations until he was arrested in 1594, and then imprisoned in the notorious Clink prison in 1597. He was taken to the Tower in the April of the same year and had to endure the most appalling tortures in this ante-chamber of hell. His hands were crippled for the rest of his life, as he had been hung up by his wrists. With the co-operation of some friends, he managed to escape from the Tower, adventurously reaching freedom by sliding down a rope from the window of his cell. He stayed 'underground' for some years in England and then left on 3rd May,1606, shortly before Mary Ward. He stayed in St Omer for six weeks and it may be that he met her there, or had at least heard of her.[27] His health needed thorough convalescence and he was sent to Tivoli, but already by 1607 he is to be found as English Penitentiary at St Peter's in Rome. Two years later, 1609, he was ordered to Flanders. There he took part in founding the first novitiate for English Jesuits in Louvain. This experience, and certainly too his proved heroism, were the reasons his Superiors entrusted him a few years later with the founding of a noviceship in Liège. Perhaps, too, the agitation caused by the Ambassador in Brussels against the continuing presence of the refugees in the Infanta's lands – embarrassing for England – may have contributed to this. Historical accounts pass rather superficially over his activity in Liège. His fellow Jesuit, Fr Nathaniel Southwell writes in his 'Catalogus primorum Patrum'[28] that he built a house from its very foundations in a fine style, and that out of alms which he had collected from the four corners. This was very delicately put, for it has already been seen that the alms consisted for the most part of mortgages. As this foundation of the English Jesuits is, however, most closely bound together with the fate of the Englishwomen in Liège, it must be studied in greater detail.

Not all Jesuits were supporters of the idea of transferring the novitiate to Liège. The weak financial state of some colleges and certainly, too, anxiety lest the flourishing house in Louvain should lose influence as a result, may have played a part.

And by no means all the English Jesuits were friends of the Master Builder, Fr Tomson. It is not easy to understand why such a deserving and courageous man could have had so many enemies within his own Order. This certainly cannot be explained, or at least not totally explained, by the difficulties that were to come in Liège. One might perhaps detect a certain instability in his character. A glance at his course of studies shows that.[29] But he was not alone in his bird-of-passage life. Many of the English refugees could not find a permanent home on foreign soil. Moreover the Jesuits had then, and still have to reckon with being moved frequently. The structure and the sphere of work of their Order demands great flexibility of each individual. Was it the non-acceptance of his flight from the Tower that made him unpopular? He had escaped the agonising death of a martyr, but it was precisely for this that the young English Jesuits were being prepared in the Roman College. Perhaps the reason simply lies in his being what he was, with a certain penchant for adventure, and nonchalance, coupled with 'modern' views about the structure of the Society and the place of women.

Fr Tomson of course came to know the Institute and its members during his stay in Flanders. In one of his last talks to the Englishwomen in St Omer,[30] Fr Lee named Fr Owen and Fr Antony (Hoskins?) and a Fr G. in Louvain. We will not be far wrong if we see the name Gerard behind this last letter. These fathers mentioned by Fr Lee stood firmly and solidly behind the structure of the Institute as it had been described in the 'Schola Beatae Mariae'.

Many of his confrères could have come into collision with the new Rector's attitude. The opinion of his successor in Liège, Fr Henry Silisdon, to be sure a small-minded and gloomy character, cannot be ignored. He writes:[31] 'I see general fear among all our men, among those of ripe judgement, at the success of the administration of Fr Nelson (= Fr Tomson). I fear that his zeal will lead him too far, unless he has a companion who can restrain him; but I fear still more because I see him disinclined to have anyone near him who tends to make suggestions against his own zealous wishes.' Unfortunately, facts were to confirm this sombre analysis of his character.

We are well-informed, for the first time, about the number of workers and inhabitants of the house. Officials were frequently newly installed in the Society of Jesus. The first Procurator of the house, Fr Henry More, was at the same time Fr Minister. It may have been a reference to this friend of the Institute which Fr Silisdon made in the last passage of his opinion given above. As Socius to the Rector were: 1617 Fr William Anderson; 1618 Fr John Falkner, and 1620/21, Fr Michael Alford.[32]

Fr Tomson became Mary Ward's confessor and her spiritual director. Whether she had the same confidence in him which she had once had for Fr Lee, is very much to be questioned, but she showed great reverence towards him as her confessor. But that is another matter. As a more mature woman, she did not make a vow of obedience. God had led her to a state of self-assurance, an essential pre-requisite for carrying through the establishment of the Institute according to his commands.

Whether Fr Tomson really helped the young foundation of the Institute in Liège must be left with a huge question mark. He certainly intended to do so, with the best of intentions. However, he was not very fortunate as financial administrator and it was precisely in this area that the two houses, the novitiate of the English Jesuits, and the new Englishwomen's foundation, had close connections.

Thomas Sackville

Benefactor of the Jesuits in Belgium – doubtful benefactor of the Institute

Not much is known about Thomas Sackville, although he was a key figure in the drama of the Liège foundation. On 25th May, 1571,[33] he was born as the fourth son of the English Lord Treasurer, Thomas Sackville, 1st Earl of Dorset, and Cecily Baker. The family had gone over to the Anglican Church but Thomas Sackville Junior seems, for at least some time, to have been a member of the Catholic Church.

During 1591–2 he studied in Padua, stayed in Venice too, and distinguished himself in the war against the Turks. Back in England, he is mentioned in 1610 as a Recusant. He was on the Continent again in the next few years – in Paris, Brussels, and Louvain and was counted as a great promoter of Catholics, and a particular friend of the Jesuits. For example, he supported the Arras College in Paris,[34] a house for catholic writers, and encouraged several Orders with large monetary donations. In a report of 1622, the Rector of Douai College, Matthew Kellison, wrote to the Nuntius in Brussels that Sackville had donated 70,000 guilders to found the Novitiate of the English Jesuits in Louvain, and is prepared to be answerable for forty people. This enormous sum may not be correct; Kellison was not well-informed about details.[35] Nuntius Bentivoglio, too, speaks of the generous help of the English Count in a report to Rome in 1611.[36] Through that alone, Sackville was no stranger in curial circles. On 15th October, 1613, a Thomas Sackville Esq., received permission to stay on the Continent for three years, on condition that he did not visit Rome.[37] But he did. Already on 26th

January, 1615, (5th February, New Style),[38] Dudley Carleton, the Ambassador in The Hague, received a report from London. This said that Thomas Sackville had been kept back for some years in Padua. His machinations needed sharp watch, but because of his father's position he was exempt from retribution. How long Sackville remained in Italy this time is not clear, nor do we know if he went from there to St Omer, in order to go South again at the end of the year.

On 29th February, 1625[39] the Englishwomen wrote to Cardinal Borghese that they had sent to Rome the very learned Count Sackville, to whom several of them were related,[40] and whose manner of life was praiseworthy, in order that he might submit a Plan of their Institute.

In defiance of the English government's prohibition, Thomas Sackville reached the Eternal City towards the beginning of 1616; at least, he entered his name on 3rd January, 1616 in the Pilgrim Book of the English Hospice in Rome.[41] He may have stayed there until his business was completed, for he left the Hospice only on 22nd April, 1616.[42] How long he remained in the South, and whether he had other business to transact is unknown. Certainly he did not undertake this journey solely for the benefit of the Englishwomen. In an address, which from internal evidence can be placed in the December of 1617, Mary Ward mentioned Thomas Sackville, who is supposed to have been an advocate of the Institute with the Jesuits in St Omer and the Cardinals in Rome.[43]

Thomas Sackville played an enigmatic and probably, too, a treacherous part in the fate of the Englishwomen's house, and for the novitiate house of the English Jesuits in Liège. This will be reported on later in far more detail.

It seems that Sackville returned to England once again in 1617, but he is in Liège in 1618, and in 1620 he is proved to have been in Louvain. The later years of his life may have been spent in England, where he went back to the Anglican church[44] and in 1625, at an advanced age, married Anne, daughter of Sir Robert Johnson. Sackville died on 28th August, 1646, and lies in the family vault in the Sackville chapel in Withyham, Sussex.

This man's restless life tempts one to consider him an agent, or someone allotted a particular task. At first extremely wealthy, his means gradually ebbed away, at least during his time in the Spanish Netherlands and Liège. That was probably the main reason why the members of the Institute, who had been dependent on him in Liège, were in the end at the mercy of his debts. It will probably never be established how or through whom he came into contact with Fr Tomson and the Englishwomen in Liège. Most probably family connections indeed played a part, with the offices of friends playing a lesser or greater role.

Notes

1. The letter was copied several times. Authorized copy BV, Fondo Capponi 47 f. 74rv. On the back, a note in a woman's handwriting: From the Busshop of St Omers to the Busshop of Leig. Further copies, ARSI Rome, Anglia 32/I, ff. 34–35v; Arch. of the IBVM Generalate in Rome; StA Munich, Kl. Lit. Fasz. 432/1, Arch of the Archdioc. Munich/Freising, Munich, A 258 III, Maria Ward; StB Munich, Cgm 5393, pp. 218–220 in German and pp. 220–221 in Latin.

2. Hendricq, Recueil Historique III, p. 40, AM Saint-Omer, Ms 808, and Deneuville, Annales de la Ville de Saint-Omer II, pp. 143–143, ibid. Ms. 1358.

3. Ambassador Dudley Carleton to Secretary of State Ralph Winwood, 1st December 1616. HMC Thirteenth Report, Appendix Part II, the Mss of his Grace the Duke of Portland preserved at Welbeck Abbey, II, London 1983, p. 66–68.

4. H. Michelant, Voyage de Pierre Bergeron en Ardennes, Liège et Pays-Bas en 1619 = Publ. de la Soc. des Bibliophiles liégeois, Liège 1875, p. 103.

5. They were recommended there by two unnamed Jesuits. See above, p. 198.

6. This letter too has many copies. Authorized copy BV Fondo Capponi 47 f. 78. The text of this copy was written in the same hand which has often been met with, and which also wrote/copied the "Relatio" of the Bishop of St Omer. Further copies ARSI Rome, Angl. 32/I, ff. 32r, 33v; Univ. Bibl. Budapest, Coll. Prayana V,48, and a copy from a later date in StA Munich, Kl. 432/1 as also in StB Munich, Cgm 5393, pp. 216–218 in German.

7. J. Grisar SJ. Das Urteil des Lessius, Suarez und anderer "über den neuen Ordenstyp der Mary Ward = Gregorianum XXXVIII/1957, p. 671–672; ditto. Ein schwieriger Rechtsfall zwischen den Englischen Fraulein und den englishen Jesuiten in Liège. 1618–1630 = Archivum Historicum Societatis Jesus XXIX/1960, p. 264.

8. AE Liège, Couvent Jésuites, Anglais, Registre p. 225. s.n.

9. ibid, pp. 234–235. s.n.

10. ibid. pp. 111–113, Nr. 31.

11. LR. p. 281, Inst. Arch. Munich.

12. PB. pp. 39–45, Inst. Arch. Munich.

13. P. General Vitelleschi to Fr Rector Knott in Watten, 12th November 1662, ARSI Rome, Anglia, 1/I, ff.164v–165r.

14. UB Budapest, Collection Prayana V, 45.

15. WA London, Vol. 16, pp. 327–365.

16. Mary Ward to Winefrid Wigmore, Letter Nr. 27 of 3rd February, 1625 and Letter Nr. 29 of 6th February, as also Fr John Tomson to Henry Lee, 8th March 1627. Old papers, Inst. Arch. Munich.

17. See above, note 7 and J. Grisar, Die ersten Anklagen in Rom gegen das Institut Maria Wards (1622) = Miscellanea Historiae Pontificiae XXII/1959, p. 33–36.

18. Grisar, Urteil, p. 681.

19. The beginning of the letter is in form of a copy in AE Liège, Conseil Privé, Depêches 18, f. 112v. In the Second World War valuable archives were destroyed by bombing. This manuscript was among those lost. The transcription had been copied before the war during the lengthy collection of the widely-scattered historical material concerning Mary Ward. A reference to the letter is to be found in AE Liège, Inventaire Conseil Privé, Depêches 1612–1792, p. 326, of 27th May, 1617.

20. " ... s'applicquante aux services de Dieu en appordant touttes choses vertueuses pour l'augmentation de l'église de Dieu en Angleterre quand il plairat au Seigneur Dieu de les rappeler ... "

21. At that time a suburb of Liège, not far from Saint-Martin.

22. Concerning this, Nuntius Albergati's report, AV Rome, Fondo Borghese II, ff. 182, 208, 327, 333, 359.

23. It is not known if the request was made verbally or in writing; there is no written evidence remaining.

24. Mary Ward was also in Liège on 25th June. At that time the English Ambassador in Brussels, William Trumbull, asked Secretary of State Ralph Winwood if it were not possible to place an agent in Liège, who could observe the English Jesuits and Mary Ward (Mistress Warde their hand mayde). PRO London, SP 77/12, Part 3, ff. 370r–371v.

25. The request was conveyed by Canon Castris. AF Liège, Collégiale Saint-Martin 56, f. 181 v.

26. "And he (a Flemish informant) said moreover, that the matrone of the Englishe gentlewomen there had (not long since) ben ympleaded, condemned and served with an execution for matter of debte, but that it was soon smothered and composed by the governor and mayor of Saint Omers in secrett for the avoydeing of scandall and saveing of the said matrones reputation, who (as I conceive), is Mistress Warde that nowe hath another house prepareing for her at Leege." PRO London, SP 77, 12/III, ff. 383–384v.

27. Fr Tomson received an order from Fr General Claudio Aquaviva to write about his life on the English mission, his imprisonment and his escape from the Tower of London. The original, in Latin, was first published by Fr J. Morris as "The Life of Father John Gerard" (3) 1881 in London and later by Fr Philip Caraman as "The autobiography of an Elizabethan", London 1951. It also appeared in German in Lucerne as "Meine geheime Mission als Jesuit" in 1954. Fr Tomson also wrote an account of the Gunpowder Plot, which Fr Morris published in 1872 under the title "The condition of Catholics under James I. Father Gerards narrative of the Gunpowder Plot." After being removed as Rector of the novitiate in Liège, Fr Tomson was first moved to Spain. After a short stay in Rome he was sent to Ghent (1624–1625), and finally, in 1627, he was recalled to Rome where he died on 27th July, 1637, aged 73. For his dates, see Grisar, Die ersten Anklagen, p. 37, note 36; do. Ein schwieriger Rechtsfall, p. 249 ff; do., Maria Wards Institut, p. 34, note 9, and the writings mentioned.

28. Fr Nathaniel Southwell SJ, Catalogus primorum Patrum, p. 32; Morris, The Life of Father John Gerard, p. 481, from Stonyhurst College Arch.

29. He studied at home for two years, then travelled to the continent and entered the college at Douai on 29th August, 1577, aged barely 13. In 1580 he attended the Jesuit Clermont-College in Paris for one year, then went to Rouen where he met Fr Robert Persons in 1581. In the spring of 1582 he returned to England and was imprisoned in the notorious Marshalsea as a recusant on 5th March, 1584. In 1585 he was released on bail. He left England at the end of May, for Paris. Shortly afterwards he travelled to Rome.

30. LR p. 96, Inst. Arch. Munich.

31. Fr Henry Silisdon to Fr Thomas Owen, 31st October, 1614. Morris, The Life of Father John Gerard, p. 489, from Stonyhurst College Arch. Angl. A. vol. IV, nr. 31.

32. ARSI, Rome, Anglia 13, f. 8v; Gallo-Belg. 24, ff. 56r.64v.

33. L. Pearsall Smith, The Life and Letters of Sir Henry Wotton I, Oxford 1907, p. 292; Charles J. Philipps, History of the Sackville Family (Earls and Dukes of Dorset) I, p. 243–244, as also DNB XVII, p. 588–589.

34. Thomas Floud to William Trumbull, 8th December 1611, in Report of the Marquess of Downshire III, Papers of William Trumbull the Elder, Ed. HMC London, 1938 p. 194.

35. CRS. 10/1911, p. 201.

36. R. Belvederi, Guido Bentivoglio Diplomatico II, Rovigo 1947, p. 212–214.

37. NS 25th October, 1613. Baker, Acts of the Privy Council of England, May 1613–December 1614, London 1921, p. 234. "Another /a pass/ for Thomas Sackville, Esquire, to travail for three yeares and to take with him two men and necessary provisions not prohibited with provisoe not to goe to Rome."

38. Calender of State Papers, Dom. Series of the Reign of James I. (1611–1618), ed. Mary Anne Everett Green, London 1858, p. 270, Nr. 10: " ... Thomas Sackville, son to the old Lord Treasurer is restrained to Padua for some years; his practises deserved a sharper censure, but he was spared for his father's sake ..."

39. Letter Nr. 28. Inst. Arch. Munich. The letter proves how little Mary Ward and her companions were aware of the Count's intrigues in Liège. Otherwise, five years after the catastrophic end of their foundation in Liège, they would hardly have described Sackville in such respectful language.

40. Thomas Sackville was related to Jane Brown, one of the first members, and perhaps also to other members of the Institute whose names are no longer known. There were several connections by marriage between families of the gentry and the nobility.

41. Foley, Records VI, p. 594.

42. Foley, loc. cit., Guilday, Refugees, p. 179.

43. "Mr Sackfeeld, commending us and our Course and telling how much it was esteemed by men of iudgement and amongst the Cardinalls at Rome ..." LR p. 216–217, Inst. Arch. Munich.

44. J.H. Pollen SJ, ed. The Note-Book of John Southcote from 1623–1637. CRS Seris 1, Misc. 1/1905; do. The English Catholics in the Reign of Queen Elizabeth, London 1920, p. 81, note 2; J. Grisar, Ein schwieriger Rechtsfall = Archivum Historicum Societatis Jesus XXIX/1960, p. 248, note 7.

XV

RUE PIERREUSE

Du Croissant

The old street – the house 'Du Croissant' – purchase of a house by Sackville for the Englishwomen – English Jesuits and the house of the Institute in Rue Pierreuse

Rue Pierreuse, or stony street, was not a street of distinction, nor is it now, but for all that it is one of the oldest streets of Liège. Today it begins behind the Law Courts, (Palais de Justice) previously the Bishop's residence, and leads up a slope to the summit of the citadel. There, at the monument to the 12th Regiment of Ligne, it meets the street Montagne Ste Walburge.

In earlier times there were gardens here, even vineyards, but already by the late Middle Ages both sides of the street had been built on. Lower down, in Basse Pierreuse close to the inner town, lived the diocesan officials, artisans and lace-makers, but not the wealthy citizens. There was no shortage of the typical Liège inns, or brasseries.

As for the Church, rue Pierreuse belonged for the most part to the parish of St Servais, whose beautiful gothic church still adorns the rue Fond St Servais, which lies close to rue Pierreuse. On the Haute Pierreuse,[1] on the right hand side of the street facing away from the town, lay an imposing property. It dated from the late Middle Ages on land that stretched over the wide terrain on the hill below the citadel and towards the town, sloping down towards the left side of the rue du Péry. In the fifteenth century it had been named after its owner – Krinkelberghe. But before that, in the second half of the fourteenth century, a Henri de Crexhant or du Croissant owned this large property, and from then on in the town of Liège's history it was named as 'du Croissant'.The owner of the actual land was the Cathedral Chapter of St Lambert. The manor house changed owners frequently. It was burnt down in 1468, rebuilt, and had several inhabitants. In 1593 the house belonged to a Jérôme de Borsut, superintendent of Liège city.There had been a coal mine on the land since the beginning of the fifteenth century, which had to be closed as it polluted the town's water supply.

It has already been mentioned that before the Englishwomen

came to Liège, there had been negotiations about founding a house and that the matter had already been discussed with the Elector of Cologne in August, 1616.[2] Moreover, we know that the English Ambassador in The Hague had reported to London on 1st December[3] that the Englishwomen had bought a house in Liège to the value of 11,000 guilders. This purchase is nowhere to be found in the Liège deeds, but the Ambassador cannot have conjured this information out of the air, as he was well-informed about the price of purchase. The deal was not transacted by the English-women themselves. Apart from the fact that it is highly unlikely they would have had permission to do so from the town, they certainly did not have the means, as on 20th January, 1614 they had bought their third and last house in St Omer. It is far more likely that the purchaser of the Liège house was Count Thomas Sackville, the same man who had taken the Plan of the Institute, altered by Mary Ward, to Rome at the end of 1615. Some years later he wrote in a disclaimer of his goods in Liège, that he had built the house in rue Pierreuse.[4] That must mean that he had arranged for its alterations, for the building was already standing on the land Du Croissant.

The purchase of the whole property must have proceeded in two stages, for it was on 13th February, 1618 only that Jérôme de Borsut relinquished it to Andrien de Fléron, Provost of the Cathedral of St Lambert.[5] It was acquired by auction. De Fléron had, however, not obtained the piece of land for himself but for the English Count, Thomas Sackville, who in turn intended to hand it over to the Englishwomen for a foundation. It is not known why Sackville could not appear for himself as the purchaser. Perhaps he could not produce enough ready money at that moment. A good six weeks later he was buying a farm at Halleux, south of Liège, but he had received payment for that from the English Jesuits, for whom this farm was destined. It may also be that Sackville was not in Liège at that time and that he had authorized de Fléron to make the purchase for him.

The Englishwomen had to wait longer before they could enter the house intended for them. On 4th August, 1618[6] Fr General Vitelleschi wrote to Fr Jean Heren, the Belgian Provincial, saying he had heard that the Englishwomen were building a house in Liège on the same hill as that on which the Jesuit house was situated. Before it was finished, care should be taken that the windows of this building were so placed that they had no view into the Jesuits' house. In case of any lack of agreement with the Englishwomen, they should then so cover the windows of their own house, that they had no view of the women's house or garden.

The building, or rather the re-building of this house, was still not finished by the late summer of 1618. Erratic payments made by Thomas Sackville may have been the reason for that. At the beginning of 1619 the garden area was defined and legally agreed on. Unfortunately this important paper is no longer available. It was destroyed in World War II by bombs which wiped out many of the Liège archives. Théodore Gobert still had access to the documents when he wrote this part of his comprehensive history of the city of Liège.[7] The Englishwomen may have been able to move into their house by the end of 1618. Most of the numerous town chronicles of Liège make mention of the place.[8] The worth of the property may be seen from the payment made to the Convent of the English Canonesses of the Holy Sepulchre in 1655 by the Prince-Bishop Maximilian Heinrich, when he set about buying the land round the citadel. On 7th April, 1655,[9] the Superior, Frances of St Ignatius and her convent, sold the Bishop the house at the top of the rue Pierreuse with all the requirements for brewing beer, and the garden and goods which they had acquired from Jacques Gal. The major part of the purchase money was paid. For the remainder, the Belgian Order received annually 250 Brabant guilders. During these years the Prince Bishop paid around 12,370 guilders for the estate.[10] If one remembers that the English Ambassador in 1616 had reported a purchase price of 11,000 guilders for the house, then about 1,370 guilders remained over as the price for the ground acquired. The Canonesses paid the then owner, Jacques Gal, annually 250 guilders' interest. The property was therefore, reckoning interest at 6¼ per cent, still burdened with 4,000 guilders in 1655. Probably the Bishop paid the nuns the entire sum, and these struck an agreement with Jacques Gal. The ground tax of 10 bushels of wheat to the Cathedral Chapter remained the same as in 1621. At that time the Chapter granted the impoverished Englishwomen, just as they had earlier owners − among them Count Sackville − full remission of the tax of 10 bushels of corn in exchange for a Philipus taler as well as the annual payment of 20 Brabant guilders. This was so that they, as religious (propter respectum personarum religiosarum) should not be forced to leave their house in the rue Pierreuse.[11] The size of these payments bears witness to the respectable amount of property owned.

It was only on 30th April (respectively 8th May) 1621, that the property came into the Institute's ownership. From then on they were obliged to pay taxes. If one looks at both the years' payments, it can be seen that the Englishwomen owned their house for a very short time; these were years of the most bitter disappointment, lived out in harshest poverty.

The distrust with which the Englishwomen and their proposed work in Liège was regarded by the Jesuits is seen in a questionnaire which, though short, had a heavily loaded content. This was put before them in writing.[12] One can hardly credit its composition by the Liège Jesuits. It is far more likely that the questions were put together by a group of Jesuits in Louvain and found their way to Liège. It is odd, to say the least, that they were written in Latin in order to be answered in English. The questions were certainly of Jesuit authorship. Internal evidence shows that, as also the presence of the document in the Fonds of the Jesuit Archives in the State Archives in Brussels.

The questions refer not only to the work of the Englishwomen in teaching girls, but to the whole Institute.

The first question runs:

'Do the Englishwomen observe enclosure in their houses, as is customary among the Jesuits? Are men allowed entry? In Jesuit houses no women are permitted.'

Answer: 'We always intend, after our houses are finished, to observe the same enclosure as that of the Jesuits. We have carried this intention out, as far as the arrangement of our houses allows.'

2nd question:

'Do you go out alone, or in twos?'

Answer: 'We will continue in the future as we have before: neither to go out alone, or to be alone with a man in the house.'

3rd question:

'Do you intend to give the girls music and language lessons, or will you arrange for a teacher (male)?'

Answer: 'We intend to give lessons in languages and music our-selves, to do away with any need for external teachers. That is why we wish some of ours to be trained. It has been the same with other subjects. If parents should afterwards consider that their children could be better instructed in music by a male teacher, rather than by a woman, then it will be possible for lessons to be given by one.'

4th question:

'Do you wish to be subject to us, to form a unity with us, or should we be independent of one another?'

Answer:

'We are so far from striving after union with the Society of Jesus, or to be subject to it, that we could never accept this if it were offered. We shall never give up our respect for them (the Jesuits) or their Institute, as we aim to follow their virtues and their work, as far as it is suited to our sex, without doing them harm. As to what concerns spiritual assistance, we should always wish to have this, but in the measure in which the Jesuit constitutions allow these to others also. We shall therefore take care that we do not keep the fathers from their important occupation by long confessions.'

The questions – and the answers! – contain more than is seen at first glance. The first two refer to enclosure. It is true that neither the Society of Jesus nor the Institute of the Englishwomen had any, but both written and unwritten conventions were stricter and narrower in those days, especially for women. The fact that the Englishwomen mentioned the unsuitability or 'incommodity' of their houses gives a pointer to the place in which these questions were answered — Liège.

The difference between the smaller house on Mont St Martin and the spaciously planned house under construction on the rue Pierreuse was considerable. It is easy to imagine that the English-women often passed this way, in order to do whatever was possible here and there.

The third question concerns teaching. At that time it was not usual for women to teach Latin and Music; it was, in fact, con-sidered improper. Peter Canisius would not even allow a Jesuit to be appointed for singing lessons.[13] Latin and Music had already been envisaged in the Schola Beatae Mariae, so within the first years of the Institute.[14]

It should not cause surprise if it is only now that the English-women refer to their own formation. It was for this reason that Mary Ward had moved the novitiate to Liège. In most instances, these young Englishwomen were not capable of teaching, however simple it may have been in those days. This answer alone indicates the approximate date of the questions, 1617, before the English-women could open their house in the rue Pierreuse for their work of teaching and education.

Neither should it be surprising that the Englishwomen make a reference to day pupils and boarders.

In St Omer their school was primarily one for girls from England, but also for English children who were resident there. From 1618, local girls had also attended the school.[15] In Liège, things were quite different. The situation of their house was most unsuitable for the teaching of Belgian girls, such as Bishop Blaes had recom-mended to the Bishop of Liège [16] in his letter of 2nd February, 1617. 'Bien haut en Pierreuse' — on the slopes of Pierreuse, the house was at least half an hour from the heart of the town and had not been planned for Belgian children. As is clear from the curriculum of the Schola Beatae Mariae, the Englishwomen carried out a full day's timetable, and teaching went on until 4.30 in the afternoon.

Was it wise to settle close to the citadel, where rough soldiery lounged, and the young girls had to go home — especially in winter — through the pitch dark rue Pierreuse where there was no street lighting, even if they did have a chaperone?

No This house behind a protective wall was intended as a novi-tiate, and a boarding school for young English women, though possibly some local girls may have attended it.[17]

En Condroz

1618

The purchase of a farm (from Jacques Lamet) by the English Jesuits under Thomas Sackville's name – foundation by Sackville in the rue Pierreuse for the English women to the annoyance of the Jesuits – various financial transactions – purchase of lands (from Marguerite de Chamont) by Edward Sackville – purchase of a farm (from the brothers Cabosse) by Sackville – the properties in the Condroz a doubtful transaction for the foundation in rue Pierreuse.

To pass judgement on the transactions that follow, we are not only dependent on the surviving documentary material but must refer to two papers from the years 1629 and 1630. One can be considered as Rector John Tomson's letter[18] of exoneration, the other[19] must have been written soon after, as a response, by Fr Michael Freeman. Both Fathers had been told to state their case by Fr General Muzio Vitelleschi, when the matter of the Englishwomen's debts in Liège, which had never settled down, flared up again.

The members of the Institute in Liège sent to their General Superior – who was then in Rome – three promissory notes which had been handed to them by the English Jesuits.[20]

Many of the statements from both sides can be interpreted differently, which does not mean that the transactions had been based on deception. Neither Fr Tomson nor Fr Freeman made use of prevarication, but they wrote from memory some years after the event and, however odd this may sound, neither may have been clearly informed. The financial affairs of the English Jesuits during those difficult years were not in the best of hands, and worse still, they were not recorded systematically. Fr Rector Tomson was generous but inexperienced in money matters; after him came Fr Edward Burton, who took office as Procurator from 4th August, 1617[21] together with a brother, George Kenix (perhaps Coninx, a Flemish name) who had extensive powers. He was in the rather unusual situation of having control over great sums of money.[22]

First, from Fr Tomson's version of the affair: soon after taking on the post of bursar with its gloomy financial situation, Fr Burton had to consider cutbacks. Some of the citizens suggested that he should buy a farm which could provide the table with good but cheaper supplies of food.[23] Fr Rector had not at first been enthusiastic about the idea, but finally agreed. When a suitable farm had been found in Condroz, some townspeople advised Fr Burton to buy the farm under another name. One is immediately inclined to ask 'Why?' It will also be remembered that the land and houses on it in Liège had likewise been bought by a foreigner – Colonel

William Stanley — but in the meantime the English Jesuits had raised a stately building on these lands which, to date, had swallowed up 34,600 guilders. It has been seen that of this sum far more than 18,000 guilders came from the wealth of some Liège townspeople. The expenditure was by no means ended. Perhaps one should frame the question this way: was Fr Tomson no longer credit worthy?

Wherever the truth lies, Fr Tomson asked Count Sackville to buy the farm for the Jesuits in his name. Some years later (1618) Sackville, urged on by the citizens of Liège, bought a house and garden in Liège to give to the Englishwomen.[24]

The citizens valued and esteemed Sackville, son of the Lord Treasurer of England, and put large sums at his disposal for the project, but, as they also wanted to protect themselves, Sackville had to stake his possessions as a pledge.[25]

Disquieted by these proceedings, Fr Tomson and the procurator Fr Burton, too, pointed out to the Count that now their farm in Condroz — bought indeed in his name — but paid for with Jesuit money, could be at risk, so they asked him to release the property. Upon which the Count answered that it was not he, but the Jesuits who had asked him to buy the farm in his name; that they had only themselves to blame if it was now mortgaged. He would willingly withdraw his dues if they would free him from them. The purchase in his name had been an act of kindness and he had not wished to hinder a good work. When Fr Burton stood firmly by his request that Sackville should release the property, the Count flew into a rage. Fr Rector pacified his procurator, asking him to consider that they really had no reason to approach (ricercarlo) or to impede him (d'impedirlo). This request shows the unlimited trust that Fr Rector had in Count Sackville.

It is of course no crime to borrow money in order to buy a farm, provided one intends to pay it back. The situation, in this case, was slightly different.

Count Thomas Sackville wanted to give a house to the Englishwomen. It has already been seen what great sums he had given to other Orders. He was well known in Liège as a benefactor. The Provost of St Lambert allowed him to use his name to buy a house in rue Pierreuse and the Liège Counsellor gave his permission for a single mortgage on the harvest on the widow Chamont's properties. The Jesuits also showed him a good measure of trust by acquiring goods in the Count's name — Fr Burton as well as Fr Tomson. But Thomas Sackville was not justified in mortgaging the Jesuits' property. It is not known why Thomas Sackville took such an unwarrantable measure to realise the endowment he had promised to the Englishwomen. He was supposed to have been expecting a large sum of money from England.[26] Perhaps this was in connection with his mother's death, as she died in 1615, but that is pure speculation.

At any rate it is a fact that the hoped-for money had not materialised at the time when he had already bought the house in rue Pierreuse. It is a plausible reason, but no excuse for fraud.

Encumbered with debts, Sackville left Liège, and with that left the Englishwomen to the demands of his creditors. These were for about 8,000 Scudi or 20,000 guilders.[27]

To turn to the document that Fr Tomson used as the basis of his report:

First: a promissory note from the Englishwomen for over 1,200 guilders,[28], which Fr Tomson had negotiated for the Superior Barbara Babthorpe in Liège.

Fr Tomson no longer remembered the occasion when the Jesuits had demanded this promissory note from the Englishwomen, but he insisted that he had never given them any such sum.

He then recalled two incidents. The Jesuits had raised 600 guilders from a Liège citizen. Fr Tomson wanted to pay the sum back initially, but when he saw the great poverty in which the Englishwomen were living, he advanced them this money, for which of course they had to repay the citizen, with interest. But the citizen was cautious. He held the promissory note of the Englishwomen for 600 guilders but did not return the Jesuits their promissory note. An odd way of conducting business. The second part of the sum of 1,200 guilders could, so Fr Tomson thought, be an amount which the Englishwomen had needed for a journey to England for some members of the Institute. An English merchant who sometimes came to Liège had offered to advance the money, but demanded assurance of its return from the English Jesuits. Only after Pater Perseus had promised by letter from England to repay in case of emergency, did the Englishwomen receive the money. This sum was paid back by them.

But in the meantime, before the Englishwomen had returned the two sums, the Jesuit brother who administered his Rector's private monetary affairs, demanded a promissory note for both sums, in another form. They used intricate methods in those days. Fr Tomson continued by saying that the Jesuits had no right to these 1,200 guilders as the Englishwomen were in debt for half the sum to a Liège citizen and had paid back the other half.[29]

Fr Tomson had racked his brain in vain. The promissory note could not refer to these two sums (under another name!), for it was only on 25th February,1621 that Anne Gage, as Superior in Liège, desposited a promissory note for 600 guilders with the Jesuits for the journey of some members to England.[30] And on 12th August, 1624[31] the Mayor Jean Woet transferred to the lay assessor Lambert de Lapidé a demand (capital and increment) of 676 guilders and 2 patakons to the Englishwomen. Moreover Lapidé accepted the demand of 40 guilders annually which, according to an acknowledgement of 5th February, 1615, had been promised through

Antoine Libert. And here is the sum which Fr Tomson advanced, but only on 25th February, 1621. On 5th February, 1615, namely, when a certain Antoine Libert promised to pay the interest of 40 guilders, there were no Englishwomen in Liège. Probably the lay assessor Libert did stand surety on 16th November, 1616, when Fr Tomson raised a loan of 6,000 guilders from the widow Gal, with his house in rue Pot d'Or. He was helping Fr Tomson at the time. The second sum from the English merchant was, as Fr Tomson himself stated, repaid. Nothing more is found in the documents. Fr Tomson, and with him Fr Freeman, confused these two sums with another sum of this amount, about which they presumably had no knowledge.

On 31st March, 1618,[32] a good six weeks after the piece of land in rue Pierreuse for a garden for the Englishwomen had been transferred to him, Sackville bought, again by auction, 'la cense de Halleux', the farm Halleux in the district of Nandrin in Condroz, about 60 km south of Liège. The owner was Jacques Lamet, the purchase price, 1,200 guilders. As highest bidder, Sackville obtained the farm. But did he pay? Not all of it, because when it came to the final settlement, the chief creditor, the widow Jeanne Gal, paid to Jacques Lamet on 16th February, 1623, 551 guilders and 12½ pakatons in redemption for a farm with appurtenances in the region of Nandrin, and she received from Lamet 36 guilders and 50 patakons rent.[33] That would have been for a paid capital of 600 guilders, if one reckons the interest at the then average sum of 6 − 6½ per cent. We are certainly not far out if we see in these 600 guilders the amount paid for the farm, which, however, had been rented again to Lamet as security.

Two months later, on lst June, 1618, Barbara Babthorpe deposited a promissory note of over 1,200 guilders. Now it would be very remarkable if this, as Fr Tomson would have one believe, had consisted of two contributions and that under a different label. It is easier to accept that this sum of 1,200 guilders contained a payment of 600 guilders handed over to Lamet. The gaping debt of 1,200 guilders belonged to the Jesuits. It was for this that the Englishwomen made a deposit of a promissory note, either with Brother Kenix or, as is more likely, with Fr Burton. He, as Fr Tomson wrote in his defence, could not be asked as he had already been dead for some years.

Secondly − the second promissory note of 2nd April, 1619 referred to an exchange of 3,000 guilders contracted by Mary Ward. Before his departure, Sackville had left behind some blank bills of exchange. This promissory note was again demanded of the Englishwomen by Fr Burton, again without the Rector's knowledge. The sum consisted of claims for the Englishwomen's house and other expenses.[34] The Englishwomen were pledged to indemnify the Fathers, but these had no claim to it, because the farm was mortgaged more highly than with 1,200 Scudi or 3,000 guilders, and because the creditors had never asked for this sum to be returned.

The promissory note was for a re-payment within two years. If this was not done, a third promissory note was drawn up.

Let us pause for a moment.

On 31st May, 1618,[38] two months after Thomas Sackville had acquired the farm, an Edward Sackville also bought land in the region of Nandrin, bordering on the farms which had already been acquired by the Count, paying 225 guilders to Widow Marguerite de Chamont. Thomas Sackville had a nephew named Edward. We do not know if the uncle bought the farm simply in his nephew's name, or if Edward Sackville was staying in Liège at this time also.[36] The yield of the Chamont estates were entered at the sum of 1,000 guilders as pledge.

The plea was conducted by the Counsel of Liège, the Bishop's representative on 19th May, therefore still before the contract of purchase had been issued.[37] If we look at the amount of 225 guilders (we do not know if more were advanced) and then consider the mortgaging of the harvest as 1,000 guilders more, which may be true, the value of goods amounted to at least double the sum, 2,450 guilders, probably still more, for we have seen that the second promissory note referred to a blank bill of exchange of 3,000 guilders.

Barely five months later, on 25th October, 1618[38] there followed the settlement of the year's rent between Thomas Sackville and the brothers Engelbert and Guillaume Cabosse in kind, for a sum of 500 guilders, a sum which Thomas Sackville had already paid as part payment of the purchase price for that farm near Halleux.

On the same day the Count paid them a further 1,000 guilders. The Cabosse brothers paid down an unnamed amount of malt wheat to the value of 95 guilders, with an additional interest of $6\frac{1}{3}$ per cent; therefore for 1,500 guilders.

In a second contract of the same date,[39] Sackville rented the yield of their lands.[40] Again, Sackville paid one part of the farm and at the same time pledged the yield of the harvest before he had paid entirely for the property.

Certainly, the Cabosse farm was the bigger one. If we think that the payment of the Lamet farm had signified 50 per cent of the whole, this one, as in the case of the Chamont estates, will have had the same total, so that we can estimate these properties likewise at 3,000 guilders.

And about another five months later, on 2nd April, 1619, the Englishwomen deposited with the English Jesuits a promissory note for the drawn blank bill of exchange already mentioned, with an upper limit of 3,000. As though that were not enough, on an unnamed day, they deposited the dowry of one of their members, Mary Talbot, again 3,000 guilders,[41] with the English Jesuits. Taken as a whole, the Englishwomen had declared themselves as debtors to the English Jesuits for the sum of 7,200 guilders, 3,000 guilders that were invested through Fr Burton as payment for the farms, and 3,600 guilders for the mortgages. Again, one would not be far wrong, if one saw these sums as payment for their house on the rue Pierreuse, which in 1655 was valued at about 12,370 guilders.

Fr Tomson was right when he said later in his paper that the Englishwomen were in debt to a total of 8,000 Scudi or 20,000 guilders.

Their heavily burdened possessions at a total value of 7,200 guilders, and the value of their house at 12,370 guilders would result in the sum of 19,570 guilders.

That was still not all, for from December, 1616, fifteen people at least had to be fed and housed, and in later years it was considerably more, even if they lived very modestly. No wonder that the foundation in St Omer was drawn into a state of shared misery. It is pointless to delve deeper into the Fr Rector's documents. However confused his report, it emerges that at one time he referred to one farm, then to two farms; about a larger one in the name of Count Sackville and about a smaller one in the name of another person (Edward Sackville). It can be shown from reliable sources, as it has been, that there were three purchases.

It throws light on the Jesuits' curious methods of keeping their accounts for the new building in the former En Royale,[42] if the Superior of the house did not even know the whole property of the novitiate, let alone the sums that were on loan.

All in all, it was a great deal of money.

Loneliness

1618

Some meditation points from the April, 1618 Retreat – imitation of Christ – fear of sin – her love of the Institute that she was entrusted to found

To turn from these unhappy financial matters for a short time: while Thomas Sackville was acquiring the first Condroz farm for the Jesuits, (31.3.1618),[43] and Fr General Vitelleschi was giving his instructions to the Visitor Fr Henri Scheren about Jesuits hearing the confessions of devout ladies,[44] Mary Ward was making a retreat. It was certainly Fr John Tomson who was her director, and equally certainly this was a time of prayer and meditation in spite of tensions from affairs outside. It was not only the number of the members in Liège that had increased, so had the loans, and the hopelessness of their financial situation.

The points, or rather the abridged version of her meditations from the Exercises for April 1618, refer to the Foundations (No 23) and Sin (Nos. 55–64), in other words to the meditation material of the First Week of the Thirty Days' Exercises of St Ignatius.[45] These extremely valuable fragments of twelve periods of meditation are the only ones which have survived. Others, such as those on the Life of Christ, have not.[46] In the following year, 1619, sinfulness and its effects were also the main material for her meditation, but it must be pointed out that these are fragments of all that have come down to us. Nor must it be forgotten that in those days sinfulness was more deeply imprinted on the hearts of prayerful christians, ever ready to do penance, than in later centuries.

It is not so much her 'fear' and 'abhoring' of sin, her discernment of the right path towards God, or that remoteness from God which she considered sinful, which we want to deal with here. It is far more that we wish to stress certain of her sentences that refer to the Institute.

In her third entry (the fourth meditation on the Foundation), she perceived with joy that Christ has marked out the best way for the right use of things, and that she too wanted to go along this path, impelled by an unrecognised inner motivation.[47] She added later: 'Afterwards,I was troubled and disturbed by some fears that imitation of our Saviour, which now I desired so much, might not agree with my election, and my chosen course of life. I would have enjoyed them both'.[48] But she ended her thoughts with 'this fear hindered, I fear, the effectiveness of my prayer for grace to follow Christ's example.'[49] Fear of sin played its role in her prayer life, certainly. In the meditation on Sin, when she placed herself before God's judgement seat, she felt 'confounded' and as though 'shrunk up to nothing'. It was only when she looked up towards God that a radiance of happiness filled her, and she had sorrow for her sins from love of him: 'In an instant I loved Him, and was very sorry for all those sins, and besought Him with love and a few tears to forgive me them all and every one.'[50]

She would have liked to have placed each individual sin before him, but she could not turn her eyes away from him or lose sight of him. Nor did she want to leave the place, and look at herself on earth. She was not even in a condition to make a confession.

A deep insight into Mary Ward's state of soul is given in the last entry of her Spiritual Exercises of 1618. It has two headings. First, one written in Elizabeth Cotton's handwriting, giving the contents correctly: 'How severly God punisheth sinne, except we doe pennance.'[51] And then the second, with an addition by Mary Ward: 'The loneliness'. The title speaks for itself. The meditation was a conversation between God and her loving soul. 'I saw', she begins in her note,'that it pleases God more if I make satisfaction in this life.' And she implored him to show her how to proceed.

She reflected that she had already decided to avoid sin, and was therefore bound to do so. To accept the fulfilment of the divine will readily, and not out of a sense of duty, would in itself be an increase of penance. As this seemed to her to be too little, she prayed again for clearer knowledge, and it occurred to her that she would, perhaps, find more difficulties in her life than she could imagine. But she prayed that she might accept with love and joy whatever might come. She prayed at the same time that nothing might hold her back from fulfilling God's will.

These considerations are shown in the Painted Life, panel No 28. Mary Ward continues her notes with some extremely important sentences. A disquieting premonition struck her and she writes: 'Presented that perchance there was some great trouble to happen about the confirmation of our course.'[52] And, to balance that — 'with this I found a great and new love to this Institute, and a near embracing or union of affection with it.'[53]

It is necessary to point out that with 'this Institute', she meant the one entrusted to her by God, and not that suggested in the form of a Pium Institutum.

In view of the past and immediate difficulties surrounding her, it was no painless request she made when she implored God to give her grace to bear this burden, and hinder any obstacle in the way of fulfilling his will (namely the establishment of the Institute entrusted to her).[54]

All her life Mary Ward was very matter-of-fact with regard to herself and she perceived that the opportunity to make her offer a reality had now come, and that God alone could be her consolation in the forthcoming troubles.[55] A deep fear of facing this Garden of Olives in her life lay behind her request that the love that she felt for this way of life might help her later, as then perhaps the possibility, or the strength, or time, might be lacking.[56] 'I requested with much love,' she concluded her notes,' that this prayer which I was now making might be a request for his grace at that time.'[57]

A great love for this Institute as the 'Instrumentum caritatis Dei', as Ignatius named his Society of Jesus, shines from these words.

A Bottomless Pit

1619 – 1621

Further mortgages of the English Jesuits in Liège — the Englishwoman's increasing poverty - eviction from the Mont St Martin — Mary Ward's refuge in God

These were the years of the large bills. Apart from the property in Condroz, which caused the English Jesuits in Liège so much anxiety and probably indignation as well, there was the new novitiate house, which could by no means be yet regarded as the Jesuits' rightful property. It has already been shown that at the end of 1617, Fr Tomson had taken out a mortgage for 34,600 guilders at an annual rate of interest of 2,220 guilders.

In 1619, only after the purchases of Condroz and the buildings in the town had been completed, Fr Tomson took out some more – some of which were for large sums: on 3rd January, 1619 [58] with the old Mayor Jean Woet, 2,250 at 150 guilders' interest per annum. It was expressly mentioned in the agreement that Fr Tomson had been 'attribué par ses supérieurs' – allowed to do so by his superiors.

In the same month, on 28th January,[59] he contracted a loan of 1,350 guilders with the widow Anne Heymont, born Woet, at an interest of 90 guilders per annum. On 1st March[60] followed the loan of 3,000 guilders at a total annual interest of 200 guilders with the organist of the college Church of St Denis, Nacek. And again a month later, on 4th April, [61] Fr Burton, accompanied by Brother George Kenix, concluded an agreement to a mortgage of 10,000 guilders, again with the widow Jeanne Gal at 540 guilders per annum interest, this time with the approval of Father General.

Fr Tomson must have had some difficulties from his creditors, for on 19th April, 1619 [62] he received a letter of protection from the Bishop of Liège, because certain people wanted to make trouble concerning the possession of the farm in Nandrin. Which of the two farms is meant here is uncertain. Both lay near Halleux in the region of Nandrin.

In the next year too, great sums of money were borrowed. On 28th January, 1620,[63] Fr Tomson borrowed 10,000 guilders from Lady Mary Lovel,[64] a rich Englishwoman, but paid 1,000 back, so that 9,000 guilders at 562,50 guilders interest remained payable annually. On 19th February[65] he borrowed 2,400 guilders at 150 guilders per annum interest, from the Jesuit College in Namur.

Together these mortgages amounted to 28,000 guilders at an interest rate of 1,692,50 guilders a year. With the loans, which had already been made up to the end of 1617, and which had reached a total of 34,600 guilders at an interest of 2,220 guilders, the Novitiate house, by the end of 1620, was burdened with a debt of 62,600 guilders, with an interest rate of 3,912,50 guilders annually. These sums have been taken from the account book of the English Jesuits. One does not know if still other amounts were borrowed and not entered. With 200 guilders a year, one person could live modestly; they were the amount of the interest from a capital of 3,000 guilders. Fr Tomson had therefore, to procure the same sum in interest which would suffice to maintain nineteen to twenty Jesuits.

The bucket was full, but it had a hole. And the Englishwomen on the Mont St Martin? As seen already, they had petitioned the

Chapter of St Martin on 13th November 1617,[66] in vain, for security on the remit of the monthly income of the Chapter. Presumably this was settled one way or another. Perhaps they borrowed again and again, smaller or larger amounts from citizens with large capital. Only very few documents of the years 1617–21 give information about their precarious financial situation and increasing poverty.

On 3rd January, 1620[67] Canon Michael de Merica, owner of their house on Mont St Martin, renewed a charge before the Chapter, filed on account of the Englishwomen's insolvency. As they did not wish to leave the house, he asked to be allowed to take out a legal order of eviction. The Chapter answered non-committally; it wished to send Canons Mernier and Heusden as deputies to both parties, in order to receive a report. We do not know if this occurred. At any rate, Canon de Merica seems to have acted independently fairly soon, for three days later, on the Feast of the Epiphany,[68] Canon Vandenroy reported to the Chapter that armed men had forced their way into the Englishwomen's house on the orders of the owner of the house, and had carried on in an arbitrary manner, hunting out the sick inhabitants and refusing admission to those who were healthy. The Chapter was silent. This rough treatment in the middle of winter will have increased the destitution, and above all the public disgrace and humiliation of these defenceless women. Whatever illness it was that the Englishwomen had was not mentioned. Plague and dysentery were constantly flaring up in Liège. According to the Parish Register of Deaths, whole familes were wiped out. It is unlikely that the heartless treatment of the women at that time was a result of the plague, for in that case no one would have dared to enter the house.

In spite of all this, one thing must not be overlooked. As far as appearances went, the Englishwomen owned a fine house on rue Pierreuse, which could have housed the growing number of members. But an outsider, even Canon de Merica, could hardly have known how things really stood with Count Thomas Sackville's splendid foundation; at all events, the women were led by a good star when they had decided not to leave the house on Mont St Martin, whatever the risk might be that for some time to come they might not be able to pay their rent.

Particularly unpleasant in this respect is the wish expressed in the English Ambassador's report. William Trumbull writes from Brussels on 11th/21st January, 1619 to Dudley Carleton that the Bishop of Liège, acting in the interests of preparations for war made by his brother (the Elector of Bavaria), had mortgaged property in the diocese of Liège. Perhaps he would also like to take possession of the property of the English Jesuits and the Englishwomen – 'their expectatives or devoted sisters of the Sodality'.[69]

It was at this time that Mary Ward wrote down: 'After a great attack of sickness, a freedom of all care of worldly affairs with so

great a hunger to go out of myself to God; if I did not take care and trouble, it would be impossible for me to behave normally'.[70]
A world of difference between the hiddenness of her interior life and her involvement in every day affairs.

Notes

1. Théodore Gobert, Liège à travers les ages, Les rues de Liège. Nouvelle Edition du text original de 1924–1929, IX Brussels, 1977, p. 362. Unfortunately, the new edition of the comprehensive town history of Liège repeated the disturbing misinformation that after the suppression of the Institute, the English women entered the order of the English Sepulchrines. This is not correct. These ladies, likewise called "English Ladies", who inhabited the Institute House in rue Pierreuse, came to Liège only in 1642, and bought the house and all appurtenances in 1644 from Jacques Gal. Between the Suppression of the Institute and their arrival there was a gap of 11 years. Moreover, the names and ages of the English Sepulchrines are known. None of them belonged previously to Mary Ward's Institute. For this, see the excellent work of Sr M. Hereswitha OSSep. De Vrouwenkloosters van het Hl. Graf in het prinsbisdom Luik vanaf hun ontstaan tot aan de Fransche Revolutie (1480–1798), Louvain 1941.
2. Dudley Cartleton to Secretary of State Ralph Winwood, 12th August, 1616, HMC Thirteenth Report, Appendix Part II, The Mss of his Grace the Duke of Portland preserved at Welbeck Abbey, II, London 1893, p. 23.
3. ibid. p. 27.
4. " ... pour édiffier la maison que j'ay fait en Pierreuse ou aultrement ..." AU Liège, Couvent Jésuites Anglais 1, Registre concernant les Pères Jésuites Anglais, pp. 83–84, Nr. 20.
5. "Le 13 février 1618 Jérôme de Borsut cédait partiellement l'immeuble du Croissant, par rendage proclamatoire au prévot de Saint-Lambert, Andrien de Fléron, pour Thomas Scaville, fils du comte de Derrester, grant trésorier d'Angleterre. Ce notable étranger n'avait fait l'acquisition qu'en vue d'en doter les "Dames Anglaises" qui furent pour ce motif connues sous la designation "Comte Scaville". Gobert, loc. cit., p. 365.
6. ARSI, Rome, Gallo-Belg. 1/II, p. 428. This order is typical of someone who has to rely on information from others and has no personal knowledge of the locality. The Englishwomen's house was on the right side of the rue Pierreuse, below the Citadel; that of the Jesuit novitiate on the rue Royale. Between the two buildings lay rue Pierreuse and the large expanse of the Jesuits' grounds. One can still overlook the house today, but a figure in a window would hardly be recognizable. The order from Rome was either motivated by exaggerated anxiety or malice.
7. "En janvier et février 1619, les voires jurés du courdeau, à la requête de ces 'dames' procédèrent aux formalitées préliminaires, pour renclore et renfermer leur jardin joindant à celui de Gerard Gordinne." Gobert loc. cit.
8. Barbara Ward writes on the other hand: "This was finished a compleat college with schooles, church and what els necessarie the same yeare it was begun which was 1617." This information is not correct. Out of the 2nd paper, Inst. Arch. Munich.
9. The list says: " ... la maison qu'elles on et possèdent en cette cité en la montaigne de Piereuse avec brassine, jardins, héritages, méliorations et impenses montantes à grosses sommes et touttes autres appartenances qu'elles ont cy devant acquis du Sieur Jacque Gal à charger de payer et acquitter par Saditte Altesse et ses successeurs à leurs descharge de

payer et indemnité au dit Sieur Gal et ses repésentans une rente de deux cents cincquante florins brabants redimibles selon les contracts, restane d'une plus grande partie redimée par ladite Mère et couvent, laquelle redemption elles cèdent aussi à Sadite Altesse et ses successeurs et ayants cause. Item d'acquitter dix muids fonciers d'espeaute de rente deus à Messeigneurs de la cathédrale de Liège comme aussi deux florin liégois de cens aux chanoines de Saint-Materne selon que d'icelles charges appert par le contract de transport que le dit Sieur Gal leurs en a fait l'an mil six cents guarante quattre le dixième jour de juin réalisé pardevant les Sieurs eschevins de Liège l'onzième du mesme mois et an ..." AE Liège, Notaires, Ruffin, J. (1654–1658), 1654–1656, ff. 59r–60v and Chambres des finances des Princes-Evêques de Liège, Chambre des Comptes 83 (82), 1651–1660, ff. 259v–261r.

10. Spécification de ce que Son Altesse Sérénissime a donné à ceux, qui ont eu des biens enclavéz dans les fortifications de la citadelle de Liège, depuis l'an 1650, p. 2: Les Angloises, ff. 12 373.6.16. BU Liège, MS Delvaulx, Annexe T.III, Nr. 64.

11. Decision of the Chapter, 21st May 1621. AE Liège, Cathédrale Saint-Lambert, A. Secretariat, Registres aux conclusions capitulaires 22 (130), 1621–1622, f. 57r.

12. AGR Brussels, Archives Jésuit., Prov. Gallo-Belg. Carton 32.

13. B. Duhr, Gesch. d. Jesuiten in den Landern deutscher Zunge I, Freiburg/B. 1907, p. 443.

14. see above, p. 165.

15. Letter of complaint from the Englishwomen to the Town council of Saint-Omer. AM Saint-Omer, CCXXXIX, Nr. 16, Filles Anglaises ff. 12–14.

16. see above, p.211ff.

17. In the Bishop's letter of 6th April, 1619 to the Ursulines: " ... Voire qu'en une ville si ample, il n'y a pas d'escoles formeles, si ce n'est depuis peu après des devotes Filles Anglaiss, lesquelles, outre leur langage étranger et leur demeure dans une extremité de la ville, ne sont seule suffisants pour y enseigner, les jour ouvriers, les filles déjà grandelettes ..." printed, J. Daris, Histoire du diocèse et de la principauté de Liège pendant le XVIIe siecle I, Liège 1877, p. 357. The testimonial from the city of Liège dated 10th September 1620 to Cologne concerning the Englishwomen's activity in Liège is summed up in a few dry words: "Itaque sicut civitati huic propter eximiam modestiam et virtutem gratae admodum fuere et propter piam puellarum educationem perutiles sic bonis omnibus charas fore minime dubitamus." The original of this letter in the Hesse State Archives in Darmstadt was lost in World War II. An authenticated copy lies in the IBVM Generalate in Rome.

18. ARSI Rome, Angl. 32/II, ff. 362r.–365v.

19. AGR Brussels, Archives Jésuit. Gallo-Belg. Carton 32.

20. J. Grisar, Ein schwieriger Rechtsfalls zwischen den Englischen Fräulein und den englischen Jesuiten in Luttich 1618–1630 = Archivum Historicum Societatis Jesu XXIX/1960, p. 246–304.

21. AE Liège, Couvents, Jésuits Anglais, Registre, p. 234, s.n.

22. Fr Burton and Brother Kenix raised a mortgage of f.1.10,000 in the name of their Rector on 4th April, 1619 from Widow Jeanne Gal. ibid. pp. 138–144, Nr. 35. Fr Tomson and a "Frer George" had already raised a capital of fl.1,350 from Widow Anne Woet on 28th January 1619. ibid pp. 164–166, Nr. 40. On 8th March, 1621, the chapter of Saint-Martin ordered the Englishwomen to repay their arrears for the house on Mont Saint-Martin. This could come, the Chapter suggested, from the sum which had been made available to them by Brother George of the Society of Jesus. AE Liège, Collégiale Saint-Martin 58, f. 124r.

23. ARSI Rome, Angl. 32/II, f. 363r. The quotations must be treated with caution; the document was extraordinarily long-winded.

24. ibid.

25. ibid.

26. ibid.

27. "Dopoi quando il detto conte ... non potte ripagare i denari, che si era fatto prestare in Liège, lassò il debito totale, e la rendita annuale, che si doveva pagar per esso, fosse pagato, et sodisfatto delle soddette signore, alle quali haveva donato la casa, e terre che con i detti denari haveva compro, et le somme non erano piccole; le quali me pare arivassero intorno à 8.000 scudi ..." ibid.

28. ibid, f. 362r.

29. ibid.

30. In the settlement of 12th August, 1624. See note 31.

31. AE Liège, Couvents, Jésuites Anglais, Registre pp. 223–224. s.n.

32. AE Liège, Officialité de Liège, Rendages proclamatoires, Nr. 17 (1615–1621), f. 303rv.

33. AE Liège, Parchemins des Eschevins de Liège Nr. 1578.

34. The amount was once again added to the Count's entire possessions, that is, on the Jesuits' possessions. For the lengthy details, ARSI Rome, Angl. 32/II, f. 363v.

35. AE Liège, Couvents Jésuites Anglais, Registre pp. 79–82, Nr. 19.

36. Edward Sackville was the second son of Robert Sackville (second Earl of Dorset). He was born in 1591 and was therefore some twenty years younger than his uncle Thomas jnr. After his brother Richard's death (3rd Earl of Dorset), Edward succeeded as 4th Earl of Dorset. He died in 1652. Edward seems to have led a fairly active life. He was on the continent in 1613 and killed a Lord Edward Bruce near Bergen op Zoom (Holland). DNB XVII p. 578–580. It may be remembered that Thomas Sackville jnr. received a pass to travel abroad on 15th October, 1613. see p. 221 ff.

37. "Officialis Leodiensis supplicatione ac testium depositionibus attentis concedimus supplicanti licentiam impignorandi bona quoran est usufructuaria pro summa mille florenorum brabantiorum semel idque ad effectum petitum et non aliter. Datum anno Domini XVIc decimo octavo mensis maii die decima nona." Insertion in the lease of 31 May, 1618. See above p. 233.

38. AE Liège, Couvents, Jésuites Anglais, Registre pp. 73–75, Nr. 17; Pierre Delrée. Nandrin et Fraineux sous l'Ancien Régime. Notes historiques = Bull. de l'Institut archéolog. Liégeois 71/1956.

39. AE Liège, Couvents, Jésuites Anglais, Registre pp. 76–79, Nr. 18.

40. It is no longer possible to assess the total value of the amounts. They would have been paid in kind. It was a matter of arable land, meadows and pasturage and a farm with garden.

41. ARSI Rome, Anglia 32/II, f. 365r.

42. Now rue des Anglais. The old part of the house was considerably altered and enlarged by large wings. The complex now serves as a hospital (Hopital des Anglais). The former garden was already built over.

43. AE Liège, Officialité de Liège. Rendages proclamatoires Nr. 17. (1615–1621), f. 303rv.

44. ARSI, Rome, Gallo-Belg. 1/II, pp. 387–388.

45. The "Exercises" or "Spiritual Exercises" of St Ignatius are spread over four weeks. The material for meditation is in the famous "Book of the Exercises".

46. It may be the case, of course, that Mary Ward made these notes available. The entries would be used for the education of the members and also copied.

47. " ... to goe that way fourth of some other motive or caus I could not find what. It was not the reward of the good nor the punishment of the bade but some other inward thing." VP/D 1, pp. 1–2, Inst. Arch. Munich.

48. "I was troubled, and unquiet after, fourth of some fears least this imitation of our Saviour, which I now desired soe much, should not agree with my election and chosen Cours of life. I would have inioyed them both." ibid.

49. "This fear hindred, I fear, the effect of my prayer for grace to follow the example of Christ." ibid.

50. "In an instant I loved Him and was very sory for all thos sinnes and besought Him with love and a few tears to forgive me them all and every one." VP/D 3, p. 4. Inst. Arch. Munich.

51. "How severly God punisheth sinne except we doe pennance." VP/D 6, Inst. Arch. Munich.

52. "Presented that perchance their was some great trouble about to happen about the confirmation of our Cours ..." VP/D 6, p. 1. Inst. Arch. Munich.

53. " ... and with this I found a great and new love to this Institute and a neer imbracing or union of affection with it." ibid.

54. "I offered my self willingly to this difficulty and besought our Lord with tears that he would give me grace to bear it, and that noe contradiction might hinder his will ..." ibid. pp. 1–2.

55. "I was as though the occation had bene present: I saw thear was noe healp nor comfort for me, but to cleave fast to Him, and soe I did, for He was their to help me." ibid.

56. "I besought Him that the love I fealt to this Cours now, might steed me then, when the trouble should happen, becaus perhaps I should not then have means or force or time to dispos my self or to call so perticularly upon Him." ibid.

57. "I begged of Him with much affection, that this prayer I now made might serve as a pettition for His grace at that time." ibid.

58. AE Liège, Couvents, Jésuites Anglais, Registre pp. 159–161, Nr. 38.

59. ibid. pp. 164–166, Nr. 40.

60. ibid. pp. 108–110, Nr. 30.

61. ibid pp. 138–144. Nr. 35.

62. AE Liège, Conseil Privé, Dépêches 1612–1792, Nr. 113.

63. AE Liège, Couvents, Jésuites Anglais, Registre pp. 168–170, Nr. 42.

64. Lady Mary Lovel may be identical with Lady Jane Lovel, the daughter of Lord John Roper, first Baron Teynham, and widow of Sir Robert Lovel Kt. In 1606 she travelled to Spa. Among the women travelling with her was her niece, Joyce Vaux, who later entered the Institute. In 1608 Lady Lovel entered with the English Benedictines in Brussels, but left them in 1609. She then endeavoured to found a convent in Malines from her own means. The Archbishop, however, raised such objections that she sought somewhere else for her foundation. In 1617 she made preparations to found an English Carmelite convent in Liège, but these came to nothing. In 1618/19 she acquired a house in Antwerp for a Carmel. Finally, she wanted to found a house for English Cistercians in Bruges, but died (between 1627 and 1629) before she could effect this plan. The house she had acquired she bequeathed to the Jesuits. Lady Lovel was also kept under close surveillance by the English ambassador. Hamilton, Chron EPC1 I, p. 199; Guilday, Refugees, p. 360–362.

65. AE Liège, Couvents, Jésuites Anglais, Registre pp. 236–237. s.n.

66. see p. 218.

67. AE Liège, Collégiale Saint-Martin 58, ff. 64v.–65r.

68. ibid. f. 65r.

69. Ambassador William Trumbull in Brussels to Ambassador Dudley Carleton in The Hague, PRO London, SP 77/14, Part 1, ff. 3r–5v. Trumbull's almost fanatical hatred against catholics is shown in the following: " ... so they must be sente beyond the equinochall lyne to encrease and multiply the holy generation of the Loyolites ... "

70. The whole text: "After a great fitt of sicknes, a freedom from all solicitude of temporal businesses with soe great a hunger to goe out of my self into God as without observation and some labour I could not carry my self in my ordinary maner, but held back as not daring, with some kind of couwardlynes and fear. Both restraint and desire were passive, and to suffer both thes at once seemed to be all that was in my power, but as I have since thought, than if I had asked courage to go, perchance ther would have followed some other effect. A hunger to goe to God with a not daring to venture in respect of His greatnes." VP/G 2, Inst. Arch. Munich (June 1620).

XVI

THE OPPONENTS

In the Society of Jesus

Government of the Order and Mary Ward's Ignatian Institute – General Vicar Ferdinand Alber – Fr General Muzio Vitelleschi – Fr Provincial Jean Heren – critical reports via Fr Young – Fr Jacques Bonfrère and many unnamed Jesuits.

Silent enemies are always the worst. The Englishwomen had bitter enemies in the Society of Jesus. Only a few names have come down to us; most remain unknown and these, perhaps, were the most dangerous of all. The motivation for their behaviour may have been various, such as strict adherence to the command not to become involved with the foundation of female religious congregations; fear that these 'Jesuitesses' could make the Society of Jesus appear ridiculous and probably, too, a rather narrow attitude to women's place in society and the Church in particular.

In 1612 an autonomous province of the Society of Jesus had been set up in Belgium with Fr Jean Heren as its first Provincial.[1] Jean Heren was born in 1562 in Douai (Flemish Doornik). In 1582 he entered the Society of Jesus and became Rector of the College of Lille (Flem. Ryssel). It was during his first term of office as Provincial (1612–1619) that the Institute was founded and began its rapid development. Fr Heren may have granted the Institute a measured and even benevolent attention at first, but letters of warning soon reached him from Fr General Aquaviva[2] though, at the same time, Fr Antonio Colasso was able to intervene on their behalf with Secretary of State Philipp Prats,[3] and Fr Roger Lee was deeply involved in promoting the Institute. Things changed after Fr Aquaviva's death at the beginning of 1615.

The brief term of office of General Vicar Ferdinand Alber, an Austrian from Innsbruck,[4] formed as it were the prelude to sharper attacks on the Institute by the Jesuits. This was at the time when Mary Ward had a free hand in her Institute after Fr Lee's death. An inevitable hardening of the front was the result. During his short tenure of office Fr Alber twice sent Fr Heren orders concerning the Englishwomen. On 21st February, 1615[5] he commanded that in future no Jesuit should have charge of the spiritual direction of the Institute. He gave Fr Provincial strict directions on the matter in the spring of the same year.[6] Fr Heren, in duty bound, passed the information on.[7] The Fathers could meet with religious sisters briefly, and by the door of the house of the Order. Visits to their houses should be only in cases of necessity and always in the company of a fellow member and after permission given by the Superior. Spiritual direction, or administration of the sacraments to these devout ladies should be given in exactly the same measure in which they were given to other ladies. Moreover, administration of their worldly possessions should be forbidden to Jesuits. These devout ladies were preferably to be discouraged from imitating the Jesuits in their work and way of life.

A further example of the Jesuits' distancing themselves from the Englishwomen lies in Fr Richard Blount's letter, 9th June, 1615[8] from England to the Prefect of the English Mission in Rome, Fr Thomas Owen. It is a direct statement: Mary Ward and her Institute in England were as sought after as if they were priests and dangerous people, and many women had been arrested on their account and were now in prison.

At that time two important facts in the history of the Institute followed one another in quick succession. Fr Muzio Vitelleschi was elected Fr General of the Society of Jesus on 15th November, 1615 and exactly one year later, 24th November, 1616, fifteen English-women left St Omer for Liège, to make a foundation that was to emphasise a different dimension of their work.

Fr Muzio Vitelleschi [9] was born in Rome on 2nd December, 1563. He was therefore almost twenty years older than Mary Ward. On 15th August, 1583 he entered the Society of Jesus, was a good preacher as a young Jesuit, and soon became professor of philosophy and theology. He was Provincial in Naples and Rome and Assistant for Italy during Fr Aquaviva's term as general. After the latter's death, the choice fell on Fr Vitelleschi, who then became the sixth General of the Society. After thirty years in office, he died on 9th February, 1645, in Rome, the scene of his life's work, only ten days after Mary Ward's death.

So much for the facts. Two passages show Fr General's attitude towards the Institute – it could have been anticipated: up to Mary Ward's first journey to Rome, he was opposed to the Institute, and even hostile during the complexities of the Liège affair. Biassed information from opponents in the Society, strict observance of the Order's constitutions and, not least, reluctance towards a congregation of women that imitated the Society of Jesus in its structure and work, all contributed to this. It may have been Mary Ward's personality, radiating her union with God together with her distinctive bearing, that changed this man's attitude from active hostility to one of understanding and benevolence. Fr Vitelleschi stood firm by his principles as a Jesuit and as General of the Society of Jesus, but this gentle and serene man let Mary Ward and, with her the Institute, experience his good will and influence during their stay in Italy, and he smoothed their path — at least as far as their educational work was concerned.

The attacks and charges gradually increased in strength after the foundation in Liège, which was in the front line. On 21st October, 1617,[10] Fr Vitelleschi wrote to Fr Henri Scheren, the Visitor, that he wished to have Decree 56 of the 7th General Congregation brought to the attention of the Belgian Province. This Decree gave directions about co-operation of Jesuits with women's Orders. There had been too much involvement in the affairs of women where there were English houses, to such an extent that it seemed they had neither heard of nor listened to the Decree. For example, a novice, Fr Anglus, had recently been sent to England as companion to Mary Ward, the Superior of the Englishwomen in Liège.[11] Fr Tailer, likewise a novice, had been sent to the Englishwomen to give them singing lessons. What was more, the women had been granted entry to the house so that an artist — at the Jesuits' expense — had done some work for them. They had also been invited into the Jesuits' garden, to have lunch there. In summer, two fathers and four Englishwomen had made a pilgrimage to Sichem in a carriage.

These were weighty, and to a certain extent slanderous charges. But the matter did not stop there. The years to come were full of admonitions and commands to Belgium from the administrative centre of the Order in Rome. On 21st April, 1618[12] Fr Vitelleschi praised Fr Scheren for carrying out instructions, and decided that these should be left in writing in the novitiate of the English Jesuits in Liège. On 5th May,[13] he allowed the Jesuits to be confessors to the Englishwomen and to give them spiritual direction, too, but only as far as they did for other women. Soon afterwards, on 26th May, 1618,[14] he expressed his disquiet at the way the confession of religious women was practised in St Omer. He had been informed that in the previous winter, before Feast Days, the Jesuit church had remained open up to three hours after sunset and that two fathers had been occupied in hearing the confessions of certain holy women during this time.

Fr Vitelleschi named no names, but it is not difficult to read 'Englishwomen' here, about whose lengthy confessions complaints had been made for some time.

On 4th August[15] Fr General sent the Belgian Provincial directions about the the new house being built for the Englishwomen in rue Pierreuse in Liège; it has already been mentioned. The fathers could visit sick members of the Englishwomen only if accompanied by a doctor or some other respectable gentleman.

Two months later, on 6th October[16] he once more impressed on the Provincial that he should not allow the Englishwomen in St

Omer or Liège to have any services other than those granted to other women. A week later, on 13th October,[17] Fr Provincial Heren received a report from Rome that the Englishwomen intended going on Pilgrimage – probably to Sichem again as they had done the year before – and that they should be dissuaded from doing so, through Fr Tomson.

What was fact and what was fiction? It is difficult to be objective, and pass a fair judgement. We do not know of any defence of those accused, who may not even have known that they were the object of such information. The truth of the reports to Rome cannot be proved. But it would be important to know what was intended by it – for example, the report of Mary Ward's journey to England in the company of the novice, Fr Anglus. Every Englishman of the time knew what difficulties were involved in sea journeys if one were forced to travel under an alias, or clandestinely. Might it not have been the case that Mary Ward and Fr Anglus travelled under the protection of a third party?

There is also a great difference between a pilgrimage made by the Jesuits and Englishwomen together in one coach, or in several coaches as part of a pilgrimage group. This information was most likely not given. It must not be forgotten that the Englishwomen were used to freer mobility in their homeland, without it being regarded as at all improper. Added to which there was the special situation of Catholics in England. Many of them together with their parents will have hidden priests, or offered them opportunities for flight. As common as the nets which spies spread across the country were the attempts to slip through their meshes.

There is no doubt that some of the Jesuits had supported the Englishwomen perfectly legitimately, and had been accustomed to routine and normal meetings with them.

However, one must also be fair to the position of the opponents. The Englishwomen's heavy debts were undoubtedly openly discussed in the town. No wonder that a number of the fathers who had been against the Institute from the beginning regarded the restored and enlarged house on rue Pierreuse with distrust. It stood four-square before their very eyes. They must also have known of the Englishwomen's predicament. If the latter's landlord, Canon de Merica, knew that Brother Kenix had obtained money for them, is it likely that the Jesuits themselves did not? Their Rector was often with the Englishwomen, he directed their affairs, or at least, so people said. He most certainly did.

How should these women have coped, drawn as they were into a labyrinth of debts. Mary Ward was in England from before 15th December, 1617 and travelled again in July, 1618. She returned to Liège shortly before 21st July, 1619. We do not know if Barbara Babthorpe, soon to be Provincial Superior, and after her Anne

Gage, who returned to the continent in 1618 and was superior in Liège, were good organisers and expert in financial matters. This much is certain. They were advised by Fr Tomson. The near future was to prove that.

It is remarkable that Fr Vitelleschi apparently never wrote his objections to Fr Tomson. It was of course correct procedure to inform the Provincial. Fr Francis Young received a word of thanks for his detailed presentation of facts[18] but he was advised to discuss the matter with his Provincial. It seems strange, though, that Fr Tomson was never addressed about the difficulties concerning the fathers of his house and his own person. Other fathers did receive an answer, as for example Fr Cresswell, who was in Liège at the end of April, 1619.[19] After his report, Fr General entrusted him with the responsibility of warding off any closer relationship between the Jesuits and the Englishwomen and, above all, of deterring these from their use of their name 'Jesuit'. (Jesuitissae dicantur). On 23rd October, 1618, this apparently zealous writer of letters to Rome received a word of praise.[20]

Did Fr Vitelleschi perhaps find it unpleasant to burden Fr Tomson – whom he esteemed highly – with such matters until it was too late? A word of warning or hint from the provincial was quite different from receiving the equivalent from the highest authority in the Society. As will be seen, Fr General protected Fr Tomson up to the very end, only abandoning him when the reputation and good of the Order were at stake, as suggested by incoming reports.

One does not know what part the provincial took, if any, in the many reports sent to Rome about the members of the Institute. But suddenly, on 2nd February, 1619[21] shortly before the expiry of his first term of office and before the establishment of the English Vice-Province, a letter from the General to the departing Provincial showed his keen dislike for the Englishwomen's Institute. The General thanked the Provincial in Belgium for the exact reports about the Englishwomen, saying that he intended to take action with the Pope against their Institute. Probably the provincial's report had the whole Institute – both the Englishwomen in St Omer and in Liège – as its object, for even Fr Jean Leclerq in St Omer, and Fr Joseph Cresswell in Liège were shortly to receive written answers from their General, which suggests a correspondence about the Englishwomen.[22] Shortly after, on 10th June, 1619, Fr Provincial wrote once more to Rome; he had meanwhile visited the houses in St Omer. This report to the General has survived [23], and its contents are reported here briefly: Jesuit opinion about the Englishwomen is divided. Their greatest benefactor is the Rector of the Novitiate house in Liège, Fr John Tomson. He administers nearly all their affairs, and visits them frequently. One cannot get anywhere with him if one does not favour the English women. That is probably the reason why officials are changed so often in his house. A distinguished Englishman has been dissuaded from entering the Society of Jesus because he could not live under the rule of this Rector. In Liège, the congregation of the Englishwomen is increasing steadily, as though their Institute were already approved; even some Belgians are being accepted. They have their novitiate in one house (Mont St Martin) and their school in another (rue Pierreuse). In St Omer, on the other hand, their number is diminishing because they do not have such influential benefactors as in Liège. The English Jesuits in particular object to this Institute, for they see it as harmful to the Society. But the Englishwomen know their benefactors and their opponents. After Fr Henry More had been removed as their confessor and other confessors appointed them in St Omer, Mary Ward had taken the members of her Institute who spoke only English to Liège. Those who stayed in St Omer went to the Walloon Jesuits to confession; but they still remain in close contact with the English fathers, particularly with Fr Tomson, who tells them everything about the Society. The ladies imitate the Society in everything, even teaching Latin, and they have recently – and secretly – had the Jesuit emblem put over the door of their chapel in St Omer.

All this information flowed from the pen of a man who wanted to make a report in the interests of his Order, and that an unbiassed one. It is, therefore, all the more significant when he ends his letter with words to the effect that the Institute of the Englishwomen should be esteemed as holy and godly, (quod sanctum piumque iudico),[24] so long as it remained within its limits, and the Jesuits, too, kept to the instructions of their Order.

Even if this letter leaves nothing to be desired as far as plain speaking is concerned, certain enquiries are justified. From whom did Fr Heren obtain his information? The Provincial of the Jesuits in Belgium had lived mostly in Brussels or Louvain; for details concerning the houses he had to rely on his visits to the fathers, or their reports. One of his informants may have been the infuriated Count Thomas Sackville; it was he who had spread the rumour among the Jesuits in St Omer that one could not get to Fr Tomson except through the English women. Two facts stand out here: only the English Jesuits, and their attitude towards the Englishwomen, is spoken of here. It was therefore from these that the disapproval and the complaints came. Fr Heren will also have visited the Walloon houses of the Society of Jesus in Liège. He will also doubtless have received letters from these Fathers, but apparently there were few or no discouraging remarks about the Institute. The French speaking members of the Institute went to confession to these fathers in St Omer.[25] Did these have no objections against their penitents, who belonged to this much-criticized Institute? Fr General's letter of 9th March, 1619 merely allows one to draw conclusions about the reports concerning the Englishwomen's dependence on the Society of Jesus. But the English Jesuits knew the Institute not only on the Continent but also from the members' work in England. It was not so much that the Englishwomen in St Omer and Liège were prejudicial to the Society of Jesus in the educational sphere – although their teaching of Latin was unacceptable – but far more in their apostolate of pastoral work among adults, a work in which women had no right to be engaged in those days.

Something else is worth noting. Fr Heren actually reported something more detrimental to the English Jesuits than to the Englishwomen. The English Jesuits, and especially Fr Tomson, were their benefactors and apparently these overstepped the limits of their superiors' decrees by devoting themselves more to these women than to others, and even gave them information from the houses.

The Institute's members in Liège had increased in numbers, probably at the expense of the St Omer house; they had accepted Belgian women, taught Latin, and went to the Walloon fathers in St Omer to confession. With their countrymen, they were in touch with the Society of Jesus. It is difficult to regard that as inadmissible, or detrimental to the Society of Jesus. Naturally, more prudent behaviour would have been possible. It did not exactly lead to mutual understanding when the Englishwomen placed the Jesuit emblem, the IHS seal within its surrounding rays, over their chapel door. It was a public chapel, and any outsider visiting it could see the sign. This would hardly have been the sole event that helped to poison the atmosphere. A more reserved attitude towards the Society of Jesus would have served them better and smoothed many a rough grain. It is not difficult to predict the future of the Rector of Liège. What the official, comprehensive report to Fr General did not and could not contain, were the basic reasons why Fr Tomson was so occupied with the English women and their business: namely, the dismal financial affairs of Count Thomas Sackville, for which he was partly, if not mainly, responsible.

It was not only the Provincial of the Belgian province of the Order who wrote to Fr General criticising the Institute which had caused so much disquiet among Jesuit ranks, but also an experienced Jesuit of the English Mission, Fr Francis Young who, in his report to his highest authority, took a critical stance towards Mary Ward's Institute.[26]

Fr Young knew the Englishwomen and their Institute in England and perhaps also in Belgium. Although his report reflects less of his own emotional judgement and more of the opinion of others, this letter is of great importance. It has two parts: first, Fr Young reviews the Institute, its aim, its course, and its foundress Mary Ward; in the second part he is concerned with the consequences that this Institute could have on the Society of Jesus. Its contents, briefly:

The Institute was founded in St Omer; it now has another house in Liège, and more foundations are planned, and there are various opinions about such plans. The congregation has eminent friends among the Jesuits in England and still more in Belgium. Their aim is the teaching and education of girls on the Continent and apostolic work and help for priests in England. Finally, Fr Young sums up the activity of the members, particularly in England, approving it thoroughly, even if with reservations. Their way of life is praiseworthy. He considered their imitation of the Society to be a drawback; they even went so far as to take the name 'Society of Jesus.' He was less sympathetic in his judgement of the foundress of the Institute, Mary Ward. Here he followed gossip. After a life of severe asceticism in her youth, she first entered the Poor Clares Order in St Omer, left it soon after and founded a house for English Poor Clares in Gravelines. Under Jesuit influence, she left the Order (rebus nondum stabilitis) as the convent wished to be subject to Franciscans. She went back to England and afterwards founded her own Institute, which was constructed totally along the lines of the Society of Jesus.

Fr Young was large in his praise of the work of the Englishwomen in their schools, both day and boarding; he utterly rejected their liberal method of education, which was likewise on the Jesuit model. He gave similar judgement to their work in England. Commendable in itself, it was far too dangerous for women; moreover, it caused gossip.

Then Fr Young moved on to the second part of his report: the effect of such an Institute on the Society of Jesus. Even if their schools were good they were imitating the Society in their teaching, and made this subject to ridicule (risum). They copied the Jesuits in everything, read their Rule in the refectory, celebrated the feast days of the Jesuits' own saints, and even used their seal, and this without papal permission, or the approval of Fr General. In all this they found support among fathers who had helped them in one way or another, although this was against orders. They were the cause of the differences that had broken out between Jesuits. It was not surprising that this had spread abroad and made the Order ridiculous to many outsiders. The letter ends with a request to Fr General to take action.

Fr Young was a mature man when he wrote this letter. He was working at the time in Douai, the centre for the English secular priests who either continued or ended their studies there and were opposed to the Jesuits. Fr Young therefore knew the contemporary opinion of the Institute and its members, but it was an extremely biassed and subjective opinion. Happily, he could not say anything harmful about the women. It was merely their adoption of the Rule of the Society of Jesus and their subsequent following of the work and manner of life of the Jesuits that caused him to complain. The danger for the Institute lay in the frequency with which their opponents' objections were sent to the curia of the Society of Jesus with the repetition of the word 'ridiculous'.

Constant dropping of water wears out a stone.

The long list of objections were not yet finished. On 28th September, 1619,[27] Fr General ordered an examination into accusations against Fr John Falkner, who had directed the pupils of the Englishwomen in some theatrical pieces in Liège. He wrote to Fr Falkner on the same day,[28] that he had at first given no credence to the charge, and that he wished to bring the contentious matter to a close. Fr Vitelleschi did not inform him how he proposed to do so.

On 14th April, 1620,[29] Fr Jacques Bonfrère[30] wrote a detailed report to Rome from Dinant. Out of love for the Society of Jesus, and concern for its reputation, so continued the writer, he was forced to pass on certain pieces of information from Liège, which he and some other fathers had learnt. Next followed attacks on the Englishwomen, about whom Fr Vitelleschi must have heard quite enough already:

The ladies copy the Jesuits in everything, even in dress, as far as women can; in the Rule too, which they have in their possession; in their order of the day, their customs, their Vow formula, and the structure of their novitiate. They base their school system on that of the Jesuits. Moreover, their manner of life is about to be confirmed by Rome as a Pius Institute.[31] But people do not understand the difference between an Order and a Pius Institute. Recently, in Spa, some of the fathers had been asked about the Englishwomen, which caused great indignation among them. The women call themselves Jesuitesses. What is dangerous is that they have benefactors even among the Cardinals, through whom papal approval of the Institute could be obtained. Then there is Fr Tomson, although a saintly man, he is very closely involved with the Englishwomen.

Certainly, as far as Fr General was concerned, this letter was yet another accusation. But what charge did it contain, precisely? That the Englishwomen imitated the Jesuits in everything was true. Otherwise the sharp observer had nothing detrimental to report to Rome. Here were some women who intended to become Jesuitesses, but apparently they were good women of high moral standing, pious, and with good intentions. If they had committed anything morally wrong, it would immediately have been brought to the attention of Rome and elsewhere. Fr General's thanks[32] to Fr Bonfrère were also accompanied by the weary statement that it had told him nothing new and he hoped that the new Vice-Rector would soon take action on his return from England.

In this context, with all these lesser and greater pieces of news, with the complaints and accusations and the general unrest that had infiltrated Jesuit houses, it is significant that in the Spring of 1619, Count Thomas Sackville left Liège and, in the spring of the following year, was to be found with the English Jesuits in Louvain.

In this year, 1620, Mary Ward wrote in her notes:

'My heart was held by some power far above myself',[33] and further on, 'but I am not so much moved to pray, as called to see.'[34]

In England

Complaints from persons unknown about the Englishwomen's open way of life – 'Only women'

A completely different style of letter is that of an Englishman dated 1st/11th June, 1619, (Old/New style respectively),[35] signed with the initials A.B. Whether these indicate Anthony Browne, 2nd Lord Montague, remains an unproven possibility. Both of Montague's daughters, Anne and Lucy, were members of the Institute on the Continent. He was a nephew of Jane Browne, one of the first members. The anonymous recipient may have been Fr Provincial Heren, for he is addressed as 'Plurimum Reverende Pater'. The letter lies in the State Archives in Brussels among the Jesuit documents. Whether it was the author himself who composed his letter in good Latin, we cannot be sure. It would appear that he was a man of good education, for the contents show that he was a member of that courageous and wealthy group of Catholics who granted Jesuits hospitality and safety in their houses, and was now obliged to write an anxious letter to the Continent because of the imprudent actions of one of the Fathers – as he wrote. For some years, members of a new Order who wished to be called 'Mothers', have been at large in England (spargitur). They do all they can to recruit new members, and are encouraged in this by the Jesuits. The letter-writer gave an example of a happening in his immediate neighbourhood, which had also involved him personally. The Jesuit chaplain in his house was a devotee of this new Order of women and, because of his dealings with them, had put his household at risk. He had even urged the only daughter of his host to enter with them but he, as the father, had managed to put a stop to that. These women had already kept a relative of his with them by force (detinuerint) so that he could get her back only after some trouble. From reasons of security and prudence, he had refused his chaplain's request to allow the women of this community to be given spiritual instruction in his house. At the end of the letter the writer asked for help in this dangerous situation, otherwise – however reluctantly – he would have to take action himself. What that would be, he did not disclose.

To pass fair judgement on the letter, which contains specific charges, we must try to see the situation from the man's point of view. He had taken on the dangerous task of providing accommodation and protection for a catholic priest and that a Jesuit, a member of the group then much suspect in England. He must have owned a large house in London, for it was hardly likely that several Englishwomen would have frequented a country house for instruction. In any case, they operated mainly in towns, where people could be contacted easily. And it was precisely for these women, who exposed themselves to the danger of ending in prison, that his chaplain was now requesting that they might have spiritual instruction or readings in his house. It is true, such gatherings of catholics were very dangerous; government agents were everywhere. But, one might be excused for thinking that the man had already placed himself in jeopardy by harbouring a Jesuit in his house. It seems that his courage only began to falter when the Englishwomen appeared on the scenes, those extremely energetic and courageous women, who could however pose a threat by infecting his one and only daughter with their enthusiasm for their Institute. That would appear to be the real reason for this letter, containing as it does an implicit request for the transfer of his chaplain.

On closer examination, he is attacking the life style of these women 'who want be called Mothers', with their unusual freedom of movement and openness towards men when God's work required it, but he is not denouncing their morals, still less their aims.

However, his letter reached its destination, was read, and carefully filed away as evidence of that infamous type of work, the Englishwomen's controversial pastoral activity, which lured even Jesuits into their net.

This letter may serve as an example of many objections which have not survived, objections which gradually created an aura of baseness or something essentially corrupt, and spread a cloud of disapproval around these women.

A totally different picture is that presented by the Painted Life in Panels 30 and 31. Both are filled with movement. Panel 30 shows Mary Ward kneeling before an open door. Against the background of open country are groups of saints, who each found different ways to holiness. To the top left there are people being beheaded, hanged and put to the stake, the martyrs of the Church. To the right, as though in the tranquillity of contemplation, stands a group of the old Orders of the Church: St Benedict, Pachomius, Francis of Assisi and Dominic and, between them, the great saints of the women's contemplative Orders: Clare, Bridget, Scholastica and Teresa of Avila. But in the foreground, close to Mary Ward, are a group of people who are evangelizing in various ways: by teaching children, or in conversation with adults. The dynamic of movement is quite different from that of the martyrs at the top of the picture. The text runs: 'In 1619, in St Omer, while Mary was fervently thanking God for the grace of her vocation, He showed her clearly that to help to

save souls is a far greater gift than the monastic life or even martyrdom itself.' As with the text for the Gloria Vision, it must be
pointed out here too that the words may be misleading. Certainly,
as far as Mary Ward personally was concerned, her apostolate was
'a far greater gift', but this was not meant as a generalisation.
The difference between the Orders can never be viewed in terms
of degree.

Panel 31 has two parts; to the left, and occupying about two
thirds of the space, is a picture of the calling of the Apostles. There
is movement everywhere; not feverish movement, but one of commitment. The Lord's inviting gesture is reflected in Peter's, as he
clambers out of a boat. Three other apostles look across towards
the Master and get ready to leave. The sea is in constant movement,
with curling waves that cover its entire surface. The sky is not
uniform blue, but broken by the wandering clouds of a summer
day. Mary Ward is kneeling to the right before a priedieu with
a picture of the Madonna. The text: 'In 1619, when Mary was
meditating on the call of the apostles, she perceived that they had
no resting place in anything of this world but were entirely at their
Divine Master's disposal. This knowledge aroused in her a renewed
desire to attain to perfect self abnegation.Suddenly she experienced
a feeling of complete liberty and detachment from earthly things,
from the world and from created things.' The same joy of commitment lies in her rousing words of December 1617 or 1618, [36]
to members of the Institute in St Omer, after a stay in England.
They were provoked by the opinion of the Father Minister of the
English Seminary in St Omer, who declared that the first fervour of
the members would soon wear off, as 'they are but women'. These
words had caught the members on the raw, and disturbed them.
Mary Ward, to whom union with God was of the essence, picked
up the remark belittling her sex not simply in order to refute it but
probably also to remove the bitter taste left behind by the Father's
statement.

'Zeal to do good is a gift of God's grace, and people − men as
well as women − grow slack in proportion to their imperfection.'[37]
She had just taken a world of trouble, in these last weeks, with a
priest whose fervour had grown tepid.[38] 'Fervour does not consist
in feelings, nor in pious narcisissm, but in the will to do good. It
is not the taking of vows, nor the approval of superiors that gives
security, but simply and solely the search for truth, and that is the
search for God.[39]

True, in marriage, woman is subject to man, and the leadership of
the Church lies in the hands of men, and it is not for women to give
the sacraments or preach in public churches, but is she of less value
because of this?'[40] Today, after more than three hundred and fifty
years, these remarks sound very moderate and not remotely radical.
But in the seventeenth century there were priests who 'would not

for 10,000 worlds be a woman', because she could not know God.[41]
Mary Ward recounted this episode and other conversations from
England, which showed that this priest was not alone in his views.

Mary Ward was no suffragette. She acknowledged the social
order of her time both in civil and ecclesiastical affairs, but
she warmly objected to any denigration of women in the religious sphere. Women too could, no − should − be considered
worthy of aspiring to union with God. 'It is not learning now that
I commend to you, but knowledge, true knowledge, which you all
may have if you love and seek it ... even in little things, lack of
true knowledge is a great lack.'[42]

These were compelling words addressed to the young members,
of whom Mary Ward said in her third talk that they would make
their mark on society.[43]

One could argue that her stance was anachronistic at a time
when the Church was reviving its strictures about the enclosure
of female Orders. History, including the history of women, is a
continuity, and every movement within it is a reaching out to the
future. It was not opposition that impelled Mary Ward to formulate her statement, but the clarification of something of supreme
importance.

'I implore you, for God's sake, to love the truth.'[44]

Again and again in these talks, there resonates 'Love verity'
echoing through other trends of thought. Love the truth; the truth
is God. That is why, for Mary Ward, truthfulness and union with
God are one and the same.

The claim of pious men that a woman could neither have fervour
nor the desire for truth, that is, a relationship with God, may have
offended Mary Ward no less than her companions. It was not by
chance that the consoling words of the Letter to the Romans were
placed towards the end of her talk:

'We know that in everything God works for good with those who
love him, who are called to his purpose.'[45]

The Worm within

1619

*Increasing opposition by unknown Jesuits against the
Institute − Sr Praxedis and her followers*

The hidden testing of strength to which the Institute had been con-
tinually subjected since Mary Ward's revelation of 1611, burst out in
a violent explosion of opposing views within the community in 1619.
It happened at the same time that Thomas Sackville left both Liège

and the fragments of his putative wealth to the Englishwomen.

We do not know a great deal about the exact circumstances which led to it, nor of the course of events. Certainly, Mary Ward's complete loyalty to her task of forming the Institute on the model of the Society of Jesus was not understood by every member of her community. There was also pressure from outsiders. The attitude of most English Jesuits in Liège had grown sharper. Their running commentary to Rome, evident from Fr General's answers, proves that. Moreover, Count Sackville's inability to pay the building expenses for their house in rue Pierreuse caused the Englishwomen to run into an alarming financial situation which was soon to end in complete collapse and do a good deal of harm to the English Jesuits. All of this may have contributed to make more acceptable Sister Praxedis' alleged visions about a change of structure of the Institute. Even Fr Burton, the procurator of the English Jesuits and their confessor, believed her.[46]

The English Vita describes Sr Praxedis with few words[47] as a simple maid from the Ardennes, who as a 'seer' became the focal point of a threatening trend in the Institute, a trend that wanted to strike out in another direction. We will not be far wrong if we see in the group around Sr Praxedis' supporters of the 'Pium Institutum', such as there had always been in the community. In her own circle, Sr Praxedis may indeed have had a great influence, particularly as she was simple and religious, but it is likely that the member Mary Alcock, who left the Institute a short time after these events and some years later was to supply material for a slanderous pamphlet against Mary Ward, was a far more dangerous opponent.

The requests of those who were dissatisfied are not known. Fridl, in his 'Tugend-Schul' [48] says they were supposed to have had negotiations with another Order for taking on their Rule, but he gives no reference in the sources.

Inner tension remained, even after the death of Sr Praxedis, which the English Vita regarded as a judgement of God.[49] The whole affair may have made inhuman demands on Mary Ward but at the same time great graces were given her.[50]

Spiritual Exercises, 1619

April and October

From Mary Ward's notes: longing for original justice — thoughts of leaving the Institute — anxiety about changing the structure of the Institute — striving for conformity with God's will — attempt to interpret some difficult notes on the structure of the Institute

It is not surprising that Mary Ward made two retreats in this year, 1619. The Spiritual Exercises meant withdrawal and tranquillity, and above all meditation and loving converse with God in prayer. At this time of interior purification and of the exterior downfall of her Institute she could have wanted nothing more than to retire to her chosen refuge – the Lord. The first sentence of her retreat note for April is: 'A quiet content, I think with God'.[51] These notes, without exception, have come down to us in Mary Ward's own writing, transcripts of which were made in the Parchment Book.[52] It is not surprising, either, that the main trend of her thoughts was concerned with God's will, with people's co-operation with it, and free will. These may have been the very themes that she was pre-occupied with for her Institute, which may indeed have forced themselves on her. It would be good to comment here on the notes referring to the Institute.

In the meditation on the sin of Adam and Eve[53] we are strongly reminded of the Vision of the Just Soul. In that, Mary Ward compared the beauty of someone who sincerely performed the duties and requirements of the Institute to the beauty of those in the state of original justice. Her longing for God breaks out: 'O my God, cannot this state be had in this life?'.[54] This state that had been captured in her preceding sentences – 'The delicacy of that state, where sense obeyed reason, and reason the divine will. Where there was neither darkness of understanding nor inclination to evil. Whose work was the will of their master, and their fulfilment, that God was pleased with them.'[55] What a picture for a hungry heart! Her request was like a supplication, showing her own needs: 'As much as it may be imparted to anyone, bestow it, my Jesus, on her whom thou has made thus, to enable her to carry out those things.'[56] It is there again, that dark fear of a discrepancy between herself and her task, between the greatness, the glorification of God in her Institute, and her own wretchedness.

Like a loving consolation, she continues: 'I know, my God, that darkness of understanding and a propensity to sin will still remain (at least in some measure), but these in themselves are sufferings, not sins, though alas those falls that come from ignorance or rashness will often be caused by them.'[57] The last passage in her notes on this meditation concentrates on her readiness to do God's will.[58]

Her notes for the meditation 'On death' are significant. Her soul was encompassed by sadness and darkness. Concern about those who were discontented and wanted to change the charism of her Institute was undoubtedly the cause, for suddenly there comes the sentence: 'As I was more careful to go into particulars, I found a disinclination to leave this company before it was confirmed.'[59]

The reason: 'those that followed might make it something else, and here (against my will) I seemed of some importance, and not to be spared without prejudice to the work.'[60] Her anxieties are clearly evident here: fear, lest the character of the Institute desired by Sr Praxedis and her followers might gain credence if she, Mary Ward, were to leave it before it received papal approval. But she, humble woman that she truly was, is almost frightened at such a thought which seemed like pride – 'this I knew to be a lie, and to proceed from no good ground'[61], and she sought refuge in thoughts of self-disparagement. Almighty God could have his will performed by anyone at all, she thought. And at the same time she reflected on former times, and how she had been brought through a world of difficulties and troubles by God, in order to do the little that she had done.[62] And she came to the conclusion that God's working was the beginning, middle and end, and was the sole reason, why this good (namely, the Institute entrusted to her), had no existence nor place in her, but was solely the work of God's grace.[63] This grace, in her own words: 'which though in me, was yet a different thing from this Me; without which, ... this good (the Institute) could not stand and which, withdrawn, I should remain as before'.[64] She found no help in confessing her own nothingness before God, 'I found ... I would still be of importance and someone who was needed.'[65] She saw herself, as she offered herself to God – 'little, and of less importance for his work.'[66] And then, 'God's will and wisdom seemed great, and his power such, and of such force, as strongly to effect in an instant or with a look, whatever he would. And before this greatness, the power of all his creatures (resisting him) altogether melted away and, in a moment, lost their being.'[67]

When once again she offered to leave everything that was dear to her, and even desired to die before everything was accomplished, because then it would be quite clearly seen as God's work, she was moved to desire God's will only, and nothing else. Not even that desire, which was in effect a loving subterfuge, was granted her. Her answer was decisive: 'moved to wish nothing else, except God's will, I said inwardly, 'neither life nor death, my God, but your holy will ever be done in me; do whatever pleases you best.'[68] How much this struggle filled those dark days in Liège is shown by some entries made in the late autumn of the same year; they are difficult to make out, and have been translated freely. In one note, which may have been written in October, and bears the title 'what I find and am drawn to practise'[69] after several reflections about her longing to fulfil God's will, are the following concluding sentences:

'An imperfect sight/ that something, or everything,/ in or belonging to our Institute was God's known will. These are all suffered,/ not sought for, nor followed further nor longer/ than by the means (the matter and manner) in which they are made known (by God) and should so remain.'[70]

On St Francis' Day (4th October), she prayed peacefully and contemplatively with 'freedom of all powers', ready to do all for

God, and ready for anything that was to come, completely committed to God's will. Next follow a few sentences about interior experiences. Finally, she reflects: 'I see in our Institute what I cannot say, and more by a certainty that there is in it what I do not see.'[71] Her struggle with selfwill is alluded to over and over again in these notes, selfwill that must be seen in the context of her fear of the acceptance of a model for the Institute other than that of the Society of Jesus. This occurs again in a short entry: 'A sight concerning our subordination, (that is, the independence of the Institute,) but less decided because I feared lest it should proceed from myself and that my own will was now mixed with it. Refusing (to accept it) God withdrew and left me idle.' [72] One can see from this how much Mary Ward feared this great responsibility, and God's inflexibility. From the same reflections are other sentences which touch on an equally difficult topic.

'Those of the Kingdom of Christ think that if I only had to ask and could act as I would wish, I would long above all else to spend my days in such work. On one such occasion I found myself persuaded to pray that I might not only live in this sort of work but die for it.'[73] By 'those of the Kingdom of Christ' she undoubtedly meant those members who, according to St Ignatius in the Second Week of his Spiritual Exercises (no.93), worked in the 'Lord's vineyard', and were active on the dangerous English mission. Mary Ward had often been engaged in it herself during her frequent and sometimes extended visits to her homeland between the years 1614 and 1620. Of these, four were recorded and there may have been more. As the daughter of a man who 'had suffered much for the good cause' and a mother who belonged to the militant Wright family, she had never lost the way of it. Mary Ward feared sin. She was also anxious about the responsiblity entailed in the office of first General Superior of the Society of Jesus for women. But when it was a matter of assisting the oppressed catholics of her own country she was the courageous woman who, as she herself said, was prepared 'to die in the same cause.' There is a glint in these words not unlike her uncle John Wright's sword when he – one of the best swordsmen of the county – defended himself to the last, back to back with his brother Christopher at Holbeach.

The same notes give us a sentence which should be remembered above all others:

'There was no love I desired or treasured like to His.' [74]

Letter to Fr John Tomson, SJ

1619

*The Englishwomen's Institute: the Ignatian charism but inde-
pendence from the Society – attempt to interpret some difficult notes – clarity concerning the structure and work of the
Institute in the letter to Fr Tomson*

One can see from the notes written in 1619 how Mary Ward
sought over and over again in prayer to obtain a clear definition
of the Institute. The very notes themselves are sometimes difficult
to understand.

'As I was doubting the words 'this Society', I had a clear insight,
accompanied by loving confidence, to ask God that he would grant
and accomplish what he had commanded and what we had endeavoured to undertake. That this was far more the same Institute of
the Society of Jesus both in substance and practice than if the same
Institute should be applied to us by any other way or in any other
manner, in which those who doubted might understand the Institute
and. . .'[75]

The difficulty lies mainly in Mary Ward's use of the same term
for different concepts, which were clear enough to her. Thus 'this
Society' signified the Society of Jesus for men and women. The
'Vision of the Just Soul'[76] has already shown this. 'The same'
refers to the Institute of the Society of Jesus or rather the Formula
of the Institute, the Rule and the Constitutions of this Order. That
is equally true of the reference 'Institute', which should be read into
the text.

The next note is even more difficult. 'In this respect we understand that God has so ordained it that our subordination, etc., must
be among ourselves. It seems absolutely necessary, if we look to
the last analysis of our Institute, that while we take the same of
the Institute of the Society of Jesus, we should leave it entire and
without doing it harm. If we understand that by 'taking the Same'
it is required that we leave 'the Same of the Society of Jesus' without
damage, and that the one of these (the Society of Jesus), cannot
stand without the other (the Institute of Mary Ward), which both
the founder and we, who now take the Institute of the Society of
Jesus upon ourselves, would cause it no harm. O wisdom of God,
who orders all things so wisely, when we understand as well that in
this respect the laws of this Institute (of the Society of Jesus) point
to the fact that this Institute (the Society of Jesus) is so constituted
that whoever wishes to take the same Institute of the Society of Jesus
must leave the Society of Jesus entirely the same and will practise as
both Blessed Father Ignatius, we ourselves, and the words of the
Institute, etc. . . . God declared what, and this Institute shows how.

The same Institute (Society of Jesus) comprises both the 'how' and the 'what'. [77]

However difficult these notes may be, it emerges quite clearly that Mary Ward learnt to regard the Society of Jesus and her Institute as a unity; that St Ignatius received the Constitutions of the Society of Jesus from God just as she had been charged with taking on these same Constitutions and the Formula of the Institute for her Institute.

Both congregations, with 'the Same' Institute and the same task, should, however, remain independent of one another. From this we see how comprehensive and worldwide the Society of Jesus was understood to be.

Mary Ward's clear revelation about the God-given commission concerning her Institute formed the basis of her letter to Fr Tomson. [78]

The passage in the Parchment Book [79] is dated simply with the year, 1619. The text lies between the meditation 'On Death' (pp. 32–37) and that on the 'Comparison of Christ with a temporal King' (pp 47–50). Both themes are taken from the Spiritual Exercises made in April, 1619, though that does not establish conclusively that the letter was written at that time.

Once again, the opening words convey fear: 'As I was today in a sea of uncertainties', she begins, 'and full of fears because of my own inability to do anything, however little, without some powerful and extraordinary help, calling on God as my last and best refuge, and receiving him (in Communion), the following proposal came into my mind. Might not Sister Praxedis write down what she has seen, and everything else that she has learnt from God concerning the Institute? What if both you and Fr Burton were to bid her to draw up an Institute as carefully as she would if she were in my position, and I were in another world, and as though this whole matter depended entirely on her?' [80]

If an aside may be permitted here, the fact that Mary Ward names the two fathers – Fr Tomson and Fr Burton – in one breath seems to indicate that Fr Tomson too, like his procurator, stood by Sister Praxedis and had welcomed a change in the matters under debate, full adoption of the Institute of the Society of Jesus by the Englishwomen's Institute and perhaps, also, the apostolate in England.

'She may also know', continues Mary Ward in her letter, 'what I had from God touching this, if this is thought useful, and would help her.' [81] And then come the words which are so familiar in every writing about her, and which should be understood as they have been written: 'Take the same Institute of the Society of Jesus. Fr General will never permit it. Go to him. These are the words whose worth cannot be valued, nor the good they contain too dearly bought. These gave light where there was none; made known to me what God would have done; gave strength to suffer what has happened since, and assurance of what is wished for in time to come'.[82]

There is an urgency and passion in these words, written by this usually reserved woman. We would like to draw attention to the expression: 'assurance of what is wished for in time to come.' Mary Ward knew that her Institute would be unacceptable, that she could not carry it through. But she also knew that one day the time for her Institute would come.

Finally, she writes 'And if I should ever be worthy to do anything more about the Institute, this is my starting point. I could say a great deal about these words, but never everything'.[83]

It has already been shown from her notes that the 1611 revelation did not stand in isolation. Again and again, alarmed at the difficulties confronting her, Mary Ward turned to the Lord for help, consolation and support, and they were given her. God never overburdens anyone. The letter continues, 'Twice doubting what kind of subordination we should have, I was sent home (I mean to your Institute) and commanded 'Do what is done there'.[84] In other words, make her Institute subject to the Pope as the Jesuits did.

Later, in her notes for 1624,[85] she counted the following illumination among those granted to her by the Lord: 'About the name. St Omer.' 'The Subordination, Grafton and Liège'. We do not know what occurred in Grafton during one of her visits to England. Panel 27[86] of the Painted Life provides a further insight about the Just Soul, while she meditated on the words 'You shall call him Jesus.' It was in Liège that she was granted confirmation of her knowledge about the Institute, as already remarked. 'Once,' she continues in her letter, 'I think I saw a general of yours who said nothing, but whose expression promised all cooperation with us.'[87] This sight of a far distant future may have been for her encouragement, she thought, for it was just at that time that some of the Jesuits were declaring that the Institute which Mary Ward believed was ordained by God would never be sanctioned by the General.[88] But neither could she believe that she would be abandoned to human power. The vision had given her the certainty that, when the time was right, Father General would not harm the Institute. Quite the contrary.[89]

There is a revealing sentence towards the end of the letter which shows how she saw herself: 'Anything else (in revelations) I have had, has been general, and in particular such an understanding of your Institute and such a love of it as only He can effect Who alone is able to do so, without any action or endeavour of mine, that is, to bring together two things that are so different: your Order and my perverse will.'[90] This letter was written, as the saying goes, with her heart's blood. It is a particularly important fact for us that Mary Ward did not deviate by one hair's breadth from her commission, in spite of the difficult situation of her Institute, in spite of sometimes tempting outside influences, and even in spite of the crisis threatening her Institute from within.

How often one comes across the words 'God's Will' in her prayers and meditations. His will was her only life-line, but it was not a painless attachment. The final words of the passage above refer to her 'perverse will', which probably hinted at an interior weakening, or perhaps even a disinclination. Who knows? Her life in God's service was certainly not easy. But she had struggled through to that loyal discipleship to which she was called. One consolation in all the opposition was that deep love which she cherished for the Institute, the 'nearness of affection' which, in the final resort, was rooted in her love for her Lord who had given her this testing yet wonderful charge.

Notes

1. Fr Elesban de Guilherny SJ, Ménologe de la Compagnie de Jésus, Assistance de Germanie, 2 Série, Partie I, Paris 1899, p. 412–413; P. Delattre SJ, Les Etablissements des Jésuites en France depuis quatre Siècles II, p. 258, 1183–1184; A. Poncelet, Nécrologe des Jésuites de la province Flandro-Belge, Wettern 1931, p. 54.
2. On 25th August 1612, Fr General Aquaviva wrote that a secular priest should take on the spiritual direction of the Englishwomen, and that the Jesuits should hear their confessions in the Jesuit church only. ARSI, Rome, Gallo-Belg. 1/I p. 12. This order was conveyed in a letter, 12th September, to Fr Jean Busleyden, ARSI Rome, Germ. Supp. 4, f. 34r, and imparted afresh to Fr Provincial as well as Fr Rector in Saint-Omer, 13th October, 1612. ARSI Rome, Gallo-Belg. 1/I, pp. 20 and 21.
3. AGR Brussels, PEA 1944. (3)
4. Fr Ferdinand Alber SJ was born in Innsbruck in 1548 and entered the Society of Jesus in 1565. He became General Assistant for the German provinces and was responsible for the business of the Society after the death of Fr General Claudio Aquaviva (31st January, 1615) until the election of the new General, Fr Muzio Vitelleschi (15th November, 1615). B. Duhr, Gesch. d. Jesuiten in den Ländern deutscher Zunge in der ersten Halfte des XVII Jahrhunderts, II/1, p. 14, note 3 and p. 17, note 3.
5. ARSI Rome, Gallo-Belg, 1/I, p. 167.
6. On 11. April, ibid. p. 175 and AGR Brussels, Archives Jésuitiques Prov. Gallo-Belg. Carton 32.
7. AGR Brussels, Archives Jésuitiques, Prov. Gallo-Belg. Carton 32. The instructions are not dated but must have been written at this time.
8. Stonyhurst College Archives, F. Chr. Grene SJ, Collectanea M. p. 95b.
9. For Fr Muzio Vitelleschi SJ see above all Sommervogel VIII, p. 848, L. Koch, Jesuitenlexikon, Paderborn 1934, Sp. 1822–1823 and Duhr, Jesuiten II, passim.
10. ARSI Rome, Gallo-Belg. 1/I, p. 332a.
11. Mary Ward had left the continent on 21st July 1617; the accusations therefore were concerned with an event which was already past.
12. ARSI Rome, Gallo-Belg. 1/II, pp. 387–388.
13. Fr General Vitelleschi to the visitor Fr Scheren, ibid. pp. 389–399.
14. ibid. p. 405.
15. ibid. 1/II, p. 428.
16. "Quod attinet ad gyniceum Anglicanum, quod Leodii et Audomari est, cum

coetus illis in unum collecti opera Societatis dissipari non possint ..." ibid. p. 444. This sentence has a waspish tone.

17. ibid. p. 447.
18. On 20th September 1619, ARSI Rome, Germ. 111 f. 100v. Fr Young was again in Douai.
19. On 27th April, 1619. ARSI Rome, Angl. 1/I, f. 88rv.
20. ARSI Rome, Germ. 111, f. 12v.
21. ARSI Rome, Gallo-Belg. 1/II, pp. 471–472.
22. Fr General Vitelleschi to Fr Leclercq, 9. March 1619, ibid pp. 486–487; ditto to Fr Creswell, 27. April 1619, ARSI Rome, Angl. 1/I, f. 88rv.
23. ARSI Rome, Gallo-Belg, 40, ff, 26r–27v.
24. On 20th July 1619 Fr General Vitelleschi thanked the Provincial for his report and promised to take appropriate measures. ARSI Rome, Gallo-Belg. 1/II, p. 520.
25. On 26th June 1619, Fr Heren made it known in an open letter that, at the wish of their superior and without any action taken by the Jesuits, the Englishwomen would be confessing to the Walloon fathers. AGR Brussels, Archives Jésuitiques, Prov. Gallo-Belg., Carton 32. The reason for this letter may be found in the displeasure of some English Jesuits, who rightly considered the appointment of fixed confessors for the Englishwomen as an infringement of personal liberty. Fr General Vitelleschi welcomed the change of confessors for the Englishwomen in a letter to Fr Provincial Heren. 27th July, 1619. ARSI Rome, Gallo-Belg. 1/II p. 524.
26. Fr Francis Young SJ (1570/75–1633) took the fourth vow. He spent the greater part of his religious life in England. As often as he was taken prisoner, he was released on the intervention of the Spanish Ambassador, Gondomar, and banished from the country. He worked for a time in Douai, and then returned to England where he died on 30th March, 1622. ARSI, Rome, Catalogus Anglia 1610, 1621–1649, ff. 7r. 16v, 48v, 76v and Foley, II, S.XIII, 95 and 100–103. His report: ARSI, Rome, Anglia 32, Historia III, Parte II, ff. 1r–2v.
27. ARSI, Rome, Gallo-Belg. 1/II, pp. 542–543.
28. ARSI, Rome, Anglia 1/I, f. 114r.
29. ARSI, Rome, Anglia 32/I, ff. 1r–2v.
30. Fr Jacques Bonfrère, SJ (1573–1642) from Dinant entered the Society of Jesus, was ordained in 1604 and solemnly professed in 1612. He was in several colleges as professor of theology and philosophy and from 1619–21 was prefect of studies in Dinant College. ARSI Rome, Flandro-Belg. 9, f. 206, Nr. 46; f. 257, Nr. 19; f. 300, Nr. 17, f. 336, Nr. 29; Flandro-Belg. 10, pp. 75–76, Nr. 8; Gallo-Belg. 24, ff. 77 and 89v; Necr. Gallo-Belg. 27, p. 233, and Sommervogel, Bibliothèque I Sp. 1713–1715.
31. Probably an allusion to the answer of the Congregation of the Council in 1616 to the Petition for confirmation, Arch.S.Congr.Concilii.Positiones (Sess) 223 f.361rv, which was recast as an approbation in the Bishop of Saint-Omer's open letter of 10th February, 1617, BV Rome, Fondo Capponi 47,f.78.
32. On 16th May, 1620. ARSI Rome, Germ.111.f.92r.
33. "My hart howlden with some powre farr above yt self ..."VP/G1.p.1,Instit. Arch. Munich.
34. "... but I am not so much moved to pray, as called to see ..." ibid.
35. AGR Brussells, Archives Jésuitiques, Gallo-Belg., Carton 32.
36. Mary Ward gave some talks to the members in Saint-Omer after her return from England. The year cannot be conclusively established but the first talk was apparently in the month of December, for she reminded her hearers of Fr Lee's death, and he had died in December 1615. For this talk, LR, pp.216–234; 234–243; 243–262; Inst.Arch.Munich.
37. "Fervour is a will to doe well, that is a preventing grace of God and a guift

geven graties by God, which we could not meritt. It is true, this fervour doeth many times growe could. But what is the caus? Is it because wee are weomen? No, but because we are unperfect weomen. There is not such difference betwen men and weomen. Therfore it is not because we are weomen, but, as I said before, because we are unperfect weomen and love not veirity but seeke after lyes." LR pp.218–219.

38. Vita E f.23rv. and the "Painted Life" T.29.
39. LR pp.223–224,225.
40. ibid.pp.227–228.
41. "Ther was a Father, that lately came into England whom I hard say that he would not for a 10,000 of worlds be a woaman, because he thought a woaman could not apprehend God." ibid.pp.229–230.
42. "Yet it is not learning that now I commend unto you, but knowledg, true knowledg which you all may have, if you love and seek it ... Even in little things, want of true knowledg is a great want ..." ibid.pp.241–242.
43. "It is certaine that God hath looked uppon you as he never looked uppon any. I say not better, nor in a greater or more excellent manner, nor with more love, for I entend not to make any comparisons. But I say: As he never looked uppon any, and this is certane," ibid.p.244.
44. ibid.pp.224–225.
45. ibid. p.261; Rome 8,28.
46. He wanted to write her life after her death. see p.354.
47. Vita E f.24r. Vita I ignores the foundation in Liège and likewise the difficulties there.
48. Fridl.I,p.179–182.
49. See above, note 46. Fridl.loc.cit., translates Arden by Artesien, that is, from Artois. That is an error. Sister Praxedis was the daughter of a farmer from the neighbouring Ardennes. Fridl embellishes things considerably. The early writers like Bissel, Lohner or Pagetti, make little or no mention of the foundation in Liège and do not advert at all to the difficulties there. Cf.Chambers E I, p.448 and D I p.356, which are based on Lohner while keeping close to Fridl.
50. Panel 33. of the "Painted Life" for example shows the infused knowledge that only few attain to eternal bliss, while many will be judged for not co-operating with grace.
51. "A quiet content, I thinke with God ..." VP/E 1, Inst.Arch.Munich. Mary Ward's union with God is recorded in panel 34, inadequately, as is understandable. She is shown kneeling in a room similar to that in panel 31. The Lord's appearance is presented pictorially; his form, diminished in size, is on her heart.
52. The little parchment bound book, called the "Parchment Book". Inst.Arch.Munich.
53. VP/E p.3.Inst.Arch.Munich.
54. "O my God, cannot this estate be had in this life?" ibid.
55. "The delicacie of that estate whear sence obayed reason, and reason the devine will. Whear was neither darknes of understandinge, nor inclination to evell. Whos worke was the will of their master, and whos satiation, that ther God was pleased with them". ibid.
56. "So much as yt may imparted to anie, bestow, my Jesus, on her whom thou hast made thus, and to doe those things."ibid.
57. "I know, my God, that darknes of understandinge and propention to sinn will still remayne (at least in some measure), but thes in them selves are sufferings, not sinns. Though alass such falles as comes by ignorance or rashnes will often happen by them." ibid.
58. As:"For the rest, my God, I will in all have a will conformable to thine, and never proceed in that which I see to be less pleasinge." ibid.

59. VP/E 4, p.1."Using more diligence do descend to perticulers, I found a lothnes to leave this Company before yt wear confirmed..."
60. "... the cause least thos that folowed might make yt some thing els, and hear (against my will) I seemed of some importance, and not be spared without prejudice to the worke ..." ibid.
61. "... this I knew to be a lye and to proceed from noe good ground ..." ibid.
62. "Lookinge backe how all the beginning of my call to this Cours had passed; I saw by perticulers ... how hardly and with how much a dow I was brought by God to doe that little I have done..." ibid. pp.1–2.
63. The whole sentence is: "That with thos grases, anie els would have byn moved as soon, and many farr sooner, and that this good had noe being, nor place in me, but by the only working of His grace." ibid.
64. "... which though in me yet a different thinge from this me, without which I would needs that this good could not stand and which, withdrawn I should remaine as before."ibid.
65. "I found... I would still be of importance and a needfull person." ibid.
66. "...I saw my self little, and of less importance for His worke."ibid.p.3.
67. "God's will and wisdome seemed great and His powre such, and of such force, as strongly to affect in an instant, or with a looke, whatsoever He would. And before this greatnes, the pour of all His creature togeather (resisting Him) melted away, and in a moment, lost yt beinge."ibid.
68. "Then moved not to desire anie thinge but God's will, I inwardly sayd: Nether life nor death, my God, but holy will be ever done in me, what pleaseth the best that doe."
69. "What I find and am drawn to practis." VP/E 12, p.2.
70. "An imperfect sight that somewhat, or all, in or belonging to our Institute was God's known will. Thes are all suffered, not sought for, nor folowed further nor longer then by means they come from that they are stayed." ibid.p.4.
71. "I see in our Institute what I cannot say and more by a certainty that ther ys in yt what I doe not see." VP/E 13, p.5.
72. About our subbordenation, but less determinately, becaus with restraint and fearfully least yt should proceed from my self at least my owne will now mixt with yt. Refusinge God withdrue and left me idle." VP/E 17,p.7. Panel 35 of the "Painted Life" should be seen in connection with this.
73. "Thos of the Kingdome of Christ so mine (meane? note) as yf I might have for askinge, and had witt to my will, I would before all things begg to spend my dayes in such labours. In one of thes ma/tters/ I found my self moved to aske, not only to live in them but to dye for the same caus.' ibid.pp.7–8.
74. "Ther was noe love I desired, or esteemed lyke to His by many degrees." VP/E 8, p.6.
75. The sentence breaks off here. "Doubting about that word '*this* Society, very clear sight accompanied with love and confidence, to aske of God that which he had commanded and we endeavoured to undertake, he would give and accomplish it, that this was farr more the same both in substance and practis then yf the same Institute should be applied unto us by anie other way or in anie other manner that thos that doubted might read the Institute and – VP/F 1, Inst.Arch.Munich.
76. see above, p.170ff.
77. Seing for such respects. etc. God hath so ordayned as that our subbordination etc. must be amongst our selves, etcc. Yt seemes altogether needfull seing our Institute to the end, that takinge the same we may leave what we take intire and without detriment. Seing that to take the same ys required to leave the same without detriment and that the one of thes

cannot stand without the other. Which both the founder and we that now undertake would noe dettriment the Institute etc. O wissdome of God that so wisly orders all things – Seeing besids etc. the laws of the Institute leads that this Institute ys so drawn as who so ever will take the same intire must leave the same intire, and will practis as both Blessed Father Ignatius, we ourselves and the words of the Institute etc. God declared what, and this Institute shows how; in that same ys included what and how." VP/F 2, Inst.Arch.Muniche.

78.   PB pp.39–45. Inst.Arch.Munich. The heading: "To Reverend Father Tomson (alias Jhon Garett), of whom she took now the exercise and in it wrott the letter following in the year 1619 at the time when Sister Praxedis busines was about our Institute and the manner of subordination she said ours were to have, which was wholy different to that our Mother had understood from God etc."

79.   The transcript is undoubtedly genuine. The style corresponds indisputably to Mary Ward's way of expressing herself.

80.   "As I was to day in a sea of uncertainties and full of tears, forth of my owne inability to doe any thing how little soever, without some powerfull and extraordinary help, calling to God for his, as my last and best refuge and receaving him to that purpose, this came to my mind to propose... Might not Sister Praxedis sett down what she hath seene, with what els she can obtaine of God touching that matter in forme of an Institute? What if she wear bid by your selfe or Father Burton to draw an Institute with as great care as she would, if she wear in my place and I in an other world so as this business rested wholy upon her."

81.   "She may likewise know, what I had from God touching this, if that be thought fitt, or would further her..."

82.   "Take the same of the Society. Father General will never permitt it. Goe to him. These are the words, whose worth cannot be valued, nor the good they containe, too dearly bought. These gave sight where there was none; made knowne what God would have don; gave streingth to suffer what since hath hapned, assurance of what is wished for in time to come."

83.   "And if ever I be worthy to doe any thing more about the Institute, heather I must come to draw. I could say a great deal of those words, but never all."

84.   "Twice doubting what kind of subordination should be, I was sent hom (I meane to your Institute) and bidden, doo as there was don."

85.   "What hath byn granted by unworthy / I / by entersestion... by our Blessed Saviour... About the name, Saint Omers. The subordination Grafton and Leig.VP/H 1, Inst.Arch.Munich.

86.   Mary Ward prayed long and frequently for grace to be free from sin. Most of her meditations are concerned with this request. Yet it cannot be the orginal "righteousness" that was meant by this prayer; probably the longing for innocence. The picture is unusually lively and offers a wealth of separate presentations. The left two-thirds shows God the Father above and a soul in human form adoring him. Close by is a crib scene. In the middle of the picture there are various figures, leading a sinful life. Below is Hell's mouth, a monster swallowing his victims. To the right below are figures from the Old Testament: Adam and Eve, King David, etc. To the far right, Mary Ward kneels in prayer. Over her, bathed in light, is a "Just Soul" in the form of a white-clad woman.

87.   "Once I thinke I saw a general of yours who said nothng but his countenance promised all concurance with us."

88.   "This was I thinke to comfort, for some of yours at that very time would needs, that the generall of the Society both could and would hinder such a thing as I did beleeve to be Gods will in us."

89. "I could never beleeve to be in the power of man. For the second this sight gave confidence (the same I saw likewise in those words: Goe to him) that, when the time should come neither would he have a will to hurt us but the contrary."

90. "What els I have had, hath bin generall or generally, and in perticular such an understanding of your Institute and such a neernes of affection to it as he can only worke who aloane is able to make without my disposing or indeavour one thing of two so farre different as is your order of life and my perverce will."

XVII

CATASTROPHE

Vice-Province of the English Jesuits in Belgium

Reasons for its establishment – Vice-Provincial Richard Blount SJ

As in the confined world of convents, so too in the larger sphere of the Belgian province of the Jesuits, complaints were being voiced with increasing loudness. Not all of these had to do with the Englishwomen. As mentioned before, it was only with difficulty that English refugees could be accommodated in Belgian houses. Apart from language problems, there were other obstacles, stemming from national differences such as food, customs and general feelings. Added to which, a good number of the English Jesuits living in Belgium sometimes worked in their own country, which involved a drift away from recent acclimatization. Superiors acted discreetly in controlling these problematic relationships in Belgium. They first introduced an English vice-province, with its own Vice-Provincial; this could later become a full English Province after a time of experiment.

Already, in a letter dated 20th July, 1619, to the Provincial Fr Jean Heren,[1] Fr General Vitelleschi made reference to the new Vice-Provincial who, he hoped would solve the problems occasioned by the Institute of the Englishwomen. This Vice Provincial was Richard Blount.[2]

Born on 6th October, 1563 into an old English family, he worked for some years in his own country as a secular priest after completing his studies. He entered the Society of Jesus on 7th September, 1596 and soon found employment in various posts connected with the establishment of an English province of the Order. He was Vice-Prefect of the English Mission from 1606–1619. He came to know the members of the Institute during his time in England and was numbered among their opponents and probably belonged to the group of those who were not exactly favourably disposed to Fr Tomson. In this man Fr Vitelleschi had found someone who was to cut away the festering wounds in Liège from the body of the Belgian Vice Province.

Fr Blount not only had his own observations and experiences, but could also count on various willing sources to supply him with incidents and details about these difficult ladies and their adherence to the Society of Jesus. Incidentally, also at his disposal were the none too gratifying impressions of Fr Henri Scheren, who had visited the province in the spring of 1618.

Fr Blount was already in office by September, 1619, for it was then that Fr General considered him fortunate to have upright young men like Fr Young, about whom he had made a reference to the new Vice Provincial when talking about the Englishwomen's affairs.[3]

Fr Blount was one of those opponents of the Institute who are most difficult to understand. His submissions to Rome, together with his whole correspondence to Fr General were destroyed after the latter's death. And yet, the hand of the Vice-Provincial − and it was a relentless and punishing hand − is evident in the measures taken against the Englishwomen in Liège.

The 'Werp'

Count Sackville in Louvain − certified disclaimer of his possessions in favour of the Jesuits in Liège

Count Thomas Sackville may have stayed on in Flanders after he left Liège, for at the beginning of 1620 he was in Louvain.[4] He is reputed not to have had a single penny and to have been living on the Jesuits.[5]

On 3rd April, 1620[6] he gave up his claim to the properties in Condroz and drew up a certification of disclaimer, a 'Werp', in favour of the Jesuits in Liège.

At first it looks as though it was merely a matter of the estates in Condroz[7] and not his other possessions, such as the house in rue Pierreuse which he had acquired by mortgaging those properties. But Count Sackville did not only waive his rights (droit et action) regardless of the amount, which he had spent on extensions (emplissement) for transferred estates, discharge of debts or other such.[8] In cold, solid fact, he waived all the debts which he had incurred on behalf of the house for the Englishwomen.

In order to leave the English Jesuits in peaceful possession of the estates (la plus paisible possession) he had pledged all his possessions in the prince-bishopric of Liège[9] regardless of the mortgage of certain estates which he, Sackville, must have transacted in order to build the house in rue Pierreuse. The farm in Halleux was mortgaged for that.

Under suitable cover of veiled language and circumstantial detail, the shady matter of the transfer of all the debts incurred for the Englishwomen were thereby shifted across to the English Jesuits' already crumbling mountain of debts.

The document of disclaimer was attested on 6th March, 1620[10] by Notary Jean Hermans of Louvain and two witnesses, Guillaume Holdin and François Thimelbe.They all signed the document, Thomas Sackville included. They had come to the College of the English Jesuits in Louvain for that purpose.

It is not known if anyone had advised Count Sackville to take this course of action or if he did this on his own initiative. He had certainly discussed it with professionals. It is strange that the lawyer's document was executed in the English Jesuit college. This does point to people behind the scenes who dared to make an attempt to save the Englishwomen from their predicament. But there is little purpose in speculation, as there is too little information about those who could have acted behind the scenes, whether they were fathers of the Society of Jesus, or acquaintances of the Englishwomen among the citizens.

In the normal run of events, Father Tomson could have effected the acceptance of the properties, the 'Saisinne', and had this certified by the civil authorities. Father Tomson did not do so.

The Last Resort

The Englishwomen as Liège citizens – Lord Talbot of Shrewsbury's petition to Duke Maximilian I of Bavaria to act as intermediary for papal approbation of the Institute – recommendation by Count Sackville (to Graf Eitel Friedrich von Hohenzollern) for the founding of a house in Cologne by the Englishwomen

It can be assumed that connections between Father Tomson and Count Sackville were not completely severed, and that contact was maintained by correspondence at least. But after their conversation with Sackville in the Spring of 1619 it must have been crystal clear to both fathers, Fr Tomson and certainly Fr Burton, that they could no longer depend on their former benefactor. They may have indicated as much to the Englishwomen, though these had probably already come to the same conclusion and were looking for a way out of their quandary. Guidance almost certainly came from Fr Tomson, who made things easier for them. It was not for nothing that he had been reported to Rome for conducting the women's secular affairs and being frequently in their house.

On 8th April, 1620 five days after Sackville had transacted his waiver in Louvain for the properties in Condroz, the Englishwomen were granted citizenship of the town of Liège,[11] having entered the Smiths' Guild on 4th April.[12] Barbara Babthorpe, Anne Buskells and Elizabeth Falkner[13] were the applicants, the first probably in her office as provincial superior, the other two as superiors of the house on Mont St Martin and rue Pierreuse respectively. Just as all members of a family were included in the rights obtained by the head of the family, so too did the superiors stand for the members of both communities. Somewhat remarkably, Mary Ward was not included in this.

As citizens of Liège they now had the right to claim protection by the town. They were soon to put this privilege to use.

On 10th September, 1620[14] the town of Liège issued a report for the town council of Cologne concerning the reputation and work of the Englishwomen. They led blameless lives, and did not burden the citizens by begging but lived on private means. They had put up a fine building and, by their virtuous life and education of girls, were an asset to the town. This was signed on behalf of the town by Servais de Fléron, Lay assessor, Secretary to the Bishop, and Privy Councillor.[15] It was not so expressly stated, but it is possible to read between the lines that the Englishwomen were now educating Belgian girls too. Perhaps not many, as there is no trace of their teaching activity in the town history of Liège, nor in their own sources. The same will be met with in St Omer. Perhaps it was forced on them by their great poverty; they would not otherwise have been able to count on co-operation from the towns. Hardly one month later, on 3rd October, 1620, George Talbot, Earl of Shrewsbury,[16] sent a long petition on behalf of the Englishwomen to Maximilian of Bavaria.[17]

George Talbot of Grafton (9th Earl of Shrewsbury since 1618), was a great friend of the English Jesuits and was one of the founding benefactors of their novitiate in Liège. It has been said that he was ordained before 1618, but there is no proof.

Before he returned home,he began his letter, he would like to make a request of the Elector. When he had stayed in Liège on his way to the watering-place Spa, he had come to know the Englishwomen, of whom he had heard previously, as three daughters from his family had entered the congregation.[18] Their Institute is formed on the charism and aims of the Society of Jesus, as far as is suitable for women. They devote themselves to the salvation of their neighbour and the education of girls, particularly in reverence towards God but also in whatever is necessary for their lives. They do for young women what the Jesuits do for young men. Their lives are exemplary, their numbers grow daily, and it is expected that after papal approval has been received for their Institute girls from other countries will apply for admission, as they do not limit their teaching and education to English girls only. The Bishop of Liège has expressed his graciousness to them on several occasions; Graf Eitel Friedrich von Hohenzollern had tried to get them to go to Cologne; the Bishop of St Omer, in whose town the Institute had begun, had written an open letter about them, and the celebrated Fr Leonhard Lessius had issued a recommendatory testimonial for their Institute. He himself, Talbot, had placed the Plan of the Institute some years previously before Duke Wilhelm of Bavaria, who had shown approval of it. The Englishwomen do indeed follow the rule of the Society of Jesus and practise similar activities, as far as these are suitable for women (Societatis Jesu regulis ac mediis quantum earum fert sexus), but are independent of the Society, who give them the same spiritual help that they give to all other christians. This consists in giving the sacraments, and spiritual guidance. They need both, as they follow the charism of the Society of Jesus. They have already brought many girls to conversion by means of moral improvement and education (in multorum vitae reformatione et morum emendatione ac iuvencularum instructione), but they could do still more, if their Institute were to be granted papal confirmation. They have great enemies, although their Institute does not present any innovation or anything particular (non est hoc novum aut iis peculiare); it is suffering the same sort of difficulties experienced by other Orders — the Society of Jesus among them — before confirmation.

The letter concludes with the request that the Elector would intervene with the Roman Curia for the confirmation of the Institute.

Let us take a look at the author of the request first of all. Although George Talbot, the great friend of the Jesuits, gave his name to the letter, it was certainly not of his authorship. Talbot, on his way from Spa to England and staying for a time in Louvain, was hardly so a good Latinist or experienced an exegete that he could have composed a long letter in Latin intermingled with passages from Holy Writ. He had certainly come to know the Englishwomen and to esteem them, but it must also be pointed out that the property disclaimer of Count Thomas Sackville and its attestation had both been composed in Liège, the latter even in the College of the English Jesuits. One would therefore not be far wrong to suppose that steps had been taken in the English Jesuit College to save the unfortunate members of the Institute from the effects of the impending financial collapse. There were great benefactors of the Englishwomen living in Louvain — as will be seen in the so-called 'Confession case', and among these were the most capable Jesuits of their time. But their most hardened adversaries lived there too.

If we look at the structure of the Institute which is here being recommended to Rome, we come up against the same obstacle which had blocked Mary Ward's Institute from the beginning, and which was destined to remain: that is, the Institute of the 'Schola Beatae Mariae'. The name was not mentioned, but Talbot had earlier handed a Plan of the Institute to Wilhelm (V) of Bavaria. Now George Talbot was in Munich in November, 1611. That can be vouched for. At that time there was no other Plan except that Jesuit draft, which had little enough in common with what had been revealed to Mary

Ward. Here again in this letter the work of the Englishwomen in the adult apostolate is glossed over, whereas their achievements in the classroom and boarding school were stressed and praised. Some facts seem exaggerated. There is no existing written testimony of the Bishop of Liège's goodwill (multis signis ac testimoniis benignissime ostendit), so one must presumably replace this by his interest in the beautiful singing in choir of the school's boarders.[19] The same holds good for the summons of the members to Cologne by Graf Eitel Friedrich von Hohenzollern (valde eis favet et Coloniam quoque traducere aliquas illarum conatur). Some time later, in Rome, he was indeed one of their benefactors, but if the Institute really was so needed in Cologne, why had so little been done for its members who were half-starved, in Trier as well as Cologne? As for the favour of the Bishop of St Omer, it has been shown that this extended to those members who remained in St Omer, whom he looked upon as members of an embryonic Order, but not to those who had moved to Liège and were being prepared for the apostolate in England.

The author's intention is revealed most clearly in his naming of Fr Lessius as the community' advocate, for this famous theologian welcomed the 'Schola Beatae Mariae' of certain Jesuits[20] but not Mary Ward's Institute, which aimed at the Society of Jesus for women. It was, moreover, not correct to state that the Institute was nothing new in the Church. It was indeed. That was the precise cause of all the trouble.

This petition to the Elector of Bavaria was yet another well-meant effort to help by those Jesuits who had tried to obtain a modus vivendi for the Englishwomen ever since the beginning of the Institute, but at the cost of the exact following of Mary Ward's revelation of 1611. This was something quite different.

In her biographical outline of Mary Ward, Barbara Ward gives a fleeting overview of the troubles connected with the foundation in Cologne. She writes that the Elector of Cologne had invited Mary Ward on her return from England (Spring, 1619) but that the Englishwomen had been unable to take this up because they had no money.[21] The lack of money was correct, but it is doubtful if the Englishwomen had enough money one year later, in 1619, shortly before the collapse of their foundation in rue Pierreuse in Liège. Far from it.

An undated piece of information about the Institute, with no details concerning the recipient and no signature but which, according to a remark on the copy, had been addressed by Count Sackville to some high personage,[22] reveals attempts made in Belgium to ensure a place for the Englishwomen in Cologne.

Hundreds of courageous men work in the English mission, reported this document. Now women have joined them, and give valuable service. In catholic countries these women have set up schools for English and indigenous girls. Their teaching is free; for board and lodging they make a modest charge. In England they are engaged in adult education, in so far as it is fitting for women. They are planning new foundations in Cologne, Lorraine[23] and elsewhere and hold out hopes of future members for themselves from these, especially since missionary connections between England and Germany have been established. They could be a bulwark of the true faith in the catholic town of Cologne, which lies, after all, in a heretic country. The women of Cologne are inclined to devotion and the single life, and the Englishwomen feel drawn to them. The town of Cologne would be as little burdened by them as the towns of St Omer and Liège, where they already have houses.

It emerges from the text that it was destined for some important person in Cologne, who was closely connected with a brotherhood for the conversion of heretics. Now, Nuntius Albergati had founded the Brotherhood of the Holy Cross in 1612, expressly for this purpose.[24] In 1620 Eitel Friedrich von Hohenzollern, Provost of the Cathedral and Archdeacon of Cologne, was Prefect of this brotherhood.[25] Through him, Sackville could have had access to influential citizens, some of whom sat on the city council. For it was not the Elector but the city which might have had reservations about the advent of a new religious community, whose presence could imply a burden for the people. Thomas Sackville did not compile this information himself any more than George Talbot wrote his petition of 3rd October,1620. This too presupposed a Latinist who also knew how to underpin an argument.He may be looked for among the Louvain Jesuits, where Sackville abandoned his claim to the Condroz properties in April/May 1620, and where Talbot allowed himself to be involved on behalf of the Englishwomen.

But the Institute presented here is essentially different.

In the document sent to Munich it is the teaching and educational aspect that is stressed, whereas here, on the contrary, the missionary task of the Institute is presented openly. For here it was possible to knot together the threads of the past with those of the present. St Ursula and her companions, who were buried in Cologne, came from England. In a council meeting of 20th January, 1621,[26] the city of Cologne appointed a commission to examine the petition, which sought to establish a foundation of the Englishwomen. Vicar Adolf Schulcken, a friend of the Jesuits and of English catholics, and Agyd Camp, Vice prefect of the Archbrotherhood of the sufferings of our Lord, had reported on the matter.

These are the only pieces of information about the foundations of Trier and Cologne which have come down to us. It is not likely that there would have been much more, as neither of these houses had much future and neither existed very long.

It may seem surprising that Count Sackville was once more active for the Englishwomen at this time. It may be that he was filled with the same anxiety for them as Fr Tomson who, inspite of the prohibitions of superiors, tried to support these impecunious women. Moreover, at this time – Autum/Winter 1620, the English women were probably not completely aware of what he had done.

The Settlement

Fr Rector Tomson unofficially renounces Count Sackville's possessions in favour of the Englishwomen in Liège – Visitation of the English Jesuits' novitiate by Father Blount – his repudiation of Count Sackville's legally certified disclaimer in favour of the English Jesuits – Fr Tomson's disclaimer certified by notary – the Englishwoman's acceptance of Sackville's properties taken to court – judgement of the process – Mary Ward's retreat notes from this time

In the summer of 1620[27] Fr General Vitelleschi sent a request in very stern phrasing to the new Vice Provincial, Fr Richard Blount. He wished him to submit a report regarding the spiritual care given by the English fathers to the women or any help in the formation of their Institute. He had received complaints of Fr Rector Tomson in particular as well as certain other fathers. This implies that several serious charges may have been sent to Rome in the first half of 1620, for on 26th October, 1619[28] Fr General had praised his Rector in Liège for being able to refute certain anonymous accusers. Fr Tomson's request to be allowed to retire from office had been turned down at that time by Fr Vitelleschi.

We do not know what the Vice Provincial answered. He probably suggested keeping an eye on the situation in Liège and of making a visitation of the house. That would have been a wise measure. He must have heard already about the extent of the debts. At all events, on 12th December, 1620[29] Fr Vitelleschi ordered him, when he next visited the Liège novitiate, to forbid Fr Tomson to give any spiritual direction to the Englishwomen, to build anything, or undertake any great expenditure without the consent of the Vice Provincial. Fr Blount was also to commission several fathers to inform him, the Vice Provincial, if Fr Tomson were to infringe the limits set to his expenses. This must also have been caused by the complaints sent to Rome. Equally clearly, it shows little trust in the Rector's management.

In the meantime the debts incurred by the novitiate had risen yet again. It has already been shown[30] that on 28th January, 1620, Fr Tomson accepted 10,000 guilders from Lady Lovel and on 19th February 2,400 guilders from the College in Namur. It is not stated whether this was with or without the permission of his superiors.

Also, there arrived in Liège both Count Thomas Sackville's declaration of renunciation of property of 3rd April, 1620, in which Fr
Tomson and Christian Blisia, his spokesman before the court, were
mentioned as authorised representatives, and their notarial attestation of 5th May, 1620. There was no further mention of these
two documents later on, however, in the former Rector of Liège's
records of 1629.

It remains an open question as to whether Sackville renounced his
property in Condroz in favour of the Jesuits or that of the Englishwomen. It had formed the sole, if precarious, foundation for the
house in rue Pierreuse. Negotations had always been between Count
Sackville, Fr Tomson and Fr Burton. The Englishwomen had never
appeared in any transaction of properties. But between 5th May,
1620, when Sackville's waiver was legally attested, and 26th April,
1621, when Fr Provincial Blount rejected this waiver, a document
of a private nature was once more issued, this time in the novitiate
house in Liège. In it, Fr Tomson waived the estates in Condroz in
favour of the Englishwomen. In his report he gave curious and enigmatic reasons for this 'Werp': in the bond of 2nd April,1619, the
English women were obliged to repay the 3,000 guilders, which Mary
Ward had accepted with a blank bill. As they were not in a position
to keep to the agreed term of two years, Fr Burton, on the advice
of the Jesuits' lawyer, had caused this third instrument, namely
the waiver, to be drawn up.[31] But, it went on, Fr Burton had not
wished to do the women any injustice. Everything was simply there
for appearances' sake and to secure possession (per sigurezza della
nostra possessione). The Jesuits had de iure renounced possession
of the estates but de facto these remained as before their property.
They managed these, and wished to keep them.[32]

To summarize: The properties were therefore to be kept in the
interest of the English Jesuits, but the Englishwomen − as Count
Sackville once before − should give their name for these now heavily
burdened estates, and that too only in appearance. When Fr Tomson
had acquired the estates in the name of Count Sackville, the question
then asked was whether he was still credit-worthy. One is now justified in asking if Fr Tomson perhaps wished to take the estates out
of the prospective mortgage when, in Spring 1621, the financial collapse of the English Jesuits' novitiate was imminent?[33]

This is hinted at in his report: the Englishwomen had to
be persuaded to accept the estates.[34] It would have been
put to them that they had already signed a promissory
note, and had deposited cash amounting to the value of
the property. What is more, the farms and lands in nominal
possession of the Englishwomen were by no means covered; they had even less money than Fr Tomson, and they
did not have the safety net of an established Order as
support.

In fact, both congregations, the English Jesuits and the English-women's Institute, were at one another's mercy as far as these properties were concerned, for better or worse.

In April, 1621 Fr Vice Provincial Blount was in Liège, accompanied by Fr Edward Rodncy who had taken over the shattered finances. The Vice Provincial may have found little to give him joy: a divided community in the house with burdensome debts and, across rue Pierreuse the Englishwomen's handsome and newly renovated house. Among the papers and the many unpaid bills in the bursar's office – we know of sixteen of them, some of them extremely high mortgages – was the disclaimer, the 'Werp', of Count Sackville's heavily debt-burdened estates in Condroz.

On 26th April, 1621[35] Fr Blount,in a legally certified document, refused to accept this declaration. That is, he refused to accept the 'Werp' and did not issue a 'Saisinne'. Servatius Geynocht and Johannes Gathy were witnesses, and Notary Martin Veris gave the document legal force.

And now comes Fr Tomson's third document in his records of 1629.

It is possible to see the situation from a different angle, realistically, and untrammelled by Fr Tomson's befuddled world of appearances: the estates in Condroz had been mortgaged for the purchase and renovation of the Englishwomen's house. As far as Fr Blount was concerned, those were the hard facts. He knew from England of the ladies' activities which caused such contention; he must now have heard the many complaints of the Fathers in the novitiate house. Granted, both as a member of the Order and as Vice Provincial, Fr Blount had to judge and straighten out the affair in the interests of his Order. Yet recourse – as Fr Tomson soothingly expressed it – was now had to a laywer. This can hardly be regarded as morally justifiable.

In 1629 Fr Tomson no longer knew the whereabouts of his disclaimer in favour of the Englishwomen. Perhaps, he said, it had remained in the hands of the lawyer or the notary, as both of them had been present.[36] One can only be astonished at such negligence, for it concerned a document which indeed may have been drawn up for appearances' sake only, but which could do considerable damage in certain circumstances. This was precisely what happened. On 30th April, 1621 the declaration of disclaimer – but in a changed form – was legally certified and and sent on to the court of assessors. The same Johannes Gathy, who had witnessed the Vice-Provincial's disclaimer, appears as witness here too. The court accepted this 'Werp' on 8th May, 1621[37] and, also, the 'Saisinne' of Barbara Babthorpe. Years later Fr Tomson said in his records that it had all happened without his knowledge and, moreover, that he had never discharged such a disclaimer.[38]

This important document requires a closer glance. First: Who negotiated at the Town Court? Fr Tomson was represented – without his knowledge – by the lawyer Philipp Wez, and Barbara Babthorpe by Servais Charles. What took place, according to the wording of the record? Advocate Wez renewed (a renouvellé) Fr Tomson's disclaimer of rights over the estates (ne veuillent prétendre aucun droit de domain à la cense ou censes) and made this disclaimer known. Servais Charles accepted the disclaimer in favour of the Englishwomen in the name of the Superior, Barbara Babthorpe. But it was not only the rights which she accepted but all the debts (tous les drois et actions et touttes obligations, tant actives que passives). Then Servais Charles disclaimed possession of the estates on behalf of the Englishwomen (reportat ... les susdittes censes) in favour of the Jesuits, and Philipp Wez accepted the disclaimer in the name of the Fathers. So, the Englishwomen were the nominal owners of the estates, the firm possession of which they handed over to the English Jesuits, and that for a tax of 200 guilders annually up to a total of 3,600 guilders, thus for eighteen years.

What Sackville, in 1620 had termed as 'quelques charges ou debte ... pour édiffier la maison ... en Pierreuse', was named in the 'Werp' at the end of April 1621 as 'in aedificiis et emptione fundorum' and was taken officially as what the Jesuits had given as investments, 'avoient emplié az édiffices des susdittes censes et en achapt des terres pour l'augmentation d'icelles.' The house on rue Pierreuse was carefully by-passed, in that it was not even mentioned that the Englishwomen held other properties from Sackville, namely, their house. Everything was put onto the estates. But it is barely credible that the Jesuits had invested such a high rate, namely 3,600 guilders, in estates which they bought by means of mortgage, and had only partly paid for. Sackville covered them moreover with similarly large mortgages and, to a large extent, had mortgaged the harvest profits. All this, while their own house was burdened with a debt of dizzying proportions?

In his report Fr Tomson took great pains to deny the request for these 3,600 guilders.[39] But he did not succeed. One remembers only too well the sums which Sackville had paid from Jesuit money: 600 guilders deposit for the Lamet's farm, 1,500 guilders' instalment and mortgage for the Chamont's lands, and 1,500 guilders deposit for the Cabosse farm. Altogether that comes to 3,600. That was the amount of the Jesuits' 'investments', which Fr Blount was now demanding back from the Englishwomen, in annual contributions from the Jesuits' debtors. But not only that – they now indeed received the farms, de iure, which however, de facto, were to be managed by the Jesuits. The unfortunate women were therefore made responsible for the entire burden of debts which Count Sackville had taken on for them – as a gift! To repeat: the house in rue Pierreuse was inextricably entangled with the lands in Condroz.

Fr Tomson was right about one thing: the promissory note, showing a sum of 4,200 guilders and Mary Talbot's dowry of 3,000 guilders, revealed the debit item of the farms which now belonged to the Institute. So the promissory note and the dowry should have been restored. This was not done. It may be, because the Jesuits had too great a mistrust of the Englishwomen; it may be that, even after the house in rue Pierreuse had been confiscated, they remained of the opinion that the women were still morally obliged to restore the payment the Jesuits had made for the farms together with the mortgages.

It is extremely difficult to make even an approximately fair picture of moral guilt. In the last resort it is God alone who can see into the heart. Nevertheless, we dare to state that it was Thomas Sackville himself who was responsible for the fraud. Whatever his financial straits, he should never have been allowed to burden the Jesuits' property. The end does not justify the means. Fr Tomson, too, in spite of all his goodness of heart and zeal for the faith – and these can never be doubted – built on too large a scale and at too great a cost, without having either the necessary business acumen or sober calculation of a property developer, as proposed in Luke 14,28-30. The financial matters of his house lay in various and not always capable hands. This department of management however was part of his office, at least in a supervisory capacity. Fr Tomson did not possess the gifts necessary for such activiies. He had, moreover, allowed Count Sackville full freedom with sums of money which belonged to the Order and had even defended him when the procurator had criticised Sackville's proceedings.

The Englishwomen's greatest enemy in Belgium, Fr Richard Blount, would appear to be far more culpable than Fr Tomson. Because of the double-dealing with the Rector's disclaimer, and the further secret transfer of the whole affair to the city authorities, he managed to place the whole of the Rector's mismanagement as well as Count Sackville's fraud on to the Englishwomen. Fr Blount, his procurator Fr Rodney, and the opponents of the Englishwomen among the Jesuits, presumed that the ladies had been aware of the whole impenetrable financial negotiations and had even approved and promoted them. Not only that. That the women even allowed their incredible acceptance of the declaration to be legalized in a court of law. From this resulted not only the destruction of the material existence of a community that was entitled to some hope, but dozens of people became destitute. Of course, regarded purely factually, the Englishwomen were given precisely what Thomas Sackville had taken on himself for their sake. But from a human point of view? Would it not have been possible, with a little good will, to have co-operated with these hard-pressed women, who had been deceived just as the Jesuits themselves? But no one was willing to concede that there had been any fraud. The Jesuits were indeed deeply in debt. They were also under distraint. Father Rodney paid 1,905 guilders[40] between years 1621–1626, for the most outstanding interest. Only after the Elector of Bavaria's[41] endowment seemed secure did he dare to pay 3,000 guilders to the Carmelites in Antwerp, to write off part of the loan of 9,000 guilders which Fr Tomson had taken from Lady Lovel on 28th January, 1620.[42] During those years the Englishwomen suffered a great deal from hunger.

Were the Englishwomen really morally guilty, as their opponents claimed? There is no proof. Perhaps Fr Tomson had written several times to Rome concerning the matter. If he had not received an answer — and that is quite possible — the existence of such a letter cannot be shown today, as Fr Vitelleschi's current correspondence was destroyed after his death. There is no single letter dating from this time among the Englishwomen's papers. We are, however, well informed about their superior, Mary Ward.

If we think back to the 'Cloasing Days' of 1616, we may recall a sentence in her notes: 'They (those who love God) feel one lack only, that they cannot be certain that they love God enough.'[43] Sentences echo from the 1618 Retreat, as: 'I was glad, when I saw that Christ had chosen the most perfect way in his use of all created things.'[44] Or, 'My soul, where now is true greatness of mind (which causes everything to be done completely in His time)?'[45] Or, 'I besought God earnestly to give me the grace never to offend Him again deliberately in great or lesser things, and that I might turn my back on sin forever.'[46]

From the Exercises of 1619 only the following are repeated: 'God was present; I had freedom to speak. Most of this hour was spent in speaking to Him with love and hope, and in listening to what he wanted, with the desire to do His will.'[47] and 'There was no love that I desired or esteemed that could come near to approaching His.'[48]

Can one isolate these soaring thoughts from the presumptuous statement that the Englishwomen — therefore Mary Ward too — had been aware of the corrupt dealings of the Count, even before the English Jesuits themselves? And is it in anyway acceptable that Mary Ward could on the one hand make a Retreat with Fr Rector — twice in one year — and at the same time trick him out of several thousand guilders? That is not easy to credit.

At the same time the Englishwomen deposited promissory notes with the Jesuits for payments that Count Sackville had made for their house. That had been a well-justified measure of protection on the part of the procurator, Fr Burton, and the women may have entered upon it with the same trust that certain rich citizens of Liège and Fr Tomson and Fr Burton too, at first, had entered into transactions with the Count.

As a result of all this: as swiftly as preparations might allow, Mary Ward left for Rome, not only to obtain confirmation of the Institute from the Pope but also to speak with Fr General Vitelleschi.

Can one seriously believe that this woman, who feared sin so much, could summon up the courage to look the Fr General of the Society of Jesus in the eye, person to person, if she had even a glimmering of moral guilt? Let us anticipate the General's significant comment: 'The Fathers there (de ces quartiers là) were deceived (ont esté trompé).[49] There was no breath of accusation against Mary Ward and her Institute in those words. On the contrary. Fr Vitelleschi promoted the Englishwomen in Italy and later too north of the Alps, as far as he could, and, in the opinion of several Jesuits, too far, for by so doing he put his reputation on the block. In conclusion, in 1629, after she had received the three documents from Liège, Mary Ward went to see not only Fr Tomson but also Fr General Vitelleschi, who once again ordered an enquiry into the affair.

Her behaviour and above all her prayer cannot be explained in any other way than by that 'sincerity', that uprightness, of which she spoke in the Vision of the 'Just Soul' and which she considered to be the most necessary, most important virtue for members of her Institute, in fulfilling the duties and tasks they undertake.

The Consequences

The difficult financial situation of the Institute in Liège – consequences for the foundation in St Omer – Fr Tomson's move

From a material point of view the settlement that had been legalized on 8th May, 1621 before the Lawcourts of Liège, was a death blow to the Institute's young and recently established community. Its financial situation in Liège had never been rosy for by the end of 1617[50] the members had difficulty in producing the rent for their house, and in January 1620[51] – to be sure after their landlord had waited a long time – they had been issued with an eviction order. Then once again, at least for the immediate future, an arrangement appears to have been made which is not documented, for the community continued to live in their house on the Mont St Martin.

The sad events which followed in St Omer lead one to conclude that the first of the Englishwomen's foundations on the continent must have come to the help of the new foundation in Liège after 1619. The difficulties that sprang up unexpectedly at the same time as those in Liège cannot be explained otherwise. Without warning there comes the report of the seizure of the Englishwomen's furniture. What happened in Liège on 6th January, 1620, happened later in St Omer, though in a different form.

Four months after taking possession of the estates in Condroz, on 3rd and 4th September, 1621,[52] the City Council of St Omer dealt with the report of Maraud Hambre, a legal officer. He had been sent to the Englishwomen to take up the mortgage of an outstanding debt of 560 guilders to one Symphorien Machin. But when Hambre tried to enter the house, the Englishwomen refused him entry. The Town Council finally ordered the Superior of the house to grant admission to their legal executor.

Another creditor, the butcher Maxime Juet, presented himself before the court. The Englishwomen owed him 345 pounds and 6 sous. The details of the mortgage as it was executed, at which a third creditor appeared, Jean Ogier, can be read in the Englishwomen's complaint to the Magistrate of St Omer.[53] It is long, and full of resentment. Although they are refugees, it states, they have been thoroughly badly treated. Their creditor Simphorien Machin had pretended to a far higher debt than that which they really owed. At his complaint their tables, chairs, beds, mattresses and kitchen pots had been taken away, so that they had literally to sit and eat on the ground. Six or seven doors had been broken, with no legal justification, for the women had defended themselves for fear of the rough men's intentions. Their equipment for brewing beer had been removed by force. This had cost 800 guilders. Indeed, even their chapel, a sacred room where the Blessed Sacrament was kept, had been in danger. Not only that, but objects which did not belong to them had been dragged away, such as pictures which the English Jesuits had put at their disposal.

A seventy year old widow who lived with them had had her bed and other objects removed and sold for a ridiculous sum. And all this had happened without the permission of their ecclesiastical superior (leur Superieur immédiat), the Bishop, and during the absence of the superior of the house. Jean Ogier had removed objects worth 500 guilders, although only 250 guilders was owing to him; he had wanted to swindle them. Moreover, so continued the complaint, they had lived in the town for fifteen years, during which more than 60,000 guilders had been poured out to the people in what they had paid for their upkeep. They would also like to mention that during the last three years they had maintained a free school with three classes for the daughters of the citizens.[54]

The very words show their bitterness at what had taken place. Creditors sometimes showed long patience for money owed them, only to follow this with an implacable demand. It is worth noting that if, in September 1621, local girls had already been taught for three years, then the Englishwomen had begun doing so in 1618. From this one may see that they had altered their original policy of teaching and educating English girls only. This cannot have had anything to do with the seizure of their goods, as the teaching was unpaid. It is more likely that Bishop Blaes (died 21 March, 1618) had influenced this course of action. He wrote something of the kind to the Bishop of Liège.[55]

Moreover, continued the Englishwomen in their petition, it should be taken into consideration that they had been recommended by the Princes of the country, and that they came from noble or at least good families. Their Institute had been approved by the Holy See (approuvé).[56] The town should reflect on the harm done them, they concluded, otherwise they would be forced to think that the persecution in St Omer was worse than that in England. They would be compelled to make the affair known in Flanders and would not hesitate to turn to the Infanta and ask for her assistance.

They requested a deferment of payment for three months, so that they might repair the damage to the house and inform their chief superior of what had happened.

Although the catalogue of complaints was signed in their own hand by the house-prefect 'Mère Anne Minors, Ministre' and the procurator, 'Mère Margaret Campian, procura', the Englishwomen certainly did not compose this unwise and cantankerous piece of writing. We cannot credit them with having sufficient French. However, they must have known the contents, for only they had experienced the actions. An equally sharp reaction was not long in coming. On 11th September, 1621,[57] Jean Ogier vindicated himself, and gave this explanation: the Englishwomen owed the hospital 'Of the Twelve Apostles', of which he, Ogier, was the bailiff, 500 guilders. This was two years' interest for a mortgage encumbring one of their houses.[58] As bailiff of the hospital he effected a writ of execution against them, but after they had repaid 250 guilders he released them from distraint. When they now came under distraint to Symphorien Machin, he took some of their possessions in lieu of the remaining debt of 250 guilders' interest, without however obtaining a new writ of execution for this amount. He then issued a receipt for 250 guilders. He had not wanted to enrich himself.

In the consequent court session of 13th September, 1621,[59] the waves grew calmer to a certain extent. John Wilson,[60] manager of the famous printing house of the English Jesuits in St Omer and representative of the English Jesuits in this court session, demanded the return of the Jesuit pictures which had been removed unlawfully. His manoeuvres also effected the restoration of the belongings of widow Margaret, who had made a home for herself with the Englishwomen. He was able to come to an agreement with the two creditors Symphorien Machin and Jean Ogier.

But the Englishwomen were obliged to write an apology. Councillor Antoine Aubrun[61] composed the letter and mentioned their lack of knowledge of the French language and of accountancy. That would certainly have been true. The intimidated women had certainly not mastered the native language sufficiently. It would have been wiser if they had composed their missive in a more moderate fashion, precisely because they were refugees and in that respect guests of the country. During the legal process it also emerged that it was not Machin but Ogier who had removed the apparatus for making beer. In their agitation the Englishwomen had confused the names. They immediately turned to the Infanta in their need. On 18th September,[62] the Princess ordered a temporary stay to the town of St Omer's coercive measures. In a session dated 28th September,[63] the town council denied the havoc which the Englishwomen claimed had taken place at the sequestration of their goods. And so the matter remained; so too did the humiliation before the town's population, though for the present this disedifying dispute was at an end.

More dangerous was the the Society of Jesus' disapproval of the Institute. This had increased, and the Englishwomen were probably unaware of its intensity for the present. In very downright terms, on 19th June, 1621, Fr General Vitelleschi refused the intervention of Fr Michael Alford, who had been asked by the Englishwomen to request some favour.[64]

On the same day[65] Fr Vitelleschi wrote a long letter to the Vice Provincial. He cherished the hope, he said, that the difficult financial situation of the novitiate house in Liège could be turned to good. With this in view, the Vice Provincial's directions were to be followed. Even by Fr Tomson.

Fr Blount had written to the General on 7th and 14th March, and we can take it that these letters, which no longer survive, were largely concerned with the burden of debts of the novitiate house and, not least, with the mortgaged estate of Count Sackville in Condroz.

In this letter the suggestion is voiced for the first time — it was soon to be translated into action — of moving Fr Tomson as Rector of the novitiate house in Liège, and replacing him with Fr Henry Silisdon from the English mission. But Fr General first wished to hear the views of his assistants on the matter.

Presumably Fr Blount was also given strict instructions concerning the bursar's office, for Fr Vitelleschi showed great satisfaction at the provincial's order that from that time forward financial matters should be left solely to the Father Procurator. A self-evident truth, one might think. No-one, added Fr General, should in future concern themselves with the secular affairs of the Englishwomen. As to what concerned the debts in Condroz which had been made on behalf of these women, the General reserved to himself a time of consideration.

The dice, however, had already fallen.

The most urgent payments, up to about 6,000 guilders, could be made from Brother Fisher's dowry.[66] One can see that the finances of the new Jesuit foundation were ominously stretched.

On 19th June,[67] Fr General also sent a letter to the Rector. He had written to the General on 7th May,[68] without any idea of what was to take place the next day in the civil court. Fr Tomson had accepted the Provincial's orders with good will, although they cannot have been easy for him. Fr Vitelleschi assured the unfortunate man of his sympathy, but added words of caution, to the effect that one should refrain from looking after the Englishwomen's property as such an occupation was not in conformity with the rules of the Society of Jesus (cum Institutio Societatis). Fr Vitelleschi did not doubt Fr Tomson's good intentions but as all Jesuits were spiritual men and understood laws, they should follow the rules of the Society of Jesus concerning love of their neighbour.

A father could not have written more benevolently to his son. It must have been during these days that Fr General was fed some information that provoked him very keenly, for in his letter of 26th June[69] to Fr Blount he said that it should be looked on as a sign of God's providence that he had uncovered the Rector of Liège's hidden machinations on behalf of the Englishwomen before it could be brought to the attention of the Holy See. The Society of Jesus would otherwise have been the object of displeasure and hostility as well as of ridicule and mockery (omnium etiam risui et ludibrio). All such undertakings were to be stopped immediately, and Fr Tomson reprimanded, without exposing Fr Latham[70] however, who had sent the letter about the matter to Rome. The fathers were once again forbidden to be involved in anything connected with the confirmation of the Englishwomen's Institute. Fr Price[71] too was to abandon his book about the Institute; it must not be printed, nor circulated in manuscript form. Fr Price should be reproved. Fr Tomson should neither be moved to Louvain without the General's approval nor be allowed to remain longer as Rector in Liège, as it was very much to be doubted if he could again be entrusted with the position of superior.

Three weeks later, on 17th July,[72] Fr General informed Fr Vice-Provincial that the General Assistants had agreed to the nomination of Fr Henry Silisdon as Rector of the novitiate house in Liège. Fr Tomson had been put under obedience (praecepto obedientiae) to stop helping the Englishwomen. He should be kept under sharp surveillance in this respect. Even the Belgian Provincial, Fr Florentin de Montmorency, received an order[73] to warn Fr Théophile Bernardin to act prudently. He was in pastoral charge of the Filles de Sainte-Agnes in St Omer, and the English fathers might take offence at this, as they had been forbidden to concern themselves with the Englishwomen.

Fr Johannes Copper, Provincial of the Rhineland Province, likewise received a command[74] forbidding the fathers in his province to give spiritual direction to the Englishwomen in Trier. It is surprising that such an amount of time and trouble was taken over this last. The Englishwomen's house in Trier was small and remained very poor and without any influence. But his letters provide eloquent witness to the flood of warnings and objections that had reached the General. In those days all these letters were subject to the Order's custom of censuring correspondence. They would not, of course, have been handed in to the Rector in Liège, but to the Vice

Provincial in Louvain. The beginning of September was to decide the future fate of the former Rector. On 4th September,[75] the same day on which the Englishwomen's mortgage was dealt with by the Town Council in St Omer, Fr General told Fr Blount to arrange for Fr Tomson's transfer from Liège to Spain or Paris. The decree of Fr Silisdon's nomination as Rector of the Liège foundation was enclosed.

And he reiterated: writings composed by Jesuits concerning the Englishwomen were to be handed in. No Jesuit was ever to take such a task upon himself. Furthermore, the translation of the Constitutions into English should also be relinquished, in case they fell into the hands of the Englishwomen.[76]

As with his order concerning the house in rue Pierreuse, Fr General came a little too late. Fr Francis Young had been able to write to Rome on 21st August, 1619,[77] that the Englishwomen read the Jesuit rule at table. Of course this may not have meant the Constitutions. But who can guarantee that they were not already in their possession? In the 'Ratio Instituti' Plan for the Institute, Constitutions had been mentioned as the Constitutions of the Institute, and that was in 1616/1617 at the latest. Also, in one of her St Omer addresses, which can certainly be dated as 1617, Mary Ward said 'But for us it is to do ordinary things well, to keep our Constitutions, and all other things that are usual in every office or any employment.'[78]

When the Englishwomen' superiors were planning a journey to Rome, Fr General suggested that it would not be of much use to their Institute, in a letter to Fr Blount dated 4th September. There seems to be a touch of hesitation in those words. On 9th October,[79] finally, Fr Vitelleschi informed the Vice Provincial that Fr Silisdon's arrival in Belgium had given him much pleasure, as he could now take up office in Liège and Fr Tomson could be removed from the proximity of the Englishwomen. The new Rector would certainly straighten out the financial difficulties and could eventually obtain outside assistance; he, Fr General, would support that. And on the same day,[80] he wrote a second letter to Fr Blount, a sign that he had the Liège affair much at heart. He was considering what measures to take against Fr Tomson, who had not withdrawn his help for the Englishwomen. He should be transferred to a distant college. If the Englishwomen should come to Rome, he would made clear his justifiable displeasure at the management of their affairs by the Society of Jesus.

Fr Tomson also received a letter.[81] The reasons he had been given, said Fr General, in connection with unauthorized help for the Englishwomen had not been convincing. It was still less comprehensible how Fr Tomson had continued to busy himself with the English women's affairs even after the prohibition which he, the General, had issued. It showed imprudence and a lack of understanding of obedience. In the interests of the Society of Jesus he, the General, had been obliged to take painful action. Fr Tomson soon learnt his fate – transfer to Madrid. The south west of Europe was far distant from the north west. But the burning question remains: what exactly had happened?

Notes

1. " ... obtulit enim mihi occasionem serio de remediis cogitandi et forte ad haec invenienda multum iuvabit declaratio viceprovincialis Angliae quem spero non ita facile huiusmodi res celari posse." ARSI Rome, Gallo-Belg.1/II, p.520.

2. Fr Blount remained Vice Provincial until 1623 and became first Provincial of the English province, from 1623–1635. He died on 13th May 1638. Sommervogel I, Sp.1549; Foley I, p.11, note 63, p.128–129; II, p.1; III, p.481–488; VI, p.163–164; VII p.892.

3. Fr Vitelleschi to Fr Young, 20th September 1619. ARSI Rome, Germ.III.f.100v.

4. Fr Provincial Heren to Fr General Vitelleschi, 10th June, 1619, ARSI Rome, Gallo-Belg.40, ff.26r–27v. "Emptorem novitiatus, qui pro virginibus etiam emere solebat, eo quod tandem hac in re difficilem se exhibuerit, non solum officio sed etiam loco movit et huc ad seminarium alio licet praetextu ablegavit dixitque neminem Leodii habitaturum, qui virginibus non faveat." In all probability this statement referred to Count Sackville, who had bought the farms for the Jesuits and the house for the English-women. See pages 227ff.

5. Fr Freeman, Responsio, Point 9; AGR Brussels, Arch.Jésuit.Gallo-Belg.Carton 32.

6. AE Liège, Couvents, Jésuites Anglais, Registre pp.83–84, Nr.20.

7. " ... les censes et biens que j'ay au quartier de Condroz à Halleux, ban de Nandren avec touttes appendices et appartennances et touts droicts dépendants en aucune façon que se soit encore que ce fuissent des pièces de terres ou prairies particulièrement acquieses sans rien excepter de ce que me peut appartennir illecque ou au environ mesme ..." ibid.

8. " ... cède et transporte toutte telle droit et action qui me pouldroit competer à l'occasion des deniers par moy ou en mon nom exposés contre quelque personne, que ce soit pour avoir emplissement des choeses transportées ou promises à l'occasion desdit biens et à raison desquels je pouldroit avoir aulcune action ou droit réelle ou personelle, soit pour extinction des charges ou aultrement et constitué icelluy à cest effect en mon lieu et place." ibid.

9. Et pour la plus paisible possession de telles biens et de rendre lesdits Pères quictes et indempnes de touttes molestations ou troubles que peuvent advenir à cause de quelques charges ou debte pour argent que j'ay prin à rente pour édiffier la maison qui j'ay fait en Piereuse ou aultrement, néantmoins que la cense de Halleux soit générallement ou spéciallement obligé pour le payement de telles rents ou debts pour leur indemnité et guarandissement de touttes molestations, j'ay obligé par quinsaine tout les aultres biens, meublés et immeublés, que j'ay au pays de Liège." ibid.

10. AE Liège, Couvents, Jésuites Anglais, Registre pp.84–85, Nr. 21.

11. AE Liège, Recès du Conseil de la Cité de Liège 7, pp.56–57.

12. " ... q'avons veu certain act authenticquement expédié procédant du bon mestier des febvres en date du quattrieme d'avril saize cent et vingt ..." ibid. This document is no longer extant.

13. It cannot be ascertained if Elizabeth Falkner was related to Fr John Falkner SJ. Fr Falkner was reported to Fr General for having directed some of the

Institute's girls in theatrical performances. ARSI Rome, Gallo-Belg.1/II, pp.542–543, and Angl.1/I, f.114r.

14. The original of the testimonial in Hesse State Archives in Darmstadt was lost in World War II. An authenticated copy is in the IBVM Generalate Archives in Rome.

15. Becdelièvre, Biographie Liégeoise I, p.459 and BNB VII, p.108.

16. Sir George Talbot of Grafton (1564?–1630) was the eldest son of Sir John Talbot of Grafton and Frances, née Giffard. In England he conducted himself most circumspectly, otherwise he would have risked losing his father's title and estates in 1618. Talbot was a friend of Maximilian I of Bavaria and spent many years at his court. The Duke helped him in his difficulties in succeeding to the Earldom. Foley IV, p.329; Doyle, Peerage, p.322.

17. BV Rome, Fondo Capponi 47, ff.66r.–67v.

18. In 1612 the Englishwomen named two Talbots as members of the Institute. Barbara Babthorpe, Anne Gage and Mary Ward to Infanta Isabella Clara Eugenia, before 8th September 1612. AGR Brussels, PEA 1894. (2) Bishop Blaes, too, in his letter of 19th March, 1615 mentioned the name of Shrewsbury among the members of the Institute. ARSI Rome, Hist.Anglia 31/II, pp.659–664.

19. "When the prince elector came thither to masse, would not heare his owne musicke but ours, as surpassing, as he said etc." Vita E, f.106v.

20. Fr Leonhard Lessius to Fr Rector Giles Schoondonck on 24th May, 1612, ARSI Rome, Anglia 37, f.117e.

21. "Whilst her stay in thes parts she was invited at her retourne (from England, note) by the Prince of thes parts to have a house at Cullen, which afterwards he provided halfe-a yeare before her going, which time of stay was on her part for want of monyes." Barbara Ward, Out of the 2nd paper, Inst.Arch.Munich.

22. This information was also in the Hesse State Archives in Darmstadt, and lost in World War II. An authenticated copy is also in the IBVM Generalate archives in Rome. Headed: Exemplar informationis de Virginibus Anglis per Illustrissimum Dominum Sacvil missae Coloniam.

23. Reference to the foundation of a house in Trier. (1621).

24. A.Jakobs OMCap., Die Rheinischen Kapuziner, 1611–1725 = Reformationsgeschichtl. Studien und Texte 62/1933, p.49–51; L.Just Beiträge zur Gesch.d.Kölner Nuntiatur = Quellen und Forschungen 36/1956, p.256–266 and 296–302.

25. Eitel Friedrich von Hohenzollern was High Steward of the Court of Archbishop Ferdinand of Cologne and as such was often entrusted with diplomatic missions. His brother Johan was High Steward of the Court, Chamberlain and President of the Privy Council of Duke Maximilian I of Bavaria. Later, Cardinal Eitel Friedrich von Hohenzollern was one of the few benefactors of the Englishwomen in Rome.

26. Council Report 67, ff.282v–283r. Histor.Archiv.of Cologne.

27. On 11th July, 1620. ARSI Rome, Anglia 1/I, f.122v.

28. ibid. f.115v.

29. ibid. f.130rv.

30. see p.239.

31. Fr Tomson's paper, f.362r.

32. ibid. f.363v.

33. The creditors may have been impatient by spring, 1619; on 19th April of the same year Fr Tomson received a "Sauvegarde", a letter of protection from the Bishop of Liège, because unnamed persons were disputing his possession of the estate in Nandrin. AE Liège, Conseil Privé Dépêches 1612–1792, Nr.113.

34. Fr Tomson's paper, f.363v.
35. AE Liège, Couvents, Jésuites Anglais, Registre pp.89–90, Nr.23.
36. Fr Tomson's paper, f.364r.
37. AE Liège, Couvents, Jésuites Anglais, Registre pp.85–89, Nr.22.
38. "In quanto allo scritto mandato hora quì in Roma non sò che fosse fatto in quell'interim, ne anco intesi mai simil cosa; et sè mi fosse stato letto, non l'havrei mai lasciato passare sicurissimamente, perchè havrei visto e dimostrato fosse stato fatto con molta falsità o malignità ..." Fr Tomson's paper, f.364r. Fr Tomson here puts the blame on the lawyer, but it is unlikely that any lawyer at court or before the authorities would proceed other or further than his mandate allowed.
39. Fr Tomson's paper, in detail f.364v.
40. AE Liège, Couvents, Jésuites Anglais, Registre pp.101–102, Nr.28; pp.111–113, Nr.31; p.137, Nr.34; pp.146–147, Nr.36; pp.162–163, Nr.39; p.167, Nr.41; pp.224–225 s.n.
41. The foundation was given documentary confirmation on 8th September 1626 in Munich. AE Liège, Couvents, Jésuites Anglais, Registre, pp.255–264, s.n.
42. ibid. pp.232–233, s.n. from 29th August, 1626.
43. "Only in this they feel a want, that they cannot be certayn that they love Him." VP/C 2, p.2, Inst.Arch.Munich.
44. "I was glad when I saw that, that way Christ tooke in the use of all created things was the perfitest." VP/D 1, p.1, Inst.Arch.Munich.
45. "My sowle, whear is now true greatnes of mind (which causeth every thing to be compleately done in His time)?" VP/D 2, p.3. ibid.
46. "I besought God earnestly to give me grace neaver to offend Him agayn advisedly, in great or litle, and that I might now for evere turne my bake of sinn." VP/D 3, p.5. ibid.
47. "God was present; I had freedome to speake; the most of this howre was spent in speaking to Him with love and hope, and in harkininge what he would, with desirs to doe his will." VP/E 5, p.1. ibid.
48. "Ther was noe love I desired, or esteemed lyke to His by many degrees." VP/E 8, p.6. ibid.
49. 'Je feu auprès le Pere Generalle de la Société et luy donneray les lettres de Vostre Altezze. Il use beaucoup de fort bonnes parolles, confesse que ces Pères de ces quartiers là ont esté trompé. "Mary Ward to Infanta Isabella Clara Eugenia, 1st January, 1622. agr Brussels, PEA, 458, ff.3r–4v.
50. see p.217.
51. see p.239.
52. AM Saint-Omer, CCXXXIX 17–18, Filles Anglaises, ff.27–28.
53. The implementation of the distraint was decided on at the Council session of 6th September 1621. ibid. f.31. The letter of complaint must have been written *before* 11th September. AM Saint-Omer, CCXXXIX 16, Filles Anglaises, ff.12–14.
54. In the text: "Trois excoilles pour enseigner la jeunesse de la ville 3 annés de longe jusques asjoir." By "escoille" is meant classes.
55. see p.211.
56. "approuver" can also mean authorise, sanction, though this meaning is not intended here. Even the word "praised" is a re-interpretation of Rome's rescript. See p. 185.
57. AM Saint-Omer, CCXXXIX 16, Filles Anglaises ff.7–8.
58. On 20th September 1619 Antoine de Grenet, Sieur de Werp donated 1,500 guilders in interest claims, among which were 250 pounds on the possession of the Englishwomen in rue Grosse, for the foundation of a hospital for twelve poor men in Saint-Omer. L'Deschamps de Pas, Recherches historiques sur les établissements hospitaliers de la ville de Saint-Omer depuis leur origine

jusqu'a à leur réunion sous une seule et même administration en l'an V(1797) = Société des Antiquaires de la Morinie, Saint-Omer 1877, p.423–439, appendix 15. If the arrears of two years amounted to 500 guilders, then, at the normal rate of interest of about 6¼% for a mortgage, the amount was 4,000 guilders.

59.   AM Saint-Omer, CCXXXIX 18, Filles Anglaises, f.32. The claim for it was issued on 11th September. ibid. CCXXXIX 16, Filles Anglaises. f.11. (draft) and ff.16–17 (copy).

60.   John Wilson (c.1575/76–c.1645) was a convert from Staffordshire. He entered the English College, Rome in 1603 and was ordained in 1605. He first worked for the Jesuits as Fr Persons' secretary. In 1608 he took over direction of the printing works of the English College in Saint-Omer. From 1610 he acted occasionally as chaplain to the Poor Clares in Gravelines. He later showed himself a benefactor to the Englishwoman. He compiled an "English Martyrologie", which appeared in Saint-Omer in 1608. It is not certain that he entered the Society of Jesus before his death. Foley, V, p.424–426; VI p.228–229.

61.   Marie Aubrun, daughter of Councillor Antoine Aubrun, encouraged Bishop Blaes to found an educational establishment "Notre Dame du Jardin" for poor girls. See Bled, Evêques, p.407. The court recognised Antoine Aubrun as the author of the apology. Document: AM Saint-Omer, CCXXXIX, 17–18, Filles Anglaises, f.30.

62.   ibid. CCXXXIX 16, Filles Anglaises, f.6.

63.   AM Saint-Omer, Registre aux délibérations du Magistrat 1621–1626, f.22v. No statement of the council's decision to send an official denial to the Infanta can be found.

64.   Fr General Muzio Vitelleschi to Fr Michael Alford, ARSI Rome, Anglia 1/I, f.139v.

65.   Fr General Muzio Vitelleschi to Fr Vice Provincial Richard Blount, ibid. f.140rv.

66.   Probably Philipp Fisher, who had entered in Liège on 23rd October 1617. In 1621 he was a scholastic in Louvain, in 1625 he was working in London. Later he was one of the early companions of Fr Andrew White, the apostle of Maryland. Fr Fisher was superior there in 1636 and died in Maryland in 1652. Foley, vii, p.255–256.

67.   ARSI, Rome, Anglia, 1/I, ff.138v–139r.

68.   This emerges from Fr General's answer. Fr Blount had sent three letters to Rome: on 22nd April, on 7th and 14th May. cf.above, note 65.

69.   ibid. f.141r.

70.   Fr George Latham, vere Mainwaring SJ (1590–1631), came from Lancashire. He first studied in Saint-Omer; in 1609 he was accepted into the English College, Rome and entered the Society of Jesus in 1612. He was professor of moral theology in Liège and died of the plague on 12th September 1631 in Malines as chaplain to the soldiers. Foley I, p.654–655; VI p.254; VII p.278. A Kenny edit. The Responsa Scholarum of the English College, Rome, I, 1598–1621 = CRS 54/1962, p.217–218. Fr Latham received a personal letter of thanks from Fr General on 26th June, 1621. ARSI Rome, Anglia 1/I, f.141rv.

71.   Probably John Price, who was professor and prefect of studies at Louvain at this time. In 1622 he was chaplain to the Earl of Shrewsbury, George Talbot, active on the English mission. Foley VII, p.632–633.

72.   ARSI Rome, Anglia 1/I f.142v. It emerges from this that Fr Blount had written to Rome on 12th June.

73.   On 7th August 1621. ARSI Rome, Gallo-Belg.1/II, f.715r.

74.   On 21st August 1621. ARSI Rome, Rhen.Inf.6, f.29r.

75.   On 4th September 1621. ARSI Rome, Angl.1/I, f.144v.

76. "Det etiam operam Reverentiae Vestrae, ut recuperat exemplaria constitutionum in linguam Anglicanam traductarum, non enim videtur expedire, ut illa in manibus faeminarum relinquantur . . .' ibid.
77. See p.250.
78. "But for us it is to doe ordinary things well, to keep our Constitutions, and all other things that be ordinarie in everie offise or imploiment." LR, p.226, Inst.Arch.Munich.
79. ARSI Rome, Angl.1/I, f.145rv.
80. ibid. f.145v.
81. likewise on 9th October. ibid. f.146rv.

XVIII

FIRST VISIT TO ROME

1621

King Philip of Spain's recommendations for the English-women and the "Brevis Declaratio" – Infanta Isabella Clara Eugenia's draft of a recommendation for the Englishwomen to the Pope – its obstruction – altered suggestion for petitions to some Cardinals – report from an unnamed Jesuit – the final draft of the Infanta's petition – petition of Nuntius Guidi di Bagno – a defence of the Institute of the Blessed Virgin Mary

There were always civil or ecclesiastical notabilities who drew attention to the English women in their correspondence, sometimes because they were their advocates and supported them with a petition, sometimes because they opposed the Institute and wished to alert other notabilities about its existence.

Even before the decision of the Congregation of the Council had been taken, Bishop Blaes of St Omer had sent an informative document to King Philip III on 3rd February, 1616.[1] He mentioned the Englishwomen who had bought a house in St Omer a short time before and were now teaching girls. They were leading devout lives, and their congregation resembled that of the Society of Jesus. Fr Joseph Cresswell, Prefect of the English mission in Belgium at that time, had written an accompanying letter.[2] He asked the king for a letter of thanks to the Bishop, who had done so much for these Englishwomen. No more is known of the effect of the Bishop's letter.

Since then five years had passed. Death had overtaken Pope Paul V, Bishop Blaes of St Omer and King Philip III of Spain.[3] But in these five years matters had gone forward. From the Institute under the Bishop of St Omer's patronage had emerged the independent community in Liège, which embodied the original mode of life, their 'first estate', according to the words of the vision of their superior, Mary Ward. This community may have been financially bankrupt but it remained ideologically sound, in spite of sharp internal discord. One thing was evident, at all events: a clear decision was long overdue. It was for this reason that Mary Ward had long intended to go to Rome, in order to present her Institute to the Pope and request its confirmation. The sources state that she had wished to travel earlier, but had been prevented by illness.[4] Perhaps it had been the transfer of her confessor, Fr Lee, and then his death which had held her back, not to mention disunity within the Institute. However that may be, on an unknown day in 1621, the Infanta Isabella Clara Eugenia was asked to write to her nephew, King Philip IV of Spain[5] and urge him to intercede on behalf of the Englishwomen in Flanders with Pope Gregory XV and his powerful nephew, Cardinal Ludovico Ludovisi. The request was accompanied by a document (papal). This was undoubtedly that draft of the Ignatian Institute of the English-women, entitled 'Brevis Declaratio', and was composed in Latin and in Spanish.[6] In this summary, in which the independence of the Institute is strongly emphasized, there is no new Plan to be seen and therefore it has not been treated as such.

As a result of the decline of the countries in northern Europe – the Netherlands, too, which must have interested the King of Spain mightily – where the Jesuits worked with profit and educated young men, the authoresses of the 'Brevis Declaratio' had jointly come to a decision, in order to work for their own and their neigh-bour's salvation with greater benefit. They were involved in the pastoral apostolate of adults and the education of young girls and had decided on the Rule or Constitutions of the Society of Jesus (vel Constitutiones). These are not being sent, as they do not wish to adopt them in their entirety, but only as far as is permitted for women, without however being dependent on the Society of Jesus or on any other authority. The women would of course always wish to accept the good advice of wise men. The work and structure of their Institute requires subordination to the Pope alone.

It was an opportune moment for the Infanta to write. The young King, not yet sixteen when his father died, and the new but elderly and ailing Pope – he was sixty seven years old at his election – had borne the burden of power for a few months only.

Neither the rough draft of the Infanta's letter in Brussels, nor the original in Simanca can be found, though it was mentioned in a letter from Philip IV to the Spanish Ambassador in Rome – Don Fernandes de la Cueva, Duke of Albuquerque. The king's letter, too, survives only in the form of a copy.[7] The king commissioned his ambassador to help certain ladies who wanted to found a new Order in Flanders. This Order was to be fashioned on that of the Society of Jesus, and bear its name. The king and his council saw nothing extra-ordinary in that, for the monarch's great-aunt, beautiful Johanna of Austria, had actually been a member of the Society of Jesus.[8] The king had already made contact with Cardinal Ludovisi and now entrusted his ambassador with this mission, which would presumably be continued in Madrid but which was to be an extraordinarily dif-ficult task for its recipient in Rome, where it could cause ripples in diplomatic circles. It is not known how long the Infanta's petitions lay in Madrid; the royal chancellery's tempo cannot be described as exactly lively. 17th September, 1621 is the date when it was sent on to Rome. Neither is it known what happened to the original of the king's letter and its enclosure. The copy, however, bears an informative remark, which may well cause amazement. It runs:

'Copy of his Majesty's letter to the Duke of Albuquerque, my master. Written in Madrid, 17th September, 1621, concerning the new Order which some English women in Flanders wish to found. To be sent to Cardinal Bandini.'[9]

No one knows who wrote it. It was probably an indiscretion on the part of some official of the Spanish Embassy. But with Cardinal Bandini, Head of the Congregation of the Council, it fell into good hands. It is uncertain whether Cardinal Ludovisi really received a letter from the king. Even should that have been the case, this paper remained in the hands of one who was guarding the infirm and fading life of the old man, Gregory XV. If we know nothing about the pre-history of this letter in Belgium, we at least know that it arrived in Madrid and could have reached its destination in Rome.

A letter to the Pope fared differently. This was not channelled through the Spanish chancellery officials of the Infanta, and was therefore under the supervision and at the discretion of another bureau. A fair copy exists, in the clear but rather uneven hand of Mary Ward's secretary, Margaret Horde. It bears the dorsal comment: Your highness may send your letter to His Holiness in Rome in this or some similar form.[10]

To summarize the contents of this letter: after the introductory formula of it being the duty of a sovereign to promote God's honour and the salvation of one's subjects, the Infanta introduced the Englishwomen's Institute to the Pope. She recommended the devout and noble lady Mary Ward who, eleven years ago, with some other noble Englishwomen, had begun a religious Institute (pium vitae Institutum) in St Omer and had continued tirelessly in her holy zeal up to the present time. She directed her institute and enlarged the community, spreading it to other regions. These women wished to devote themselves to the salvation of the whole world, and especially the northern countries, where morals had deteriorated. They wished to visit Rome to try to obtain papal confirmation, so that their work could be established. In their schools they teach noble girls the fundamentals of the faith and christian morals and also devote themselves to the conversion of adults by means of religious discussions. Not a few had already returned to the catholic church. Their aim is to do for women what the Jesuits do for men. Their Institute has already been commended by the Cardinals of the Congregation of the Council in 1615 (!) and his approbation anticipated. The letter ended with a request for confirmation.

At last. One might be tempted to breathe a sigh of relief, that at last Mary Ward's God-given task had been expressed unequivocally.

But it would be dangerous to rejoice too soon. This letter never left the old palace of the Princes of Burgundy in Brussels. Who leaked the information it contained will never now be known. What happened here in Brussels was to happen later to the King of Spain's letter in Rome. We may recall Fr General's letter of 26th June, 1621[11] to the Vice Provincial in Belgium, that it could be taken as a sign of God's Providence that Fr Blount had uncovered Fr Tomson's secret efforts on behalf of the Englishwomen before they had been able to cause havoc in Rome.[12]

One or two statements in the Infanta's draft seem, on closer examination, to be strangely expressed. First of all one is forced to ask: was Mary Ward's original Institute really the same as that of the congregation commended by the Cardinals of the Congregation of the Council, and whose confirmation was anticipated? Likewise the fact that Mary Ward had begun a Pius Institute in St Omer from which she had in no way deflected. That was not so. If one were to consider the beginning of the Institute, therefore the first steps before the vision of 1611, that would be the 'Pium Institutum', so it cannot be said that Mary Ward had changed nothing. She had not, of course, deviated from her task of pastoral work among adults and educating girls. This coincided largely with the work of the Jesuits. But, as has been shown, after the vision, the members wanted to form the spiritual structure of their Institute according to the Jesuit model. It would have been truer to say that Mary Ward had continued on her way without change. Something else: the description given above says a good deal about the work but not about the basic Ignatian charism or of the Constitutions of the Institute.

Perhaps the 'Brevis Declaratio' was also enclosed with this petition, but there is no mention of it in the text.

It must have caused no little embarrassment in the Court Chancellery when the Superior of the Society of Jesus in Belgium involved himself in the matter.

Only a few pages still exist in the Brussels' State Archives of the Infanta's draft of a letter.[13] The handwriting is strong and masculine. It is the draft for a petition to Cardinal Robert Bellarmine SJ. To this was appended a list of the names of important people in Rome, to whom similar petitions could possibly be sent.[14]

And now appears another, more familiar Institute: the memory of the great Jesuit Cardinal is first refreshed by a reminder of that Institute which had been presented to the Pope and the Cardinals of the Congregation of the Council six years previously (in 1615). In these letters from the Congregation to the Nuntius in Belgium, the Institute was commended to the Bishop of St Omer and a promise was given to those who received it that, provided the members of the community would continue along the path they had undertaken, they would have the rights and the name of an Order bestowed upon them. The members of the Institute had done their part, for in their places of education they had instructed girls in the fundamentals of the faith and christian morals, as well as in other subjects valuable and necessary for life. The Infanta hopes that the promised confirmation would now be forthcoming, as no one could be ignorant of the fact that the education of girls was highly necessary, above all in the Spanish Netherlands, though it would be beneficial for the church in general. To this end the Infanta requests the Cardinal to intercede with the Pope on their behalf and to give all possible assistance to the Superior of those ladies who are to travel to Rome for the confirmation of their congregation.

It is clearly evident from the enclosed document, partly repeated verbatim, that it was once again a matter of the bishop's 'Pium Institutum' of 1616, in which girls were taught in St Omer, but which had hardly anything in common with the Jesuits. But this draft was not used once in the Infanta's many petitions. As in 1616 in St Omer, so in 1621 in Brussels, an invisible filter was interposed between what went in and what came out.

Among Jesuit papers [15] in the State Archives in Brussels lies a relatively short report, little more than three sides long, written in a fine masculine hand. It may have been a compilation of various items of news, collected by the author, for he knew of contemporary details from three cities: Brussels, Liège and Louvain. The first item of news communicated was the text of the Infanta's two petitions – to the King of Spain and to Cardinal Bellarmine – to serve as the basis for confirmation of the Englishwomen's Institute by the Pope. The summarized contents of both these letters is given here: The letter to the King of Spain concerns an Institute of certain Englishwomen who have followed a conventual manner of life (religiosum cursum) for about twelve years and have the approval of princes and high ecclesiastics. They requested the Infanta to intercede on behalf of their congregation with the King, with the aim of obtaining papal confirmation. Parents hesitate to pay the dowry of certain members while approbation is lacking. The Infanta does not doubt the king's wholehearted interest in this matter in Belgium and sends a brief plan of the Institute with her letter (Brevem eius Instituti Formulam), which has already been approved and reported on by reputable scholars.

The Petition of the Infanta to her nephew, Philip IV of Spain should be recalled. This had in fact reached the king and showed quite a different slant. First, one is struck by the undoubtedly important but totally incomprehensible reason given for the confirmation of the Institute: the matter of dowries. This financial detail was a curious point of departure to lay before the head of christendom in so important a matter as the confirmation of a congregation! Besides, the Englishwomen had not fallen into a state of poverty because of the lack of dowry money, but because of Count Sackville's double dealing. It is equally odd that the old, well-known 'Pium Institutum' raises its head once again, but not Mary Ward's

Ignatian Institute, which the Infanta had in fact supported.

The second letter was addressed to Cardinal Bellarmine, but shows only a vague awareness of the contents, which have already been made known. Again it must be assumed that the Cardinal was au fait with the circumstances of 1616. For after a few sentences about the Englishwomen's progress, which had not passed unnoticed, we read the stupefying statement, that the fruits of their work would be significantly greater after they had received the confirmation of their Institute from the Pope and could be freed from the complaints and reproaches of their adversaries.[16] This leads one to believe that the Infanta used the ceaseless disputes and friction between the English-women and their unnamed opponents as a springboard for a petition to a famous Cardinal, a member of the Society of Jesus, moreover. An unreasonable expectation. Still better is to come.

These two letters, as the report continues, were sent to the Infanta with a brief summary of the Plan of the Institute — named the 'Brevis Declaratio' — in Latin and in Spanish, and with a letter in French written personally by Mary Ward but composed by Fr Tomson. Even the trusted Lady in Waiting, Madame de la Feira, received a letter. The contents of the enclosed document were written from memory and cause certain questions to surface. Fr Lessius was given as reference for judging the 'Brevis Declaratio'. That could not possibly have originated with Mary Ward, for she knew very well that Fr Lessius had defended the Institute at Fr Burton's request, but not the 'Brevis Declaratio'. Had Fr Tomson really undertaken this task? But then he too must have been as well acquainted with the facts as Mary Ward. And is one really expected to believe that Mary Ward had copied this, without query?

To continue this imaginative account, there now follows a passage dealing with Brussels. There the Infanta, together with Madame de la Feira, devoted herself to the study of the 'Brevis Declaratio'; even Archduke Albrecht was drawn into it. But it was not the Ignatian character of the Institute, nor the adoption of the Rules and Constitutions of the Society of Jesus by the members of the Institute that shocked the Archduchess, but the independence of this congregation, which did not wish to pay obedience even to the Apostolic Nuntius. And when the name of Lessius was mentioned in the accompanying letter, the Infanta sent Madame de la Feira to the old scholar, who lay at the point of death in Louvain. As she conducted her anxiously guarded commission in the confessional, nothing further can be known about it. But the reporter knows exactly what has happened in Louvain! He even knows Fr Lessius's words of rejection. It is to be hoped that he does not want to make us believe that the seal of confession was broken, even if it was not a matter of conscience. In addition to which, in April, 1621 the twelve-year truce 'het twaalfjarig bestand' between North and South Netherlands came to an end, and hostilities flared up again that were to last for eighty years.

Is it likely that the Infanta Isabella Clara Eugenia, who was an outstanding politician, would really have found the time to study the plan of a women's congregation, together with her Lady in waiting? And would she have had the basic knowledge for such a study? Lessius, presumably, would have praised her abilities in this respect.[17] Archduke Albrecht was mortally sick during this time. He died on 13th July of the same year. Could the Army Commander, Archduke Albrecht, have taken part in consultations of this sort? It is more likely that the Archduchess would have spent any moments of free time by the bedside of her beloved husband.

It must be asked — if the whole story has any truth at all — would not the Infanta have pointed out the dangers in the 'Brevis Declaratio' to the Society of Jesus before? It would have been a simpler solution.

Finally, the reporter gives the contents of two letters, again from memory: Madame de la Feira's letter in answer to Mary Ward, dismissing the 'Brevis Declaratio' and a sharp letter from Fr Lessius to Mary Ward.

Then the author dashes back to Liège, while reporting on the Englishwomen's consternation at Fr Lessius' letter. It would be interesting to know if the letter to the General Superior of the Institute, who was in Cologne at the time, had been opened in Liège. Or was this addressed directly to Fr Tomson and then publicly enlarged on?

To return to the text: in a letter drafted in French by Fr Tomson, Mary Ward rejected the disputed point of the exemption of the Institution from episcopal jurisdiction. She wished to present this matter herself in Rome. But she reproached the Rector for having mentioned it to Fr Lessius. With that the report comes to an end and we ask: How could Mary Ward reproach Fr Tomson — had she not herself (as we have just been informed) written the letter drafted by the Rector in her own hand? Might not the name Lessius have struck her then, even if she had been writing the letter absentmindedly?

The report abounds with inconsistencies to such an extent that one is inclined to ignore it, but that will not do. It is not known who compiled it. Fr George Latham[18] had sent information to Rome in the same year, but it is difficult to imagine that he would present such nonsense to the highest authority in his Order. One must not overlook the fact that Fr Blount had been praised by the General for having discovered the involvement. Probably it was because of Fr Latham's statements that the negotiations behind the scenes in Brussels had come to light. It has been shown that the King of Spain's letter was still able to reach its destination, but not that addressed to the Pope. Presumably a completely distorted aide-memoire, shaped by rumours and things imagined, had been used as a basis for this. Rumours that were passed around in the English Jesuit novitiate and those in rebellion against Mary Ward within the Liège community, may have been responsible.

On the same day that final legal negotiations in St Omer about the English women's goods and possessions had taken place, and they had presented a written apology for their unconsidered complaint to the Town Magistrate, busy scribes in the princely chancellery in Brussels were completing drafts for petitions to six Cardinals.[19]

The text of the draft submitted was not taken as a model. The old school of Habsburg diplomacy knew better than most how to shade nuances according to the person addressed.

Cardinal nephew Ludovico Ludovisi was requested to support a Pius Institute, which devoted itself to the teaching of girls. His influence with the Pope was mentioned politely, and incidentally. Cardinal Eitel Friedrich von Hohenzollern had his attention drawn to the still very young foundation of the Institute in Cologne. Shortly before accepting the purple, he had shown an interest in the matter. He too was reminded of the educational aspect of the Institute. For Cardinal Guido Bentivoglio, to whom the first Englishwomen in St Omer had been introduced in 1611, heavy stress was laid on their school activities in a country which he had known as Nuntius. Even more pressingly, an appeal was made to the famous Jesuit Cardinal, Robert Bellarmine, and his fervour for the glory of God and for the general good, as these were the same aims which had led Mary Ward to Rome. That is the unvoiced, hidden motive. The emphasis in this instance was that, under the Pope's authority, the Englishwomen wished to educate English and Belgian girls as a congregation confirmed by the Pope. Only the merest trace of a suggestion of the Society of Jesus is visible in this formulation.

A further explanation of the Petition was presented to two Cardinals by the Belgian Ambassador, Juan Bauttista Vives, and these were Cardinal Scipio Borghese, Protector of the Spanish Netherlands and Odoardo Farnese, Cardinal Protector of England.

Cardinal Borghese was presented with an Institute which, greatly strengthened by papal confirmation, could therefore be entrusted with the enormous field of educational work in teaching Belgian girls. It was only in the letter to Cardinal Farnese that the Englishwomen were introduced as 'Dames Anglaises', English Ladies, who had a foundation and congregation in St Omer. Because they are English, the Archduchess has placed the matter in the Cardinal Protector's care. This petition is the only one which makes no mention of their work in education and teaching in St Omer. This small variant – one might be led to consider it an unintentional omission – speaks more loudly than a careful selection of words. It was not by chance that the Belgian Ambassador was sent to those Cardinals who were, specifically, the Cardinal Protectors of the countries concerned, the Spanish Netherlands and England.[20] And not only to these two was the harassed Ambassador sent. He had to address the Congregation of the Council and clarify certain matters which are not disclosed here. Moreover, the confrontation with the General of the Society of Jesus was still to come. No easy prospect.[21] It was only next day, 14th September, that the draft of the letter to Pope Gregory XV was finally ready.[22]

Our dear and well-beloved Mary Ward, it begins without preamble, is travelling to Rome to seek the confirmation of her Institute, humbly kneeling at the feet of Your Holiness, an Institute which she founded to the greatest glory of God (la plus grande gloire). The Infanta feels herself obliged to bear witness to the progress, devotion and other praiseworthy qualities of this woman and her companions who, for eleven years in St Omer, have taught girls and educated them in the fundamentals of the faith, giving them a moral basis for their lives. Her Institute now has houses in Liège and Cologne, where they are much in demand.

As this congregation could prove of inestimable service in raising the moral standards of the country, the Archduchess requests the Pope to be pleased to confirm the Institute as an Order (religion).

In spite of the somewhat baroque style of the letter, it radiates an honest and well-intentioned desire to help by recommending a congregation which is serving a country threatened by war and deprived, in many aspects. Yet, somewhere in this varied correspondence with the Cardinals, a door remains open, if only by a hair's breadth. This may be seen in the Archduchess' letter to Cardinal Farnese, the Roman Catholic protector of a country not under the Infanta's jurisdiction, but which she well knew was the heart of the matter for these Englishwomen.

Ambassador Vives received a copy of the royal letter to Cardinals Ludovisi and Borghese. As though anticipating her Ambassador's reluctance, she casually mentioned, for his consideration, that he should keep before his eyes solely the glory of God and the good of the country as she used her royal authority in the affair. And then came the charge: 'We desire you to undertake this (commission) earnestly and zealously, in that when you present this letter which you have received to his Holiness, the Cardinals, the Cardinals of the Congregation and the General of the Society of Jesus, you stress the necessity for this country of the confirmation of the Institute, which has begun here so successfully. Although most of the present members are Englishwomen, if they develop along the right lines, they will accept Belgian girls too and, to my mind, that will be of tremendous advantage to our young people of Belgium.'

The Ambassador could add other reasons when speaking with individuals, the Infanta continued, but above all he was to emphasize the need for such a Pius Institute in Belgium.

In the letter accompanying the royal petition to the Pope, probably prepared by Secretary of State Carlos de la Faille, Vives received, into the bargain, the task of proposing to the General of the Society of Jesus that he should put a stop to the intentions of certain fathers who were trying to put obstacles in the way of the confirmation of the Institute of the Englishwomen, and their stay in Rome.[23] If Vives was even remotely familiar with the multi-facetted intrigues of the Roman Curia's procedures, as he certainly was, then he could hardly have regarded the approaching group of women as cause for celebration.

Even the Nuntius wrote petitions. Five Cardinals, Ludovisi, Borghese, Farnese, Millini and Ubaldini,[24] received a letter clothed in skilful, though neutral language in which requests were presented for the noble English Lady Mary Ward. A few years previously she had established a community of women in a Belgian town with the permission of the Bishop. She now wished to go to Rome in order to obtain papal approval for her congregation. The 1616 appeal for a decision from the Council of the Congregation and the Infanta's petitions made to him, the Nuntius, were not lacking from any of these requests. True, Nuntius Giovanni Francesco Guidi di Bagno[25] was active in Belgium for a short time only. He entered Brussels on 20th July, a week after Archduke Albrecht's death, so he could hardly be expected to exert himself in the matter of a community which he did not know at all. He had been Vice Legate in Avignon since 1614, sufficiently far enough from Flanders not to have heard of the Englishwomen. Probably the new Nuntius was presented with a list with the names of the Cardinals to whom he was to write. That emerges clearly in a letter of his to the Cardinal Protector of England, Odoardo Farnese.[26] It was only to Cardinal Millini, who was soon to show himself a strong opponent of the Institute in Rome, to whom the Nuntius wrote that the Englishwomen's work would be very valuable for an England riddled with heresy, though he did not expatiate on their kind of work. Nuntius Guidi di Bagno stayed in Belgium for a short time only; he was transferred to Paris by 1627, so it was not he who had to bring things to their bitter conclusion.

Without having any demonstrable connection with the preceding papers, or indeed of belonging to this time and matter, there is a later statement about the Institute of the Englishwomen which can, perhaps, be seen as a defence.[27]

Neither the time of its composition nor its author are known. The headings is:

Rationes quibus demonstratur non convenire his virginibus subordinationem aliquam episcopis, praelatis, superioribus religionum aut ulli alteri comm/entarius/. In another hand on the back has been added: De Virginibus Anglis. The contents summarized:

The aim of the Institute of the Englishwomen, the salvation of its members and the exercise of apostolic activity, especially by teaching and educating girls as the Jesuits do boys, presupposes mobility and, therefore, the possibility of its members being transferred from one place to another. Such flexibility can only exist if the Institute has its own central authority. The bishop of the place, for example, would hardly be able to find time to order the internal matters of the community. The interests of his diocese must have priority. In the matter of extra-diocesan expansion, the concerns of the Institute would be subordinate to different bishops, and this would inevitably destroy its internal unity and coherence. Local connections sometimes pose a threat to expansion. That is why the Institute desires to be subordinate to the Pope.

This new but opportune type of work done by women in the apostolate requires a new form of community. It was God who gave the instruction to model the Institute entirely on that of the Society of Jesus. As for possible, future difficulties, such as the government of such an organisation by women, or the convening of a general chapter, the election of a general superior, religious instruction by women and the possibility of disorders arising from this community, these point to the Society of Jesus and the opinion that women could be better governed by women.

Certain lines of thought, such as the transfer of the generalate to Rome, the convening of a General Congregation, or even the extending of the Institute to other continents, could hardly have been conceivable in those days, yet the possibility for them in the future was nonetheless left open.

As to the matter of the date, one can only point now to the alleged reservations of the Infanta Isabella Clara Eugenia concerning the independence of the Institute, which is so strongly stressed here – to such an extent that they did not wish to be subordinate even to the Nuntius. And this poses the question of the author. He may have been one of the English Jesuits. The text is compactly and clearly constructed. The Ignatian Institute for women, Mary Ward's Institute, does indeed form the basis of it but that does not signify that Mary Ward had composed and suggested the opinions it contains. The use of scriptural texts (the Book of Daniel, Numbers,) concrete statements about Jesuit methods, considerations about future General Congregations, the seat of the Generalate, etc, point to the contrary, for that most certainly did not flow from Mary Ward's pen, but from that of a man who was versed in the matters under discussion with all their problems. It was certainly not written by Fr Tomson. Such clarity or precision of language could not be expected of him.

Even the question of the recipient cannot be answered with certainty. It could have served as the groundwork for a consultation concerning the independence of the Institute, say for a discussion with the fathers in Louvain, or for Fr Blount, who was extremely opposed to the Institute, even hostile. But that is pure supposition.

Mary Ward's letter to Nuntius Antonio Albergati in Cologne

Liège or Cologne, before 4th August, 1621

Mary Ward's letter to Fr General Vitelleschi and to Nuntius Albergati − source and significance of the letter − history of her vocation − her Institute

At the end of September or beginning of October, 1621, during her stay in Cologne,[28] Mary Ward wrote what was probably her first letter to Fr General Vitelleschi. It has not survived. It may be assumed that it contained explanations and readiness to cooperate, for Fr General's answer of 6th November, 1621[29] was particularly courteous, even welcoming. He expressly asked Mary Ward to understand his position and the instructions he had given to the superiors of his Order, as Jesuits were forbidden by their Constitutions to assume the care and control of female Orders. Possibly, too, her letter may have contained a reference to the many attacks made by Jesuits, for Fr Vitelleschi assured her that the fathers would no longer obstruct her project. [30] This undoubtedly was a reference to the proposed journey to Rome.

A detail, which throws light on the situation − Fr General used the term 'Perillustris' in his answer to Mary Ward, one generally reserved to members of the nobility. This form of address roused a protest from the English Jesuits: Mary Ward was not noble, so such a title could lead to misunderstandings. Fr General answered by way of explanation that he had merely used the continental custom.[31] Some indiscretion must lie behind this − on the part of the English women − for obviously Fr Blount in Belgium, to whom the General's answer was addressed, could not have known how his General Superior had written to Mary Ward. But in Cologne, or perhaps in Liège before her departure there, Mary Ward had written a far more important letter which has been mentioned repeatedly: to Nuntius Antonio Albergati in Cologne, concerning her Institute.[32]

The source of this letter, of such importance in Mary Ward's life, is not certain. The English draft must undoubtedly have been written by Mary Ward herself. Only she could have known her interior experiences so exactly, and conveyed them with so personal a touch in her own style. There are several copies of this draft, however. The original for the Nuntius would probably have been in Latin, and is no longer extant.

It is possible that the English text, being there, was used as the basis for a consultation, as could have been the case in St Omer with Bishop Blaes' 'Relatio' for Nuntius Ascanio Gesualdo of Flanders. This has already been suggested.[33] The letter could also have been composed somewhat later as the written foundation for a discussion.

The sources do not give adequate grounds for passing any definite judgement.

The text, as compared with the original, may have been abridged slightly. That is true at least of the opening sentence, for the sudden reference to the accompanying enclosure is rather remarkable when one considers that the letter was addressed to a Nuntius. As to date — the letter offers scanty interior indications. Bishop Blaes' death has already been mentioned; he died on 21st March, 1618. That is not particularly informative when seeking an exact date. Albergati was mentioned as being still Nuntius of Cologne. He left this city on 4th August, 1621 for Rome.[34] Here at least is a date ante quem. Fridl[35] and Chambers[36] set the time as after June, 1620. As their source for giving a date they quote the Parchment Book, in which the letter was entered after Mary Ward's notes for this month. In relation to everything else, but with some scepticism, the date should rather be placed as the summer of 1621, when the departure of the Nuntius was imminent, and Fr Tomson's endeavours to achieve confirmation of the Institute had been discovered.

It is clearly apparent from the text that Mary Ward had previously been in contact with the Nuntius concerning the formation of her Institute, and that Albergati too had raised objections to it. Certainly, both houses in Liège as well as the new foundatiuon in Cologne lay within Albergati's jurisdiction, but this Nuntius was transferred and he was on the point of leaving for Rome in the summer of 1621.

Albergati's opinions about the Institute were, consequently, of especial importance at this precise time. Added to which, Nuntius Albergati was closely related to Gregory XV's influential nephew, Cardinal Ludovico Ludovisi. He could, therefore, be an important negotiator in Rome. It is not clear if Mary Ward knew that the King of Spain's correspondence with the Curia had been blocked.

The aim of this letter, the contents of which dealt exclusively with Mary Ward's spiritual development and God's guidance, is patently obvious: to provide evidence that her Institute, the construction of which was enclosed, was the result of divine revelation and not that of personal whim. Nevertheless, a deeper reason why this normally reserved woman was so expansive may be sought on the personal level, although there is too little information about the relationship between the Englishwomen and Nuntius Albergati to allow any conclusive statement.

As for the all-important letter, it bears the superscription 'Written to be delivered to the Nuntius Apostolic of Lower Germany, Monsignor Albergati.'[37] This 'to be delivered' does not necessarily imply an instruction to the post, but rather points to a personal handing over.

Without any introduction, Mary Ward mentions the enclosure to the letter, which contains the Englishwomen's desire, namely: 'the same to which God in a particular manner had called them.'[38] So

Margaret Garret at Babthorpe.

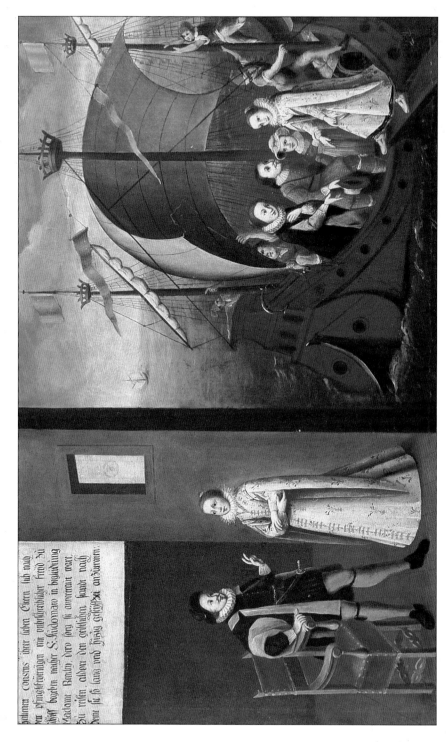

Mary Ward leaving for St. Omer.

Harewell House across the fields.

Newby, Yorkshire.

Winefrid Wigmore.

Mount Grace Chapel.

these were not two separate things, but a unity. The next sentence echoes the impotence of the mystic to explain her experience. 'If I could express myself in words, I do not doubt that your grace would approve the reasons which I would like to cite why this Plan appears to be God's will for us.' As already mentioned, the Nuntius may have rejected the Ignatian charism of the Institute, for she continues: 'And as I do not wish, except for the most pressing reasons, to give the appearance of contradicting Your Grace's suggestion and desire, I will say a little of the great amount that could be said concerning this intention.'

There follows, as if ranked in sections one after another, the history of her spiritual life: her vocation to be a religious, parental opposition, her crossing to Belgium and entering the 'most austere' Order, which reflected her total surrender to God. At that time she had not even considered an active life for God in the world. Of the first four years of her life in St Omer she mentioned only briefly the foundation of a convent for English Poor Clare's, the stay of the first Englishwomen in a rented house and their interior peace, in order to give more space to the event of St Athanasius' Day (2nd May, 1609). She parted from the Poor Clare Order in obedience to God's command, and returned to England in order to 'do all the little I could for God and the good of those there.'

She also devoted much attention to the 'Gloria Vision' and its consequences. Then followed the second crossing to Belgium, this time in the company of some Englishwomen who had joined her in order 'to be religious women where I should be living'. Clerical friends urged 'some Rule already confirmed' upon this small community and were nonplussed when all their endeavours were refused.[39]

Only with the revelation of 1611 was there full certainty. She wanted to adopt the Institute of the Society of Jesus for her congregation. It is not necessary here to repeat this presentation.

Her confessor resisted, and 'all the Society opposed' it. Plans were drawn up, and even 'pressed upon us'. And then comes the incontrovertible sentence 'there was no remedy but to refuse them, which caused infinite troubles.'[40] Mary Ward explains this problem in greater detail. The Jesuits wished her to choose at least a different name, not that of 'Jesus' and in this respect the fathers were immovable. They would allow them to have the Constitutions of the Society of Jesus in general but not literally ('that forme which these Constitutions and Rules are writt in'). This was neither essential nor necessary, thought the fathers. Mary Ward quickly complied with the opinion of her confessor, Fr Roger Lee, SJ, who had been placed in a difficult position in his Order on her account.[41] There follows an important statement: 'As to what concerns the name, I have twice, in different years, understood in as particular a manner as those other happenings which I have recounted, that the name of this Institute must be Jesus.' [42]

She frequently experienced the inconveniences that were to result if her Institute should be dependent on the Society of Jesus in any way.[43] As a seal to what had gone before, she said finally, God granted her 'continual light' about 'the true practice' of the Institute. The progress of its members in the spiritual life were a sign that God's hand was at work, and that the manner of life observed up to then had his approval. This, however, was no other than that which she presented in the enclosed document 'is no other than what in this other paper I humbly here present.'

It is unnecessary to waste time in surmise: the enclosed paper was undoubtedly the 'Formula Instituti' of the Society of Jesus. [44]

Ten years had passed since God had imprinted this on her heart. The letter reveals three main points, which are clearly highlighted; the enlightenment on St Athanasius' Day, the 'Gloria Vision', and the 1611 revelation. Their cumulative impact cannot be overlooked. With her directness, Mary Ward never deviated from this orientation, and certainly not on the eve of her first journey to Rome.

The Journey

November/December 1621

Audience with Infanta Isabella Clara Eugenia in Brussels — Pilgrims' clothes — route and group — arrival in Rome

Fr General's answer of 6th November, 1621[45] did not reach Mary Ward in Liège. It may be that she had guessed its contents already; perhaps she entrusted her representative to read and keep the letter.

The English Vita records that Mary Ward was occupied until 18th October with the foundations of both Cologne and Trier; on 21st October, the feast day of St Ursula and her companions, she began her journey to Rome. Both the English and the Italian lives mention a visit made by Mary Ward to the Infanta in Brussels. Probably she had already had an audience earlier, for it would have been impossible with her contemporary forms of transport to have covered the 100 km between Liège and Brussels (18–21 October) in three days, to have a conversation with the Archduchess, and then make final preparations for the long journey to Rome. The advice given her by the Archduchess, for safety's sake to wear pilgrim's garb on the way to Rome, was followed. And such clothing had to be made ready. It must also be remembered that the letters of recommendation had already been drafted on 13th/14th September and probably soon after had been turned into fair copies. One is justified in doubting the report given first by Fridl and taken on board by Chambers, which states that Mary Ward was in Brussels between 18th and 21st October and began her journey to Rome from there.[46] It is far more likely that the visit to Brussels took place at the end of September or the beginning of October.

No single source gives any inkling of what the two women discussed. Without doing violence to history, it may be assumed that the audience led to open and friendly conversation. Mary Ward may have revealed the situation of the Liège house to the Archduchess, who was very well-disposed towards her. That can be seen in a letter from Rome.

On 18th September, very quickly for the normal practice of her chancellery, the Infanta wrote to the town of St Omer, to obtain a stop to the forceful measures against the Englishwomen there, whose possessions for the most part were mortgaged. The Infanta will have made it clear to Mary Ward that, since the death of her husband, she alone had to carry the burden of governing a country constantly at war with its northern neighbours and that she had to give pride of place to the good of the country. Moreover, the dismissive attitude of the Society of Jesus towards the Institute may have warned the Infanta to be cautious. Someone in her Council of State, or several of her immediate retainers may have taken part in building up a negative position. There is a portrait of Mary Ward, relating to this time, though it can hardly be an original dating from 1621. The Englishwomen would not have had the means to have such a portrait painted during a time of such need. Hunger was staring them in the face in Liège. If the pilgrim clothing was made only after the Brussels' audience, there would have been relatively little time left for it.

This portrait shows Mary Ward in dark brown clothing with a fine ruff and lace cuffs as the only accessories brightening its monotony. The little cap, reminiscent of the head-covering of the Augsburg portrait [47] is likewise trimmed with lace. On top of this, Mary Ward wears a large, broad-brimmed hat. It is the same pilgrim hat which is still preserved in the Institute house in Altoetting. In her right hand she holds a pilgrim's staff. In contrast to the prematurely worn (she was thirty-six years old) but finely-featured countenance with the deep-set, thoughtful eyes, are the awkward hands. Under the picture is: 'Maria, 1621, travelled from Trier to Rome on foot, in Pilgrim's dress.' If the picture had been painted in Belgium or in the circle of the first members, the title would have been in English. Of course, it may have been added later. But then the indication 'Trier' is doubtful which, as has already been seen, first appeared in Fridl in the first quarter of the eighteen century.

Up till then, the Englishwomen had limited the work of their Institute to England, Flanders and Liège. It had been a time of maturity and, too, one of purification. Now, Mary Ward and some of the first members were setting off for the heart of christianity.

That involved a journey of two months, straight across a war-torn Europe. Geographical difficulties apart, there were almost unimaginable dangers for any small unarmed group of travellers, half of which were women.

There is little information about the route taken. The English Life mentions three towns: Nancy, Milan and Loreto.[48] Nancy was a halting place for rest; from there Mary Ward wrote to the Infanta.[49] In Milan the travellers visited the grave of St Charles Borromeo, and in Loreto, the Holy House. Bissel[50] and Khamm[51] describe the landscape of Lorraine instead of Nancy. Only Chambers [52] draws − unfortunately without source-references − an approximately exact route: Brussels − Trier − where they visited the new foundation of the Institute, then through Lorraine to Nancy. From there the journey continued through Basle, Lucerne, over the St Gotthard to Lake Maggiore, to Como, Milan, Piacenza, Bologna, Ancona, Loreto, Rome.

If one tries to follow this route on a map, one's doubts are justified. It would have been a murderous journey on foot in November directly across Switzerland and in winter. The well-known St Gotthard hospice lies at a height of 2,100 metres. Would it not have been more practical to follow the valley of the Meuse from Liège to Namur, Sedan, Verdun and thus reach Nancy?

There is no other place in the written sources that gives Mary Ward as having journeyed to Italy via Trier. What would have been the sense in making such a detour? She had been in Cologne in the autumn and perhaps Trier too. At all events, she had seen the members of the new foundation only a short time before. From Nancy the shorter and more comfortable route would have passed through the upper Mosel valley, and the Saone and Rhone valleys in order to reach southern Europe. Three further arguments militate against the route given by Chambers: the travellers had no German but probably French, as they had lived for some years in a French-speaking region. Moreover, dressed as pilgrims, they were fairly striking, which could have posed a threat among the anti-Roman Calvinists of Switzerland. They never needed to pay toll, as they had the Infanta's recommendation. That would have been possible in France, as the Queen, (Infanta Anna) was Infanta Isabella Clara Eugenia's niece.

In 1637, when Mary Ward was making her last journey across Europe, she took the route out of Rome via Sienna, Florence and Bologna towards the north.[53] At that time the sick woman could not expect to make another visit to Loreto. The journey continued beyond Milan, Vercelli and Turin, crossing the mountains in a westerly direction towards Lyon. From there she made for Paris.

Would not this route, but in reverse direction beginning from Liège and via Nancy, have been better in 1621? There is a similar uncertainty about the composition of the travelling group. The English

Vita[54] names four members of the Institute as well as Mary Ward, then a serving maid, a priest, a secular companion and a manservant. Nine persons in all. Of the two horses, one was a packhorse, the other at the service of anyone who was tired out.

The Italian Vita [55] gives five members as well as Mary Ward, a priest, a secular companion and a manservant. The serving maid may have been a lay sister. Pagetti[56] names Mary Ward and five Englishwomen but no further companions. Bissel[57] totals eight people: four Englishwomen. Fridl alone [58] has a guess that among the four Englishwomen there were Mary Ward's sister Barbara, Winifred Wigmore, Susan Rookwood, and Mary Poyntz. Chambers[59] names Mary Ward and her sister Barbara and Winefrid Wigmore, Margaret Horde and Mary Poyntz. In the parish register of San Lorenzo in Damaso in Rome,[60] before Easter 1623 (16th April) the following Englishwomen are entered: Mary Ward, Margaret Horde, Susan Rookwood, Winefrid Wigmore and Anne Turner, in whom perhaps we may see the serving maid. Barbara Ward had alread died on 25th January in Rome.[61] The priest is named in later sources as Henry Lee[62] but his real name was Fines. He had first of all studied for three years in England, came to the continent in 1600, and was then won over to the Catholic faith by his uncle Roger Lee SJ. Subsequently he studied for six years in St Omer and then went to Rome, where he was accepted on 23rd October 1606 into the English College. He was also ordained there. Henry Lee must have been long acquainted with Mary Ward and the Englishwomen, for he would only have undertaken such a long, arduous and dangerous journey for someone who meant much to him. The same holds good for the secular companion who, according to tradition,[63] was Robert Wright. He must have been related to Mary Ward and remained in the service of the Institute until his death.

Although finances were low, it was an imposing party of nine people who made their way south in the usually unfriendly and rainy season of the year in western Europe. It is not known why Mary Ward chose precisely these people and one can therefore only point to their personal connections and probably too, to considerations of prudence. It is understandable that she would take her lovely sister Barbara with her. Of the other Englishwomen, Margaret Horde was her secretary and Winefrid Wigmore was personally close to her; Anne Turner may have had medical capabilities, for she accompanied Mary Ward when sick on all her journeys. One can only surmise why Susan Rookwood travelled with her − perhaps, like Winefrid Wigmore, she was linguistically gifted.

As to the servants: it was an absolute necessity to have men attendants in those times of war, with rough roads and rough hostelries. Added to which, it would have been utterly unfitting for those of high birth, however poor their circumstances, to have undertaken a journey without some retainers. Henry Lee was a priest.

With his presence, Mass and the sacraments were assured. Moreover, he had spent a long time in Rome as a student. He would certainly have remembered streets and possibly places where they could find accommodation. He knew the city of Rome itself, and would have had some Italian. But, it may well be asked, why did Mary Ward choose precisely this time of year to make such a journey? She herself was ill, and made almost unreasonable demands of herself and her companions. A glance at Liège – the situation of the Englishwomen there had become utterly untenable. They were literally forced to live on the dowry of each one. If they had been able to free their house from debts – 20,000 guilders! – they could at least have drawn on the income of the fees of their boarding pupils. A slow but at all events steady cure for their financial ills would have been possible. For that, however, the confirmation or at least the approval of the Institute was a prerequisite, for several parents hesitated to pay their daughter's dowry, when they joined the as yet unconfirmed congregation. There is yet another reason, the Englishwomen were deeply in debt to the Society of Jesus, through no fault of their own, as has been seen, but they were to learn gradually what had been reported to Rome and what had not. It may indeed be assumed that a visit to Fr General Muzio Vitelleschi was just as important as an audience with Pope Gregory XV. Nor must one overlook the fact that Fr Tomson left Liège at the same time. The General's letter to him, dated 2nd November, 1621[64] was sent to Bordeaux. The Father was, apparently, to pass that way.

From one of Mary Ward's letters to the Infanta[65] it is known that the journey was made on foot and without any illness. The whole journey from Liège to Rome – far more than 2,000 km – was accomplished in seventy days. They averaged thirty kilometres a day, an astonishing achievement if one considers that Mary Ward was suffering from gall stones and had need of rest, warmth and suitable food. It was probably for reasons of discretion that Mary Ward said nothing in her letter to the Infanta that she had been robbed on her journey.[66] This fact explains why she arrived in Rome with no money. Material considerations apart, the journey was taken for other reasons with great seriousness. Mary Ward, and certainly the other members too, knew that everything was at stake. The Italian Life reports rather proudly that Mary Ward took letters of recommendation with her to Rome [67] but among those letters which were in favour of a 'Pium Institutum' devoted to the education of Belgian girls, she carried in her luggage a different petition for the Pope. This request was to present the Ignatian Institute as it was understood after the revelation of 1611. It was her personal contribution to the future of the Institute.

Some kilometres outside Rome, Mary Ward knelt when she saw the cupola of St Peter's and gave witness to her respect for that reliquary of the prince of the apostles and her willingness to be at the

Pope's disposal.[68] Both her petition and her reverence reflected her integrity.

Notes

1. AG Simancas (Spain) E 906. Further copies are in widely scattered archives and libraries: Bibl.Ambrosiana Milan, G.222 Inf.f.182r; AV Rome, Fondo Borghese Series II 448 ab, ff.308v–309r; PRO London, 31/9/121 A.f. 139–141, Roman transcr. Borghese T 448.
2. On 22nd February, 1616. AG Simancas E 906 with the heading in another hand: El Padre Cresvelo 22 de hebrero. Recibada en 29 de marco. A juicio de causa. Sant Omer 1616. Marginal in a third hand: Que se le responda, y de quenta de todo muy particularmente al Senor Archiduque, y procure que Su alteza escriva ello a Su Magestad.
3. Pope Paul V died on 28th January 1621, Bishop Blaes on 21 March 1618 and King Philip III on 13th March, 1621.
4. Vita E f.18r refers twice to Mary's Ward's intention of going to Rome. The first was after receiving the "Laudatio", therefore in spring, 1616. She was ill then, having caught measles from a child. In a letter of 29th February, (!) 1625 the Englishwomen still gave bad health as Mary Ward's reasons for postponing her journey to Rome in a letter to Cardinal Borghese. Letter Nr.28. Inst. Arch. Munich. Vita E f.24r. says that she wished to travel to Rome before the foundations in Cologne and Trier but had been hindered because of business concerned with these two foundations.
5. The letter was written in Madrid on 17th September, 1621. At that time Philip IV had succeeded his father, Philip III. The King names the Infanta as "mi tia." She was his father's sister.
6. Only the Latin version remains: "Brevis Declaratio earum rerum, quae ad maiorem Dei gloriam ab hac minima surgente Societate intenduntur." There is a copy in the university library, Budapest, Collect. Prayana V, 42. It is not complete. A copy in the Inst. Arch. Munich is probably of a later date. There is a fair copy in the handwriting of Margaret Horde, Mary Ward's secretary, in the IBVM Generalate Archives in Rome.
7. BV Rome, Fondo Capponi 47, f.82rv.
8. Infanta Juana (1535–1573) was accepted by St Ignatius as a 'Scholastic' into the Society of Jesus at her request in 1555. She later founded her own convent, the Descalzas Reales, in Madrid, where she is buried. Hugo Rahner, Ignatius of Loyola, Letters to Women, Freiburg/BR.1956. pp.62–80.
9. "Copia de carta de Su Magestad para il Duque de Alburquerque mi Senor. Escrita en Madrid en 17 de setiembre 1621 sobre la nueva religion que unas mugeres Inglesas quieren fundar en Flandes. Para remitir a Senor Cardinal Bandino."
10. AGR Brussels. PEA 456, ff. 224rv. 228v.
11. ARSI, Rome, Anglia 1/I, f.141r.
12. A letter from Louvain to Rome probably took a month's delivery. The Vice Provincial must therefore have written to Rome towards the end of May. The composition of the letter for the Englishwomen to Brussels would in all probability have coincided with the date of acceptance of the debt-encumbered estates in Condroz. The same date could be given to the Infanta's letter to the King of Spain. No wonder that Rome received exasperated letters from the Liège Jesuits about their Rector's activities on behalf of the Englishwomen, which caused more mischief than was justified.
13. AGR Brussels, PEA 456, ff.225rv, 226v.
14. ibid. f.227rv.
15. AGR Brussels, Arch. Jésuit.Prov.Gallo-Belg.Carton 32.
16. " ... et fructus sine dubio legeremus in dies copiosiores, si confirmatio

eas apostolica ab invidorum calumniis et obloquentium machinis redderet immunes."

17. "Miratus sum altum principis iudicium". According to the report under consideration: Fr Lessius to Mary Ward.

18. Fr General Vitelleschi to Fr Vice Provincial Blount, on 26th June, 1621, ARSI Rome, Anglia 1/I, f.141r. and ditto to Fr George Latham similarly on 26th June, ibid. f.141rv.

19. On 13th September, 1621. AGR Brussels, PEA 456, ff.231r–237v.

20. The Infanta to Vives, 13. September, 1621. AGR Brussels, PEA 456, f.223rv.

21. The Infanta to the Cardinals of the Congregation, 13th September 1621, ibid. f.239rv; and to Fr General Vitelleschi, 13th September 1621, ibid. f.238r.

22. AGR Brussels, PEA 456, f.240rv.

23. On 13th September 1621, ibid. f.230r.

24. The Petition of 17th September, 1621 to Cardinal Ludovisi. BV Rome. Barb.Lat.6812 f. 71rv. The other petitions of 23rd September 1621 in the Registro di lettere volgar della Nunciatura di Fiandra Bd.5, 1621–1623, s.p. in the Archivio dei Marchese Guidi di Bagno, Mantua.

25. Giovanni Francesco Guidi di Bagno was born in 1578 in Florence. In 1614 he was Vice Legate in Avignon, in 1621 Nuntius in Brussels, 1627 Nuntius in Paris. 1631 he became a cardinal and subsequently bishop of Cervia and Rieti. From 1639 he was Cardinal of the Curia in Rome, where he died in 1641. Biaudet, Nonciatures, p.210 and 225; B.de Meester, Correspondance du Nonce Giovanni-Francesco Guidi di Bagno (1621–1627) I (1621–1624) = Analecta Vaticano Belgica, 2e.series Nonciature de Flandre V, Bruxelles-Rome, 1938 s.v-x, 136; L.Gnockaert, Giovanni-Francesco Guidi di Bagno, Nuntius te Brussel (1621–1627). Enige aspecten van zijn opdracht en van zijn persoonlijkheid, Bibl. de l'Inst. histor. Belge de Rome VII/1956, p.1–135.

26. On 23rd September 1621. Registro di lettere volgari della Nunciatura di Fiandra vol.5, 1621–1623, s.p. in the Archivo dei Marchesi Guidi di Bagno, Mantua.

27. AGR Brussels, Arch.Jésuit.Prov.Gallo-Belg. Carton 32.

28. Her stay in Cologne is suggested by Fr General's letter, see below, note 29.

29. ARSI Rome, Germ.113, pp.46–47.

30. " ... ita etiam diligenter providebo, ne quisquam nostri ordinis se consiliis vestris quae pia et sancta essent, opponat."

31. Fr General Vitelleschi to Fr Vice-Provincial Blount on 5th March, 1622, ARSI Rome, Anglia 1/I, f.153v.

32. StA Munich, K1.432/I Nr.16–19, handwriting of Margaret Horde. Another copy: PB pp.123–141, handwriting of Elizabeth Cotton, Inst.Arch.Munich. German translation, StA.Munich, K1.432/I, Nr.13–15, 20 is considerably more recent.

33. See above p.180 ff.

34. Biaudet, Nonciatures 198, 213; Hier. Cathol. IV, p.368; L.Just, Die Quellen zur Vorgeschichte Kölner Nuntiatur in Arch.u.Bibl.des Vatikans = sources and researches made in Italian archives and libraries 29/1938/39/p.260.

35. Fridl, I, Add.Litt.ad Nr.104.

36. Chambers E I p.476 ff; D I p.380 ff.

37. "Written to be given to the Nuntio Apostolicio of Lower Germany Monsignore Albergato etc." PB f.123.

38. "In that other paper is contayned the summe of what we doe desire, as the same which God in a perticuler manner hath called us unto ..."

39. "Great instance was made by diverse spirituall and learned men that we would take upon us some rule already confirmed. Severall rules were procured by our frinds, both from Italy and France, and we earnestly urged

to make choyse of some of them. They seemed not that which God would have done and the refusall of them caused much persecution, and the more, because I denied all, and could not say what in perticuler I desired or found my self called unto."

40. " ... ther was noe remedy but refuse them, which caused infinitt troubles."

41. " ... they urging him in many things to say as they sayd, though against his own iudgment and knowledg, as after I understood ... "

42. "Concerning the name I have twice in severall yeares understood, in a perticuler a manner as these other things I have recounted, that the denomination of these must be Jesus ... " In her notes, Mary Ward wrote that she received illumination concerning the name of the Institute in Saint-Omer: About the name, Saint-Omers, VP/H 1, 8th January, 1624, Inst.Arch.Munich.

43. Concerning the independence of her Institute from the Society of Jesus she received clarification both in Grafton and in Liège: "The subordination Grafton and Leig." ibid.

44. The only copy of the Formula Instituti of the Society of Jesus for the Englishwomen's Institute written in Margaret Horde's hand, is in BV Fondo Capponi 47, ff.56v–63v. On f.56v it bears the heading: Institutum Virginum Anglicarum. Materia monialium Anglicanarum. On the reverse the comment: Donne Inglese in Fiandra.

45. ARSI Rome, Germ.113, pp.46–47.

46. Vita E f.24 rv; Vita I pp.23–24; Fridl I, p.192; Chambers E I p.478–479; D I p.385–386.

47. This portrait of Mary Ward hangs in the Provincialate of the Augsburg house of the Institute, together with her portrait in pilgrim's dress.

48. Vita E f.24v. Vita I, p.24. names Loreto only.

49. Vita E f.24v. The letter has not survived.

50. Bissel, p.97.

51. Khamm, p.11–12.

52. Chambers E I, p. 492; D I, p.392.

53. Vita E ff.57r–59r; Vita I pp.38–39.

54. Vita E f.24v.

55. Vita I p.24.

56. Pagetti, p.10.

57. Bissel, p.97. Unterberg, p.16–17.

58. Fridl I, p.193.

59. Chambers E I, p.485; D I p.386–387.

60. Archivio Generale del Vicariato San Lorenzo in Damaso, Rome. Stat d'animo 1623–1624, f.12v.

61. ibid. Book of the dead, Morti (1591–1643), f.99r.

62. The Responsa Scholarum of the English College, Rome I, ed. Anthony Kenny = CRS 54/1962, p.174, Nr.440.

63. Robert Wright died at a great age on 9th December, 1683 in Augsburg. Chambers E I, p.487–488; D I, p.389–390.

64. ARSI, Rome, Anglia 1/I, f.147r. Fr Tomson received orders to change his destination from Spain to Rome, in order to report on his affairs. Fr Vitelleschi still did not know then that the Englishwomen were already on their way to Rome.

65. Mary Ward to Infanta Isabella Clara Eugenia, Rome, 1st January, 1622; AGR, Brussels, PEA 458, ff.3r–4v.

66. Vives to Infanta Isabella Clara Eugenia, 31 December 1621, AGR Brussels, PEA 456, ff.378r–379r.

67. Vita I, p.24.

68. Vita E, f.25r.

XIX

NEGOTIATIONS WITH POPE GREGORY XV

The Pope and his Curia
1621 – July 1623

Gregory XV – his nephew Ludovico Ludovisi

Rome was and remains one of the most beautiful cities in the world. Pope Gregory XV had been lord of this city and of the extensive papal states which covered a large part of central Italy since 9th February, 1621.[1] Alessandro Ludovisi was born on 9th January, 1554 in Bologna to an aristocratic Florentine family. When only thirteen, he entered the Germanicum in Rome but was a delicate and sickly boy and could continue his studies only after a long stay at home. In 1575 he became Doctor of Law in Bologna university.

This quiet, scholarly man was a gifted diplomat and had already won the attention of Popes Gregory XIII (1572-1585) and Gregory XIV (1590-1591) and had often been drawn on for consultation by them. At first Alessandro held various offices, was Referendar of the chancellery of Justice and Grace, Auditor of the Bologna rota, Vice-Regent of the Cardinal Vicar of Rome and finally, in 1612, was appointed Archbishop of his native Bologna. Four years later he was raised to the College of Cardinals. Cardinal Ludovisi conducted his diocese on excellent lines. His principal desire was for zealous clergy, as well as the implementation of the decrees of the Council of Trent.

On 9th February, 1621, he emerged from a brief conclave as Pope, and chose the name of his predecessor Gregory XIV, whom he had greatly admired. The old, delicate man, who was somewhat indecisive and opted for political neutrality, had the good of the Church as his sole aim, and needed a capable aide in order to carry out the multiplicity of tasks demanded by his position. This he found in his highly-gifted nephew, Ludovico Ludovisi, forty years his junior. He too had been educated by the Jesuits and studied Law in Bologna. During Alessandro's time as Archbishop of Bologna this nephew had been of great assistance to him. Immediately after his election, Gregory XV created the twenty-five year old Ludovisi a Cardinal and soon afterwards ordained him. His extraordinary diplomatic skills and great knowledge made him indispensable in the Vatican; all important papal transactions passed through his hands. Although the obverse side of nepotism was present too, such as the enormous prosperity of relations and the Ludovisi family, Pope Gregory XV, whose pontificate was brief, achieved much that was significant for the Church. As far as Mary Ward was concerned, only two need mention: the setting up of the Congregatio de Propaganda Fide (1622) and the nomination of a Bishop for England (1623).

When Gregory XV received the papal tiara, he had a college of seventy cardinals, many of them aged. Within two years the new pope had added eleven new cardinals, some of whom, however, died during his pontificate.[2]

It is extremely doubtful if the small group of travellers who entered Rome's inner city through Porta del Popolo on 24th December, 1621, had the slightest idea of the many varieties of difficulties they were soon to encounter. Until then, Mary Ward had not been able to convince the Jesuits in St Omer and Liège of the need for her Ignatian styled Institute. On the contrary, they had turned it down. A minimum of spiritual direction within the confessional was either denied her members or made difficult, and the possibility of developing their activities had been destroyed by the financial ruin of their houses. This was one aspect of things which was, so to speak, left behind her in Belgium and yet which she carried with her in her own petition to the Pope, and − more than that − in her heart. Another, and totally unfamiliar aspect of their problems confronted them: Rome, with its strange people, and strange language, its many offices and countless officials, and its innumerable congregations.

For every English Catholic, the faith signified loyalty to the pope (as distinct from the national church) and was interwoven with the conflicts resulting from this loyalty. Now however, in a few days, the Englishwomen were to see the pomp of the papacy and the sophisticated luxury of the papal court. This grandeur was composed for the most part of highly-placed clerics; they were often aristocratic youths, sometimes without priestly ordination, who received rich benefices for little service. The Englishwomen may have lived at a time when the world was monarchical and they themselves had a certain social standing, but their stark experience of the bitter reality of poverty and absolutism made them more keenly sensitive to such contrasts.

The Ambassador

Juan Bautista Vives – his negative attitude to the Institute

The Spanish Habsburgs were represented at the Holy See by two ambassadors: Spain by Don Fernandez de la Cueva, Duke of Albuquerque, and the Spanish Netherlands by the prelate Juan Bautista Vives [3] who was born in 1542 of Spanish nobility.

Since 1618 Vives had held the office of Resident in Rome, which he continued to hold after the death of Archduke Albrecht (d.13th July, 1621). The Ambassador had therefore lived in Rome during the last years of the Borghese Pope, Paul V. Whether he was in favour with the new Pope, Gregory XV and his nephew Ludovisi who had both been Jesuit students, remains to be seen. Vives was no friend of the Society of Jesus. He had assuredly been informed by his Spanish colleagues about the Englishwomen who had founded an Ignatian Institute in Belgium and for whom King Philip IV of Spain had wished to mediate in the September of the now rapidly passing year, 1621. At the same time the Infanta Isabella Clara Eugenia in Brussels was burdening her old agent in Rome – Vives was almost eighty at the time – with tasks for these Englishwomen who were soon to come knocking on his door.

Even before he met the women personally, he had already taken up a defensive attitude towards them, which he was not to relax.

For confirmation of their Institute, he wrote to Secretary of State de la Faille on 23rd October,[4] it was absolutely necessary to have the local Bishop's approval of the work of their congregation and his report concerning the virtuous way of life of the members. Moreover, he added zealously, would it not be better if they joined the Ursulines? He had heard of such foundations in France. The Flanders community could attach itself to that in France. In any case, a copy of the papal approbation of the Ursulines should be produced.

When Vives wrote this letter to Brussels, the Englishwomen were already two days' journey on their way to Rome. No one knows where they spent their first nights in Rome. Christmas – their first Christmas in Rome – was probably spent praying in St Peter's and in the Gesù, where Ignatius Loyola, founder of the Society of Jesus had once lived and worked on the Constitutions of his Order.[5]

One of the gentlemen-companions must have announced their arrival in Rome to the Belgian Ambassador. Mary Ward wrote shortly afterwards in her first letter from Rome to the Archduchess Isabella Clara Eugenia, 'On the following Sunday (after their arrival) we had ourselves announced at Your Highness's Ambassador. On Monday, Monsignor Vives honoured us with a visit.'[6]

Their appearances may have filled the old gentleman with dismay, accustomed as he was to the rich attire of the clerics of the papal curia and the southern charm of the Roman ladies. How did these distinguished Englishwomen appear to other eyes? Like religious sisters? No – they wore no habit, but a simple black dress, as was usual for widows in northern countries. Secular ladies, therefore? That neither – for they all wore the same. People of standing in Rome, however, wore the manto, a long veil, which stretched from the forehead to the feet. In this strange sort of attire which had, it is true, a vague resemblance to religious dress, with a strong hint of the Jesuit gown and biretta, these women walked openly in the streets before the appraising Roman eye. Extremely embarrassing.

The Audience

28th December, 1621

Mary Ward's report to Infanta Isabella Clara Eugenia – Ambassador Vives' petition for a 'Pium Institutum' – continuation of the Englishwomen's affairs before the Congregation of Bishops and Regulars – Vives' report to the Infanta – the Englishwomen's petition to the Pope

Vives had obtained an audience with the Pope for 28th December. This was with almost suspicious speed, when one considers that for the Head of the Church the Englishwomen were not only modest but also of little importance.

The audience probably took place in St Peter's, perhaps in one of the rooms close to the Basilica. Mary Ward would have known too little of the labyrinthine Vatican buildings to make a close approximation

The tenor of the audience is relatively well documented. We first learn of it from Mary Ward herself in a letter dated lst January, 1622[7] to Infanta Isabella Clara Eugenia: 'Tuesday (28th December) he (Vives) took us with him to St Peter's where he explained in detail and excellently who we were, while we knelt at the Pope's feet: the reason for our visit, the results of our small endeavours and the good impression we make in the places we live in, the favourable disposition and love of Your Highness to us, and Your deep desire for the confirmation/of our Institute/ by means of a papal bull. Graciously, the Holy Father answered: 'God supports his Church in need'. And he added that the raising of the moral values of the female sex in these regions (Belgium) was very necessary. He asked some questions about our dress, our accommodation, the number of our members and the order of the day. Monsignor Vives answered very well or even better than we could have done.' Mary Ward added with what seems like amazement: 'Your Highness must have coached him well in everything.' Vives was spokesman because the audience would have been conducted in Latin.

One is tempted to ask which Institute was here being recommended to the Pope. Mary Ward's Ignatian Institute? Not at all. A good word was being put in for the Institute as it existed then in St Omer – for a community exclusively occupied with the education and instruction of girls, and, in the future, of Belgian girls. It was for such an Institute only, on Belgian soil and for Belgian aims, that the Infanta could involve herself as Archduchess of the country. This was the Institute for which Vives handed in a Petition.[8] It was customary to hand over a brief summary of the matter referred to in the audience, as an aide-memoire for the Pope or rather, for the Congregation appointed to deal with the matter. In this petition too the familiar reasons are produced: eleven years have passed since certain Englishwomen have settled in Flanders who, when they saw the decline of morals in this country, began to instruct young girls in the christian faith and good morals. They had obtained excellent results and were also known and loved in neighbouring countries.

What follows next is an utterly fatuous reason for the ambassador's request. Verbatim: 'And so that this Institute may not pass into oblivion, if the foundress should be no more (no longer be alive), and so that this Institute may increase for the common good, the Infanta sends your Holiness a chief person of this (Institute), Mary Ward, to give a report to the Holy Father, and (the Infanta) requests the Confirmation of the Institute as an Order (religione)'.[9]

So the Englishwomen had not undertaken this terrible journey in the middle of winter, from Flanders to Rome, of their own initiative? No, the Infanta Isabella Clara Eugenia had sent them there, simply to add weight to her request. The Princess had acted out of a certain anxiety lest this Institute, on the death of its foundress – the formula cannot be understood otherwise – should be forgotten. A broader and deeper chasm between Vives' version and reality can hardly be imagined.

A second question: had Mary Ward understood what had been said in Latin? Certainly not all of it, though it can be assumed that several matters had been discussed when the ambassador had paid them his visit – as far as language difficulties allowed and Vives was able to guide the conversation. 'His Holiness,' continued Mary Ward in her letter to the Infanta, 'promised his 'faveur', and that the matter should be handed over to the congregation of the Cardinals, in which Cardinal von Hohenzollern would have some weight. This was because we had mentioned his name and desired that he should be asked concerning our manner of life, as he had seen it in practice.'[10]

Thus far Mary Ward's report of the papal audience. From this it emerges that the Pope had made it known, at that time, that the Petition was to be given to a Congregation for further consideration, as was customary. He probably did not name the Congregation – or at least Mary Ward could not give the name. It was only in the letter dated 8th January, 1622[11] that she wrote to the Infanta that the Petition was to go before the Congregation of Bishops and Regulars.

It is also very likely that Mary Ward mentioned the name of Cardinal von Hohenzollern in conversation with the Pope, and that Gregory XV had acted on it. On their departure, he bestowed some unspecified indulgences on the Englishwomen with benevolent words which raised their expectations and were yet non-committal: 'Whoever perseveres to the end, will receive the crown.'[12]

Resident Vives wrote about the audience to his Princess on the same lst January,[13] merely saying: 'People at this Court were astonished by the Englishwomen, particularly by their large hats. Even the Pope remarked on these and asked about them pointedly. I told him that this was part of their dress and that they always wore them.'

That was the sum of what Vives reported to the Infanta about an audience which was to be decisive for the future of the young congregation in the Church.

Even his answer to the Pope was not entirely correct.

But it was not simply the Infanta's Petition, and the written summary about the Englishwomen's affairs from the Chancellery of the Belgian Embassy in Rome that were presented to the Pope. Mary Ward had also brought with her a Petition composed by the Englishwomen, which, according to the dorsal comment, was in fact handed in to the Holy Father. A fair copy of this letter in Latin lies in the Fondo Capponi in the Vatican Library; a fair copy of the original English draft is in the Institute Archives in Munich. Both petitions were written by Margaret Horde, Mary Ward's secretary. The Petition, it is true, is undated, but was undoubtedly presented at this audience. Later, there would have been no sense in doing so.[14]

The first passage of the Petition is given in full, even though it is long and florid in style:

'Holy Father, according to God's will, we wish to adopt the same Institute and way of life already approved by several Popes... for the fathers of the Society of Jesus. During these twelve years we have endeavoured to practise and test ourselves in this, according to the measure of divine grace given us and as far as the constant persecution, laid on us by both bad and good men ever since we began, has allowed us to do. Therefore, to remove these and other similar obstacles, and for our greater confirmation and strengthening in this course, for the more certain guidance of the Holy Spirit in our progress and for the greater encouragement of those who will join us later, we humbly request that this Institute referred to above, with its Constitutions, its way of life and recognized practice (even if independent of the said fathers), may be confirmed and approved by the authority of the Apostolic See in the same way for us. We wish to follow the Rule of the same Institute in its entirety (as the necessary means for the same end, which is the greater glory of God and the salvation of souls, which we have in common with the previously mentioned fathers), as far as God has not forbidden this by the difference of sexes, as, for example, the giving of sacraments, public preaching or disputations about theological questions and such functions which are the preserve of priests alone according to law.'

Certain points deserve consideration.

First, one is struck by the length of time mentioned. Vives spoke of the eleven years' sojourn of the Englishwomen in Flanders, which is not exact. They had been on the continent since the beginning of 1610. The Englishwomen, on the other hand, mentioned twelve years during which they had followed the Jesuit form of life and the prescripts of the Society of Jesus. The revelation given to Mary Ward on this point was granted, as we know, in 1611. Reckoning with different dates for the beginnings and endings of the years, as was then customary, we come to 1622 and twelve years. The Englishwomen had certainly calculated on 1622 for their Petition when in Liège, where it was composed; they had not expected to be received in an audience by the Pope in 1621. But it is not only that which is interesting. It goes on to say that according to the measure of grace granted them, they had endeavoured, as far as this was possible on account of the obstacles occasioned by both bad and good men, to follow this way of life. This reason was also given in the letter allegedly written by the Englishwomen to Cardinal Bellarmine, which has already been met with in the involved summary of the correspondence.[15]

It is unnecessary to dwell at length on the clear and unambiguous contents of the Petition. The Society of Jesus for women is openly presented as the way of life which the Englishwomen had observed for the past twelve years under Mary Ward's guidance. Finally, the petitioners pass on to their work in few and comprehensive terms: their help towards the salvation of their neighbours' souls. Next follows the request for recognition as religious, and for the authority to admit members to probation and later to profession, according to the custom and practice of the Society of Jesus. They submitted themselves to the Pope in obedience, praying for special protection, so that they might not be subordinate to the jurisdiction of a local bishop or any other person as director of their congregation. Religious jurisdiction, it went on to explain, though holy and helpful to communities with another, enclosed type of life, would not be compatible with the Institute with which they had been charged and would, on the contrary, be a hindrance to the spiritual life of the members and their proposed sphere of work.

It may seem curious that two Petitions were drawn up, each apparently concerning another Institute. The Infanta's petition deals simply with the excellent teaching and educational abilities of the Englishwomen in Belgium and the hopes cherished by the Archduchess for this praiseworthy work. The Englishwomen's petition, on the other hand, concerned itself with the structure of the Institute which was to be for all the members. Not a single word more was said about the Englishwomen's activities. Briefly and by way of generalities, mention was made of the fact that they would prepare souls for the ministrations of priests. That happened then and still happens today in a variety of ways – say, by religious education in schools, careful instruction and, too, the open apostolate.

It may be taken as certain that the Englishwomen went to this audience equipped with the 'Formula Instituti' of the Society of Jesus, altered for their Institute. A fair copy of it lies in the Fondo Capponi of the Vatican Library.[16] This copy was thoroughly studied. The text has been underlined in places, even a summary of it has been made.[17] It is not known whether the Englishwomen left the audience in an optimistic mood. Mary Ward probably did not. In Loreto she had been shown the weight of sufferings to come. Vives reported rather pessimistically to the Infanta.[18]

The exemption demanded by the Institute, and freedom from enclosure, would pose the greatest difficulties. The negotiations – that is evident – could be long-drawn out. With regard to the length of the Englishwomen's stay in Rome, one could count on several months. There would be no decision before May. The women had no money at their disposal, either. Vives had already had to help them, but he awaited instructions from the Infanta. The English-women had made their appreciation clear by giving him a pair of fine goatskin gloves, which he had passed on to Cardinal Ludovisi.

The women must indeed have found themselves in an embarrassing situation, dependent on the ambassador, not only for his goodwill, but also for material goods and his generosity which, however one may sympathize with his dilemma, was not pronounced.

The first visits

To the Spanish Ambassador Albuquerque – to nephew Ludovico Ludovisi – to Father General Muzio Vitelleschi – to Cardinal Ottavio Bandini

The next days in Rome were filled with visits to make initial contacts. Before the end of the year they had met with the Spanish Ambas-sador, Albuquerque, and Cardinal-Nephew Ludovico Ludovisi, but for the eager Englishwomen it was far too slow. During the festive season the Cardinals were too busy, she wrote to the Infanta on New Year's Day,[19] and it was, moreover, raining ceaselessly.

Already, years before her first meeting with Fr General Vitelleschi, Mary Ward had learnt, in one of her spiritual experiences, that her request for permission to model the Institute on that of the Society of Jesus would be refused. And now, on one of the last days of 1621, a momentous year for the members, they came face to face: the naturally retiring but determined Englishwoman, and the cautious, conciliatory Roman, personally kindly but officially dismissive, in loyalty to the Constitutions of his Order.

Very little is known of their conversation. Vives, who was present, hid behind vague generalisations in his letter to the Infanta.[20] He merely mentioned a lengthy consultation, the only result of which, seemingly, was an agreement to meet again several times to consider the matter well and often. It is possible that the ambassador was not present at the whole discussion, for Mary Ward told the Infanta details which throw a proper light on the mutual friendliness which, so to speak, broke the ice.[21] 'I visited Fr General of the Society of Jesus', she wrote, 'and gave him Your Highness' letter. He spoke very kindly and admitted that the fathers of that place (Liège) had made a mistake, and he promised his own help and that of the fathers. We will inform Your Highness of the effects.' Mary Ward may not have placed too much hope on this co-operation. She continues: 'I noticed that he had received another letter from Your Highness, and that he would take care not to displease you.'

From these ambiguous words, it can be seen that at this first conversation with Fr General, Mary Ward had immediately referred to the unhappy matter of the debts of the Jesuits and her own congregation in Liège. Equally, it emerges that she had been able to bring the head of the Order to see things differently, and that he had changed his mind in certain respects. Nonetheless, Fr Vitelleschi remained steadfastly opposed to Mary Ward's Liège foundation, even to the extent of being callous. In a letter to Vice Rector Knott, he regretted the imprisonment of some of the Englishwomen in Liège, as a result of their enormous debts, but he killed off this touch of sentiment with his final remark that the Society of Jesus would not fall into disgrace, as it was well-known that they had no connection with the Englishwomen.[22]

It must be recognized that Fr Vitelleschi was, personally, very kindly disposed towards Mary Ward, and it transpires that he helped her Institute in as much as this continued to be involved in the teaching and education of girls, and remained a 'Pium Institutum', but that constitutionally he opposed a congregation of women 'in the matter and manner' of the Society of Jesus. Fr Vitelleschi was not the person Mary Ward had described in 1619 to Fr Tomson, when she said she saw a General of the Society who said nothing, but whose expression promised co-operation with her Institute. This sighting was for a still distant future.[23]

Finally, all the petitions were placed in the hands of Cardinal Bandini. He was born in Florence in 1558, and when the Englishwomen came to Rome he was already elderly, sixty-three years old. Bandini had come to Rome in Pope Gregory XIII's time, and acquired great respect. Clement VIII made him a member of the Congregation of Bishops and Regulars, the direction of which he had from 1623 to his death. (1st August, 1629) Paul V called him to the Holy Office, and Gregory XV placed him in the new Congregation, Propaganda Fide, where he was Vice Prefect.

Gregory XV in particular valued Bandini very highly as an adroit diplomat.

The Cardinal, although following the party line in his attitude to the Church, was a somewhat vacillating character and endeavoured to be all things to all men in confrontational situations without losing face. In Roman circles he was considered unreliable and frequently earned himself mordant comments.[24]

How little the open and straightforward English woman understood the psychology of this man may be seen by a passage in the English biography: 'She (Mary Ward) was highly esteemed by all the Cardinals and Prelates, particularly however by Cardinals Bandini, Ginnasio, Trescio, and Hohenzollern. The first-mentioned was head of the Congregation which was to deal with her matter. He therefore had more means and opportunities to deal with her and learn her great and sterling qualities. She stood so high in his estimation that he told one of his friends that if it had not been for his position, he would have knelt before her and asked for her blessing.'[25]

In odd but significant contrast to this statement is the following occurrence, which can be better vouched for than an effusive gesture which never took place. For a chronological course of events, we must go back a few weeks.

At the beginning of February, the Englishwomen had been invited to a consultation with Cardinal Bandini. Vives was also present. On 10th February,[26] Mary Ward thanked the Cardinal for an unspecified gift — it may have been financial. She had probably been received by him a short time before on this account. In a letter to Secretary of State Antonio Suarez in Brussels, Vives describes the course of the conversation in a few sentences.[27] The greatest difficulty, the Cardinal made clear to the Englishwomen, was exemption from enclosure. This demand would destroy their Institute totally. It would be impossible for the Pope and the Congregation of the Cardinals to confirm any congregation which did not have enclosure. He suggested that they should obey this decision in some form or another. The members could, after all, live in their own house, with the boarders in a connecting house, as the Ursulines did in France. Upon which the Englishwomen had answered emphatically that the work on the English mission was their greatest concern (el mayor provecho). The Cardinal retorted: that was not woman's work. Still less was preaching. In other words, implying that they had done so in England, although they contested this.

It is rare that contradictory views are given such clearly barked-out expression as in this, the first conversation between the Englishwomen and the very Cardinal who held the fate of their Institute in his hands. After the audience,[28] the Cardinal continued the discussion with the Belgian and Spanish ambassadors. They dealt mainly with the paper which had been handed in to the Pope, and which could do the Englishwomen great harm. They considered how to withdraw this line of approach. Cardinal Bandini's dilemma is obvious. John Bennet, the new representative of the English secular clergy, had been in Rome since 21st November, 1621, and had become friendly with Cardinal Bandini. Bennet formed, so to speak, the channel by which attacks on the Institute could flow into Rome from England. These pieces of paper, which acquired great influence in Rome, will soon come under scrutiny.

Dead End

Congregation of Bishops and Regulars and their style of work — suggestion of the Belgian and Spanish Ambassadors to set up a particular congregation — more diplomatic help from Vives — the insuperable difficulty: freedom from enclosure — the Englishwomen's poverty

Pope Gregory XV passed on the Englishwomen's petition, together with the plan of the Institute (Formula Instituti) to the Congregation of Bishops and Regulars. Mary Ward and Vives knew this on 8th January.[29]

If one bears in mind the end of year festivities and receptions between 28th December and 8th January, one must realise that the document was handed over with little time for deep perusal.

In 1616, in the first draft of the Petition, there had been a request for confirmation of a Pius Institute for Englishwomen exclusively occupied with the education and instruction of girls, both within England and abroad. This underscoring, presupposing freedom from enclosure, was subsequently brought before the Congregation of the Council, which was also responsible for the implementation of the decrees of the Council of Trent concerning enclosure. Now, however, came the Englishwomen's request for the confirmation of their Institute as an Order. This shift of emphasis — and the problems resulting from it — made it subordinate to the Congregation for Bishops and Regulars.

The Congregation was founded in 1586 and consisted of thirty cardinals, according to Mary Ward's account in her letter to the Infanta. It was, therefore, a powerful piece of bureaucratic machinery, by its very nature imposing long-drawn out consultations and debates. This may soon have been made clear to Mary Ward in conversations and briefings. In her letter to the Infanta she mentioned Cardinal Millini as someone who delayed the proceedings. She asked the Belgian Ambassador if there were any possibility of hastening matters. This was probably not caused by impatience so much as by the dire material needs of the English women in Rome, as well as in the houses north of the Alps. On 7th January, Vives presented a request to the Pope,[30] suggesting that negotiations might be placed before a special congregation of two cardinals. The Spanish Ambassador also submitted a request on the same day,[31] far more detailed than that of his colleague, and differing essentially from the petition which King Philip had wished to endorse in Rome in the autumn of 1621.

Here the Englishwomen appear as teachers and educators of Belgian girls and of great benefit to the country, as in the Infanta's altered Petition and, moreover, under the protection of their Bishop. So that this congregation should not disintegrate on the death of the foundress — one is reminded of the phrasing of the Belgian Ambassador's first petition — six members of this Institute have come to Rome and submitted their request, which has been passed on to the Congregation of Bishops and Regulars. As this, however, would consist of a long process, and the Englishwomen have to support twelve people in the present costly times, they ask if their business could be shortened by the setting up of a special congregation for two or three cardinals, among them Cardinal von Hohenzollern, who could best give an account of their Institute.

Things did not move as rapidly as the penniless Englishwomen hoped. This alarming request also came before the Congregation of Bishops and Regulars, which they dated 15th January, nine days later. From there it was sent to Cardinal Bandini. In the Session of 21st January, — another seven days later — it was decided that the Secretary of the Congregation, Monsignor Nicolo Zambeccari, should present the request to the Pope — to whom it had been addressed on 7th January![32]

1622 was fourteen days older.

Nothing further happened. On 8th January,[33] Mary Ward had again written to the Infanta, and Vives had shared his misery with the Secretary of State, de la Faille,[34] though the ambassador had once more recommended the Institute to the Congregation,[35] and Cardinals Farnese and Borghese, Protectors of England and the Spanish Netherlands respectively, had been entreated for favours. It did not help.[36]

On 15th January,[37] a gloomy Vives reported on his vain attempts to the Secretary of State in Brussels, and Mary Ward wrote once more to the Infanta.[38] Disconsolately, she said that the Congregation had not even begun to consider their affair, and every attempt to have a special congregation set up to deal with it had been fruitless so far. She was now thinking of enlisting the help of the Duchess of Fiana, the Pope's sister-in-law. This was grasping at a straw. Mary Ward over-estimated the Duchess' position. True, Gregory XV had bought the Duchy of Fiano for 200,000 scudi — 500,000 Brabant guilders[39] — for his brother Orazio, but neither he nor his wife had any significant influence on the Pope's decisions. Henry Wotton, English Ambassador in Venice, wrote scornfully to his colleague, Dudley Carleton in The Hague, and the Secretary of State in London, George Calvert,[40] that Rome at last had an order of Jesuitesses, whose odd attire had drawn comment from all sides. These wanted to give catechetical instruction to girls just as the Jesuits did for boys. Needlework and embroidery would be more suitable. For the Englishwomen, there were thanks for letters received [41] and due promises of help, and thus the matter remained.

Perhaps the judgement of the anglican Ambassador Wotton was not so different from that of the higher catholic clergy in the Vatican. There was an unbridgeable gulf here. Later, Father Vitelleschi was to write consolingly to Father Silisdon in Liège, that the Englishwomen's efforts to obtain confirmation of their Institute must be taken as shipwrecked.[42]

It was not only Father Vitelleschi who thought this. Considerably earlier, John Bennet, agent for the English clergy, had information on that point. He had already written to England on 22nd February, 1622[43] that the Englishwomen could not expect to receive confirmation of the Institute without enclosure. Moreover, the fourth vow to the Pope, missioning members for the conversion of Turks and heathen had come up against a flint wall.

That was understandable. The Curia was better informed than these well-intentioned Englishwomen about the Turks and the grisly practices they perpetrated on captured christians. The latter came from a country in which there was persecution, but they probably knew little of women's social status among the Islamic Turks. The 'Formula Instituti' for women was a concept for a far distant future, at least as to what concerned missionary activities in pagan countries. Negotiations about material support for the Englishwomen dragged on.[44] Vives saw there was no way forward, and saw no point in exerting himself; he soon gave up even the appearance of doing so.

On 15th January,[45] Mary Ward had already written to the Infanta, acknowledging the old man's attempts, but also presenting the Infanta with some requests for her agent. Vives might, she suggested, be more active in a work of such importance for Belgium. He might also speak out in the Infanta's name and inform her, Mary Ward, of what was happening in all the discussions. This really meant that Vives was no longer interested in their affairs, and was going his own way, about which Mary Ward knew nothing. Obviously someone must have warned her of the ambassador's dangerous attitude towards the Institute; it would otherwise be difficult to explain this request to the Archduchess of the Spanish Netherlands, which sounded like a call for action.

Infanta Isabella Clara Eugenia interpreted the message and acted exactly as Mary Ward had wished.[46] The Princess' subsequent instructions[47] must have caused Vives no little discomfort, as they implied criticism of his negotiations. The rift widened.

The government in Brussels remained benevolent towards Mary Ward. On 22nd March,[48] the Infanta again sent a petition to the Pope. It was more in the nature of an urgent note, which was intended to set the faltering machinery into motion once more. Nothing would please the Infanta so much, it said, as to be sure of the Pope's interest in the fate of christianity in Belgium. It was for this reason that she was once again recommending the matter of the Englishwomen,namely the Confirmation of their Institute, which he had praised in his letter (12th February) to the Infanta. This was perhaps stating the matter too highly.

At that time the Pope was a very ill man and for weeks had not been in a fit state to grant audiences.[49] The Englishwomen changed course slightly. In a new petition,[50] they asked for Confirmation of their Institute in England, Belgium and Germany. In these countries, they considered, they had worked devotedly and without scandal. Communities could exist there without enclosure. The character and customs of those countries presented no obstacles (si per la natura di quelle nationi, come anco per l'uso di quel paese). This assertion, that there were no obstacles in the northern countries, was gainsaid by serious accusations against the Institute in England itself. The Curia listened to these, and not to the Englishwomen's statements.

Meanwhile, Vives had an audience with the Pope on 6th May, and handed him the petition.[51] The next day he informed the Infanta of his lack of success.[52] The Pope had insisted on enclosure and even thought that this should be observed everywhere (en todas partes). Reports from England had come to his ears of abuses which strongly confirmed the Church's stand on enclosure. Vives had gone so far as to ask the Pope to give him these reports, so that the Englishwomen might defend or justify themselves. Grevory XV declined to do so, ending the conversation with: 'If you were Pope, sitting in this chair (St Peter's), as I am, you would not grant that either.'

Vives' next piece of well-meant advice to his Archduchess was to recall the penurious Englishwomen to Belgium. These, however, went one step further. In a petition to Cardinal Bandini, they declared themselves ready to accept a further limitation, namely, that of the number of members to be admitted to their enclosure-free work in England, Belgium and Germany.[53] But the Cardinal was no longer prepared to a raise his little finger in the matter.[54] Then the Infanta made a proposal for negotiations which could accommodate both opposing opinions: she suggested a limited form of freedom of enclosure for the Institute. This should be for superiors, not subjects.[55] Mary Ward was to decide on the matter.

All these suggestions and pieces of advice were kindly meant, but none of them touched the nub of the matter. It concerned the Institute, and this particular Institute. Mary Ward expressed this very clearly in giving the reasons why the Institute could not be altered. She wrote it on two pages,[56] perhaps as an aide-memoire for a consultation, or as the rough workout of a letter. The manuscript is not dated but certainly comes from 1622, as Mary Ward refers to foundations in three countries and of their twelve-years activities, 1611–1622.

The reasons fall into four categories:

1. The Englishwomen had chosen the Institute of the Society of Jesus, which had already been approved by the Church and had proved itself suitable for the apostolate.
2. Social changes and their own experience had caused them to choose this model.
3. A trial period of twelve years in following the Jesuit Rule (the same Rule)[57] had guided the members to their own and their neighbour's salvation.
4. They were called to this Institute above all, and it had been confirmed in them by the exercises prescribed by St Ignatius. This Institute offers women a place in the Church in working for their own and their neighbour's salvation. It embodies a striving for God's greater glory, which is the personal right of the vocation of anyone called to an Order. As the choice of a partner is free in marriage, so is the choice of an Order free for those called.

These words may sound glorious and liberating to the ears of christians of later centuries. They were tantamount to blasphemy to the clergy and the Curia in the early seventeenth century. Noted prelates granted few rights to women, and even less powers of understanding. Moreover, in contrast to the views expressed here, the Curia adhered rigidly to the decrees of the Council of Trent, including those concerned with enclosure. It was, after all, the question of a new stage of development, one that was not yet recognized and then, sceptically, condemned.

During this time, on 12th March, 1622, St Ignatius Loyola, founder of the Society of Jesus, was canonised.

The Roman Foundation

1622

The Englishwomen's request to found a house and school – the curriculum – opposing views about the school in the sources – the Englishwomen's poverty – support from the Belgian Ambassador

The Englishwomen's final suggestion, that of limiting their members north of the Alps in order to achieve confirmation of their Institute, was as much as Mary Ward was able to concede. She could not deviate from the structure of the Institute, or she would have been false to the charge entrusted to her.

There remained one final possibility: to put their way of life, with its freedom from enclosure, to the proof. It is only in this way that one can view the foundation in Rome, and soon afterwards those of Naples and Perugia, unless it was also to save the members in Liège. For at that time such an involvement of the whole Institute (adult pastoral work included) by Mary Ward was not actually necessary in the catholic south, especially in the Papal States. There were sufficient priests to take care of pastoral work and these were not trained for female help. They would probably not have accepted it, either, or been allowed to do so. The social status of women in Latin countries was very different from that in northern and western Europe, as has been said. True, this attitude stretched all the way from London to Rome. But one can hardly believe that the southern countries had replaced the Institute's work in Flanders or England.

With hindsight, one might still question whether it was wise to expand the still unconfirmed structure of the twelve-year-old Institute on unknown religious terrain.Certainly, considering the situation of the Englishwomen just then, a foundation in Rome made sense. Towards the middle of 1622 they presented a request to be allowed to settle in Rome.[58] They had gradually been made aware that Confirmation would not be granted by the end of May, although Vives had forecast that as possible.[59] In this request they mentioned that they had not received an answer to several enquiries. They now suspected that their good intentions and works undertaken for the common good and salvation of souls would be hampered by the effects of adverse information about the Institute.

They were not far wrong, as will be seen later.

They therefore wished, so they went on, to continue their particular form of life in Rome itself for the good of the people and at their own expense. No specific work is mentioned in this petition. This, it appears, was because those making the request were thinking only in terms of an enclosure-free foundation. It is stated expressly 'in which we may retire and devote ourselves to our spiritual life and the salvation of our neighbour, as we have done in other countries.'[60] If by 'these other countries', only Belgium was meant, or England too, was not clarified. That can be taken as a sure sign that the structure of the Institute and the spiritual formation of its members were seen as a unity, whether these were to be employed later in the English mission or in educational work in Belgium.

At the same time[61] the Englishwomen also sent Monsignor Lorenzo Campeggi, Secretary of the Congregation for Bishops and Regulars, a letter requesting that he might use his influence to delay the Congregation's proposal to alter their Institute. Two points form the

basis of this letter: first, the offering of a counter-sign to the accusations against them, and concern lest their Institute be channelled
along different lines, as had happened in Belgium. As Grisar says,[62]
it is very unlikely that the Curia would have seriously considered their
adoption of the way of life of the Oblates of the Torre de' Specchi.
The request followed the usual bureaucratic course. On lst July[63]
it reached Cardinal Bandini, who passed it on to Cardinal Millini,
the Cardinal Vicar of Rome. He authorized any new foundations
by immigrants to Rome. On 19th August[64] the request was placed
before a session of the Congregation of Bishops and Regulars. That
was seven weeks after the request had been handed in.

The Englishwomen did not know what it was to be idle. They set
up a school in Rome just as they had on their arrival in Belgium.
Teaching and education was then and remains today an essential
work of the Institute, which they continued. The curial procedures
dragged on. In the middle of July[65] the women wrote to Bandini
that they had learnt (hanno inteso) that, before any decision could
be made, the Cardinals wanted to know what they would be teaching
the girls during the time they were awaiting settlement of their affairs
in Rome. This shows clearly that the women were not considering a
permanent foundation

The information was soon imparted. Reading, writing and
needlework of all kinds. This was probably all that their Italian
vocabulary permitted. The renewed petition of 19th July, 1622[66]
shows that Cardinal Bandini was not satisfied with this modest
description. Perhaps he merely wished to gain time. The Englishwomen expanded their project in a more detailed answer: they wished
to teach every kind of work, as well as good behaviour and morals
fitting the female sex. They thought this sort of work was suitable
for women, yet they would find it difficult to explain to the Cardinal. He probably would have had difficulty in understanding it.
As to judging their activities, the petitioners continued, supervision
could be at their expense. Distrust of these women must indeed have
been profound. And what were they proposing to pay with? One
week later Mary Ward asked the Nuntius in Brussels for a donation
of four or five gold pieces monthly for one year.[67]

Apparently the Englishwomen received no report from Cardinal
Bandini, for they repeated their request before 18th August.[68] On
19th August the desired answer was finally given. The General Vicar
of Rome, Cardinal Millini, in virtue of his authority, was pleased
to grant permission and stated that there was no bar to the Englishwomen's request. This was written on the back of their Petition in
the second half of June, to the Pope.[69]

Autumn was approaching. Mary Ward asked Cardinal Bandini for
an audience.[70] She probably wanted to make something clear about
the school situation. There is no information about her request being
granted.

The first foundation of the Institute in Rome, from November 1622 [71] was at the corner of Via Monserrato/Vicolo Montoro. That was then opposite the Corte (Curia) or the Savelli prison, a large building which served as court of law into the seventeenth century and was connected with the prison of the same name. The English College was in the immediate neighbourhood.

On 16th April, 1623, the following were members of the community: Mary Ward, Margaret Horde, Susan Rookwood, Winefrid Wigmore, Mary Radcliffe, Elizabeth Cotton, Margaret Genison, Elizabeth Keyes, Anne Turner, Esterguoccer Gua (probably written phonetically) and a Maria Caslone. A certain Margaret was added (with no other description) who had died. There was no further mention of Barbara Ward, who had died on 25th January, 1623. A Mauritia, whose name implies she was Italian, was a servant.[72] It is not established if the two men who had travelled with them, Henry Lee and Robert Wright, lived elsewhere. They do not appear as living in the house in Via Monserrato in the Status Animarum of San Lorenzo in Damaso.

The sources report relatively little, and often inconsistently, concerning the community and their work, depending on who was giving the information. The Belgian ambassador was soon to write to Brussels[73] about the now approved foundations of the Englishwomen. Vives concluded his report to the Infanta with the rather sceptical remark that the foundation of a house in Rome would not greatly help the women. Time would soon open the eyes of these self-assured ladies (son personas que so goviernan por su).

The representative of the English Secular clergy in Rome, John Bennet,[74] wrote with unconcealed disgust to London: the Englishwomen in England have spread the rumour that the pope welcomed their Institute benevolently (lor vagabondo Instituto), but the fact is that they are merely tolerated by Rome. Their schools for the poor are insignificant, and they themselves are despised by the people.[75] Some time later,[76] he wrote to Edward Clifton in London that the rumour that the Pope had given two houses to the Englishwomen was not true. They had rented a house at their own expense. Before he left Rome he would teach this diabolical Institute a lesson (there Institute I detest as follish and diabolical).

In contrast to this whipped-up hatred, Mary Ward's news to the Infanta sounded hopeful,[77] and true to fact. On 25th February, exactly one month after her sister Barbara's death, she wrote that three months before, the members had been installed in a spacious house in which they could hold a school. About one hundred and twenty girls of various ages and social backgrounds were brought to school daily, which caused no little surprise in the city. The friends of the Institute were delighted at the good reception of their teaching methods, and the mouths of their enemies were stopped, for the time being. Perhaps the older convents were stirred to object.

The Englishwomen began first of all with a day school. The pupils did not spend their time in an enclosure as had been customary before, but were taught in a classroom. The people of the neighbouring cities such as Perugia, Mary Ward continued, had voiced their wish to have such schools. The members had even been offered a house and a church but for the present they had neither the money nor suitable staff for it. In any case, papal confirmation was their chief aim. The English Vita mentions the remark of some wits who said that there would soon be too few stews left in Rome, and poor parents were now relieved, knowing that their children were educated and prepared for life, and trained in virtue.[78]

The truth probably lies somewhere in the middle of these attitudes. Exaggeration was certainly rife in the circles round the Englishwomen, less from the need of parading their poverty than from hope of success. It must surely have been an exaggeration when Bennet wrote to London that the school was insignificant, for it would not have shown such an intake of pupils. Of course the newly founded project could not compare with the well-directed schools and well-appointed teaching staff of St Omer and Liège. In the first place, there were no teachers who spoke or even understood Italian among the few Englishwomen in Rome. But for primary teaching such as reading, or guiding a small child's hand to write, or for simple handwork and the making of an Italian meal, there would have been sufficient understanding. A higher level could not have been expected. But a beginning had been made in teaching girls from the poorer quarters of Rome. That was a courageous undertaking.

The unhappiest side of this unplanned foundation, which must have posed a challenge for Mary Ward, was the financial situation. In his first letter to the Infanta after their arrival in Rome, the Belgian Ambassador had reported that the Englishwomen needed her support, but that he would await her instructions in the matter.[79] Vives had to wait until August for a clear mandate, although he mentioned the Englishwomen's penury in every one of his many letters to Brussels.[80]

It is true that the Infanta, on 26th February of the same year had already granted[81] support for the Englishwomen in case of emergency – but what was supposed to constitute an emergency? It is understandable that he, a man of few needs and modest life-style, did not act on such vague directions in case he left his beneficence open to reproach. So Vives handed out only small amounts, which must have seemed like alms. And yet these amounted to a total of 150 scudi, or 375 Brabant guilders by 9th July.[82] That was almost the salary of two average officials. Vives stopped his donation. Finally, on 6th August,[83] he received written agreement to make a substitution of the present contribution, giving the Englishwomen greater support.[84] Vives now set the monthly donation at ten scudi.[85] Ten scudi or 25 Brabant guilders per month were insufficient to feed a dozen people even frugally. And who knows if the women did not share this meagre amount with their hungry pupils from the poor quarters of Rome whom they were teaching how to cook? From another, unspecified source, the Englishwomen received a hundred Real a month. That too was painfully little. It is not surprising that some of the members fell ill, starving, and unaccustomed to Rome's summer heat.[86] Besides, it is not even certain that the women did receive this support every month. For the second half of 1622 the Belgian Embassy's account of donations in Rome records two items for the Englishwomen, on 1st November, ten scudi, and on lst December, ten scudi. That was twenty scudi or 50 Brabant guilders in half a year. Receipts were always signed by Maria della Guardia.

Vives wrote to Secretary de la Faille[87] truly enough when he said that the amount settled on was by no means enough for a community of thirteen. In May, 1623, the donation was discontinued at the Infanta's command.[88] That is only understandable. In the same month of May the Institute made a second foundation in Naples, or at least, preparations were made for a foundation. The opening of a third house in Perugia was only a matter of time. The Belgian authorities, who had to tax their people in order to finance the expensive war in the Northern Netherlands, were no longer willing to pay for teachers of Italian children. The state of affairs was similar to that after the financial collapse of the Institute in Liége. When the foundation ran into danger, the two houses of Trier and Cologne were opened.

The Accusations

1621/1622

The 'Informatio' of Archpriest William Harrison – the petition of Fr Robert Sherwood, OSB -Mary Ward's rulings about dealings with externs – Dr Matthew Kellison's article – reasons for these accusations

The poverty was bad enough but the uncertainty was worse. Up to the last moment Mary Ward did not know if her request to open a school in Rome would be granted. She must certainly have been aware that it would take some time to consider her Plan, and formulate a position. But everything took so much time, and she did not have any information as to how things were progressing. It was only in the second half of August that she learnt that the foundation and opening of a school had been granted. Even if one did not need much in those days for setting up a classroom, something had to be done. It was, too, relatively late for parents to be told that their children could be accepted.

The Church authorities' attitude in this was similar to their handling of the Englishwomen's most cherished desire – the confirmation of their Institute. The latter did not know, at least officially, whether their Institute would be refused or not. This uncertainty was to have painful consequences in the years ahead. They were also in the dark as to the assertions and opinions about them which were being passed to the Curia from abroad in the form of grave accusations.

Up till then, Mary Ward had always been able to conduct affairs openly, quickly and directly, in St Omer with Bishop Blaes, in Brussels with Infanta Isabella Clara Eugenia, and in Liège and Cologne both with the bishops and the civil authorities. None of that was possible in Rome. There the women did not even have a partner with whom to dialogue. The Curia preserved silence, and by doing so denied the Englishwomen even the possibility of defending themselves as honest brokers.

At the first talks about their concerns, hints had already been made about a document delivered to the Pope. It was regarded as a great drawback to the continuance of negotiations.[89] Presumably this was a reference to the 'Informatio' of Archpriest William Harrison, written in England before 11th May, 1621, but which was sent to Rome later only, at the time when Mary Ward personally was seeking confirmation of her Institute.

An extract of the undated Archpriest's article is in the Vatican Library,[90] a further one in the Archives of the Congregatio de Propaganda Fide[91] and a third in the Westminster Archives in London.[92] The original cannot be found; the three copies are of the same date. The Vatican Library copy bears the title: Informatio de Jesuitissis ad Apostolicum Sedem per Reverendum Archipresbyterum Angliae nuper defunctum et ab assistentibus post eius mortem subscripta.[93]

This paper fixes the date ante quem of the time of writing. Archpriest William Harrison,[94] who had held office since 11th July, 1614, died on 11th May, 1621. As to why the article remained in England then, there is no satisfactory answer. Perhaps the Archpriest was already too ill to send it to Rome; perhaps there was no opportunity to send a document of such importance shortly before his death, as it could not be entrusted to everyone. For that, someone of note was needed, who had contacts with the Curia or high curial officials. The opportunity came a few months after the Archpriest's death. In the autumn of 1621 John Bennet,[95] previously assistant to the Archpriest, left England to take up office as Roman Agent of the English secular clergy. He arrived in Rome on 21st November, 1621. This was almost exactly a month to the day before the Englishwomen arrived. It must certainly have been publicly known that Mary Ward was preparing to go to Rome, and the reason would not have been unknown either. It may therefore be assumed with some certainty that the new agent in Rome, whose signature was no longer to be regarded as that of a mere Assistant, took with him the seriously compromising article written by the dead prelate, in order to present this or at least introduce it, after the Englishwomen had had their first audience with the Pope.

The author had already been dead some six months but his opinions were and remained those of the secular clergy of his country; they even gained in value when, after his death, they were signed by the representative Archpriest and his Assistant. It cannot be verified to whom the document was addressed. Probably not to the Pope personally. Its form would not have been suitable for that. Still less was it destined for the General of the Society of Jesus. The English secular clergy were unfortunately hostile to the Jesuit Order, who saw the English mission as their particular task, and acted accordingly.[96] It may be presumed, cautiously, that Bennet presented it himself, perhaps as grounds for a papal audience, or presented it to the Head of the Church through an intermediary.

For a closer study, in summarized form:

Up till now, Harrison begins his 'Informatio', the catholic faith had been spread by serious men of tested virtue and steadfastness. However, a short time ago some women had involved themselves in this work. They belong to a congregation which has devoted itself to the conversion of England and have taken on priestly activities. The clergy refuses to recognize this Institute, and yet there have been several members in England for some years. The Institute of these 'Jesuitesses' is modelled on the Society of Jesus and receives direction from the Jesuits. The foundress Mary Ward was with the Poor Clares for a short time, then some young women gathered round her and she founded her own Institute. The members make a two-year novitiate, and afterwards take the three simple vows of the Order, like the Jesuits. They learn Latin, they practise speaking in public in order to hold religious conversation with externs and take on temporary direction of a family; they are being prepared for missionary activity in England (ad missionem Anglicanam) in which they see the aim of their Institute (in qua earum Instituti finis positus videtur). In England they live as they like. They are like seculars, they help families and want to be taken for religious sisters. If Paul V had really known this Institute, said Harrison and his assistants with him, he would never have praised them.

The Archpriest gave a whole range of offences in seven points:

1. Up to now it has never been known that women undertook apostolic work. They are not capable of it.
2. Such an Institute, without enclosure, is canonically forbidden. The English women call themselves 'religiosae' but not 'moniales', and refuse to accept enclosure.
3. They dare to speak on religious topics and give public 'exhortationes' even in the presence of priests, whereas women should keep silent in church. Here Harrison not only quoted St Paul's famous passage, 1.Cor.11,34-35, but also several Fathers of the Church, and named passages in Canon Law.
4. It is not yet possible to prove the danger of heresy. The Archpriest calls to mind the history of the Beguines.
5. The 'Jesuitesses' gad about all over the country, creep into houses of the aristocracy, put on different sorts of dress, consort with men among others and talk with people of ill-repute. Sometimes they travel to and fro between Belgium and England.
6. Not only are they not needed in England by the Church, they are a danger to its reputation.
7. Several of these female Jesuits are held to be of bad repute, frivolous and shameless, and a scandal to the catholic faith.

The 'Informatio' expresses the author's wonder at the Jesuits' acceptance of these women, as the fathers had been forbidden to concern themselves with female congregations after convents in Louvain and Gravelines had complained that the Jesuitesses deprived them of future members.

In trying to understand Harrison, one has to admit that he was well-briefed about the Englishwomen, who tried to model themselves in their spiritual life and work as much as possible on the much-disliked Jesuits. Perhaps he himself had met some members of the Institute of whom he did not approve. Even if one were to go so far as to take the rumours of misbehaviour among their members as true — likewise from hearsay, with Harrison — this could only be with the same proviso which the Lord made, 'Let him who is without sin among you throw the first stone,' and with a reference to the strict observances of their superior Mary Ward.

However, the question arises: What actually caused the Archpriest to write his 'Informatio'? The Englishwomen's shameful deeds? Hardly. Harrison remains very vague in his hints. Even presupposing considerable discretion, the author could be expected to produce concrete evidence. He does not. The question should be: How did Harrison, as a man, regard these women? At the very beginning of his article stands the assertion that wise men in the Church have not supported these women's unnecessary ventures. This doubtful generalisation may be disregarded, and cause us to glance at the word woman, 'Mulier'. It stands there as 'muliercula', little woman. The very word is significant. These little women pour into England together and are called Jesuitesses (Jesuitissae), among other mocking names. They have undertaken this work under the pretext of love.

Harrison brusquely rejects women's co-operation in the Church. In his eyes the female sex is frail (mollis), fickle (flexibilis), treacherous (lubricus), inconstant (inconstans), prone to error (erroneus), always seeking novelty (novitates semper affectans) and subject to thousands of perils (mille periculis obnoxious). For such a creature, the words of St Paul, the Fathers of the Church, and the decrees of the Councils are easily applicable. After which comes the Archpriest's opinion, which he had evidently formed during his theological studies: it was not Adam but the woman who had been tempted (by the serpent) to sin. (Adam non est seductus, mulier autem seducta in prevaricatione fuit). The Englishwomen, who put themselves at the risk of teaching heresy, are garrulous little females (garrulas mulierculas) whom others call runaway nuns (moniales cursatrices) and apostolic viragoes (apostolicae viragines).

They recall those words which had stung Mary Ward so sharply, spoken by a priest; he had voiced his joy at not being a woman, for a woman could not apprehend God. The views of that priest, and the charge entrusted to Mary Ward, were worlds apart, unbridgeable at that time. The way to mutual understanding was blocked by centuries' old traditions in society, which had not stopped at the walls of the Vatican.

This sharply expressed 'Informatio' probably did not fall on deaf ears. News of the unusual work of the Englishwomen must have penetrated curial circles already, spread by those English Jesuits who did not favour the Institute, by Vives, and by their real enemy, John Bennet. Last of all, there were the Englishwomen themselves, who led a totally blameless life but presented, however, a totally unusual sight in the holy city – religious women outside the enclosure.

The charges in this article can hardly have given the Curia any new information but did confirm the increasing disaffection towards these women on the Roman scene.

Shortly after Archpriest Harrison's 'Informatio' had been presented in Rome, a much shorter but more dangerous accusation against the Englishwomen reached Pope Gregory XV. It was the pamphlet-type petition of the Benedictine, Fr Robert de Sancta Maria, written before the end of May in Rome, 1622. Like several other denigratory documents, this 'smear campaign' against noble women – one cannot describe it otherwise, also lies in the Vatican Library.[97]

Not much is known about Fr Robert Sherwood, OSB,[98] alias Sherington. He was born in Somerset in 1588 and in 1612 entered the Benedictine Order in Douai. In 1615 he was ordained. At the

Chapter of the Order dated 2nd July, 1621, he was elected Procurator of the English Benedictine Congregation, which was confirmed
by Pope Paul V but remained dependent in certain details on the
Spanish Congregation. Up to 1622, Sherwood represented his Order
in Rome, returned to Douai and, soon after, was moved to the
English mission. There is evidence that he was there in 1624. Between
1633 and 1641 he was Provincial of the English Congregation of his
Order. He died on 17th January, 1665. At the beginning, Sherwood
gives his name: Frater Robertus de Sancta Maria. The petition is
not dated but, from internal evidence, must have been composed
between 24th December, 1621 and the end of May, 1622. At that
time both Mary Ward and Robert Sherwood were in Rome. Perhaps
his petition is among those writings which Mary Ward mentioned in
her letters to the Pope and Cardinal Bandini before 7th May.[99]

Sherwood wrote on behalf of his Order, which felt itself shoul-
dered aside, as did many secular priests, by the Jesuits in England. He
will certainly, too, have made his views known by word of mouth[100]
in Rome.

It is no well planned 'Informatio', like that composed by Archpriest Harrison, but a superficial and unfortunately, also, an ignoble
petition.

Briefly, for ten years certain Englishwomen have been following
a new way of life. Their community had been founded by the Jesuit,
Fr Roger Lee, which is why they were also called 'Rogerianae' in
England.Their superior (primaque faemina), who was at present in
Rome, had first been an outsister in the Poor Clare Order in St
Omer, but had to leave, (extracta fuit) so that her chastity on her
begging trips in this very catholic city should not be endangered
(ne in petendis eleemosynis in civitate illa valde catholica castitas
eius periculo exponeretur). At all events, there was no fear for her
chastity in her dealings with heretics, to whom these women preach
and whom they prepare for confession, which is a matter of scandal
to catholics and one of utter ridicule to the heretics. Under the pretext
of the greater perfection of their Institute, they entrap pious girls, give
hopes of the confirmation of their congregation and their way of life
(vivendi modi perfectissimi), and swallow up their dowries in the
meantime so that these can neither enter a convent nor get married.
There are constant rumours that several members (aliquas inter ipsas)
have suffered moral shipwreck (in castitate naufragium fecisse). It is
known from reliable sources that some of them, for dubious reasons,
have eaten meat on fast days. Other Orders complained about them
that they took away their postulants from England, which they were
able to do by their free mode of life (ex libera, quam habent, vagandi
licentia). Their pupils, sent to them to be educated, publicly produce
immoral plays (publice et non satis verecunde), so that later they may
consort with seculars or preach in churches in this bold manner (hoc
modo audacius). It is commonly stated in England that these women

are supported by the Jesuits and that they prepare the ground for them, so that the houses are open only to the Jesuits and not to the secular clergy or priests of other orders.

In the name of his Congregation, Sherwood asked the Pope either to send these women into an Order already confirmed, or to impose enclosure upon them or (coetum prorsus dissolvere) to dissolve their congregation out of hand, or to forbid them their dangerous work in England (periculosas in Angliam missiones).

Few words need be added to these. They are their own condemnation. Like Harrison, Sherwood continued to spread rumours. The whole range of accusations against the women — gadding about, public preaching, snatching candidates from other Orders, once again highlights the alleged scandals. Sherwood, however, had a different emphasis.

Harrison, the traditionalist, chiefly rejected the apostolate for women; Sherwood stressed the immoral life-style of the Englishwomen. Mary Ward's departure from the Poor Clare convent was sufficient to constitute a threat to her virginity. He probably did not know that her predecessor had been guilty in this respect. And Mary Ward did not decide to leave the Order — extracta fuit. In England, according to Sherwood, the Englishwomen lived extravagantly, contrived admission for themselves into grand houses, ate meat on fast days, took others to confession, and allowed the children entrusted to them on the Continent to produce plays of little moral value, publicly. Fed from dubious sources, Sherwood sketched a caricature of the members of the Institute as operating out of inclination and frivolity. This picture was to rob the women of the last vestige of sympathy in the Roman Curia.

But it must be questioned whether Fr Sherwood's suggestion to place these women, whom he described as morally evil, into an already approved Order, or at least to have enclosure imposed upon them, could really have been taken seriously.

In the face of these grave accusations, which remained unknown to the English members and which could not therefore be rebutted, we recall Mary Ward's address which was perhaps written in Liège.[101]

'Visits: I will sometimes visit externs, either for their use or the good of our congregation, if God's greater glory seems to demand it.

Our Neighbour: I will never do or say anything from false human respect, though I think the result could be helpful for my own soul or for that of my neighbour.

Externs: In conversation with externs I will often think of God and refer everything to Him.' These words were not intended for publication, and were not written to make an impression, but to keep firmly directed towards God in her dealings with the outside world and to make it similarly more aware. It is unthinkable that such principles could have brought about the results described by Sherwood.

In the middle of October, 1622,[102] an order was sent from the Nuntiature in Brussels to the President of the English Seminary in Douai, Dr Matthew Kellison,[103] for a report about the status of the seminaries and the English men's and women's convents and monasteries in Flanders, for the information of the newly-erected Congregation of the Propaganda Fide.

Within ten days, on 26th October, Kellison sent the Nuntius a report in which the Institute was included. Kellison offers a survey, merely, which at first looks objective and free of animosity. On a closer reading, however, it reveals that Kellison had drawn his information about the Institute from the accusations already known, and from rumours. That was not really good enough.

Kellison wrote the following report, which reached Rome via Brussels.[104]

The Englishwomen live like Jesuits in everything, as far as is permitted to the weaker sex (infirmiori sexui). Their Institute was founded one year after the establishment of the Gravelines' convent by the Jesuit, Fr Roger Lee, a man of moderate gifts (in doctrina modicus). The General Superior, an extraordinarily gifted and graced lady (singularis ingenii et facundiae), who was now working for the community in Rome was first, shortly before Profession, in the Poor Clare convent in Gravelines, but changed her mind and joined the new Institute with its Jesuit charism. The Institute spread to the diocese of Cologne – probably the diocese of Liège was intended here.

The first task of these women consisted in the education of young girls but then they devoted themselves, under the pretext of business matters, to the catechesis of noble ladies and even of men, in England. At first the Jesuits furthered these missionary tasks, as the women were of assistance in their pastoral work, but then they met the resistance of many catholics, secular as well as regular clergy. They have no conventual life (vitam non nimis religiosam) but are similar to seculars in everything (laicis per omnia similem), with the exception of their prayers, which they practise privately. Sometimes (interdum) they lead a life that is even unworthy of the laity. At first they were protected by the Jesuits, but they have gradually withdrawn from the fathers. The reason for the journey to Rome must lie in this uncertain relationship between the Institute and the Society of Jesus, although they are trying to obtain the confirmation of their congregation there. A year ago they were under distraint but the Bishop of St Omer is supposed to have helped them. Since then only fourteen or sixteen members are active in St Omer; the greater part of the community moved to Liège. The foundation can have little future, as with the rejection of the Institute, the source of income in the form of dowry is diminishing.

This shows how fact and fiction were closely interwoven. It is true that the Institute was under Fr Lee's influence for several years, but he was certainly not the founder. Mary Ward's subsequent entering is a falsification of fact. It has already been seen that the first task of the Englishwomen was not the education of girls but that the Institute developed out of adult pastoral work in England, and that this work continued uninterruptedly together with the school simultaneously founded in St Omer. Kellison did not even assess the Jesuit's attitude correctly. Rejection of Mary Ward's Ignatian Institute had been there from the beginning, and the Society of Jesus had always refused to guide the Institute. Kellison was, of course, dependent on the opinion of others when it came to judging the Englishwomen in England and, consequently, he is negative. Even if the fatal turn of events in Liège may have determined the time of Mary Ward's first journey to Rome, it was not the sole reason for it. She had certainly grasped the fact that she had to take this step. Of the real situation of the Institute, which showed its effects in St Omer too, Kellison seems to have known nothing.

As well as official accusations, there was a regular private correspondence from the most disparate sort of people who busied themselves about the members of the Institute. The final report[105] of the departing Venetian Ambassador in England, Girolamo Lando, is also erroneous, although the reports of this capable dimplomat are in other respects a mine of information for historical researchers. The report is not a private letter in the usual sense but it did not reach the Vatican, at all events. Lando knew only enough about the Englishwomen to state that they were gadabout women (donne vaganti), that they devoted themselves to teaching young people (figliouole e figliuoli) but that without accepting enclosure they would never have papal approval. Their Abbess (una abadessa) lived in Liège but travelled every year under a Spanish name and with princely pomp (pompa più da principessa) to England.

A William Farrar wrote on 5th April, 1623[106] to John Bennet, that the English women were swarming around (swarme) in London and other places. Their provincial, Barbara Babthorpe, had recently travelled via Dover to St Omer in the company of two other members of the Institute and a young man. They give out the opinion that their affairs in Rome are going well and will soon be settled.

All these opinions and points of view – certainly only a small number of these have survived – twisting and disapproving, stemming from rejection, or enmity, streamed towards Rome. It can be seen that the main part of the most dangerous of the accusations concerned the free apostolate of the members in England, a task of which Mary Ward said to Cardinal Bandini that it was on account of this that the Institute could not accept enclosure.

It may cause surprise that, apart from three surviving letters[107] from earlier days, it was only somewhat later in the Institute's history that such weighty accusations were raised against the Englishwomen by highly placed priests. Grisar[108] rightly points to the depressing controversy between the English Secular clergy and the Society of Jesus, into which the Englishwomen were drawn as an Ignatian Institute.

Nevertheless the question remains, why was it that the secular clergy of England formulated such damaging words against the Englishwomen after 1621 and sent them winging to Rome? The struggle against the influence of the Jesuits in England was considerably older, as also the activities of the Englishwomen in their home country.

If one looks back at the confusion of the house of the Institute in Liège, it has already been seen that on 25th February, 1621, Fr Tomson had advanced Anne Gage, Superior, a sum of 600 guilders to enable some members to travel back to England.[109]

It was only when the belief that any successful activity in Liège was extremely unlikely, and such a large community could barely exist, that the exodus of members of the Institute began. On 15th July, 1622 there were about fifty Englishwomen living in rue Pierreuse.[110] Eight years later, when the Liège house was suppressed, there were seven members of the Institute, in the house on Mont St Martin.

It was in England also, and not only in the new foundations in Cologne, Trier and shortly afterwards in Rome, Naples and Perugia, that the many enthusiastic young women who had attached themselves to Mary Ward's Institute, found themselves without even a roof. They must be seen as full members of the Institute, and not as people stranded and abandoned by it. Their return had serious consequences, though. It was only when a greater number of members were active in England that they became conspicuous to the secular and regular clergy. The reasons for the rejection of the Institute by these were various. Some of the secular clergy did indeed dislike the Jesuits and similarly any jesuit-influenced community of women. The Jesuits defended themselves against the imitation of their Institute by women. Finally, both came together on one point: a refusal to co-operate in pastoral work with women, however subordinate these might be. The meeting place of their complaints: Rome.

Notes

1.   Pastor, History of the Popes, XIII/1, p.27 ff. (German edition)
2.   Pastor, loc.cit. p.68ff.
3.   Grisar, Institut, p.38, note 16.
4.   AGR Brussels, PEA 456, f.281r–282v.
5.   Vita E f.25r and Vita I, p.24. The oldest writings follow the Italian, if they deal with it at all.
6.   Mary Ward to the Infanta Isabella Clara Eugenia, 1st January, 1622. AGR Brussels, PEA 458, ff.3r–4v.
7.   ibid. Also, Vita E f.25rv and Vita I p.24.
8.   Between 24th and 28th December, 1621. BV Fondo Caponi 47, ff.11r–12v.
9.   "Et perchè detto Instituto non svanisca, mancando le fondatrici et acciò si possa propagare in beneficio generale, La Serenissima Infanta manda

Donna Maria de la Garde, una delle più principali di esse, per informar di esse, per informar la Santità Vostra et supplicarla resti servita approvare et confirmare detto Instituto in forma di religione." ibid.

10. see above, note 7.
11. AGR Brussels, PEA 458 f.11 rv. In her letter to the Nuntius of Flanders dated 8th January 1622, she still did not know the name of the Congregation. Bibl. Nat. Paris, MSS Lat.5175 I, pp.437–438. She may have received the news that her matters were to be put before the Congregation for Bishops and Regulars only in the course of the day.
12. AGR Brussels, PEA 458, ff.3r–4v.
13. AGR Brussels, PEA 458, ff.1r–2r.
14. BV Rome, Fondo Capponi, 47, ff. 50v–51r in Latin; Inst.Arch.Munich, Letter Nr.6 in English. The unimportant sentences in parentheses are not included here. Also: Vita E f.25v: "Her ambition as well as her fidelity in her part of labours would not permit her to loose time, wherefore she immediately presented to His Holynes and the Congregation he appointed for her busines to be treated in, what her intentions were and petitions for them, and this was all simplicity and integrity which many politicians condemned her for."
15. " ... et fructus sine dubio legeremus in dies copiosiores, si confirmatio eas apostolica ab invidorum calumniis et obloquentium machinis redderet immunes." AGR Brussels, Arch.Jésuit.Prov.Gallo-Belg. Carton 32. see also above p. 300.
16. BV Rome, Fondo Capponi, 47, ff.56v–63v.
17. ibid. ff.48r–49v.
18. On 1st January 1622. AGR Brussels, PEA 458, ff 1r–2r.
19. AGR Brussels, PEA 458, ff.3r–4v.
20. ibid. ff.1r–2r.
21. "Je feu auprès le Pere Generalle de la Societé et luy donneray les lettres de Vostre Altezze. Il use beaucoup de fort bonnes parolles, confesse que ces Pères en ces quartiers la on esté trompé et promet tout avancement par soy et les siens, ce que trouverons par effect Vostre Altezze entendera. J'apercoy qu'il a receu des autres lettres de Vostre part e s'en prendera garde qu'il ne vous déplaise." Mary Ward to Infanta Isabella Clara Eugenia, 1st January, 1622. ibid. ff.3r–4v.
22. On 14th January, 1623, ARSI Rome, Anglia 1/I, f.167r.
23. "Once I thinke I saw a Generall of yours who said nothing, but his countenance promised all concurrance with us." PB pp.39–45, Inst.Arch.Munich.
24. Grisar, Instit. p.78–80 and note 95.
25. Vita E f.28rv; Vita I p.25 repeats this. With almost childlike naiveté these Englishwomen accepted this southern courtly artificialities as genuine.
26. BV Rome, Fondo Capponi 47, ff.15r–16v. In this letter Mary Ward promised to bring the Cardinal their Constitutions personally, as soon as these were ready, with the words: "J'entend par Monsignor Vives, que nostre Institut (c'est à dire les papiers qu'il donnoit à Vostre Illustrissime) vous plait bien, qui est une grande consolation à nous toutes, ne doubtant du tout que nos constitutions qui s'escrivent maintenant vous donnera beaucoup plus grande sattisfaction comme tractant plus amplement de chasque particulier, lesquelles quand elles seront aschevées. Je vous suppleray de me vouloir faire la faveur que les pouvoir porter à Vostre Illustrissime moy mesmes ..." It is very doubtful if the Constitutions of the Society of Jesus adapted for the Englishwomen's Institute ever were handed in. They have never come to light. One suspects that difficulties, and Fr General Vitelleschi's objections prevented this.
27. On 12th February, 1622. AGR. Brussels, PEA 458, f.49 to rv.

28. ibid.
29. Mary Ward to Infanta Isabella Clara Eugenia. AGR Brussels, PEA 458, f.11 rv.
30. ibid. Ambassador Vives' petition. BV Rome, Fondo Capponi 47, ff.9r, 10v.
31. BV Rome, Fondo Capponi 47, ff.13r, 14v.
32. These dates are taken from the dorsal remark on the Petition of 7th January: "Fiandra. 15th januarii 1622. Ad Illustrissimum Bandinum. Nicolo Zambeccari from Bologna was secretary to the Congregation of Bishops and Regulars in 1621. He died on 14th April of that year. Antonio di Paolo Masini, Bologna Per illustrata II, Bologna 1666, p.166–167.
33. AGR Brussels, PEA 458, f.11rv.
34. ibid. ff.12r–13v.
35. Probably soon after 8th January. BV Rome, Fondo Capponi 47, ff.22r–23v.
36. Vives to Cardinal Odoardo Farnese, ibid. ff.28r–29v and to Cardinal Scipio Borghese, ibid. ff.30r, 31v.
37. AGR Brussels, PEA 458, f.18rv. Vives moaned about the Englishwomen's need of money and his own lack of means to help them in every letter to Brussels.
38. Also on 15th January, ibid. ff.19r–20r.
39. Pastor, History of the Popes, (German) XIII/I, p.53–55.
40. Venice 11/21. January 1622. PRO London SP 99/24, part 1, f.5rv. The letter to Secretary of State George Calvert ibid ff. 7r–8v. uses the same wording. One can see how the Englishwomen were engaged in talks. The reference in this letter to a vow to teach religion may originate from the earlier Schola Beatae Mariae.
41. Fr General Vitelleschi to Infanta Isabella Clara Eugenia on 8th January, 1622, AGR Brussels, PEA 458, f.9rv. In this letter too Fr General indicated politely but clearly the Constitutions of the Society of Jesus; Cardinal Ludovico Ludovisi to Nuntius Guidi di Bagno in Brussels, on 22nd January, Archivio dei Marchesi Guidi di Bagno, Mantua, Lettere del Signor Cardinale Ludovisi 1621–1622, Nunziatura di Fiandra C.2; Cardinal Ludovico Ludovisi to Infanta Isabella Clara Eugenia on 12th February, 1622, ibid. Cc.2; Pope Gregory XV, to Infanta Isabella Clara Eugenia on 12th February, 1622, AGR Brussels, PEA 458, f.57v.
42. On 23rd April. ARSI Rome, Anglia 1/I, f.156v. On the same day and with the same content Fr General wrote to Fr Provincial Blount, ibid. f.157r.
43. John Bennet to /William Bishop/, WA London, B25, p.53; John Bennet to /Edward Bennet/, on 18th March 1622, ibid. p.54.
44. On 26th February Secretary of State de la Faille wrote to Ambassador Vives that the Infanta had not yet come to a final decision about support for the Englishwomen in Rome. AGR Brussels, PEA 458, f.68rv. On the same day the Infanta wrote to Vives that when necessary (en cas de nécessité) he should help the Englishwomen financially. That did not amount to an order, which was that Vives was waiting for. ibid. f.70rv.
45. ibid. ff.19r–20r.
46. On 10th February the Princess thanked Vives for his report of 31st December and instructed him to continue to help the Englishwomen. ibid. f.46r.
47. On 26th February, ibid. f.70rv; to Mary Ward on 27th February, ibid. f.72r.
48. BV Rome, Barb.lat.6800 f.40. In an accompanying letter to Vives of 18th March, the Infanta likewise commanded Vives to contradict the calumnies spread about the Englishwomen. AGR Brussels, PEA, 458, f.78r. An accompanying letter from Secretary of State de la Faille to Vives, ibid. f.83rv.

49.   It was only on 21st April that the Pope could go from the Vatican to the Quirinal. Giacinto Gigli, Diario Romano (1608–1670) pub. Giuseppe Ricciotti, Rome, 1958, p.63. Vives wrote on 16th April to the Infanta that he had not yet been able to speak to the Pope in an Audience. AGR Brussels, PEA 458, f.105r.

50.   BV Rome, Fondo Capponi 47, f.34r–35v. An identical petition went to Cardinal Bandini. ibid. f. 32r–33v. Both documents were compiled before 6th May.

51.   On 7th May Vives wrote to the Infanta "A hyer fue la primera audiencia, que me ha dado Su Sandidad despues de convalecido ..." AGR Brussels, PEA 458, ff.122r–123r.

52.   ibid.

53.   Before 17th June, 1622. BV Rome, Fondo Capponi 47, ff.38r–39v.

54.   Mary Ward to Cardinal Bandini, 18th May, 1622. The Englishwomen had submitted a synopsis of the plan for their Institute. BV Rome, Fondo Capponi 47 f.20r, ff.48r–49v. At the beginning of June they handed in certain amendments to their customs. ibid. ff.46r–47v. The Institute was dealt with in the Session of the Council of 31st May 1622, and the matter of enclosure was already causing problems.

55.   The Infanta to Vives, 10th June, 1622. AGR, Brussels, PEA, 458, f.146rv. In a letter to Mary Ward on the same date the Infanta referred her to Vives. ibid. f.145r. It is clear that this suggestion could satisfy neither party.

56.   This important text should be adhered to in extenso. Reasons why we may not alter, etc.

First. Becaus what we have chosen ys already confirmed by the church and commended in severall bulls and in the councell of Trennt as a most fitt Institute to help soules.

2ly. Becaus experience and the great mutation of manners in the world in all sorts of people doth show yt to be so.

3ly. Becaus we have proved now this 12 years that the practis of the same rule doth most conduce to our owne profitt in perfection and noe less to the help of our neighbour.

4ly. Becaus that ys the vocation unto which we wear first called and which hath byn confirmed in us by the assured trialls prescribed in the booke of blessed father Ignatious his exercises, and therein approved and commend to all by the highest authority. Therfore, as Our Lord sayth that none can come to him unless his Father draws them, and that every plant which his Father hath not planted shalbe rooted out, we therfore, haveing used of clensinge our harts that we may see Gods will the better, of retirment and prayre, and the best advice we could find for our help ther in, have all ways found this choyce of ours to be the only way to gyde best to our end, and most to secure and advance our owne salvation and perfection, and therwith to serve also the church in procuringe the good of soules by all means posible for woemen to the greater glorie of God, a quo omne datum optimum et omne donum perfectum, from whom all vocations to religious perfection must come and not from man, as we se yt hath proved in all precedent orders. And yf yt wear a wronge to force anie privat man to marrie a wife whom he can not affect, much more must the election of every ones vocation in this kind be free, which ys not only more sure to last all the tirme of our life (sith the other party never dieth), but ys for ever to indure and doth determin our place with Christ for all eternity. Now as yt ys free for every privett man to chuse for him self, so much more yt must needs be fitt for princes to be ther owne chusers. This ys the reason of that was sayd before, and good reason that the king of kings should chuse his own spowses, and that God and not man should give vocations. And yf so to every privet soule, how much more to a begginninge order and

so much importinge the service of his church and good of souls. Vocations. For England, Flanders and Germany, in which 3 kingdoms we have
practised the same for this 12 years space to the great satisfaction of thos
inhabitants, as wittneseth the commendations of princes and testimony of
besshopps, which wear delivered to the commendations of princes and testimony of besshopps, which wear delivered to the illustrious cardinalls of
the Congregations of Regulers. IHS. Proved by all the assured trialls prescribed by learned men and commended to all by highest authority to be
the only way to gide best to our end and conduceinge most to our owne
salvation and perfection and the same which at the howre of our death we
should wish to have chosin." Inst.Arch.Munich, letter Nr.5.

57. That was therefore since 1611.

58. BV Fondo Capponi 47, ff.1ar–2v. The Petition should be placed in the
second half of June.

59. The Ambassador had already expressed this thought on 1st January, 1622.
AGR Brussels, PEA 458, ff.1r–2r.

60. " ... licenza di star in Roma alle spese nostre, ove potiamo ritirarci et
attendere al nostro bono spirituale et al beneficio de prossimo come havemo
fatto in altre paese e con il nostro buon esempio turare la bocca a tali male
dicenti." as above, note 58.

61. Before 1st July, 1622. Letter NR.8. Inst.Arch.Munich. The date is taken
from the dorsal comment written in another hand: dedit the 1 of july 1622
5 congregacion.

62. Grisar, Institut, p.103 ff. Rightly, Grisar connects the Englishwomen's
anxiety with the above report on their way of life, as the English Vita also
commented. ibid. p.97 ff. For the English Vita, ibid. p.103. note 154.

63. Dorsal comment on the Englishwomen's letter to Secretary Campeggi.

64. Mary Ward to Cardinal Bandini (20th August) 1622, BV Rome, Fondo
Capponi 47, f.21r. " ... in congregatione hesterna ... "

65. ibid. ff.5r–6v. " ... nell'ultima congregatione ... " This session had taken
place on 1st July, but the Englishwomen's matter was not dealt with. There
was not even mention of the letter addressed to the Pope.

66. ibid. ff.7r–8v.

67. On 27th July 1622. AGR Brussels, PEA 458, f.201r.

68. BV Rome, Fondo Capponi 417, ff.3r–4r.

69. "Ad Illustrissimum Millinum uti Vicarium qui auctoritate sua ordinaria
permittat et observet, cum eorum, quae petuntur, nulla sit prohibitio. Die
19a augusti 1622." ibid. ff.1a–2v.

70. On/20/August 1622. ibid. f.21r. An unknown, masculine hand wrote this
letter which was signed by Mary Ward.

71. Mary Ward to the Infanta Isabella Clara Eugenia on 25th February, 1623.
AGR Brussels, PEA 459, ff.60r–61r. The address comes from the official
entry in Status Animarum. See note 72.

72. The names, echoic of their sound, are in Stato d'anime 1623–24, f.12v,
Archivio Generale del Vicariato Roma, San Lorenzo in Damasco. "Maria
della Guardia, Madre Principale, Margherita Orde, Susanno Rucuo,
Guenifreda Corpigna, Maria Rocchelf, Elisabetta Cotton, Margherita
Geneson, Elisabetta Chiees, Maria Rorchilf, Esterguoccer Gua, Maria
Caslone, + Margherita (?), Anna Tornor, Maritia serva."

73. Vives to Infanta Isabella Clara Eugenia, on 3. September, 1622. AGR
Brussels, PEA 458, f.251r.

74. ARSI Rome, Anglia 32/II, f.169rv. The letter was written towards the end
of 1622. Translation and archive deposit point to an indiscretion.

75. "Sono ridicolisissime et la gente sene burla del fatto loro, quando le veggono
andare intorno per le piazze come se fossero huomini maestri e le chiamano
le moglie delli Gesuiti."

76. On 6th March, 1623. WA London, B.25, Nr.86.
77. See above, note; 71. In his letter of 1st April, 1623 to Secretary of State Carlos de la Faille, Ambassador Vives named 150 girls attending the Englishwomen's school. AGR Brussels, PEA 459, ff.112r–113r, 116r.
78. " ... she (Mary Ward) obtained to doe in Rome as in other places, that was both in their owne personall practise and assistance to others, teaching gratis those of our sexe both vertue and qualityes which produced such effects, as the wicked sayd if this went on, the stewes in Rome would fayle and poore parents felt the pleasing benefitt of having their children made fitt by qualityes to gaine their livings honestly and by vertue made capable to know it was their duty so to doe." Vita E, f.26r.
79. On 1st January, 1622. AGR Brussels, PEA 458, ff.1r–2.
80. Vives to Sec. of State de la Faille, 8. January 1622, AGR Brussels, PEA 458, ff.125–13v; likewise on 15. January, ibid. f.18rv; to the Infanta, 10. February, ibid; the Infanta to Vives, 10 February. ibid. ff.46r. respectively 47r.; Vives to Secr. of State Suarez, 12. February, ibid. f.49 to rv; to the Infanta, 16. April, ibid. f.105r; to Secr. of State Suarez 16. April, ibid. f.106 to rv; to the Infanta, 7. May, ibid. ff.122r–123r. The list could be extended.
81. AGR Brussels, PEA 458, f.70rv.
82. Vives to the Infanta, ibid. f.179rv.
83. /Secretary Carlos de la Faille/to Vives, ibid. f.216rv.
84. The Infanta to Vive, ibid. f.217r.
85. Enclosure in Vives' letter to Sec. de la Faille, 21. January, 1623, AGR Brussels, PEA 459, f.26r respect. 27r.
86. On 25th January, 1623 Barbara Ward died aged 31. Archivio Generale del Vicariato S. Lorenzo in Damaso, Morti I (1591–1643), f.99r.
87. On 25. March, 1623. AGR Brussels, PEA 459, f.96r–97r.
88. Vives to Sec. de la Faille, 1. April 1623. ibid. ff.112r–113r, 116r and de la Faille to Henry Lee, 3 June, 1623 ibid f.167r. Lee had turned to the Sec. of State for more support for the Englishwomen on 6th May. ibid. f.147rv.
89. Vives to Secr. of State Suarez on 12th February 1622, AGR Brussels, PEA 458, f.49 to rv.
90. BV Rome. Fondo Capponi 47, ff.68r–72r.
91. APF Rome, Belgium sive Fiandra, Jesuitissae ad 1648 incl. Vol.205, ff.304r–408v.
92. WA London, Vol.16 (1617–1622) pp.213–220.
93. WA London: Copia Informationis; APF Rome: "Copia Informationis" struck through and replaced with "Informatio".
94. William Harrison (1553–11th May 1621) was Archpriest in England from 11th July 1614 until his death. He studied in Rome and lived there from 1603–1608. In the controversy against the Jesuits he tried to obtain independence for the secular clergy. The "Archpriest" with twelve assistants was not a normal structure in the church. In England the Archpriest was a substitute for a bishop. The office had been set up on 7. March, 1598. For Harrison, DNB IX, p.47; Gillow III, p.150, and W. Kelly ed., Liber Ruber ven. Collegii Anglorum de Urbe = CRS 37/1940; Grisar, Die ersten Anklagen in Rom gegen das Institut Mary Wards (1622) = Misc.Hist.Pont. XXII/1959, p.52, note 9 and the writing referred to there.
95. John Bennet from Wales, studied theology in Douai and Spain and was active as a secular priest in 1591 on the English mission, where he was soon imprisoned for a time is Wisbeach. Later he and his borther Edward were among the Assistants to the Archpriest, William Harrison. After the latter's death he was sent to Rome as representative of the English secular clergy, to work for nomination of a bishop for England. Soon after his arrival he made influential friends and succeeded in having Dr William

Bishop appointed as apostolic vicar for England. At the end of May, 1623 he returned to England, where he died in August. He was among the fiercest opponents of the Jesuits and therefore opposed Mary Ward's Institute violently. Gillow I, p.184–185; Guilday, p.185; E. H. Burton and Th. L. Williams, The Douay College Diaries I, 1598–1654 = CRS X/1911, p.212, 216.

96. A. O. Meyer, England and the catholic church under Elizabeth = Bibl. of the Royal Pruss. Hist. Inst. in Rome 4/1911.
97. BV Rome, Fondo Capponi 47, ff.64r–65v.
98. Grisar, Anklagen, p.56. note 16 and the writings referred to.
99. BV Rome, Fondo Capponi 47, ff.32r–33v, resp. 34r, 35v.
100. Grisar, Anklagen, p.61, n.19.
101. VP/E 25 Inst. Arch. Munich.
102. Guilday, p.317.
103. Grisar, Anklagen, p.63, note 21. and the writings referred to.
104. The report undoubtedly reached Rome, although it has not been discovered. The Congregatio de Propaganda Fide was a new establishment at the time, so it is perhaps understandable. Two copies of the report are in WA, London.
105. Venice, 21 September, 1622. Nicolo Barozzi e Guglielmo Berchet, Le Relazioni degli Stati Europei. Lette al Senato dagli Ambasciatori Veneziani nel secolo decimosettimo, Serie IV, Inghilterra I, Venedig 1863, p.260.
106. WA London, Vol.17, pp.71–72, Nr.19. The recipient was not named, it is true, but the letter, filed in the Westminster Archives, could only have been addressed to a representative of the English secular clergy in Rome.
107. The first letter was mentioned in Bishop Blaes of Saint-Omer's open letter, 19th March, 1615; the second letter written at the beginning of 1615 and the third on 1./11 June, 1619. All three came from England.
108. Grisar, Anklagen, p.6 ff.; do. Institut. p.179.
109. see p.233.
110. AE Liège, Cathédrale St Lambert, A. Secretariat, Registre aux conclusions capitulaires 22 (130) 1621–1622, f.250v.

XX

THE HOUSES NORTH OF THE ALPS UP TO THE DEATH OF GREGORY XV

England 1621–1623

The libellous pamphlet 'Godfather's Information' – Mary Alcock's participation – the pamphlet's influence – Sister Dorothy's report – mode of operation of the Englishwomen in England – influence of the report – Fr John Tomson after his move from Liège – Fr General Muzio Vitelleschi and the Englishwomen

How exactly did the English women carry on their work in England? It must be assumed that men like Archpriest Harrison, President Matthew Kellison and Fr Robert Sherwood, OSB, who all took up positions against the Institute, did not wish to be economical with the truth. There are two documents still extant which take up diametrically contrasting views. One is the report of a Sister Dorothy of the Institute[1] and the other, the libellous pamphlet by an unknown author, 'Godfather's Information.'[2] Both statements appeared in the latter part of Gregory XV's pontificate, and both are significant for an interpretation of the adult apostolate of the Englishwomen in their own country. Moving in chronological order, 'Godfather's Information' must be examined first.

As distinct from the attacks on the Institute already dealt with, 'Godfather's Information' is a case of downright libel aimed at the destruction of Mary Ward personally. Even the heading: 'Certain observations, delivered me by Mistress Mary Allcock' betrays the fact that this is no homogenous work. It rests on statements made by Mary Alcock, which seem to have been considerably distorted by the author and compiled with mischievous intent. The date is certain: March, 1623.[3] Rightly, Grisar[4] calls attention to the fact that the agent John Bennet wrote to England at the end of 1622,[5] that the English women were spreading rumours about the forthcoming approval of their Institute. He would like to know if they could prove that in an enquiry. It would also be good policy to produce written declarations of contrary rumours. By that means the suppression of the Institute by the Pope could be hastened. It is possible that just such a demand had led to an interrogation of Mary Alcock. Very little is known of her, the Institute's first house-prefect. The office of 'oeconoma domus', house prefect, was mentioned in Bishop Blaes' letter of 19th March, 1615. Mary Alcock must therefore have been one of the first members.

In this interview she mentioned the names of Fr Roger Lee, who left St Omer at the turn of the year 1614/15, and of Fr Richard Gibbon and John Choyd, who were active in St Omer until 1612/13.[6] Mary Alcock died in 1627, having left the Institute a few years earlier.[7]

The charges can be listed under nineteen points:

1. Mary Ward had always been directed by the Jesuits in every respect. She favoured these alone and criticized the secular clergy. She had the whole community summoned if a Jesuit were to celebrate mass, but if it were a secular priest then only a few pupils might be present.

2. After the death of Fr Lee, who had been able to keep her in check to a certain extent, she began to take her meals with only a few favoured members. She wanted to eat English food, and if there were not enough, the Mater Ministra (Mary Alcock) was blamed.

3. When she returned from even a short journey, there had to be a three days' celebration, with a feastday meal on the first day.

4. She was so obsessed by good food that she did not abstain on Fridays or during Lent and even in public did not keep the rules of fasting.[8]

5. She was particularly extravagant when travelling.

6. Whenever she put in an appearance, the order of the day was disturbed.

7. The members of the Institute had to make their requests kneeling; only shortly before she left England for the last time did she desist in this.

8. Escorted like a duchess, she visited the Jesuits imprisoned in Wisbech and scattered largesse liberally.

9. She gave similar gifts even when staying overnight in a manor house.

10. She also wrote about her lavishness to St Omer, where it was received with mixed feelings, as she was squandering more than belonged to her.

11. She led a dissolute life in London with her companions, wearing expensive clothes of the latest fashion at Hungerford House in the Strand.[9]

12. She dressed so as to be taken for a maid, and was sought as such by the authorities. There are witnesses to this.[10]

13. She later lived in the same manner in Knightsbridge,[11] where musicians from London serenaded her.

14. She allowed her sister Barbara to be dressed in a way that was downright immoral and sent her with a similarly dressed companion into a hostelry in order – so she said – to win souls.[12]

15. In imitating the 'boys from St Omer' (the Jesuits' pupils), she organised games and called them 'activities', at the expense of her murmuring creditors, who had to pay for her diversions.

16. Mary Ward contributed to the entertainment of the Prince Bishop of Liège. In a perfumed room there was an artificial tree which sprinkled scented water on passers-by as they touched it, and may have cost at least a hundred pounds.[13]

17. Certain Jesuits urged her to extend her Institute to Liège, Trier and Cologne. She gave the members money for two or three months to take with them. Afterwards these had to settle with her creditors. When these asked for their money back, Mater Ministra (Mary Alcock) had to refuse them with harsh words.

18. She encouraged the members of the Institute to listen to her, Mary Ward's, instructions rather than those of their confessors, and likewise to use their own intelligence. If anyone objected to this, she was left to herself.

19. She often said that after the Pope had confirmed the Institute, the members would be sent to other convents as reformers. That was why they had to proceed courageously and show themselves as more than 'only women.'

We do not wish to engage in a war of words about the pamphlet, and deliberately refrain from a detailed criticism of its crude and transparent accusations, limiting these to a minimum in the notes. But it must be asked: what is Mary Alcock actually proving? She is denouncing the splendid clothing, the dressiness of Mary Ward and her companions in England, her vanity, even in spiritual matters, her fastidious palate and in connection with that, her extravagance and hard-heartedness. These are typically feminine remarks, arising from years of pent-up jealousy of the elegant, colourful life-style of the great. Perhaps Mary Alcock would have liked to participate in the English mission, which carried with it clothing befitting the occasion and a presence in social life. But she was house prefect in St Omer and some years later Ministra in Liège. It was a position of trust, but the management of the more than simple household of the Englishwomen in a provincial town can have offered little advancement and, in the given situation, little joy.

It is possible, and more than probable, that Mary Alcock was one of those dissatisfied members of the Institute who disapproved of the expansion of the work of the Institute in the English mission. In addition there is the disunity of the community in Liège, the subversive influence of Sister Praxedis and her followers, enemies among the Jesuits, and finally her own departure or dismissal from the Institute. All these impulses may have built up in Mary Alcock's embittered heart, which proved too small for the great vision of the Institute, and turned into a destructive hatred, precluding a sense of proportion or calm reflection.

That this woman, her life in tatters, was a welcome tool for the ever-watchful enemies of the Institute to give usable information, is enlightening. The taint of slander — and it is a serious one — cannot be lifted from Mary Alcock.

Her partner is not known. The title 'Godfather' can have several connotations. It states nothing and can, if it comes to that, refer to both the author or the receiver of the information. It was certainly a man; it is unlikely that a woman would have analysed the details in such a way. It is disputable that he was a priest. None of the great accusatory documents, whether they were from Harrison, Kellison or even Sherwood, who was not prudish, contains the word 'whores' (hoores). Only the layman, Michael Branthwaite, secretary in the English Embassy in Venice, names the house of the Englishwomen in Rome as a 'burdello', a brothel.[14]

John Bennet operated in Rome, an avid and merciless collector of accusations about the Institute he detested, and its foundress. In his circle of accomplices the author of 'Godfather's Information' may be sought, men who were not shy of obscene tale-bearing. The interview, or interviews, with Mary Alcock provided an information service for anyone defending society's stand with regard to the position of women, and supplied Bennet with grounds for his impassioned outbreak: 'There Institute I detest as follish and diabolicall'.[15]

Whether 'Godfather's Information' actually reached Bennet and, even if it did, whether he could use it, is doubtful, for the pamphlet produced no remarkable results. The sources for Mary Ward's biographies are silent about this unworthy lunge at her honour. Even Francesco Ingoli, secretary of the then newly founded Congregatio de Propaganda Fide, who was to prepare the destruction of her Institute some years later, cannot have known anything about it. And yet complaints and statements of this kind were current and polluted the atmosphere. They could neither be proven nor contradicted.

As a counterblast, so to say, to this obscene report, the course of time has preserved for posterity a quite different history of the apostolic activity of members of the Institute; it covers the years 1621 to 1623 in the county of Suffolk, and London. Up till now there have been only sparse indications in the sources about the pastoral activity of the Englishwomen in their own country and these have come almost without exception from the pens of their enemies. The report of her activities from 'one of ours, that live in villages in England'[16] gives a graphic insight into the almost breath-taking way in which the English women operated in England and, makes a highly interesting contribution to the position of English catholics under James I.

The oldest surviving copy in Margaret Horde's writing[17] may fairly certainly be ascribed to 1623. It forms a contemporary counterpart to 'Godfather's Information.' Margaret Horde was Mary Ward's secretary between 1621 and 1624, as can be proved. From 1625 onwards her handwriting is missing, and it can be assumed that she died in this year.

The authoress is named as Dorothy and in a dorsal note is given as laysister. Her family name is unknown.[18] From the manuscript text it emerges clearly that she was a member of the Institute. Her position as laysister tells us nothing about her background. This lady, versed in the ways of the world and accepted in noble circles, may have belonged to a family of good standing. There are other examples – Bridget Talbot, of the Earl of Shrewsbury's family, was also a laysister and performed the service of portress in St Omer; Isabella Laiton, whose father was Lord Mayor of London, likewise entered the Institute in 1638 as laysister.

The account is addressed to an unnamed superior.[19] It is possible that this was Frances Brooksby, who worked together with laysister Dorothy in England in 1621 and was living in the Cologne foun-dation in 1624. The report was certainly not intended for Mary Ward. She is mentioned several times but always in the third person.

Was this report customary in the order?

Hardly, for although Dorothy says at the beginning that she has received an order to write, her account lacks all the characteristics of a report both as to content and form.She does not comment on matters such as the situation of other members of the Institute, or their work, or of any difficulties which have appeared, the state of new members, relationships with authorities, and so forth. Nor is the tone of her report businesslike, it is a straightforward personal account.

One question is obvious – could it possibly be taken as a defence of the Institute's apostolic work in England? Against that is the fact that Dorothy – unconcernedly, moreover – is talking of her work and its dangers, exactly what the Institute was being condemned for undertaking – tasks unsuitable for women. Although the writer knew of the attacks of their enemies, her account can not be taken as biassed or in the nature of an apologia, nor was it used as such. It never appeared outside its own circles, and its author never attained great renown within the Institute. Not even the name of her family is known. She was probably one of many who spent her life defending the faith of the catholic church without making any claim for thanks or recognition. She clearly wrote for a superior who had asked her to do so. It is perfectly possible that this account is a compilation of several reports, the interpolations indicate this. Not that this lessens its value. The letter, or letters, must have found their way to Rome at some later time, for the report is in Margaret Horde's hand-writing, and she was then in the eternal city. It is possible that this unbiassed commentary was shortly afterwards used here to give the members in Italy – who were certainly not blessed with temporal goods – a picture of the extreme conditions under which other members of the Institute had to live in their English homeland. Certain criteria of the manuscript point in this direction: the letter bears no address, no salutation, no introduction, and no ending, not even a greeting. It simply describes the dangerous conditions of the work, the difficult position of catholics in general. Twice a sort of heading is inserted, which certainly did not come from Dorothy. And then comes the sentence of such importance for every member: 'If all our work should be lost here, it would not be lost in Him for whom we have performed it.' These words, written in their severely tried homeland, expressed the final aim of those Englishwomen who could have been discouraged by the hopelessness of their endless negotiations.

Now for the contents:

Dorothy lives in the house of a poor woman and identifies her as a relative. Through a certain Lady Timperley[20] – who alone knows who she was – it is possible for herself and others to receive the sacraments occasionally. Deprivation of the sacraments is Dorothy's greatest suffering. She dares not instruct children openly, as do the members abroad, but she goes to their parents' houses and can so serve both the little ones and the adults pastorally. She also teaches simple people and prays with them. Those who are afraid of per-secution or of loss of their property cannot at first be transformed into really active members of the catholic church but she endeavours to share faith in the way of salvation. As a rule those go rarely or under compulsion to the Anglican church and have an abhorrence of receiving the sacrament in that rite. Dorothy can sometimes gradu-ally turn them from their sinful way of life and their misguided practices.

She visits the sick, bringing them home-made medicines, and reconciles those who are separated. She performs these works of love in several villages. It is difficult to find a priest for peni-tents. There are few in England and sometimes their hosts are in great fear. Once there were three people in great spiritual need but Dorothy could not obtain a priest for them for six months until finally she secured the Benedictine, Fr Parker,[21] who rec-onciled one of the three with the catholic church. Another time she found a secular priest some twelve miles away (about twenty kilometres). Six people were converted and several catholics from the neighbourhood received the sacraments with Lady Timperley's help. Certain other people were helped by a Benedictine through Dorothy.

Three points strike one in this work of reconciliation:

a) She was constantly winning people back to the Catholic Church.

b) One person was reconciled to the Church at death, the others were alive.

c) The conversion of some people always resulted in violent persecution.

Now, excommunication from the Anglican church was prepared for Dorothy.[22] Sometimes, however, the opponents were like 'barking dogs which do not bite'. Just as the churchwarden who flew into a passion when he found Dorothy's first name only on the excommunication form of the Anglican church, but took no steps against her.

On 19th April, Lady Timperly asked her to visit a convert lady, whose mother had taken the Oath[23] and her husband had been a lukewarm catholic who was soon to die. Dorothy went, and at first did not speak about God but tidied up the neglected house and so won general approval. In this way she was able to reconcile the master of the house to the Church, shortly before his death for which a Jesuit prepared him. Dorothy was also able to win over the relatives of the dead man. After her departure, she continued to work with the Jesuit father.

One day Lady Timperly, the Benedictine Fr Parker, and a large party came on a visit. Later, Lady Timperly told her that the Jesuit and the Benedictine had spoken highly of her. The Jesuit wished that there were thousands like her in England. Dorothy was afraid that she had been recognized as a member of the Institute but Lady Timperly thought that in that case neither of them would have expressed such high praise, as they were enemies of the Institute.

Once the authorities appeared unexpectedly and searched the house, but found nothing incriminating. Afterwards, Fr Parker recommended Dorothy to a lady, saying that she worked miracles. She gave religion lessons here as well, praying with the people, encouraging them to receive the sacraments, striving against their bad practices and looking after the household. Six weeks later she wanted to return to her poor people but the Jesuit persuaded her to remain a little longer, as the lady concerned was not yet strong enough in her faith.

In spite of all their precautions, the conversion of the householder could not be concealed from the heretics, and Dorothy was summoned to court, though the Jesuit was able to save her from the worst through his connections. The judge asked her why she did not go to the Anglican Church. Dorothy answered courageously:

'Because I am a catholic.' When the judge then said that that was against the law of the land, Dorothy replied, 'Yes, but it is in conformity with the will of God.' That was enough for her. The judge wanted to know if she was a widow, or married. When she told him that she was not married, he answered: 'All the better, as I hope that a good husband will bring you round to change your religion.' But Dorothy retorted that he would certainly not do that. Finally, the judge regretted that she did not belong to the Anglican church. He was a peaceable man and let her go, but not without a warning of the possible consequences of her proselytising. Dorothy went off to a sick women and brought her into the lady's house where she herself was living, so that she could look after her better.

On 16th October she accompanied her hostess to Lady Timperly. During the two days of their stay she was able to procure a priest for the poor friends in the first place where she had been. She then went to London, where there was the greatest danger of being recognized. Lady Timperly had warned her, and said that in that case she would have just as many enemies among priests and catholics as she now had friends. By a miracle she was not recognized. After she had returned from town, she visited her poor people and found a priest about eight miles away (thirteen kilometres) for them and for a lady who had not been to the sacraments for about six or eight years. She had married a heretic and been badly treated by him. She procured a piece of land from an acquaintance of Dorothy's in order to build a house in which Dorothy wanted to set up a chapel and dwelling place for a priest.

On 24th December she accompanied her lady to Lady Timperly, to celebrate Christmas. There too she had some success. In a little chapel Dorothy treated the theme: 'of helping to the conversion of some, and of others who bore the name.'[24] The result: the Benedictine recommended her to Lady Arundel[25] as a helper in the work of reconciliation, though she could not achieve much. Under the title of 'Statements concerning the Institute'[26] there follow some extremely interesting episodes in Sr Dorothy's report. The Benedictine Fr Parker and other priests often spoken about the Institute, and thought Mary Ward might well seek to send members of her Institute to England, to do work like Dorothy. Only then would they have use for the Institute and its superiors. They thought that the members lived in large houses for their own benefit and to promote the Society of Jesus. Others again thought that it was unsuitable for religious women to live outside their convent. Retirement and recollection were more suitable. On such occasions, Lady Timperly defended Mary Ward and the Institute and refuted the critics. The Englishwomen, she said, were admirable women, people of prayer, of mortification and of exemplary life.

Another priest, who wished to become a Jesuit, spoke slightingly about Mary Ward and her Institute but this time too Lady Timperly defended the members. Sometimes visitors feared that she would persuade Dorothy to enter the Institute! They told her that Mary Ward had gone to Rome in order to seek the confirmation of her Institute but that she would never obtain it. Once Fr Parker asked Dorothy if she would like to be a 'galloping nun', 'a preacher'. She avoided the question by saying she was satisfied with her present condition, upon which the priest said that he would be glad if she took the vows of obedience and chastity.

The report ends there. There remains little to be added. A comparison of these two accounts should be sufficient. It must be emphasized that this style of life was extremely dangerous, not just in the physical sense of imprisonment or other deprivations but in that of moral and spiritual dangers; undoubtedly God gave the graces necessary for this sort of vocation.

Even if one admits the possibility of failings in this type of life, one cannot approve of its opponents' desire to blot it out of existence. In that case whole Orders of the Roman Catholic church would have to be banned,for where are there any communities of men and women without failings? In the second half of May, 1622, the English Vice-Province held a provincial congregation in London. Vice Provincial Richard Blount was the chairman, Fr John Salisbury, then superior of the English mission in Wales was secretary, and Fr Henry Silisdon, rector of the novitiate in Liège, procurator. None of these names boded well for the English women.

Only those submissions which concern Mary Ward's Institute will be mentioned here. One point dealt with was the question as to whether Fr John Tomson should be moved to Rome, after the Englishwomen had left there, or to Madrid. This question vibrates with the desire of the proposer – or proposers – to make sure that this uncomfortable member should be removed as far as possible from Belgium. It may be remembered that Fr Tomson was in Florence at the time, and that a final decision about his future fate had not yet been made. But Fr General Vitelleschi decided otherwise. It may be anticipated here that he had already decided on 8th February, 1623[27] to place the well-deserving man, in spite of his failure in Liège, in another position in Belgium. From the beginning of 1623 Fr Tomson was to instruct the tertians in Ghent. They were not to be easy years.

Fr General reacted quite differently over the question of the Englishwomen in England. On 28th May,[28] a submission about their confessors had to be dealt with. As in Belgium, the confessors in England were appointed by superiors. It is enlightening to know that in practice the suggestion came close to withholding the sacrament of penance. England had become a missionary country. To create opportunities for confession, or to hear confessions, entailed severe legal penalties, if discovered. Relatively few Jesuits worked in the wide-spread area of the English mission, and these rarely had a permanent address.

Fr General praised the circumspection and vigilance of the provincial congregation, which protected the good of the Society of Jesus by confronting a danger unnoticed by less prudent fathers. One should be on guard, that this question should be given more attention in future, and the Father Provincial was to decide on the confessors for the Englishwomen. A marginal note: I praise and recommend this highly (valde laudo et commendo).[29]

If we consider that Mary Ward was able to write to Infanta Isabella Clara Eugenia after her first visit to Fr Vitelleschi that this man had spoken to her kindly and promised every sort of help,[30] then we are presented with two different people. At the same time it must not be overlooked that it is a matter of two different spheres of work. Fr Vitelleschi protected the 'Pium Institutum' with its sole task of teaching and boarding school, but refused to consider the Ignatian Institute which, like the Society of Jesus, undertook pastoral work among adults.

At the end of the provincial congregation Fr Silisdon left for Rome. He would, of course, have made a report about the Englishwomen.[31] He arrived there on 9th November, 1622.[32]

Saint Omer

1621-1623

The material position of the community — threat of distraint — the Infanta's assistance

The situation of the Englishwomen in St Omer had become less complicated but not less unfortunate. There was no longer any question of friction with the Jesuits. The community was subject, willy nilly, to Bishop Blaes' successor, Paul Boudot,[33] with whom they probably had little contact. Those members who understood French, confessed to the Walloon Jesuits. The community may have just managed to eke out a scanty living. They hardly even appear in the sources, at most they are mentioned on Rogation Days, as on 4th January, 1622, when it was the turn of their church to pray for the whole Church as part of the prayer of the diocese of St Omer[34] or, some years later, on 29th August, 1624, when the citizens of the town celebrated mass in their church for the victory of the Spanish army over the northern Netherlands.[35]

Otherwise there were only accounts of their financial situation, and these were bleak.

In the autumn of 1621 the Infanta was able to help the Institute by ordering the townsmen to cease their coercive measures against the Englishwomen.[36] At that time the two creditors, Symphorien Machin and Jean Ogier could recoup from their debtors. The butcher Maxime Juet had apparently left empty-handed or had temporarily suspended his demand, as there was nothing to gain.

Because the Englishwomen remained unable to pay, the problem of distraint was again acute. The Infanta's intervention was a temporary respite only. On 18th February, 1622[37] the butcher Maxime Juet once again made representation to the town and requested a new distraint on the Englishwomen, who still owed him a residual sum of 315 guilders. In autumn of the previous year the sum owed had been 345 guilders. Seemingly the Englishwomen had paid 30 guilders and for future meat deliveries, or perhaps they had bought little.

This time the town was more cautious. It immediately turned – although somewhat sharply – to the Privy Council in Brussels with the request to be allowed to take up the distraint already approved against the Englishwomen.[38] Juet, wrote the Magistrate, had always sold his English customers good wares, indeed, he had even bought meat from other butchers at his own expense, as the quality of his wares did not satisfy the Englishwomen.

Usually the town granted twenty-four hours to take up a distraint. So far they had been restrained by the government. Perhaps this was because the Englishwomen were not considered as religious sisters? They had not been, when they settled in St Omer some years ago. They were secular refugees, and as such were accepted by the town and into the town. They had presented themselves as secular persons and could have legal action taken against them as such. On their acceptance by the town they had promised not to cause any difficulties, on the contrary, that honour would be paid to St Omer for having given refuge to people who had left their country for religious reasons.

The Privy Council kept its head and let time pass. Only on 2nd May[39] did it answer the query and not even this opinion could satisfy. The town should, so it ran, grant the Englishwomen a further month in which to pay. Proper care should be given to those unable to pay.

The letter reached St Omer on 25th May, together with other closed letters for the Englishwomen, which were to be handed to them.[40]

The town understood; a month passed quickly. But the term of payment was barely past when the Englishwomen asked for yet another postponement, this time for two years.[41] Once again, in their petition to the Infanta they told the sad course of events. Im September of the previous year they had been 'fort rigoreusement' treated, but the Infanta had protected them from further molestation. The Privy Council had granted them a month to pay the open accounts of Maxime Juet. They were doing their best to pay their creditors gradually. In the past year they had settled several debts, and they would do all that was possible in the future. Could the Infanta save them from complete ruin and effect a further postponement, say for two years. Otherwise great disgrace would come on her little community. As refugees they hoped for the assistance of the princess of the country. At that time the community totalled not more than fourteen or sixteen members.[42]

Once again the Infanta had pity on the needy.

At the same time the Infanta received an agitated letter from her ambassador in Rome, who was expected to protect twelve people from hunger with scanty means. On 6th June[43] she left it to the town of St Omer to make an arrangement between the Englishwomen and their creditors. There was little possibility of that happening. The postponement for a further month, which they had requested, was to be granted. During this time, also, they were to be safe from arrest. Once again Maxime Juet practised patience and once again the town court delayed action. Before the 21st March, 1623,[44] ten months later, the Englishwomen once again addressed a petition to the Infanta and once again requested a respite of six months, and protection against force. And once more the Privy Council tried to gain time, by asking the town for its opinion on the matter.[45] The Privy Council must have been adequately informed by this time.

With this, the sources peter out. Whether the Englishwomen ever paid their debts, cannot be verified. Perhaps they did manage to pay the outstanding bills in very small instalments over a lengthy period of time, and with great retrenchments. Otherwise, Juet would surely have repeated his demands for the gross amount.

Liège

1621–1623

Material predicament after acceptance of the debt-encumbered farms in Condroz – Fr Rector Henry Silisdon and the Englishwomewn – Fr Tomson's journey to Rome – the Englishwomen's 'Confession case' – Fr Lessius' opinion on the Englishwomen's debts

1621 had brought about great changes for the Institute in Liège. One thing only remained the same – their fearful poverty.

It seems that the community, which had grown steadily, had rented a second house on Mont St Martin, for on 8th March, 1621,[46] shortly before the great disaster struck, the Chapter threatened them with seizure of their movable goods if they did not pay the arrears outstanding to Canon Servais Meys.[47] It was now possible for them to do so, the Chapter said, as they had received a larger sum from

Brother George Kenix. Canon Meys must therefore have been rapidly informed about the 600 guilders which Fr Tomson had obtained for the English women and for which the superior, Anne Gage, had given a promissory note to the Jesuits. But this money was urgently needed by the superior for a group of members of the Institute who were to leave Belgium in order to seek refuge in their home country.[48]

In May, 1621, shortly after their acceptance of the farms in Condroz, which were encumbered with debts, the Englishwomen requested the Chapter of the Cathedral of Saint-Lambert for a reduction of the ground tax for their house in the rue Pierreuse. It was granted them out of recognition for their status as religious.[49] Then the sources remain silent for some length of time about the predicament of the Liège community. It was only on 15th April, 1622[50] that Canon Meys renewed his complaints to the Chapter about the Englishwomen's payment of arrears. The Chapter issued a warning of seizure within eight days, but this remained a warning only.

Three months later[51] the Chapter of the Cathedral of Saint-Lambert granted the Englishwomen, at that time numbering about fifty in Liège, assistance in the form of an unspecified sum. They had asked for it. One can imagine how hard it was for these Englishwomen to request alms.

The depths had still not been plumbed.

Two months later, on 23rd September,[52] the Chapter once more gave them a donation. This time they received 250 guilders which came from penal fines accruing to the Cathedral, though the women were not aware of its provenance. In those days, 250 guilders was a tidy sum. But what was that among fifty people? A drop of water on a hot stone. One person could live − on the bread line − for two or three days on one guilder.

A week later, on 30th September,[53] there was another complaint, from Canon Merica to the Chapter of Saint-Martin. It was to be feared, he said, that the Englishwomen would move without repairing his house. The Chapter then stated in that case he could insist on his rights, that is, he could place them under distraint. It seems that the landlord had become impatient and threatened them with a new warning of seizure, for on 29th October[54] the Englishwomen asked the Chapter to intercede. The Chapter sent two Canons, Jean Heusden and Thomas a Sarto, to accomplish a settlement. This cannot have come about, for hardly one month later, on 26th November, 1622,[55] Merica was once again at the Chapter, making representation about the Englishwomen's arrears in rent and their inability to repair his house. What the damage amounted to, is not clear.

As well as all this, there was the tricky relationship with the English Jesuits. Fr Tomson's sucessor, Fr Henry Silisdon, was the son of John Bedingfield, Esq., and Margaret, nee Silisdon. Fr Bedingfield adopted his mother's family name as cover. His brother, Rector of the tertians' house in Ghent, Fr Edward Silisdon, did likewise. Henry Silisdon was born in 1584 in Redlingfield, Suffolk, and was one year older than Mary Ward. He first studied in London, then in St Omer and then from 31st October 1599, in the English College in Rome where he was Prefect of Studies. In 1602 he entered the Society of Jesus. Before he was made Rector of the novitiate house in Liège, he had worked on the English mission.

Although his nomination came in July, 1621,[56] the decree was sent to Belgium on 4th September only.[57] He took up office in Liège in October.[58] Extremely ascetic,[59] suspicious and gloomy, Fr Silisdon was by temperament an utter contrast to Fr Tomson's cheerful confidence. This man, of all people, was to pick up the baton of the deposed rector, a feat difficult to accomplish on the human level. He was, moreover, to put everything to rights. Fr General mistakenly expected great things from Fr Silisdon, who was now to set another course for the Englishwomen.

Strict measures and harsh principles are not, however, a universal panacea.

Towards the end of November 1621,[60] Fr Vitelleschi made an ungracious criticism of the Englishwomen to the new Rector and warned him to send frequent reports to Rome. He was to have no cause for complaint on that score.

The General remained in close contact with Fr Silisdon[61] and the Englishwomen surface again and again in reports. It was they who shared responsibility for the unhappy financial situation of the Jesuit novitiate, their enemies stated. On 23rd April, 1622[62] Fr Vitelleschi was able to console his Rector in Liège with the assertion that papal confirmation of the Institute must be considered as having foundered. This may have been a relief to the General in Rome; it was none to the Fathers in Liège, for the Institute was not suppressed, even though confirmation had been withheld. It seems that the Walloon Jesuits in Liège attempted to put an end to the disedifying quarrel which had certainly spread outside the walls, by wanting to release from debenture the mortgaged farm of the English Jesuits — that was probably Jacques Lamet's, to which Widow Gal had laid claim as creditor. They soon received sharp instructions from Rome not to intermeddle in the affairs of their English brothers.[63] Their Rector, Fr Pierre Bouille, liked the Englishwomen. Unnoticeably at first, but steadily, matters came to a head. Assurances from the General, that he was keeping the Englishwomen in Rome under observation, and that Fr Tomson, who had had both feet on Italian soil since Spring, 1622, would be kept far from them, did not altogether convince Fr Silisdon.[64]

At the same time, Fr Vitelleschi was keeping up a lively correspondence with Fr Tomson. He had addressed his first letter to the deposed Rector on 2nd November,1621, to Bordeaux.[65] Presumably Fr Tomson was to pass that way. He was to change his destination, Fr General now ordered, and come to Rome instead of Spain, to state his case before the curia of the Order. On the December 28th,[66] the same day the Englishwomen were received in audience by Pope Gregory XV, Fr Vitelleschi wrote to Fr Tomson in Madrid that he was to remain in Spain for the time being until the Englishwomen, who had arrived in Rome, should have finished their business. No one could foresee that this business would take so long, and that the days would turn into years.

On 10th December, Fr Tomson was in Valladolid, for he wrote from there to the General.[67] It seems unlikely that he had received the letter in Madrid from his chief superior, for on 16th April, 1622,[68] Fr Vitelleschi wrote to him in Genoa. In an extremely friendly tone he once more forbade him to continue to Rome, and added that a meeting between him, Fr Tomson, and the Englishwomen, would be undesirable in the interests of the Society of Jesus. The Father should remain in Genoa until the Englishwomen had returned to Belgium. He was not to write to them, either, as all occasions of upsetting the Fathers were to be avoided. Fr Tomson however, had probably asked the General to receive him, for Fr Vitelleschi wrote on 30th April[69] – this time unequivocally – that as he had taken himself to Genoa, he could stay there. On no account was he to travel to Rome. That,however, did not keep Fr Tomson in Genoa. On 13th May,[70] he obtained permission to go to Florence and wait there until he was summoned to Rome. So there he waited, ante portas Urbis, in order to be on the spot as quickly as possible. It was on 31st December, 1622[71] that he received permission to put the last short stretch of his long journey behind him, and enter the Generalate of his Order. It was not only the Fr General and the General Assistants whom he was to meet there, but also his greatest adversary, Fr Henry Silisdon, who, as already mentioned, had arrived in Rome on 9th November and had certainly made his views known. Fr Tomson would possibly have preferred to have got there first.

As in Mary Ward's case, it can be assumed that Fr Tomson had no moral guilt to conceal. Otherwise he would have stayed in far-distant Spain, or at least not been so importunate in his requests for an interview with his General. His progressive travels, which may seem to border on non-compliance, sprang from the desire to open up a fresh and truer angle of perspective on past events. There was never any question of deliberate disobedience. Fr Vitelleschi continued to be kindly towards the not always prudent but ever open-hearted Fr John Tomson.

Fr Edward Knott, Rector of Watten, conducted affairs during the absence of the Rector of Liège. The situation in the house was so difficult and the community so divided that it was not possible to suggest appointing one of its members as a substitute.

In the meantime reports had reached Mary Ward in Rome of the intrigues against the Liège house of the Institute. She complained to Fr Vitelleschi about the false rumours spread by Fr Burton, then in Liège. In a letter to Fr Knott,[72] Fr Vitelleschi pointed out that the former procurator had even written a biography of Sister Praxedis, who was said to have died in the odour of sanctity (cum opinione sanctitatis). Fr Knott was to enquire discreetly (clanculum) into these rumours, and put a halt to Fr Burton's project. It emerges clearly from this how dearly Fr Vitelleschi wished to keep the peace between the Fathers. Yet, he could still add a clause to his letter, that Fr Silisdon had informed him that the material for the biography had already been destroyed.

The taunting and the friction did not cease. The announcement of the former Rector's return possibly added to the ferment in the English province of the Society of Jesus. Fr Tomson may have been severely blamed for not following instructions in his attitude to the Englishwomen, yet here he was being installed once more in Belgium.[73] He had solid adversaries among his brethren. Fr Vitelleschi at first considered their fears that he would again become involved in the English women's affairs as groundless. All the same he found it advisable to place the Father far from the Englishwomen, and to keep him under observation (diligenter advigilent).[74]

In the April of 1623[75] Mary Ward made another representation to Fr General. The complaints of the Englishwomen, he subsequently wrote to Fr Provincial Blount, were about certain unnamed Jesuits who were trying to prevent young English women from entering the Institute, even going so far as to obstruct the payment of their dowry. The Fathers were not to question the Englishwomen about their debts, nor to refuse them absolution in the confessional on account of them.

The financial state of the community on Mont St Martin grew considerably worse. It is only from a letter dated 14th January, 1623 from Fr General to Fr Edward Knott[76] that we learn the members in Liège had been imprisoned on account of their debts. This may not have been a result of prosecution by their landlords Merica and Meys, but because they could not pay the bills of the tradespeople from whom they bought their supplies, or perhaps because they were no longer able to pay the high interest on the mortgages which they had accepted through Count Sackville for their house – and therefore for the Condroz farms. On 16th February, 1623,[77] their main creditor Widow Gal, paid Jacques Lamet 551 Brabant guilders as transfer fee for his farm with appurtenances in Halleux in the region of Nandrin, and she received 36 Brabant guilders as rent from him. With that, the first farm which Sackville had acquired for the Jesuits became the Widow's property. One week later[78] the Englishwomen on Mont Saint Martin received fifteen litres of rye as alms from the Chapter of the Church of Saint Martin.

Parallel with all this, the so-called 'Casus Conscientiae', the Englishwomen's confession case took up a good deal of time just then for the Liège foundation. They may have known very little about the problems under discussion between the Jesuits' Roman Generalate and the English fathers in Liège, or between these and the English fathers in Louvain.

To put things in their context, one is justified in repeating certain facts:

The problem of the Englishwomen's confessions was older than that of their debts. On 25th August, 1612,[79] in the first years of the Institute, Fr General Claudio Aquaviva had written that the Englishwomen in St Omer should receive the sacrament of penance in the Jesuits' church. It would appear that their spiritual adviser, Fr Roger Lee, had given them absolution in their own house. It was more practical, when the confessor visited the English women's house, to hear the confessions of some dozen women than for them to come to the Jesuit's church. However that may be, after Fr Lee's move,[80] General Vicar Fr Ferdinand Alber, temporarily in charge of matters after Aquaviva's death, decided that only those Fathers appointed by the superior should hear the confessions of the Englishwomen in the Church, and Fr Provincial Heren limited this to the then customary days of confession.[81]

The new General Fr Muzio Vitelleschi allowed counselling and spiritual direction in the confessional[82] – it would have been difficult for him to forbid it – but soon stated[83] his disquiet at the Englishwomen's custom of occupying two Fathers up to three hours in the confessional of their church after sunset. After Fr Lee's transfer, Fr Henry More became their confessor, yet he – presumably because the Englishwomen occupied him too – was likewise transferred. After which the Englishwomen confessed to the Walloon Jesuits. Longer conversations, which might have amounted to the direction of a member of the Institute by a Jesuit in the confessional were certainly not facilitated by the language barrier.

That was in St Omer. One is struck by the following: after Fr Roger Lee's transfer when the Englishwomen had been deprived of direction, even if a very limited one, they apparently received spiritual guidance as budding religious in Jesuit confessionals. Such dialogues took considerably longer than the normal time of a confession. It is stressed that this guidance could not constitute the regular direction of the Institute, which had been strictly forbidden the Jesuits, and which had certainly not been sought by Mary Ward. It would have been difficult, if not impossible, to separate the spiritual life of a person exercising the usual practices of religion from that as a member of the Institute. It is quite clear from the measures of the curia of the Order in Rome, that the most detailed reports were being sent to the General, which showed their effect in the decrees of the Order to the Belgian province.

At the end of 1616 the Englishwomen gained a foothold in Liège, where Fr Tomson was directing the new novitiate house for Englishmen and Fr Henry More was procurator from November 1616 and minister. Outwardly at least there were at first no difficulties concerning confession of the Englishwomen in Liège. But here too sharp observers gave biassed information to the General. Then came the business of the Rector's unfortunate financial stewardship coupled with Count Sackville's treacherous behaviour, which placed the whole of the debt on to the Englishwomen. The part played in this by Fr Vice Provincial Blount has already been dealt with in detail.

Fr Silisdon came from the English mission. He will certainly have heard criticisms about the Englishwomen, and may even have rejected their method of work from his own experience. His mistake in Liège lay in the fact that he did not want to learn the true facts from the women. Perhaps, inclined as he was to scrupulosity, his heart had become hardened in this respect. Apart from this, the fact that they were in debt can hardly have been the real reason for the measures that Silisdon now took, as his own house was three times more in debt than that of the Englishwomen. No one, apparently, had thought of denying Fr Tomson or his procurator Fr Burton the sacrament of penance because of their debts. No, Fr Silisdon was striving for the total repudiation of the Englishwomen, who still had friends in the Society of Jesus. He went about it with a heavy hand. First, he wanted to refuse them the choice of confession to the English Jesuits, but this was declined by Fr Vitelleschi, who had meanwhile come to know Mary Ward and her companions in Rome. However, he did not given any personal suggestion, but directed Fr Silisdon to the specialists in the Order.[84]

The spring of 1622 was approaching, and Fr Vitelleschi was doubtless thinking of the forthcoming English vice-provincial congregation; he will have been on his guard against saying anything decisive on such a knotty problem, which had become an apple of discord to the English Jesuits in Belgium. This gentle and conciliatory man undoubtedly knew that the English vice-province was about to ask to be raised to the status of a province.

On his return to Liège from the discussions in London, Fr Rector Silisdon immediately followed his General's advice and placed certain questions before well-known theologians of the Order in Louvain.[85] Whether it was he who turned to Fr Leonhard Lessius, is not known. It may be that the division of labour went through the normal channels of superiors. As mention was made in the questions of the six or seventh months spent by the Englishwomen's Superior in Rome, we may assume that these were written in June or July, 1622. Fr General's instruction to Fr Silisdon of 26th March, 1622 referring to the women's confession could have reached Liège at the earliest by the end of April. Although no sender or author is named, this can be assumed to be Fr Silisdon, as it was he who carried on the correspondence with Fr Vitelleschi. His presentation of the facts, however, was not impartial. Certain pious ladies, he wrote, who wished to found a religious Institute and hoped to receive speedy confirmation of their congregation, have run into serious debts. There is the risk that they will never be able to repay these. They have already suffered distraint and there, where the secular princes protect them (in St Omer), are openly called deceivers who have deprived the poor of their money. They have also been threatened with imprisonment. Meanwhile they do not even have the means to support themselves and are therefore forced either to close their community or continue to incur more debts without any guarantee of ever being able to pay these. They believe that their Institute will be confirmed by the Pope. Knowledgeable friends have attempted to convince them that they must borrow money for two or three months, and continue to survive during this time. Their superior has been in Rome now for six or seven months and they still believe that she will be successful. Nonetheless there is the danger that they will lose their house. They no longer dare go into the streets in case they are accosted by their creditors. And yet they cling to their opinion that they would rather borrow money than lose their Institute, especially as their superior, who has been consulted, has encouraged them to do so.

The facts mentioned were, unfortunately, true. The amount advanced by Fr Tomson of 8,000 scudi or 20,000 Brabant guilders were in connection with their house, and the farms forced on them in Condroz. Added to which there were now the standing bills of their suppliers. These are not known, but they must have far outpassed the demands of the tradesmen in St Omer, as the community in Liège had grown considerably greater than that of the oldest foundation, which had diminished markedly.

At first glance, this position statement seems objective enough, but on closer study it is seen to be heavily weighted against the Englishwomen.There is not a single ray of light or hope, and nothing beautiful to be found in this portrait. Everything is dark, destined to failure, despicable and morbidly sinful.

Fr Silisdon may have known how to report in detail, but he was silent about one very important fact. What was the origin of these debts incurred by the these Englishwomen in Liège? He simply said that the Englishwomen wanted to found an Institute and hoped for its confirmation. But should such a project eo ipso carry heavy debts?

It has been seen in some detail how the matter came to be, and it is amazing that there is no word in this report of matters contributing to the course of events.

Next came the questions Fr Silisdon presented to the theologians:

1.   May the Englishwomen continue to amass debts, although they know that they cannot meet them?
2.   Can the older members and the superiors, who have an overview of the financial situation, obey their Chief Superior, assuming that everything was discussed beforehand? How far are the younger members of the Institute guilty, who have no full knowledge of their situation?
3.   The confessors are doubtful if they can give these women absolution in confession. Are they permitted to do so, although the affair is publicly known and condemned as deceitful and unjust?

It is not known if Fr Lessius gave his opinion on these questions, but it must have been in the second half of 1622, as the scholar died on 15th January, 1623.

Fr Lessius' answers are distinctly remote:

To the first point, he thought: If they were convinced of their inability to pay, the Englishwomen should incur no more debts – that would be theft – unless they were so placed that further loans of money should be granted them. With these limitations Lessius followed the line of several moral theologians, who granted everyone the right to exist and to grasp at the means of existence when in extremity.

To the second question Lessius considered that office-holders, and such people who have an overview of the financial situation and know that they can no longer repay money lent them, should borrow no more, even if the Superior had pledged them to do so. The Superiors had no moral guilt for their conduct in the past over money matters. They acted on the instructions of their highest superior, convinced that they would be able to make repayment. But as they could now have no hope of the confirmation of their Institute, they should accept no more money in the future.

Younger members had no moral guilt.

To the third question, Lessius answered that the confessors should first of all warn the Englishwomen and only if they did not obey, refuse them absolution.

Moreover, the women should be advised to request the secular and ecclesial authorities for help, so that their Institute and their work should not perish.

When one considers that, in his 1621 judgement on the Institute, Fr Lessius wrote a sharp and dismissive letter about Mary Ward, then here, hardly one year later, he was cautious and factual. His mention of the highest superior – Mary Ward – was coupled with the assumption of her conviction that the debts could be repaid. Finally, he even advised the Englishwomen to obtain help through influential people.

It must not be overlooked that Fr Lessius is still, even here, considering an Institute occupied with the education of girls (opus inchoatum ad instructionem · puellarum), and not Mary Ward's Institute, which had imposed on itself the task of the English mission.

However that may be, Fr Silisdon did not achieve his aim. This affair continued to vex both parties.

When Pope Gregory XV died on 8th July, 1623, the house of the Englishwomen in rue Pierreuse, which suited all their requirements, had passed into the hands of Widow Gal. The members on Mont Saint Martin were starving, and the much-needed personal spiritual guidance of the English Jesuits was under discussion.

In Rome, negotiations concerning confirmation of their Institute limped along. On 8th July,[86] Vives sent Brussels his customary half-annual account of donations to the Englishwomen made by the Belgian Embassy. This financial contribution amounted to 40 Scudi or 100 Brabant guilders for more than a dozen people. Each time it arrived Mary Ward signed for its receipt.

Notes

1. WA London, Vol. 17, pp.59–62.
2. NS Nr.8. Handwriting of Margaret Horde, Instit. Arch. Munich.
3. "Certaine observations delivered me by Mistress Marie Allcock, the first minister of Mistress Wardes Companie att Leeds (Liège) yea the first of all who was publicklye so called. March 1623".
4. Grisar, Institut, S.379–380.
5. ARSI Rome, Anglia 32/II f.169rv. Italian copy.
6. P. Richard Gibbons SJ (ca. 1549–1632), professor and writer. Foley, Records IV, p.484–485; Gillow, English Catholics II, p.439–442. Fr William Flake SJ (ca 1563–1637) actually the founder of the English Seminary in Saint-Omer, in that he spent practically the whole of his religious life there and held positions of authority. He was well-disposed to Mary Ward and her Institute. The letters of recommendation which Mary Ward brought with her to the continent in 1606 were addressed to him. Fr Flake died on 13th December 1637. Foley, Records VI, p.167, VII, p.XXX VII and 261; Sommervogel, Bibliothèque III, Sp.768. Next paleographically follows John Choyd, perhaps Fr John Floyd SJ (1572–1649) from Cambridgeshire. He entered the Society of Jesus in 1592 and was frequently on the English mission. After being exiled, he was a professor in Saint-Omer from 1607–1610, where he died on 16th September 1649. Fr Floyd was a well-known and prolific author. Sommervogel, Biblioth. III, Sp.812–818.
7. Mary Ward to Winefrid Wigmore, on 29th September, 1627. Letter Nr. 42, Inst. Arch. Munich.
8. Sherwood reported the same about the Englishwomen. It is possible that they had to eat meat publicly on those strictly observed fast-days, to avoid recognition as catholics and imprisonment.

9. Now Hungerford Market and Hungerford Street near Charing Cross. It is not possible to find when the members lived there. It is more than probable that those who worked in London lived in several small communities and changed house often. A larger community of women living together could have aroused the attention of the ever-vigilant Watch. Hungerford House at that time belonged to Sir Edward Hungerford, a relative of Lucy Shelley, a member of the Institute.

10. "Godfather's Information" names Mary Ward's brother, George Ward, SJ, who went under the alias of Ingleby. He could hardly have had detailed knowledge of his sister's life, as he was in the Jesuit College in Valladolid from 1615–1620, in Louvain briefly in 1621 and from 1622–1625 was again in Valladolid. He was on the English mission in 1626. The English vita f.22v–23r describes the incident more credibly. See above, p. 162

11. Knightsbridge, now between Picadilly and Kensington in London, was then a disreputable quarter outside the city walls, but offered some security for catholics.

12. The Englishwomen also endeavoured to help fallen girls. Acceptance into their school in Saint-Omer granted to some young people who had thus fallen is even in paragraph 55 of "Schola Beatae Mariae", admittedly only in individual cases. They must have sought out such girls in England and did not always find them in respectable surroundings. This sort of apostolate is distortedly presented here.

13. Even if the Englishwomen paid due respect to a visiting bishop, and perhaps received him with hand-made offerings, they will have had other things to think about!

14. Michael Branthwaite to Ambassador Dudley Carleton, Venice, 9th January 1623 (st.v.) Lamport Hall Archive, Northampton J.C.3501.

15. John Bennet to Edward Clifton, 6th March, 1623, WA London, B.25, Nr.86.

16. Dorsal comment: A relation of one of ours, a laysister, one of those that live in villages in England.

17. Letter Nr.8. Inst. Arch. Munich.

18. The family name is not in the "Calendar of Members", nor in the French Death Register, nor in the handwritten abstracts. All are in the Inst. Arch. Munich.

19. The report begins without any introduction: "According to your command I intend in the best and breefest manner I can to relate my proceedings and manner of living ..." Only a superior could have given her the order.

20. At that time Sir Thomas Timperly, Esq, was owner of Hintlesham Hall near Ipswich, Suffolk. He was married to Elizabeth, nee Shelley of Michelgrove in Sussex, whose relative Lucy Shelley had entered the Institute. For Lady Timperly see J. G. Nichols, the Herald and Genealogist, III, London 1866, p.420.

21. The name was spelt variously in the manuscript (Pammer, Paumer, Palmer, Pamlmer) but undoubtedly refers to the Benedictine Fr William Parker (1575–1655), who made his profession in the Italian monastery of the congregation in Montecassino and then went on the English mission. There is evidence to show he was active in Hintlesham Hall (1632–1633) in Suffolk. He died on 31 May, 1655 in Longwood, Hampshire. H. N. Birt OSB, Obit Book of the English Benedictines 1600–1912, Edinburgh 1913, p.35; B. Weldon, Chronological Notes containing the rise, growth and present state of the English Congregation of the order of St Benedict, London, 1881, p.190 and App. p.5.

22. The government considered every English citizen as a member of the Anglican church. Excommunication or exclusion from the national church therefore made him fair game.

23. The Oath of Supremacy, by which a citizen recognized the King as head of the English Church, and therefore abjured the Roman Catholic Church.
24. "Of helping to the conversion of some and others bore the name."
25. Not supported by documentary evidence.
26. "The coneceite and opinion had of our Companie and daily disputes against it and Mylady definding it."
27. For the interrogation: ARSI Rome, Anglia 32/I, f.123v.
28. The Congregation's report: ARSI Rome, Congr.57, f.46v, Session 18. The decision of Fr General: ibid. f.55v. and as revised copy: Anglia 32/I, f.126r.
29. Already some time earlier, on 26th March, 1622 in a letter to Fr Richard Banks who was engaged in the English mission, Fr General disapproved of the Englishwomen in their missionary work. "In posterioribus fuit etiam mihi valde gratum iudicium Reverentiae Vestrae de Instituto Virginum Anglicanarum de quo, si omnes ita prudenter et ex sensu sancti Patris nostri Ignatii iudicassent ..." It is evident from this that this was his personal opinion of the Institute, and not a moral judgement on the Englishwomen. ARSI Rome, Anglia 1/I, f.155v. On 26th November, 1622, Fr Vitelleschi referred Fr Alexander Fairclough to Fr Vice Provincial Blount for his attitude towards the Englishwomen. ibid. f.165v.
30. On 1st January, 1622, AGR Brussels, PEA 458, ff.3r–4v.
31. Memoriale for Fr Silisdon, ARSI Rome, Anglia 32/II f.133rv.
32. Fr Vitelleschi to Fr Knott, 12th November, 1622. ARSI Rome, Anglia 1/II, ff.164v–165r.
33. Paul Boudot, 1618–1619, Bishop of Saint-Omer, then transferred to Arras, where he died in November 1635. Hier. Cath. IV p.99.
34. Prières publicques pour les nécessités de l'église dans tout le diocèse de Saint-Omer. 4 janvier /1622/: Les Damoiselles Angloises de Saint-Omer. AM Saint-Omer, Ms.806; Annales Bertiniana ca.1545–1655 by Gérard d'Haméricourt, Abbe de Saint-Bertin, f.125v, 126v.
35. Règlement touchant les prières à faire au diocèse de Sainct Omer pour l'heureux succez de nos armées contre les ennemys ... Les jour destinés aux messes solenelles pour les villes de chaque mois: Aoust et novembre. Sainct Omer.4 Dimanche les Pères Dominicains, jeudi les Damoiselles Angloises.
36. See above, p. 461. 286
37. AM Saint-Omer, CCXXXIX Nr.17–18 Filles Anglaises, p.29.
38. The Council session, 25th February, 1622, AM Saint-Omer, Délibérations du Magistrat 8 (1621–1626) f.36rv, and the draft of a letter to the Privy Council with the same date. AM Saint-Omer CCXXXIX Nr. 17–18, Filles Anglaises, pp.20–6.
39. AM Saint-Omer, CCXXXIX Nr.16, Filles Anglaises, pp.18–19.
40. Dorsal comment to the letter mentioned in note 39.
41. The Englishwomen to Infanta Clara Eugenia, between 25th May–6th June. AM Saint-Omer, Correspondance dué Magistrat 38 (1622), Nr.133.
42. Matthew Kellison, Rector of the Seminary in Douai, to Nuntius Francesco Guidi di Bagno on 26th October 1622. Kellison gave as reasons for this their moving to Liège. E. H. Burton, The Douay Diaries (1598–1654) I = CRS 10/1911, p.195–206.
43. AM Saint-Omer, Correspondance du Magistrat 38 (1622) Nr.131.
44. ibid. 39A Nr.89.
45. ibid. Nr.87. The letter reached the town only on 13th April, 1623.
46. AE Liège, Collegiale Saint-Martin 58, f.124r.
47. Servais Meys, Canon of Saint-Martin, died in 1632. AE Liège, Collégiale Saint Martin 84, f.282.
48. Memorial, Fr Tomson, ARSI Rome, Anglia 32, f.362v.
49. " ... propter respectum personarum religiosarum ..." On 21st May, 1621.

AE Liège Cathédrale Saint-Lambert. A. Sécrétariat. Registre aux conclusions capitulaires 22 (130) 1621–1622, f.57r.
50. AE Liège, Collegiale Saint-Martin 58, f.178r.
51. "Ad supplicationem Virginum Anglarum numero hic personarum plusquam quinquagenario." On 15th July, 1622. AE Liège, Cathédrale Saint-Lambert A Sécrétariat. Registre aux conclusion capitulaires 22 (130) 1621–1622, f.250v.
52. ibid. Registre aux conclusions capitulaires 23 (131) 1622–1624, p.17.
53. AE Liège, Collegiale Saint-Martin 58, f.195r.
54. ibid. f.197v. Already on 3rd January 1620 the Chapter had decided on two Canons, Heusden and Mernier, as intermediaries. ibid. ff.64r–65r. Canon Thomas Goddeus a Sarto died in 1681. A E Liège, Collégiale Saint-Martin 84, Clauses extraites du livreaux testaments 1510–1759, f.36rv.
55. AE Liège, Collégiale Saint-Martin 58, f.199v.
56. Fr Vitelleschi to Fr Vice Provincial Blount on 17th July 1621. ARSI Rome, Anglia 1/I, f.142v.
57. ibid. f.144v.
58. On 9th October Fr Vitelleschi expressed his joy to Fr Blount at Fr Silisdon's arrival in Belgium. ibid. f.145v. Fr Silisdon remained in Liège until the end of 1628. He was Rector in Watten. He occupied several positions of responsibility. He was Rector in Louvain, Superior in London, Novice Master in Liège and Watten, Instructor of the Tertians in Ghent and Provincial of the English Province in Belgium from 1646–1650. He died on 28th August, 1659. Foley, Records VI, p.211–212, and Grisar, Ein schwieriger Rechtsfall, p.263, note 25.
59. It was said that he shortened his life by excessive penitential practices. Summarium defunctorum provinciae Anglicanae Societatis Jelsus anno 1659 and 1660, AGR Brussels, Arch. Jésuit. Prov. Gallo-Belg., Carton 31.
60. ARSI Rome, Anglia 1/I, f.148rv.
61. On 23rd April Fr Vitelleschi commented on three letters from the Rector: of 25th February, of 11th and 15th March, ibid. f.156v.
62. Fr General Vitelleschi to Fr Rector Silisdon, on 23rd April, 1622. ibid. f.156v. He wrote to Fr Blount with similar words, ibid. f.157r.
63. Fr General Vitelleschi to Fr Rector Pierre Bouille, on 30th April 1622. ARSI Rome, Gallo-Belg. 1/II, p.766. Fr Pierre Bouille SJ (1576–1641) was a member of the Society from 1592. He became Rector in Dinant and from 1619–1622 Rector of the Walloon College in Liège. ARSI Rome, Gallo-Belg. 24, ff.46v, 63v, 74r, 85r, 92r, 224r, and Delattre: Le collège de Lille = Etablissements II, p.1217–1218. On 27th August, 1622 Fr Vitelleschi thanked Fr Bouille for sending in his report about the Englishwomen on 8th June; unfortunately this has not survived. However he complained also that he had not been sufficiently informed about the matter. ARSI Rome, Gallo-Belg. 1/II, p.789. This admission was, unfortunately, somewhat late.
64. Fr Vitelleschi to Fr Silisdon on 21st June 1622. ARSI Rome, Anglia 1/I, f.158v. Fr Creswell, too, at that time Superior in Watten, wrote concerning the Englishwomen, as did other fathers. On 21st June, 1622, Fr Vitelleschi thanked him. ibid. f.159v.
65. ibid. f.147r. On 6th November Fr General thanked Fr Blount for his help in moving Fr Tomson to Spain and added, that he would summon him to discuss the matter in Rome. ibid. f.147v.
66. ibid. f.149v.
67. Fr Vitelleschi to Fr Blount, 12th February, 1622. ibid. ff.151v–152r.
68. ibid, f.156r.
69. ibid. f.157v.
70. ibid. f.158v.
71. Fr General Vitelleschi to Fr Tomson, ibid. f.166r.

72. On 12. November, 1622. ibid. ff.164v – 165r.

73. Fr General Vitelleschi to Fr Blount on 28th January 1623. ibid. f.168rv. The congregation of the English vice-province, held in May 1622 in London, effected its elevation to the status of Province. On 21st January, 1623, Fr Blount was named as Provincial.

74. Fr General to Fr Provincial Blount, on 8th April, 1623. ibid. f.169v.

75. ibid. f.173rv.

76. " ... Quod scribebat de Virginibus Anglicanis ob debita a creditoribus captis esse sine dolore non legerim, minus tamen molestum fuit, quod existimam inde nullam ad nostros infamiae notam pervenisse, cum credam nunc satis palam omnibus esse Societatem cum illis nihil commune habere ..." ibid. f.167r.

77. AE Liège, Parchemins des Eschevins de Liège. Nr.1578.

78. On 23rd February, 1623. AE Liège, Collegiale Saint-Martin 58, f.208r; Domini annuerunt Dominabus Anglicis triginta sextarious wassindii. Wassin (seigle), rye. Jean Haust, Dict. Liégeois, Liège 1933, p.707.

79. Fr General Aquaviva to Fr Provincial Heren, ARSI Rome, Gallo-Belg. 1/I, p.12.

80. Fr General vicar Alber to Fr Provincial Heren, 21st April 1615, AGR Brussels, Arch. Jésuit. Prov. Gallo-Belg., Carton 32.

81. The order. ibid.

82. Fr General Vitelleschi to the Visitor of the Order, Fr Scheren, 5th May, 1618, ARSI Rome, Gallo-Belg. 1/I, Epp. Gener. p.398 – 399.

83. Fr General Vitelleschi to Fr Provincial Heren on 26th May, 1618, ARSI Rome, Gallo-Belg. 1/II, p.405.

84. On 26th March, 1622, ARSI Rome, Anglia 1/I, f.154v.

85. Stonyhurst Archives, Codex A-J-40.

86. AGR Brussels, PEA 459, f.215rv.

XXI

NEGOTIATIONS WITH POPE URBAN VIII UP TO THE SUPPRESSION OF THE FOUNDATIONS IN THE PAPAL STATES AND NAPLES

The new Pope

Curriculum vitae – character – political leanings – nepotism

It took a long conclave, from 19th July until 6th August, 1623, before Maffeo Barberini was offered the tiara. The new pope, Urban VIII, was born on 5th April 1568 in Florence. After ending his studies in the Roman College, he studied Law in Pisa and after ordination to the priesthood entered on various services in the Church. First he was Referendar in the Commission of Justice and then in that of Grace. In 1602 he was consecrated Archbishop of Nazareth and two years later was appointed Nuntius in Paris. After another two years, in 1606, he was elevated to the purple. Briefly back in Rome, he was made Protector of Scotland, and in 1608 Bishop of Spoleto. There he was an excellent prelate but was appointed Prefect of the Commission of Justice, which meant that he had to move back to Rome. Pope Gregory XV summoned him to the newly founded Congregatio de Propaganda Fide; he may have become acquainted with the Englishwomen and their affairs there.

On that 6th August, 1623, the Roman Catholic Church was presented with a capable pope; he was also relatively young, at fifty six, and of robust health. Urban VIII was highly educated, gifted both poetically and musically, and extremely active, but he had a difficult character. Pastor[1] writes: 'One had the feeling of being confronted with a self-assured, sharply observant man who could not endure contradiction.' Urban VIII was not only extremely cautious and slow in making his decisions, but also distrustful and therefore easily irritated. 'His self-confidence', concludes Pastor,[2] 'was so strong that he disdained to accept, even to hear, another point of view.'

In foreign affairs the Pope showed a preference for France – although he was not in the same league as those two unscrupulous statesmen Richelieu and Mazarin. His lapse in the Thirty Years' War may be explained by his Franco-phile attitude.

At home his nepotism was almost unlimited. His elder brother Carlo became Captain-General of the Papal States, his younger brother Antonio, the Capuchin, was made Cardinal. His young nephew Francesco, too. The same dignity was bestowed on another nephew, Lorenzo Magalotti. Only those Barberinis are named here who play a part in the history of Mary Ward and her Institute. All these nephews gained great prestige and rich benefices. They lacked one thing only: any controlling influence over their benefactor.

It was with this Pope – so totally different from his predecessor Gregory XV – that Mary Ward now had to conduct her affairs. That did not happen at once.

There are proofs that she sought an opportunity to meet Urban VIII,[3] but the founding of two houses prevented this.

Naples

Reasons for founding a house – Fr General Vitelleschi's recommendations – difficulties at first – Susan Rookwood, superior – success of the foundation – the great necessity for a school for the people

It is impossible to explain why Mary Ward planned and established a second foundation so soon after her arrival in Rome. According to the English Vita, it was the result of a divine impulse.[4] As a counterbalance, are Fr Vitelleschi's words of caution: if he had known about it before, he would not have advised this foundation.[5] Apostolic zeal would certainly have been Mary Ward's prime motive; her whole life was devoted to God and his kingdom. But Fr Vitelleschi was right in many respects. The house in Rome was only just finding its feet and the members were lacking most things. Moreover, negotiations with the Curia were making no headway. Naples was 'abroad', it belonged to the Spanish crown. Perhaps Fr Vitelleschi did not know all the difficulties confronting the English women in Liège, or that Mary Ward hoped to close that foundation.[6]

Mary Ward left Rome on 12th May, 1623, going on foot to Naples. Her companions were a member from Rome and a laysister, the priest Henry Lee and Robert Wright, and provisions – 'a small viaticum'.[7] On her arrival Mary Ward found simple accommodation in an inn. She fell ill. Hunger and exhaustion may have brought on an attack of gallstone.

Inspite of his earlier reservations, Fr Vitelleschi sent recommendatory letters to the superior of the house of professed fathers in Naples, Fr Carlo Mastrilli, who had been in office since the beginning of the year.[8] In particular, Fr Vitelleschi praised Mary Ward's piety and the worthwhileness of her proposal. He recommended the Jesuits most warmly to give her assistance, admittedly, in the confessional in the Jesuit church.

The Jesuits could not act as intermediaries with the Archbishop, for Decio Carafa objected to the Institute, and any recommendation would have done more harm than good.[9]

Fr Mastrilli did not react immediately, and Fr General had to repeat his request.[10] This time it was even clearer: 'It is necessary that they are helped, where possible, with means of livelihood without interfering in their affairs. They deserve to be supported because of their exemplary life.' It is more than probable that the house was placed at their disposal because of Jesuit action. Mary Ward stayed a fairly long time in Naples, a sign that initial difficulties kept her there.

How bitterly the Englishwomen suffered from poverty in Naples can be seen from Mary Ward's letter of 16th September, 1623[11] to Barbara Babthorpe in Liège. It is not only the fact that she asked for 30 pounds for Henry Lee, who was starving as they all were, and had hardly anything to wear; she also asked for 20 or 30 pounds from England or elsewhere. When one considers how well Mary Ward knew the Liège situation, it does not take much imagination to grasp the sort of deprivations being endured by the Englishwomen in Naples. There was also the blazing heat. This had such an effect on them that they could not begin to teach in the school as planned. 'To live or die for God is all gain, when he wills it,' Mary Ward said in conclusion. Those words were not written by a well-nourished woman in comfortable circumstances, but by one with an empty stomach in a totally empty house.

The situation improved in the autumn. They probably received larger donations from the people.[12] They also received a great deal of help from the Jesuit procurator, Fr Francesco Corcione. He was their confessor and his solace may not have been only spiritual.[13] By the end of the year the Englishwomen in Naples were even able to send a gold coin to the house in Rome[14] and on 20th January, 1624 they managed three gold pieces for Perugia.[15] It was rare that the Naples' house had anything over for the two houses, in Rome and later for Perugia, but this small measure of support is a sign of their close unity.[16]

Perhaps a significant event during the time of this foundation may be traced back to Fr Corcione. The English Vita states: The house of the Englishwomen in Naples was located in good air − so it was probably a little away from the city centre − but that was absolutely all. The members slept on straw, Mary Ward even when she was ill. When a priest saw their poverty, he went off to a rich lady who was one of his penitents and told her that it was a disgrace that she had so many good beds in her house, while the Englishwomen had to sleep on the ground. So Mary Ward had a bed, at least.[17]

On 15th November, 1623, after installing Susan Rookwood as superior of the new house, Mary Ward returned to Rome.[18] The relationship with the Jesuits in Naples had been used to revitalise the lethargic negotiations in Rome. The Papal Chamberlain, Virginio Cesarini, one of the most capable men in Urban VIII's curia, told his relation Fr Carlo Mastrilli that he was prepared to recommend Mary Ward to the Pope.[19] It is not known if he actually did so.

It was not only at the beginning of the Naples foundation that the Jesuits gave their help; they continued to do so. There are continual expressions of thanks in letters from the Englishwomen, but there are, too, in those of Fr General.[20] By way of return, the members willingly undertook small services for the Jesuits, such as the conveying of letters.

Unwillingly, Bishop William Bishop admitted from England to his agent in Rome that the information of the 'surrounding sisters' (galloping girls) in England had not been exaggerated; they had indeed managed to found a house in Naples.[21] How close Mary Ward remained to this foundation, which had originally presented such hardship, may be seen from the words she wrote to Winefrid Wigmore on 16th April, 1624:[22] 'How is your work proceeding? Is my presence needed or desired by those outside? By whom? Tell me honestly, without thought of my health or illness or any reservations.'

It says much for the Englishwomen that, in spite of their poverty, young women soon asked to be admitted to the Institute. 'Devotes', those who already belonged to a community in the world, would not have been accepted, so this must refer to those who intended to enter.[23]

The first great blow fell on this small but potentially promising community on 25th May, 1624 with the early death of Susan Rookwood, one of the first members, who had followed Mary Ward to the continent.[24]

Some months later, on 27th October, 1624[25] in the same letter in which she gave an account of her audience with the Pope in Mondragone, Mary Ward wrote to Winefrid Wigmore about moving Mary Ratcliffe and Jane Brown to Naples; on 25th January, 1625 she informed her of the transfer of Lucy Shelley.[26] Fr General Vitelleschi had already recommended these three travellers to Fr Corcione on 14th December, 1624.[27]

At the beginning of 1625, Mary Ratcliffe took up office in place of Susan Rookwood; until then Winefrid Wigmore had been vice-superior.[28]

It was to be a short period of office, for in spring of the same year, 1625 came the final blow to the growing community. Pope

Urban VIII ordered the suppression of the house.[29] The English-women's school had soon become very useful to the city, and it is a matter of great regret that it did not have a longer existence.[30]

Perugia

Reasons for founding a house — Fr General Vitelleschi's recommendations — the journey — arrival, fact and fiction — Bishop Napoleone Comitoli — adversaries among the Jesuits — Mary Ward in the spa of San Casciano — brief activity of the members in Rome, Naples and Perugia

The English Life[31] lays the responsibility for the expansion of the Institute in Italy on the shoulders of the Bishop of Perugia, Napoleone Comitoli, who expressed a wish to have a house of the Institute in his episcopal city. He had given a pressing invitation to a hesitant Mary Ward, obtained a dwelling, and had even received the first members in full regalia, having written a poem in their honour.

Some scepticism is needed here, and a comparison with other sources.

It seems that Mary Ward had come to know a lady from Perugia, Ottavia Caimi, widow of a Dr Oddi Sforza, a university professor who had died in 1611. This lady urged her to travel out of Rome, but Mary Ward was ill[32] and had to postpone the journey until the end of 1623.[33] By 13th January, 1624 she had still not decided on a date; an audience with the Pope took precedence.[34]

But the following week, on 18th January,[35] she wrote before daybreak to Winefrid Wigmore that on this very day she had covered the 20 miles — that is 30 kilometres — to Perugia, where objections were soon raised against the project.[36] Two days later[37] Fr General Vitelleschi wrote a cordial recommendation for Mary Ward to Fr Rector Giovanni Maria Camoggi, saying that the Society of Jesus in Perugia might help the 'Donne Inglesi' who taught girls, without becoming involved in their Institute.

The journey was hard; the weather cold, and windy. Whoever has lived through an Italian winter knows the dreaded Tramontana. We know little of the travelling group though Mary Ward[38] names Mother Minister, probably Elizabeth Cotton, Mary Claton and Hester (most likely Hester Claton), all of whom were frail, or at least not in robust health. Consequently, they suffered from the hardships of the journey and did not make rapid progress.

Henry Lee was certainly with them and perhaps Robert Wright as well. The state of health of the travellers was such that they could not undertake long marches, and yet they covered the 180 kilometres between Rome and Perugia in six days,[39] for they arrived on 23rd

January,[40] which implies an average daily stretch of 30 kilometres.

Unlike the Naples' journey, there is a contemporary account of the arrival of the Englishwomen in Perugia – 'Effemeridi Perugine' by Ottavio Lancelotti.[41] His entry for the 23rd January says: 'Certain noble widows from England came on foot from Rome; by their clothing as well as their vocation they were taken for Jesuit tertiaries. Frau Ottavia Caimi, a very pious noble lady from Milan, wife of the famous late Doctor of Law Doddi (Oddi) Sforza, induced them to come here in order to found a school for girls in this town as in others and teach good behaviour and reading and beautiful handwork. Their superior is Maria della Guardia. For some days they were accommodated in the house of Donna Ottavia, then, with the Bishop's permission, they withdrew to San Bartolomeo near Porta Burnea. They will live there on their own means, as they are very rich and of good standing (commodus)'.

It is worthwhile spending a little time on this, to see the full range of phantasy in the earliest statements about the members.

First – the arrival: The women did not travel all the way from Rome to Perugia on foot for reasons of pleasure, but because they were as poor as churchmice and could not have paid for any other type of travel. From their long black clothing, which resembled the Jesuit gown, and the fact that they taught girls, Lancelotti took them to be tertiaries of the Society of Jesus. The author of 'Effemeridi Perugine' had probably heard the 'Jesuitesses' spoken of, but he did not seem to know that the Society of Jesus had no Third Order.

They first stayed with Donna Ottavia Caimi, their negotiator, and then waited for the Bishop to provide their accommodation. This he did with a house and church. In 1615 Bishop Comitoli had closed the parish of San Bartolomeo. He had granted the church and certain houses belonging to it to a brotherhood called 'Dell' Annunciata'. The land with the buildings was to the south of the old town of Perugia, by Porta Burnea. The Bishop may have given the English-women one of these houses. Lancelotti added, moreover, that the Englishwomen would live on their own means, as they were wealthy. He must obviously been ignorant of the true state of their affairs, or else his statement was extremely sardonic.

One thing is true. Bishop Napoleone Comitoli composed a poem for the arrival of the members.[42] In it he sings of Perugia's famous christian history, which in times past had welcomed foreign reli-gious, such as the Japanese Brothers.[43] Now, it continues, Cardinals and other influential personages have recommended the English-women and he, the Bishop, has placed a house and a church at their disposal.[44]

Bishop Comitoli was an educated man. He wrote some poetry, and occasional verses which, while not perhaps revealing a poet, possess a certain historical worth. This is true of the poem entitled

'On the arrival and reception in Perugia of the servants of Christ from England, on the feast of St Constantine, 1624.' This feast was celebrated on 29th January, when a solemn procession made its way through the town.

From these strophes it may be seen that the Bishop was in full regalia because of this procession, in which the Englishwomen must have taken part a few days after their arrival. His ceremonial dress was not, however, for the tired, dusty women who climbed the hill to the town of Perugia on that 23rd January, 1624, when Mary Ward was thirty nine years old.

The Bishop had received them with great kindness. On the very day of their arrival[45] he had sent his chamberlain and his secretary to escort them to a reception in his palace. During the two to three hour conversation, he informed himself about their way of life and teaching methods and was pleased with both. They were again his guests on the following Sunday.

There were shadows, however, in the form of adversaries of the Institute, close to the Bishop.[46]

'Now we are as poor as Job', Mary Ward had written a week earlier to Winefrid Wigmore.[47] The three gold pieces from Naples had provided them with supplies. The house would be habitable only after the Bishop arranged for it to have doors and windows 'hath made yt windows and some dours'.[48]

Then the foreseeable happened after all that effort: Mary Ward suffered another attack of stone. She told Fr Coffin[49] that it was really because of the many lady visitors from town, who had filled the whole room and had stayed over into the afternoon. This last may indeed have been the final straw to the inevitable results of a strenuous journey. Mary Ward, the sober northener, gives a description of the temperamental southern ladies: 'these ladies from Perugia, effusive in their politeness and conversation, are not only articulate but of such endurance that, filling a room, they do not usually come to an end from one o'clock until six, when their customary parting words are: If you need anything at all, dear Lady, count on me. I will help you to the last drop of my blood.'

In spite of these helpful avowals, the situation remained difficult. The Jesuits of Perugia in particular showed little affability to the Englishwomen. Mary Ward wrote to the General about this on 22nd January.[50] Fr Vitelleschi regretted the unfriendliness. A pointer to the Jesuit's attitude is that on the same day[51] Fr General wrote to the Rector, Fr Camoggi, that the Englishwomen could choose their own confessor in the Jesuit church. One can see that here too, far from St Omer and Liège, difficulties arose immediately in connection with the confessional practices of these women. Fr General's attitude, if looked at superficially, was not consistent. On the one hand he was pleased that Rector Camoggi had made it clear to the Bishop that the Englishwomen were independent of the Society of Jesus[52] and on the other, he repeated over and over again his regret at being unable to help them.[53] There is no doubt that it pained the good man to be bound by the constitutions of his Order and perhaps even more keenly by the sharp vigilance of those Jesuits who disapproved of the Institute.

Once again, on 23rd April,[54] Mary Ward wrote to Naples: her health was bad, the gold piece sent from Naples to Rome had been lost; Robert Rookwood[55] was with them in Perugia. She then visited San Casciano between 15th May and 23rd July, to find some relief for the pain of gallstone. On 23rd July[56] she was back in Perugia. To Winefrid Wigmore she expressed her desire to go to Naples before Christmas, but that she was kept in Perugia until October, and then had to spend a short time in Rome.

Her doctor had ordered rest.

The enemies of the Institute — it might have been anticipated — penetrated Perugia too.[57] We might not have known much about the house otherwise. The English Vita[58] names Elizabeth Keyes as a member of the community. On 16th April, 1624,[59] Mary Ward reported to Susan Rookwood in Naples that seven girls had presented themselves for lessons; there were no boarders. On 23rd July[60] she wrote to Winefrid Wigmore that she was considering putting Joyce Vaux in as superior of the young foundation. It is not known if she did so. On 25th April, 1625, Pope Urban VIII suppressed this house, fifteen months after it had been opened.

Before the decree of suppression was known, Fr General Vitelleschi wrote twice to the Rector that he might help the Englishwomen in the matter of a house.[61]

At the end of August,1624, Bishop Napoleone Comitoli died. He was succeeded by Cardinal Cosimo de Torres,[62] no friend of the Institute. From Fr General's words it is clear that the new Bishop did not allow the Englishwomen to remain in the house granted them by his predecessor. There is a hint of this in Fr Vitelleschi's second letter when he tells the Rector that, no matter how others might judge, he could give assistance to the Englishwomen just as he would to other people.

None of the three foundations in Italy were of long duration. In Rome the members worked for two and a half years (October 1622 — April 1625), in Naples for two years (May 1623 — April 1625) and in Perugia only fifteen months (January 1624 — April 1625).

One might ask if there had been any point in founding them in the first place.

The only answer is that Mary Ward could not see into the future. To put the question differently — why were the houses founded?

Mary Ward's Ignatian Institute, which included the work in the English mission, was rejected in Flanders and Liège by most Jesuits and by the Bishop of St Omer. The Roman house was intended to demonstrate their way of living and working without enclosure. It may also be added that these Englishwomen were extremely active people with a horror of remaining idle in the service of the Church and their neighbour during a long period of waiting.

One must not forget that in April, 1623[63] there were thirteen Englishwomen living in the eternal city; these all came from the houses in St Omer and Liège. In the same month the Infanta Isabella Clara Eugenia adjusted her meagre financial support for the members in Rome.[64] Then, virtually the same thing happened as once before, after the collapse in Liège. Two little houses were founded, in Naples in May 1623 and in Perugia in January, 1624, hardly eight months later.

Six months later the Secretary of the Congregation of Propaganda Fide, Ingoli, gave the total of Englishwomen in the Papal States and Naples as thirty.[65] In London alone there were known to be thirty members of the Institute.[66] It is difficult to assess the numbers in Cologne and Trier. Both houses remained small and had little influence.

Now comes a previously unnoticed consequence. After the financial downfall of the house in Liège, which brought about that of St Omer too, the Englishwomen lived in four cities, Cologne, Trier, Rome, Perugia, belonging to the lords spiritual. Material conditions in these houses were extremely harsh. Things were different in the realms of the secular princes, as in Naples, where initial problems had soon been overcome and in England, where they worked in family circles or served with people of similar mind. Sister Dorothy's account has proved that.

In a letter to Barbara Babthorpe,[67] Mary Ward expressed the hope of closing the house in Liège and in the same letter she enquired after the members whom she had summoned south. But she had not closed the house in Liège. On the contrary, as will be seen, she later wished to return there.

Without discounting Mary Ward's zeal for souls and her longing to make the work of the Institute more widely known, it is also possible to see the foundations in Italy as an attempt to obtain less daunting living conditions for the young people who had joined her and her Institute.

The members had, of course, entered the Institute freely and they could have left equally freely, but for the Chief Superior there also remained the huge responsibility of caring for them materially. Nowhere could Mary Ward offer any guarantee of an assured existence, but no other foundation experienced the poverty of those in Liège, where the rage of their creditors exposed them to the dangers of legal action.

Thomas Rant's petition

The first half of 1624

Adversaries of the Institute in Rome: Ambassador Vives –
Ambassador Branthwaite (in Venice) – Agent Bennet – Agent
Rant – the Congregatio de Propaganda Fide – Rant's petition
for the destruction of the Institute – the petition in the
Congregatio de Propaganda Fide – Secretary Ingoli's par-
ticipation – the Congregation's decree for Cardinal Millini

Clear, outspoken hostility is less dangerous than the kind that is concealed and unseen. The English Life makes this clear when it says
that of all Mary Ward's powerful enemies not one of them had the
courage to admit this to her face, or even to appear as one.[68] It
may be that her sincerity, together with the dignity of her person,
commanded their respect. But this unvoiced and invisible hostility
had been a great danger for the Institute in Rome from the very
beginning. As a minor example: in January 1624 Vives became the
Roman representative of the King of the Congo. Soon afterwards he
set up a college in his palace for the formation of black seminarians.
He wrote to the Secretary of State in Brussels [69] that he had turned
down a request from the Englishwomen to have accommodation in
his palace, as his house was intended for the propagation of the Faith
and not that of the human race. This witticism, frivolous in the mouth
of a highly-placed prelate, was received with loud amusement in the
Roman court, as Vives later reported to Brussels.[70] Naturally enough
this somewhat ungentlemanly answer found its way to England.[71]

The trifling episode reveals that Mary Ward and the members of
the Institute had turned to Vives with confidence in time of need,
hoping to pick some crumbs from his well-covered table. They presumably had no idea that the old man had become hostile, or they
could have saved themselves a humiliation.

Far to the north, in Venice, there was another unknown adversary,
Michael Branthwaite, Secretary in the English Embassy in this city
of lagoons between 1621–1623,[72] who trumpeted aloud the current
gossip concerning the Englishwomen. He wrote to the Secretary of
State, George Calvert in London[73] that it was known in Venice that
about sixty Englishwomen were living in Rome, whose superior was a
certain Mary Ward. They were building castles in the air, as the Pope
would never allow them to have a single house on earth, even if they
had sufficient means for it. Later, Branthwaite contradicted himself
when he wrote to Ambassador Dudley Carleton in The Hague[74] that
twelve – not sixty! – Englishwomen were trying to establish a community in Rome on the model of the Society of Jesus, but had been
refused by the Pope.

These foreign women from a heretical country in the north of

Europe, who were so sure of what they wanted, and so tireless of pleading their cause in Rome, were the butt of similar and certainly more important and dangerous stories which created a climate of distrust and disapproval, at first barely perceptible but destined to endure. John Bennet, the agent of the English secular clergy in Rome actually hated the Institute. The Rector of the English College in Rome, Fr Thomas Fitzherbert, said once that this was due to Bennet's attitude towards the Jesuits,[75] and his statement was probably well-founded.

For more than a decade, news about the Englishwomen had found its way across the Channel. John Bennet had not succeeded in bringing the Pope to the point of suppressing the Institute, but his influence had contributed in great measure to the underminining of the Englishwomen's position. In catholic circles in England they were held to be immoral, in Rome, ridiculous.

At the end of 1623 John Bennet left Rome and Thomas Rant, perhaps less temperamental but all the more dangerous for that, was his successor. Rant entered upon a formidable inheritance. The wrangling concerning the government of the English College in Rome, the rehabilitation of those students inimical to the Jesuits and, above all the organisation of an ecclesial hierarchy in England, kept tensions high. Every inch of the way was marked by the constant and hardly edifying proceedings of the secular clergy against the Jesuits.

The Englishwomen probably did not recognize their opponents. Towards the end of 1624[76] Rant wrote to England that they had approached him for a contribution for their superior, who was ill. He had told them that they were in Italy to look for confirmation of a Jesuit invention (namely, their Institute). He had no money for such plans. Such was the brusque, dismissive treatment which the Englishwomen experienced in their poverty from members of the clergy in Rome.

Shortly before his death Pope Gregory XV had established the Congregatio de Propaganda Fide, a sort of papal watchdog entrusted with the guardianship of promotion of the faith. The new Congregation limited its work at first to the countries which had fallen into heresy: to the protestant parts of the Continent, to Anglican England and the Islamic Near East. In the session of 8th March, 1622, Cardinal Odoardo Farnese was made responsible for the propagation of the faith in England and Ireland. The Nuntius in Brussels, whose sphere of work, in the geographical sense, was closest to it, was appointed as his assistant. All the agendas of the Congregation were presented through its bustling, efficient Secretary, Francesco Ingoli. Given certain conditions, the decisions taken had the validity of apostolic constitutions. Other decisions, for which its faculties did not suffice, were reserved to the Pope. In its early years he presided over the monthly discussions.

It was under this new triumvirate – Pope Urban VIII, Secretary Francesco Ingoli and his friend Thomas Rant – that Mary Ward's enterprise moved into a decisive phase of what was to be its short existence. Poison from many veins, collected at first in such accusatory writings as those of Harrison, Sherwood and Kellison, flowed into the artery of the papal administration at the beginning of 1624 with the Petition of the new representative of the catholic church in England.

Rant wrote the request himself. The original lies in the archives of the Congregatio de Propaganda Fide.[77] According to a remark on the back, it was addressed to the Pope and soon reached the Congregatio de Propaganda Fide.[78]

Why did Urban VIII send the petition there, precisely? After all, the matter had been put before the Congregation for Bishops and Regulars in 1622.

When Mary Ward had handed in her Petition, she had asked for papal confirmation of her Institute, a matter which certainly lay within the competence of this congregation. Now, however, Rant was aiming at the suppression of the community because the members were pastorally active in England in work which, it was said, women should not take part because of its attendant dangers. This therefore became a matter concerning England as a missionary country.

As for the contents of his request:

The 'Jesuitesses' (faeminae Jesuitissae) lead a loose life. They run about all over England and associate with men. They refuse to pray in choir or to follow conventual practices and, on the Continent, they train their pupils for just such a daring way of life by the production of plays. In doing so they are a threat to the women of England and a scandal to catholics. Might the Pope consider the following suggestions?

1. He should either confirm their Institute as an enclosed Order for teaching girls within the enclosure, or
2. Forbid their pastoral activities in England, as their form of life there is fraught with danger, or
3. Suppress their community as it is, so that they cannot admit any new members, deprive devout girls of their goods and chattels, and rob other Orders of their much-needed candidates.

The suggestions have a crescendo effect: point one demands the confirmation of the Institute as an enclosed Order. That, eo ipso, would have been the end of the pastoral apostolate of its members in England. Point two demands the end of the apostolate in England and point three is an outright request for the suppression of the congregation.

Rant was therefore not lashing out against the teaching and educational work of the Institute – apart from his attack on plays for the pupils – but on the women's apparently unholy influence on young people by catechesis, by their undignified and even immoral practices, such as their life without enclosure or prayer in choir, or wearing a religious habit. He was therefore not attacking the Institute from the point of Canon Law (he would not have got as far in two years if he had) but in one of the two great branches of his own sphere of work – the active apostolate.

Seen from Rant's point of view, it was a clever move. In this way he was able to reach the sharp ear of the Roman Curia.

His petition, which dealt with unauthorized innovations in propagating the faith in a heretical country, was passed on by the Congregatio de Propaganda Fide with unusual speed for Rome, naturally without reference to the other party concerned, and exactly as Rant had written it. However, matters did not proceed as swiftly as he hoped. Even Urban VIII waited for years before he annihilated the Institute with one of his sharpest Bulls. But with this request, the axe had been put to the tree, to bring it down some years later. The request was brief in construction. The dorsal comments however, if not more important, are all the more significant.

The Congregation decided on Rant's first suggestion: the English-women should be compelled to adopt enclosure. Cardinal Giovanni Garcia Millini was charged with consulting the Pope on the matter.[79] Ingoli's supplementary information for Cardinal Millini was considerably more pointed. The writing refers, says Ingoli, to the scandals and improprieties of the Jesuitesses in England, where they roam freely, their behaviour is unwomanly and a disgrace to the catholic faith, for they consort with young men. They have sought out the richest young girls for their Institute, consumed their dowries so that these have been left without means and their future placed in jeopardy. To encourage their pupils in audacity, they allow them to produce plays.

These three points were already in the petition, but Ingoli underlined them more darkly by his hints. Ingoli must have taken the next point out of Matthew Kellison's book, that is, attempts by members of the Institute to distance women in England from the secular clergy in order to guide them towards the Jesuits, whom they praised to the skies. They even tempted the serving-staff in the houses of the wealthy in the same way. Three assistants of English secular clergy had written to agent Rant about the matter.

From this, and above all from the very tone of Ingoli's personal additions, it can be seen that Rant, who was in a far better position to gain information from England than was Ingoli, had provided the latter with details which strengthened his request.

The two last comments may originate from other sources, that in the three Italian houses there were thirty Englishwomen. In London, too, there were thirty. The founders of the Institute were the Fathers Tomson, Lee and Talbot, three Jesuits of little education.

On 23rd July, 1624, the Congregatio de Propaganda Fide held its eighteenth session, at which five cardinals were present.[80] Even less accurate statements were written into the report: the Fathers Campion, Lee and Talbot founded the Institute in England. It was from there that the missionary 'Jesuitesses' came to Belgium, Rome, Naples and Perugia, where they taught and educated girls. The Congregation's decree was sent off to Cardinal Millini.[81] One might ask why to this cardinal in particular? Perhaps it was in connection with his office as General Vicar of Rome. The suppression of the Institute – and this was both sought and expected – devolved upon this man, probably the Englishwomen's greatest adversary in Rome.

As far as is known, there is no written record of Cardinal Millini's conversation with the Pope. His attitude towards the Jesuits remains equivocal. Even as an opponent of the Englishwomen, precise evidence is elusive. His notes, which are not carefully dated, give only a few facts about the turn of events.[82]

The Englishwomen, of course, learnt nothing of all this. Mary Ward was undergoing a cure in San Casciano. It was 23rd July before she was once more in Perugia.[83]

The audience in Mondragone

October, 1624

Mary Ward before Urban VIII, speaking without fear – her request for confirmation of her Institute – the Pope's noncommittal answer

Anyone looking at the magnificent building of Mondragone, near Frascati, can hazard some guess at the luxurious life of the Papal court in those days. Today the badly neglected building lies in the middle of extensive grounds, and on clear days, both east and westwards, the sea is visible as a narrow, glittering strip. In those days this peaceful estate belonged to Cardinal Scipio Borghese, who had placed it at the Pope's disposal for his period of convalescence. Urban VIII stayed in Mondragone from 17th to 30th October.[84]

No one knew of Mary Ward's preparations for a journey to Frascati, which took place soon after the Pope's departure from Rome. Neither the Jesuits nor the members were informed of it, with the exception of Margaret Horde, Elizabeth Cotton and Mary Poyntz, who were to accompany her. This visit to Frascati was a risk, even assuming that she did reach the Pope, for Urban VIII was known to be difficult. It must also be assumed that she had an intercessor within the doors of Mondragone, for it was not possible to approach the Pope unannounced. She took with her a Petition and supporting documents, and these were not written in Frascati but in Rome, even if only a short time before.

She received a private audience in the strict sense of the words, for the following description breathes with a personal atmosphere, not an official one.[85] She must have taken one of her companions in with her; she would not have been allowed an audience by herself. That was normal. Only anxiety about the members of her Institute and fear of suppression would have given this otherwise reserved woman courage to make such an address, clearly and simply. She told the Pope that she had come to petition for the confirmation on earth of what had already been confirmed in heaven, namely their way of life (course), which they had now led for sixteen years in various countries, and which Pope Paul V had approved with the promise of confirmation. As confirmation had not yet been granted, parents of members of the Institute hesitated to pay their daughters' dowries, and for this reason they were suffering bitter poverty, especially those who were dying. For sixteen years most Orders had been trying to prevent the establishment of the Institute.

Let us stop for a moment. Mary Ward spoke frankly and with conviction to the pope about the divine confirmation of the way of life which they had led for sixteen years. She was therefore reckoning from 1609, when the first members of the Institute came together in England. When she spoke of the divine confirmation, she was undoubtedly referring to the revelation of 1611 which had given her the spiritual basis for their way of life in the Institute.

It may seem strange that Mary Ward referred to the laconic 'Laudatio' of the Institute by the Council of the Congregation in 1616.[86] But it must not be forgotten that she also knew of the embellishments it had received while in the Bishop of St Omer's office.

It may also appear odd that Mary Ward gave lack of confirmation as the cause of the members' dire poverty, no dowry being offered by their parents for such an insecure form of life. The most driving reason for this was the financial collapse of the Liège foundation only three years before, falling victim to the same lack of dowry. For it was certainly the temporizing attitude of several parents that played a part in the impoverishment of the Institute. The main reason, however, she did not mention, as it would inevitably have done harm to the Society of Jesus. Mary Ward would never have committed such an indiscretion, for that would have meant abandoning part of that Institute which she had once been allowed to glimpse as a spiritual unity of men and women members.

One cannot be certain which Orders Mary Ward charged with opposition to her Institute. As well as most of the Jesuits, the Benedictines had shown little friendliness. Fr Sherwood,[87] with his coarse attacks, was not alone. What sort of answers would Pope

Urban VIII give to these direct and – one might say – incontro-vertible statements? Mary Ward reproduced them:[88] 'He answered mildly that he had heard about us, that he could not, himself, deal with it (namely, confirmation of the Institute), that he knew our concerns were being looked into, and that after his return to Rome he would be informed by the Cardinals who had dealt with the matter.'

Quite apart from her sacrosanct love of the truth, there is no reason why Mary Ward should have distorted or misrepresented the Pope's words when she was writing to her friend Winefrid Wigmore, to whom this letter was addressed. It is also impossible to believe that the Pope gave a lie as an answer. There remains only one inference, therefore, that the Congregatio de Propaganda Fide, after attending to Rant's application, had attempted to bring about the suppression of the Institute in Italy, but had not succeeded. Perhaps Urban VIII, who knew of the model life of these Englishwomen in his city, hesi-tated, and the Congregation's petition was unanswered for the time being. This supposition would explain the sudden silence after the Congregation had charged Cardinal Millini with discussing their decision with the Pope.[89]

To look more closely at the text: Mary Ward pursued the Pope's line of thought, as he had given her a cue by mentioning the Car-dinals, and asked him to entrust the treatment of her business to a special congregation ('somefew, not such a number as before'), since most of the Cardinals who had been occupied with it up till now, could be named as its opponents. They had misunderstood the nature of the Institute and stood by their repudiation of it.

Even if these words were extremely courageous, the concluding sentence, for someone like Pope Urban VIII, was little short of censure. 'I begged him very earnestly to trust the matter to God, for we had entrusted it entirely to God and his Holiness.'

The Pope could be certain that the suppliant was not at all satisfied with the way his Curia operated, still less with their understanding of her Institute. Only a few cardinals should be appointed, who under-stood the Institute well. Today, one would say specialists, familiar with the subject, and far-sighted.

Only a woman who was utterly convinced could have spoken in such a fashion to a pope in the seventeenth century. Only a woman totally given to God would have dared to suggest to this particular pope that he turn to God.

Mary Ward did not report what the pope answered. Perhaps he did not say anything, perhaps it was only his last words that were important, 'His last words were, he would act as God granted him to act.'

This time it was Mary Ward who had given the pope a cue. Finally, she requested that they might be allowed a chapel in their Roman house. Probably they had an oratory only. The pope was evasive.

When he returned to Rome, he would commission Cardinal Millini to see to that. It is true, the latter was General Vicar of Rome, and such matters lay in his province. None the less, Pope Urban VIII was the Bishop of Rome. All in all, Mary Ward was content with the audience. The Pope's attitude had been pleasant, condescending and satisfactory.

It was her mistake that she took this exterior appearance of benevolence as genuine.

At this audience Mary Ward may also have handed in a petition for confirmation of her Institute. There is an undated manuscript in the Fondo Capponi in the Vatican Library, which can be drawn on here.[90] This Petition was written by a woman — certainly a member of the Institute — and bears no date, though the reference to having lived sixteen years according to the Jesuit model gives the correct date of 1624. In essentials this Petition with its request is identical to that which the Englishwomen had handed in to Pope Gregory XV at the end of 1621. Perhaps only its vocabulary had been changed. The text may be referred to in the extract.[91]

The Special Congregation

1624

The Englishwomen's petition to Cardinal Bandini — rejection of the Institute by the Cardinals of the special congregation — letter to Cardinal Borghese — Cardinal Millini's records

Pope Urban VIII did indeed concern himself with the resumption of negotiations. No one can tell if this was a result of the audience granted to Mary Ward, or to forces among his own entourage, or from his own deliberations.

At the end of 1624 a special congregation was set up, consisting of four cardinals: Bandini, Millini, Cobelluzio and Antonio Barberini. The names speak for themselves.

Once again the Englishwomen composed a petition to Cardinal Bandini, in an attempt to support their cause.[92] The letter is similar to the foregoing Petition. Neither the mention of the divine origin of the Institute, nor the 'Compagnia's' broad sphere of work, nor the experience of sixteen years is left out. However, there is a new tone: the Englishwomen now knew of their alleged misdemeanours. It is doubtful if they also knew the land of origin, or from whom the attacks came. They would otherwise not have been able to count England as one of the countries in which they had been able to work without hindrance. It was precisely from there that the sharpest rejection of the Institute came.

They may no longer have hoped for confirmation of their foundations in the Papal States and Naples, for they asked for an Institute
of about a hundred members, as they had done in 1622, in England,
Flanders and Germany. It is an indication to the fact that in 1624
there were not many more than that number of members, for certainly Mary Ward would not have dismissed anyone to attain this
round sum.It has already been seen in Ingoli's statement that there
were thirty members in England, and as many again in Italy. The
remaining houses north of the Alps may have had as many as forty,
from which it may be seen how far the two foundations in Belgium
had diminished in number. On 15th July, 1622, there had been about
fifty members of the Institute in the rue Pierreuse in Liège alone.[93]

Mary Ward's congratulations on the promotion of the Cardinal
at the end of the letter may have been a reference to Bandini's nomination as head of the special congregation.

The Cardinal had probably barely answered, when a few weeks
later[94] Mary Ward made enquiries about the time of the Cardinals'
next session. She confided her disquiet openly: the terrible poverty,
which the Liège community especially was suffering. The members
there were dying, she wrote, because they could not buy the necessary medicine and food for them. With some bitterness the usually
optimistic woman pointed out the length of time they had spent
in seeking Confirmation of their Institute. In that week the Englishwomen had been in Rome for three years and they had as yet
achieved nothing.

By the end of January, 1625, Mary Ward knew that the Cardinals
of the special congregation had spoken out against Confirmation,[95]
but she was determined to continue to defend the Institute. 'Everyone
tells me,' she wrote to Winefrid Wigmore in Naples, 'I should continue with the negotiations, particularly since it (the Institute) has
been condemned to death ('to strike yt dead').'[96] One wonders who
spurred her on. These sentences show that her attitude was not
directed against the Pope, to whom she had shown trust in her
audience in Mondragone, but against those cardinals and influential
people in the papal court who rejected the Institute. She now knew
that Thomas Rant 'who makes himself horse' against the Englishwomen, had handed in a memorial against the Institute to the Pope
and to the Bishops of Naples and Perugia.

Now came the bad news for the others.

A week later Mary Ward wrote to Winefrid[97] that the four cardinals were solidly set against the Institute. Three days later[98] that
the cardinals were doing 'the worst they can' against the Institute,
and in another two days,[99] she wrote that there were no more consultations but that the cardinals had decided 'to doe there worst.'

The rising tenor of the news reflects the rising tension in the ailing
woman.

Negotiations had to be broken off during Lent. Mary Ward wrote on 6th April to Winefrid Wigmore[100] that since the Monday of Passion Week there had been 'hot businesces' between the cardinals and the Englishwomen. This was most probably about the work of the members in England and the demand for them to accept enclosure. One cannot otherwise explain the words 'especially in cases where God only is served and sought'.[101] 'But',she thought, despite the heavy fasting, 'the gain will be ours every way in the end.'[102] In those days of grave and hopeless debate, the Englishwomen sent a long letter to Cardinal Scipione Borghese.[103] This letter, or rather petition, has come down as a copy only; it was most likely written for Winefrid Wigmore. The date on the back — 29th February, 1625 — is wrong, for 1625 was not a leap year. One should perhaps place the letter in March, for it contains references to the imminent suppression. The papal decree was written on 11th April, 1625.

In studying the letter, the familiar history of the Institute can be by-passed: only certain items should be considered. The development of the community was rightly stated here as having taken place in England. It is significant that Infanta Isabella Clara Eugenia, but not Bishop Blaes of St Omer is named as protector of the Institute in St Omer. Count Thomas Sackville, who in 1616 had taken 'il loro Instituto e modo di vivere' to Rome with him, was described as 'una persona . . . di gran santita'. (The Englishwomen were soon to leave out this sentence). The answer of the Cardinals of the Congregation of the Council of 1616 was named, true to facts, as 'certe lettere di raccommandatione'.

The Institute, it continued, was kindly received by Pope Paul V and Gregory XV, but the devil had sown discord. Certain priests and religious had attacked the Institute with its Ignatian charism. That is why Pope Gregory XV had hesitated to confirm it.

The permission to make foundations in Italy was stressed. That was probably on account of the accusation that the Englishwomen had crept in.

Also mentioned was the resumption of negotiations under Pope Urban VIII, negotiations for an Institute which had worked for sixteen years without any suspicion of disfavour in northern countries, in education (edificatione) and pastoral work (aiuto del prossimo) and that without any enclosure. Yet Cardinal Millini had informed them that the Pope and four cardinals of the special congregation had decided not to confirm the Institute, and to banish the Englishwomen from the Papal States (che ogni una andasse . . . a casa sua).

Then follows the Englishwomen's actual request to Cardinal Borghese, into whose charge the church in Flanders had been entrusted since 1609.

The letter found other uses. Other people, not closely connected, were to read it. This emerges from an appendix added by Mary Ward, possibly some time later. She had marked out the essential part of the letter between two lines and she added that only that part was to be shown. This should also show that the text was indeed written to Cardinal Bandini, and with the intention of convincing Cardinal Millini of his mistake. It was he who had attacked the concession to the Englishwomen to live as communities in Rome, Naples and Perugia.

Giovanni Garzia Millini was born in 1563 to an old Roman family. He received the cardinal's hat in 1606 during the pontificate of Paul V Borghese. Under this pope he became General Vicar of Rome (1610) and Vice Protector of England (1612). Mary Ward's unambiguous words indicate this most dangerous though inexplicable opponent of the Institute in Rome.

There remain a few of Cardinal Millini's notes about the Englishwomen in copies of his lost 'Libri Manoscritti'.[104] Unfortunately, the dates are missing but internal evidence from the manuscript gives its time of writing as after 11th April, 1625.

It is worth bringing together the Cardinal's grievances, which were in line with Archpriest Harrison's statement.

The Englishwomen do not only teach Latin, it said, but they preach publicly and devote themselves to apostolic tasks ('far l'ufficio apostolico'). That was not unusual; it was also both ridiculous and dangerous, as scandal could come of it. Such a manner of life ran counter to the decrees of the Council of Trent, which ordered enclosure and retirement for the conventual life of women. It was also unusual and against modesty for women to preach or teach the truths of the faith.

So far the accusations correspond in general with Harrison. But then follow certain considerations from the Cardinal himself. Pope Paul V had recommended this work in 1616 to the bishops and nuntios. Mary Ward, the foundress of the Institute had indeed come to Rome in 1616 (!) where she had merely obtained letters of recommendations for bishops. Neither Paul V nor Gregory XV would have confirmed her Institute.

One can see how the 'Laudatio' was interpreted!

The Englishwomen have now founded a house in Naples and intend to have one in Perugia, but Pope Urban VIII has ordered the suppression of their community there, and their return to Flanders, as many of them have fled out of England.

Neither the many letters of the Englishwomen to Cardinal Bandini, nor their letters to other cardinals or even to the Pope, could have the slightest effect on this rampart of rejection and reproach. Not even the model life-style in Rome, obvious to everyone, was able to do that.

If one compares General Vicar Millini's incriminating items with Archpriest Harrison's objections, the anti-Jesuit attitude of the English secular cleric is lacking in Millini. That is striking. Nor was it important for the Curia in Rome in its conflict with the Institute. Apart from Latin and catechesis in their schools, it was above all the open pastoral apostolate of the Englishwomen which was completely repudiated. Millini had no understanding of the needs of catholics in England.

Of course Millini and the other adversaries of the Institute could appeal to the Tridentine precepts on enclosure, and to the subordinate position of women in society, especially in the Church. Contemporary attitudes must not be forgotten, but it must also be pointed out that the letter of the law had killed an irreplaceable way of life in the suffering Church of its day.

Notes

1. Pastor, Popes XIII, 1, p.251 (German ed.)
2. ibid. p.252.
3. On 29th November, 1623, the papal Chamberlain, Virginio Cesarini declared that he was prepared to recommend Mary Ward to the Pope, but he died in 1624. Cesarini to his relative, Fr Carlo Mastrilli SJ in Naples. "Old Writings" Nr.IX Inst. Arch. Munich. At the beginning of 1624 Mary Ward was considering an audience with Urban VIII. Mary Ward to Susan Rookwood, 13th January 1624. Inst. Archiv. Munich. Letter Nr.14.
4. Vita E, f.26v. An association with the Infanta Isabella Clara Eugenia who was one of the Spanish Habsburgs is not really tenable, as Chambers E II, p.92 thinks, for this had been broken off since the middle of 1623. Neither does the suggestion that the Englishwomen could have worked there without molestation carry weight, for the Roman house was founded precisely to demonstrate their way of life. Moreover, Mary Ward founded a house in Perugia, likewise within the Papal States, within a year.
5. Fr Vitelleschi to Mary Ward, 10th June, 1623, ARSI Rome, Naples. 14/I, f.86r. Nr.557.
6. Mary Ward to Barbara Babthorpe, 16th September 1623: "When shall I hear, ours are out of leig and settled well elsewear and thos on the way I have written for." Inst. Arch. Munich. Letter Nr.9.
7. Vita E, f.27r.
8. Fr Carlo Mastrilli (1550–1624) of noble family in Nola, entered the Society of Jesus in 1569. He had been Superior of the house of Professed Fathers since 21st January 1623. He died on 16th August, 1624. ARSI Rome, Naples. Hist. 73. ff.190r–196r.
9. Fr Vitelleschi to Mary Ward, ARSI Rome, Naples 14/I, f.94r. Nr.609. Carafa had been Archbishop of Naples since 1613.
10. Fr Vitelleschi to Fr Mastrilli, 24th June, 1623, ARSI Rome, Naples 14/I, f.92v, Nr.600. Cf. too Fr Vitelleschi to Mary Ward, 1st July, 1623. ibid. f.98v. Nr.643.
11. Letter Nr.9, Inst. Arch. Munich.
12. Vita E, f.27v. and Fr Vitelleschi to Mary Ward, 7th October 1623. "La pietà di cotestà citta non mi è nova ..." God's service, he said later, presented difficulties initially, but these lessened when patience and humility were shown.
13. Fr Vitelleschi to Fr Corcione, 9th December, 1623. The proviso is here once more: "secondo il modo nostra senza entrar ne'loro disegno e Instituto". ARSI Rome, Naples 14/I, f.169r.
14. /Elizabeth Cotton/ to /Winefrid Wigmore/ Inst. Arch. Munich, Letter Nr.11 of 30th December, 1623.
15. Mary Ward to Winefrid Wigmore, 30th January, 1624. ibid. Letter Nr.16.
16. Mary Ward to Susan Rookwood, 16th April, 1624. The money was lost in transit. ibid. Letter Nr.18. Mary Ward on 10th September 1624 from

Perugia, thanks for 12 crowns. ibid. Letter Nr.22. Mary Ward to Winefrid Wigmore, 20th December, 1624. ibid. Letter Nr. 25. Mary Ward also turned to Winefrid Wigmore for her cure in San Casciano. ibid. Letter Nr. 32. of 26th April, 1625.

17. Vita E, f.27rv.
18. Mary Ward to Winefrid Wigmore, 25th November 1623. Letter Nr.10, Inst. Arch. Munich.
19. Virginio Cesarini to Fr Carlo Mastrilli, 29th November 1623, "Old writings" Nr.IX, Inst. Arch. Munich.
20. Say Fr Vitelleschi to Fr Corcione, 9th December 1623. ARSI Rome, Naples, 14/I, f.169r. Mary Ward to Susan Rookwood, 13.January, 1624, Letter Nr.14, Inst. Arch. Munich; to Winefrid Wigmore, likewise on 13.January 1624. Letter Nr.13. ibid.
21. WA London, Vol.17, p.325.
22. Letter Nr.19, Instit. Arch. Munich.
23. Mary Ward to Winefrid Wigmore: "Our colliges are only for our owne", 23rd July, 1623, Letter Nr.21, Inst. Arch. Munich; and in a letter after 15rd August 1624. Letter Nr.12, ibid.
24. Susan Rookwood was one of the first members of the Institute. She probably travelled to the continent with Mary Ward or soon after, as at her death she is given as having been a member fifteen years. She died aged forty-one, and was therefore born in 1584. She may have worked for a long time on the English mission, where she was superior for three years and imprisoned five times. She was one of the group accompanying Mary Ward on her first journey to Rome in 1621. She was installed as superior of Naples in October 1623. These dates have been taken from a lead panel intended for Susan Rookwood's grave, but replaced by a more durable pewter tablet, put into the grave with the corpse. Inst. Arch. Generalate, Rome. Unfortunately, Winefrid Wigmore's letter about the death of her superior is not extant. It must have been deeply moving. Mary Ward to Winefrid Wigmore, 23rd July, 1624, Letter Nr.21. Inst. Arch. Munich.
25. Letter Nr.23. ibid.
26. Letter Nr.26. ibid.
27. ARSI Rome, 14/II, f.357v, Nr.852.
28. Mary Ward to Winefrid Wigmore, 20th December, 1624, Letter Nr. 25, Inst. Arch., Munich.
29. Urban VIII to the Congregation of Bishops and Regulars. AV Rome, Sacra. Congr. Epic. et Regul. Letters G – O, Anno 1625 s.f. of 11.April, 1625 and its transmission to Cardinal Decio Carafa via the Congregation on the same date. ibid. Registrum Regularium 34, f.109v.
30. In a letter to Winefrid Wigmore dated 10th September 1624 Mary Ward spoke about "lower and higher schools", which should be read as classes for beginners and more proficient.
31. Vita E, ff.29v – 30r.
32. Mary Ward to Winefrid Wigmore, 25th November, 1623. Letter Nr.10, Inst. Arch. Munich.
33. Mary Ward's postscript to Elizabeth Cotton's letter to Winefrid Wigmore, Rome, 30.December, 1623. Letter Nr.11. ibid.
34. Mary Ward to Susan Rookwood, Letter Nr.14, ibid.
35. Letter Nr.15, ibid.
36. "You would marvell to see how much opposition there ys already against that beginninge." ibid.
37. On 20th January, ARSI Rome, Rome, 18/II, f.431r, Nr.68.
38. On 6th February, 1624 to Fr Edward Coffin, Letter Nr.17, Inst. Arch. Munich.
39. Mary Ward speaks of 5½ days in her letter to Fr Coffin.

40. See below, note 41.
41. Biblioteca Augusta, Perugia Ms G 39, p.x.
42. State Library, Munich, Clm 1971, pp.207–208.
43. Four Japanese princes came to Perugia from Portugal in 1585. F.Briganti, Principi Giapponese a Perugia e Foligno = Bolletino delle Regia Deputazione di Storia per l'Umbria, fasc. 3, vol.10, 1904, p.485–493.
44. Neither name nor indication survive. Fr General Vitelleschi probably helped.
45. Mary Ward in her letter to Fr Coffin, see above, note 38.
46. "I dare say the good ould man loves and esteems us very much, and desirs our settlinge in Peruge with his whol hart but he hath people about him and certaine favourits in the town, who will I fear me, keeps him from doinge much for us." See above, note 38. This statement is reported in the English vita.
47. On 30th January, 1624, Letter Nr.16, Inst. Arch. Munich.
48. ibid. Mary Ward expresses herself somewhat more optimistically in her letter of 6th February: after viewing the house, she wished the community in Rome could have such a rent-free house in such good air. She hoped that the house would be ready for occupancy within a week.
49. See above, note 38.
50. Fr Vitelleschi to Mary Ward, 10.February, 1624. ARSI Rome 18/II f.439v. Nr.145.
51. ibid. f.439v, Nr.146.
52. Fr Vitelleschi to Fr Camoggi, 17th February, 1624. ibid. f.441v, Nr.163.
53. Fr Vitelleschi to Fr Camoggi, 2nd February, 1624, Rome. 18/II, f.446r, Nr.206; to Mary Ward, 13th April 1624. ibid. f.457v. Nr.308. Apparently Mary Ward had complained in a letter dated 2nd April.
54. Letter Nr.18, Inst. Arch. Munich.
55. One of Susan Rookwood's five brothers.
56. The dates are taken from the letter.
57. Thus Thomas Rant, the representative of the English secular clergy in Rome, a violent adversary of the Institute, wrote a letter against the Institute to the Bishop of Perugia, as will soon be seen. Mary Ward to Winefrid Wigmore, 25th January, 1625. Letter Nr. 26, Inst. Arch. Munich.
58. Vita E, f.99r.
59. Letter Nr.18, Inst. Arch Munich.
60. Letter Nr.21, ibid.
61. Before 29th October and on 15th November, 1625. ARSI Rome, Rome, 19, f.116v, Nr.264 resp. f.122r, Nr.1013.
62. Cosimo de Torres from Rome. On 5.September 1622 he was raised to the College of Cardinals; on 16. September he became Bishop of Perugia. He died on 1.May, 1642 in Rome. Hier. Cath. IV, p.277, note 16.
63. Vives to de la Faille, 1st April 1623. AGR Brussels, PEA 459, ff.112r–113r, 116r.
64. ibid.
65. Notes for Cardinal Millini, 23rd July, 1624. APF Rome, vol.205, f.442r.
66. ibid.
67. On 16th Sept. 1623. Letter Nr.9. Inst. Arch. Munich.
68. "It is not of small consideration that of all her powerfull, great and violent enemyes, never any one had the courage to professe it to her face or make other semblance then of friendship." Vita E, f.28r.
69. Vives to de la Faille, 18th May, 1624. AGR Brussels, PEA 460, f.144v.
70. On 21st February 1626. ibid. PEA 462, f.74v.
71. Paul Overton to Thomas Rant, 5th March 1625, St v. WA London, B 47, f.194rv. Nr.170.
72. L. Pearson Smith, The Life and Letters II, Appendix III, p.464–465

and A. B. Hinds, Calendar of State Papers and Manuscripts relating to English Affairs 18, Venice 1623–1625, London 1912, p.111, Nr.141 and p.545, Nr.749.

73. On 18th October 1623, St v. PRO London SP 99/25, Part 1, ff.109r–110v.

74. On 19th January, 1624, St v. Lamport Hall, Northampton, JC.3501, likewise to Secretary of State George Calvert, PRO London, SP 99/25/Part 2, ff.139r–140v.

75. Peter Biddulph to John Bennet, 3rd July 1623. Biddulph was then a student at the English College, Rome. In 1623 he was dismissed with four other students because of their rejection of the Jesuits. He continued his studies in Douai and was ordained in 1625 in Cambrai. First he worked on the English mission, then he became Agent for the English secular clergy in Rome. Foley VI, p.291.

76. Thomas Rant to /Paul Overton/, WA London B 25, Nr.102.

77. APF Rome, vol.205, f.435rv. Enclosure: The information of Archpriest William Harrison, ff.436r–441v.

78. Dorsal: Sanctissimo Domino Nostro. In another hand: Alla Congregatione De Propaganda.

79. First as a dorsal comment on the Petition submitted.

80. Decree of the Congregation of 23rd July, 1624. The only names given were those of Cardinal Magalotti and Monti and Fr Dominicus a Jesu Maria. APF Rome, Acta vol.3, ff.122r, 124v.

81. BV Rome, Fondo Capp. 47. f.83rv. The copy is headed: Copia Supplicationis in causa Jesuitrissarum. Apart from two slight grammatical alterations it is a verbatim replica of Thomas Rant's petition. It is not, however, addressed to the Pope who is spoken of as "Sanctissimus Dominus Noster". The writing is composed in "We" form.

82. A copied extract from the missing "Libri manoscritti" of the cardinal. Arch. di Stato Rom. Arch. della Famiglia Santacroce, B.21 (63) f.55rv.

83. She wrote to Winefrid Wigmore from Perugia on this date. Inst. Arch. Munich, Letter Nr.21.

84. BV Rome, Barb. lat. 2818, Diarium Pauli Alaleonis a die 4. maii 1622 ad diem 17 februarii 1630, ff.146v–147r.

85. Mary Ward to Winefrid Wigmore, Rome, 27th October 1624, Inst. Arch. Munich, Letter Nr.23.

86. See p.178.

87. See the Petition he submitted for the suppression of the Institute, p.543ff. Added to which, the letter of Don Tomaso OSB, Monte Cassino, to his confrère Don Anselmo OSB on 21st March, 1622.

88. As above, note 85.

89. See p. 390.

90. BV Rome, Fondo Capp. 47, ff.42r–43v.

91. See p. 321.

92. November–December 1624. BV Rome, Fondo Capp. 47ff. 24r–25v.

93. AE Liège, Cathédrale St Lambert, A. Secretariat, Registre aux conclusions capitulaires 22 (130) 1621–1622, f.250v.

94. On 2nd January, 1625. BV Rome, Fondo Capp. 47ff. 26r–27v.

95. Mary Ward to Winefrid Wigmore, 25th January, 1625. Letter Nr.26. Inst. Arch. Munich.

96. ibid.

97. On 3rd February 1625. Letter Nr 27. Inst. Arch. Munich.

98. Mary Ward to Winefrid Wigmore, 6th February, 1625. Letter Nr.29, Inst. Arch. Munich.

99. Mary Ward to Winefrid Wigmore, 8th February, 1625. Letter Nr. 48, Inst. Arch. Munich.

100. Mary Ward to Winefrid Wigmore, Letter Nr.30. Inst. Arch. Munich.
101. " ... espetially in cases whear God ys only served and sought ..." ibid.
     Apparently the Englishwomen in Rome were still in contact with the former
     Nuntius in Cologne, Pietro Francesco Montorio, who was friendly towards
     the Institute, for Mary Ward wrote in the same letter, Montorio had just
     visited her.
102. "The gaine wil be ours every ways in the end."
103. Letter Nr.28. Inst. Arch. Munich. Dorsal note: A copy of a memoriall sent
     to cardinal Burghese the 29 of february 1625.
104. Archivio di Stato Rom, Arch. della famiglia Santacroce B 21 (63)f. 55rv.
     The reference to the proposed house in Perugia indicates the beginning of
     1624, that of the rejection of the Institute by Urban VIII to the time of
     development after 11th April, 1625.

XXII

SUPPRESSION OF HOUSES IN THE PAPAL STATES AND THE BRIEF CONTINUATION OF THE HOUSE IN NAPLES

Papal States and Naples 1625

The papal decree of 11th April, 1625 – the English agent Thomas Rant and the Englishwomen – implementation of the decrees of suppression, November 1625 – fresh complaints by English secular clergy – the English agent Thomas Blacklow – the Naples' house – attempt to found a house in Catania in Sicily

On 11th April, 1625[1] Pope Urban VIII ordered the Congregation of Bishops and Regulars to suppress the Englishwomen's houses in Italy. As reasons for this the Pope names their type of congregation (vita commune), their following of a rule (alcune loro regolo), their uniform clothing (habito uniforme), and above all, their refusal of enclosure.

It should be noted that reasons of canon law were the decisive factors for the suppression of the Institute, and not its Ignatian charism.

The Congregation wrote forthwith to Cardinal Decio Carafa,[2] Archbishop of Naples. They used almost exactly the same form of words as that in the papal text, and concluded their mandate with the remark that the same commands had been issued for the foundations in Rome and Perugia. It is unlikely that Mary Ward was informed of the papal rescript. The sharp words in her letter to Winefrid Wigmore[3] were directed against unknown adversaries in the papal court, and not against the Pope, who had received her in the October of the previous year in Mondragone with such affability. 'I do not believe,'she wrote, 'that we will be sent away from Rome, for we will have to be expelled, otherwise we shall stay here.' Mary Ward was waiting for the Pope's final word, and she had not received this by 19th April, when she was writing her letter.

Certainly, the Pope's command was not implemented in the spring of 1625. Apart from Mary Ward's letter, this may be deduced from the following considerations:

1. It is remarkable that it is only the papal rescript to the Archbishop of Naples, who lived outside the Papal States, that has been preserved, but not the mandate for the Bishop of Perugia, or even that of the actual suppression of the foundation in Rome itself.
2. The episcopal visitation, awaited by the Englishwomen, which one might assume to be appropriate, never took place.[4]
3. In the middle of May, Mary Ward left for a cure in San Casciano. Under the circumstances, it would have been unthinkable behaviour towards her community in Rome. She had never avoided difficulties.

At this time of paralysing uncertainty, the English agent Rant doubled his intrigues. He read into Mary Ward's second journey to San Casciano the departure of all the Englishwomen from the Papal States.[5] Their Institute might be ludicrous, he thought, but they did not want to relinquish it, because they thought their congregation was good and of divine origin. Some weeks later, Rant committed a culpable indiscretion. Probably by some mistake in delivery, some letters from England for the Englishwomen, addressed to Mary Ward, fell into his hands. Correct procedure would have been to send them on to their addressee with an explanatory note. Rant did no such thing. On the contrary, he sent the letters to Cardinal Lorenzo Magalotti[6] and asked him to show them to the Pope. The letters were addressed to Mary Ward, General Superioress of the Institute. Rant found this offensive. They call themselves religious sisters (religiose), he said in his accompanying letter; members of the English clergy had complained about them several times, and on this occasion, too, were turning to the Pope personally.

Cardinal Magalotti, however, was not in Rome. Rant therefore went to Cardinal Bandini, on 17th June, and showed the letter to him. The Cardinal kept it. Rant remarked on that in a marginal comment on his letter. But not only that, the agent had also shown the letter to others: Giovanni Ciampoli, Secretary of the Latin Briefs, who was a friend of Urban VIII; Cardinal Scipione Cobelluzio; Claude Bertin, Superior of the Oratorians in Rome, and the English Benedictines, Don Anselmo, Don David and Don Robert, probably all opponents of the Englishwomen.[7] The incivility with which the members of the Institute were treated here is particularly offensive.

It is not clear when the school in Rome was closed. Most probably the Englishwomen gave the mothers of their pupils timely warning of the suppression of their house, for these reacted quickly and made representations to General Vicar Millini, to Donna Costanza, the Pope's sister-in-law, and to other influential people.[8]

The sole authority for a date ante quem is the Rant letter to Cardinal Magalotti mentioned above.[9] The marginal note has been referred to. Two other sentences, expressly omitted before, are pertinent: 'Their school will be closed. They may remain in Rome if they wish but must remove their dress. Their houses in Perugia and Naples will be closed.' Rant did not make these notes on 15th June, when he wrote his letter to Cardinal Magalotti, but some time later.

Why did he write them, anyway? They had nothing to do with the contents. As an aide-memoire for himself? Hardly. He kept a diary, and moreover, what he wrote about the Englishwomen's school was under his very nose. But if it was not Rant himself, who else could have an interest in Rant's notes? Who, except himself, would have access to the documentary material of the English agency in Rome? On 26th September,[10] shortly before he left for England, Rant wrote to his successor, Thomas Blacklow, concerning the Englishwomen: 'It is neither enough, that they no longer teach, nor that their particular type of habit is forbidden them and that they may not live in community, for they observe the first point only.'

These notes were attached to the letter shortly before Rant left Rome, when he was looking through the documents for Blacklow. He told Blacklow several times in his 'Instruction'[11] of the importance of studying it carefully.

Viewed from this angle, George Muscott's words about the Englishwomen, written on 5th August from London to Rant, have another import: 'I hope that the Englishwomen in Rome will retire on their own and be warned in good time.'[12]

A decree of suppression had not, at that time, been issued, neither for the community nor the school.

A word about the date of the decree: in 1625, Easter fell on 30th March. The implementation of the Decree of 11th April should have followed after the Easter holidays. But the time after Easter was the worst possible time to move house. At this time of year there were – and still are – the greatest number of pilgrims in Rome, still more in the Holy Year of 1625. Perhaps Cardinal Borghese had considered this fact, certainly the practical mothers of the Roman children had, and taken it up with Cardinal Millini. It was different with the papal mandate of 12th November, which was enacted after the long holidays. The new school year would not yet have begun. One cannot make any separation between school and community in Rome, when it comes to the suppression. Both were decided on 11th April, 1625, but for practical purposes executed only in the autumn of the same year. There were two different dates given: the new school year was not allowed to open; in Italy that was in October. The Englishwomen had to leave their house, that was at the beginning of November.

Once again the English secular clergy aimed a written charge against the Jesuits and Jesuitesses.[13] The Jesuits were taking the benefices of the secular priests in England from them, as they stayed especially in the houses of the nobility. The Jesuitesses who were running about, helped them by recommending the fathers to well-to-do people, and considered the secular clergy incapable.

Cardinal Magalotti read out this objection in a session of the Congregation of the Propaganda Fide. The Cardinals decided to intervene between both parties.

It has already been seen that before Rant left Rome he wrote instructions to his successor[14] in which not only the tasks of an agent of the English secular clergy were recorded but also the very manner in which the hidden agenda could best be achieved. He saw its main work as that of the struggle against the Jesuits. The instructions are therefore for the most part concerned with them. From these emerge some special items, from which only those of importance for the Englishwomen have been taken.

The affair of their Institute should be brought to a conclusion with the Curia. Blacklow was obliged to work for the total suppression of the Englishwomen and to call a halt to every one of their activities. Referring to his successor's working methods, Rant urged steady and forceful action on the Curia. He himself had always carefully recorded important events of his diplomatic activities, and a careful perusal of the documents could only be of advantage to his successor, as he would have to continue the negotiations. Personages with whom Blacklow would have to make contact were listed in a separate enclosure, and their diplomatic usefulness evaluated. This last was destroyed on Rant's command; it cannot, unfortunately, be drawn on here.

The declaration of the departing agent has already been recorded, that neither the rejection of the Institute by public decree of the Special Congregation, nor the closing of their schools, the ban on their type of clothes and communal life was sufficient to bring the activities of the twenty or thirty English women in Italy to a stop. It can further be shown that the main motive of the secular clergy in destroying the Institute was the pastoral activity of the members in England. Bennet and Rant may both indeed have taken up their attitude towards the Institute because of its Ignatian charism. However, the 'matter and the manner' are inseparable from one another.

It is impossible to know how far this renewed attack of the English secular clergy influenced the course of events. Blacklow did not need to do much more, after all, for the final blow fell on 12th November, 1625.[15] On the Pope's orders, General Vicar Millini sent an order to both the landlord of the house in the Corte Savelli and the Englishwomen, that the latter were to leave the house within three days. Every sign of a convent was to be removed; they were to stop teaching. If they did not comply with this order, they would either be placed in an enclosed convent, or imprisoned, or banished from the country, and the landlord, Seno, would have a fine of 500 Scudi imposed upon him. The community of the English-women in Rome – not their Institute – was thereby suppressed.

This second papal mandate, much sharper than the order of 11th April, was carried out with southern tempo. For six days later[16] Pontio Seno gave reasons why it was impossible for him to turn the Englishwomen out into the street at once, especially in the Jubilee Year, 1625. They had already paid their rent in advance. It was a well meant but vain attempt to gain time for the harassed foreigners. The communities in Rome, Naples and Perugia were closed according to instructions, though the Englishwomen might continue to live in the Papal States.[17]

The suppression of the Naples' house could not be effected as rapidly as the Roman authorities wished. Naples, politically con-nected with the island of Sicily, was subject to the Spanish crown. It had to be considered that the Englishwomen had sought pro-tection from King Philip IV, whose aunt, the Infanta Isabella Clara Eugenia, had helped them so often in Belgium.[18] Also, the English-women had the energetic support of the Jesuits in Naples.

Towards the end of 1625, Cardinal Bandini sent the mandate of suppression to Cardinal Decio Caraffa, Archbishop of Naples.[19] It contained the same conditions as for the community in Rome. Should the Englishwomen not comply, they were threatened with enclosure in a convent, and the landlord with a fine of 500 Ducats.

One must differentiate here between the suppression of a reli-gious community, which the Pope has the right to do for good reasons, and compulsory eviction. In secular territory this could not force citizens loyal to the pope to leave their house or accom-modation. This will be seen later, and not only in connection with the Englishwomen.

Mary Ward was urged to go to Naples. On 27th December, 1625[20] she wrote to Winefrid Wigmore that she would like to celebrate her birthday (23rd January) there. It is not certain if she arrived in time, for on 24th January, 1626,[21] Fr Vitelleschi sent a recommendation for her to Fr Corcione, in a letter which had already gone ahead.

Unexpectedly,[22] there is a recommendation for Mary Ward from Fr General to Fr Vincenzo Galletti, confessor in the house of the professed Jesuits in Palermo, who had a good command of English. Mary Ward was intending, it said, to make a foundation of the Institute in Sicily. Fr Galletti might help her, especially with the authorities without, however, becoming involved in the Institute.

Whatever could have induced Mary Ward, one is inclined to ask, to move to this beautiful country? It would have been extremely foreign for Englishwomen. They must have had enough language dif-ficulties in Naples. One must remember that after the suppression of the houses in Rome and Perugia, Mary Ward must have been forced to think of where she could go with the members. To Liège or St

Omer? Both these communities were at the end of their financial
tether. In Cologne and Trier the houses were bitterly poor and could
hardly have accepted refugees from the papal states. To England?
Catholic women were fleeing from it to the Continent, as the Secretary of the Congregatio de Propaganda Fide already knew well
in 1624. Several members of the Liège community had returned to
their own country, it is true, but it is very doubtful if they all had
the means to do so.

The Naples' house was the only one to flourish soon after its
foundation. Perhaps it was still possible to save it, if they did not
at first live like a religious community. How would it be, if the
members of the two suppressed houses could be accommodated in
Spanish Naples and Sicily? Perhaps Fr General had been thinking
along those lines, too, because this time he did not warn Mary
Ward as he had when she founded the house in Naples, but on
the contrary prepared the way for her. It cannot be stated how
much Fr Galletti did in Palermo, but at all events he received a
letter of thanks from Fr General for his efforts.[23]

For more than a year Mary Ward considered a foundation in
Sicily as a possibility for her Institute and its members, and Fr
Vitelleschi helped her during the whole of this time.

Then something happened, which changed her plans geographically by a hundred and eighty degrees.

The Pius Institute once again

1625

*The Englishwomen's morale after the suppression of their
foundations in the Papal States and in Naples — the 'Pium
Institutum' of 1625 — author and time of compilation — justification of the Institute as a 'Pium Institutum'.*

The suppression of the houses of the Institute in the Papal States
and in Naples affected the morale of the members. Until then
they had always managed to hope. Now they were confronted
with questions such as, has the Institute been suppressed, along
with our enclosure-free existence in the Papal States? Is this type
of service of our neighbour and the church, which we have tested
so long by prayer and penance, really to be considered sinful, as our
adversaries have claimed so successfully before the Curia? Perhaps
their enemies had indicated as much. The Englishwomen would certainly have wanted a clear answer to such questions, and awaited
a decision about them from theologians working on their behalf
within the Society of Jesus.

There is an assessment of the Institute which bears neither date nor signature. Only a few inner criteria point to its time of writing and its author.

It was undoubtedly a Jesuit who wrote the 'Votum', for he called the Society of Jesus 'Societas nostra'. He may have been English; the expression 'de nostris Virginibus Anglis' which he used at the end of the work, could simply refer to the subject-matter. It is assumed that it was written in Rome. The author also showed that he was well-informed on Belgian matters, but that was likewise true of his knowledge of the religious situation in the Italian states. He cited Lessius' paper as 'pro his ipsis virginibus quod exstat apud illas'. This would have been put at his disposal by the Englishwomen. But who else could have done that except Mary Ward?

As to dating, one is first alerted by the mention of Urban VIII, proclaimed pope in August 1623. Then follows: 'on 3rd and 6th February, 1625[24] Mary Ward urged Winefrid Wigmore to send the report which Fr Burton had once written about the Institute and which was now in the hands of Fr Corcione in Naples.' For whom else could Mary Ward have needed this particular tract, except for that unknown Jesuit who was writing an authoritative report about the Institute, who quoted the Lessius' document possessed by the Englishwomen, and who, moreover, had the 'Laudatio' of 10th April, 1616 before him? He cited the latter in its entirety. This document, therefore, can be placed shortly before the suppression of the Institute houses in the Papal States and in Naples. Mary Ward could not really have believed in their continuation in the south[25] and she must have been tortured by the problem of where the members could go. She had been able to move some thirty members to Rome, Naples and Perugia. They had all made the same long and wearisome journey south as she had. These human considerations must never be left out of Mary Ward's anxieties; they were present, and a daily burden.

It is perhaps daring to suggest that this report was written at Fr General's request. At all events, Fr General must have been informed, for it not likely that a task involving papers of Jesuit authorship and mentioning the relevant canonical literature could have been written without his knowledge, in the very place where he lived. How otherwise can one view Fr Vitelleschi's attitude, which *after* the decision to suppress the houses of the Institute in Italy and *after* the execution of this decision against the same Institute, granted its members help which had hitherto been unavailable? This cautious man, who always acted on principle, could only have done so out of the conviction that this Institute, despite the suppression of its houses, should have its existence recognized as a Pius Institute in the north. Not long before, Mary Ward had turned once more to Cardinal Bandini with the same question.[26]

Only two manuscripts of this 'Pium Institutum' survive. One, which may be the original, is in the archives of the Society of

Jesus in Rome[27] and a copy is at Stonyhurst.[28] The report had no influence on the negotiations which had been going on in Rome since 1622; it appears not to have left the archives of the Order. Whether the copy arrived in Stonyhurst College archives by way of some leakage or at a later date, is difficult to say. It would be natural enough for it to have been made for the English Jesuits in Liège, and travel to Stonyhurst after the suppression of their novitiate; that was the history of many documents.

Briefly: there is the usual presentation of the Institute's members who educate girls (specialiter vacant institutioni puellarum quae a parentibus ad ipsas mittuntur), who do not wish to be subject to the local bishop, and whose enclosure-free Institute was regarded as inadmissible without papal approbation. We have been surfeited with accounts of it from earlier reports, likewise liberally sprinkled with quotations from canon law. It is asked whether the women have committed mortal sin by living in a religious community without papal permission. The author gives, as had Lessius and Burton before him, several reasons against such an accusation. Something illuminating emerges here: the statement that their Institute is permitted, as long as it is not forbidden by the Pope.[29] The author goes back to Lessius and Burton, when he states that the community could be seen as 'on the way to confirmation'. As a 'pia congregatio' they do not need the confirmation of either the Pope or a Bishop.

So, shortly before the suppression of the houses in the Papal States and Naples, the Jesuits had not moved one hair's breadth in their attitude towards Mary Ward's Institute. They merely agreed to a Pius Institute, a community of women occupied in the education and teaching of girls. In no way was this to be regarded as the Society of Jesus in any shape or name.

Fr General Vitelleschi and the Institute

His dislike of the Institute in Liège and England – his recognition of the communities in the papal States and in Naples – his respect for Mary Ward

In addition to what has been written in the preceding chapter, certain comments are made here on the attitude of the man who was of immense importance to the Institute, Fr General Muzio Vitellschi.

If one compares the warm sympathy he showed to the communities of the Institute in Italy with his cold dislike for those in Liège and England, it is tempting to conclude that he had a Janus-like attitude to the Englishwomen. That would be a mistake.

In the first place, a distinction must be drawn between the Englishwomen and their Institute. Fr Vitelleschi never accused a single member of evil intent or sinful style of life. On the contrary, he felt compassion for all they had to endure.[30] He was still praising Mary Ward's integrity and her purity of intention years later.[31] His first encounter with her in Rome was auspicious[32], and his subsequent meetings were characterised by dignified respect.[33]

It was a different matter where the Institute was concerned. Until he made the personal acquaintance of the Englishwomen at the beginning of 1622, Fr Vitelleschi showed a thorough dislike of their congregation.[34] The objections of the Provincial Fr Blount and the English Jesuits in Belgium against both the women and Fr Tomson were undoubtedly the cause. Perhaps Fr Vitelleschi could not quite fathom the English Jesuits' attitude towards Fr Tomson. Belgium was far from Rome, and communications were unreliable.

After the Englishwomen had settled in Rome, however, a remarkable change was noticeable in Fr Vitelleschi's stance towards the Institute.

To turn for a time northwards. Fr Richard Banks,[35] an opponent of the Institute in England, was praised by the General for his attitude towards the women, which was certainly far from cordial. Already, on 23rd April, 1622, Fr Vitelleschi told the new Rector in Liège, Fr Silisdon, that the Englishwomen had failed in their attempt in Rome. The relief in his words is almost palpable.[36] Fr Bouille, Rector of the Walloon Jesuits in Liège, received a sharp rebuff when he tried to help the Englishwomen there in their desperate situation.[37] The restrictions surrounding the Englishwomen's confession imposed by the London Provincial Congregation has already been mentioned, and Fr General's pleased concurrence.[38]

It was only after the sharp separation had been effected between the Jesuits and the Jesuitesses, particularly in the matter of spiritual direction within the confessional, that Fr Vitelleschi had a free hand.[39]

Thus it was that on 2nd December, 1623, he was able to send a recommendation for the Englishwomen together with a request for assistance – as far as the constitutions permitted – to Fr Rector Wilhelm von Metternich in Trier,[40] and Fr Rector Jacques Deullin of the Walloon Jesuits in Liège.[41]

These examples should be sufficient to show the negative aspect of the General's attitude. How did matters stand in the South? On 10th June, 1623 – therefore fourteen days after his letter to Nuntius Montorio – he recommended Mary Ward to Fr Superior Mastrilli in Naples,[42] of course with the same now-familiar prohibitions against becoming involved in the internal affairs of the Institute.

Matters did not end with this recommendation.

The same attitude is to be seen when the house was founded in Perigua.[43] Here too the Englishwomen, who wished to establish a school for girls, were given a good reference. He even went so far as to grant them freedom of choice of a priest in the confessional of the church of the Order.[44] Yet at the same time Fr Rector Camoggi was praised for making it crystal clear to the Bishop of Perugia that the Englishwomen's community had nothing to do with the Jesuits.[45]

As will soon be seen, Fr General continued to recommend the Englishwomen in their new foundations north of the Alps.

The key to the understanding of this apparently schizophrenic behaviour lies in Mary Ward's words in a letter of 18th January, 1624,[46] written to Winefrid Wigmore in Naples, where the English-women had been helped by the Jesuits at Fr General's request. She writes: "In England ours are despised. Fr General is much more dry. Fr Blount has written to him all that he has in his head."

It should first of all be remembered that Fr Vitelleschi was confronted with a complexity of currents within the Society. The slow-moving revolution in social structures was towards a liber-ating effect on women's place in society. One cannot suppose that the tensions of such an eventful epoch passed by the Fathers of the Society of Jesus without a trace. The history of the Institute of the Englishwomen is a glaring example of this, for within the Society of Jesus there was no agreement on this point. It is remarkable that it is almost solely Englishmen[47] and not only the Jesuits among them, who opposed the Institute. They did not obstruct the teaching and educa-tional activities of the Englishwomen but their hitherto unheard-of work in the English mission. Jesuits, generally of a conservative cast of mind in their attitude to woman and her position in society, strove against the Englishwomen especially in England and Liège, where they were being trained for this work in the missionfield. Fr Blount and Fr Silisdon were among such Jesuits and, moreover, they were superiors.

The conservative Jesuits could, of course, appeal to the strict injunctions of their constitutions which forbade a feminine form of the Order and the regular direction of womens' congregations. Followers of this opinion scented danger even in the act of con-fession, suspecting that assistance or support was being given to such congregations. Several of them feared that these "muliercules" or "little wives" could make the Society of Jesus appear ridiculous. Ridicule has a demoralizing impact.

By no means all Jesuits shared this judgement, however, and the Englishwomen knew who were their benefactors among the fathers of the Society of Jesus.[48] Among these it is not the names of Fr Roger Lee or Fr John Tomson that spring first to mind, whose influence on the Institute cannot be sufficiently affirmed, but rather that of Fr Andrew White from Louvain, who tried to obtain a foundation for the Englishwomen in England,[49] or Fr Corcione in Naples. These refused to become entangled in litiginous dispites, created no Plans, but offered solid help. The most important task for Fr Vitelleschi, as General, was to put up the barricades against the eye of the storm, the allegedly scandalous work of the Englishwomen in England and their foundation in Liège, which had, moreover, brought so much anxiety and harm to the English Jesuit novitiate there. Or so he had been told. Fr Vitelleschi could justify his defensiveness by citing his duty to keep the peace between Jesuit communities and protect the constitutions against these women who had adopted the "Institutum Societatis Jesu" for the basis of their congregation. One might add that in all probability Fr Vitelleschi agreed with them about the place of women in society.

It is the reasons given above, and not schizophrenia, that caused Fr General's repudiation of the Institute in England and Liège, while according them a helping hand in Italy, as he was soon to do on the mid-European scene. In those days the population of the Papal States and Naples was catholic. Here, women who lived according to "the matter and the manner" of the Society of Jesus were not acceptable. Fr Vitelleschi was doubtless of the opinion that much cause for discord in his Order would be removed if the women transferred their aim from England to the Continent. He was soon proved to be right.

Mary Ward and Rome

Her correspondence with Winefrid Wigmore about illness and poverty – prayer in the Roman churches according to the 'Painted Life'

Two facts in particular highlight Mary Ward's life in Rome: her illness and her poverty. There are a series of letters from these years, a mere fragment of the active correspondence she carried on in the interests of her Institute and its members.

In those addressed to ecclesiatics or dignitaries, it is rare that there is any remark of a personal nature. Very probably these letters were written, or at least corrected, by external friends or acquaintances for language reasons.

It is from her letters to Winefrid Wigmore, the only correspondence with a member of the Institute, with a few exceptions, which has survived, that much is learnt of her personal life. This exchange could begin only after Mary Ward left Naples and Winefrid Wigmore had to stay behind, therefore from the end of November, 1623.

The first words[50] she wrote to Winefrid are characteristic of this really humble, great-hearted woman. 'According to the measure of affection which I do and shall always have for you, you may have felt the parting. But my shortcomings were and are so many that my absence can be no loss to anyone except you'. The warmth of her feelings shines through the words. It cannot be mistaken for dependence or faithfulness. For a parallel between men, there is that of Ignatius and his friend Francis Xavier, whom he sent as an apostle to the Far East and never saw again.

She dismisses her state of health in a few sentences. For about ten days a painful abcess forced her to stay in bed, and her visit to Perugia had to be postponed. She was physically weak during the whole of December. Elizabeth Cotton wrote on 30th December[51] to Winefrid Wigmore that Mary Ward was not feeling well, suffering from headaches and stomach pains. Probably the migraines were connected with her sufferings from stone. Elizabeth Cotton laid the blame for it on her long, cold stay in church during the wintry Christmas night, and all her writing. Mary Ward never drove an easy quill; her piles of correspondence were sometimes burdensome. The cold and overtiredness were not conducive to her good health.

In her first letter from Perugia[52] she only talks about their poverty, but her attack of gallstone soon after their arrival has already been mentioned.[53] Her state of health remained poor.[54] Headaches recurred constantly, though she paid little attention to them.[55] She spent some time in San Casciano between 15th May and 23rd July, 1624 at a water cure.[56] The English Vita speaks of her frightful and almost unbearable pain,[57] as one can well believe. The pains of gall or kidney stone are among the worst one can have. Mary Ward must have known that her life-style was unlikely to help alleviate her pain. She remarks jokingly to Winefrid Wigmore that she has recovered well from the cure in San Casciano but her virtue is not strong enough to keep her in health.

On 10th September, 1624,[58] she caught a bad cold and her whole body was in pain. A little later her secretary Margaret Horde[59] was bemoaning her frailness. During the next year she was hindered from writing in greater detail to Winefrid Wigmore[60] on account of weakness as well as lack of time. She went to San Casciano again in the second half of May, 1625.[61] One can see from these references how ill Mary Ward was between the age of thirty five and forty. Added to which were deprivations as a result of their grinding financial plight. They would hardly have been able to carry on without the occasional gold coins from Naples, and probably donations from friends of the Institute as well. But it must have cost the daughter of the old and once wealthy Ward family an effort to have signed receipts for the meagre pittance from the Belgian embassy. She knew that a Jesuit − and therefore a Jesuitess − must be ready to beg when need demands it. Perhaps her signature indicated more humiliation than a word of thanks for a gift from a friend would have done. Everything would have been more bearable, if there had been even a glimmer of hope of success. Her hopes for the confirmation of the Institute remained high during several years of patient waiting; but that was not enough for the Englishwomen. She must have suffered acutely, warm-hearted woman that she was, with her members in both the houses in the Papal States, and the sufferings caused by their deprivations. They too were courageous and above all devoted women, loyal to Mary Ward and the Institute, but the austerity of their life and the gnagging uncertainty persisted.

The spiritual dryness she experienced in both 1624 and 1625 must have been a crushing weight to bear. She once[62] wrote to Winefrid Wigmore about her loneliness: 'I think, dear child, the trouble and long loneliness you heard me speak of, is not far off. Whenever it comes, happy success will follow.' From these few rather diffident words we can measure Mary Ward's ability to conceal or perhaps ignore what were certainly distressing interior sufferings. She was not self-regarding, but directed towards God and his will for her Institute as she knew it. The only source of strength in all her anxieties and troubles, fears and disappointments was God. She sought him in the many and beautiful churches of Rome.

The 'Painted Life' devotes five panels to Mary Ward praying in Rome. Panel 38[63] portrays a revelation on the feast of St Peter in Chains (1st August) 1625. The picture is divided. To the right Mary Ward kneels before a picture of the Madonna and Child. The left half of the picture is covered for the most part with regalia carelessly thrown together: an emperor's crown, a papal tiara, two ducal hats, a mitre, a cardinal's hat, books signifying scholarship, instruments of war, a chest with gold. All of which is worthless trash compared to God, who is represented in the middle high on a throne, and whose light falls on Mary Ward at prayer. The mystical experience of free access to God unburdened by worldly dignities and advantages as the one true way, must have been of great consolation to Mary Ward.

Panel 39 shows Mary Ward in the Church of San Gieronimo de la Carità, in which she asked God for understanding, so that she could use her sufferings most gainfully. Here the mystical experience showed that she would give God greatest pleasure if she could be well pleased with it. Her suffering undoubtedly stemmed from the rejection of the Institute by the church authorities. It is true that God takes no pleasure in our pains, but attempting to carry out his will may cause personal suffering.

On panel 40 Mary Ward, and a companion who turns her face away from the mystical happening, are in the church of Maria del Orto, Trastevere, on 11th April, 1625. She sees her own insignificance and God's omnipotence.

Panel 41 takes us to the church of St Eligio, on 26th June, 1625, where Mary, kneeling before the Blessed Sacrament, was given to understand the value of forgiving the injuries done her by her enemies. This showing strengthened her love of her enemies.

Panel 42,[64] finally, takes the observer to 1626. Mary Ward is in a Marian church – perhaps Maria Maggiore. She had been praying for the Institute and thinking of the words: 'Can you drink the chalice whereof I shall drink?' And she was shown the reproaches and hostility she would have to endure in carrying out God's will. She was ready to do so, with gladness.

The two oldest biographies give several churches where Mary prayed: Madonna di Scala, where she prayed for the cure of Dr Alfonso Ferro;[65] St Michaele in Borgo, to which she made a pilgrimage for forty days, to keep the Quarant' Ore devotion.[66] St Giovanni in Laterano and St Gregorio.[67] Without exaggerating, it can be assumed that Mary Ward and her companions visited most, if not all, of the Roman churches, not as museums but to pray there.

All these pictures of the 'Painted Life' — with panel 32[68] there are six — refer to the years 1624–1626, so to that stretch of time when Mary Ward was undergoing the hardest struggle for her Institute. The texts are full of references to opposition, interior sufferings and conflict. But, however serious their subject may be, there is a total lack of gloom. Every picture shows kneeling figures, one might almost say in a monotone, set against phantastically decorated church interiors. Yet it is precisely this that reinforces what those five years meant for Mary Ward personally. Her great, serene love of God, found expression above all in her loyalty to his commission. And this loyalty entailed certain consequences.

Once, the well-known and saintly discalced Carmelite, Fr Dominicus a Jesu Maria, who had been present as observer at the sessions of the Congregatio de Propaganda Fide, said of Mary Ward and her companions that it was inevitable that they were crushed underfoot. They had to have the same dependence on God as young crows, abandoned by the older ones because they did not have the same feathers.[69]

Notes

1.   AV Rome, S. Congr. Episc. et Regul. Lett. G-O, Annot 1625 s.p.
2.   Likewise on 11.April 1625. AV Rome, S. Congr. Episc. et Regul. Registrum Regularium 34, f.109v.
3.   On 19th April 1625, Letter Nr.31, Inst. Arch Munich. "I doe not thinke we shalbe sent from Rome, because by force we must be expullered or els we stay still hear."
4.   Mary Ward in the letter cited in Note 3.
5.   Thomas Rant to Bishop Richard Smith, 20th May 1625. WA London, vol.19, p.105, Nr.32. The bishop officiated obviously without being recognised as bishop or priest.
6.   On 15th June, 1625. WA London vol. 19, pp.151–153, Nr.50–51. Lorenzo Magalotti, born in Florence like Urban VIII, rose rapidly in the ranks of the Curia and was made Secretary of Briefs. Although Cardinal-Nephew Francesco Barberini was not well-disposed towards him, Magalotti remained friendly with Urban VIII. His sister Costanza was married to Carlo Barberini.
7.   The letter of Don Tomaso the English Benedictine of 21st March, 1621 from Monte Cassino to his confrère Don Anselmo shows that he was

no friend of the Englishwomen. Arch. dell'Abbazia S.Pietro, Cong. Cass.
Perugia SS (PD 42), p.429.

8.   Vita E, ff.27v–28r. Mentioned in Vita I, pp.24–25.

9.   Grisar, Institut, p.201ff.

10.   WA London, vol.19, pp.247–249, Nr.82.

11.   ibid.

12.   WA London, B 47, f.183, Nr.160.

13.   Entry of the Congr. de Prop. Fide on 19th September 1625. APF Rome
I, Anglia 347, ff.230r–231v.

14.   See above, note 10. Dorsal note: "Don David, the Benedictin munck asked
a coppye of the gravamina."

15.   AV Rome, S. Congr. Episc. et Regul. Lett. G-O Anno 1625. s.p.

16.   On 18th November 1625. Arch. del Vicariato Rome, Notari, Silvestro
Spada. 1625, f.1108rv. Entry in the Register.

17.   On 20th May 1627 Mary Ward wrote to Winefrid Wigmore that four
members of the Institute should remain in Rome, as otherwise in case
of sickenss it would be impossible to attend Sunday Mass – this was
in accordance with the custom of going out in twos. Letter Nr.39, Inst.
Arch. Munich.

18.   Already in 1624 the members were in contact with the Vice-King of Naples.
Margaret Horde to Winefrid Wigmore, 30th November 1624, Letter Nr.24,
Inst. Arch. Munich.

19.   AV Rome, S. Congr. Episc. et Regul., Registrum Regularium 34,
ff.386v–387r.

20.   Letter Nr.35, Inst. Arch. Munich.

21.   ARSI Rome, Neap. 15/I, f.77v, Nr.612.

22.   On 12th March, 1626. ARSI Rome, Sicula 9/I, Epist. Gener. 1625–1628,
f.119rv, Nr.803. On the same day Fr Vitelleschi wrote atol Fr Marotta in
Naples also. ibid. Naples. 15/I, f.105v, Nr.30, and to Mary Ward, ibid.
f.107r, Nr.42.

23.   On 14th May, 1626. ARSI Rome, Sicula 9/I, Epist. Gener. 1625–1628,
f.135r. Nr.17.

24.   Letter Nr.27 and 29, Inst. Arch. Munich. On 8th February Mary Ward
wrote to Naples that it was no longer necessary to send it, as she had
already found a copy. Letter Nr.48. ibid.

25.   Letter Nr.26 of 25th January 1625 to Winefrid Wigmore. ibid.

26.   (November/December 1624) BV Fond. Capp. 47, ff.24r–25v.

27.   ARSI Rome, Anglia 31/II, pp.667–674.

28.   Stonyhurst Archives, Anglia VII, Nr.66.

29.   According to the statement of various canonists: "Verum his et similibus non
obstantibus absolute dicendum videtur, licite potuisse hucusque huiusmodi
virgines in sua congregatione aut societate convivere et licite posse convivere
etiam in posterum, nisi prohibeantur a Sede Apostolica." And somewhat
later: " … nemini potest esse dubium, quod hucusque fuerit licita, et sit
futura etiam in posterum, donec ab Apostolica Sede, quod Deus avertat,
reiiciatur."

30.   As, say, the imprisonment of some debt-encumbered Englishwoman in
Liège. Fr Vitelleschi to Fr Knott, 14th January, 1623, ARSI Rome, Anglia
1/I, f.167r.

31.   On 10th June 1623 to Fr Mastrilli in Naples. ibid. Naples 14/I, f.86r.
Nr.555; on 20th January, 1624 to Fr Camoggi in Perugia, ibid. Rome
18/II, f.431r, Nr.68.

32.   See p.325ff.

33.   See p.19ff, p.247ff.

34.   We indicate his active correspondence with Fr Blount and Fr Silisdon.

35.   On 26th March, 1622, ARSI Rome, Anglia 1/I, f.155v.

36. ibid. f.156v.
37. On 30th April, 1622, ARSI Rome, Gallo-Belg. 1/II, p.766.
38. On 18th May, 1622, ARSI Rome, Congr. 57, f.53v – 54r and ibid. on 8th Feb., 1623, ff.55v.
39. See p.???.
40. ARSI Rome, Rhen. Infer. 6. f.105r.
41. ARSI Rome, Gallo-Belg, 1/II, p.870.
42. ARSI Rome, Neap. 14/I, f.86r, Nr.555.
43. On 20th January 1624 to Fr Rector Camoggi, ARSI Rome, Rome 18, f.431r, Nr.68.
44. On 10th February 1624 likewise to Fr Camoggi, ARSI Rome, Rome 18, f.439v, Nr.146.
45. On 17th February 1624 to Fr Camoggi, ibid. f.441v, Nr.163.
46. "In England ours are much contemned. Father Generall much more drye, Father Blunt hath writt him his mind at large." Letter Nr.15, Inst. Arch. Munich.
47. We draw attention mainly to the charges of William Harrison, Robert Sherwood and Matthew Kellison in the written accusations.
48. Thus Fr Provincial Jean Heren to Fr General Vitelleschi on 10th June, 1619. ARSI Rome, Gallo-Belg. 40, ff.26r – 27v.
49. On 14th February, 1622. Old Writings, Nr.VI Inst. Arch. Munich. Still in January 1624 he tried to gain a further confessor for the Englishwomen in Liège from Fr General. ARSI Rome, Anglia 1/II, f.165r and Fr Vitelleschi to Fr White, 20th April 1624, ibid. f.195r.
50. "Accordinge to the measure of the affection I doe and ever shall bear you, you might have some feilinge of our partinge, but my wants wear and are so many as my absence can be noe loss to anie but for your perticuler." Letter Nr.10 of 25th November, 1623. Inst. Arch. Munich.
51. Letter Nr.11. ibid.
52. Mary Ward to Winefrid Wigmore, 30th January 1624. Letter Nr.16, ibid.
53. See p.???
54. On 16th April 1624. Mary Ward to Susan Rookwood in Naples. Letter Nr.18, ibid.
55. Mary Ward to Winefrid Wigmore, 16th April 1624, Letter Nr.19. ibid.
56. Mary Ward to Winefrid Wigmore, 23th July 1624, Letter Nr.21. ibid.
57. " ... for the excessive payne she suffred of the stone." Vita E, f.28v.
58. Mary Ward to Winefrid Wigmore, Letter Nr.22, Inst. Arch. Munich.
59. On 30th November from Rome, Letter Nr.24, ibid.
60. Mary Ward to Winefrid Wigmore, 6th April 1625, Letter Nr.30, ibid.
61. Mary Ward to Winefrid Wigmore, 19th April, 1625, Letter Nr.31, ibid.
62. "I thinke, dear child, the trouble and long lonlynes you heard me speak of ys not farr from, which when soever yt ys, happie succes will follow." On 27th October 1624. Letter Nr.23. ibid.
63. The text: "On the feast of St Peter-in-Chains 1625, in Rome, as Mary was fervently commending her Institute to God, He made known to her that its prosperity, progress and security did not depend upon wealth, dignity and the favour of princes, but that all its members had free and open access to Him from whom proceeds all strength, light and protection." This text is taken almost word for word from Vita E, f.97rv.
64. The text: "In the year 1626, when Mary was praying for the Institute in St Mary's Church in Rome, God reminded her interiorly of the words of Christ: 'Can you drink the chalice that I shall drink?', showing her what great adversities, persecutions and trials she would have to encounter in accomplishing His holy will. She joyfully declared herself ready to accept everything."
65. Vita E, f.99rv.

66. Vita E, f.97r; Vita I, p.53.
67. Vita I, p.53.
68. In the text for this panel Mary Ward is similarly occupied with suffering: "When in 1625 Mary felt inwardly troubled at living without sufferings, trials or opposition ..." These words seem extraordinary to us, as it is precisely in 1625 that Mary Ward's Institute in the Papal States and Naples were suppressed, so she had little occasion to complain of lack of suffering.
69. Vita E, f.30 rv. "He would also often tell us how much she and hers must suffer, and would use those very words: That we must be trampled on and have that dependence on God Almighty like as the litles crowes, left by the old ones because not feathered like themselves ..."

XXIII

THE HOUSES NORTH OF THE ALPS
The old foundations 1623–1625

It is almost exaggerated to talk of houses. Certainly they were there, the foundations in St Omer, Cologne and Trier, and then of course the places where the Englishwomen lived in England, but they are hardly mentioned in the sources. The activities of their members had possibly been reduced to a minimum, at least in educational work on the Continent. It was different in Liège, where the bitter struggle of the English Jesuits against the unacceptable Institute still continued.

Liège

The Englishwomens' confessions and their debts – use of dowries and the validity of their vows – opinion of certain Jesuits concerning the acceptance of further loans by the Englishwomen – their poverty – change of confessor – the Bishop of Liège's letter of protection – recommendation by Nuntius Montorio

On 8th February, 1623[1] Fr General Vitelleschi had approved of the suggestion made by the provincial congregation in London to limit the possibilities of confession by the Englishwomen working in England. It was to have consequences for Liège too, for on 29th April, 1623,[2] Fr Vitelleschi wrote to Fr Blount that Mary Ward had complained to him because the Jesuits had been asking members of the Institute in Liège about their debts, wanting to refuse them absolution on account of them. The Fathers were to stop doing this. He warned Fr Silisdon once more and advised him to appoint other confessors for the Englishwomen.[3]

This shows quite obviously that Fr Vitelleschi did not accept the reasons submitted him for refusing the sacrament of penance – they could have held good for priests too – but that he saw a connection between this and the wretched financial mismanagement of the deposed Rector, Fr Tomson.

The authorities in the Order were not any the less severe, however. On 19th July, 1623[4] Fr Blount categorically repeated his decision that the superiors of the houses in Belgium were to appoint confessors to the Englishwomen.

It was during this time that Lessius' 1622 statement on the Institute was put before certain theologians for a fresh review. There were serious reasons for this. On 8th July, 1623 Gregory XV died; he had not confirmed the Englishwomen's Institute, but then neither had he suppressed it. The possibility of its being confirmed, with moral implications for granting the Englishwomen further loans, appeared even less likely under a new pope, or even of postponing this to a dim and distant future.

And now come the opinions of 3rd August, 1623.[5]

The fathers Giles de Coninck[6] and Peter Wading[7] did not voice any opinion of their own but joined Lessius by appending their signatures to his judgement of 1622.[8] Frs Thomas Southwell[9] and John Crathorn[10] also kept to Lessius for the most part, though they added modifications. For the first question, they thought that the Englishwomen should incur no more debts, as there was so little hope of the confirmation of their Institute, unless a creditor were to grant them a further loan out of consideration for their plight. They also broadened their answer to the second question by adding that the superior of the house should not give out any more money at the command of her chief superior, should certain well-informed advisers be able to convince her to do so.

To the third question they remarked that the confessor could refuse absolution to those Englishwomen who did not follow his advice, unless other counsellors had persuaded them to another point of view.[11]

As can be seen, doors were left open, if only by a chink.

Fr George Morley[12] was more independent and considerably more sweeping in his opinion. Like all individuals in great need, he wrote, the Institute should be allowed to accept money. If the members considered their desire for confirmation of their Institute to be hopeless, they could leave the Institute, to be sure, only in order to better their personal predicament. If, however, they were able to continue their essential work in the Institute by means of a loan, they should improve their situation by doing so. The decision as to whether their Institute should be suppressed or whether they should remain in their community without approval, must be left to suitable men or ecclesiastically appointed arbitrators. But then the Englishwomen should accept their decisions and follow these.

To such consideratons, Fr Morley added certain other pertinent remarks: any decision concerning the suppression or, respectively, the approbation of this Institute, should be dependent on the usefulness of the community. In the first case, that of suppression, then the members should borrow no more money; in the second, they could. The confessor should assess their situation prudently, not from his own judgement, nor that of his superiors − that was a clear hint -but should draw on experienced arbitrators and follow their suggestion. Until then they should act as formerly. The confessor should, of course, warn the women to cut down their expenses to the minimum, but should not refuse them absolution, even if they did not follow his personal advice or the judgement of an expert. Jesuits, continued Fr Morley, were hardly fitting persons to be involved in such a difficult case. The Englishwomen had the right to reject a judgement given them, and to await the Church's dictum. If that were the case then the Jesuit confessor could certainly use his power to withdraw from them.[13]

With similar independence and a certain gentle irony, the great apostle of New England, Fr Andrew White, gave his judgement.[14] The Englishwomen should be allowed to receive loans, he considered, just as a family was allowed to borrow in great need, even if there were little hope of being able to return it. Always presupposing that there was this intention.

The suppression of the Institute could, according to Fr White, be equated with a betrayal of the creditors, for there would then be no prospect of settling their demands. It would be better for these to wait and hope for payment as, with the possible distribution of the property, they would have to be satisfied ·with a small part. Further, he thought that the Englishwomen were acting in good faith and that it was adverse circumstances which had made them fall into debt.

This disgrace, however, should not compel the suppression of their Institute. That would be a greater evil than the acceptance of further loans. Fr White referred to the plight of princes who had fallen into debt, yet accepted loans repeatedly, in order to preserve their dignity or be able to hand out alms. He was right on that score. Secular and religious princes were often in debt for enormous sums. Fr White then pointed out Jesuit houses that were equally heavily encumbered with debt, and could not immediately repay their loans. To bring the apostolate to a halt would do more harm than the acceptance of money, especially as one could trust in God at the beginning of a new undertaking. One can read between the lines as to what he meant by that. At all events, Fr White thought, the decision of the new pope should be awaited, even if the examination of this new type of Institute were to take a long time because of the tenacity of the its members in holding out for a new style of life. If they were to be approved, they would be able to resolve their situation. Fr White added[15] a few other remarks: the Englishwomen should not follow their own judgement, but act in obedience to the decisions of their prudent superiors, who advised them wisely. The confessor should not refuse them absolution, and the women should buy only what was most urgently needed for sustenance.

The questions about novices' dowries were even more pressing.[16] These were:

1. Could the Englishwomen, in this desperate situation of their Institute, accept a dowry from unsuspecting parents and use it, thus inflicting them with a loss
2. Could the novices take vows and offer their dowries to the demands of the creditors?
3. Did not their predicament invalidate their vows? They are not a mendicant order.
4. After taking their vows, they bind themselves to their Institute by means of a civil contract. This is probably invalid, useless and reprehensible, for it leaves it to the Institute and not to cogent reasoning to decide whether to keep a member or dispense her from the vows.

Lessius judged:

1. They were not allowed to use the dowry, as their parents could then sustain a loss and possibly they themselves could be in moral danger.
2. While there was any danger of the dowry being lost because of a loan, the novice should make no vows.
3. The vows taken could not be invalidated, as they were not religious vows.
4. The civil contract, for good reasons, allows the removal, or departure of a member from the community and the dispensation from vows.

Fathers Southwell and Crathorn followed Fr Lessius' answer to the first three questions, but to question four stressed the validity of the civil contract, from which members could obtain a dispensation for good reason.

Fr Morley[17] differentiated between novices who were of age and those who were minors, and said that those Englishwomen who were of age should have the dangers of losing their dowry brought to their attention; the parents of those who were minors should be given advice. If those of age accepted this danger, then they could take their vows. The minors were dependent on parental permission. Furthermore, the difficulties in which the community now found itself should be made clear before the civil contract was entered into. Full knowledge of the situation carried the obligation of agreeing freely to the disposal of the dowry and to remaining in the Institute, in which case the person concerned could be harmed by the contract from a religious point of view.

Father White's opinion was the same.[18]

One wonders whether the Englishwomen knew of these deliberations of moral experts among the Jesuits in Louvain. Probably they simply experienced the humiliating refusal of a confessor.

Fr Vitelleschi in his letter to Fr Silison dated 29th July, 1623[19] showed his gratification at the testimony of one superior of the Institute – we are not informed who this was – stating that none of the Confessors could be said to have transgressed. But Fr General still hesitated to give his opinion.

This unedifying and shaming situation was soon altered. Mary Ward may have told the superior in Liège at this time to change the confessor for the community. On 11th November[20] Fr Vitelleschi expressed his satisfaction that the English women in Liège were now going to confession to the Walloon Jesuits, and he added that Mary Ward should have suggested this earlier.

As in St Omer, the Institute in Liège was now completely rejected by the English Jesuits, although some members may have kept to an English confessor.

If one considers the hopeless situation in Rome, and the two houses in St Omer and Liège, it is clear that the members of the Institute and Mary Ward in particular, were sitting on a time bomb.

The material situation of the house in Liège remained gloomy.[21] From the documents one has the impression that the Englishwomen who stayed there were living on alms, in so far as they had not consumed their dowry. But alms were not always given[22] and even when the beggar's pleas were heard, donations trickled in slowly and thinly.

On 19th April, 1624,[23] they received a bushel of corn from the Chapter of the Cathedral of Saint-Lambert, on 7th February 1625[24] the Chapter of the Collegiate church of Saint-Martin granted them a donation of four Sextaria of beans and rye each. On the same day[25] this Chapter refused Jérôme Gherinx the confiscation of their movable goods. Three weeks later, on 28th February,[26] the Chapter of the Cathedral of Saint-Lambert showed them goodness of heart and allowed them to beg within the cloisters of the cathedral. However, fear of insult and molestation from their creditors was so great that they did not dare go into the street. The Walloon Jesuits were allowed to enter their house for a short time in order to hear their confessions.[27]

The English Ambassador Henry Wotton wrote scornfully towards the end of 1623[28] to Lord Edward la Zouche, that he had nothing more entertaining to report than about the English Jesuitesses in Liège, who think that with the help of St Paul's 'grace', they can share in the work of the church, as though this were women's work. The allusion to St Paul's view of women's position and co-operation in the church, as it is in l.Cor.14; v.33–34, is clear.

From these years there are only two friendly testimonies, which are like a gleam of light against the backdrop of the gloomy Liège relationships: these are the letter of protection from the Bishop of Liège for the Englishwomen in his diocese, and the recommendation of the Englishwomen by the Nuntius of Cologne, Pietro Francesco Montorio.

The Bishop's letter of protection, dated 5th March 1624,[29] exists now only as a copy. The five surviving examples indicate his meaning, which is also emphasized by the form in which it is presented. The Bishop wrote, as had Bishop Blaes of St Omer a few years earlier, a letter patent for his episcopal city, which boasted a flowing title, an introductory statement of contents, and an imposing seal. When one reduces the customary bombastic turn of phrase down to essentials, the letter offers protection and recognition for the Englishwomen.

The Bishop took them under his paternal care, as Bishop Blaes of St Omer before him. The Englishwomen, the Bishop continued, led an impeccable and exemplary life and taught young girls, particularly English girls, the truths of the faith and other useful subjects. Their Institute also, which, under God, was destined especially for the conversion of England, was being taken under his protection until its confirmation by the Pope. He granted its members, who live according to the approved rule of the Society of Jesus, all the privileges which clergy and members of religious orders possess in his see. Their Institute and manner of life are to be seen as ecclesial, (modo pro ecclesiastico habentes) in spite of attacks from others.

The letter was written in Liège and by the Bishop's General Vicar, Jean de Chokier,[30] and also signed by secretary Henri Muno. That does not lessen its value; the General Vicar had episcopal powers and will certainly have acted according to the mind of his Bishop. It is not known if Chokier compiled the letter. The author of the text knew of the recommendations for the Englishwomen, perhaps too the 'Relatio' of the Bishop of St Omer. It is at least remarkable that in both papers there is mention of women who have destroyed England as well as those who are leading the country back to the church.[31]

If the recommendation of the Bishop of Liège is compared with that of the Bishop of St Omer, one can notice an essential difference. Certainly, the chief aim of Bishop Blaes consisted in making known the charge given him by the pope as shepherd of his flock. That has already been referred to. But it dealt rather less with the author's opinion about the Institute.

In St Omer a 'Pium Institutum' was shown, subject to the Bishop, whose members were devout and lived for the good of their neighbour and he, the Bishop, wished to raise it to the status of an Order. Of rules, tasks and names there was no mention. Bishop Blaes in his recommendation of the Englishwomen in Liège at least hinted at their great ability as teachers. The Bishop of Liège on the other hand spoke clearly and simply about Englishwomen, who lived according to the rule of the Society of Jesus, whose Institute was directed to the conversion of England, and who were occupied with the education of English girls and young women.

It is a pleasing though astonishing fact that the Bishop recognized them as Jesuitesses for his diocese — even if this title was not expressly used. The Nuntius of Cologne's recommendation is far more superficial.[32] As an eye witness he could testify to the blameless life of the Englishwomen, who had devoted themselves to the instruction and education of girls from England and other heretical regions. Perhaps he meant Dutch and German girls by this, for Liège borders on both countries, though these foreigners can only have been isolated cases.

Why these two recommendations were written can no longer be established, for they stand alone and seemingly without reason in the middle of the unfortunate happenings in Liège. Only when one looks for a connection and sees that Mary Ward was having an audience with the Pope at this time, does anything become clearer. Admittedly, she could not foresee that the pope was to be in Mondragone in October, 1624 though the precise date is not important. Mary Ward needed support for the audience planned for Urban VIII. Neither of these letters, written with the best of intentions, had the slightest influence on the course of events, whether in Rome nor Liège. The community there was quite literally at its last gasp.

Mary Ward's letter of 2nd January, 1625[33] to Cardinal Bandini has already been mentioned; this contained the news that a short time before some sick members of the Institute had died in Liège, because they could not pay for the medicines ordered by the doctor, or the necessary food supplies. They had probably died of the plague or dysentry, which raged in Liège during the years 1623 and 1624. The death registers of the church of Saint-Remacle en Mont, the parish church of the Englishwomen on Mont Saint Martin, were kept only from 1626. There is no record of how many members had died in the previous years. Those whose death was mentioned by Mary Ward were the first of a sad little group.[34]

Notes

1. With the words 'Valde laudo et commendo". ARSI Rome, Congr. 57, f.55v.
2. ARSI Rome, Anglia 1/I, f.173rv.
3. On 27.May 1623, ibid. f.174r.
4. PRO London, SP 16 ff., 40r–41v, and British Library London, Ms. Add. 5506, p.67.
5. Stonyhurst Archives, A I 40, pp.83–100, Nr.13–17.
6. P. Giles de Conick (1571–1633) was a pupil of Lessius. As his colleague he taught theology for eighteen years in Louvain. Sommervogel II, Sp. 1369–1371.
7. Fr Peter Wading (1583–1644) Irish by birth, taught theology in Louvain from 1623–1630 and later in Prague. In 1641 he was the first professor of canon law in Graz. Sommervogel VIII, Sp.928–951.
8. Stonyhurst Archives A I 40, pp.87–89. Nr.14.
9. Fr Thomas Southwell, vere Bacon (1592–1637) worked for eight years in Liège and several years in Louvain. Sommervogel I, Sp. 755; Foley V, p.520–521, and VI, p.259. In 1629 he was apparently procurator in

Liège, for on 20th March of that year he paid 200 fl. interest on a capital of 3000 fl. which Fr Henry More had borrowed on 3rd April 1617. AE Liège, Couvents, Jésuits Anglais, Registre concernant les Pères Jésuites Anglais pp.225 and 228–229.

10. Fr John Crathorn from Yorkshire, born c.1590, was prefect of studies 1622, and confessor in the English College in Ghent and in 1623 was professor in Louvain. According to Foley IV, p.569, he worked on the English mission in 1642.
11. Stonyhurst Archives A I 40, pp.83–86, Nr.13.
12. Fr George Morley (1585–1664). From 1622–1623 he was professor of theology in Louvain, then active on the English mission, and afterwards professor of theology in Liège, Sommervogel V, Sp. 1326–1327.
13. Stonyhurst Archives A I 40, pp.91–93, Nr.15.
14. Fr Andrew White, born in London in 1579, he studied from 1595 in Valladolid, Seville and Douai. He was ordained in 1605 and went on the English mission. Arrested in 1606, he was ordered to leave the country. In 1607 he was professor of theology in Louvain and Liège. From 1629 he took part in founding a colony in North America (Maryland), to which he travelled again in 1634. He worked among the colonists and the Indians. In 1644 he was brought forcibly back to England with others. He was accused there, but not condemned. However, he was not allowed to return to his missionary territory. He died in 1565 near London. Sommervogel VIII, Sp. 1091–1093.
15. Stonyhurst Archives A I 40, pp.99–100, Nr.17.
16. ibid. pp.95–97, Nr.16.
17. ibid. pp.91–93, Nr.15.
18. ibid. pp.99–100, Nr.17.
19. ARSI Rome, Anglia 1/I, ff.175v–176r.
20. ibid. f.185r.
21. "Briefly, all goes in extremity ill at Leige." Mary Ward to Winefrid Wigmore, 18th January 1624. Letter Nr. 15. Inst. Arch. Munich.
22. On 28th February 1624, the Chapter of Saint-Lambert refused the Englishwomen's request for a donation. AE Liège, Cathédrale Saint-Lamber, A. Sécrétariat, Registre aux conclusions capitulaires 23 (131), 1622–1624, p.201.
23. ibid. p.220.
24. AE Liège, Collégiale Saint-Martin, 59, f.10v.
25. ibid. Jérôme Gerinx died on 11. September 1630 as Dean of the Collegiate Church of Sainte-Croix in Liège. E. Poncelet, Inventaire analytique des cartres de la collégiale de Saint-Croix a Liège, Brussels 1922, p.207, Nr.2474.
26. AE Liège, Cathédrale Saint-Lambert, A. Sécrétariat, Registre aux conclusions capitulaires 24 (1624–1625), f.51r.
27. Fr Vitelleschi to Fr Heren on 20.January 1624 ARSI Rome, Gallo-Belg. 1/II, f.877. On 6th April this favour was rescinded. Fr Vitelleschi to Fr Deullin, ibid. f.894. Fr White's request, to provide another confessor for the Englishwomen was brusquely refused by Fr General on 20th April, 1624. ARSI Rome, Anglia 1/II, f.195r. On 1 June 1624 Fr Vitteleschi stated that he agreed with Fr Heren's decision, that the confessions of the Englishwomen should not take place in their house. ARSI Rome, Gallo-Belg, 1/II, p.901.
28. On 25th November 1623 " ... save the Englishe Jesuitesses at Liège, who by St Pauls leave meane to have theire share in church service as well as in needle-worcke ..." PRO London, SP 14/154, St 80.
29. BV Rome, Fondo Capp. 47, f.81rv; Archives of IBVM Generalate, Rome; Archives of the Metropolitan Chapter, Munich A 258/3; StB Munich Cgm 5393, pp.233–236 and pp.229–233 (in German).

30. Jean de Chokier (1571–1656) Canon of the cathedral of Saint-Lambert and since 1622 General Vicar. J de Theux de Montjardin, Le Chapitre de Saint-Lambert de Liège, III, Brussels 1871, p.247–250.

31. In the Relatio: " ... cum per faeminas in illo regno maxime haeresis inducta fuit et propugnata per faeminas vult etiam oppugnari et tandem extingui." BV Rome, Fondo Capp. 47, ff.76r–77v. In the letter above " ... ad Angliae omnino ... deperditae et depravatae conversionem praedestinatum ut quod faemina distruxit per faeminas reparetur ..."

32. 28th June 1624. Archives of the Metropolitan Chapter, Munich. A 258/3.

33. See p. 395, note 94.

34. In this letter Mary Ward mentioned first of all that parents were hesitating to pay dowries for members of the Institute. The chief reason for this was the heavy burden of debt of the Liège house, about which Mary Ward remained discreetly silent.

XXIV

THE NEW FOUNDATIONS NORTH OF THE ALPS

The predicament 1626

Reasons for the journey north — Recommendations of Fr General Vitelleschi and of Cardinal Gabriel de Trejo

The sources are not clear about the reason for Mary Ward's departure from Rome, which was to be a matter of great importance for the expansion and development of her Institute, however.

If we take the writings in chronological order, the English Vita informs us laconically but truthfully that Mary Ward no longer had any reason to stay in Rome, whereas her presence was needed in the Netherlands and in England. She could return to Rome at any time, if God's service required it.[1]

The Italian Vita is briefer: she left Rome in 1626 because of business (per suoi affari) in Flanders and England.[2]

Later writings reveal a fumbling for more cogent reasons why Mary Ward and her company are to be found at the beginning of 1627 in Munich, far from the west. Pagetti (1662)[3] puts forward reasons of poor health, which demanded a health cure in Flanders. Then maybe, an audience with her great benefactress, Infanta Isabella Clara Eugenia, might have taken her there. Spa was obviously intended here, where Mary Ward had received treatment some years before. In those days Spa was in the diocese of Liège and not Flanders, but that difference would probably not have been registered by the Italian author of the little volume in Rome. What is more remarkable is that he accepted this reason, when Mary Ward could have taken the cure in San Casciano more cheaply and with less exertion. She had found relief for her pain of gallstone there. As for the Infanta Isabella Clara Eugenia, she had broken off all contact after the Englishwomen had made a foundation in Rome. Pagetti's other attempt to explain the journey to Munich, an invitation from the Elector, is not true either.

Twelve years later Bissel[4] confined himself to the statement of the English Vita.

Lohner wrote in 1689 that Mary Ward, after a stay of five years in Italy, wanted to do valuable work in the northern countries.[5] The only question is, where would that have been possible? The deplorable conditions of the impoverished and debt-ridden houses in Belgium and western parts of Germany have been described.

Fridl[6] puts practically everything together, suggesting the Curia's refusal of confirmation of the Institute, the Englishwomen's better possibilities of work in the Netherlands and England, and Mary Ward's zeal for souls, especially for a member of the Institute in Liège who wanted to leave the Institute.

Unterberg[7] stayed on safe ground by simply mentioning the Institute's many enemies in Rome.

Chambers[8] points to Mary Ward's longing to spread the Institute in Germany, slipping in a suggestion about the influence of the much esteemed Fr Dominicus a Jesu Maria with the Emperor and the Elector of Bavaria, but there is no proof whatsoever of this statement. Finally, Panel 45 of the 'Painted Life' shows the tiny group of Englishwomen in a coach, drawn by six strong greys, travelling through an idyllic landscape. A shimmering ray of light from heaven reaches down to Mary Ward and the text: 'When Maria travelled for the first time to Munich, God had made known to her, as she told her companions not far from the Isarberg, that His Highness the Elector would give them a comfortable dwelling in his city and annual support, which happened soon after their arrival.'

None of these statements is satisfactory, for they do not give the reason why these Englishwomen chose this difficult detour over the Alps in the dead of winter, without proper equipment and miserably poor, in order to reach western Europe

Looking at Mary Ward's situation objectively, we see that at the end of 1625 her foundations in Italy had been suppressed; at the same time the members in the oldest houses north of the Alps were suffering unimaginable deprivation. This must never be left out of consideration if Mary Ward's subsequent actions are to be understood. It was she who carried the crushing responsibility of almost a hundred young women who remained true to her and the Institute.

To turn to the statements in the documents.

Barely one year after the suppression of the foundations in Italy, on 8th September, 1626[9] Elector Maximilian I of Bavaria and his wife Elisabeth gave the debt-encumbered novitiate of the English Jesuits in Liège an extremely large donation, namely 200,000 guilders, which, at an interest rate of five per cent annually, resulted in 10,000 guilders for the Jesuits.

Shortly afterwards[10] – the news of this could just about have reached Rome – Fr General wrote to Fr Edward Knott, who was acting as Fr Provincial's representative in Belgium, that Mary Ward had set off from Rome some days previously. He had granted her request to make the Exercises with her former confessor, Fr

Tomson. This seems utterly astonishing, when one considers the precautions the General had taken in 1622 to prevent them even meeting.

From Mary Ward's letter to Winefrid Wigmore, 31st October,[11] a few days before leaving Rome, it can be seen that she intended going to Liège.

But at the same time, 3rd October, Fr General wrote kind recommendations for the Englishwomen in quite another direction, to the confessor of Emperor Ferdinand II, Fr Guillaume Lamormain,[12] to the confessor of Empress Eleonore, Fr Luca Fanini[13] both in Vienna, and to Fr Adam Contzen,[14] confessor of the Elector Maximilian I in Munich. There is no mention of any particular type of work in any of these letters, only a 'negotiorum causa' is mentioned as the reason for the long journey. Naturally enough, the by now stereo-typed prohibition was not omitted: the Jesuits should refrain from interference, particularly with regard to the matter of the adoption of the Society of Jesus by the Englishwomen. Two days later, on 5th October,[15] Cardinal Gabriel de Trejo, who was once cured from a serious illness thanks to Mary Ward's prayers, issued a testimony at the Englishwomen's request. They were travelling, it said, to Germany and other northern countries on business.

What was put under separate cover in Fr General's letters appears here in one sentence: 'To Germany and other countries north of the Alps.' That was correct.

These two facts, according to the sources, the proposed visit to Flanders and the route via Munich and Vienna cannot be seen as separate from one another, but should be closely connected.

We are convinced that Liège and St Omer, those two first houses of the Institute which acted as a springboard for the work in England, were Mary Ward's destination but only after she had tried in Vienna and Munich to obtain financial help for them. It was for this that Fr Vitelleschi wrote his recommendations. No monetary interest should be attributed to the General here − for the settlement of the English-women's remaining debts in Liège would benefit the Society house there − but it should rather be assumed that he wished to free Mary Ward from a moral burden. He, far more than the others involved, would have known how much this upright woman suffered from the fact that it was her Institute, even though innocent, which had caused material damage to the novitiate of the English Jesuits in Liège. For, from her ideal perspective, Mary Ward regarded her Institute as part of the whole body of the Society of Jesus.

It was a breakneck undertaking, such a long journey on foot at that time of year. But perhaps it is this very fact that spells out the terrible situation of the Institute, and of Mary Ward's longing to help her poverty-stricken members. These journeys must never be seen as reckless acts of bravado. Their most impelling cause was always poverty; this was true of her journey to Rome at the end

of 1621 just as it was for her second crossing of the Alps at the
end of 1626.

The Journey

1626–1627

*Departure from Rome – reception in Florence and recom-
mendation of the Grand Duchess Christina to Maximilian I of
Bavaria – Parma and the recommendation of Duchess Marga-
rita – Milan and evidence of Cardinal Borromeo's favour –
Christmas in Feldkirch – Innsbruck and the recommendation
by Archduchess Claudia – Hall in Tyrol – Munich*

On 10th November[16] the small group left Rome. Mary Poyntz,
Elizabeth Cotton and a laysister are named as Mary Ward's com-
panions,[17] together with the priest Henry Lee and Robert Wright.
Panel 45 of the 'Painted Life' shows both men on horseback.

In Italy the way chosen was over Florence, Parma, Milan and
Lake Como. From there it lay directly north, through the Calvinist
region of the Grisons, which was dangerous for catholics, and then
veered towards the east where their route covered a short stretch of
Habsburg territory.

It is not known why the travellers took this route and not the
shorter and less dangerous one in north Italy over Lake Guarda,
through the Adige. Perhaps Mary Ward wanted to meet the
Ursulines in Parma and Milan, as Grisar thought.[18] The toll in
terms of exertion and danger must have been considerable. The
English Vita gives detailed coverage of certain events during the
journey.[19]

In Florence the Grand Duchess Maria Magdalena[20] showed the
travellers great honour, granting them a viewing of the famous
picture of the Annunciation,[21] usually uncovered only on feast
days. This, according to legend, was painted by an angel and now
occupies a small marble shrine in the church of Sa.Annunziata in
Florence.

On 24th November,[22] Grand Duchess Christina, mother-in-law
of Grand Duchess Maria Magdalena and sister of the Electress
Elisabeth of Bavaria, issued a testimonial for Mary Ward. The
Englishwomen were therefore in Florence on that day, for they
would doubtless have accepted this letter personally as they went
on their way.

They took almost fourteen days for the relatively short journey
from Rome to Florence, and probably had to wait a little before
receiving an audience. No recommendation to the Viennese court
was issued in Florence.

Now for the document itself: in this, Grand Duchess Christina recommended the noble Englishwoman Maria della Guardia to her brother-in-law on the occasion of a visit on her way from Rome to Bavaria. The princess commended her pious intention of founding a house of the Order in Bavaria according to the Rule of Saint Ignatius (qualche casa di religiose della professione di santo Ignatio) – with the permission of the Elector – as she had done in Flanders, Cologne and in also Italy.

Even if the recommendation is seen as a general one, as it was, it is none the less surprising that this was the first mention of any foundation of a house of the Institute in Bavaria. Had Mary Ward already intended this before she left Rome? It seems unlikely, as there is nothing in the testimonials taken with her to allow one to conclude this. Mary Ward wanted to travel westwards. From her long letter of 16th February, 1627[23] to Barbara Babthorpe, which will be dealt with later on, it emerges quite clearly that she had not forgotten the needs of the members in Liège even after the friendly reception in Munich, and was weighing up the difficulties attendant on the longer journey.

It must be pointed out that nothing is known of what took place in the audience Mary Ward had in Florence, and nothing either of the views of counsellers behind the scenes, whose influence on the princes one should never under-estimate. It seems more likely that here in Florence, so close to Rome, Mary Ward would point out the difficulties she would encounter if she were to request financial help from the Elector for the houses in Liège and St Omer. The princesses, familiar with and influenced by the realpolitik of the Medici, are more likely to have thought in terms of the Elector's aid for the Englishwomen in his own country, and given their support to that. This seems very probable. The Englishwomen had experienced something similar – nowadays we would call it nationalism – from the Infanta Isabella Clara Eugenia, who was certainly well disposed towards them, until they made a foundation in Rome.

In the Duchy of Parma too they were received with esteem. The Farnese family had ruled there since 1545. Mary Ward was invited to bless Duchess Margareta's children.[24] These were the eleven year old Maria, eight year old Victoria, and the six year old Francesco, later a cardinal.

An even greater honour, in its own fashion, was granted by the austere Cardinal, Federigo Borromeo, nephew of St Charles Borromaeus and Bishop of Milan, where they had arrived on 11th December. The Cardinal rarely gave an audience to women. He would talk to the female members of his family in church only. But, according to the English Vita,[25] he talked to Mary Ward for more than an hour about important matters in his bishopric and invited her to stay longer in Milan. He also spoke kindly to her companions about their vocation in the Institute and their superior Mary Ward.

On 15th December they continued travelling northwards from Milan. On Christmas Eve, 1626 they entered Feldkirch.[26] The 'Painted Life' devotes two panels of its series to their stay here. Panel 43 shows the Englishwomen during Mass, surrounded by the local congregation. The text explains: 'Maria, in 1626, arrived late on Christmas Eve in Feldkirch in the Tyrol; although it was bitterly cold and she was exhausted by travelling, she stayed motionless from eight o'clock in the evening until three o'clock in the early morning, totally absorbed in God.'[27]

Panel 44 shows details taken over by the later writings. Here again the members are depicted kneeling. The text here: 'Maria, in 1626, when she was in the Capuchin Church at Christmas, praying most earnestly for the conversion of the King of England to the new-born saviour, was clearly shown the infinitely tender love with which he embraced him and longed to have him share his glory with him, but that his cooperation alone was lacking.' The English Vita says, however: 'She never said anything further about her experience in prayer.'[28]

However that may be, one can see from the text that even when close to Munich, the Englishwoman in her was still occupied with the conversion of her homeland.

On 4th January, 1627 they were in Innsbruck, the capital of the Tyrol, where they received another friendly welcome.[29]

Only shortly before, in 1625, the ruler of the country Archduke Leopold V had resigned from his bishopric of Passau and Strasburg, and assumed the government of the Tyrol. He had never particularly liked his crozier and never received higher orders. In the year following (1626) he married Claudia di Medici,[30] the sister-in-law of Grand Duchess Maria Magdalena of Tuscany.

It was not the lord of the land, but his wife Claudia who held a reception on 4th January[31] for 'Maria della Guardia, Madre Generale delli collegi delle Signore Inghilese' and her companions. There it was given out that the women were bound to a community by a rule 'di molta perfectione', and were returning to Flanders (se ne ritorne in Fiandra). It was for business reasons that they had to pass via Munich (deve passar da Monaco per alcuni negotii).

It can be seen that here, close to Bavarian territory, no foundation was mentioned, in contrast to the statement made in Florence. Here, more than anywhere, it could surely have been expected. Apparently the young princess, who had only spent two years in her new home, had less objections than her relations in Florence. Even in Innsbruck no arrangement was made for a testimonial to the Emperor in Vienna. In spite of her marriage connections, the young Florentine woman with her Medici influences was not particularly welcome at the Viennese court. The Englishwomen travelled in one of the Prince's coaches and reached Hall in Tyrol,[32] where they were invited to make a long stay by the 'Stiftsdamen'.[33] But Mary Ward was urged onwards. Although it was winter, they travelled north from Hall partly by boat along the Inn and reached Munich on 7th January, 1627.

Munich

1627 – 1628

Elector Maximilian I and the political situation of Bavaria – annual allowance for the Englishwomen – the Paradeiserhouse – opening a school – Jesuits in Munich – their first contact with the Englishwomen – trouble about use of the Holy Cross chapel – discord among the Jesuits – Fr Silisdon's letter – Fr Vitelleschi and the new foundation – 'Jerusalems'

For the next part of Mary Ward's story, no detailed discussion of the prevailing confused political situation in Germany is to be expected as that would be outside the scope of this work; a few remarks are needed for the sake of the context.

In the religious troubles of the sixteenth and seventeenth centuries, which caused so much strife and suffering across Europe, the duchy of Bavaria remained catholic. It became a champion of catholicism under its Wittelsbach overlords, admittedly without prejudice to any of their rights as rulers, or without furthering the centralising plans of the house of Austria.[34]

When Mary Ward arrived in Munich, Elector Maximilian I had already ruled for a period of thirty years. He was born in 1573 in Munich, son of Duke Wilhelm V. He studied for some years in Ingolstadt – he was therefore a Jesuit pupil. He began ruling in 1598. He inherited a country which was a financial ruin, but with economic measures and careful husbandry he improved matters relatively quickly. Politically, he first remained neutral, but later joined the counter-reformers, and in 1609 became head of the catholic league. Emperor Ferdinand II, a brother-in-law by his first marriage with Maria Anna, Maximilian's sister, gave him the position of Elector. Maximilian was both politically and by personality one of the most important princes of his time. His kindliness could sometimes be severe, but never unjust. His first marriage to Elisabeth of Lorraine, the younger sister of the Grand Duchess-Mother Christina of Tuscany, was a happy one.

The city of Munich had experienced much cultural development under Albrecht V and Wilhelm V; under Maximilian I it was counted as one of the most beautiful cities of Germany. In church matters, this capital city of Bavaria was in the diocese of Freising, which dates back to St Corbinian. Freising, not far from Munich, has been the bishops' place of residence for more than a thousand years. (742–802) When the Englishwomen founded their house in .Munich, Veit Adam von Gebeck[35] was bishop; he had been in office since 1618. In 1599 he studied in Dillingen – like his prince, a former Jesuit student. There is nothing in the sources to show that he ever had any connection with Mary Ward or the first members. If one omits St Omer – where the Institute had its beginning but also its end – and Naples, the Englishwomen found themselves for the first time in secular territory. Mary Ward's way of proceeding leads one to suspect that she did not fully understand the authority possessed by a bishop without territory in countries which had remained catholic under princely absolutism. That will be seen again later in Vienna, where there were difficulties with authority.

The Elector not only made a shrewd assessment of the English-women's desperate need, but also the possibilities they offered for the people of his capital. On 21 April, 1627[36] he gave an order to his treasury to pay the Englishwomen 2,000 guilders annually. This sum was estimated as provision for ten people, and was to be paid from 23rd April, quarterly. The treasury registered the order for the sum of 2,000 guilders on 24th April.[37]

It was not only this annual allowance that gave ten members of the Institute a secure existence, but the Elector put the Paradeiser House at their disposal and even restored it for them.[38] The large, spacious house owed its name to its former owner, Christoph Paradeiser, Lord of Neuhaus and Gradisch, chamberlain and adviser to Elector Maximilian and curator of Crandtsperg. In his will dated 1621, Paradeiser had bequeathed this house to the ducal family for pious purposes. Its position in Weinstrasse near Wilprechtsturm was an ideal situation for the Englishwomen's work.

With such prompt assistance, the foundation could expect nothing short of rapid success. Immediately after receiving the first payment of their allowance in April the Englishwomen opened a school for local girls, which soon had a very good reputation and offered excellent instruction to the first boarders and many day pupils. To the primary subjects of the three 'R's, foreign languages were added (Italian, French and Latin) and all manner of handwork. This teaching establishment for girls was the first of its kind in Munich.

Naturally, German-speaking teachers were the first essential, and the Institute had none. Even before the lessons had begun,[39] Mary Ward complained to Winefrid Wigmore about the lack of suitable teachers. She could use twenty, she said, and good ones 'for God will not be served with other than good ones'. Winefrid was to do her best by training the young members.

Barbara Babthorpe in Liège was also to hear of Mary Ward's problems.[40] In Munich, Mary wrote, they are 'crying out for ours', but they can only say that they have not yet had an answer from the superiors. The letter contains suggestions for the transfer of some members. The holy zeal of a holy woman!

It is evident that Mary Ward sank all her energies into making the new foundation a success. For this it was important that German girls should enter soon. Some young members from Munich will be met with in the house in Vienna, which helps to establish dates.

It was delightful but dangerous for the Englishwomen – as time will show – that the Society of Jesus had been in Munich for more than fifty years, and was highly respected. Duke Albrecht V had summoned the first Jesuits to Bavaria. The Order founded universities in Dillingen and in Ingolstadt, which soon achieved fame. In 1559 the Duke consulted with Fr Peter Canisius concerning the beginning of a school in Munich; it was opened towards the end of the same year.

Albrecht V's successor, Duke Wilhelm V, built the beautiful church of St Michael for the Jesuits between the years 1583 – 97, and a large house with a college. A princely letter of exemption (1590) ensured them privileges and the financial basis for their large university establishment, which totalled more than 1,400 students at the beginning of the seventeenth century.

When one remembers that the fathers also practised an active pastoral apostolate, one can well understand why they were held in high repute by the Bavarians. In addition, the Order had great influence on the princely family, as confessors.[41]

Mary Ward had undoubtedly heard in Rome about the influence of the Jesuits in Bavaria, although that was not the reason she had been drawn to its capital. But both the position of the Elector, and Fr General's charge to the Jesuits were of decisive importance for her plans. One must assume that it was the Jesuits who had arranged an audience with the Elector and his wife soon after their arrival, for on 14th January,[42] about a week later, she wrote to Father General that she had met with a good reception in Munich. That may not only have referred to the Jesuits, but also to the princes, for Fr General had sent his recommendations to the confessors of both Maximilian and his wife. In the following weeks Mary Ward continued to send satisfactory reports to the General.[43]

The attitude of the Jesuit fathers in Munich was of equal importance to the Englishwomen, who were now settling down in their city. That was especially so in the case of Fr Walter Mundbrot,[44] Provincial of the Upper German province since 1624, Fr Johann Manhart,[45] from 1623 Rector of the College, and Fr Kaspar Hell,[46] his minister. It is difficult to decide on these men's initial attitude to Mary Ward's Institute. They must have heard of the Englishwomen and their Institute. Even if they had not known about the

Petition in 1621 to the prince, in which Maximilian's advocacy in the matter of papal confirmation of the Institute was sought,[47] something must have travelled along the grape-vine about the problems in Liège.

But none of them could have defended themselves against the advent of the Englishwomen, for one of their most influential members, the Elector's confessor, had received a recommendation for these women from the General at the end of 1626.

Very soon, hardly a month after the Englishwomen had arrived in Munich, the Jesuits received directions from Rome. The General's letter to the Provincial stated that Mary Ward and her companions had come to Munich in order to negotiate their affairs with the Elector and his wife.[48] Then followed Fr Vitelleschi's prohibition: the Jesuits were not to judge the Englishwomen's Institute according to their personal opinion, but on the contrary, show the utmost reservation. They need not be silent about the virtuous lives of the women, but they should allow themselves no further spiritual service to them than to other women in their churches. It was the old, well-known formula, stating the prescripts of their Order.

But something incompatible with this must have happened soon afterwards, as Fr General had to repeat his instruction to Fr Mundbrot on 13th March.[49] A week later,[50] Fr Contzen not only received repeated thanks for his efforts on behalf of the Englishwomen but a warning that he should not be involved in any propaganda for the Institute while, however, praising the women's virtue. On the same day[51] Fr Vitelleschi drew the Provincial's attention to Decree 56 of the seventh General congregation and explained in addition that the Jesuits were not to give the last sacraments to the Englishwomen and that they should behave towards them when visiting just as they did to the Ursulines or the Stiftsdamen in Hall in the Tyrol.

The same old song was being sung yet again. 'Modern' Jesuits, who were interested in the Englishwomen and their Institute, associated with them and were, as a result, reported to their General by opponents.

Soon after this a specific complaint reached Rome: the Englishwomen had been granted the use of the chapel of the Holy Cross by the Elector and his wife.[52] It is not clear if they had made a request to do so. This is a side chapel in St Michael's church, which had been built for the Jesuits. It had always been regarded by the Wittelsbach's as a family chapel, and they therefore considered they had some say in its disposal. Rector Manhart, however, thought otherwise. The affair raised stormy waves. On 17th April,[53] the General asked the Provincial, Fr Mundbrot, to suggestion names for a new rector, as Fr Manhart had behaved imprudently towards the Electress. Fr Vitelleschi made enquiries of Fr Contzen as to what should be done to soothe the vexed princess.[54] At the same time the first rifts appeared among the Jesuits, from which the General was not excluded.[55]

A letter from the General shows[56] that Fr Manhart submitted but had to accept the rebuke that the Jesuits had not followed their General's orders.

The letter to Fr Mundbrot was severe, too.[57] The provincial was to look further into the matter, inquire into the reasons for the Englishwomen's use of the chapel and then try to have a discussion with the princess. Once again: the Jesuits could praise the Englishwomen's way of life, but they should not speak about their Institute, nor recommend it, but practice the utmost reserve.

Probably Fr General was overwhelmed with accusations against the Englishwomen, for within a week[58] he felt it necessary to repeat his instruction to the provincial that the Jesuits in Munich were not to give the last sacraments to the Englishwomen in Munich, any more than in Cologne or Trier. Even the Elector's confessor, Fr Contzen[59] was reproached, in that the Jesuits had done more for the Englishwomen than was allowed, or as accorded with Decree 56 of the seventh General Congregation.

The Englishwomen received an order too – in a letter to Fr Mundbrot[60] – to consult their chief superior in future on matters that concerned both themselves and the Jesuits, and not the rulers directly.

The internal squabble continued.[61] Mary Ward in Vienna[62] received a request from Fr General to avoid, if possible, the regrettable state of affairs in Munich.

One thing attracts attention. At the end of 1627, when the Englishwomen had been working for some months in the Paradeiser House, certain of Fr Silisdon's slanderous manoeuvres came to Fr General's ears. The former Rector of the novitiate house in Liège, who was now Rector in Watten, had warned the Elector about the Englishwomen. Fr Vitelleschi demanded explanations, and a justification.[63] He himself, he wrote, had always been impressed by the commendable life of these ladies and supported them, even though he could not approve of their Institute. In Spring, 1628 Fr Vitelleschi once again requested enlightenment about Fr Silisdon's information to the Elector.[64] He did not receive it.[65] Perhaps the case was inconclusively discussed on Fr Provincial Edward Knott's visit to Rome, for the exchange of correspondence about this continued[66].

These internal squabbles appear small and insignificant when compared to the fearful situation of Germany, where lands were being turned into a theatre of war, and whose people had to endure indescribable sufferings. The amount of space granted them here has been in order to show the sort of difficulties the members of the Institute also had to face in Munich, where there was a large community of Jesuits and where the happenings in Liège stalked them like a black shadow.

Relations between the two communities never became entirely pacific. The Englishwomen must have suffered because of it. A sign of this is the cover name which they gave to the enemies of the Institute: 'Jerusalems'.[67]

The expression was fittingly chosen and certainly shows no bitterness or dislike; on the contrary. This can be shown by its connection with scripture, from which it was undoubtedly taken. In his lamentation over the holy city, the Lord said: 'Jerusalem, Jerusalem, you that kill the prophets and stone those that are sent to you! How often have I longed to gather your children, as a hen gathers her chicks under her wings, and you refused!' (Mt.23,37) In another passage, (Lk.19,42) when the Lord looked down on Jerusalem: 'If you in your turn had only understood the message of peace! But alas, it is hidden from your eyes!' Jesus spoke these words with great sadness.

Mary Ward must have known regret, too. The structure and work of the Institute had been shown her so clearly, and she had always founded houses with the best of intentions. But 'Jerusalem' and the 'Jerusalems' had not accepted her, and her endeavours had been falsely interpreted, struck at, and mocked. A world of sadness lies behind that expression, 'Jerusalems'.

In spite of all this, and despite Winefrid Wigmore's transfer to Munich,[68] the Institute's centre of gravity was moved from Naples to Rome. The Englishwomen had worked for five years in the Papal States and Naples.

Before we follow Mary Ward to the Emperor's countries, it seems necessary to draw attention to a problem, in case it should be overlooked. The Munich foundation was to become the cradle of the Institute in Europe. For the first months of its existence, when nothing had changed in its development, one might have asked: what actually is happening here?

The English Vita outlines the princess's rather arbitrary plans when it says: 'Her highness did not want to let her pass, unless with the condition that she return and others (Englishwomen) should settle there. The princess said that she had long planned and waited for what God had now sent her, and this would not be allowed to slip away easily.'[69] Mary Ward wrote much the same in her letter to Barbara Babthorpe on 16th February, 1627. Her letter was in answer to alarming news from Liège. 'God knows,' she said, 'how we will hold out with the money, if I come to you to do business; what shall I do about the money, in order to get from hence, for I must not beg of the Duke and Duchess for that matter, on any account, much less is it a time to suggest the foundations of Liège or Trier.'[70]

These sentences show quite clearly that Mary Ward could not carry out her original plan – the support of the houses in St Omer and Liège and, eventually, those of Cologne and Trier –

after her arrival in Munich, and could not even suggest them. She was simply offered the possibility of beginning a work for Bavaria, when the Ursulines had also wished to make one there and that at the same time.[71] Mary Ward's Institute with its Ignatian charism had been rejected by both the Society of Jesus and the Curia; now, for the first time, it found acceptance in Munich, and paid the fee for admission, to put it bluntly. For its advantages, certainly the expression of goodwill, rested on the favour of the rulers in Bavaria as was also the case soon after in the Emperor's lands. In those days, absolutism in government implied that freedom of decision was confined to the wishes of the prince and the needs of the country. All that the Wittelsbachs and the Habsburgs wanted from the Institute in their countries was the education of girls. They had not the slightest understanding of the apostolate of these women for the conversion of England, still less money for it.

Teaching and education were indisputably important areas of work in Mary Ward's Institute, and were to remain so. But, as has been explained before, they were not its only activity, if this Institute were to remain Ignatian. One wonders whether Mary Ward had seen the danger which must inevitably result for the whole work of her Insitute, when she associated it with the affairs of middle European princedoms. For the further Mary Ward withdrew from the west coasts of Europe, the more she distanced herself from her Institute's point of departure, for which she had once rejected enclosure[72] that is, the conversion of England and with it the active apostolate among adults.

It is doubtful if this woman, who always had 'the matter and the manner' of the Society of Jesus before her eyes, could ever have seriously considered this unilateral orientation of her Institute. It must not be forgotten that she could not have foreseen the further development which is clearly visible to us today. Nor must the impoverished conditions of most members of the Institute be overlooked either. We have tried to show why the foundations in the Netherlands and in western parts of Germany were so rapidly established: Liège would have been unthinkable without the rejection of the Institute in St Omer, and the houses in Cologne and Trier without the collapse of the foundation in Liège. The journey to Rome in the winter of 1621 must be considered together with the predicament of the members of the Institute in Liège. Again, the lengthy negotiations in Rome occasioned or at least hastened the foundation of three houses staffed with members from the beleaguered houses in St Omer and Liège. The houses in Italy were established with such feverish haste that even so reserved a person as Fr General expressed his qualms.[73]

After the suppression of the houses in the Papal States and Naples, the same pattern was repeated just as five years before, when Mary Ward left Liège: in January, 1627 the Englishwomen arrived in Munich and in the next weeks a foundation followed. In July, 1627 we find Mary Ward already in Vienna occupied with setting up the house 'Stoss am Himmel'. At the beginning of 1628 there followed a foundation in Pressburg, and in the summer of the same year negotiations for a house in Prague were set in motion, though these came to nothing. If one counts the attempt in Prague, that comes to four houses within about two years.

No wonder that Fr Tomson, that old friend of the Institute, warned of excessive haste.[74]

It is not only the suddenness of the Institute's development, but the very geographical situation of the new foundations which is significant. Munich was the capital of Bavaria and place of residence of Elector Maximilian I. Vienna was the capital of the Archduchy of Austria and residence of the Emperor; Pressburg, since the siege of Budapest by the Turks, had been the seat of government for all that remained of royal Hungary, and Prague was the capital of Bohemia. A house of the Institute was to exist in each one of the capitals of the most important crownlands of Ferdinand II. It was a strategy for spreading the faith. There would indeed have been great schools established, but there is no way of knowing how the future of the whole Institute would have been shaped, if it had grown deeper roots in these countries. In many places, protestantism had won a hold on the population. The missionary task of the Institute, such as was implemented by them in England, could have been equally fruitful under the best conditions. Incipient signs of this work were there; they will be referred to later.

It must be assumed that Mary Ward, with the help of the Elector and the Emperor, had originally intended to give material help to the houses in Flanders and in Germany. She was forced to change this plan, however, and anchored the Institute still more strongly in those countries where she could count on material help in order to support the foundations in western Europe, and gradually make them self-supporting. In the south she had made the foundation of a house in the secular lands of Naples able to offer such assistance to the houses in the Papal States. These views cannot be supported with documentary evidence from the sources. But there are two facts of great importance in this respect: Mary Ward did not suppress either of the communities in Belgium or western Germany. She herself, years later, when all prospects of continuing the Ignatian Institute had been annihilated, returned to England to work there quietly until her death, true to her principles.

Vienna

1627 – 1628

Recommendation of the Englishwomen by Maximilian I to Emperor Ferdinand II – the Archduchy of Austria – the position of the Imperial residence and its diocese – Nuntius Carlo Carafa – 'Stoss am Himmel' – annual allowance to the Englishwomen – return of Bishop Klesl, Bishop of Vienna, from prison – the first episcopal visitation of the English-women on 17th November, 1627 – Klesl's first attacks against the Englishwomen's foundation.

Barely six months after the effortless opening of the house in Munich, Mary Ward asked the Elector for a recommendation to the Emperor. Maximilian wrote to Vienna about the Institute on 19th June, 1627[75] in an extremely benevolent and warm-hearted letter. He said that Mary Ward wished to travel to Vienna to have an audience with the Emperor, in order to promote the greater growth and development of her Institute. He, Maximilian himself, had been recommended her Institute which was esteemed, and held a good reputation for its education of young girls. The Englishwomen led a blameless life, had begun teaching girls in his city and gave reason to hope for a solid and healthy enterprise. Mary Ward and her companions probably took this letter with them and handed it in personally.

Vienna has always been a fortress from time immemorial, and has kept this character throughout the centuries. The centre of the city, still known as the 'inner city', lay behind protective walls until the middle of the nineteenth century and therefore remained rela-tively small.

Outside these walls stretched broad, undeveloped countryside, which hostile attacks had not left unscarred. Behind those levels lay the suburbs, tiny villages which today have long been engulfed by the city but which, centuries ago, had to be left to the mercy of the enemy. For the enemy was constantly there, the enemy from the East, the powerful migration of the peoples in the early Middle Ages, then the Magyars, the Osman and, since the sixteenth cen-tury, the Turk. It was above all the latter, marching against Vienna for the first time in 1529, who kept the different ethnic groups along the Danube in tension, and incidentally, kept the Habsburg financial resources modest. Judged from the viewpoint of internal politics, the situation of the Habsburg countries was not very different from those of Bavaria. But in the case of the Habsburgs there was also the loss of the greatest part of Hungary, whose crown Ferdinand also bore. This implied a constant threat to his German-speaking inheritance, which was in turn weakened by religious discord and peasant unrest.

The women may have chosen to travel by water along the Danube, for the country of Upper Austria was disturbed at that time by an uprising of the peasantry. The route by land would have been too dangerous for this small group of Englishwomen who could only have made themselves understood with difficulty. They reached Vienna towards the end of June or the beginning of July.[76] It is not known when they had an audience with the Emperor, but it may have been fairly soon, thanks to the intervention of the Jesuits.

With Emperor Ferdinand II, a branch of the Styrian line of the house of Austria had once more returned to the Hofburg in Vienna. The inheritance of his predecessor, Emperor Mathias, was in many respects a difficult one, even within the circle of the imperial family. One of Austria's greatest poets – Franz Grillparzer, has portrayed this powerfully in his drama 'Bruderzwist in Habsburg.'

On the ecclesial scene, however, the unwitting ladies found a situation that differed completely from that of Munich. Unless its development is sketched here, however slightly, much that took place during the short but significant stay of the Englishwomen in Vienna would be difficult to understand.

It was already in the days of the Babenbergs that the Dukes had designs on diocesan property in Austria. This plan was only realised when in 1469 the Habsburg Emperor Friedrich III founded the small diocese of Vienna and Wiener Neustadt in the middle of the Passau diocesan district and this without the approval of the bishop concerned. Although Pope Paul II gave recognition to the foundations, Passau never withdrew its claim to its purloined rights. Ever since the fourteenth century, Passau officials and general vicars had lived near the church of Maria am Gestade in Vienna and from there had conducted a battle of jurisdiction between the two dioceses. It may only have been fought with feather quills, but it left many a scar, until in 1783/85 Emperor Joseph II changed the situation by new arrangements of the diocese, which was at the same time the end of the diocese of Passau in Austria.

A short time before the Englishwomen entered Vienna, the battle of jurisdiction had reached a climax, in which the energetic official Karl von Kirchberg in Rome went so far as to demand the suppression of the small and still insignificant diocese of Vienna. At that time, Cardinal Melchior Klesl, bishop of Vienna, had been removed from his diocese.

From the enormously interesting life of this Viennese convert, only the following may be related: this otherwise tolerant man was among the most violent political adversaries of Ferdinand II. He was arrested in 1618 and taken to the Tyrol, and had been in honourable constraint since 1622 in the Castel Sant' Angelo in Rome. In the meantime his General Vicar, and faithful supporter, Tobias Schwab, was Administrator.

Vienna is one of the oldest nunciatures. On her arrival, Mary Ward found Carlo Carafa as Nuntius. He came from the same family as Archbishop Decio Carafa of Naples, and Nuntius Pierluigi Carafa of Cologne. The Englishwomen had not had good experiences with Decio Carafa in Naples; with Carlo Carafa in Vienna and Pierluigi in Cologne they were not to be any more fortunate. Into these three spheres of power: the imperial court, the bishop's court and the nunciature, the Englishwomen now entered in the summer of 1627 with their petition, and were graciously received by the Emperor – and by him alone. The information given in the English Vita, that the Emperor would have allowed Mary Ward to choose from all the houses in Vienna,[77] must not be taken literally. On the contrary, the offer carried strict conditions.

The merchants among the citizens of Vienna were now and then influenced by their protestant business partners in Germany, and the greater part of them had turned to the new denomination and were therefore considered guilty of crimen laesa majestatis, or enemies of the Emperor. To a great extent this was directed against those who had sympathised with the Bohemian uprisings and had been brought to account after the imperial success at the Battle of White Mountain of 1620.

Confiscation of the goods of political opponents has everywhere and in all ages been a proven means of rendering them harmless.[78] This is exactly what happened here.

Among the buildings appropriated during these years were two houses mentioned in connection with the Englishwomen: the house 'by the Golden pillars' in Judenplatz[79] and 'Stoss am Himmel', opposite the Church of Maria am Gestade. Mary Ward decided on the latter. The building was more suitable. A few years previously the Emperor had sold this house with the deduction of the mortgage sum of 6,000 guilders to the Lord Chamberlain, Hans Jacob von Khisel. Since 1612 the house had belonged entirely to the Viennese cloth merchant Leopold Pruckner,[80] and was reckoned on confiscation as worth 10,000 guilders. Shortly afterwards the house must have been sold again, to the former Chancellor of the Regiment of Lower Austria, Hans Ruprecht Heegemuller. The exchange was executed quickly and with short shrift in 1627.[81]

The Emperor wrote to Heegemuller that the 'religious ladies, as the Mothers of Jesus are called', whom he wished to establish in his town, 'so that their Institute could best exercise and practise for the catholic faith', had decided on this house. Heegemuller could hardly refuse such a request, which was little other than an order, as the Emperor had thought of buying it himself. On 18th September,[82] Hans Graf Tobias Helfridt von Khayserstain received the command to place the purchase money ready from the Emperor's income.

It is not clear from the deeds whether it ever really was purchased. Perhaps a different arrangement was agreed on,[83] as Heegemuller continued to pay tax for the house and it was never legally in the ownership of the Englishwomen.[84]

In Vienna too the Englishwomen received an allowance: 600 guilders annually from the Emperor and 400 from the Empress.[85] That would have been for the support of five members of the Institute. By the time of the Bishop's visitation in October 1629 they numbered eleven.

The house 'Stoss am Himmel' was spacious, as it had accommodated eight families,[86] who now had to seek dwellings elsewhere. During the course of the following year the house must have been enlarged considerably, as the tax was raised from 800 to 1,000 guilders.[87]

In the same summer the Englishwomen opened a school for girls, which was soon well attended. But at the same time a shadow fell on the foundation, which revealed the outlines of the diocesan, not the imperial, court.

At the intervention of Pope Gregory XV and his nephew Cardinal Ludovico Ludovisi, Bishop Klesl's return to Vienna was made possible. Before the Bishop left Rome, the Viennese consistory court sent a survey of the Viennese diocese to the Pope. At that time there was no house of the Institute in Vienna. It was founded only after Klesl had left Rome but before he reached his diocese. Hardly had the elderly man stepped onto Austrian soil, (on 18th December, 1627 he celebrated his entrance into Wiener Neustadt) but the General Vicar, Tobias Schwab, gave the choirmaster of St Stephan's Cathedral, Stephan Zwirschlag, and the curate of St Stephan's, Christian Schumayr, an order[88] to visit the Englishwomen, who had not appeared on his report for Rome. Without permission from the diocesan curia, they had founded a religious community in Vienna and opened a school for girls. As advisory expert, the two cathedral priests took with them Dr Johann Baptist Lindenberg, Rector and teacher for many years in the Burger school for boys at St Stephan's. The report made on 18th November[89] contains nothing to the discredit of the Englishwomen. Information had been given in German by the Superior, Margaret Genison. Present too were the General Superior and three members of the house in Vienna. First of all the Visitors showed their mandate. Then the Englishwomen presented the commission with recommendations for their Institute from highly-placed eccesiastics and secular persons. Only after these formalities did they say that their community was based on that of the Jesuits, naturally only as far as was possible for women. They took the three vows privately, but they could be dismissed by their superior. They were not members of a religious Order but 'ecclesiastici faeminae' – which could be translated as 'women in the service of the Church', whose life and work were directed to the greater honour of God and the salvation of their neighbour. Their rule of life – conscriptas suas regulas – could not be produced, as these were in Rome, awaiting confirmation. They taught girls reading and writing and sewing, and prepared them for the sacraments.

To the question as to why they had not applied to the diocesan curia, they answered that they had not done so in Munich or anywhere else.

Already, the very fact that a Visitation had been ordered, suggested a whisper of reproach about the independence of the women in founding a house of their Institute in Vienna. The hapless answer of the General Superior, that she had done the same elsewhere could, if one wished, be taken as an excuse but not as solid information. Far more important, however, was the fact that this first contact of the Englishwomen with church authorities in Vienna was characterised by a frosty aloofness on the part of the Visitors. They felt that they had been ignored and insulted by the Emperor's procedures. There was an exchange of authorisations and recommendations, there were language difficulties, and statements were reduced to a minimum. Nothing passed unnoticed: these strange Englishwomen in their gown-like attire, the house full of lively young Viennese girls, and the General Vicariate of Passau on the other side of the Church of Maria am Gestade, which was being used by the Englishwomen.

On January 25th, 1628, Bishop Melchior Klesl entered Vienna with due solemnity. Perhaps the Englishwomen were among the show-loving Viennese, who greeted the Bishop along the sides of the streets.

Cardinal Klesl had already informed himself about this new congregation – from the most competent source – the Jesuits[90].

It does, however, seem strange that a short two weeks after his return to Vienna, he gave vent to violent accusations against the Englishwomen in a letter to Cardinal Bandini.[91] He formulates his sentences sharply: 'In Vienna there are certain women, who call themselves Jesuitesses, take three vows and, without the previous knowledge or permission of the Bishop, have opened a school for girls in the city. They do not wish to be subject to the episcopal court, but only to their own superior general and are dependent on the Emperor alone. The Jesuits do not support them. A few days ago their pupils produced a play. The General Superior has gone to Hungary, in order to found a house under the Emperor's protection. As scandals are feared, could Cardinal Bandini possibly send him, the Bishop of Vienna, instructions as to how to handle this matter.'

We can see that from a moral point of view there is nothing concrete against the Englishwomen Only the independent founding of a school could be produced as an objection against them.

But in the middle of the statement is one phrase which would send alarm bells ringing in Rome: the Bishop of Vienna saw in the foundation, so much esteemed and protected by the Emperor, a purely political matter – mere politica. That was a dangerous allusion, for after the death of Duke Vincent II of Mantua (1627) Emperor and Pope opposed one another fiercely to protect their influence on northern Italy.[92] Again, not to be overlooked – the Congregatio de Propaganda Fide received yet another accusation against the Englishwomen which required further action. The Congregation of Bishops and Regulars had the competence to suppress the houses of the Institute in Italy at the command of the Pope. Here it was a matter of a wider field, one which had been seized by the spirit of the reformation and which to a great extent had turned from Rome. Moreover, in this instance it was in the Emperor's own place of residence.

If the Bishop of Vienna expected to receive a personal and precise charge to take up arms against this apparently dangerous community, then he made a basic error. The official curial nag went its accustomed way, and it trod daintily.

When no answer came from Rome, Klesl repeated his apprehensions.[93] Neither to his letter of 29th April,[94] nor that of 6th May [95], did he receive any guidance.

However, it must be clearly understood that the members of the Congregatio de Propaganda Fide who had received Bishop Klesl's information on 21st March, 1628, had taken certain decisions after reading his letter. They simply did not inform the Bishop.

Pressburg

1628

The rest of Hungary – Countess Maria Palffy – trouble over the Zerdahély house – the Andreas benefice by the Cathedral – Cardinal Peter Pázmány – school curriculum,

At that time only the western part of Hungary belonged to the 'free world'. This was merely a narrow strip of land in comparison to the vast area that surrounds the Hungarian plain and the capital Budapest, in which the Turks lived for a hundred years and more.

Pressburg, today's Bratislava, then a small town, is situated on Austria's eastern border, only sixty kilometres from Vienna. It was the seat of government for the rest of Hungary. Cardinal Peter Pázmány, Archbishop of Gran (Estergom) and primate of the country, had his residence there. As with many other European towns, a great deal of it belonged to the Church, to the Cathedral Chapter, and to religious houses.[96]

The godmother of the new house of the Institute was Countess Maria Pálffy, née Fugger.[97] It was probably she who negotiated with the church authorities on their behalf, and was a support to the women after their arrival in Hungary.

The situation was totally different from that in Vienna; here, Mary Ward could count on the Cardinal and the clergy, although to begin with she was drawn into a conflict caused by the catholic archbishop's position in a town that was mainly Lutheran. Cardinal Pázmány had allotted the Englishwomen a house in Langengasse, which had been bequeathed him by a certain Gyorgy Zerdahély. This was shut, and the parish priest, Provost Nagy,[98] apparently possessed no key so he allowed it to be broken into, to enable them to see it.[99] There was an immediate protest from the Town Council. Nagy tried to explain the circumstances by referring to the Archbishop's legal position, adding that the Town Council ought not to put obstacles in the way of a girls' school.[100] This, in fact, was exactly what the predominantly protestant Town Council intended. A commentary from the Archbishop shows what was going on here.The house may indeed have been bequeathed to the Archbishop, the councillors conceded, but the Town insisted on an ancient privilege, its right to acquire religious houses by purchase. Upon which the Archbishop suggested that a building called the German school in the Pfaffengasse might be put at the Englishwomen's disposal, as this had always been inhabited by catholics. The councillors did not want that either. A German schoolmaster had always lived there, they countered, and the house should be kept as residential property. The Town Council had nothing in principle against the establishment of a girls' school, it affirmed, it was a simple fact that there was no building available, and no benefice.

The Archbishop lost that round.

But he was able to give the Englishwomen a place near the cathedral, in the benefice of St Andreas.[101]

In a detailed letter dated the first half of March, Mary Ward thanked Cardinal Pázmány.[102] Propst Gyorgy Nagy had installed her in the house (quale di tutti i luoghi in Posonio fu da me il più desiderato). All had been in order, except the kitchen, which was poorly equipped, but the small community would manage. They had acquired their own beds and bedclothes.

Mary Ward had appointed Barbara Babthorpe as superior of the house.[103] The latter had, she continued in her letter, a good deal of experience in the Institute's affairs. That was certainly true — Barbara Babthorpe had endured years of misery and distress in Liège. Two teachers had also been appointed: an Italian, Ursula Maggiori,[104] and a German, possibly Veronika von Maxlrain, who was on the register as being in Pressburg until 1631. Another German, whose name is not given, was the portress; the cook was a secular.

The situation was not as rosy as Mary Ward had indicated in her gratitude.

Barbara Babthorpe described it in different terms on 6th July, 1628[105] in a letter presumably to Winefrid Wigmore. It must have been a very rainy summer, as the superior began her letter with little more than a weather report. The house was a building site; partly under repair, partly for the Englishwomen's use. The superior thought it would have been more to the purpose if it had been rebuilt from the very foundations, but the archbishop did not have the money.

On 29th June, Barbara Babthorpe had sent him greetings, as it was his name day, and she received 600 taler as thanks. Archbishop Janos Telegdy of Kalosza had sent her 400 taler a few months earlier. In a delightfully described exchange between the Cardinal and this brother in office from Kalosza, Pázmány acquired Telegdy's cooperation in the form of an even larger donation for the Englishwomen, namely 1,000 taler, which came from Telegdy's salary as Imperial Councillor.[106] The Hungarian Treasury reacted sourly, and informed the Court Treasury in Vienna of their disapproval, as religious councillors to the Emperor rarely received a salary and in any case Archbishop Telegdy was a wealthy man. However, they endorsed the donation.[107] In the end, the Emperor approved 400 Hungarian guilders from the income of the Hungarian Court Treasury, instead of 1,000 taler from the councillor's salary of the Archbishop of Kalosza.[108] It was cheaper.

On 3rd July, Barbara Babthorpe, another unnamed member, and Countess Palffy, were guests of Archbishop Pázmány. The conversation was conducted in Italian, which resulted in language problems. The Archbishop asked who was to be appointed as secretary. The superior answered that this was one of her members, from Italy. Upon which the archbishop asked her nationality. The answer came, she is German. Laughing, the cardinal exclaimed, 'An Englishwoman, an Italian, and a German!' And in Pressburg the language was predominantly Hungarian.

At this charming meeting, which gives a good picture of the great Hungarian Pázmány, the archbishop also asked what sort of food was offered the members. Provost Nagy answered for them: cabbage, soup, beef, sometimes a small hen which had to do for four people. Bacon did not appear on their menu. They received a supply from the archbishop's larder. Wool, too, was given them with which they could improve the bareness of their accommodation.

Archbishop Pázmány remained a good patron to them, and promised to encourage Hungarian girls to enter their community. It is not known if anything came of this in the short time they were in Pressburg.

There remains an invaluable witness to the brief educational work of the Institute in Pressburg: the school curriculum.[109] It carries no date, but as one can assume that it was prepared for this foundation, it must be from about 1628. The handwriting points to male authorship. After almost two decade's experience in teaching, the Englishwomen would have been capable of a practical arrangement of subjects, but the logical and compact form of the curriculum indicates a man, and moreover, an expert in schools. That is true especially for the religious education, and the out of school religious care of the girls during the week-end.

The assistance of a Jesuit would seem obvious. It is, of course, perfectly possible that the curriculum had already been prepared for the school in Vienna or even in Munich. The Englishwomen would not have had a great deal of variety between their different schools.

The main emphasis was on religious teaching, in accordance with the aim of the Institute and the needs of the Church. The elementary subjects of reading, writing and arithmetic bear witness to the laborious first steps of girls's education in general. Latin was an option; the beautiful handwork and painting techniques conformed to the educational pattern of women in those days. For details:

First Form:
Religion: First and foremost the prayer-life of the young girl was to be formed.
All necessary prayers for a christian were to be learnt, such as morning and evening prayers, grace at meals, prayers before and after work, rosary, and the celebration of Mass. Further, there was an introduction to the sacrament of penance. In addition, the learning of hymns, understanding of reverence for God, for one's parents and persons in authority. Lessons in the basic subjects comprised reading and writing in the vernacular or, if this was already known, in Latin. If the parents did not want this, the girls could learn various types of handwork.

Second Form:
Religion: Repetition of the prayers learnt, ongoing understanding of the sacrifice of the Mass and of the rosary; a deeper preparation for reception of the sacraments and the beginning of catechism lessons; honouring of Mary and the saints, learning of hymns.
In secular subjects, teaching was in the vernacular or Latin, or carried on in Italian for handcrafts.

Third Form:
Religion: Once more repetition of matter already learnt, Holy Mass, spiritual communion, the rosary, spiritual books, arousing of contrition, general confession, the devout and worthy reception of communion, the Marian Office, the Holy Spirit, learning the catechism, spiritual songs and hymns.
In secular subjects the girls to be taught in Latin were introduced to the grammar of this language, or they learned the fundamentals of arithmetic or various handcrafts.

Form Four:
Religion: Repetition of material, continuation of catechism learning, the Breviary, examinination of conscience, Holy Mass and church

ceremonies, indulgences, penances, honour due to saints, pilgrimages and the practice of virtues. Overcoming one's faults, meditation and interior prayer.

In secular subjects the syntax of Latin was dealt with, as well as simple Latin reading matter, or wider knowledge of arithmetic was taught, or finer craftsmanship in handwork.

Seen from the viewpoint of the pedagogy of later centuries, there is much room for improvement, but it must not be forgotten that girls' education was then at its beginning. These girls, for the most part with none of the pre-conditions for a regular education, were instructed according to the principles of their day as good catholics.

No less important was formation during the week-end, and this was solely concerned with religion. On Saturdays, explanations were given for the Mass of the following day, and the week-day Masses to come. On Sundays the girls were present at the public catechism classes.

It was the boarders at the Englishwomen's school in particular who received comprehensive religious education, but songs and music played their part in it too.

Great value was laid on painting, but also on preparations of medicines made from plants, on the making of fruit drinks and cordials. Household economics were not forgotten.

The beginning was hard. In the letter mentioned previously, Barbara Babthorpe[110] writes that the school had a good number of pupils but that the girls did not attend regularly. Many of them were needed at home at the time of the wine harvest, and missed lessons. Archbishop Pázmány advised patience: educationally, he said, the people were unschooled and backward.

In spite of this somewhat pessimistic opinion, on 25th April, 1628, seventy of the Institute's pupils took part in St Mark's procession through the streets of the city.[111] A fine achievement for a short time.

Prague

1628

The confused religious situation in Bohemia – Archbishop Harrach of Prague – Fr Valerio Magni – Count Althan's foundation for the Institute – trouble over the use of an empty church – letters of Nuntius Carafa and Pallotto against the Englishwomen to Cardinal Barberini – Pallotto's further attacks – his discussions with the Englishwomen – Mary Ward in audience with Archbishop Harrach

In marked contrast to Vienna and Pressburg, where the Englishwomen had found ready acceptance, Mary Ward met with difficulties on the politically fiery soil of Prague which were to hasten the eventual downfall of her Institute. To sketch in the external situation: there were as many religious differences as there were nationalities in the Habsburg lands in the middle of Europe. That was particularly true of Bohemia, where Hussites, Utraquists, Bohemian Brothers and Moravian Brothers, as well as emigrants from Germany: Anabaptists, Lutherans, Calvinists and Zwinglians, lived together or sometimes lived in conflict with one another. Counter-Reformation forces were not idle, either. In 1555, Peter Canisius preached in Prague, where the Society of Jesus made its first foundation in the following year. But the Counter-Reformation gained momentum only after the victory of the imperial troops over the Bohemian uprising on White Mountain in 1620. All this coincided with the Church's efforts at reconciliation and the relentless methods of the secular arm.

The Imperial Court had left Vienna in September, 1627, to attend to urgent government business in Prague. Emperor Ferdinand II, King of Bohemia, arrived in a country which had not only been reconquered with difficulty, but one in which he found the churches in a difficult situation. It was not only the restlessness of the population that was a problem; the Archbishop of Prague, Ernst Adalbert von Harrach, was not particularly well-disposed towards his king. Harrach had been born in Vienna in 1598, son of the chief court dignitary of Emperor Ferdinand II. This Bohemian family, Harrach, like most of its peers, had held a high position at court, in the civil service or in the army. Ernst Adalbert had been a Jesuit pupil and studied at the German College in Rome, and in 1623 at the age of twenty five, was made Archbishop of Prague. One year later he received the cardinal's hat.[112]

As a young man this archbishop was faced with difficulties which, with his lack of experience, he could hardly have been expected to navigate satisfactorily without some help. This he found in Fr Valerio Magni, an Italian from Milan, who had entered the service of Emperor Rudolf II, usually living in Hradcany Castle in Prague. In 1602 Magni entered the Capuchin Order and was soon briskly active. It was this man, politically involved and hostile to the Jesuits, who developed an influence over the young archbishop; he was his confessor.[113] One important ingredient of this small melting-pot must not be overlooked. A few years previously the Emperor had given the Presidency of the University of Prague to the Jesuits. (1622) The same had happened in Vienna at the same time, but in Prague this attempt by the Emperor to raise academic standards was to have unfortunate effects, for Archbishop Harrach was Chancellor of Prague University and felt that his rights had been ignored. This delicate situation also had consequences in resolving matters for the three Englishwomen for, as Cardinal Klesl had put it, they were 'mere politica' — absolutely political. Even in Prague.

Both of the first biographies of Mary Ward leave us high and dry about the short time the Englishwomen spent in Prague. The Italian Vita refers to the need for a foundation in Bohemia; the English Vita acknowledges such good progress made by the members in Munich and Vienna that the Englishwomen were invited to Pressburg and Prague; it even mentions the opposition of Archbishop Harrach and his adviser,[114] but then turns to a detailed description of the pious Countess Neuhaus and makes no further mention of the sad course of events. Only from a relatively late report of March, 1629,[115] after the Englishwomen had already left, do we hear that Count Althan had promised Mary Ward a sizeable house with a church, and an allowance for the support of thirty people. This would seem too good to be true, as, combined with the allowances for Munich and Vienna, this would have meant a firm material basis for the entire Institute. But to look at the scanty contemporary sources first: at the beginning of May, 1628,[116] Mary Ward wrote from Prague to Winefrid Wigmore in Munich − a revealing letter: 'Where God will have you, I do not know, nor whether we shall have a beginning here in Prague or not, a foundation, I mean. I am determined either to be well placed here ('in very good tirms') or not at all.'

If one considers that on 6th May Mary Ward had been in Prague only a very short time, one can argue from these words that something had gone awry from the very beginning. 'In this region there is no lack of work for us,' she continues, but then, 'there will be fine times, a great persecution in all likelihood is at hand from the Cardinal of this place, and the Nuntius, as also from the Cardinal Archbishop of Vienna. Their letters to the Pope deal with what jurisdiction they should have over ours, etc. . . .' So Mary Ward knew some of the dangers surrounding her.

'If I were sure,' she goes on, 'that we were not to have a college here, I would write with this post to Mother Rectrix,[117] to ask her, and leave you as Vice Superior for a month in Munich.' Elizabeth Cotton seems to have had a letter enclosed in this with items of information about the situation, but unfortunately this has not survived.

The next sentences concern the Institute in Munich and are omitted here; then we find Mary Ward once again making a request for German-speaking members. These would have been of great importance for Vienna, Pressburg and Prague, for even if the native tongue in the last two was Hungarian and Bohemian, the Englishwomen had found that a knowledge of German opened doors to them more quickly in the Danube countries, especially with the authorities.

Two letters,[118] one from Nuntius Carlo Caraffa and one from the Nuntius extra-ordinary, Giovanni Battista Pallotto, to Cardinal Nephew Francesco Barberini, develop Mary Ward's rather vague references. Both letters were composed on 7th June, one month after Mary Ward had written her letter to Winefrid Wigmore. First,

Caraffa's letter: by way of introduction, the Nuntius describes the rapid growth of the Institute, the foundation in Vienna under the protection of the Emperor, where the Englishwomen had founded a school on the same lines as the Jesuits', wore clothing similar to the Fathers, a dark long garment, and allowed themselves to be called 'Jesuitesses' everywhere. Their similarity to the Jesuits pleased the Emperor. In Pressburg the Archbishop had provided them with a house. Now, some two months ago, they had come to Prague to find a foothold, accompanied by two gentlemen appointed by the Emperor. They laid claim to a filial church in Teyn parish, which carried with it a house and benefice of 300 talers annually. The church lay empty just now because of a shortage of priests. The two gentlemen had called on Harrach and asked for this benefice to be placed at the disposal of these women. He, however, had turned to him, the Nuntius. Carafa had drawn Archbishop Harrach's attention to the fact that the women belonged to a congregation not yet approved by the church and could not be given any church, let alone a parish church (molto meno che fussero parochiali). In Italy, so Carafa said, they had no church at all. Cardinal Harrach, caught between the Emperor's protegées and the statutes of Canon Law, hedged, and the Nuntius had had to apply the full force of his authority to prevent him handing over the property. Upon which, Carafa continued, the women wanted to return to Vienna.

Then the Nuntius turned on the Institute, revealing his reason for rejecting the Englishwomen. The Church should exercise proper care, he warned, and refuse an unrecognised congregation admission to a land shaken by heresies like Bohemia. These women did not want to be subordinate either to the Bishop of the place or the Nuntius. They sometimes called themselves religious sisters, sometimes not, as was convenient, but they behaved like religious sisters.

Just as Cardinal Klesl in Vienna, so now the Nuntius feared the possibility of scandal from these women in Prague. They obeyed their superiors only, had no enclosure, and the girls in their school would only attract the attention of young men. Nuntius Carafa also had grave misgivings about the freedom of speech which the Englishwomen had with seculars, as a result of their educating older and marriageable girls. Such a letter was, of course, successful in Rome where many complaints of this type about the Institute had already been received and gained a ready ear.

The letter from Nuntius-extraordinary Pallotto was written in much the same vein but was more incriminating. He had his information from Nuntius Carafa, as he freely admitted in his preface.

Pallotto was in Vienna in the second half of May only, and had arrived in Prague on 26th May. He could not yet have had much insight into the problems of the Viennese Nunciature nor been at all familiar with their modus operandi. It can be taken as fact, however, that he had come to know Mary Ward and her Institute in Rome, or had at least heard of her unsuccessful attempts to obtain approbation. Although Pallotto recorded the same information as Carafa, his letter had a very different tone and certainly too, a very different object. The Jesuitesses, he said, had withdrawn from Rome without receiving ecclesiastical recognition for their Institute, and had obtained houses and churches in parts of Germany, where they were called religious sisters by bishops and archbishops. They were now laying claim here to a parish church in Prague. They were not satisfied with a house and an oratory where Mass could be celebrated. Supported by the Emperor, they were burdening the Archbishop of Prague with requests for this church. The Superior allowed herself to be called the General Superior and used a seal similar to that of the Father General of the Society of Jesus, although the Jesuits did not want to have anything to do with them.

Pallotto endorsed Carafa's arguments in his negotiations with the Archbishop, and also warned the authorities in Rome about these women: their sex was inconstant, and inclined to error (un sesso tanto fragile e facile a cader in errori d'intelleto e di volontà). He, Pallotto, had advised Carafa to refer to appropriate authorities in Rome who could keep an eye on these women and − warning!-could take action before it was too late. The concluding remarks were significant, that the Archbishop had wanted to appeal to the Propaganda Fide, but the Englishwomen had shown great aversion to this and preferred to leave Prague. It seemed remarkable to Pallotto that the Englishwomen dedicated themselves to service in God's kingdom, and yet fled the supervision of the Holy See.

As can be seen, Carafa's accusations, certainly not to be treated lightly, took on a pointed emphasis here.

First, it must be asserted that neither the Bishop of St Omer nor the Bishop of Liège had ever looked upon the Institute as an Order. The Englishwomen had been allowed the rights of an Order in their respective dioceses until papal confirmation of their Institute had been received but that was something quite different, and the bishops had acted within their rights.

Again, the assertion that the Englishwomen laid claim to a parish church is an exaggeration. This church had been offered them by Count Althan, though it is not known which was intended. But even if the Althan family had the patronage of this church, the Count would still not have had the right to suggest its presentation to the Englishwomen, as this benefice was founded for a secular priest. It is understandable that the Archbishop resisted its handing over to women, whether they belonged to a recognised congregation or not. The bishops always intervened in order to protect such benefices for the secular clergy. But in this case it was not a matter of a parish church but a filial church which, moreover, was standing empty. The Englishwomen will certainly not have claimed this as belonging to their Institute, but for its use by their own members, and the school they intended for girls.

It was extremely dangerous for the Englishwomen that Pallotto emphasized their supposed rejection to the Roman authorities so mercilessly. The contrast – the Institute's work for the Roman Catholic Church, and the Englishwomen's fear of the Roman authorities – was very likely intended to strengthen the negative attidude of the Cardinals of the Propaganda Fide. Mary Ward never wished to avoid supervision by the Holy See. On the contrary, she had made a foundation in Rome precisely so that the Curia might pass judgement on the Institute and its manner of life. Nor had the foundations in Naples and Perugia been conducted secretly. Courageously, and not like a woman acting surreptitiously, she had presented herself before Urban VIII in 1624 to discuss the concerns of her order. Her attempt to stabilize the Institute beyond the Papal States, unencumbered by troublesome accusations to the Curia made by her enemies, ought not to be held against her. The pleasant meeting with the Pope in Mondragone will have remained bright in her memory. Her Institute had not been suppressed, and it could continue perfectly legitimately, according to the concept of 'Pium Institutum' of 1625.

This extremely denunciatory letter from the pen of the Emperor's Nuntius extraordinary, a man highly esteemed in Rome, probably made a powerful impression and strengthened the authorities in their view of the Institute and its members.

For the time being, Mary Ward knew nothing of these grave accusations. On the contrary, her letter of 10th June[119] to Winefrid Wigmore – three days after these two letters had been written – has an optimistic ring. She writes: 'It was decided today that we shall have the church which the Emperor has granted us, at all events for a short time.' Winefrid was to prepare for the journey to Prague after the return of the Superior, Mary Poyntz. According to this, it seems that Archbishop Harrach had been prepared to hand over the church in question to the Englishwomen.

These three letters show how information can differ. At the beginning of May, Mary Ward was not yet certain that the foundation would be approved at all. As a result, she actually summoned Mary Poyntz to Prague. The Archbishop, originally dismissive towards them, seems later to have agreed to their proposal and that of their advocates, which caused Mary Ward's optimistic letter of 10th June, and goaded the two Nuntios to increased opposition and serious complaints to Rome.

All of which came to a head just as the Court prepared to return to Vienna, as can be seen from two further letters from Pallotto to Cardinal Barberini. The first was written by the Nuntius on 28th June,[120] in Znaim during the Court's return journey, the other on 8th July, from Vienna.[121] From these letters it can be seen that Pallotto, while still in Prague, had had a conversation with the two counts appointed by the Emperor, Althan and Martinitz. Both were as friendly to the Jesuits as Pallotto himself, so the conversation could therefore have taken place in a relaxed atmosphere. Pallotto told the two that the Englishwomen had been badly advised if they thought they could continue without the approval of the Holy See. It would be best if they concentrated their energies on obtaining recognition for their Institute. Pallotto seems to have presented his opinion so plausibly that Mary Ward's imperial counsellors were convinced of the need for a conversation with the Nuntius extraordinary in Prague. Accompanied by Elizabeth Cotton and probably Mary Poyntz, who was now in Prague, Mary Ward went to this portentous audience. In this, for the first time, we meet Pallotto's diplomatic language, much at variance with his real mind.

The intention of the Ladies was good, he said, but first they must take steps in Rome for the approval of their Institute. Mary Ward must have hesitated. First she agreed to meet the Nuntius extraordinary again in Vienna, but she was not against travelling to Rome. In the end, Pallotto advised Cardinal Barberini just the reverse: the Institute should be remodelled in Rome, but the women should not be allowed to return to Bohemia with its dangerous situation.

The last sentence of his encoded letter gives Pallotto's real opinion of Mary Ward: 'If the head of this woman is not properly bridled and checked, I am more than ever fearful of that hour of which I have spoken, for it seems to me that she considers herself better than most women and esteems herself more highly than a human being.'[122]

But Mary Ward thwarted Pallotto's simple calculation. Irritably, he wrote again on 8th June from Vienna to Cardinal Barberini, that Mary Ward (who allowed herself to be called the General Superior of the Society) had, in spite of her promise to meet him again in Vienna, had a further discussion in Prague with Archbishop Harrach in order to acquire the parish church.

The Archbishop had answered that Nuntius Carafa had forbidden this and that he had threatened to excommunicate Mary Ward should she set foot in the church. Upon which she had answered the Archbishop that the granting of a church lay within the archbishop's jurisdiction. If the Nuntius were to excommunicate her for that reason, she would not heed it, as this exclusion from the church community would not be legally correct.[123] But Cardinal Harrach stood firm.

It is difficult to pass a fair judgement on this point.

This passage of the letter about the Englishwomen was written in a testy frame of mind. But we do not know who reported Mary Ward's words to Pallotto and it would above all be important to know the tone in which they were uttered. From an objective point of view, Mary Ward was correct, as the Nuntius had brought his influence to bear on a matter in the Bishop's sphere of authority. It is also questionable whether excommunication – exclusion from receiving the sacraments – could really have been imposed for so slight a cause. But it painted the disquieting portrait of a woman with an over-weening self-assurance, if one reads rebellion and scorn into her words, as they did.

Despite attempts to be objective, it is not easy to accept that Mary Ward, who had always been modest, and never questioned the authority of those in a position of responsibility in church or state, would have allowed herself to adopt such an attitude.

The founding of a house in Prague came to nothing, although Mary Ward sought to do so for a short time.

Certain lesser matters have come to our attention in this final battle against the Institute. It is, for example, remarkable that Mary Ward did not make any contact with Fr General to ask him for introductions, either when she was seeking to make a foundation in Pressburg or to obtain a house in Prague. She had done so before, in Rome, when she had left to conduct negotiations in Munich and Vienna, and Fr General had given full support in Munich. He had even been criticized for doing so by some of the fathers of the Society. There is nothing of the sort for these last two foundations. On the contrary, Fr General sounds a dry note on 27th May, 1628[124] to Fr Lucia Fanini in Prague, when he regretted that certain of the Prague Jesuits had been unfriendly towards the Englishwomen, adding, however, that it would be difficult for him to intervene as he did not know of any actual dispute that had taken place. He gave the usual admonition to the Jesuits, to treat the Englishwomen as they did all other women who entered their churches.

It has been stated that when she left Rome, Mary Ward had certainly no intention of founding a house in Munich or Vienna, but went north to appeal for help for those houses already existing north of the Alps. Father Vitelleschi had given his support in the form of recommendations to the influential confessors of princes. But when the possibility arose of founding two houses with great potential, he remained true to his word, and continued to help within the limited framework at his disposal. Admittedly, one foundation suceeded another very rapidly. But this can hardly be proposed as an excuse for lack of time for correspondence. Fr Fanini could write to Fr General, for his letter dated 27th May was the answer to information from the Prague Jesuit. Neither could it be that Fr Vitelleschi had left a query of Mary Ward's unanswered, for he stayed in touch with her, even during the darkest days of her Institute, by prayer and with words of consolation.

It should be pointed out that neither in Pressburg nor in Prague was there an autonomous government, for Emperor Ferdinand II was both apostolic King of Hungary and King of Bohemia. Mary Ward, probably certain of imperial protection, was supported by contacts which she had made in Vienna. For Pressburg she relied on the efforts made by Countess Pallfy, and the members were able to occupy a house put at their disposal by Archbishop Peter Pázmány in spring, 1628. The same happened when Count Althan invited them to Prague. She had no cause to fear serious difficulties with the Jesuits in either city. Conversations with superiors and confessors of the imperial couple would have reassured her in this respect.

In Pressburg the Englishwomen undoubtedly collaborated well with the Fathers in the short time of their activity on Hungarian soil, just as in Prague there was no special difficulty, or Father Vitelleschi would have given a different answer to Fr Fanini than that recorded. Not even in Munich, where the waves had risen higher, were any difficulties looked for from the Jesuits about the foundations in Pressburg or Prague. Fr General answered Mary Ward's query concerning this, dated 8th March − at the time of the Pressburg foundation, therefore − that the Jesuits in Munich would have no anxiety at the growth of her Institute, for it could not be considered a liability for the Society of Jesus.[125] Of course, Father General had to order extreme precautions to be taken when Propaganda Fide suppressed, first the houses north of the Alps, and then the Institute itself, but he was never one of Mary Ward's enemies.

The good offices of the Emperor and certainly those of Counts Althan and Martinitz seem, as far as one can judge, to have been unsuccessful.

Secular rulers and potentates could dispense gold, goods and privileges, but it was with difficulty that they carried any weight in the sphere of canon law or ecclesial jurisdiction, especially if political tensions played a role, as it is more than probable that they did during this brief stretch of time.

It was not, however, in Prague that the Institute was finally broken. That had already happened some years before, on that inconspicuous hill in Liège: in the rue Pierreuse.

Notes

1 "She found there was not what needed her presence in Rom and a necessity of it in the Low Countreyes and England niether could her magnanimous courage apprehend it hard or any way unfactable to returne to Rome when God's service should require it." Vita E, f.30v.
2.   Vita I, p.26.
3.   Pagetti, pp.10−11.
4.   Bissel, p.114.
5.   Lohner, p.130.
6.   Fridl, p.252ff. Mary Ward was extremely anxious on account of Helen Wigmore, whose vocation in the Institute had become shaky. Fridl refers to two missing letters from Mary Ward, written from Rome on 19th September and 31rd October, 1626. ibid. 254.
7.   Unterberg, p.20.
8.   Chambers II E. p.198ff; II D S 163ff.
9.   AE Liège, Couvents, Jésuites Anglais, Registre pp.255−264 s.n.
10. On 11th October, 1626. "Domina Maria della Guardia quae post paucos dies hinc in Belgium discedit." ARSI Rome, Anglia 1/II, ff.245v−246r.

The dating must be incorrect, as the Englishwomen left Rome on 10th November, 1626.

11. Fridl, p.252 ff: "Your Maimb (cousin? trans. note.) will travel with me for other reasons as well as this, that I truly love your sister." See above, Helen Wigmore was in the Institute in Liège; she left the Institute in 1627. Mary Ward to Winefrid Wigmore, 29th September 1627. Letter Nr.42. Inst. Arch. Munich.
12. ARSI Rome. Austria 3/II, pp.747–748.
13. ibid. 748.
14. ibid. 747–748.
15. " ... in Germaniam et alis ultramontanas partes ad perficienda quaedam sua negotia." St B Munich, Cgm. 5393, p.239.
16. Vita E, f.30v. Vita I, p.26, gives the year only, and the important places on the route.
17. For Mary Poyntz see Mary Ward's letters from Rome mentioned by Fridl, p.254. Elizabeth Cotton wrote the letters as Mary Ward's secretary at this time.
18. Grisar, Institut, p.279–280, note 15.
19. Vita E, f.30v.–33r.
20. The daughter of Archduke Karl II, who ruled in Styria. In 1608 she married Cosimo II de Medici, who died in 1621. Together with her mother-in-law, Grand Duchess Christina, she ruled during the minority of her son Ferdinand II. Wilhelm Karl v. Isenburg, Stammtafeln z. Gesch. d. Europaischen Staaten II, Berlin 1936. T.120: Die Gross herzoge von Toskana aus dem Haus Medici. In 1626 Maria Magdalena was 37 years old.
21. Vita E, f.30v; Vita I does not mention this.
22. The original was lost in World War II. Copy in IBVM Generalate, Rome.
23. Letter Nr.37, Inst. Arch. Munich.
24. Vita E, f.31r. Vita I does not mention the incident. Duchess Margareta was born Aldobrandini. In 1600 she married Duke Rainutio I Farnese from Parma, who died in 1622. Isenburg, loc. cit. table 127, Die Herzoge von Parma aus dem Hause Farnese.
25. Vita E, f.31v; Vita I, p.26. For the rather florid account of this visit and the Cardinal's attitude, see Bissel p.115; Fridl I, p.255–257 and Chambers II E, p.203–205; II D, p.167–169.
26. Vita E, f.31r, errs in saying that Feldkirch was under the Archbishop of Innsbruck. The town belonged to the Diocese of Chur until 1816. Politically however it was subject to the Tirolese line of the House of Habsburg. Its overlord, Archduke Leopold V of Tirol, was Bishop of Passau until 1625. Perhaps there was a confusion here between "Arch" – Archduke and Archbishop.
27. Panel 43 shows four members of the Institute among the local people, during Mass. The text on the picture does not match the representation. Cf. Vita E, f.32rv. Vita I does not mention the visit to Feldkirch.
28. "Particulars she would never tell but in generall tearmes that it concerned the conversion of England." Vita E, f.32v.
29. ibid. Vita I says nothing of this visit.
30. Born in 1604, she married first Francesco della Rovere, Prince of Urbino (murdered in 1625) and in 1626 Archduke Leopold V of Tirol. Isenburg II,. loc. cit. table 120.
31. The original in the Privy Registry of the Ministry of Culture in Munich was lost in 1944. An authenticated copy is among the documents of the diocesan process for the canonisation of Mary Ward in Munich, vol. II, f.220rv.
32. Vita E, f.33r.

33. The reference here is to the imperial foundation in Hall, Tirol, founded by the three daughters of Emperior Ferdinand I: Magdalena, Helena and Margareta. It had similarities to the Jesuits.

34. Reigning concurrently: Wilhelm IV. (1508–1550), Albrecht V (1550–1579). Wilhelm V. (1579–1597) and Maximilian I (1598–1651).

35.. Before consecration as Bishop he was Canon in Freysing. The war seriously affected his time in office. He died on 8th December, 1651. Hier. Cath. IV, p.190.

36. StA Munich, Kl.434/10, f.9r–10v.

37. StA Munich, HZR 1627, f.270. The Prince did not provide the English-women with a foundation but with an annual allowance which could be revoked. This sum was minimal when compared with what the English Jesuits in Liège had received, for regarded simply as interest, at 5%, this would have meant an original sum of 40,000 guilders. The Jesuits in Liège received a donation of 200,000 guilders. But there was no question of anything like that here, and moreover the Institute's work at the time could never have guaranteed results such as the Jesuits had achieved in Munich.

38. In the first decree. The Institute was responsible for the maintenance, but the Bavarian treasury paid the first expenses. Sta Munich, HZR, 1627, s.f.

39. On 4th February, 1627, Old Writings Nr.36, Inst. Arch. Munich. On 20th May, 1627 Mary Ward summoned Mary Ratcliffe and Magaret Genison to Munich. Letter Nr.39, Inst. Arch. Munich. However Mary Ratcliffe remained as superior in Naples while in the same letter, Winefrid Wigmore who had been named as superior in Naples was soon moved to Munich. See below, Note. 68.

40. On 16th February, 1627. Letter Nr.37. Inst. Arch. Munich.

41. B. Duhr, Gesch. d. Jesuiten in den Ländern deutscher Zunge im XVI Jhdt. I Freiburg/Br. Above all, p.183ff, 246ff, and II, p.204ff.

42. This date is supplied by Fr General's letter to Mary Ward of 13th February, 1627. ARSI Rome, Epp.NN 2, f.305v. Nr.675.

43. In his answer 3rd April he mentioned her letters of 21.January and 12th March. ibid. f.308v, Nr.688.

44. Fr Mundbrot (1576–1645) was Provincial of the Upper German Province from 1624–1631 and from 1634–1636, and German Assistant at the curia of the order in Rome from 1636–1645. Duhr I, p.1200; Sommervogel V, Sp 1402–1404.

45. Fr Manhart (ca.1571–1647) was first of all Rector in Ingolstadt, Ensisheim and 1623–1628 Rector in Munich. ibid. p.486.

46. H. Thoellen, Menologium oder Lebensbilder der deutschen Ordensprovinz der Gesellschaft Jesu, Roermond 1901, p.610–611.

47. See p. 275ff.

48. On 6th February 1627. "de quibusnam suis negotiis cum Serenissimis Ducibus tractatura. " ARSI Rome, Germ. Super. 5, f.469v.

49. ibid. ff.476v–477r.

50. On 20th March ibid. f.480v.

51. ibid. f.481r.

52. Fr General Vitelleschi to Fr Rector Manhart, 10.April 1627. ibid. f.483r. Fr General had no objection to the Englishwomen's use of Holy Cross chapel.

53. ibid. ff.483v–484r.

54. ibid. f.484r.

55. A letter was circulating in Munich, accusing Fr General of being inconsistent. Cf. Cf. Fr Vitelleschi's letter of thanks to Fr Daniel Feldner and Fr Heinrich Lampartner of 24th April 1627. ibid. f.464rv.

56. Fr General to Fr Manhart on 24th April, 1627. ibid. f.486r.

57. Of 1st May, 1627. ibid. ff.486v–487v.

58. On 7th May 1627, ibid. f.492r.
59. On 15th May 1627. ibid. f.489r. On the same day Fr General asked Fr Provincial's Socius, Fr Peter Gottrau, for information about the Jesuits' compliance with his orders, ibid. f.489r. The Fathers must certainly have sent some explanation to Rome. Fr General's letters of 22nd May to Fr Manhart and 5th June to Fr Contzen allow this interpretation. ibid. f.491rv respectively f.492v.
60. On 12th June. ibid. f.496rv.
61. On 12th June, 1627, ibid. f.49rv; on 17th June 1627, ibid. f498v; on 17.July 1627, ARSI Rome, Germ. Super, 6, pp.5−6; on 31st July 1627, ibid. p.8; on 21st August 1627, ibid. p.13; on 28. August 1627, ibid. pp.14−15; on 4th September 1627, ibid. p.19; on 11th December 1627, ibid. pp.40−41; on 12th February 1628, ibid. p.50.
62. On 12th February 1628. We do not know what exactly was referred to here. ARSI Rome, Epp. NN2, f.323v, Nr.992.
63. On 11th December 1627, ARSI Rome, Anglia 1/II, f.165r.
64. On 1st April 1628. ibid. f.271r.
65. An express letter 15.April 1628. ibid. ff.271v−272r, and 22nd April. ibid. ff.272v−273r.
66. The last unsatisfactory reference was in Fr General's letter, 1st July 1628 to Fr Silisdon. ibid. f.278rv.
67. The term "Jerusalem" is found three times in the sources: on 6.May 1628 in a letter from Mary Ward to Winefrid Wigmore. The attempt at undermining the good relationship between the Englishwomen and the sovereign, referred to in the letter, could indicate enemies of the Institute among the Society of Jesus (Letter 50). The same could be true of the enemies Mary Ward wrote about on 16th February, 1631 from the Anger convent: "Noe, noe, it is not the friers nor clergy but the Hierusalems etc." (Letter 56). In a letter at the end of February or the beginning of March, she wrote of Rome as "Jerusalem". (Letter Nr.70).
68. On 9th February, 1628. Letter Nr.49, Inst. Arch. Munich.
69. Vita E, f.33r; Vita I, p.27. Similarly, Pagetti, p.11; Bissel, p.117, Lohner, p.131−133, Fridl I, p.265−266, Unterberg, p.21, Chambers II passim which in the main are based on Fridl.
70. Letter Nr.37. Inst. Arch. Munich. " ... for I must not begg of the Duke and Duches for that busines in noe case, much less ys yt a time now to propound to them the foundation of Leig or Trevers."
71. Above all the Prince Bishop of Basel, Wilhelm Rinck von Baldenstein, who advocated the Ursulines. See State archives of the Canton Bern. Furstbisch. Baselsches Arch. Abt.A.113, Ursulinae Bruntruti. Grisar, Institut, p.282−285 treats of these events as well the attempt to unite both congregations.
72. In a conversation with Cardinal Ottavio Bandini. VIves to Secret. of State Suarez, 12th February 1622. See above p.327.
73. Fr General Vitelleschi to Mary Ward about the foundation in Naples. 24th June, 1623. ARSI Rome, Naples. 14/I, f.94r, Nr.609.
74. Fr Tomson to Henry Lee, 8th March 1627, Inst. Arch. Rome, transcript. "And better it were to have that house well and fully furnished ther to strive and strayne others thoughe they were offered even by the emperour, for yf that house where you are doe florishe, the fame and opinion of that good which there is donne will make (them to be) desired in other places, that the best will thinke they rather receave than doe a pleasure to beginne a house in their states." Mary Ward however desired a foundation in Vienna.
75. StA Munich, K1434/10. The Electress had written a similarly warm recommendation on 16th June. A copy of this letter lay in the Privy Register of the Ministry of Culture in Munich. "Union und Abredung zwischen

denen Englische Fraulein in Munchen and denen Ursulinerinnen zu Basel",
1616–1629. In the World War II the document was lost. Authenticated
copy in Inst. Arch. Rome.

76. Fr Vitelleschi addressed his letter dated 10th July 1627 to Mary Ward in
     Vienna. ARSI EPP NN2, f.312v. Nr.717. On 14th July negotiations were
     already taking place in Vienna about a house. HA Wien, Niederösterr.
     Herrschaftsakten, convents of the "Matres de Jesu, 1627–1632", W.61/B32.
     On 17th July 1627 Fr Vitelleschi wrote to Fr Provincial Dombrinus. ARSI
     Rome Austria 3/II, p.866. This order concerning the Jesuits' dealings with
     the Englishwomen in Vienna corresponds to Fr General's instructions to Fr
     Provincial Mundbrot in Munich.

77. It says: Emperor Ferdinand "bidd our dearest Mother (to) take her choyse
     of all the houses in Vienna, for which she would should be hers." Vita E,
     f.34r; Vita I, p.27 covers the foundations in Vienna and Pressburg in gen-
     eral terms only.

78. See the "Verzaichnuß aller declarierten rebellen heyser und grundtstuckh
     benebens auch theils deroselben vahrnuß, welche alhie in unnd ausser
     der stadt confisciert und eingezogen, auch wohin deroselben guetter schon
     verfwendet worden. HA Wien, Niederösterr. Herrschaftsakten W61/C42,
     pras/Datum 4th Januar 1621.

79. ibid. W 61/B 32. On 14th July 1627 the Emperor commissioned both his
     Vice-Domos Christopher Strauss and John Marienbaumb to view the house
     belonging to Paul Gold, for the "Matres de Jesu."

80. 1622. Pruckner received 809 Guilders. The Emperor had allowed Khisel
     more than 1,000 guilders reduction. ibid. W.61/C 42.

81. AStW Grundbuch 1/13 (Stadt/Gewährbuch K), f.125rv and HA W 61/B 32
     of 17th July 1627. On 12th June 1627 Mary Ward wrote to Fr Vitelleschi
     of the good progress. The letter does not survive.

82. ibid.

83. ibid.

84. Vite E. f.34r, allows that conclusion.

85. ibid. of 25th September 1627 and the Englishwomen's assertion on the epis-
     copal visitation see below, p.753.???? The Empress's 400 guilders probably
     came from her private income.

87. AStw, Ste uerbucher, 1625, f.24r, Nr.611 and 1627 f.20v, Nr.911.

88. DA Vienna, Suppressed convents, Jesuitessses, 5th November 1627.

89. ibid. The visitation took place on 17th November.

90. This emerges from the letter mentioned.

91. On 5th February. APF ROME, SOCG. 69. Letter di Germania et Polonia
     ff.123v–124rv.

92. The quarrel about succession was first of all betwccn the immediate heirs,
     Karl von Gonzaga-Nevers and the younger line of the Gonzaga family in
     Guastalla. Because France took the part of Gonzaga-Nevers, and Spain
     that of Conzaga-Guastalla, the quarrel turned into an affair involving the
     major powers; what was at stake was the sphere of influence in northern
     Italy. Urban VIII, a francophile all his life, stood on the defensive with
     the French against the encirclement of the Papal States by the Habsburgs.
     Emperor Ferdinand II, who wished to seize the Duchy as a feudatory into
     his realm, sided with Spain.

93. Klesl to /Bandini/ 18th March 1628. SOCG 69, Lettere di Germania et
     Polonia, 1628, ff.133v. 140v.

94. ibid. ff.142r, 149v.

95. ibid. ff.144, 147v.

96. This can be established from old town plans.

97. Vita E, f.36rv. One of Countess Palffy's daughters is supposed to have been
     cured of a fever by Mary Ward when she visited them. The Countess gave the

Englishwomen in Pressburg 400 Hungarian guilders. Grisar, Institut, p.300. Note 58.

98. Provost von Also Feher, Canon of St Martin in Pressburg from 1613. He died in 1636. Carolus Rimelyt, Capitulum insignis ecclesiae collegiatae Posoniensis ad S. Martinum ep. olim ss. Salvatorem, Pressburg. 1880. p.267.
99. Protocollum Actionum 1622–1633, p.209 of 15th January 1628. StA Pressburg.
100. ibid. p.210.
101. The house within the benefice of St Andreas stood between the Cathedral and the Wodritz Gate. The foundation, which also had a vineyard, dated back into the 14th century. See: Theodor Ortvay. Gesch. d. Stadt Pressburg I, Pressburg, 1903, p.81–82.
102. With the wrong date 15th March, 1628. UB Budapest, Collectio Prayana V 32, 71/44.
103. The exchange of letters in this connection continued in the months following.
104. Barbara Babthorpe to (Winefrid Wigmore), 6th July 1628. Old Writings, Letter Nr.6. Inst. Arch. Munich.
105. See above, note 104.
106. In addition the petition from Superior Babthorpe, July 1628 to the Emperor. HA Vienna, Court Treasury Hungary, Nr.135 red and MOL Budapest, Kamara E21, Benignae Resolutiones, ff.1r–2v.
107. HA Vienna, Court Treasury, Hungary, Nr.135 red.
108. Benignae Resolutiones, ff.1r–2v. MOL Budapest.
109. UB Budapest, Collection Prayana V, 42.
110. See above, Note 104.
111. Historia Collegii Posoniensis 1622–1635, p.15 and Acta irregistrata Collegii Posoniensis 6 Memorabilia Collegii Posoniensis 1622–1656, both in MOL Budapest.
112. Eubel, Hier. Cath. IV. p.19, 288.
113. For Archbishop Harrach and Fr Valerio Magni, see Grisar, Institut, p.324 ff.
114. Vita E, f.34v.; Vita I, p.28.
115. AV Rome, Miscell. Arm. II, 37, ff.213r–215r.
116. On 6th May, 1628, Nr.50 Inst. Arch. Munich.
117. Mary Poyntz, who was superior in Munich.
118. BV Rome, Barb. lat. 6945, f.83rv, respect. Barb. lat. 6956, ff.36r–38v.
119. Letter Nr.51. Inst. Arch. Munich.
120. Codes and decoding, BV Rome, Barb. lat. 6957, ff.62r–63v.
121. Codes and decoding, BV Rome, Barb. lat. 6956, ff.95r–101v.
122. " ... quanto il cervello di detta donna non sia ben frenato e regolato, teme hora, che gli ho parlato, più che mai, parendomi che sia piàdi donna, e che essa lo reput più che di huomo." Grisar, Institut. p.342. translated somewhat variously. The sentence is difficult to understand.
123. " ... gli havesse replicato che gli desse pur Sua Signoria Illustrissima la chiesa, che quando per questo l'havesse scomunicata, non se ne saria curata essendo scomunica ingiusta ..."
124. ARSI Rome, Austria 3/II, p.1011–1012.
125. On 8th April 1628. The date letter was received emerges from the contents. ARSI Rome, Epp.NN 2.f.326rv, Nr.1013.

XXV

SUPPRESSION OF THE HOUSES IN NAPLES AND UNDER THE VIENNESE NUNTIATURE

Negotiations in Rome 1628

Results of Bishop Klesl's letter — decisions of the Congregatio de Propaganda Fide, 21 March, 1628 — abuses in the Institute according to Secretary Ingoli's inventory — Letters of the Nuntios Carafa and Pallotto from Prague — Session of Propaganda Fide of 7th July, 1628 and the statement of the decisions of the special congregation of 13th April, 1628 — decree of suppression of the houses of the 'Jesuitesses'

After Mary Ward left Rome in November, 1626, the church authorities took no action for the present against the Institute. The two houses in the Papal States had been suppressed. In Naples things had taken somewhat longer, but it was only a question of time. Mary Ward had left for the north; the members of the curial congregation did not even know her exact destination, otherwise they might have reacted differently two years later.

It is not known if the Englishwomen left their house in Rome immediately after the eviction order, but it is most likely that they did.

Cardinal Bandini must have been astonished when he received Bishop Klesl's[1] news from Vienna, that the very same Englishwomen who had pestered him regularly for some years with petitions and visits, were now living under the protective hand of the Emperor in Vienna, had established a school there and allowed their pupils to produce a play. The General Superior had even travelled on to Hungary, in order to obtain entry there too, near the dangerous frontier of the archfiend of christianity. And all this without the approval of the Bishop of Vienna. It seemed as if one had to begin all over again.[2] This letter from the Bishop of Vienna informing the Cardinal of all these facts, fell into Ingoli's hands, and was produced before the 89th session of the Congregatio de Propaganda Fide on 21st March, 1628 — probably by the secretary himself.[3] Five Cardinals were present: Gaspare Borgia, Guido Bentivoglio, Ludovico

Ludovisi, Cornaro Federico Cornelius and Francesco Barberini, as well as the two prelates Corsius and Tornielli, and Fr Dominicus a Jesu Maria. The assembly made three decisions:

1. To set up a special congregation, which should inquire how the suppression of the Englishwomen's Institute could be achieved. Appointed for this were: Cardinals Millini, Borgia, Ludovisi and Zacchia, as well as the two prelates Maraldi, secretary of Briefs, and Fagnano, secretary of the Congregation for Bishops and Regulars. Not much is known about their attitude towards the Institute, with the exception of Cardinal Millini, though that was not important. Their task, the destruction of the Institute of the Jesuitesses, had already been made known to them.
2. Fr General Vitelleschi was to be warned against promoting the Institute.
3. Cardinal Lorenzo Magalotti should be charged with finding out the connection between the Institute of the Englishwomen and the Belgian 'Angelicae', and the Beguines. The ignorance of the congregation and of their secretary Ingoli is here made abundantly clear.

There were 'Angeliche' in Italy, but not in Belgium. Perhaps the word was used in error, a spoonerism for 'Anglicanae'. That there was no connection between the once suppressed and then reinstated Beguines and Mary Ward's Jesuitesses, the members of the Congregation should have known, for they had kept the Englishwomen under observation for some few years now. The Congregatio de Propaganda Fide should at least have been informed about the Institute; it would have wasted less time and been less awkward than later inquiries. The worst was to yet come.

It is not clear if Fr Vitelleschi immediately received the warning, or only after the papal decree of 7th July had been confirmed.

In the same week, Fr General sent four letters with instructions to the Jesuits in Naples and Vienna,[4] but it is doubtful if these were in connection with the decision of the Congregation; a week before,[5] the Provincial in Naples had received an instruction concerning the fathers' visits to the Englishwomen.

In blatant contrast to Father Vitelleschi's opinion, who knew the women and their Institute well, credence was given to a memorandum written by someone who hardly knew the women, who may even have never set eyes on them, and their Institute judged on the vituperative documents which had been circulating in Rome for the last few years. The person concerned was the secretary of Congregatio de Propaganda Fide, Francesco Ingoli, and the memorandum, his catalogue of abuses in the Englishwomen's Institute. It was probably intended as an aide-memoire.[6] It is undated, but without doubt can be placed in 1628.[7]

Secretary Ingoli wrote and corrected this in his own hand, and had it brought before the papal Secretary of State. There it was used by the Nuntios as an appendix in their task of the suppression of the Jesuitesses. Ingoli's attitude to the Englishwomen, whose fate was largely in his hands, is clearly evident.

The inventory shows little order and reveals little that is new, being derived from the already familiar accusations which had accompanied the Institute from the beginning. The accusations of 1615, and those of Harrison, Sherwood, Kellison and Rant, perhaps Godfather's Information and certainly current gossip wagged by tongues in Rome, together formed the material for this hotch-potch of a summary. Like the background material, Ignoli's 'Relatio' had the tragic result of producing apparent justification for the suppression of such a depraved community.

The points alleged are given in order:

1. The Institute was founded by a Jesuit of little education who was succeeded by a former Poor Clare nun of a masculine cast of mind. (vergine d'animo virile – originally it said – giovane d'animo virile).

2. The main work of this Institute consists in preaching in missionary countries, in spreading the faith especially among women and even the heathen; in teaching girls, and that in all subjects, as do the Jesuits. Like these, they also take three vows, have no enclosure, and can be dismissed by their general superior although they themselves are bound to the congregation.

3. They are proud, with a mania for liberty, and garrulous.

4. In England and Flanders the general superior drove around in a four-in-hand, and pretended to be a duchess incognito.

5. In England she preached publicly before the altar. In Louvain she gave explanations of the Our Father.

6. She blessed the Abbess of the Poor Clares in Gravelines.

7. The 'Jesuitesses' show preference to their Institute and prevent young girls from entering Orders.

8. They are so heavily in debt that their houses in St Omer and Liège have been confiscated by their creditors, although the first (in St Omer) was rented from the Bishop. They are so poor that they eat roots to stay alive. But the Jesuits help them, even in Rome.

9. They wish to teach theology in their schools, at least moral theology, so that their pupils may not be misled by their confessors.

10. They are obliged to confess their sins to the superior, particularly those concerning the sixth commandment, and must give the name of their partner.

11. They set spies to watch over the length of confession of indi-

viduals, and force them to say if the confessor attempted to turn them against the Institute.

12. They invent revelations and marvels, to obtain confirmation of their Institute.
13. They allow plays to be performed.
14. In England they sometimes wear the dress of the upper classes, sometimes that of servants.
15. They make long and expensive journeys, covering the costs from alms received.

    These journeys are dangerous for their chastity, as proved in the case of one of them in Bruges in Flanders. In Naples they were given a house by a distinguished man, offered on the condition that he might choose five of them and have them at his disposal.
16. They feign sickness in order to avoid the laws of fasting.
17. In England they have a bad reputation, and in the Jubilee Year (1625) they were publicly called whores.
18. One of them had a child. Her name and her partner in sin can be given.
19. Their depraved chaplain, who does not pray the breviary and leads an immoral life, has ruined their reputation.[8]

These incredible assertions do not deserve long consideration. Most of them have already been met before in the lengthy accusatory documents. The points have been given here in full, to show the concentrated impact of Ingoli's attack against the Englishwomen and their Institute.

A few observations may be permitted. It is remarkable that Ingoli could testify to the depravity of the Englishwomen in other parts of the world, but not of those who lived under the eyes of the Curia in Rome and to whom, as Cardinal Millini once said,[9] twenty-five spies had been allocated.

In general, Ingoli judged from hearsay but gave no names, as in the instance of the alleged offence of a member in Naples (item 18). Discretion was hardly his priority in these discreditable revelations. Here, collected together, were the supposed offences which had found credence in Rome together with the accusations already mentioned, which had been discussed ad infinitum. What is one supposed to make of the offence against chastity committed by a member near Bruges? There was no house of the Institute in the neighbourhood. That was true of Louvain, too, where Mary Ward was supposed to have given a commentary on the Our Father. And what is one supposed to make of these accusations in the face of Fr General Vitelleschi's words, written at the same time? It has already been explained that Fr General rejected Mary Ward's Institute in so far as it resembled the Society of Jesus and practised missionary activity, but he never attacked the women, for he was convinced of their goodness. 'I have always hoped that the Society of Jesus will give all the satisfaction it can to these women; they deserve it because of their virtue', were his words in a letter of 25th March, 1628 to Father Corcione.[10]

No, this inventory is little more than a broadsheet. It is incredible that it should come from the hand of a priest; still more incredible, that one who held high office in the Curia should put such defamatory statements on paper in order to use them as a weapon against women who could not defend themselves, because they were not called to account.

Towards the middle of 1628, the letters from Carafa and Pallotto arrived from Prague. A glance at the map is sufficient to show that the Englishwomen had managed to win the favour of the Elector of Bavaria and the Emperor for their work in a short time.

On lst July, 11[11] Cardinal Francesco Barberini answered Nuntius Carafa in Vienna that the affair of the Jesuitesses would be given mature consideration, and that the Pope's intentions on the matter would be sent him.

Proceedings against the Institute were conducted with unusual rapidity for Rome. On 7th July, 1628[12] the Pope presided over the 94th Session of the Congregatio de Propaganda Fide in the Quirinal Palace. The fifth item on the agenda dealt with the Jesuitesses. Present were Cardinals Millini, Borgia, Bentivoglio, Ludovisi, Antonio Barberini, Francesco Barberini, the prelates Corsius and Tornielli, and Fr Dominicus a Jesu Maria. At this session the findings of the Special Congregation of 13th April were confirmed. Cardinal Borgia reported on this.[13] The Cardinals allocated to this had been Millini, Borgia, Ludovisi and Zacchia, as also the secretary of Briefs, Maraldi. In accordance with the Pope's command (iuxta Sanctissimi Domini Nostri mandatum) they gave it as their judgement that a community of women like the Jesuitesses, who lived without any enclosure but took vows, was forbidden by canon law and should on that account be suppressed; all the more so because they taught girls according to the Jesuits' teaching curriculum and even, as it was asserted, intended going on the mission to preach the gospel, if not to distribute the sacraments. A directive should be sent to the Nuntius in Vienna giving him the special task of informing the Emperor and Empress of the Church's judgement. A somewhat delicate matter.

The Ordinaries concerned should be ordered to suppress the Institute in their dioceses. The same should be done in Belgium where, as Rome still thought, the Infanta Isabella Clara Eugenia supported them. Here, too, it is evident how little the Congregatio de Propaganda Fide knew about the Institute in Belgium.

Cardinal Magalotti should have consulted the papal archives, which prove that it was more than two years since the Infanta had handed in a petition on behalf of the Englishwomen. A short enquiry of Vives would have sufficed to learn the position of the Belgian government. But this was not done.

The Pope approved the Decree of the Special Congregation and charged Cardinal Millini, in his name, to advise the General of the Society of Jesus against advocacy of the Jesuitesses, either personally or through the fathers of his Order.

Again, a somewhat sensitive task.

Naples

1628 – 1629

The new Archbishop Buoncompagno – Nuntius Bichi – Decree of Suppression of 1628 – fate of the Institute members decided by Congregatio de Propaganda Fide – help given in vain by Fr Vitelleschi and the Neapolitan 'Council of Six'

Even after the suppression of the houses in the Papal States, the foundation in Naples was able to continue, as already mentioned. Archbishop Decio Carafa, no friend of the Jesuits, died in 1626. His successor Francesco Buoncompagno,[14] a great nephew of Gregory XIII, was, however, a friend of the Order. Fr Vitelleschi promised Mary Ward to intercede with the new pastor;[15] the help of the Fathers was already assured them.

But the situation changed when the harshly-worded Decree for Suppression of the Jesuitesses from the Congregatio de Propaganda Fide was forwarded to the Nuntius of Naples, Alessandro Bichi[16] on 14th July, 1628. The Nuntius was told to advise the Archbishop. But the Nuntius preserved silence. The Congregation then turned to Archbishop Buoncompagno.[17] This letter about the 'Sectresses' (questa donnesca setta) was equally sharp, but did not have the desired effect. On 9th September,[18] Secretary Ingoli wrote to Nuntius Bichi.

In the session of 17th October,[19] the Congregation gave their decision about the eight members of the community: the four Italians were to be sent home to their parents, the other four were to be accommodated in the town for the time being, at the discretion of the Nuntius and the Archbishop. There was talk of Belgians, but the four foreigners were actually Englishwomen. Those moved to Naples had been Mary Ratcliffe, Jane Browne and Lucy Shelley.[20]

From then on everything moved quickly. On 24th October,[21] the Congregation thanked Nuntius Bichi for his help in the affair. The 'harmful Institute' (questo dannoso Instituto) had been uprooted from Naples.

'They have no other refuge but your love', Fr Vitelleschi wrote compassionately to Fr Corcione,[22] on New Year's Day, 1628. At the beginning of February of the same year, Mary Ward sent a greeting[23] from Vienna to Winefrid Wigmore in Rome, and transferred her to Munich.

There are some letters from Fr General about this affair[24] but the commission given the new archbishop[25] by the Congregation must have marked the end of the community. A later intervention by the city was unsuccessful.[26]

Fr General Vitelleschi, who had originally doubted the wisdom of the Naples' foundation, wrote towards the end of the year[27] to the superior Mary Ratcliffe the following words of consolation: 'You know very well that anguish is the daily bread of the Lord's servants, and that his divine Majesty is pleased to be near those who are undergoing sufferings out of love for Him.'

In his instructions to the Provincial, Fr Vinzenio Carafa,[28] Fr Vitelleschi proposed that the homeless women might live in Bovino, in the College 'Monteleone', without payment. There is no mention of how long they remained in Naples.

Intermezzo in Brussels

1628 – 1629

Instruction of Congregatio de Progaganda Fide to the Nuntios in Vienna and Brussels about the 'Jesuitesses' – Belgian 'Jesuitesses' – Nuntius Fabio de Lagonissa of Brussels and his difficult position after receiving the decree from Rome – opposition of the Belgian bishops and the attitude of the government – the suppression of the house 'St Catherine's' of some Belgian 'Jesuitesses' – the English 'Jesuitesses' in Liège and St Omer from the viewpoint of Congregatio de Propaganda Fide

As a result of the 7th July Session of the Congregatio de Propaganda Fide, towards the middle of 1628 a directive was prepared for the nuntios in Vienna and Brussels. This had originally been intended only for Nuntius Pallotto in Vienna. There are two versions of the directive, both entered by the same copyist in the register 'Istruzioni diverse degli anni 1623 – 1628' of Congregatio de Propaganda Fide'.[29] These two differ, both as to content and form.

The first is strictly itemized, the second composed as a letter. The first, in spite of its heading,[30] was intended only for the Nuntius at the Emperor's court, the second to the Nuntius in Brussels. The Infanta is mentioned at the beginning of the text.

From a letter of Cardinal Millini's dated 13th July[31] to the Secretary of the Congregation, it emerges that it was he who had prepared the draft of an directive against the Englishwomen's Institute to Nuntius Pallotto. Accordingly, the first draft must be seen as Ingoli's, and the second as that of Millini. The final version, which went to two different addressees, has not been preserved, although it must have been sent. Cardinal Millini was the official in charge.

It should not cause surprise that both documents were preserved. They show marked differences – not a daily occurrence during Ingoli's term of office – and that not only from a formal point of view.

Ingoli kept to the points decided on by the Congregation in his statement. Millini, however, added an accusation extremely damaging to the women, that of disobedience towards the Pope, and mentioned two letters written by Father General Vitelleschi to the Jesuits. Ingoli may have anticipated difficulties caused by these alterations and thought it better not to depart from his own draft.

A brief summary of Ingoli's main grievances:

1.   Freedom from enclosure is not allowed by canon law for women's congregations.
2.   It constitutes a constant danger for the moral life of its members.
3.   The independence of the Institute from episcopal authority is likewise unacceptable, both as regards its community life and teaching activity.
4.   The consumption of their dowries has placed those members who have left in moral danger.
5.   The Jesuitesses take a vow binding them to the instruction of girls and uneducated women. Without permission from the local bishop, however, no teaching may be undertaken.

Rejection of the two most important struts in the construction of this new type of congregation, namely, freedom from enclosure and exemption of the members from episcopal power, was almost as old as the Institute itself. The consumption of dowries, which had indeed happened, was occasioned by the extreme poverty of the Englishwomen in Liège, by no means through riotous living or irresponsible financial dealings, as represented by Ingoli.

Of no less significance were the accusations of immorality – although unproven – which did enormous harm to the Institute and hardened the Curia in its opinion.

The complaint that they had taught without authorization could only have referred to Vienna, and they were saddled with this because of the political disagreements between the Emperor and the Bishop. Bishop Blaes of St Omer encouraged the Institute precisely because of its teaching activity, as had Bishop Wittelsbach of Liège and Archbishop Pázmány in Pressburg. Moreover, as mentioned previously, the houses in Liège, Cologne, Trier, Rome and Perugia, lay within the jurisdiction of religious overlords. Any abuses would have involved them in appropriate penalties. But the suppression of the houses in Italy did not happen in 1625 because — as one might be led to expect from the foregoing — they had educated girls with no authorization, and presumably under vow, but because they lived together as a religious community without enclosure. Besides which, a vow to educate girls and women was not customary with the Englishwomen. This appeared only in the Plan of the Institute 'Schola Beatae Mariae', which had been rejected by them. From Cardinal Millini's directive,[32] only those points which vary from those of Ingoli are given here. Millini conveyed his information in the form of a letter.

After the Pope had banned the Institute of the Jesuitesses in the whole of Italy, begins Millini, he also intended to suppress their foundations in Germany, Flanders and elsewhere. The Nuntius could help to suppress it in the Infanta's lands, respectively the Emperor's, by urging the Jesuitesses to enter an Order already recognised. They consort freely with men, independent as they are. This will lead to scandals. In England it has already been seen that moral dangers have faced those members who have left, their dowries having been consumed. These dangers will become even greater, for they recognise their own superiors only, and wish to be independent of the authority of the local bishop and the Holy See. The suppression of their Institute should be carried out soon, for their congregation is growing rapidly. They bring religious life into disrepute, above all that of the Society of Jesus, whose name they have adopted. The method of procedure is left to the prudence of the Nuntius concerned. As to his, Millini's, conversation with the Father General of the Society of Jesus, the latter has already written to the Jesuits and will do so again.[33]

As we have seen, Millini gave his directive an additional and dangerous twist by referring to the Englishwomen's independence of the Holy See. This was totally absurd. Mary Ward had sought for years to obtain the Pope's approval for her Institute and one of the basic concepts in her draft of the Institute was that of the vow of obedience to the Pope.

This directive makes one question whether the Congregatio de Propaganda Fide arrived at its decision objectively or if it was not, in fact, the target of biassed reporting. Or did it close its eyes to signs of the needs of its times by maintaining traditional conventions? The Nuntius in Brussels, like Nuntius Pallotto in Vienna, received the Decree of the Congregation about the suppression of the Jesuitesses' houses, as well as the directive.[34] To turn next to Flanders.

The Decree objected to 'Jesuitesses', intending the Englishwomen, as the Congregation knew of these only, and their instructions were therefore concerned only with them. They did not know of the existence of the small group of Belgian Jesuitesses which had no connection with Mary Ward's Institute. By 1628, however, the number of Englishwomen in Belgium had diminished. In Liège there was still a community on Mont St Martin, and these were under the Cologne Nuntiature. The community in St Omer lay within the jurisdiction of Nuntius Fabio de Lagonissa, this too comprised a very small number of members. It so happened that Nuntius Lagonissa [35] had been working in Portugal until 1627, and had held office in Brussels for a short time only, so knew hardly anything about Belgian Jesuitesses and still less about Mary Ward's Institute. He therefore extended his enquiries, as demanded by his task, to all the Jesuitesses in the Spanish Netherlands. When he reported his findings to the Congregation he included communities not intended by the Decree at all.

The Congregatio de Propaganda Fide cannot be exonerated from all blame in this indiscriminate destruction of small communities by their misleading directive, communities of whose existence they had never been informed and could therefore pass no judgement as to their actual worth or lack of it.

Nuntius Lagonissa reported cautiously (solamente significar).[36] In Brussels, he wrote, there were six Jesuitesses. Some English Jesuitesses, who had gone to Rome some years before to obtain approval of their Institute, had apparently returned to their country. This is where Ingoli should have stopped listening. He did not; nor did he when Nuntius Lagonissa warned him about acting precipitately, as the Belgian Jesuitesses did much good with their educational work and had many benefactors.[37]

Meanwhile, Lagonissa turned to the bishops of his area for information. Their answers were inadequate and not very reassuring.

In the diocese of Antwerp[38] there were no Jesuitesses, but there were 'devout ladies'. In the diocese of Bruges[39] however, and above all in Bruges itself, several groups of Jesuitesses were living, though their connection with the Society of Jesus was not exactly clear. The Jesuits were said to praise their way of life, which, to be sure, precisely because of their co-oooperation with the fathers, did seem to be rather prejudicial to the secular clergy and the enclosed Orders. These women take a vow of chastity, some of them also a vow of obedience to their confessor. They sometimes live in community and sometimes alone.

In the diocese of Tournai[40] there were no Jesuitesses. In the town of Tournai there were some sisters who led a devout life and taught girls, for which they received financial support from the town council. On Sundays the Jesuits preached to them and gave religious instruction. These woman are called 'Jesuitesses' by the people.

Even before Lagonissa's warning could have reached Rome,[41] the Congregation sent an urgent message to Brussels.[42] A long tug-of-war began between the harassed Lagonissa and Ingoli, stiff-necked in his obstinacy.

On 25th November, 1628[43] the Nuntius wrote a long letter to Cardinal Bandini about the affair, showing the difficulty of his position. In the first place, he wrote, the suppression of the Jesuitesses was rejected out of hand by the Infanta and her government. For reasons they gave the women's teaching activity, which was a great blessing for the country, and that Rome's intervention would be seen as a violation of long-standing and well-protected privileges. In any case, there were few Jesuitesses in Belgium. There were several Ursulines, and certain other communities who devoted themselves to various good works as lay people. Upon which he, the Nuntius, had answered that every sort of life which resembled an Order had been forbidden by decrees and councils of the Church and required the approval of the local bishop and the Holy See. Finally, the Infanta had yielded and agreed to the suppression of those communities which had no enclosure but had taken vows, and which had not been approved.

The Nuntius had not yet been able to speak to the Archbishop of Malines. This time Lagonissa mentioned five Jesuitesses in Brussels. Their congregation, he thought, could be suppressed without causing much stir. The Jesuitesses had not received any instructions from the general of their order, although it would be important to gain her co-operation for the suppression.

On the same day, Lagonissa addressed a letter to Secretary Ingoli,[44] saying that he had followed the example of the Archbishop of Naples, but one could not always do what one wished in Belgium. That was true enough.

Hardly a month later and the Nuntius excused himself once again to Ingoli:[45] he had not been able to do much, as the Infanta was ill. The counsellors had suggested forbidding the Jesuitesses their conventual lifestyle, but not their educational work. Lagonissa had apparently attempted to reach a compromise, for he recommended this solution.

A week later[46] the Nuntius made excuses to Cardinal Barberini: he would have carried out the suppression of the Jesuitesses long ago, if these did not have hidden benefactors, clever and scholarly men, who were so long in the service of Holy See that it posed no problem to them. It is quite clear who was meant here. In his letter of 13th January, 1629 to Ingoli[47] he again says that the absence of the Archbishop of Malines had postponed the suppression of the Jesuitesses.

A week later[48] Lagonissa reported to Cardinal Bandini that the Infanta and her council had given their agreement to the suppression of those Jesuitesses who wished to be taken as religious sisters, but not those who taught girls as lay people and were indispensable for the country.

It was already February, 1629[49] before the Congregation had to admit to the Nuntius that the General of the Society of Jesus had not complied with their request to co-operate in the suppression of the Jesuitesses. We know that on the contrary Fr Vitelleschi promoted the women, and precisely the English Jesuitesses in other countries with his recommendations and words of consolation.

It was almost Spring[50] before Nuntius Lagonissa once again fended off Ingoli with the prospect of the imminent suppression of Jesuitesses in Belgium. The Flemish, he thought, were slow to make up their minds. As an Italian speaking to an Italian, he was right.

Once again[51] the Congregation's order to suppress the Jesuitesses in Belgium reached the Nuntius. Communities without enclosure and without solemn vows were canonically forbidden. On the 10th May, 1629[52] the position was this: Archbishop Jacques Boonen of Malines signed the decree of suppression for the Jesuitesses in his diocese, who lived in the house 'St Catherine's' in Brussels.

As shown in this exchange of letters, not much was known about the Belgian Jesuitesses. In the land where Beguines were traditional, there were several communities of women who formed a sort of 'Pium Institutum' and taught girls and doubtless contributed much to their homeland with their constructive work. They confessed to the Jesuits, received some spiritual direction from them, and were called 'Jesuitesses' in local parlance.

One such community lived in Brussels, in Guldenplatz, in a house known as 'St Catherine', opposite the Jesuits. In addition to the foundress, Marie de la Lamnie, there were seven members. They had devoted themselves to teaching girls since 1608 and were permitted to do so by the Council of Brabant and the Archbishop of Malines. They enjoyed a good reputation among the people because of their way of life and their work. They took vows of chastity, and a promise of obedience to their superior but had not taken a vow of poverty, as each one lived on her personal income. They gave 220 guilders annually for the support of poor girls; their oratory was endowed with two mass stipends. Marie de la Lamnie had provided her own house for this work and for the community.[53]

The Archbishop's decree showed his unwillingness at the enforced suppression of the Jesuitesses in Brussels. This was to be carried out on the orders of the Nuntius, it ran, as the previous visitation had shown nothing but good of the women, who were not Jesuitesses but simply called that by the people. The only valid reason for their suppression was that they had founded a community according to ancient practice – without ecclesial approbation, nothing to do with freedom from enclosure.

What was actually suppressed here? The Archbishop expressly approved of their teaching activities – and as Ordinary he was justified in doing so – he even took over the management of their endowment for poor pupils. They could continue to teach as lay people.

But what had they been before? Their vows had been dissolved. Which had they actually taken? Their obedience was a promise, they managed their own finances, and they simply took a vow of chastity, a private vow therefore, which could never be in conflict with canon law. The loose union of their community had been destroyed − their oratory and their mass stipend had been taken away from them, but no Roman authorities could stop subjects of the Infanta, on Belgian soil, from living together as lay people in one house. Canon van Wachtendonk, who visited them once more on 15th November, spoke in his report of 'aliis in dicta domo commorantibus', of others who lived in the house. This dissolution, achieved with such difficulty by Nuntius Lagonissa, and held up later as a model by the Congregatio de Propaganda Fide was, de facto, a purely external compromise between the Belgian government's defensive demands, and the Congregatio's determination to ensure the implementation of its canonical decrees.

It must not be assumed that the matter ended here. By no means. First of all, those who took part in the suppression had to be thanked for their efforts.[54] Secretary Ingoli praised Lagonissa's actions as an example for other nuntios.[55] Archbishop Jacques Boonen of Malines received a papal letter of thanks.[56] One wonders if he had joy of it. In a letter to Ingoli[57] the Nuntius of Flanders admitted that some Jesuitesses lived in the Archdiocese of Cambrai, but Archbishop Francois van der Burch was causing difficulties about the matter. Thereupon the Congregatio commissioned the Archbishop to follow the example of the Archbishop of Malines, and suppress the Jesuitesses in his Archdiocese.[58]

Nuntius Lagonissa seems to have been spurred on by the praise he had received, for on 28th July,[59] he enquired of Ingoli if he, as Nuntius, could make a visitation of the Archdiocese of Cambrai against the will of its Archbishop. In the same letter he informed the Secretary of something that was not known to him which was to have far-reaching consequences for Mary Ward's Institute, namely the fact that there were also Jesuitesses in Liège.

A great deal of Lagonissa's letter was taken up with an ornately worded request that Ingoli might convey a hint to the Pope concerning gratitude for his efforts. Lagonissa did not like Belgium, and Infanta Isabella Clara Eugenia made frequent representations to the King of Spain in order to have this difficult, fiery man transferred. When one considers, however, that Lagonissa's request rested on the questionable suppression of a tiny community of pious teachers, his words touch a sore nerve. The cardinal's hat desired by the Nuntius was not granted. It would have been thirty pieces of silver.

Lagonissa's remark directed the attention of the Congregatio de Propaganda Fide to southern Belgium. Probably as bait, the Nuntius sent a copy of the papal letter of praise for the Archbishop of Malines, to Archbishop van der Burch in Cambrai.[60] He even went to meet him.[61] Unfortunately, there is no record of what they said, but the Archbishop had to begin clearing his archdiocese of Jesuitesses. He invited the superiors of the community of Notre Dame sisters from Mons, Valenciennes, Ath and Maubeuge, and several other communities and tried to persuade them to accept enclosure. This cannot have helped matters much, for the women defended themselves and answered that no one could be forced into the religious state. Nor could they. The elderly members of their community would not be able to endure the unaccustomed form of life within an enclosure. Neither were their houses suitable for enclosed convents, and any extension would cost a lot of money. Their work with the children would be hindered by the change.[62] Upon which the Archbishop wrote a long and emphatic letter to the Belgian Ambassador in Rome, to Vives.[63] In the diocese of Cambrai there were no Jesuitesses, but of course there were communities whose members taught girls as, for example, the Daughters of St Agnes and many others who had been active for a long time in Belgium, most rewardingly. But they were no Jesuitesses. There were some, it appeared, in Liège. These took vows, travelled around, were active in the apostolate, and preached.

The letter came into the archives of the Congregatio de Propagatio Fide. Van der Burch justified his inaction to the Nuntius by referring to a letter expected from Rome and, more to the point, the threatening attitude of the civil authorities, who stood firmly behind the communities and their work.[64]

But the Congregation did not leave Lagonissa in peace. He was first of all to await the Archbishop of Cambrai's actions, and only if he hesitated to cooperate, to visit the Archdiocese. Information had reached the Congregatio from Germany that the Jesuitesses in Brussels were still living in their house, and teaching girls. The Jesuitesses from Mons were to be suppressed.[65]

Lagonissa parried the blow, and wrote to Ingoli[66] that he had come to an agreement with the Infanta's Privy Council to bide his time with the Archbishop of Cambrai before he made another move.[67]

All the same, he wrote to Cardinal Gaspare Borgia[68] that the Archbishop of Cambrai was obstructing the suppression of the Jesuitesses, and had won over the Magistrate of Mons to intercede for them with the Infanta; the Jesuitesses in Brussels had in fact been suppressed.

Lagonissa probably felt impelled by these constant hints about the Jesuitesses still living in Brussels to arrange another visitation for the women in St Catherine's. Canon Johannes van Wachtendonk was commissioned with this, but on 10th November he could find nothing that was contrary to the decree of the Congregation: the mass stipend had been transferred, the community's oratory removed. The visitor could not find any sign indicative of a religious community.[69] But the women still lived in the house. It was made clear to Nuntius Lagonissa that this visitation was outside his competence in Belgium.

Finally, after extensive researches and countless letters, and with the help of information given by the Englishwomen's ancient enemy Vives, who lived in Rome, the Congregatio de Propaganda Fide learnt the difference between the 'English Ladies', 'Ursulines' and 'Daughters of St Agnes'. The decree of suppression against the English Jesuitesses, so the Ambassador wrote to the Infanta,[70] remained in force, but not against those Belgian Jesuitesses, about whom Lagonissa was to receive new information.

1629 had grown old. Vives erred if he thought the Congregation and, above all, its Secretary, would leave the Belgian Jesuitesses in peace.[71] Now for the fate of the Englishwomen.

Vienna

1628 – 1630

Nuntius Pallotto, a secret but most dangerous opponent of the Institute in Vienna – Mary Ward in Eger at a cure – her return to Vienna and audience with Pallotto, who persuades her to visit Rome – Mary Ward in Munich, Autumn 1628 and her hesitation to leave for Rome – her second audience with Pallotto and decision to go to Rome – farewell from Vienna – Nuntius Pallotto and Cardinal Klesl of Vienna – attitude of the Curia – episcopal visitation of the house 'Stoss am Himmel' of 7th October, 1629 – the 'informatio Generalis' of the Vienna consistory – the decree of suppression, a draft – Jesuits and Jesuitesses in Vienna

The suppression of the Institute house in Vienna, whose foundation had been made possible by the Emperor and which depended on his favour materially, was not to be undertaken lightly by the Curia in Rome. It proceeded with its time-honoured diplomacy, very cautiously. A distinction is to be made between the part played by its representative, Nuntius Pallotto, and that of the bishop of the place, Cardinal Klesl. Each had their specific role in the dramatic turn of events.

Carlo Carafa was still Nuntius, when the Court returned to Vienna from Prague in July, 1628. There was also the specially commissioned Nuntius-Extraordinary, one Giovanni Battista Pallotto. Carafa may have found the division of labour hard, as this clearly showed that Rome considered he had not come up to expectations.[72] Cardinal Francesco Barberini wrote to Nuntius Carafa on 1st July [73] saying merely that the matter of the Jesuitesses would be considered carefully, and that Carafa would be informed of the Pope's intentions on the matter. This was probably in answer to Carafa's censorious letter from Prague about the Englishwomen.

However, it was not the departing Nuntius, but the Nuntius-Extraordinary who received the commission from the Congregatio de Propaganda Fide to suppress the Institute.[74]

Scarcely fourteen days later[75] Pallotto received a laudatory epistle from Rome. He had acted wisely, it said, in dissuading the Jesuitesses from their proposal to found a house in Prague, and in advising their General Superior to return to Rome where an end could be made to this dangerous movement (queste pericoloso movimento).

It will be remembered, however, that Pallotto had intimated something quite different concerning the competent authorities in Rome when he had met the women in Prague.[76] The letter had been addressed to Cardinal Francesco Barberini, who therefore recognised Pallotto as a master of devious diplomacy.

Meanwhile Mary Ward had set off for Eger[77] for a water cure, in total ignorance of what was going on. Her last notes come from there, headed 'Various Papers' in the collection of writings relating to her life. A few sentences from them are given here:

'I had a great clear and quiet light or knowledge of what God does in and by his creatures (my poor self especially), and what they are or do towards him. I saw these two parts so distinctly, and what was particular to each, but am incapable of expressing it... Here I had a clear sight of much that is good, hindered, deferred, or perhaps lost wholly and forever, with greatest ingratitude to God, who ordained it through his immense love. This is an infinite loss to both doer and receiver.'[78]

Back in Vienna, Pallotto began a busy correspondence. His reaction to the directive from Rome was somewhat restrained – probably anticipating what it would entail.[79] If the order were carried out, he considered, it might harm the negotiations connected with the conflict in Mantua, as the Englishwomen depended on the Society of Jesus, and these are said to have a great influence at court. Pallotto was also in touch with Fr Valerio Magni, who was in Rome at this time.[80]

Cardinal Barberini wrote with unusual sharpness to Pallotto [81] that the impudence (l'impertinenza) of the superior of the Jesuitesses was increasing steadily and that Pallotto should try to discredit (sceditar) her Institute. The reports from the two Nuntios from Prague had not failed in their aim.

But Pallotto waited for Mary Ward's arrival in Vienna,[82] which Cardinal Barberini understood. At the beginning of September,[83] in answer to Pallotto's rather hesitant letter of 5th August, he gave the flattering information that his, Pallotto's, nomination as Nuntius of Vienna and Archbishop of Thessalonica was imminent. It was for Pallotto, to decide when to carry out the injunction against the Jesuitesses, but he must not do anything prejudicial to the Pope's matter in Mantua. As to whether the Fr General of the Society of Jesus had been spoken to, Cardinal Barberini did not know.

Mary Ward returned to Vienna from Eger at the beginning of September. On Sunday, 10th September, as had been arranged in Prague, 'the Englishwoman Maria della Guardia, who allows herself to be called the General Superioress of the Society of Jesus', went to her audience with Nuntius Pallotto.

The gist of the conversation is known from his letter to Cardinal Francesco Barberini.[84] Mary Ward, he said, was aware of the letters against her which had been written from Prague to Rome, as did the Father General of the Society of Jesus, but had done nothing about it so far. She also knew that a decision had been taken by Rome, and that Nuntius Pallotto was to carry it out. She would have liked to know what Pallotto was about to do but he, the Nuntius, had evaded her question by remarking that Mary Ward had broken the agreement which she had made with him in Prague.

It is doubtful if Mary Ward realised what he was like. In Prague he had not acted as brusquely as Carafa. However, it is even more doubtful that she informed him so readily of her knowledge of the letters directed against her; she was a reserved person, as we have seen. One wonders, incidentally, how she could have learnt about them. Archbishop Harrach would have beem careful not to reveal the contents of the Nuntios' letters to the Englishwomen – even supposing that he knew them. Fr Valerio Magni is still less likely to have done so. The Jesuits in Vienna would probably not have known about them either. Most likely it was from Rome that Mary Ward learnt the facts, from members who had remained there.[85] That would also explain why Fr Vitelleschi was marking time.

Did Nuntius Pallotto feel his way by cautious allusions, without arousing Mary Ward's suspicions? After all, she had asked him trustingly what he was going to do. That would not have been possible if she had regarded Nuntius Pallotto as hostile towards her.

However that may be, instead of an answer she was given a reprimand for acting independently in Prague. That was a remarkable affront, for Mary Ward and the Englishwomen were not Pallotto's prisoners. Mary Ward had not even gone over his head, for the allocation of a church lay within the competence of the bishop of the place, not the nuntius.

And then began the great debate about Mary Ward's return to Rome. Pallotto had written to Cardinal Francesco Barberini on 13th September in a letter already mentioned, that the Institute should not be allowed to expand any further. Yet the Jesuitesses had powerful benefactors, not only in the persons of the Emperor and the Elector of Bavaria, but also in Cardinal Franz Dietrichstein, Bishop of Olmutz, in Cardinal Pázmány and in influential Jesuits. He had done nothing so far, continued Pallotto, as he would first of all like to learn from the Provincial, Fr Dombrinus, what Fr General Vitelleschi had ordered them to do in the matter.[86] He would like to hear from Nuntius Lagonissa in Brussels how he had dealt with the problem.[87] Finally, there was the Emperor, the Empress and the Elector of Bavaria and their connections with these women. Pallotto would act with the necessary severity.

Nuntius Pallotto had a full programme before him in his new career at the Imperial Court.

It must be assumed that Mary Ward did not give the Nuntius sufficient assurances of returning to Rome during this audience of 10th September. Pallotto would otherwise have informed Cardinal Francesco Barberini in his letter of 13th September.

Soon after her conversation with the Nuntius, certainly after 20th September, 1628,[88] Mary Ward left Vienna. The exact date is not known, nor that of her arrival in Munich. She probably did not see this departure from Vienna as final, for there is nothing about her taking leave of the Emperor and Empress, and that would have been customary. It can be taken for granted that she travelled first to Munich. Before undertaking a journey to Rome that was of such consequence for the Institute, it would have been essential for her to consult with the oldest members of the Institute. Again, it was only there and not in the house in Vienna that she could gather her companions and make preparations for the weeks' long journey over the already wintry Alps. One must not forget that her most trusted companion had been left behind in Munich. A great deal had happened in the meantime.

It was a different matter for Nuntius Pallotto. What would happen, if Mary Ward acted as independently on her arrival in Munich as she had in Prague? There was no Cardinal Harrach to obstruct her. On the contrary, Elector Maximilian would support both her and her Institute, which offered such excellent educational opportunities to the girls in his city.

Pallotto therefore ordered this delicate woman, who had hardly set foot in Munich, to return to Vienna for a further meeting. At the end of October she told him that she had not finished the preparations for her journey.[89] This could have set alarm bells buzzing.

In the meanwhile the Nuntius had been staying as the guest of Cardinal Franz Dietrichstein, Bishop of Olmutz, in his castle at Nikolsburg.[90] He had used the opportunity by advising Dietrichstein to wait until their Institute had been examined in Rome [91] before allowing the Englishwomen into his diocese. Apart from that there are no references to a foundation in Moravia, though that is no proof that there had not been any negotiations. Here, too, Pallotto did not reveal what he knew, or what he had been ordered to do. Cardinal Dietrichstein, who knew nothing of the facts of the case, quite naturally agreed. What is significant is Pallotto's appendix, which sounds like an excuse for his behaviour in Nikolsburg: the Englishwomen were held in high esteem by the Emperor, the Elector of Bavaria and the Archbishop of Gran (Peter Pázmány), as well as

by their friends among the Jesuits. These were the champions of the
Roman Catholic Church against the forces of the Reformation in
the middle of Europe.

Mary Ward must have left Munich comparatively soon after
receiving Pallotto's invitation, for she was already in Vienna when
the Nuntius arrived from Nikolsberg and made an appointment for
an audience on 4th November. But Pallotto postponed this until
5th Novemer. The next detailed letter from the Nuntius was on
11th November[92] to Cardinal Francesco Barberini, which includes
a report of his last meeting with Mary Ward. The relevant passage
is given verbatim:

'On Sunday and on Thursday (that was 5th and 9th November),
I spoke for a long time with Donna Maria della Guardia. She is at
last prepared to go to Rome as soon as possible, to negotiate concerning the approval of her Institute. She submits to the disposal,
the decision, and the will of the Holy See and of the Pope. I have
refrained from comment, all the more so as I have seen that this
is what your Grace wishes and approves. My consolation lies in
the effect of my endeavours, for it is likely that, as she said, she
will take her leave of their Majesties this week. Although she is a
woman, she has many advisers at her disposal. I shall only feel safe
when I know that she is there.'(in Rome). [93]

Comment would be superfluous.

The next days, however, did not bring the Nuntius the fulfilment
of his desire.

His letter to Cardinal Bandini shows that.[94] But by 18th November
there was no turning back. Mary Ward had taken her leave of the
Emperor and Empress.[95] On the afternoon of November 22nd she left
Vienna, to treat of the confirmation of her Institute in Rome.[96]

Nuntius Pallotto now had his hands free to take up another
delicate task: Mantua.

Two short letters to Mary Ward from these last days before she
left Vienna say a good deal more than the whole correspondence
between the Viennese nuntiature and the Roman authorities put
together. One of them is a personal letter of thanks'from Pallotto,
the other contains Fr Vitelleschi's words of consolation. Mary Ward
had obtained a biography of St Edmund for the Nuntius, a little
book about the saint whom Pallotto revered. On 16th November[97]
he thanked her for it in a stylistically impeccable letter and promised
Mary Ward his prayers for her intention (et à suoi pii intenti nelle
preghiere, che indegnamente offrisco ne miei sacrificii). He also
thanked her for the trust she had shown him. Up to the last,
the letters of this urbane diplomat were full of flowery phrases.
It cannot be denied that he abused Mary Ward's trust. It would
be interesting to know which St Edmund was referred to. The calendar of saints has two Edmunds: the martyr king, who lived in the
ninth century and was murdered by the invading Danes for being a

christian, and Edmund Rich, who lived in the early Middle ages, was Archbishop of Canterbury, and had to leave the country because of his struggle with Henry III over the rights of the Church. He died in 1240 in the monastery at Soissy in France. Perhaps one of these names had been mentioned in the conversation between the Nuntius and the Englishwoman. At all events, the little volume dealt with a saint who had worked for the faith and the church in England. That in itself is significant.

Far simpler, and far more sincere, are the few sentences written by Fr General on 18th November,[98] which did not reach Mary Ward in Vienna. She had obviously written to the General on 29th October about her anxieties and the dangerous predicament of her Institute. In his short reply he said: 'From your letter of 29th of last month, I see that you have not lacked an opportunity for practising patience, and I think that the Lord has sent you this as a sign of his love. It is well known that his divine Majesty spurs on his servants to perfection in this way. I think that those who thwart your plan with an honest motive, are convinced as all are, that they are doing the Lord's will. That is why it is necessary that we help ourselves by praying, so that his divine Majesty may condescend to reveal his will, in order to remove the difficulties which stand in the way of achievement. I will implore his divine goodness to take you under his protection, and end this letter...' Fr Vitelleschi could not have expressed his esteem of Mary Ward more tenderly.

Meanwhile Bishop Klesl of Vienna has been abandoned since 6th May, 1628, when he asked Cardinal Bandini for the fourth time for guidance in his war with the Jesuitesses.[99]

On 14th July,[100] the same day as that on which the enclosed directive about the suppression of the Englishwomen's Institute was written to Nuntius Lagonissa in Brussels and Nuntius Pallotto in Vienna, the Congregatio de Propaganda Fide likewise composed an answer to Bishop Klesl. His was a humble role, for he was merely informed that Nuntius Pallotto had been put in charge of the affair. Klesl would be kept informed. He could be of assistance to the Nuntius with his experience and wisdom (sperimentata prudenza). Apart from keeping strictly to official paths, the Curia probably did not wish to put this man, once the Emperor's prisoner, in a key position in such a delicate matter; there was too much at risk in the Mantua affair. Pallotto promised,[101] moreover, to negotiate with Cardinal Klesl and Nuntius Carafa.

How far did Cardinal Klesl comply? Although the Bishop of Vienna must have received the Congregation's letter of 14th July, he repeated his request to Cardinal Bandini on 12th August[102] for instructions about the Jesuitesses, as he did not know the Pope's intentions concerning those women who were teaching girls in his diocese without his, the Bishop's, permission. Bishop Klesl had probably spoken with the Jesuits, but not, apparently, with

Nuntius Pallotto, for he does not mention any such conversation in his letter. It is remarkable that Cardinal Klesl always sent his letters to Cardinal Bandini, the oldest member of the Congregation and not, like Pallotto, to the Secretary of State, Cardinal Francesco Barberini.

It was already Autumn[103] when Cardinal Klesl turned once more to the Congregation, this time with a very unambiguous letter. He had still not received any directives about the Jesuitesses, he said, and once more complained that he knew nothing about these women, even whether they were religious sisters or not. The Jesuits refused to govern their community, there were daily unpleasantnesses, and there was fear of scandal (potra esse ... delle scandali). It would not be his, Klesl's, fault if the Congregation continued to shilly-shally and more problems were to follow. The Englishwomen were teaching 465 older girls and so causing harm to other orders.

It can be judged by this large number − for those days − that the school had developed rapidly in one year. The difficulties with the other convents may simply have been the result of the English-women's life without enclosure, and not because of girls entering with them; there is not a single instance of a candidate entering the Institute in Vienna.

The irritated bishop had obviously made some impact on the Congregatio de Propaganda Fide with his letter. In its session of 17th October,[104] it empowered Cardinal Klesl to take action, as the Archbishop of Naples had already done, namely, to suppress the Jesuitesses's foundation and dissolve their community. Bluntly, the large school 'cum maximo scandalorum periculo', with the greatest danger of scandals, was the reason given for the suppression.

But the autonomy of the Bishop was not ipso facto recognized on this occasion.

In the Congregation's answer of 26th October to Vienna,[105] it said that the directives against the Jesuitesses had been made known to the Nuntius. Should the disorders (disordini) become greater, then he, Bishop Klesl could take action against them with full episcopal power, as the Archbishop of Naples had done.

One can understand why Nuntius Pallotto advised Mary Ward to pay a farewell visit to Cardinal Klesl before she left Vienna for the last time.[106]

Apparently no one was eager to be the first to take action against this house full of young girls, the 'Stoss am Himmel'. In the middle of 1629[107] Secretary Ingoli had to alert them to the example of Nuntius Lagonissa, who had suppressed the Jesuitesses in Brussels. Pallotto might consult with the Bishop of Vienna, who had been the first to take up arms against the Englishwomen, and was now to effect the dissolution.[108] This hint left nothing to the imagination. But Nuntius Pallotto was still obtaining information from abroad,[109] and Cardinal Klesl kept silence.[110] The Bishop showed an inclination to have a second visitation of the Englishwomen's house, so Pallotto reported in September, 1629 to Rome,[111] but he must have run up against difficulties. Not even Pallotto had been able to get the Emperor to agree with him in several conversations, as he not only had support from Munich, but also from the edifying manner of life and the excellent teaching of the Jesuitesses (ma per la relatione della vita esemplare e del frutto, che fanno in questa città dove la buona educatione et instrutione delle donne), for which freedom from enclosure was essential.

This praise raises a question. If a strict catholic like Emperor Ferdinand II gave such witness to the exemplary life of the Englishwomen, where was the danger of scandals?

Finally, Cardinal Klesl was able to make use of his rights as Bishop of Vienna, though details are lacking. After much effort, the episcopal visitation of the house 'Stoss am Himmel' was carried out on 7th October, 1629.

The report of the Visitation[112] is in duplicate form. It is a revised fair copy, partly compiled by the diocesan secretary Matthew Sengler and corrected by Tobias Schwab. No copy of the finished document has survived. The questions concern the Institute as well as individual members.

The house 'Stoss am Himmel' in Vienna was not the most important of the foundations, but it is one about which a good many details are known – more than most. This enquiry gives valuable details about its construction and the people in the house. Undoubtedly it was the superior, Margaret Genison, who answered the general questions. The answers to the individual questions offer a unique source for information about the different members of the community.

The Vienna foundation was one of Mary Ward's later ones. It has the characteristics of such: three of the eleven members were English, the remaining eight coming from south Germany.

All of them were therefore foreigners. That was no disadvantage as the city of Vienna had for years been the repository of many nations. More to the point was the age of the members: three were under twenty, three were novices; one of them, although she had belonged to the Institute for two and a half years, had not yet made her profession. As well as that, of the eleven members only four were occupied with teaching and educational work: the Englishwoman Helen Clifford was prefect of the four boarders (the charge was 120 guilders a year), Anna Maria Mehrin from Constance was prefect of the schools, Anna Redlin from Mosberg and the 17 year-old Margaret Zimmerin from Munich were teachers. Maria Grainwoldin and the 18 year-old Klara Knellin may also have been involved in the school, but they were not entered as teachers. Even for the seventeenth century that was an extremely small staff for 450 pupils. One can quite understand Mary Ward's call for personel for the work of the Institute in Vienna.[113]

The sources do not reveal how long the Englishwomen's school was in existence, but it is unlikely that teaching could have continued long after the suppression of the Institute in January, 1631.

The Visitation was conducted by Tobias Schwab as official, Johann Augustin Zwerger and Stephan Zwirschlag from St Stephan's, and the diocesan notary Matthaus Sengler. Stephan Zwirschlag had conducted the first Visitation.[114]

Now to the questions and answers, given here in somewhat shorter form :

1. When did they come to Vienna? – Two years ago.
2. Are they an Order or an Institute? – They are an Institute and follow the Rule of the Jesuits as far is possible for women. They teach about 400 girls in Latin, reading and writing German, and sewing.
3. Are they religious sisters or lay people? Which Rule do they follow? – After confirmation of their Institute they will be religious sisters, their Rules are written in English.
4. Do they live in community? Why? – Yes. For their own salvation and that of their neighbour, as far as women are able.
5. When, where and through whom was their Institute founded? – About twenty years ago, in St Omer, by their General superior Mary Ward.
6. Has their congregation been confirmed by the Holy See? – It gained the approbation of Pope Paul V, who also promised to confirm it.
7. To whom are they subject? – In Vienna to the superior and at the same time to the Mother General Superior. The General Superior must answer for herself as to whom she is subordinate.
8. What offices are there in the community? – The Superior, the school prefect and the procurator, as in the Society of Jesus.
9. What is their official (ratione statuti) name? – Mothers of the Society of Jesus.
10. Who gave them permission (facultas) to set up a community in Vienna? Did the Pope? The Bishop? – The General Superior. From whom she received permission, they do not know; she herself will answer.
11. Do they take vows? Which? Simple or solemn? – The three vows: poverty, chastity, obedience.
12. Who can release them from these vows? – The General Superior, for good reason.
13. How are the vows taken? – According to a certain formula, before the Blessed Sacrament. After profession they pray the Roman Breviary.

14. Is their vow of obedience (promissionem obedientiae) entered in a book? – Yes.
15. Who gave them their house? Who pays their expenses? – The Emperor.
16. Do they have allowances? – Yes. 600 guilders from the Emperor annually and 400 guilders from the Empress.
17. Are the expenses paid in common? By whom? – Yes. The superior does this together with the Procurator.
18. Have they an Oratory? Is Mass celebrated there? – Yes, but no Mass is said there.
19. In what part of the house do they come together for prayer? – Generally in the Oratory.
20. What confessors do they have? – Fathers from the Society of Jesus. At present Fr Guldin.
21. Are they subject to the Society of Jesus? Who gave them permission to follow the Society of Jesus? – The answer to these items should be made by the General Superior.
22. Do they have their own precepts and rules (statuta et ordinationes)? Who has approved of these? They should produce them. – They know them.
23. How many years of probation do they have before profession? – Two.
24. What age is prescribed for admission to vows? – Sixteen years of age.
25. Is their dress one special to the Institute or a secular dress? – It is one particular to the Institute, but it is not blessed, and may be altered according to the judgement (placidum) of the General Superior.
26. Do they allow men entry into the house? – None, except for confessors, doctors and workmen.
27. Who is the English priest who goes in and out? Is he their confessor? – No, he is a relation of the Mother General Superior (the priest Henry Lee). He sometimes takes the outgoing post and supplies.

Some explanations are added here. Several items as, for instance, how long the Englishwomen were in Vienna, what they are called and what Rule they follow, should have been known by the Viennese diocesan office, but the Visitors were trying to construct a complete picture of the congregation; the questions had been prepared before the Visitation; the writing specimens reveal that. Margaret Genison answered all the general questions openly, sometimes even in more detail than was demanded: the Englishwomen follow the Rule of the Society of Jesus, they are lay people until the confirmation of their Institute and lead a communal life. But when it was a matter of ambivalent questions, the Superior referred these to Mary Ward. These were, for example, item 7 which treated of subordination to the General superior or item 10, about permission to found in Vienna, or 21, the dependence of the Institute on the Society of Jesus and the adoption of their constitutions. When they were questioned in item 3 about the their type of life and rule, Margaret Genison was evasive and merely replied that their rules were in English. Apparently this satisfied the Visitors, as it is unlikely that they would have understood the language. When, in item 22, they enquired about 'pecularia statua et ordinationes', their own particular prescripts and rules, the Superior answered briefly that they were known to each one of them. She passed over the request to inspect them.

It may be remembered that on the first Visitation on 18th November, 1627[115] Mary Ward spoke of 'suas regulas...versari Romae'. She meant the constitutions, without a doubt. It is not possible to say if these Visitors had these in mind, without further information. At any rate, the superior withheld a more explicit answer. She was perfectly justified, for as long as the rules and constitutions of the Institute had not been confirmed by the Pope, the members could remain silent about a matter under discussion in Rome.

By and large, the Visitors could have made more detailed enquires on their first visit, but they did not.

Up to this point, the general questions were directed to the Superior, Margaret Genison. The personal questioning of the members has been laid out in the form of a table.

The atmosphere may have been rather chilly, but there is nothing in this report that suggests hostility, or aggressiveness in the questioning. Both parties will have known the outcome was inevitable.

A total contrast in ecclesiastical attitude is revealed in an undated document,[116] which most probably originated from the Viennese Diocesan Consistory. It has survived as a fair copy revised by General Vicar Tobias Schwab, and also as a revised copy. Except in a few instances, Schwab sharpened the textual statements considerably by his interpolations. On 12th January, 1630,[117] Cardinal Klesl wrote to Secretary Ingoli that, as he requested, he was prepared to let Nuntius Pallotto have his 'Informatio' about the Jesuitesses, and had already given orders to that effect to his Consistory Court. It does not seem likely that the Cardinal could have been referring to the Decree of Suppression by this, for the Decree was too important, but he could have meant items of information, such as are contained in the forgoing document.

Briefly: the title carries the long-winded heading: 'Informatio generalis super Instituto seu congregatione mulierum Viennae commorantium, quae se Jesuitissas vocant.' Immediately on arrival in Vienna the Jesuitesses boasted of their successful educational enterprises in other countries. Novelty-loving Viennese mothers had sent their children to their school, but soon found that they learnt

NAME	NATIONALITY	AGE	ENTERED	PROFESSION	POSITION
Margaret Genison	English London	29	1620, Liège	1622, Rome in hands of Mary Ward	Superior
Helen Clifford	English Oxford	30	1621, Liège	1623? Liège in hands of Provincial	Head of Boarding School
Johanna Hausin	English?	c.27	1621, Cologne	1623? in hands of Provincial	Progress
Anna Maria Mehrin	/Swiss/ Constance	39	1627, Munich	/1629/Vienna in hands of Mary Ward	Prefect of Studies
Anna Maria Grainwoldin	German Munich	c.20	1627 Munich	/1629?/Vienna in hands of Superior	–
Anna Redlin	German Mosberg	31	1627 Munich	/1629/Vienna in hands of Superior	Teacher of Reading and Writing
Margareta Zimmerin	German Munich	17	1627 Munich	–	Teacher
Klara Knellin	German	18	?Munich	–	–
Anna Rea	(German) 'Golicensis'	26	1628 Munich	–	House work
Margareta Fischerin	German Augsburg	c.28	?Munich	Vienna in hands of superior	Procurator
Magdalena Erstbreckhin	German Pfrentsch/Pfalz	33	1627	–	Cook

more from secular teachers, so sent them back to these, all the more so as the Jesuitesses often visited the parents and demanded gifts. Their boarders were not well looked after. The number of pupils diminished because the government of their community lay in the hands of Englishwomen who did not know the language of the country or Austrian teaching methods.

To pause by the passage concerning their school. The Englishwomen could be justifiably proud of their teaching. There had never been a single attack of such a kind made on their schools, even by their most hardened opponents. The teaching was free; Mary Ward was also insistent on the correct placement of the members of her Institute.[118] It is also unacceptable that the Englishwomen damaged the good reputation of this school by ignorance of their pupils' own tongue. It has already been said that there were only three Englishwomen in the Viennese community of the Institute. The Superior spoke a certain amount of German. On the visitation of the house, she answered for Mary Ward, who probably understood German only with difficulty. We do not know if Margaret Genison was also engaged in teaching. Johanna Hausin was the portress, and Helen Clifford Prefect of the boarders. Again, it is not known if the latter knew enough German to teach or help the children in their tasks. But in the school itself, Anna Maria Mehrin, Anna Redlin, and Margareta Zimmerin were all teachers, and all were German-speaking.

As to whether there was at that time any definite Austrian teaching method, (modum instituendi puellas Austriacas) is extremely doubtful. Girls' education was in its first stages, in Vienna as everywhere else. The accusations which follow are directed against the Englishwomen personally, and do not actually present much that is new: they sweep through the streets in twos, visit their pupils' parents and eat with them without invitation. In summer they visit churches which are far outside the city and, so they say, visit the sick in the neighbouring villages. They do not wish to be subject to either ecclesiatic or secular (!) authority, and follow the rules of the Society of Jesus, though they are not subject to these. As to their morals, nothing is known to their disadvantage, but women in enclosed religious Orders are scandalised by their freedom of behaviour, which is praised to the skies by their accompanying priest and their superior.

So much for the contents of the 'Informatio'.

As with earlier criticisms of the Englishwomen, no immediate counter-evidence can be produced, except for the hint about the correspondence between the Bishop of Vienna and the Congregation of the Propaganda Fide. It was simply neglect of his jurisdiction and the possibility of scandals – not scandals themselves – that Cardinal Klesl was able to produce, but never inadequacy of their teaching or any questionable conduct.

Moreover, the author contradicts himself when he has to admit, after all his complaints, that nothing immoral can be brought against the Englishwomen (de moribus et vitae honestate nihil certi quod sciamus contra eas). Malice is always a questionable source of information. It is most often those who state or repeat something detrimental about another who appear in an unfavourable light rather than the person concerned, who may present no defence because he or she knows nothing about it.

There were occasional small quips, which had stung the easily-roused Viennese. It was not wise of Henry Lee, in the presence of General Vicar Tobias Schwab, already disinclined towards the English-women, to talk of sins allegedly committed in Rome precisely because of enclosure. The same holds good of Margaret Genison who, when the General Vicar quoted the Italian proverb 'A woman should either have a convent or a husband' (per la donna ò muro ò marito), came back with the riposte: 'I can serve God without a cloister or a husband' (si puo servire a Iddio senza muro e senza marito). It must of course be understood that all of this was taken out of context, but it would have been wiser to have avoided such jests in their conversation.

The 'Informatio', which was not public, would not have had a large circulation. There is nothing to show that Cardinal Klesl passed it around, as a fair copy does not seem to have been made.

At all events, from this spiteful recital it emerges that the English-women did certainly not visit people in order to eat at their expense but to talk to them in order to know their needs, to speak with them about God and the Church's religious teachings, and while doing so may have accepted some refreshment.

They visited the parents of their pupils and the sick. Perhaps there were those among them who were not catholic, as a high percentage of the population of Vienna had fallen away from the catholic church. They visited churches in the neighbouring villages, it stated. There were hamlets in those days which lay outside Vienna and had hardly any connection with the city within the walls. The pilgrimage church of Maria in Hietzing lay in one of these, in today's thirteenth district.

It is the first time, with the exception of the contact they had with their pupils' mothers in Rome and Perugia, that we hear of the Eng-lishwomen's work in adult education on the Continent, an activity which undoubtedly stood their neighbour in good stead and was in tune with the whole work of their Institute.

It was probably soon after this second Visitation that a draft was compiled for the Decree of Suppression[119] of the Institute in Vienna. There are four versions of it, not merely one. Two revised drafts were written by the same hand, as a copy of the report of the Vis-itation of 7th October, and a copy of the 'Informatio Generalis'. A fair copy was again revised, until it finalised in a version which closely followed the decree of the Archbishop of Malines for the Belgian Jesuitesses in Brussels. There are two dates mentioned, 18th October 1629 and 12th January, 1630. The final version has neither signature nor seal; it never left the Bishop's court.

Cardinal Klesl protected himself carefully: after Nuntius Pallotto had acted as intermediary of the Decree of the Congregatio de Propaganda Fide, the Bishop had arranged for the Visitation of the house 'Stoss am Himmel' by his General Vicar. This disclosed that for two years eleven women had been living there, whose congregation had been approved neither by the Pope nor the Bishop of Vienna. 'They are illegal, and are to be suppressed by the Decree; the members are to be released from their vows. With the permission of the Bishop, however, the women may continue to teach girls as lay people (nec in communi vel forma congregationis viventes).'

Although, as already remarked, there was a fair copy ready by 18th October, 1629, Cardinal Klesl did not send his decree to Rome. Instead, one month later[120] he wrote to Secretary Ingoli that Pallotto had indeed provided him with a decree from Brussels, but this did not refer to the same community of Jesuitesses who lived in Vienna. Moreover, he, Cardinal Klesl, had not received any commission either from the Pope or from the Congregatio de Propaganda Fide to suppress this community. It would be advisable if the Pope were to take action against Mary Ward who was in Rome, or were to send a clear order to the bishops about this suppression. If, however, the Nuntius were judged to be better suited for this, the Pope could give him the task, as the Congregatio de Propaganda Fide had previously dealt with Nuntius Pallotto. Since he, as Bishop, had received no express command, he would take no action.

By 8th December[121] Ingoli had received no solution from Vienna. The decree remained a draft which was never fulfilled. Three months after Pallotto had left Vienna,[122] the Bishop of Vienna requested Cardinal Ludovisi for directions concerning the Jesuitesses. Another two months later, on 12th October, 1630,[123] the Congregation commissioned the new Nuntius in Vienna, Ciriaco Rocci, with the suppression of the Institute of the Englishwomen who were under his jurisdiction. They could not forward a copy of their now stereotyped formula to the Bishop[124]; Cardinal Klesl had died in Wiener Neustadt on 18th September, 1630.

Not even the Emperor had been able to bring pressure to bear on Cardinal Klesl to make him give the slightest appearance of carrying out the Curia's mandate by subordinating himself to the Nuntius and supporting him. He would not do it. His actions supply the answer to the question as to whether Cardinal Klesl saw the suppression of the Institute as a priority for the good of the Church in Vienna.[125]

Unlike Munich, relations between the Jesuits and the Englishwomen remained unclouded. There were of course some adversaries of the Institute who sent their observations to Rome,[126] particularly those concerning Fr Paul Guldin the confessor, but these had no negative effect.[127]

Mention must be made of a letter from Fr Vitelleschi to Fr Lamormain of 15th July, 1628[128] in which the General made known the disapproval of the Holy See of the Englishwomen's style of life. He asked Fr Lamormain to bring his influence to bear on the women and to inform the Emperor of the Curia's opinion. The Jesuits in Vienna were to continue to keep a distance between themselves and the Institute, and not visit the women. Fr Lamormain might have a word with the Superior. These instructions apparently had no effect. Perhaps one should rather view them as a feeble attempt to conform to the warning from the Congregatio de Propaganda Fide: the General and the Fathers of the Society of Jesus were not to promote the Englishwomen's Institute.[129]

Pressburg

1628 – 1629

Archbishop Pázmány's frustrated efforts to save the English-women's Institute in Pressburg from dissolution – relentless attitude of the Congregatio de Propaganda Fide

The suppression of the small foundation in Pressburg, which had consisted of only four members since the spring of 1628, took place without much publicity.

At the beginning of May, 1629[130], Archbishop Pázmány was in Vienna and had a conversation with Nuntius Pallotto about the Institute; the bishops in Hungary were under the Viennese nuntiature.

Back in Pressburg, Pázmány at first waited, apparently to see what action Cardinal Klesl would take, who resided in the Emperor's line of fire. It was the end of July 1629[131] before the Archbishop turned with a long letter to his agent Camillo Cataneo in Rome. Cataneo was to go to Cardinal Millini, it said, and inform him how very highly he, Pázmány, esteemed the Englishwomen. The founding of their establishment had been very difficult as he, the Archbishop, did not own a house and had no money with which to help the women. Moreover the protestant town council had tried to hinder the foundation. In spite of this, the Englishwomen had soon been able to begin their teaching. Perhaps, Pázmány said, such an Institute was not needed so much in Italy as in Hungary, where there was the threat of heresy. On the contrary, as Archbishop of an oppressed country, he was of the opinion that this Institute was a gift of the divine Wisdom (existimo maximus esse istud (Institutum) divinae sapientiae inventum). The education of girls seemed to him almost more important than that of boys.

Neither the name 'Matres Societatis Jesu', nor the unenclosed lifestyle caused any opposition in this great Hungary; the blameless life and apostolic efforts of these women were of prime importance for the Archbishop, who would also have liked to have the Institute in Tyrnau.

Cataneo may have executed his commission, at all events without success, for in the 115th Session[132] the Congregatio de Propaganda Fide decided on an urgent letter to Nuntius Pallotto, who was to exhort the Archbishop of Gran to suppress the house of the Englishwomen in Pressburg. The execution of the decision resulted in an unfriendly letter from Ingoli to Archbishop Pázmány.[133]

On 20th October,[134] after the suppression of the house in Vienna 'Stoss am Himmel' had taken place, in theory, at least, Pallotto asked Archbishop Pázmány for information about the directive concerning the Englishwomen's house in Pressburg. After his conversation with the Archbishop he should have known all about it. Once more[135] Secretary Ingoli warned the Nuntius in Vienna and repeated the charge to suppress the Jesuitesses in Vienna and in Pressburg.

At this point there is a petering out of sources concerning the foundations of the Institute, which had made a good but modest beginning.

No exact date is given for the members' departure from Pressburg.[136] The Hungarian Treasury kept accounts for the allowance given to the Englishwomen from Archbishop Telegdy of Kalosza's salary as imperial councillor[137] until the end of 1632. They had been paid something more than the half of the salary, namely 568 guilders.[138]

Notes

1. 5th February, 1628. APF Rome. SOCG 69, Lettere di Germania et Polonia ff.123v–124v.
2. For the continuation of negotiations with Propaganda Fide, see p.470.
3. APF Rome, Acta 6, 1628–1629, ff.36v–37r, 44v.
4. On 25th March to Fr Corcione in Naples. ARSI Rome, Naples 16, f.40rv. Nr.267. It concerns the confessions of sick and dying members of the Institute. Letters to Fr Bartel have the same date. Austria 3/II, p.988, to Fr Mercurian, ibid. p.989, and to Fr Provincial Dombrinus, ibid. p.990. All these letters deal with the friendly relationships between the Jesuits and the Englishwomen.
5. On 18th March, ARSI Rome, Italia 72, Responsa pro Italia 1616–1645, f.34.
6. (July 1628) AV Rome, Miscell. Arm. III/34, f.485rv. For Ingoli's characteristic judgement, see Grisar, Institut. p.238–247.
7. See Grisar: Institut, p.365 ff.
8. Grisar, Institut, p.371,ff. gives an exact analysis of the material used for this inventory.
9. Vita E, f.26v.

10. ARSI Rome, Naples, 16,f. 40rv. Nr.267.
11. BV Rome, Barb. lat. 6223, f.89v.
12. APF Rome, Acta 6, 1628–1629, ff.78rv, 85v–87r.
13. "Referente Illustrissimo Domino Cardinali Borgia decretum particularis congregationis habitae in Vaticano die 13 aprilis 1628 de Jesuitissarum Instituto . . ."
14. Hier. Cath. IV. p.16.
15. On 4th April 1626. ARSI Rome, Naples, 15/I, f.118r. Nr.125.
16. APF Rome, Lettere Volgari 7, 1628, f.96rv.
17. On 17th August, ibid. ff.115r, 116r.
18. ibid. ff.131v–132r.
19. In this session a letter from Nuntius Bichi was discussed. (letter now lost) APF Rome, Acta 6, 1628–1629, f.158v, Nr.30.
20. See p.381.
21. APF Rome, Lettere Volgari 7, 1628, f.148rv. Only two days later Ingoli pointed out the good example of his brother in office in Naples to the Bishop of Vienna. ibid. ff.154v–155r.
22. ARSI Rome, Naples 15/II, f.464nv. nr.756.
23. On 9th February 1628. Letter Nr.49. Inst. Arch. Munich.
24. On 2nd January, 1628. ARSI Rome, Naples 16, f.5r, Nr.25; on 18.March, ibid. f.38v, Nr.249; and Italia 72, Responsa pro Italia 1626–1645, f.34r; on 25th March, Naples, 16. f.40rv. Nr.267, and on 8th April, ibid. f.48r, Nr.323.
25. On 17th August 1628. APF Rome, Lettere Volgari 7, ff.115r, 116r.
26. The "Council of Six" handed in a petition to Cardinal Francesco Barberini for the Englishwomen. There had been such good and essential teaching given in Naples. Now, to the great dissatisfaction of the city (con grandissimo disgusto di detta citta), it was to be withdrawn by command of the Archbishop. Old writings, Copy, Inst. Arch. Munich.
27. On 30th December 1628. ARSI Rome, Naples, 16. f.195v, Nr.211.
28. Likewise on 30th December 1628, ibid. f.196r, Nr.216.
29. APF Rome, Istruzioni diverse degli anni 1623–1628, ff.117v–118v.
30. Instruttione per li Nuntii di Germania e di Fiandra circa l'Istituto delle Giesuitesse.
31. APF Rome, Lettere d'Italia, 3 ff.88r, 89v.
32. APF Rome Istruzioni diverse degli anni 1623–1628, ff.125r–126r.
33. Page 717, note 4 and 5 some letters from Fr Vitelleschi were mentioned and it was remarked then that these perhaps were not connected with the warning.
34. On 14th July, 1628. APF Rome, Lettere volgari 1628, 7.ff.92v–93r. resp. f.93rv.
35. Fabio de Lagonissa, 1622 Archbishop of Consa; he was Secretary to the Congregation of Bishops and Regulars, in 1626 Nuntius extraordinary in Spain, in 1626–1627, Collector in Portugal, 13th March 1627–20. January 1634, Nuntius in Flanders. He died 1653. Biaudet, p. 270, Hier. Cath. IV. p.160.
36. On 8th August 1628 to Cardinal Ludovisi. APF Rome, SOCG 102, Lettere d'Inghilterra etc., ff.57r, 62v.
37. On 14th October 1628, ibid. ff.73r. 76v.
38. Report of Bishop Johannes Malder of 22nd August. APF SOCG, 205, I.Belgium sive Flandria Jesuitissae ad anno 1648 incl., f.430rv.
39. Report of Bishop Dionysius Stoffels, 27th August. ibid. ff.430v–431r.
40. Report of Bishop Maximilien Vilain, 19th September. ibid. f.429rv.
41. Lagonissa to Ingoli, 14th October. APF Rome, SOCG 102, Lettere d'Inghilterra etc. 1628, ff.73r. 76v.
42. On 24th October. APF Rome, Lettere volgari 7.f.152.

43. APF Rome, SOCG 131, Lettere di Francia etc. 1629, ff.261rv, 268v.
44. ibid. ff.255v–256v.
45. On 23rd December. ibid. ff.190rv. 197v.
46. On 30th December AV Rome, Nunziatura Fiandra 20, f.116rv.
47. APF Rome, SOCG 131, Lettere di Francia etc. 1629, ff.191v. 196v.
48. On 20th January. ibid. ff.193r. 194v.
49. On 8th February. APF Rome, Lettere volgari 1629, 8, ff.23v–24r.
50. On 17th March, 1629. APF Rome, SOCG 131, Lettere di Francia etc. ff.206r, 213v.
51. On 17th March. APF Rome, Lettere volgari 1629, 8.f.51v. In the 106 session of the Congregation, Cardinal Bentivoglio had requested that the Nuntius be told to take final measures.
52. APF Rome SOCG 131, Lettere di Francia etc. ff.220r–221v. Two days later Nuntius Lagonissa informed Cardinal Bandini of the suppression of "St Katharina". ibid. ff.219rv, 222v.
53. Cf. above, note 52.
54. This suggestion came from Lagonissa on 12th May. APF Rome, SOCG 131, Lettere di Francia etc. ff.218rv, 223v.
55. On 30th June, APF Rome, Lettere volgari 1629, 8, ff.105v–106r.
56. On 14th July. AV Rome, Epistolae ad Principes, 43. ff.156v–157r.
57. On 7th July. APF Rome, SOCG, Lettere di Francia etc. 131, ff.229r, 232v.
58. Decision of the Session on 22nd June, 1629. APF Rome, Acta 6, 1628–1629, ff.289r. 294v–295r. Written on 10th July. APF Rome, Lettere volgari 1629, 9. ff.11v–112r.
59. APF Rome, SOCG 131, Lettere di Francia etc. ff.228v, 233v.
60. On 11th August. ibid. ff.237r–240v.
61. Lagonissa to Ingoli, 25.August, ibid. f.238r.
62. Van der Burch to Lagonissa. 5th September. ibid. ff.246r. 247v.
63. On 6th September. APF Rome, SOCG Fiandra, 205, ff.471r–420v. 422r.
64. On 9th September. ibid. ff.421v–432v.
65. APF Rome, Lettere volgari 1629, 8, f.156r.
66. On 17th October. APF Rome, SOCG 131, Lettere di Francia ff.252rv, 259v.
67. The Ursulines of Dole were anxious about the survival of their congregation. Infanta Isabella Clara Eugenia to Vives, 20.October, AGR Brussels, PEA 467, f.115r.
68. On 3rd November. APF Rome, SOCG 205, Lettere di Belgium, sive Flandria, Jesuitisse ad 1648 incl. ff.427rv, 434v.
69. Report of the Visitation. 23 November. APF Rome, SOCG 132, Lettere di Francia etc. 1636, ff.114rv, 119v.
70. On 8th December AGR Brussels, PEA 467, f.191rv.
71. Cf. AGR Brussels, PEA 467, f.193rv, 238rv, 468, f.15r/23.II. 1630/108r, 115r, 135rv, 141rv, 165r. APF Rome, Lettere volgari 1629, 8, f.181rv, 1630, 10, f.4v; ibid. Lettere Latine 1630–1646, 9, f.12v; all between 1629–1630.
72. This emerges from Carafa's letter of 16th September 1628 to Ingoli. APF Rome, SOCG 69, Lettere di Germania et Polonia, f.111r.
73. BV Rome, Barb. lat. 6223, f.89v.
74. On 14th July, APF Rome, Lettere Volgari 1628, 7, f.93rv.
75. On 29th July. AV Rome, Nunziatura di Germania, Register 116, ff.34v–36r. On 2nd August Pallotto promised Cardinal Ludovisi to implement the Congregation's order as required. APF Rome SOCG 69, ff.81r–84v.
76. See p.458.
77. Elizabeth Cotton and Mary Ward to Winefrid Wigmore, Letter Nr.52 (no date) Inst. Arch. Munich.

78. VP/H 4 of 20th August, 1628 from Eger. Inst. Arch. Munich.
79. Pallotto to Francesco Barberini, 5th August 1628. Bibl. Comm. Giovardiana Veroli (Frosinone) 42.3.13.f.95rv.
80. Fr Valeriano to Ingoli, 5th August 1628. APF Rome, SOCG 69, Lettere di Germania et Polonia 1628. ff.319rv. 321v. Pallotto to Cardinal Ludovisi 10th August 1628. 10.August 1628. ibid. ff.82v – 83v. Pallotto sent a copy of this letter to Francesco Barberini, BV Rome, Barb. lat. 6953, f.52r; Pallotto to Harrach, 7.August, Bibl. Comm. Giovardiana Veroli, (Frosinone) 42.3.13.f.105rv.
81. On 12th August 1628. BV Rome, Barb. lat. 7061, Lit.12.
82. Pallotto to Francesco Barberini, 19 August 1628. BV Rome, Barb. lat. 6953, f.59rv.
83. On 2nd September. AV Rome, Nuntiatura di Germania, Register 116 ff.78v – 79r. On 23. September Pallotto thanked the Cardinal for the nomination. BV Rome Barb. lat. 6957, ff.52r – 53v.
84. Pallotto to Francesco Barberini, 13th September 1628. ibid. ff.40r – 43v. Cardinal Barberini's affirmative answer to Pallotto of 7th October. BV Rome, Barb. lat. 7061, Littera 25.
85. Francesco Barberini wrote to Pallotto on 7th October that the English-woman knew of the Decree of Suppression. BV Rome, Barb. lat. 7061, Littera 25.
86. Pallotto to Fr Dombrinus, 30th September. Bibl. Comm. Giovardiana Veroli (Frosinone) 42.3.11.f.301r.
87. Pallotto wrote to Lagonissa on 26th September. ibid. 42.3.12.f.170r.
88. Mary Ward wrote another letter from Vienna to Fr Vitelleschi. This date is taken from his answer of 21st October, which he sent to Munich. ARSI Rome, Epp.NN.2.f.336v, Nr.1087.
89. Pallotto to Francesco Barberini, 4th November 1628.
90. Pallotto to Francesco Barberini, 4th November. BV Rome, Barb. lat. 6957 ff.130v – 136v.
91. The text runs: " ... che si compiacesse sospendere il dargli luogo e chiesa finchè il loro Instituto fusse essaminato in Roma, dove sin hora non era molto accetto." Apparently Cardinal Dietrichstein had also promised the Englishwomen a house with a church in his diocese.
92. BV Rome, Barb. lat. 6957, ff.140 – 144r.
93. " ... Ho parlato domenica e giovedi lungemente con Donna Maria della Guardia e si è finalmente disposta di vernirsene quanto prima à Roma, per trattare della confirmatione del suo Instituto, sottomettendolo alla dispositione censura e volunta di cotesta Santa Sede e di Nostro Signore. In che tanto più hò premuto, quanto hò veduto esser approvato e desiderato da Vostra Signoria Illustrissima e per il medesimo rispetto mi sarà si somma consolatione, che me segua l'effetto, com'è probabile havendo detto, che questa settimana se licenziarra da queste Maestà sebene donna e potendo haver molti consultori non me n'assicuro senon quando saprò che si trovi costà ... "
94. On 18.November. APF Rome, SOCG 70, Lettere di Germania e di Boemia ff.81rv, 86v.
95. Pallotto to Cardinal Francesco Barberini. On 9th December the Cardinal praised the Nunitus for his persevering actions. BV rome, Barb. lat. 7061, Nr.38. BV Rome, Barb. lat. 6957, ff.155r – 156r.
96. Pallotto to Giovanni Battista Barsotti on 22nd November, Bibl. Comm. Giovardiana Veroli (Frosinone) 42.3.11.ff.381v – 382v and to Cardinal Francesco Barberini on 25.November. BV Rom. Barb. lat. 6957 ff.161r – 166r.
97. Bibl. Comm. Giovardiana Veroli (Frosinone) 42.3.11.f.384r.
98   ARSI Rome, Epp.NN 2, f.339r. Nr.1103. Even a letter from Fr General,

dated 9th December to a letter from Mary Ward shows his compassion: " ... ho molto materia di compatirli come for cordialmente, e ben vero che la virtù di Vostra Signoria mi consola, et ella si consolarà con l'esempio de santi, che con gradissime contradittioni, e fatiche hanna tirato à buon' esito l'opera di servitio di Dio." ibid. f.339v, Nr.1108.

99.· See p. 448.

100. APF Rome, Lettere volgari 1628, 7, f.94r.

101. On 2nd August. Pallotto to Cardinal Ludovisi. APF Rome, SOCG 69, ff.81r–84v. The letter was laid before the 97th Session of the Congregation on 5th September.

102. ibid. ff.169r, 176v. This letter too was produced on 5th September.

103. ibid. ff.171r, 174v. This was produced in the 99th Session, on 17th October.

104. APF. Rome, Acta 6, 1628–1629, f.155v. Item 20.

105. APF Rome, Lettere volgari 7, 1628, ff 154v–155r.

106. Pallotto to Cardinal Francesco Barberini, 18.November, 1628. BV Rome Barb. lat. 6957, ff.155r–156r.

107. On 30th June 1629. APF Rome, Lettere volgari 8, 1629, ff.102v–103r. Decision of the Congregation regarding this in 111th Session on 22nd June, 1629. APF Rome, Acta 6, 1628–1629, ff.289r, 294v–295r.

108. "Sicome egli fù il primo promotore di quest'importante negotio, cosi veda il felice successo che comincia ad havere la dissolutione delle suddette Giesuitesse ..."

109. Pallotto to Nuntius Pierluigi Carafa of Cologne. 8th November 1628. Bibl. Comm. Giovardiana Veroli (Frosinone) 42.3.11.f.355v. To Cardinal Bandini, 4th August 1629. ibid. 42.3.13. To Nuntius Lagonissa, 14/15.August. ibid. 42.3.12.f.435rv. To Nuntius Carafa, 15th August. ibid. 42.3.12.f.436rv.

110. It was only on 4th August that Pallotto wrote to Cardinal Bandini about discussions with Bishop Klesl on 3rd August. Bibl. Comm. Giovardiana Veroli (Frosinone) 42.3.13.f.629rv.

111. On 15th September. Bibl. Comm. Giovardiana Veroli (Frosinone) 42.3.13, ff.693v–694r. The answer to this letter, on 6th October 1629, BV Rome, Barb. lat. 6223, f.172rv.

112. DA Vienna, Suppressed convents, Jesuitesses.

113. Mary Ward to Winefrid Wigmore, 1st December 1627. Letter Nr.46. Inst. Arch. Munich. On 10th June 1628 Mary Ward told Winefrid Wigmore to transfer 3 members to Vienna. Letter Nr.51. ibid.

114. See p.446

115. See p.446

116. DA Vienna, Suppressed convents, Jesuitesses.

117. APF Rome, SOCG 71, Lettere di Germania e di Boemia 1630, ff.81rv, 88v.

118. In 1636 Mary Ward was still telling Winefrid Wigmore to teach children without charge. The letter is lost. Chambers was able to see it. Chambers II E, p.441, D, p.367.

119. DA Vienna, Suppressed convents, Jesuitesses.

120. On 17th November, 1629. APF Rome, SOCG 70, Lettere di Germania e di Boemia 1629, ff.26rv, 29v. The letter was produced in 118. Session of the Congregation, on 19th December 1629.

121. Ingoli to Pallotto. APF Rome, Lettere volgari 1629, 8, f.180v. After the 19th December session, the Congregation referred the Bishop to the Nuntius once more. APF Rome, Acta 1628 and 1629, 6, ff.372, 376v, respect. Lettere volgari 1629 8.ff 191r. Klesl answered on 12th January that Pallotto would certainly find a way out. Should the Nuntius need the Cardinal's information, he would give it him immediately. ibid. SOCG,

Lettere di Germania e di Boemia, 1630, 71.ff.81rv. 88v.

122. On 17th August 1630, ibid. ff.62r-63v.

123. ibid. Lettere volgari 1630, 10, ff.121v-122r.

124. With the same date and the remark: "Non, andò, perchè s'intese la sua morte. ibid. f.121rv. Resolution to this letter of 130. Session of the Congregation of 1st October, 1630. APF. Rome, Acta 1630, 1631, 7, ff.133v, 134v, 135r.

125. Nuntius Rocci wrote to Cardinal Ludovisi on 28th October 1630 that Pallotto, his predecessor, had received instructions to suppress the Institute in Vienna but had met difficulties and been unable to conclude the matter. APF Rome, SOCG, Lettere di Germania e di Boemi 1630, 71.ff.47r, 56v.

126. Fr Vitelleschi to Fr Dombrinus, 25th March, 1628. ARSI Rome, Austria 3/II, p.990.

127. Fr Vitelleschi to Fr Guildin, 3rd March 1629. ibid. Austria, 4/I, pp.67-68.

128. ibid. Austria 3/II, p.1028.

129. See p.467

130. Superior Barbara Babthorpe congratulated the Archbishop on 11 May on his retirement and recovery from an unnamed illness. Old writings. Inst. Arch. Munich.

131. On 28th July, 1629. APF Rome 57, Lettere di Ungaria etc. 1629, ff.1r-2v. It appears that Pázmány rightly saw Millini as the Institute's greatest enemy in the college of cardinals.

132. On 2nd October, 1629. APF Rome, Acta 1628-1629, 6.ff.334r, 336v.

133. On 12th October, APF Rome, Lettere volgari 1629, 8.ff.161v-162r.

134. Bibl. Comm. Giovardiana Veroli (Frosinone) 42.3.12.f.553rv.

135. On 8th December 1629. APF Rome, Lettere volgari 1629, 8, f.180v.

136. On 4th June 1630 the Englishwomen's confessor, Provost György Nagy of Alsó Fehér, and Viscount Wolfgang von Bekefalva testified before the Cathedral Chapter of Pressburg to the sale of vineyard Fang, half the produce of which had been appointed for the Englishwomen by Archbishop Pázmány; sold for 632 Hungarian guilders. MOL Budapest, Camera E 151, Acta Eccl. Ordinum et monialium, Posoniensium, Fasz.14, Nr.44.

137. See p. 450

138. MOL Budapest, E 150, Acta Eccl. irregistrata Fasz. 80, ff.281r-282v. 6 July 1633.

XXVI

THE SUPPRESSION OF THE HOUSES IN ST OMER AND IN THE JURISDICTION OF THE COLOGNE NUNTIATURE

Negotiations in Rome 1629–1630

Mary Ward's second journey to Rome – her enemies there – audience with the Pope at Castelgandolfo – discussions with Cardinal Millini and Father Vitelleschi – Mary Ward before the Cardinals of the Special Congregation – the proceedings of 25th March, 1629 – the 'Compendium' of Secretary Ingoli – the Decree of Suppression of 30th November, 1629

It almost baffles belief that Mary Ward could be on her way to Rome to treat of the confirmation of the Institute just when her enemies struck the fatal blow against it. This was the result of manipulation by the Nuntius of Vienna.

She had not been able to set off on her journey as quickly as Pallotto had hoped, however. She lay exhausted and ill in Munich for four weeks. The English Vita[1] describes her agony plainly: Mary Ward could move forwards only 'with her breast even down to her knees'. She could not keep down any food and slept only if she were rocking as though in a cradle. Although the doctors had prophesied that, humanly speaking, she would not even live to pass the city gates, she left Munich towards the end of 1628/29, after the Christmas season.[2]

While travelling[3] she was asked rather sceptically by one of her companions if she really thought that she would survive the journey. She gave an answer that is so typical of her: 'It does not matter to me when or where I die, whether it is in a bed or behind a hedge, if only I am found faithful.' She had several times made a general confession, and had in fact done so recently, as though it were to have been the last of her life. That had been her usual practice for some years whenever receiving communion. 'For the rest, living or dying, she was certain that she served a good master'.

The small party consisted of four women and two serving men.[4]

From Munich to Innsbruck they were able to travel in a sedan belonging to the Electress.[5] A four-in-hand was put at their disposal by Archduke Leopold V of Tyrol to take them over the toughest part of the journey, the crossing of the Alps, and then on to Trent.[6] They arrived there on 12th January.[7] Having passed through Mantua and Loreto, they reached Rome on 10th February.[8] The journey must have been a martyrdom to the ailing woman, made in the middle of winter, in jolting conveyances or sometimes on foot on the snow-rutted roads, and exposed to the biting cold. That the Englishwomen had no idea of what was awaiting them in Rome is apparent from Mary Ward's letters to Nuntius Pallotto. Not a single one of these remains, but from his answers one learns that she wrote to him three times before she left Munich[9] and reported again from Rome on 17th February.[10] Pallotto's answers, exuding compassion at her pain and with affable wishes for her negotiations in Rome were glib and empty phrases which, since he knew the true state of affairs, do him no credit.

It was not only Mary Ward who was in Rome in February, 1629. Her enemies were also there.

First to be mentioned are the old enemies of the Institute from England. A petition has survived from this time which was probably written by the English agent, Thomas Blacklow.[11] It has come down as a copy only, and as the manuscript testifies, originated from the Belgian office of agent Vives. That is a sign that she had not only been handed over to Rome, so to speak, but was also handed around in Rome. The petition is neither dated nor signed, and is filed among the Papiers d'Etat et de l'Audience des Archives Générales du Royaume in Brussels among the documents of September 1629. Thomas Blacklow held office only until 1626[12] but remained in Rome until January 1630.[13] The petition did not contain anything new: the aping of the Society of Jesus by the Institute, preaching, and teaching of theology by the members, who entice young girls into their community and call themselves religious sisters. All of these are complaints with which we are long familiar. But constant drops had begun to wear away the stone. Dangerous, too, were hints about the untroubled attitude of the Jesuitesses towards the decree issued by the Congregatio de Propaganda Fide.

Fr Valerio Magni, Archbishop Harrach's trusted adviser at the Curia, joined the attack. He came from the storm-centre, Prague. This fierce enemy of the Jesuits had probably left the Bohemian capital in August, 1628[14] for Rome. He had to undertake certain duties for his Archbishop and for Nuntius Pallotto.[15] Mary Ward must have expected enemies among the Roman Curia, some of whom were unknown.

Two facts must be remembered in connection with Mary Ward's stay in Rome in 1629. First, that Nuntius Pallotto had had to persuade her to undertake the journey. She herself had not seen much point in further negotiations, but changed her mind after her conversation with the Nuntius.

Secondly, she was never informed personally of where she stood, with the result that she travelled south at the beginning of 1629 with freshly awakened hopes. She found a totally different situation. Between the 17th and 24th October, 1628 the foundation in Naples was suppressed.

For the events which follow we are almost entirely dependent on the oldest biographies and a few supplementary documents.

On her arrival in Rome the enfeebled woman broke down and had to spend three weeks in bed.[16] It must have been the middle of March before she had recovered. But she gave herself little real rest, for during those weeks of enforced idleness, she dictated a report on the development of her Institute which evoked great admiration from the Pope and the Cardinals.[17] One must treat such categoric statements from the first biographies with some reserve, as the facts were in all probability quite the reverse, although they cannot be ignored.

Before this is dealt with in greater detail, there is still more from the English Vita. This states that Mary Ward had an audience with the Pope.[18] That is correct, for she wrote of it on 19th June, 1629 to Nuntius Pallotto.[19] Grisar[20] takes May as the time of this sign of favour. Once again, the Pope allowed Mary Ward to leave his presence with hopeful expectations.[21] It is inconceivable that she told lies to Nuntius Pallotto. She was a sober woman, who suffered a great deal for her Institute. But at the audience in Castelgandolfo she made the same mistake that she had a few years before, in Mondragone. She responded to the outward affability of the Pope, and counted on it. The English Vita reveals one detail of the meeting with Urban VIII. It says that the Pope had taken the matter of the Institute out of the authority of the Congregatio de Propaganda Fide and entrusted it to his Vicar General, Millini, as well as the General of an Order – doubtless Fr General Vitelleschi.

And then came a difference of opinion. The Pope was convinced that this General was an influential friend – 'mightily a friend' – of the Institute. Mary Ward, on the other hand, tried to explain to the Pope that this was not so at all. But she could make no headway, the Pope over-ruled her – 'persuaded her of the contrary' – which most likely means that Mary Ward was unable to move the Pope from his opinion and had to capitulate. It next adds:[22] 'When she had contributed her part, she remained calm and dealt steadfastly with them (namely Millini and the General), but not according to her personal opinion.'

The cause of the difference will not be long to seek. Mary Ward clung to what had been revealed to her in 1611, and refused to accept the offer to alter her Institute, which might have had some hope of confirmation as a Pius Institute, possibly with certain rules of enclosure, but certainly without the active pastoral apostolate.

It is impossible to know if such a conversation really took place. Grisar[23] doubted it, as no other source refers to it except the English Life, which tells us even more:[24] anonymous enemies were powerfully at work but they did not gain the upper hand. On the contrary, the Pope ordered another special congregation of four cardinals only, at the head of which was Gaspare Borgia. Antonio Barberini, the Pope's brother, Laudivio Zacchia and Desiderio Scaglia, the Commissar of the Holy Office, were the other members of the small assembly. At a sign from Cardinal Borgia Mary Ward was allowed to speak freely before this Forum for three quarters of an hour. She was interrupted once only, and briefly, by Cardinal Barberini. Her cold did not prevent her from giving her address.

In her speech Mary Ward made it clear that her Institute was not only lawful, but also laudable and necessary; that neither in theory nor practice did they do anything that had not been done before by holy women. The Church had approved such tasks for individual persons, but not yet for communities of women. She was not surprised that the Church was advancing difficulties. On the contrary, she had great respect for their vigilance. Then she told of the long years of striving and suffering which she had gone through in order to know God's will. Now nothing could seen hard to her. She only wished to be found true at the hour of her death and was ready to give up everything at the Church's command. She could not alter the Institute. The Cardinals could dispose of her as they would any of God's creatures, for it was a matter of the good of the Church and not of her own interests.

As Grisar says,[25] a measure of scepticism is necessary here. Officially, in those days, a woman was not asked for her opinion, let alone at a session of Cardinals. This was far less likely for a woman whose life's work had already been condemned by the very same cardinals. Those cardinals whose names are given formed no special congregation in the strict sense, for such a commission is nowhere registered during this time. For the Congregatio de Propaganda Fide and probably for the Pope too, the suppression of the Institute was a matter already decided upon; the implementation of this decision was merely a matter of time. The Cardinals knew this. So did Pope Urban VIII.

As Grisar says,[26] it is unlikely that Mary Ward attended the Cardinals' deliberations, but was called upon to answer questions. The four members of this small commission came from the Holy Office, which of itself was highly indicative, though Mary Ward may not have been aware of it.

Concerning the paper which Mary Ward composed immediately after her arrival in Rome on 25th March, 1629, Grisar[27] talks of a petition to the Pope, which seems unlikely.

As to outer criteria, there are two copies. One of them, perhaps the original, lies in the Vatican Archives[28] among the documents entrusted to Cardinal Francesco Barberini. Another copy is to be found in the Archives of the Discalced Carmelites' Generalate in Rome.[29] These must have been for the use of Fr Dominicus a Jesu Maria, who both knew and esteemed the Englishwomen.[30] Grisar thinks that the original must have been handed into the Pope, as it was signed by Mary Ward. Against this alleged proof, however, it should be pointed out that not a single petition from the Englishwomen to the Pope had a signature.

It is of no particular significance that some of these petitions have been preserved as copies only. If Mary Ward had signed the original there would undoubtedly have been a signature on the copy also. A petition to the Pope, especially the original, should have borne a title. This document has none.

In addition, there are several interior criteria: the beginning has been taken verbatim from the Englishwomen's petition to Cardinal Borghese on 29th February, 1625. What is odd is that the 25th March, 1629 copy begins in exactly the same place as the anonymous letter of 1625, which Mary Ward had offered for inspection. The address, and part of the text which had been placed under a line in the old letter (1625), were omitted in the 1629 letter. Something else: the 25th March document is far more cautious in the title it gives to Mary Ward. The 'Chief Superioress of the said ladies' of 1625 has become the 'the first of the aforementioned Englishwomen.'

Still more significant is that the Pope is not addressed directly. He is referred to, as in the formulation '...un 'anno del pontificato di Nostro Signore Papa Urbano VIII...' or, at the end of the manuscript, where the members of the Institute 'alli piedi di Sua Santità' ask for enquiries to be undertaken on their behalf into the calumnies made against them, so that 'alla Santità Sua' could be spared great vexation. A turn of phrase in the sentence – 'ma per tornare alla materia' is stylistically little suited to a letter directed to the Head of the Church. Let us look at the contents of the proceedings, since the beginning is already known.[31]

Following this comes the history of the Institute since 1624 – in which the Perugia foundation is passed over: the journey northwards towards Flanders; the foundation in Munich (passando per Monaco!) where a school for girls had been requested; the spreading of the Institute to Vienna and Pressburg, where a similar task awaited the Englishwomen, this time in an area where religion was in danger,[32] and the refusal of Archbishop Harrach of Prague to grant admission to the Institute. Mary Ward recognised Fr Valerio Magni quite clearly and with unusual sharpness as her adversary. She knew of the complaints he had brought to Rome, of the objections of Archbishop Harrach, Nuntius Carafa and Bishop Klesl. It is Pallotto's name only that she does not mention, one more sign of how little she knew of this man's real attitude towards her Institute. She was silent about her shock at the suppression of the house in Naples, and at the treatment the members there had received, but showed most concern at the calumnies to which the innocent members of the Institute were exposed and which, as she thought, could give the Pope cause to suppress the Institute. And now, at last, comes the request.

All the members of the Institute (di detta Compagnia) who, for twenty years, 'all' edificatione et aiuto del prossimo' have worked in this Institute, earnestly ask the Pope not to abandon them as evil women, but to have the accusations against them examined. If they were found guilty, then they should be punished. If they were not – and they felt that they were innocent before God and in their own conscience – then possibly their Institute might be granted confirmation. This was the only effective means to spare the Pope inconvenience, the Institute (detta Compagnia) undeserved suffering, and their opponents remorse of conscience.

As can be seen, this is not a request for confirmation, at least, not primarily so. It is rather a request for an examination to be made into the calumnies issued against the members and their Institute; the confirmation of the Institute is to be seen as a 'remedio', a cure. So one should not regard this document as a petition, but as the basis for Mary Ward's justification before some cardinals selected by the Pope. The paper itself must be assumed to be an abridged version; it is possible that the enquiry lasted for some of time. Probably Mary Ward represented her enterprise satisfactorily and made a good impression on the cardinals. She certainly felt, after this meeting with them, that there was still reason to hope.

Grisar writes:[33] 'The matter could have been resolved quite simply if the Congregation had issued a decree that Mary Ward was to be told that her Institute was banned and must therefore be suppressed.' It did not do so. There are still eight letters extant from the Congregatio de Propaganda Fide to the Nuntius and Bishops, but none of them mention that Mary Ward had been informed of the decision by the church authorities in Rome. Nor, in these letters, is there any request to anyone to inform her of the suppression of her Institute.[34]

This final struggle was a test of strength for both sides. For the ever-active Mary Ward there began a time of waiting, one of gruelling uncertainty, and for her fiercest enemy, the Secretary of the Congregatio de Propaganda Fide, a time for rapid re-deployment of ammunition.

In the manner of all meticulous officials, he once more drew up a list of defects from among the rank and file of the Englishwomen. As with Mary Ward's position paper, just mentioned, so too Ingoli's proceedings show a continuation of the discussion.

The 'Compendium'[35] was written by Ingoli personally and therefore undoubtedly also compiled by him. It is based mainly on the information he gave to Cardinal Millini in 1624[36] and on his list of 1628[37] concerning the deplorable state of affairs in the Englishwomen's Institute.

In addition, he broadened the scope of his attacks with the most recent information, the 'Relatio' – not yet examined – from Andreas Trevigi, Isabella Clara Eugenia's personal physician, who was hostile to the Jesuits, from Bishop Klesl's letters from Vienna and those of the two Nuntios, Carafa and Pallotto, as well as from other untraceable sources. The addendum in another hand, with corrections by Ingoli, is concerned with a possible interview with Joyce Vaux, who had been dismissed from the Institute. Ingoli obtained his statements this time also from sources which were extremely biassed, whose clear intention was the destruction of the Institute.

The reason Ingoli tried yet again to reinforce his arguments against the Institute is not immediately plain; it can only be seen in the context of the session of the Congregatio de Propaganda Fide.[38]

Ingoli did not offer much that was new. This time three Jesuits were named as founders of the Institute: Fr Campion, Fr Lee and Fr Talbot, none of them highly-educated Jesuits. Ingoli also reported on the Englishwomen's association with men, of their gadding about and enticing young women to their way of life. His contribution, that the Englishwomen did not wish to be subordinate either to the Bishops or the Nuntios was an inflammatory statement in curial circles. It was an allegation which Ingoli had undoubtedly extracted from the letters of Carlo Caraffa.

A second part of the 'Compendium' reports on 'particular cases'. In one, Ingoli remarks on the story told by Trevigi of a nineteen-year-old girl from Flanders, who lived in a Jesuit college, dressed as a man. She was supposed to have been a 'Jesuitess'. The Prague complaints were there, too: the demands made by the 'Jesuitesses' for a parish church, their frivolous reaction to the threat of excommunication, the use of a seal by the General Superior bearing the inscription: 'Praeposita Generalis Societatis Jesu.' Supported by information from Vienna, Ingoli pointed out the dangers attendant on a rapid expansion of the Institute in the middle of Europe, where they had highly-placed benefactors; one should take action before they spread false teachings or could give cause for scandal. Their active apostolate was particularly dangerous in those countries where heresies abounded, especially as they had easy access to the relatives of their pupils. From Flanders one hundred and thirty items had been drawn up against their establishments.[39] Ingoli had even raked up the story of Sister Praxedis, more than ten years old by then. Enquiry should be made into the truth of her allegations.[40] Finally, Ingoli recorded a slightly risqué remark made by Mary Ward. When a prelate told the Englishwomen of the Pope's command to them to take off their habits (sic), Mary Ward is supposed to have said, in the presence of some other members, that the Pope and the Cardinals would probably prefer to see them go round half-clad, like street women.

From all this, it emerges quite clearly that we have two worlds confronting one another – and they were whole worlds apart.

On the one hand – strenuous efforts to form a new type of congregation for women as co-workers in the Church; on the other, the ungracious dismissal of such a way of life for women.

Here, signs of a worthwhile apostolate by this congregation both in the sphere of girls' education and help for one's neighbour; there, fear of scandal as a result of women's free activity on the religious scene.

One the one side, dismay at the slanders brought against them; on the other, the collecting and cataloguing of just such slanders.

Here, the request for an enquiry into their innocence; there, dubious and unproven sources accepted as evidence of guilt.

Here, care to avoid giving the Pope and enemies of the Institute cause for remorse of conscience; there, assiduous care taken to make sure that these 'scandals' had the widest publicity.

It is no longer possible to estimate the influence of Dr Trevigi's document and Ingoli's 'Compendium'. They may not even have been necessary, as the matter had already been decided. The Decree of the Congregation of 30th November, 1629[41] was directed expressly against the Institute of the English 'Jesuitesses'.

St Omer

Ignorance of the church authorities in St Omer about the Englishwomen – Nuntius Lagonissa's orders regarding the suppression of their house – implementation of the decree – the Englishwomen's reaction

Before following Mary Ward's next steps in Rome, attention is drawn to the fate of the houses in St Omer and the jurisdiction of the Cologne Nunciature. In his Ad Limina report of 28th August, 1625,[42] Bishop Boudot[43] had very little to impart about the Institute in his city. He simply wrote about certain Englishwomen, who taught girls and belonged to some sort of new congregation. Their superior had already been in Rome for some two or three years, in order to obtain confirmation for her community. The Bishop, by way of final remark, considered their lives edifying and religious. It took another five years before the tiny community was mentioned again in the sources. Neither the church nor the civil authorities seem to have known of their humble existence. How and through whom Nuntius Lagonissa discovered them is not known. On 6th January, and on 29th April, 1630,[44] he demanded the suppression of these English 'Jesuitesses' by Bishop Pierre Paunet, who had succeeded Bishop Paul Boudot in St Omer in 1627.[45] It does not emerge from his answer of 15th May, 1630[46] when the bishop carried out this task. He merely wrote that he had sent the Archpriest of the cathedral of St Omer to the Englishwomen concerning the suppression of the house, and that these had accepted the Pope's instructions immediately (molto presto) and followed the bishop's orders. These did not differ much from those to the rest of the Institute: their public chapel was to be closed, and the altar broken down. There was to be no bell rung for times of prayer, or any other practices which might bear a resemblance to a religious Order. They were not to go out in pairs, as religious women were accustomed to do, nor were they to wear a veil.

This command, not to go out in twos, may cause some mystification, for in those days women in religious Orders were known to be enclosed. However, the Bishop was able to mollify the Nuntius by reporting that the Englishwomen were already attending the parish church. This remark is probably an indication that up to the time of the suppression, Mass had been celebrated in their own oratory. In St Omer, too, the Englishwomen lived in great poverty (vivono assai meschinamente) on the small income obtained from their teaching. They had therefore probably been forced to ask a certain amount of money for their school, which had previously been free. Ten days later[47] on 25th May, Nuntius Lagonissa reported to Rome that he was awaiting news from the Bishop of St Omer concerning the suppression of the few Jesuitesses who were still in the city. On 6th July[48], the Nuntius wrote to Cardinal Ludovisi, that in his area there was only one establishment of the English Jesuitesses, and that was in St Omer. This community, after he had twice ordered the Bishop to do so, was now suppressed. Lagonissa's letter arrived at the 127th Session of the Congregation of the Propaganda Fide on 5th August, 1630.[49] Shortly afterwards,[50] the Nuntius was praised by Rome for what he had done. Bishop Paunet did not receive an individual letter, but the Nuntius was asked to convey thanks for his co-operation.

It is difficult to show exactly how long this small group of Englishwomen remained in St Omer. In his final report, composed in 1634,[51] in which Nuntius Lagonissa wrote about his seven years' service in Flanders, he spoke of the events between the months of May and August, 1630, saying that in spite of the suppression of their Institute, there were still some Jesuitesses living in St Omer. But here too these poor women should not be accused of disobedience to the Pope, for this was certainly not the case. As with the Belgian 'Jesuitesses' in Brussels, it can be repeated here that the Pope could suppress all the outward signs of a religious community, but not that of a purely secular house community.

Liège

*The situation of the community — the sick and the dead —
Nuntius Pierluigi Carafa — the order of the Congregatio de
Propaganda Fide of 8th December, 1629 — the Decree of
Suppression of 30th April, 1630 — the attitude of the Eng-
lishwomen — Anne Gage*

Liège had always been the most difficult and least fortunate of all
the houses of the Institute, for the community was unable to free
itself from its enormous burden of debts. It has already been mentioned that many of the Englishwomen had returned to their own
country after the financial collapse of the house.[52] Many of them
had been moved to newer foundations, but a few still remained, to
maintain the establishment on the Mont St Martin. It is not known
why they stayed. One can only surmise that some of them had no
other prospects, or perhaps preferred to hold out, as representatives
of this burden of debt which they had to carry through no fault of
their own, and were prepared to do so.[53] It must also be remembered
that there were older members and sick members in the house. Fr
Vitelleschi allowed Anne Gage to have a burial place in the English
Jesuit's Church,[54] probably a sign that she was seriously ill. As well
as the sick, there were the starving, who lived on small supplies and
smaller incomes.

On 12th June, 1626[55] the Chapter of St Martin gave them 12
patakons (small coins); on 22nd January, 1627[56] they received a
bushel of rye from the Chapter of St Lambert. On 15th February,
1630[57] four sextaria of wheat are listed as a gift for the Englishwomen from the Chapter of St Martin, on 25th October, 1630[58]
from the same Chapter, 2 patakons in money. The contributions
were sparse, and it must have been hard for the class-conscious Englishwomen to accept them, or even perhaps to request them.

Their creditors did not leave them alone, and the roof over their
heads could hardly any longer be called a protection — in the non-
literal sense. In the autumn of 1628[59] the Chapter of St Martin
informed them of the order to pay Canon Servatius Meys his outstanding rent within eight days, as he would otherwise be given the
right to take action as he saw fit, that is, that Meys could then
summon the authorities to evict them. But Meys chose another
method. He declared himself prepared[60] to sell the house in which
the Englishwomen were living to the canon who offered most for it.
One such person came forward.

Then there were those who had died. Already in 1625[61] Mary Ward
had written of deaths within the community on Mont St Martin. It is
unfortunate that the death register of St Remacle en Mont, the parish
church, was kept from 1626 only. The names of the Englishwomen
who died there are not known, but they belonged without doubt to

the community of the Institute. People belonging to an Order were not generally mentioned by name in the death register. It would be difficult to explain why it was always an Englishwoman and never an English man, who had died in such a small parish as St Remacle en Mont. On 18th September, 1627[62] a member of the Institute died. In March and November, 1628[63] likewise, two Englishwomen died. Not much later, the Institute received permission for a burial place in the collegiate church of St Martin.[64] It is not known if they used it. In 1630 three more members of the Institute died.[65] Things were not much better for the community, now much smaller; in the years that followed, between 1627 and 1635[66] they mourned nine sisters, which is a member a year, on average. And most of the members of this foundation were still young. Possibly they had succumbed to the plague, which snatched its victims in these years. It is in these pitiable conditions that the Congregatio de Propaganda Fide found the English Jesuitesses in Liège. It had been informed of the Jesuitesses from several sources.[67]

But it was only in the 115th Session, on 2nd October, 1629[68] that the cardinals decided to send the same instructions which had been prepared on 14th July, 1628 for the Nuntius in Brussels and Vienna to the Nuntius in Cologne. Secretary Ingoli carried out the order of the Congregation with extreme rapidity.[69] Nuntius Carafa was told in his letter that he could act in his own capacity or in the power of the Bishop. The decision of the 117th Session of the Congregatio de Propaganda Fide, on 30th November[70] was aimed expressly at the English 'Jesuitesses'. It said that the Nuntios in Belgium and Germany should go to extremes against them. On 8th December,[71] Secretary Ingoli forwarded these instructions to Nuntius Pierluigi Carafa of Cologne. The Englishwomen were once more confronted by a member of the Carafa family.

Pierluigi Carafa was born in Naples in 1581. In 1624 he was made Nuntius in Cologne and Bishop of Tricario, being then already forty three years old. This Carafa too was a man who rejoiced in reform. He established a seminary in his diocese which promulgated the decrees of the Council of Trent. As Nuntius of Cologne he resided a considerable amount of the time in Liège. The bishop himself lived on the Rhine, either in Cologne or in Bonn. Carafa knew the Englishwomen in Liège. It may be assumed that they were not exactly the apple of his eye.

With great resolution he informed the Elector of Cologne of the mandate of the Congregation concerning the suppression of the Englishwomen.[72]

With the cooperation of the local bishop he was to see to it that these were either expelled from their houses or accepted the rule of an enclosed and already approved Order. That would concern two of the Elector's suffragan bishops in Liège and Cologne, but he, the Nuntius, was more than ready to cooperate, so that the Pope's command could be carried out forthwith. The Nuntios in Vienna and Brussels had received the same decree; the Jesuitesses there were likewise suppressed by reason of the decisions on enclosure made by the Council of Trent. Eight days later[73] Carafa promised Cardinal Ludovisi his cooperation in the suppression of the English Jesuitesses. His zeal, however, pales in comparison to that of Secretary Ingoli.[74] The suppression, he considered this time, would involve difficulties, as the position of a bishop in the northern countries was not to be compared with that of a bishop in Italy. Although those in Cologne and Trier were princes, they had to deal with their subjects and reckon with their privileges. It has already been made clear that Nuntius Carafa erred in his opinion that the situation of the Nuntios in Vienna and Brussels would be more favourable than those of Cologne and Trier. Finally, Carafa requested the faculty of releasing people from their vows, in case some of the Englishwomen did not wish to enter one of the approved Orders.

He did not obtain this as rapidly as he would have liked. In the middle of February,[75] the Nuntius had to write a somewhat subdued letter to Secretary Ingoli, explaining that the English Jesuitesses were subject to the Electors of Cologne and Trier, and that these latter were protecting their canonical rights jealously and with some suspicion. He, the Nuntius, had therefore been forced to proceed with caution in the matter. For instance, the Elector of Cologne wanted a breathing space of twenty to twenty-five days. The Jesuitesses had asked for this, as they were expecting a favourable sign from the Pope through their General Superior in Rome. But, as Carafa ended his letter grimly, should the Elector hesitate again after this period of time, he, Carafa would himself take the necessary steps and implement the suppression. In Rome there was no retraction possible once a decision had been taken. And once again he requested faculties to be allowed to release the Englishwomen from their vows.

The Archbishop of Trier found reasons for delay, too. He was occupied in laying siege to his disobedient city of Trier, and was therefore prevented from carrying out the decree from Rome concerning the Jesuitesses.[76]

The Congregatio de Propaganda Fide contained itself in patience, and merely informed Carafa[77] that the Englishwomen's requests had been refused in Rome. Impatiently Carafa asked[78] whether the Congregation had come to a decision about his report. By then the time stipulated by the Bishop of Liège had expired. On 30th April, 1630[79] the Decree of Suppression of the Englishwomen's foundation in Liège was enforced. This decree has come down in the form of a copy only. The text is similar to that of the Archbishop of Maline's decree of suppression for the Belgian Jesuitesses in Brussels, and to that of the draft for the decree for suppression composed by the Bishop of Vienna, who had, after all, asked for the text from Brussels. Here too the Bishop acted on the Pope's command and on the directions of the Nuntius, not on his own initiative. The phrasing is brief and concise: the congregation of the Englishwomen must be regarded as suppressed; its members may not in the future have any external sign which resembles that of a religious congregation, they are therefore not even to wear the same sort of clothing, nor to have a church or oratory, where Mass could be celebrated; there was to be no convent bell, and no common burial place. They could not receive charitable funds. If they would not enter an approved Order, they would have the status of lay people. The clergy were to pay particular attention to this, otherwise, they are threatened with excommunication. The author of the decree is unknown. It was certainly not the Bishop of Liège, for he, Ferdinand von Wittelsbach, was not in his diocesan city at the time. However, the decree was issued in Liège.

In spite of its brief, clear language, there is still one unanswered question: what exactly was it that the Bishop of Liège, like Archbishop Boon of Malines, was suppressing?

The Englishwomen, after the promulgation of the decree of suppression, were to be regarded as lay people. But had they not been so before, according to canon law? Their Institute had been unable to obtain papal approbation. Moreover, the vows of the now-declared lay women were not dispensed. Neither the Bishop nor the Nuntius had the right to do so, and Rome was silent on the matter, even after a second request from the Nuntius.

It is from the enclosed report that a more exact description of the Suppression has come down to us.

On the afternoon of 30th April – it was a Tuesday – the Decree was read out by the General Vicar of Liège. This took place in the presence of Adrien de Fléron, Canon of St Lambert and of Sainte Croix, as well as the Provost of Maubeuge, Giovanni Battista de Ninis, General auditor of Nuntius Carafa, Zacharias Cools, Chaplain of St Martin, and Matthias Delbrouck, notary. The religious commission consisted of five, the members of the Englishwomen's community, eleven. Their names were given: Anne Buskells, Provincial, Mary Copley, Superior, Anne Gage, Elizabeth Hall, Bridget Heyde, Catherine Smith, Anne Morgan, Elizabeth Tapne, Helen Pick, Frances Fuller and Frances Lametz. After the Latin decree had been read out, the French translation followed. They took the decision calmly and in obedience to the Pope, only requesting the time necessary to order their affairs. The General Vicar granted them this, a period of forty days, – therefore until Sunday, 9th June. How must General Vicar de Chokier have felt, when he read out the Decree? Six years before, on 5th March, 1624, he had described the Englishwomen on behalf of the Bishop as 'religiosae et ecclesiasticae personae' and recognized them as such.

On 3rd May[80] Carafa informed Cardinal Ludovisi about the execution of the Suppression. This had been announced in Cologne, but the Decree had not yet been issued. There was no answer from

Trier yet. Perhaps Carafa meant that the affair could now be considered closed, but such was by no means the case. It is difficult to imagine the situation of the eleven Englishwomen; there are hardly any sources which tell of their lives. Something is known about Anne Gage, who had a tragic fate.

In 1615[81] she had been made superior of the community in London by Mary Ward. On her return to the Continent she ran into danger of shipwreck.[82] In the difficult years 1618 − 1621, she was superior of Liège. Now, in 1630, she asked to be released from the vows she had taken as a young woman, so as to enter an Order.[83] He request to the Pope concerning this has neither date nor signature. In his letter of 3rd May to Cardinal Ludovisi, Nuntius Carafa describes the suppression of the foundation, but Anne Gage's request was sent to Rome by him on 10th May only. The petition was therefore written *before* this day, most probably in Carafa's office, for the author knew neither the exact age of the petitioner nor the length of time she had belonged to the Institute. Anne Gage, we read, was about fifty years old, and a member of the Institute for sixteen. It is known, however, that she already belonged to the community in St Omer on 8th September, 1612, and therefore was one of the first members of the Institute. She had already taken a vow of celibacy in England with the intention of entering an order. Through her membership of the Institute, and in good faith that this was approved by the Pope, she assumed that her vows were valid. Now, however, disappointed in this by the Decree of Suppression, she requested dispensation from her vows as religious, without however being released from her vow of chastity. The sentences which then follow afford a glimpse of Anne Gage's situation − apparently without future. She will not have been the only one. Although she came from one of the landed families, she had no one in England who could help her; her parents were already dead; she could not enter another order because she was too old and too ill. She had even used her dowry to support herself and the other members of the Institute.

Anne Gage's vows were dispensed only in the 126th Session of the Congregatio de Propaganda Fide on 9th July, 1630.[84] On 20th July[85] this information was sent to Nuntius Carafa.

Cologne

The difficult situation of the house − Suppression in May, 1630 − the Englishwomen's objections − the Archbishop's attitude

The downfall of the Cologne house began with a warning about taxation. On lst March, 1630[86] the town decided to send certain officials to the 'Englischen Jungfrauwen' who lived in the house of Arnold von Krufft in Breitenstrasse but paid no contributions. An entry of 6th March,[87] makes it clear that the Englishwomen – as though belonging to religious status – refused to pay the city tax. They would have found this difficult. The town thereupon turned to the owner of the house. Because of the suppression, which followed shortly after, further prosecution by the secular authorities was superfluous. On 22nd May[88] the Archbishop of Cologne wrote a report about the suppression to Nuntius Carafa. From this some details about the implementation of the decree and the Englishwomen's attitude have come to light. The General Vicar was appointed to carry out the suppression by the Archbishop. However the Englishwomen complained that they were far more strictly dealt with in Cologne than in other cities. One can only think that they had been given no time, or a very short time only, to leave their house in Cologne in comparison with arrangements in Liège. They also referred to the suppression of their houses in Munich, Vienna and Pressburg, which had not been conducted so rigorously. Their community in Liège, they asserted, was even allowed to have the Blessed Sacrament in the house, and were also permitted religious practices.

In their extremity they asked the Archbishop to intercede on their behalf with the Nuntius, so that he might intervene for them in Rome. This request shows once more how little the Englishwomen knew of the Curia's intentions with regard to their suppression, and how trustingly they hoped for the Nuntius' intervention. He could not deny them his protection, the Archbishop considered at the end of his letter, as they were tolerated in Rome and other cities, and could accept novices.

That was something of an overstatement, for the Englishwomen had had to leave their house in Via Montorio. Their novitiate was in Munich, which had not been suppressed. In the end the Archbishop did request the Nuntius for some relaxation of the orders. Carafa even forwarded the petition.[89] But it was all a mere formality, for neither the Nuntius nor the authorities in Rome wished for any other solution than the one already taken.

Trier

The Archbishop's difficult political situation – the delayed suppression of the house in August, 1630 – objections from the Englishwomen

It has already been mentioned[90] that the Archbishop of Trier had not been able to implement the suppression of the foundation of the

Englishwomen in the chief city of his principality because of internal politics.

On 24th May, 1630[91] Nuntius Carafa had not yet received an answer; on 7th June[92] he was still unable to report any happening to Rome, and on 10th July[93] he was expecting news from Trier daily.

Finally, on 26th July,[94] wheels began to turn. The impatient Nuntius had contacted his agent in Rome, Francesco Paolucci, in order to speed things up. Then came the consoling information. On the morning of 20th August, 1630[95] the suffragan bishop of Trier, George von Helfenstein, the official and signatory of the Archbishop, went to the Englishwomen's house and made the papal decree known, in German. Neither in St Omer nor in Liège nor Cologne had the Englishwomen offered any resistance. It was quite another matter in Trier. We learn from a letter from the suffragan bishop to Nuntius Carafa[96] that the eight Englishwomen, after hearing the decree, declared that they could not leave the Institute without the approval of their General Superior. From the beginning of the year, wrote the bishop, he had tried in vain to make the Englishwomen conform to the decree. There are questions which must be asked here about his dates. The Decree of Suppression was dated 30th November, and written to Nuntius Carafa on 8th December, so can only have reached Liège towards the end of January, 1630. On 15th February, Nuntius Carafa wrote to Rome that the Archbishops of Cologne and Trier were suspicious of their canonical rights. On 15th March,[97] and also on 5th July,[98] he indicated the political difficulties of the Archbishop of Trier. According to that, it was not the disobedience of the Englishwomen that was responsible for the delay, but the shaky and beleaguered position of the Archbishop. One really cannot accept that the archiepiscopal curia of Trier, or even Nuntius Carafa, feigned political difficulties, for it would have been even more effective to indicate the Englishwomen's disobedience. These may indeed have had prior knowledge of the suppression of their congregation, but this would not have been realised until 20th August. Who can dispute with them if they attempted to delay the annihilation of their house?

The religious princes of the territory of Liège, Cologne and Trier made no difficulties with the Congregatio de Propaganda Fide about the suppression of the houses of the Institute of the Englishwomen. They may have hesitated a little, maybe out of consideration for the innocent women, or for canonical reasons, or whatever one may wish to think. Ultimately, they were bound by the decree of the Congregatio de Propaganda Fide and their obedience to the Pope as princes of the church. This explains why the Englishwomen's communities could expect less protection in the ecclesiastical territories than in the realms of the secular princes, who could at least save them from eviction.

Notes

1. Vita E, f.36v; Vita I, p.28.
2. On 2nd January, 1629. ibid.
3. Vita E, f.37r.
4. Chambers II, E p.285; II D, p.237 without references names Mary Ward, Winefrid Wigmore, Elizabeth Cotton, Anne Turner, Henry Lee and Robert Wright.
5. Pallotto to Ingoli, 3rd February 1629. APF Rome, SOCG, Lettere di Germania e di Boemia 70, ff.103r, 105r–106v. Vita I, p.28/29, names the wife of Duke Albrecht of Bavaria.
6. Health certificate of Duke Leopold V of Tirol, 6.January 1629, Landesregierungs Archiv for Tirol, Innsbruck, Hofregistratur 629, V/1, and Mary Ward's letter of thanks to the Archduke of 13th January. ibid.
7. Letter of thanks, see note 6.
8. Pallotto to Mary Ward, 3rd March 1629, Bibl. Comm. Giovardiana Veroli (Frosinone) 42.3.12.
9. ibid.
10. ibid.
11. Brussels, PEA 467, ff.63r–64v.
12. DNB XXI, Sp.79–81; Gillow V, Sp.578–581.
13. J. H. Pollen SJ The Note Book of John Southcote 1623–1637, CRS 1, Misc.1., London, 1905, p.106.
14. On 2nd August Nuntius Pallotto wrote to Cardinal Ludovisi that the father had been recalled from Vienna to Prague and would soon leave for Rome. APF Rome, SOCG 69, ff.81r–84v. On 5th August Fr Valerio, from Prague, allowed Ingoli to inform the Congregation about the conversations between himself and Nuntius Pallotto ibid. ff.393rv, 321v. Fr Valerio was present at the Session of the Congregation on 29th November, 1628, APF Rome, Acta 6, f.193r. Cited by Grisar, Institut, p.445.
15. Grisar, ibid. also quotes a letter from Fr Vitelleschi to Fr Lamormain, in which the General shows himself well informed about the Capuchin's intrigues against the Jesuits.
16. Vita E, f.37v; Vita I, p.29.
17. " ... which when presented to His Holynes and the Cardinalls of the Congregation was both admired and praysed in so much as some of them sayd, it must have been dictated by the Holy Ghost." Vita E, f.37v; Vita I, p.29.
18. Vita E f.38r. The following events are lacking from Vita I.
19. Pallotto in his answer to Mary Ward 9th July, 1629. Bibl. Comm. Giovardiana Veroli (Frosinone) 42.3.12.
20. Grisar, Institut, p.577.
21. "lascivi ... in quella buona dispositione che ... significata." Pallotto to Mary Ward, about note 19.
22. "When she had done her part she rested satisfyed and treated with them as holding the place, not conform to their private opinions." Vita E, f.38r.
23. Grisar, Institut, p.577.
24. Vita E, f.38v.
25. Grisar, Institut, p.581 ff.
26. ibid. p.588 with a pointer to Vita I, p.31.
27. ibid. p.439–444, and Druck, appendix VIII, p.763–770.
28. AV Rome, Miscell. Arm. III, 37, ff.213r–215r. Writing of Elizabeth Cotton.

29. Generalate Archives of the Discaled Carmelites, Rome. MS. Nr.106. Writing of Winefrid Wigmore.
30. See his statement p.648.
31. see p.396.
32. " ... di più molt'heretici et assai infetti di vitii ..."
33. ibid. p.595.
34. Thus Grisar, ibid. p.596.
35. APF Rome, SOCG 205, ff.4417r − 448v.
36. see p.395 ff.
37. see p.467 ff.
38. The date 14th January 1630 may point to use by the Congregation. On 30th November, 1629, the Congregation decided on the suppression of the Institute of the English "Jesuitesses". On 26th February, 1630 it decided to hand over the Nuntius of Cologne's letters with other writings to a Special Congregation. It is for this that Ingoli could have compiled his "Compendium", although the Special Congregation was not convened.
39. By Andreas Trevigi.
40. The sister, who died with a reputation of sanctity, had told Mary Ward that her Institute was not pleasing to God. Upon which Mary Ward had requested the other members no longer to regard her as holy, but to oppose her.
41. APF Rome, Acta 1629 − 1630, 6, ff.358r, 361v.
42. AV Rome, S. Congr. Visit. ad limina Audomarensis, f.166rv.
43. Paul Boudot, Bishop of Saint-Omer since 1618, was moved to Arras in 1627. He died in November 1635. Hier. Cath. IV, p.99.
44. Bishop Paunet to Nuntius Lagonissa on 15th May 1630. The letters named were never discovered.
45. APF Rome, SOCG Lettere di Francia etc. 1630, 132, ff.187r, 192v. Pierre Paunet, OMObs, 1627 − 1631 Bishop of Saint-Omer, died 31th March 1631. Hier. Cath. IV, p.100.
46. See above, notes 44. and 45.
47. Lagonissa to Ingoli. APF Rome, SOCG 205, Belgium sive Flandria, Jesuitissae and 1648 inclusive, ff.428r, 433v.
48. APF Rome, SOCG, Lettere di Francia etc. 1630, 132, ff.186r, 193v.
49. APF Rome, Acta 1630 − 1631, 7, ff.105v, 108v.
50. On 17th August 1630, Ingoli to Lagonissa. APF Rome, Lettere volgari 1630, 10, f.93rv.
51. BV Rome, Barb. lat. 2677, f.59v.
52. See p.346 ff.
53. On 26th April 1630 Fr Rector Stafford wrote to Fr Courtenay in Rome that the Pope wished to suppress the Englishwomen's Institute but it was doubtful if he could do so without enabling the women to have money to repay their debts. Stonyhurst Archives, Anglia A IV, 81.
54. On 21st September 1625, Fr Vitelleschi to Fr Blount, ARSI Rome, Anglia 1/II f.223v. The approval was repeated on 11.October, 1626. Fr Vitelleschi to Fr Knott, ibid. f.245v.
55. AE Liège, Collégiale Saint-Martin 60, f.10v.
56. AE Liège, Cathédrale Saint-Lambert, A., Sécrétariat, Registre aux Conclusions capitualaires 26 (1626 − 1628) f.89r.
57. AE Liège, Collégiale Saint-Martin 60, f.61r.
58. ibid. f.75v, and 61, f.9r.
59. On 22nd September 1628. ibid. 57, f.128v.
60. On 22nd February, 1630. ibid. 60, f.61v.
61. On 2nd January 1625. Mary Ward to Cardinal Bandini. BV Rome. Fondo Capp. 47, ff.26r − 27v.
62. AE Liège, Registres Parroissiaux, Liège, Église Saint Remacle-en-Mont, Décès 234, f.90v.

63. ibid.
64. On 22nd June 1629. AE Liège, Collégiale Saint-Martin 60 f.52v.
65. Before 5th February on 5th February and on 17th February. AE Liège, Registres Parroissiaux, Liège, Elgise Saint Remacle-en-Mont, Décès 234, f.91r.
66. Before 22.August 1632. ibid. f.61v. and once again with the same date, ibid. then June 1635, ibid f.92r.
67. Nuntius Lagonissa to Cardinal Ludovisi, 8th August 1628. APF Rome, SOCG 102, Lettere d'Inghilterra etc. ff.57r, 62v; the Archbishop of Cambrai to Vives on 6.September 1629, APF Rome, SOCG Fiandra 205, ff.417r–420v, 422r; Vives to the Infanta on 8th December 1629, AGR Brussels, PEA 467, f.191rv.
68. APF Rome, Acta 1628–1529, 6.ff.334r, 336rv, Nr.11.
69. On 12th October 1629. APF Rome Lettere volgari 1629, 8, f.161rv.
70. APF Rome, Acta 1629–1630, 6, ff.358r, 361v, Nr.9.
71. APF Rome, Lettere volgari 1629, 8, f.181r.
72. On 20th December 1629. Copy WA London XXIIII, Nr.150, pp.532–533.
73. On 28th December 1629. APF Rome, SOCG Lettere di Spagna etc. 1630, 98, ff.202r, 211v.
74. ibid. ff.214rv. 223rv. Both letters were dealth with in the 120 Session of the Congregation on 26th February, but placed among the documents for the time being. APF Rome, Acta 1630–1631, 7.ff.20r, 21r; Ingoli to Carafa on 9th March 1630. APF Rome, Lettere volgari 1630, 10 ff.17v–18r.
75. On 25th February, APF Rome, SOCG Lettere di Spagna etc. 1630, 98, ff.218r–219v.
76. Carafa to Ingoli on 15th March, 1630. APF Rome, SOCG Lettere di Spagna etc. 1630. 98, ff.230rv. 235v.
77. On 26th March 1630. APF Rome, Lettere volgari 1630, 10, f.34rv. The resolution concerned with this in the 121st Session of 19th March, APF Rome, Acta 1630–1631, 7, ff.31r–32rv. Nr.8. On 25th April 1630 the Congregation informed Nunitus Lagonissa also that the Englishwomen's request, in spite of their General Superior's efforts, had been refused. APF Rome, Letter volgari 1630, 10, f.45rv.
78. On 5th April 1630. Copy SOCG Lettere di Spagna etc. 1630, 98, ff.236r, 245v.
79. cf. below, p.540 ff.
80. APF Rome, SOCG Lettere di Spagna etc. 1630, 98, ff.237rv, 244v. Carafa's information was produced in the 124th Session of the Congregation on 15th June, 1630. APF Rome, Acta 1630–1631, 7.f, 75rv.
81. see p.161.
82. see p.163.
83. Before 10th May, 1630. APF Rome, SOCG Lettere di Spagna etc. 1630, 98, f.247r. Accompanying letter dated 10th May 1630. ibid. ff.246rv., 250v.
84. APF Rome Act 1630–1631, 7.ff.246rv., 250v.
85. APF Rome, Lettere volgari 1630, 10, f.81v.
86. Hist. Arch. of Cologne. Council Report 76. f.91v.
87. ibid. f.100v.
88. APF Rome, SOCG Lettere di Spagna etc. 1630, 98, ff.252r, 256v.
89. Carafa to Cardinal Ludovisi on 7th June 1630. ibid. f.254r–255v.
90. see p.513.
91. Carafa to Cardinal Ludovisi. APF Rome SOCG Lettere di Spagna etc. 1630, 98, ff.248r, 249v.
92. ibid. ff.254r. 255v.
93. ibid. ff.260rv, 263v, and Carafa to Ingoli, ibid. ff.259r, 264r.
94. Carafa to Ingoli. ibid. ff.266rv, 277v. The letters were submitted to the

128th Session of the Congregation on 5th September 1630. APF Rome, Acta 1630–1631. 7.ff.117r, 122r, Nr.22.
95. APF Rome, SOCG, Lettere di Spagna etc. 1630, 98, f.268rv.
97. ibid. ff.230rv, 235v.
98. ibid. ff.258rv, 265v.

XXVII

INTO THE UNKNOWN
Munich 1629

Elector Maximilian and the Englishwomen – Cardinal Francesco Barberini's accusations and the Elector's answers

It must not be assumed that the foundation in Munich was without its troubles. Fr Silisdon had written to the Elector[1] about the Englishwomen's debts in Liège. There were several Jesuits in Munich who rejected the Institute, although two highly-placed men supported the women: Fr General Vitelleschi and the Elector, Maximilian I. Over and above this was the serious attempt by the Congregatio de Propaganda Fide to destroy the Institute in Munich.

At that time there was no nunciature in Munich. In case of necessity one had to turn to the Nuntius in Lucerne or the one at the imperial court of Vienna.

That may have been a reason why Cardinal Francesco Barberini turned relatively late to the Elector of Bavaria, in comparison with the other countries.

Without the approval or confirmation of the church, the Pope's powerful nephew informed the Elector on 6th January, 1629,[2] a congregation of Jesuitesses had been founded; this had to be thoroughly examined by the church. Some of the members of this congregation had found support with the Elector. They may even have believed they would thus be able to continue their form of life without the Pope's approval.[3] The Elector, as a loyal son of the Church, would certainly exhort the women to submit to the papal decision.

The phrasing of this letter quite obviously presupposes the Englishwomen's open disobedience to the Pope. Nor must it pass unremarked that on 6th January, 1629, there could not have been any question of a thorough examination of the Jesuitesses' way of life. The suppression of the houses in Naples, Vienna and Pressburg had been decided on during the 94th Session of the Congregation de Propaganda Fide, which had taken place on 7th July, 1628 under the presidency of the Pope on the Quirinal. Cardinal Barberini should have known that, as he had been present. The Englishwomen did not know this, any more than the Elector.

Maximilian answered briefly and to the point.[4] It was only after examination of a glowing testimony that he had accepted the Englishwomen into his country. They were doing first class work with girl's education, and led exemplary lives. As to church matters which were the Pope's concern he, the Elector, would never interfere. He needed no hints in that direction.[5] That was clear enough.

It can be seen that here too — as with the Belgian 'Jesuitesses' in Brussels — there was a clear distinction between the power of the Pope over a religious community, and a mere community, seen to be of benefit to the people. Maximilian adopted exactly the same attitude as had Infanta Isabella Clara Eugenia, and with her, the city of Brussels.

The Cardinal, however, insisted. The Englishwomen, he thought in a letter of a later date[6] were conducting themselves well in Bavaria because they were under the Elector's surveillance. The Councils and Apostolic Constitutions, however, forbade any communities of women which did not have solemn vows and were not enclosed. The Church wished to protect women from constant dangers by its legislation.[7]

The Elector answered still more briefly.[8] He was of the same opinion as before concerning the 'Donne della Compagnia di Gesù.'

This time, however, Maximilian could not refrain from making a remark to the Cardinal. He asked him to understand the position of catholics in England, with particular reference to Bishop Richard Smith.[9] Smith was one of the keenest critics of the Society of Jesus among the catholics in England. It should have become clear enough to Cardinal Barberini: the situation in Vienna, where the Nuntius and the Bishop could not work in harmony, showed great difficulties. The situation was all the more problematic in Munich, where there was no resident Nuntius and no Bishop who had any influence worth mentioning. The Englishwomen's houses were not to be so easily suppressed in the secular territories.

A brief and insignificant correspondence shows efforts behind the scenes. Towards the end of the year,[10] Privy Councillor Aurelio Gigli of Munich tried to get Francesco Crivelli, the Bavarian agent in Rome, to smooth over the affair. Crivelli was in good standing with the Pope and his nephew. The Elector, Crivelli said, had simply praised the Englishwomen's way of life and educational abilities; the 'Madre del Gesù' had not been expressly praised by him. Some weeks later[11] the agent Crivelli promised to follow his prince's opinions.

Second Journey from Rome to Munich
beginning of 1630

Final wait in Rome − the journey

There is little documentation for the following events. It is not
known exactly how long Mary Ward remained in Rome after her
conference with the Cardinals, but she must have left the Papal
States soon afterwards.[12] The two oldest biographies mention only
a visit made by Mary Ward to the Pope's sister-in-law, Donna
Costanza,[13] who probably knew more about the negotiations or
rather, about the mood among the Cardinals. It was from her that
Mary Ward received the news that she should have no further expectations, and probably also, the advice to leave Rome. After this
totally unofficial information, Mary Ward wrote to Munich that
she was intending to travel.[14] We know only the year of departure:
1630. This time the journey lay via Venice: the plague was in full
force in various places in the northern princedoms of Italy. Neither
the names of those who formed the group of travellers, nor their
numbers are known. The only name mentioned in the writings is
Winefrid Wigmore's. The women had a horse for those who became
tired on the journey, as the greatest part of the way was on foot.
They had ONE pair of good shoes among them, although they had
different-sized feet.[15] Their cash amounted to 200 crowns. When
one of them expressed doubts about this, Mary Ward answered jokingly that they knew of a good way to stretch their money, namely
not to refuse alms to any poor person. And they practised generosity, even at the expense of their weakened bodies.[16] And yet −
in Venice they bought expensive silk. It puts one in mind of sewing
and embroidery, silk and brocade. There were gifted needlewomen
among the Englishwomen and what is more, they taught sewing. At
the time of purchase of these serviceable treasures, they could well
have used the money for their frugal provisions.

The Letter of 6th April, 1630

*The text − attempt to interpret it − significance of the
letter for Mary Ward's integrity towards the Pope and the
Church − Nuntius Pierluigi Carafa's accompanying letter to
Secretary Ingoli*

Among the letters about 'Relatios', petitions, and accusations which
accompanied the downfall of the houses of the Institute in western
Europe, a letter from Mary Ward has survived, the contents of
which are difficult to explain.[17]

For a better understanding, the text is given in full:[18]

'From the letter of the Superior of the Englishwomen. 6th April, 1630.

I am very astonished that Ours have allowed their courage to sink so quickly while they have so much cause for hope. But patience! On my return, I found six weeks' old letters from you and others. As to what concerns the orders for the suppression of our Institute and others of this sort, you are to know that what has been decided against us has been based on false accusations, and that the decrees have come from and been written by Cardinal Bentivoglio, an old enemy of our Institute. The orders came without His Holiness's knowledge. You must not be surprised that I have not written sooner. None of the Cardinals of the Congregation, to whom the Pope entrusted the business, knew of it, except the one just mentioned, who is the sole originator and promoter of the directive. It was Mater Campiana who first gave me news of it. The Cardinal himself wished that I should first hear of it after it had been carried out. Whatever is ordered in virtue of this command, and by whomsoever it is ordered, does not have to be accepted by Ours. They must excuse themselves with all modesty and reverence and answer that they knew from me that the author of this decree is hostile to our Institute, but that he wrote it on his own accord, without the commission of His Holiness, and without the foreknowledge of the other cardinals to whom the business was entrusted as a whole. What I wrote before remains valid: should Bishops or Nuntios – which I do not believe – go so far as to excommunicate, let them do so. Help will be at hand. Ours should remain true to the Institute, and even bear persecution on its account, although one must admit, that persecution of this kind is one of the severest punishments, when one considers where it comes from. As to the teaching, which seems to absolve Ours from obedience towards their superiors, I at all events do not know who brought that matter up; but experience will show that only loss of God's grace can separate us from that undeserved bliss.'

First of all, some comments in general about the way the letter has come to be preserved. It is a copy in Latin that has survived, though there can be no doubt that the Englishwoman Mary Ward wrote to the English members of her Institute in their mother tongue. In this connection it would be important to know who translated it. It could only be someone with a good command of both Latin and English, so it is no good looking for someone from the small community in Mont St Martin; such knowledge of Latin cannot be looked for among them, as it was necessary to produce a grammatically correct end result. Still less must it be assumed that the Italian, Carafa, or his personal office, would have had sufficient command of English. No, between the Englishwomen and the Nuntius was a third person who knew both languages. We do not have to go far in Liège to find this person or – to put it more cautiously – to suggest someone among the English Jesuits with whom some of the English members still had connections. It will be seen that Fr Rector Robert Stafford was helpful as interpreter when Nuntius Carafa interrogated the Englishwomen. This is not to be taken as a firm statement that the Rector translated the letters; this cannot be proved.

The title of the letter is also worth noting: E litteris Matris Superioris Virginum Anglarum scriptis 6.aprilis 1630. Thus: from the letter of 6th April 1630 from the superior of the Englishwomen. That means that the letter was not wholly translated, but extracts from it only were passed on. It could be, and one has the impression that only the most dangerous sentences, compacted tightly together, were translated and strung together so that explanations or qualifications were omitted. One cannot be sure. One can only wonder that Nuntius Pierluigi Carafa never wanted to send the original of the letter, or at least a complete copy to Rome, together with the date and place of issue. He entrenched himself behind the excuse that he had only received the letter in friendship and confidence (via d'amicia e confidenza).[19] It would seem to have been a somewhat doubtful friendship. Involuntarily, one's thoughts turn to that letter of the former rector of the English Jesuits in Liège, Fr Silisdon, to the Elector of Bavaria. It was written shortly after the Englishwomen had entered their house in Munich, and its intention was to deprive the Englishwomen of the Elector's favour. Fr General Vitelleschi had never seen the complete text of that letter, despite repeated requests.

To turn to the contents: in the first sentence given here, Mary Ward shows that she is astonished at the lack of courage of the members of her Institute. This, however, arouses *our* astonishment, as she must have known well enough what these women in Liège as well as in other houses had endured since the autumn of 1621, when she went to Rome. She had been told about the misery caused by the huge debts and the English Jesuits' withholding of the sacrament of forgiveness. She also knew of the sick and the dead. Nine years had passed since. 'So quickly' was not the right phrase to describe the community's loss of courage, above all in Liège. Where were they supposed to have found 'many reasons to hope?' It was far more understandable if this hope had turned into a dull depression. The sentence is only understandable if it is measured in other terms. In someone who was so totally given to God as Mary Ward, the virtue of hope had another dimension. Whether those who received the letter thought as she did, we may have good reason to doubt.

These recipients are not named. On her return, it went on, Mary Ward found letters from the last six weeks. That meant the weekly letters with news from the houses to the General Superior. The statement does not imply that all these letters came from one house.

It states'from you and others'. Theoretically, that could mean one letter from each of the houses in St Omer, Liège, Cologne, Trier, Vienna and Pressburg. But one must not forget that only *one* letter of Mary Ward's has survived, and this was obviously addressed to the community of the Englishwomen in Liège. The accompanying letter from Nuntius Carafa proves that. One thing is certain: all these letters to Mary Ward, from whatever house they came, had reported the imminent suppression.

To come to the essential point: the letter, in the form that has come down to us, does not state *where*[20] Mary Ward found the reports from the houses, and subsequently composed her answer of 6th April, 1630. Perhaps the place where it was written was not mentioned in the original, perhaps it was deliberately omitted in the translation. To have known the place of composition would have been of great significance. From that one could tell whether Mary Ward wrote the letter while still in Rome, or in Munich. To put the question bluntly — when did Mary Ward leave Rome in 1630? From the first two Lives[21] it can be recapitulated that Donna Constanza convinced Mary Ward that future attempts would be fruitless. Further, it is said there that Mary Ward wrote to Munich and informed them of her departure from Rome. Only the year is given, 1630. It must have been the beginning of the year, though, for in the session of 19th March, 1630,[22] the Congregation decided to inform Nuntius Carafa that he should make known to the two archbishops of Cologne and Trier the refusal of the petition for approval of the Englishwomen's Institute. It must be emphasized: this was mention of the refusal of a petition for approval, and not of the suppression of the Institute.

The basis for the decision against their Institute, as Mary Ward's letter of 6th April, 1630 states, was to be found in false accusations. The decrees were issued by an old enemy of the Institute, Cardinal Bentivoglio. The Pope knew nothing at all about it, and not even the Cardinals of the Congregation either. If one looks[23] at the composition of the sessions of the Congregatio de Propaganda Fide, it can be seen that Cardinal Bentivoglio did refer to the Institute in the sessions between 30th January, 1629 (Mary Ward came to Rome at the beginning of February, 1629), and 1st February, 1630. Thus much Mary Ward seems to have learnt in Rome. But these facts, probably heard in roundabout ways or rumours were, as already remarked, centred round February, 1630, therefore very early in 1630.

To which may be added the following: soon after her arrival in Munich, Mary Ward took herself off to Vienna.[24] There, so says the Italian Vita, she was able to talk to the Nuntius, Pallotto (nuntius ordinario). Now Pallotto was called from Vienna on 18th May, 1630.[25] He remained some time in the city, but the Italian Vita, written some decades later, could hardly have called Pallotto the Nuntius of the time if he had not been that officially at the time of the audience in 1630. If one considers that Mary Ward was in Vienna by the latest in the first half of May, then it must be admitted that it would not have been possible for her to have written a letter on 6th April of the same year in Rome. The distance between Rome and Munich was too great and the Englishwomen's mode of travel − on foot − would have made that impossible. For the sake of the context, we bypass certain sentences in Mary Ward's letter and a little later find the information that it was Mater Campiana who first gave her the news, in writing, of the decree of suppression (primo ad me scriptum est Matre Campiana). This Mater Campian or Campiana must not be confused with Margaret Campian[26] who in 1621[27] was the procuratrix in St Omer, and in 1622[28] and 1627[29] was mentioned as living in Liège, but who was not any longer among those present at the suppression of the house on Mont St Martin on 30th April, 1630.[30]

Nor can Winefrid Wigmore be considered as the person concerned. It is said of her that she had made the journey to Rome with Mary Ward. It can be taken for granted that the members of the Institute − and quite certainly the superiors of the houses − were in communication with one another. That was certainly the case in those days of danger to the Institute. Events and anxieties could have been known in Munich which Mary Ward did not yet know on her arrival in Bavaria. In 1630 Mary Poyntz was the superior in Munich. She too bore the alias of Campian, much-loved by the Englishwomen. There does not seem to be much doubt but that this Mater Campian referred to was Mary Poyntz, the superior. Mary Ward wrote to her concerning her journey from Rome.[31] So much for the place of composition of the letter, which would seem to have been Munich. But what was happening regarding the suppression of the houses at this time, on 6th April?

It was known, but executed only later. To recapitulate briefly: in St Omer the suppression was carried out shortly before 15th May, 1630. In Cologne the Englishwomen were negotiating at this same time with their Archbishop. Only on 7th June could Nuntius Carafa write to Cardinal Ludovisi that this house had been suppressed. In Trier, negotiations dragged on even into August, 1630. It was in Liège alone, where Nuntius Carafa resided, that matters moved somewhat more quickly. There the suppression was carried out on 30th April, 1630. But that was three weeks after Mary Ward's letter.

There are certainly statements in this letter which could cause trouble for Mary Ward: the accusations against Cardinal Bentivoglio, then the suggestion that the Pope had allowed himself to be out-flanked, and her statement about excommunication. If one takes the text as corresponding to its original form, one does not desire to minimise or play down these statements in the least, but to propose certain lines for consideration. For Mary Ward, the great

danger at that time, namely the beginning of 1630, lay in uncertainty. She knew nothing of what had, in fact, been *decided*. She
clung to her own experience, and that was not alarming. Quite the
contrary. Pope Urban VIII had greeted her with kindliness. It was
he, in that private audience in Castelgandolfo in May, 1629, who
had suggested re-considering her matter with Cardinal Millini and
the'friendly General of an Order'. Had she not been able to state
her case before the Cardinals? Even if she had hardly been able
to believe in its success, there still remained before her eyes this
rare benevolence of the Pope, as she wrote in her letter. What she
did not know was the fact that the Pope gave her reason to hope
in her audience and at the same time listened to the Congregatio
de Propaganda Fide in its discussions as to how the Institute of
the Jesuitesses was to be suppressed, first in Belgium and then in
Germany. Was it not Cardinal Bentivoglio, heavily criticized in her
letter, who between January 1629 and February 1630, had reported
to the Session of the Congregatio de Propaganda Fide, with only
one interruption? On 30th November, 1629 the decision had been
taken to issue the decree of suppression against the Institute of the
English Jesuitesses. On that occasion, too, the Pope was presiding
and Cardinal Bentivoglio gave a report.

We do not wish to leave the matter there, simply, but to offer,
at the end of this section, a survey of the sessions in which the
Congregation acted against the Jesuitesses. Some things seem to
have leaked out: perhaps these were certain remarks made by
Bentivoglio about the Institute. Who knows? The question has
to be asked – to whom could the Englishwomen have gone for
information in Rome? Could or should they have spoken to
one of the Cardinals of the Congregatio de Propaganda Fide?
Did they even know that their business was being dealt with
by this Congregation? The Nuntios were informed, but not the
persons concerned. And as a result Mary Ward saw the 'orders
to suppress our Institute' as concocted by an enemy, although
they had been decided officially by the competent commission
and sanctioned by the Pope. It may be that Pope Urban VIII,
from reasons of respect, for he esteemed Mary Ward, allowed
her a glimmer of hope. His forbearance would otherwise be difficult to explain. In reality, in this he did her no favour. It is
not our business to sit in judgement on a pope, but we think
that Urban VIII, in spite of his obligation to preserve silence
about the conference of the Congregation, should have let Mary
Ward know his own clear decision. He should have seen that
a sincere woman stood, or rather knelt before him. Or did he
perhaps shy away from this final, personal decision and left it
to the multi-headed and elusive Congregation until the information reached him that Mary Ward had resisted his decision?
We hope not.

But perhaps Urban VIII should not be burdened with the entire responsibility of this matter. For what exactly did these English-women intend, with their strange ideas about women as co-workers in the Church, among the innumerable issues of the many congregations and special congregations of the official Church in those days? Did not the Pope, over and above that, as the ruling Prince of the Papal States, have weighty political concerns as well? We must not be blind to the facts. The Institute of the Englishwomen has been much written about, and much of that abusively, but for the Curia it was de facto a matter of secondary importance, which could become dangerous only in so far as it stood in relation to the powers of secular princes.

After the accusation raised against Cardinal Bentivoglio in Mary Ward's letter, there follows the strict command to members of the Institute to be obedient to their superior, as she knew the true state of affairs. In doing this, Mary Ward took enormous responsibility on herself. The members should remain loyal, even 'to the point of excommunication'. This is a strong statement, certainly, and hardly in accordance with the Church's teaching. But it must not be forgotten that Mary Ward was convinced the Decree had been issued without the Pope's knowledge and with evil intent, and was therefore not binding. Carlo Carafa's threat of excommunication of the Englishwomen in Prague – spoken as a mere pretext – must have been fresh in Mary Ward's memory. How often had excommunication been threatened already! The Bishop of Liège's open letter of 1624,[32] which assured the bishop's recognition until papal confirmation was received, threatened all those acting contrarily with unnamed heavy penalties (sciat se multum et graviter puniendum). Six years later however, the same prelate would be threatened with excommunication in the Decree of Suppression, if he were not to carry out the decree![33] Or on 2nd April, 1630 Nuntius Pallotto threatened – without the previous knowledge of Bishop Klesl – the superiors of the monasteries in Vienna Diocese with this Church penalty if they gave communion on Good Friday, as was customary in Vienna, and as Bishop Klesl had granted permission.[34]

The same question holds good for Mary Ward's letter as it had in Prague: did a Nuntius have the power, in his own right, to exclude a christian from reception of the sacraments? In this case, admittedly, Mary Ward mentioned bishops too, but from none of these local ordinaries, either in Liège, Cologne or Trier, would such a rigorous penalty have been feared. None of these wanted to see the Institute suppressed, or be deprived of the work of members of the Institute. Mary Ward certainly did not treat the threat lightly. Later in the letter, she says that persecution of such a kind was to be regarded as the most severe of measures.

As long as the Pope said nothing, the matter was not yet decided. This opinion of hers lies in the final sentence: 'as to the teaching which seems to absolve ours from obedience towards their superiors, I at all events do not know who brought that matter up'. Probably these words were directed particularly to those members of the Institute who no longer wholly supported Mary Ward. In her Ignatian Institute, the chief superior, the General Superior, was subject to the Pope alone. There is no arrogance to be detected in these words. It is known how much Mary Ward had suffered for the full realisation of the charism of the Institute with which she had been entrusted. It is precisely the last part of the final sentence which has no connection with what went before, that makes one assume that the text has been cut.

Nuntius Pierluigi Carafa added an accompanying letter to this, on 10th May,[35] to Secretary Ingoli. After the suppression of the English Jesuitesses, he said, a letter from the so-called General Superior of the Englishwomen had appeared (comparsa). In it the members of the Institute were ordered with fiery words (arditamente) not to obey any order of suppression, whoever ordered it, as the Pope knew nothing of any such order and she, Mary Ward, would be able to obtain help. Carafa had taken the trouble to see this letter; he had received it, also, and made a copy of it (e m'e venuto fatto d'haverla, di farne copia), which he enclosed to Ingoli. The Englishwomen had obeyed the Nuntius, however. From this statement we hold firmly that the letter was a month on its way, and that there was a monstrous indiscretion, or that the Englishwomen had acted with incredible stupidity. The letter was addressed to them alone. None of them was justified in handing over for examination by outsiders an instruction written by a general superior – especially on such a serious matter.

From the house on Mont St Martin, the letter found its way to the translator. It arrived as translated and probably, too, as a much-abridged version in Rome where, inevitably, it was to be the prelude to a new and final movement against the Institute and above all, Mary Ward.

The Journey to Vienna

Its cause – the outcome

As has already been shown in detail, it was only in Munich that Mary Ward received the news of the threat to the houses in Belgium and the western parts of Germany.

From the two first biographies[36] we learn that she set out for Vienna shortly afterwards. It has also been mentioned that Munich, at that time, had no nunciature. Mary Ward had never had any contact with the Nuntius in Lucerne – later to be Pallotto's successor in Vienna. It had not been necessary. She had known Nuntius

SESSIONS OF THE CONGREGATIO DE PROPAGANDA FIDE

NO.	DATE	PLACE	CHAIR	SPEAKER	SUBJECT
89	1628 21.3.	Vatican	Pope	(Ingoli)	Creation of Particular Cong. of Supression; Warning to SJ General; further enquiry about Jesuitesses.[1]
94	7.7.	Quirinal	Pope	Borgia	Report of Partic.Cong.; Suppression of Jesuitesses in Vienna, Naples, Brussels.
99	17.7.				Closure of House in Vienna; Decision about 8 Englishwomen in Naples.[2]
103.	1629 12.1.	Vatican	Pope	Borgia	Pallotto's correspondence.[3]
104	30.1.	Bandini Palace	–	Bentivoglio	Advice to Lagonissa, Suppr.of of Jesuitesses in Belgium.[4]

Before the arrival of Mary Ward in Rome on 12th February 1629.

106	6.3.	Bandini Palace	–	Bentivoglio	Lagonissa charged with total Suppression of Jesuitesses.[5]
108	7.5.	,,	–	Bentivoglio	Copy of Lagonissa's letter to Millini.[6]

Middle of May, audience for Mary Ward in Castelgandolfo; Mary Ward's talks with Millini and Fr Vitelleschi's justification of Mary Ward before Borgia, Antonio Barberini, Zacchia and Kommisar Scaglia.

111	22.6.	Quirinal	Pope	Bentivoglio	Praise to Lagonissa & Archbp.of Malines. Pallotto's reference to Decr. of Suppression/Malines. Suppression of Jesuitesses in Archd.of Cambrai.[8]
115	2.10.	Quirinal	Pope	Bentivoglio	Orders to Lagonissa re Archb.of Cambrai.Trevigi's paper;Decree of Suppr.to Carafa in Cologne.[9]
117	30.11.	Quirinal	Pope	Bentivoglio	Decree against Englishwomen to Nuntios in Belgium & Germany; postponed decision re Belgian Jesuitesses.[10]
118.	19.12.	Capponi Pal.	–	Caetano	Negotiations with Card. Ginetti re Jesuitesses.[11]
1630 119	1.11.	Quirinal	Pope	Bentivoglio	Visitn.of Belg. Jesuitesses in Brussels; Praise to Lagonissa, Copy of his letter from Pallotto.[12]

120	26.2.	Capponi Pal.	–	Capponi	Filing of Carafa's letter until Gen.Congregation.[13]
121	19.3.	Quirinal	Pope	Capponi	Commission to Carafa; more about Suppr.of Englishwomen;dismissal of their Petition for Confirmation.[14]

6.April 1630 Mary Ward's letter to the Englishwomen April – May 1630 Mary Ward in Munich

124	15.6.	Capponi Pal.	–	Capponi	Anne Gage released of vows; Suppr. of Liège; Mary Ward's letter 6.4. passed on to Holy Office.[15]
126	9.7.	Quirinal	Pope	Capponi	Continued suppr. of Jesuitesses by Caraffa; Archbp.of Cologne informed of rejection of Jesuitesses, Rome; Gen. Superioress' request refused; Anne Gage released from vows.[16]
127	5.8.	Capponi Pal.	–	Bentivolgio	Laginissa'a letter re suppr. in St. Omer; praise for Nuntius & Bp.;[17]
128	5.9.	Borgia Pal.	–	Caetano	Carafa's letters about Trier.[18]

Winefrid Wigmore in Trier, Cologne and Liège
The interrogation of the Englishwomen in Liège

| 130 | 1.10 | Borgia Pal. | – | Capponi | Klesl's letter; Planned action with Ginetti re total surrp. of Engl. Jesuitesses in Rome; letter to Klesl re suppr. in Vienna, and to Rocci, Nuntius.[19] |

Summary of the interrogation; Ingoli's report

| 132 | 22.11 | Quirinal | Pope | Trivulti | Carafa's letter; the Liège interrogation; transfer of the Engl.Jesuitesses affair to the Holy Office.[20] |

1. APF Rome Acta 6.1628–9,ff.36v – 37r,44v.
2. ditto.ff.78rv, 85v–87r.
3. ditto.ff.155v,158v.
4. ditto.ff.191r,195r.
5. ditto.ff.206v,214r.
6. ditto.ff.233rv,239v/
7. ditto,ff,253rv.257v.
8. ditto.ff.289r 294v–295r.
9. ditto.ff.334r,336rv.
10. do.ff.358r,361v.
11. ditto.ff.372r,376v.
12. do.Acta 1630–31,7.ff.3rv,14.
13. ditto ff.20r,21r.
14. do.ff.31r,32rv.
15. ditto.ff.75rv.
16. APF Rome, Acta 7.1630–1,ff.92r,93r.
17. ditto ff.105vv,108v.
18. do.ff.117r,122r.
19. ditto.ff.133r,134v,135r.
20. do.ff.162rv,178r.

Pallotto, on the other hand, since 1628 though once again reservations must be made as to whether she ever really understood this man's character.

Mary Ward had an audience with the Nuntius, but little is known of the conversation. Pallotto was shortly to leave Vienna and up to the last he never saw eye to eye with Bishop Klesl. It may well be assumed that he withdrew more and more from the discreditable affair of the Englishwomen. He was not even able to tell Mary Ward that, despite all his endeavours, the suppression of the house 'Stoss am Himmel' had failed, and that by the personal intervention of the Bishop of Vienna, who had prevented it. Up to the last weeks of Pallotto's term of office, Cardinal Klesl defended his rights as local bishop with all possible vehemence.[37] No, Pallotto could say nothing of that. He simply informed Mary Ward that it was the protection of the Emperor alone that had restrained her many enemies from closing the foundation of her Institute in Vienna. Of the fact that he himself was one of those enemies, he will prudently have remained silent.

Still less could the Nuntius speak of the decisions of the Congregatio de Propaganda Fide against the Institute. If the Englishwomen had not been informed in Rome, the departing Nuntius was not going to get his fingers burnt by doing so. It is unlikely that Pallotto knew of the most recent happenings in Belgium, above all in Liège. But even had that been the case, he would certainly not have made any reference to it. That was far outside the Viennese sphere of his jurisdiction. Mary Ward's journey to Vienna was fruitless.

Amidst all these almost insuperable difficulties, Mary Ward did have the joy of meeting her members again, for the Vienna house, like the one in Munich, continued under the protection of the sovereign. This fact could have confirmed her conviction: if the Pope had really promulgated an edict against the Institute, then the houses north of the Alps would have been affected too, and not only those in the west of Europe. No wonder that she was strengthened in her conviction that Cardinal Bentivoglio had played his part in the game.

It is not known how long Mary Ward remained in Vienna, but it can be taken that her stay was short. On account of the danger threatening the Institute, Mary Ward was compelled to return to Munich.[38]

It is difficult to find out if she returned to Vienna again in 1630. On 17th August,[39] Cardinal Klesl wrote to Cardinal Ludovisi that the Englishwomen were said to have spoken boastfully about confirmation of their Institute by the Pope. On 27th September,[40] the Nuntius of Cologne wrote to Secretary Ingoli about the foundations in Munich and Vienna, where Mary Ward was to be found at present 'di presente'. Neither pieces of information are very convincing. The 'boastings' of the Englishwomen in Vienna could have been matters of the past: Nuntius Carafa named the towns of Munich and Vienna in one breath. In addition, he mentioned the acceptance of novices. That could not refer to Vienna, as no girl had entered there. It is not possible to agree with Chambers' statement[41] that Mary Ward had stayed longer than a year in Vienna.

After each one of her longer journeys, which were connected with matters causing great tension, Mary Ward's physique collapsed. Violent attacks of gallstone accompanied these mounting efforts on behalf of the Institute, and the sick woman then needed a few weeks to recover.

This is what happened when she entered Munich on her return from Vienna. She had to spend three weeks in bed, three weeks which she urgently needed for pressing matters concerning the Institute. That answers the possible question: why did she not go herself to the houses that were in danger? The ill woman had been practically two months on her journeys, mostly on foot, and exposed to all kinds of hardship from the weather. The brief interruptions in Munich and Vienna were not taken to relieve exhaustion. She may also have seen her presence in the middle of Europe as of prime importance, for she could not possibly have imagined to what lengths the arms of her enemies would reach.

Notes

1.   See p.435.
2.   BV Rome, Barb. lat. 6728, ff.1r–2v. Mary Ward was at that time already on her way to Rome.
3.   "forse pensando di mantener l'incominciato corso senza altra consideratione di decreti ò dichiarationi di questa Sacra Sede sopra di ciò."
4.   On 25th January, BV Rome, Barb. lat. 6706, ff.67r–68v.
5.   " ... anco senza il sui amorevole ricordo, io non me ne sarei ingerito di questa maniera come in cosa ecclesiastica et che immediatemente dipende dalla Santità Sua ..."
6.   On 17.February, 1629. BV Rome, Barb. lat. 16728, ff.12r–13v.
7.   " ... hanno per fine di provider alli pericoli, a quali stganno continuamente eposte ..."
8.   On 8th March 1629. BV Rome, Barb. lat. 6717, ff.15r–16v.
9.   " ... L'intempestivo zelo del Calcedonense, causa estremo pericolo a lui medesimo et ad altri senza minimo frutto della religione ..."
10.   On 6th December 1629. Secret Archives of State, Munich. Black Box. 7413, ff.435r–454v.
11.   On 22.December 1629. Crivelli to Gigli. ibid. f.472rv.
12.   See below, p.527.
13.   Vita E, f.39v; Vita I p.29.
14.   Vita E, f.39v. The letter has not survived.
15.   Vita E, f.40r. twice.
16.   ibid.
17.   APF Rome, SOCG vol.98, ff.240rv, 241v; BV Rome, Barb. lat 6202 ff.134v–135r; AV Rome, Nunt. of Cologne, vol.12, f.227rv.
18.   Grisar, Institut, p.612–615, which contains the Latin text also.
19.   Ingoli's demand of 26th June 1630. APF Rome, Lettere volgari 1630. 10, ff.66v–67r. Carafa's answer of 19th July 1630 to Cardinal Ludovisi. APF Rome, SOCG Lettere di Spagna etc. 1630, 98, ff.260rv, 263v.

20. Grisar, Institut, p.613, note 127, accepts that the letter was written in Rome and that the Englishwomen left Rome only after 6th April, 1630.
21. See above, p.524.
22. APF Rome, Acta 1630–1631, 17, ff.31r, 32rv.
23. see p.532.
24. Vita E, f.40r, Vita I, p.30.
25. Biaudet, Nonciatures, p.278.
26. Thus Grisar, Institut, p.614, note 130.
27. The Englishwomen to the town of Saint-Omer before 11th September 1621, AM Saint-Omer, CCXXXIX Nr.16, ff.12–14. See also p.460.
28. Mary Ward to Barbara Babthorpe, 29th October 1622. Letter Nr.7. Inst. Arch. Munich.
29. idem. 16th February, 1627, Letter Nr.37, ibid.
30. See. p.514.
31. Vita E. f.39v.
32. March 1634. BV Rome, Fondo Capponi 47, f.81rv.
33. On 30th April 1630. APF Rome, SOCG Lettere di Spagna etc. 1630, 98, ff.238rv. 243v.
34. Jos. Kopallik, Regesten z. Gesch d. Erzdiose Wien II, Wien 1894, p.207, Nr.519.
35. AV Rome, Nunt. of Cologne 12, ff.226r, 239v.
36. Vita E, f.40r. is not clear. Vita I, p.30: " ... ando à Vienna, ove allhora era nuntio ordinario il Signore Cardinall Pallotto, quivi trovo, che i suoi avversarii prevalsero molto, mà però non poterno esequir'il lor disegno contro di lei in Vienna per la gran'bonta di quel santo imperatore ... "
37. In 1630 Easter fell on 31st March, therefore Good Friday was on 29th March. In Vienna it was customary to receive communion on that day. After the festival there was a sharp disagreement about jurisdiction between Cardinal Klesl and Nuntius Pallotto, which lasted some months and rumours of which reached Rome. The Bishop of Vienna was defending the custom of the people of his diocese, and above all, his episcopal rights to pass judgement in the matter. Nuntius Pallotto, on the other hand, referred to liturgical rubrics – and won. Jos. Kopalik, Regesten zur Gesch. d. Erzd. Wien II, Wien 1894, p.207, Nr.519ff. see also p.760ff. and p.806.
38. The nursing of a woman sick with the plague, probably a member of the Institute, could not have kept Mary Ward in Vienna much longer. The incubatory period of this fearsome sickness took between two to five days. Most fatalities occurred within two or three days.
39. APF Rome, SOCG Lettere di Germania e di Boemia 1630, 71, ff.62r–63v.
40. APF. Rome, SOCG Lettere di Spagna etc. 1630, 98, ff.261r–262v, 274v.
41. Chambers E II, p.318, D II, p.264ff.

XXVIII

THE VISITATIONS IN TRIER, COLOGNE, AND LIEGE

Statement of the causes

In order to pass a fair judgement on the following events, it must be remembered that Mary Ward did not emerge much wiser after her visit to Nuntius Pallotto in Vienna, and that not even in Munich did she receive any mandatory information about the position of the houses in western Europe. This is based on the fact that by the time Mary Ward arrived in Munich, no definite report about the suppression of any house can yet have reached there. True, the suppression of the Institute had long been decided on in Rome, but the dilatory attitude of a l l the bishops indicates some differences of opinion. Taking the postal system of those days into consideration, it could easily have been the end of May at the earliest, or the first half of June, for reports from the various houses to have reached Munich.[1]

What is more, Mary Ward was convinced that her difficulties did not originate with the Pope. One should add that Mary Ward, who bound the members of her Institute to the Pope by a fourth vow of obedience, would have been incapable of acting against the Head of the Church.

It was not simply the houses that were at risk; so too were several members of the Institute, who were in danger of losing their vocation. This was especially true of superiors, who had to carry the heaviest burdens. Mary Ward would not have hesitated long before sending her representative to western Europe on so important a mission. But, before the latter reached her destination, it was already too late.

The Visitor

Winefrid Wigmore — her route

Winefrid Wigmore was possibly Mary Ward's sole real confidante. She was the same age, came from the same sort of background, was one of the first members of the Institute and shared her joys and sufferings until 1621. She does not appear to have worked on the English mission. She was one of the group who went to Rome at the end of 1621 and took over the functions of prefect of schools and novice-mistress in the new foundation in Naples. She proved her worth there. In 1628 she was summoned to Munich with the intention of making her superior of the foundation planned in Prague. Nothing came of that, however. It can be assumed[2] that she accompanied Mary Ward to Rome and perhaps also to Vienna in 1630, though there is no proof of this. At all events, Winefrid Wigmore was the person who was most familiar with Institute matters, and with the mind of her General Superior.

These few dates from her life, however, do give some guidelines to her personality. Winefrid was not afraid of facing difficulties and showed a great deal of character. She was musical, had a gift for languages, and was sociable and imaginative.[3] Winefrid Wigmore esteemed Mary Ward highly, and preserved her letters carefully. Mary Ward returned this affection without letting it lapse into favouritism.

However, like Mary Ward, Winefrid Wigmore had lived almost nine years far from the misery experienced in St Omer, Liège, Cologne and Trier. The houses in the Papal States and Naples had not been blessed with worldly goods − quite the contrary − but Winefrid Wigmore had travelled though the princedoms of Italy, the emperor's lands, and Bavaria. She had gained new perspectives. She had been able to spend some years by Mary Ward's side. This cosmopolitan experience must have resulted in distancing her somewhat from the members of the dying Institute in the western part of Europe.

For this reason it is possible that Winefrid Wigmore would have met several young members of the Institute there who did not know her, or at least had never seen her.

Winefrid and her companion Mary Wivel covered most of their more than a thousand kilometre long journey on foot. It is not known when they left Munich. They left Liège in the middle of August.[4] If one considers that they stayed in Trier as well as Cologne in order to have consultations and discussion, then one may be justified in giving an approximate time of departure from Munich as the beginning of June. In 1621, the group of Englishwomen had made the journey of two thousand kilometres between Liège and Rome in two months.

Were Winefrid Wigmore and her companion still capable of such forced marches in 1630? This time they probably had no horse, and they were ten years older.

The Visitation in Trier and Cologne

*The arrival of the Visitor, probably in the middle of July –
adverse reporting by the Nuntius to Rome concerning the
Visitor's actions – the journey to Liège*

It is not known when Winefrid Wigmore and her companion
reached Trier. If they had left Munich at the beginning of June –
and certain things point in that direction – they would have covered the eight hundred kilometres between Munich and Trier in forty
days. That would mean they would have arrived in Trier about the
middle of July.

Winefrid Wigmore found eight Englishwomen there who had
struggled not to give in to the Decree of Suppression since the
beginning of the year. When finally, on 20th August, 1630[5] before
an ecclesial notary and in the presence of witnesses, they had the
decision of the Congregatio de Propaganda Fide read to them, the
superior said that they could not leave the Institute without the
approval of the General Superior. Nuntius Carafa was informed
of this on 25th August, 1630[6] by the suffragan Bishop, Georg von
Helfenstein, in a covering note. By 20th August, however, Winefrid
Wigmore had long since gone on her way. The bishop did not
mention the alleged subversive action of the Visitor. The matter
took on a different aspect in Nuntius Carafa's letter to Secretary
Ingoli.[7] In this account, Mary Ward was held chiefly responsible
for the members' attitude, for the Nuntius wrote that Mary Ward
had sent a Visitor to Trier who was authorized to influence the
Englishwomen (le havea fatto sedurre). The Visitor had made it
clear to the women in Trier (hà loro apportate per la sedutione)
that their Institute had not been suppressed, as the decree of dissolution was the result of intrigues by their enemies. The members
of the Institute were not doing any missionary work of the sort intimated to the Pope in such a misleading manner.[8] Winefrid Wigmore
had certainly been right about that.

The Visitor persuaded the Englishwomen to be loyal to their vows
and especially in their obedience towards their General. It is worth
noting the words used: 'sedurre, sedutione', seduction, temptation.
According to this interpretation, by sending a Visitor, Mary Ward
tempted the Englishwomen in Trier to disobey the Pope. Nuntius
Carafa wrote the same to Cardinal Ludovisi,[9] though this time the
main guilt was laid on Winefrid Wigmore: it was only after the
Visitor had spoken to the Englishwomen in the manner shown
above, that they refused to obey.[10] There is a remarkable difference in the accounts.

If she had not been informed already in Munich, then Winefrid
Wigmore certainly learnt in Trier that a Decree of Suppression had
been sent from Rome to the Nuntius in Cologne. But it must not

be forgotten that Mary Ward — and Winefrid Wigmore with her — took this as no papal decision, but an attempt to deceive the Pope by their enemies. The women had never at any time been informed personally.

It is also worth remarking that at this same time Bishop Klesl of Vienna was seeking, in vain, for some personal order from Rome as to how to proceed against the Englishwomen. But in Vienna, apparently, no one had uttered dark hints as to Cardinal Klesl's insubordination. Here, however, in the prince-bishopric of Trier, and very soon in the prince-bishoprics of Cologne and Liège, matters were different.

A Nuntius bent on reform could soon make the religious gentlemen of this princedom submissive. The Nuntius was able to label the opposition of a few women, who had never been clearly informed about the accusations against themselves, as 'seduction'. The actually greater recalcitrance of a bishop and cardinal who expected personal information while knowing what was at stake, was apparently passed over without comment.

The distance between Trier and Cologne measured some 90 kilometres; perhaps Winefrid Wigmore and her companion arrived in Cologne on 25th July. Hardly anything is known about the visitation of this tiny foundation.[11] It is perfectly possible that they had an audience with the Elector, as Ferdinand von Wittelsbach was the brother of the Elector of Bavaria. Winefrid may have been able to speak with the Elector's General Vicar. But not a single source mentions it.

One thing is certain: the Englishwomen in Cologne reported the Elector's great objection to the dissolution. They had dealt personally with him about it.[12] Nonetheless, the suppression was effected in the middle of May, 1630 by the General Vicar. Although the Elector's promise was not thereby broken (that the Englishwomen were under his protection), Winefrid Wigmore found herself for the first time in a house which had been suppressed by the Nuntius. Nothing is known of her actions there, though we can well imagine that she urged the members of the Institute in Cologne to hold on, just as she had in Trier.

Cologne lies about one hundred and twenty kilometres from Liège. It was the middle of August when the small group reached the town that was so crucial in the fate of the Institute.

The Visitation in Liège

The sources — Winefrid Wigmore and the Englishwomen's community on Mont St Martin — the Visitor's way of proceeding — her confrontation with Fr Ducket, SJ and with Nuntius Carafa

Before turning to the disastrous events in Liège, it seems appropriate to refer to the sources from which the information originates. Everything comes from reports made by adversaries of the Institute, a fact not to be ignored.

Certain letters have been mentioned in connection with the proceedings in Trier and Cologne, but the fullest accounts are those dealing with the Visitation in Liège.

Chronologically, the first who wrote, on 8th December, 1630[13] was Fr George Ducket,SJ to Fr Michael Freeman SJ, in St Omer. Fr Ducket was the confessor of some of the Englishwomen in Liège. His attitude as an opponent of the Ignatian character of Mary Ward's Institute emerges clearly from the intention, as also the phrasing, of his letter. Fr Freeman has already been met as a sharp critic of the former rector, Fr Tomson.[14]

On 13th September, 1630,[15] Fr Rector Robert Stafford wrote to Fr General concerning this Visitation and the subsequent events. The letter has survived as an incomplete copy in Italian only. Fr Stafford was Nuntius Pierluigi Carafa's interpreter at the interrogation of the Englishwomen on Mont St Martin.

From Nuntius Carafa's correspondence mention is made here only of his reports to Cardinal Ludovisi and Secretary Ingoli, both dated 27th September, 1630[16] and his letter of 15th November, 1630.[17] The official report of the interrogation of the Englishwomen by Nuntius Carafa is known only from a summary made by Secretary Ingoli, who also wrote a statement. The last two articles are undated but must have been written about 22nd November, 1630.[18] The biography of Urban VIII[19] by Andrea Nicoletti, Canon of San Lorenzo in Damaso, is not drawn on for examination here. Nicoletti used the Roman sources, but his work is biassed and based on documents already mentioned.

Even before the Bishop of Liège – or rather his General Vicar – had finished preparing the Decree of Suppression for the house of the Englishwomen on 30th April, 1630 on the orders of the Nuntius of Cologne, Fr Rector Stafford was able to inform Fr Thomas Courtenay SJ in Rome[20] that there were indications in Liège that the Pope intended to dissolve the Institute – 'dissolving our gentlewomen'. But, Fr Stafford considered, he did not understand how the Pope could do this without giving the women the means to pay their debts.[21] 'What will happen to their creditors?' he asked. The Englishwomen owed the English Jesuits some ten thousand pounds. The Rector ended his letter with the words 'God grant we feel not some part of the storm (when) they dissolve. I must confess I have a horror of it.'[22] One would have thought that the truly princely donation of Elector Maximilian I of Bavaria, granted to the English Jesuits in Liège on 8th September, 1626 would have been more than sufficient to preserve the Rector from any such fears. One ought, perhaps, to add by way of extenuation that Fr

Stafford had been in office for a short time only and perhaps had not yet formed a clear picture of the debts that did actually encumber his house.

In spite of Fr Stafford's fears, the Englishwomen's Institute in Liège was dissolved on 30th April, 1630. That has already been fully dealt with.[23] There has also been mention of Mary Ward's letter of 6th April, which reached Liège at the beginning of May.[24] The space of 40 days grace granted the Englishwomen[25] had expired by the time Winefrid Wigmore and her companion arrived in Liège in the middle of August.[26]

Rightly, Fr Ducket wrote to Fr Freeman[27] that 'it ever hath been a hurlyburly amongst the English gentlewomen.' The Visitor certainly found a divided community, if one can even call it that. What was extremely disquieting was the fact that it was precisely the superiors, that is, the Provincial Anne Buskells, the superior Mary Copley and the house-prefect Elizabeth Hall, who had been shaken in their vocations.[28] One of the oldest members, Anne Gage, had made haste to obtain a dispensation from her vows in Rome, in order to become a religious.[29]

There were four groups of adversaries who confronted the Visitor: Carafa the Nuntius, a small number among the community on Mont St Martin, the creditors, and the English Jesuits. Winefrid Wigmore trod delicately, in that she first of all assessed the situation, and did not immediately present herself as the Visitor. It was spiteful of Fr Ducket[30] to write that Winefrid had idled away the time while she negotiated with creditors; that she had roused these to such an extent that they would not sleep without obtaining a settlement of the Englishwomen's debts; that she would not be able to discharge this burden of debt; that she had even been obliged to come to Liège on foot from Cologne, only to find an empty and dilapidated house.[31] Such was the way the unspeakable poverty of these few women was spread abroad – with easy heartlessness and exaggeration.

It goes without saying that someone from a later century will regard the actions of the Visitor quite differently from those who were involved at the time. Far from agreeing with Fr Ducket's disparaging words, one has to admire Winefrid Wigmore's courageous demonstration of honesty in speaking openly with the creditors. She will certainly not have acted on her own initiative, but will have discussed this important part of her mission with Mary Ward in Munich. It must also be remembered that Winefrid had not known, at first, how far she could burden the members who were wavering in their vocation – the superiors among them – with such matters.

Nothing is known of her negotiations with the creditors. They cannot have been very sanguine. In the meantime, continued Fr Ducket once more in the letter to Fr Freeman, the Visitor could 'measure the pulse of the Institute' through some of the Englishwomen who had gradually become distrustful, especially the superior Mary Copley, and the house-prefect, Elizabeth Hall. That is understandable, as these two women had been concerned with the administration of the house. The following proceedings are known only from the letters of these two English Jesuits. In his account to Fr Freeman, Fr Ducket remarked that the superior as well as the house-prefect were providing themselves with security:[32] 'Mistress Copley and Mistress Hall, their rectrice and minister, full of suspicions, cast their matters so, that upon any sudden tempest they might have in naufragium tabulam.' As the distrust of the remaining members towards Winefrid Wigmore mounted, she broke her silence and admitted that she was the Visitor. That was during the 5th September. She deposed Mary Copley as Superior and named Elizabeth Hall as her successor. Fr Ducket remarked that Winefrid Wigmore had not seen through Elizabeth Hall. On the evening of the same day, the Visitor assembled the members, and called on them to renew their vows and their promise of obedience to Mary Ward (the civil contract). According to Fr Stafford's report, Winefrid Wigmore had explained to them that the Pope could not dissolve their vows against the wishes of the individual concerned, nor without the approval of the Superior General. Also, that the civil contract had its own validity. Winefrid went even further: that the Englishwomen should dare to accept excommunication from the Nuntius, as redress could be found. This bears a strong resemblance to Mary Ward's letter of 6th April, 1630. Further, Winefrid Wigmore said that the members of the Institute could rely on their General. After all, it was God who had granted her the revelation concerning the Institute.`

Winefrid gave her listeners a short time to consider. They were to have made up their minds by the next day. Until then, no one was to leave the house. It can be imagined that not one of those women − Winefrid Wigmore included − had a peaceful night, hoping that the Lord would provide them with a solution in prayer.

Partly from fear of the creditors, partly from a moral dilemma,[33] 'partly also with the burden of conscience wherewith I had charged them not to renew any vows', Mary Copley and Elizabeth Hall left the house early in the morning of the next day (6th September). The housebell was rung on this day by order of the Visitor; it was an audible sign that the usual community routine had begun. Of the five members in the Liège house who were to be interrogated in September by Nuntius Carafa, two renewed their vows: Bridget Heyde and Catherine Smith. The die was cast.

Fr Ducket wrote that he had played little part in the decision of the superior and the house-prefect, but that was not strictly true. He had quite an influence on both women, and even excused their slightly curious departure which bears a close resemblance to flight.

The same could be said of his behaviour to Winefrid Wigmore.

After mature consideration, as he wrote to Fr Freeman, he had come to the conclusion that he could no longer give Winefrid Wigmore absolution, under the circumstances.[34] It seems almost incomprehensible to us that Winefrid Wigmore, who had adequate French, did not confess to the Walloon Jesuits. Several members of the Liège community did so, after Mary Ward had suggested it.[35] But perhaps this is another sign of how little the Englishwomen understood the enemies of their Ignatian Institute. He had further suggested to the Visitor, that if she would refrain from demanding a renewal of vows, and quietly comply with the Decrees, he would not reveal her intentions.[36] Winefrid Wigmore did not agree, and so Fr Ducket went to see her. The ensuing conversation must have been violent, with an exchange of blunt words. He told Winefrid in no uncertain terms that she could not act in this manner, as the Institute had been suppressed and therefore the renewal of vows was contravening the Pope's orders. Fr Ducket summarized the Visitor's answers under three headings:

1. Winefrid Wigmore did not wish to have any conversation with him. She did not think it necessary, as she stood on firm ground, namely her obedience to Mary Ward. He could not persuade her to change her mind.
2. Winefrid Wigmore's exact words were that no one on earth had the power to release her from her vows against her will, for no one could prevent her from doing good.
3. Marriage between husband and wife was indissoluble, even if the two partners were prevented from living together.

    Upon which Fr Ducket refused her absolution, and Winefrid Wigmore accepted the fact. Fr Rector Stafford approved the confessor's decision.

Like red tape, the constricting words 'Father General will never permit it', run through the history of Mary Ward's Ignatian Institute. Opposition to the Englishwomen's principal decisions came from the Jesuits in the first place, and then from the Church authorities. One only has to think of their work in England, or the formation of the Institute on the model of the Society of Jesus. It is not surprising then that Winefrid Wigmore − apart from the distressing negotiations with creditors − had to settle matters with the Jesuits before giving her attention to Nuntius Carafa.

If the behaviour of the Visitor is studied with this in mind, then her answers to Fr Ducket take on a different quality. Winefrid did not wish to have any conversation with him because she represented a different point of view from his, and wished to remain true to her own convictions. These were in conformity with the will of her General Superior, Mary Ward.

The second point is concerned with the indissolubility of the vows they had taken ('no power can hinder me from doing well'). If Winefrid used the comparison with marriage, and added that a consummated marriage could not be dissolved by anyone, although of course the partners could be forced to live apart, then that is the opinion of the theologian, Fr Leonhard Lessius, whose fame reached far beyond the boundaries of Belgium.[37] As in that instance, the Institute was indissoluble in conscience (in foro conscientiae) for loyal members, as far as their vows were concerned. Of course the Pope could dissolve their congregation (the cohabitation), but not the vows, unless that was desired by the head of the Institute. But Winefrid Wigmore did not even believe in the suppression of the Institute by the Pope, let alone by Mary Ward.

Fr Rector Stafford wrote his letter after the superior Mary Copley and the house-prefect Elizabeth Hall had been questioned by the Nuntius. He therefore drew his knowledge from the doubtless negative statements of these two Englishwomen and certainly also from Fr Ducket's information.

Fr Stafford wrote more composedly, and therefore with far less emotional emphasis than Fr Ducket; this was all the more dangerous for Winefrid Wigmore, who explained that in accordance with the text of letter, she had come to bring help to an intolerable situation. The deposition of the superior, Copley, had first of all taken place privately and then before the community. Her statements on behalf of the General were more sharply and incriminatingly phrased in Fr Stafford's letter: keeping the vows which had been taken before the suppression of the Institute by the Nuntius; strict obedience towards the Pope; obedience towards the General which was connected to commitment to the Institute; loyalty to the Institute, even to the point of excommunication.

However their friends and foes may have construed the news of the suppression of the Institute in Liège, for all of these it was a decree commanded by the Pope. It was not so for Mary Ward and her representative, Winefrid Wigmore. To repeat: neither of the two women had received a clear statement either in Rome or Vienna. There had always been talk about the many 'enemies' of the Institute, and they had never received a command from the Pope or anyone authorized by him about the suppression of their congregation or had even caught sight of such a document. Moreover, the houses in Munich and Vienna had remained unmolested. The Nuntius in charge had given them no indication of a Decree of Suppression. Is it to be wondered at, that Winefrid Wigmore clung to her conviction even in the west of Europe, that it was enemies of the Institute who were at work, causing the wrongful dissolution of their houses? It is far from our intention to offer a subjective defence for Winefrid Wigmore. She may not have been equal to her complicated mission, but it must be pointed out that the possibility of equivocation by the Papal Curia in dealing with her General

Superior never entered her head. It was, however, precisely what had happened.

It is more than probable that Nuntius Carafa heard the sound of the Angelus from the Englishwomen's house on Mont St Martin on the morning of 6th September from his episcopal palace. The Visitor had allowed this to sound again on the previous evening.

But even without this audible sign of insubordination, Nuntius Carafa would have gone to the Englishwomen. It was to be expected that the general tension would come to boiling point. It did indeed.

The Nuntius himself twice threatened the members with excommunication; on the third occasion he had the threat conveyed by the Rector of the Walloon Jesuits. In vain.

From the letters already mentioned from Fr Ducket to Fr Freeman, we learn some details of the stormy proceedings. Fr Ducket passes over some 'absurdities' in the women's behaviour, as to when and with what words they paid him reverence, etc.[38] When the conversation turned on Mary Ward, the Nuntius committed a serious blunder — which only goes to show how little the Neapolitan Carafa knew of the mentality of these Englishwomen. He said, namely,[39] 'that Mary Ward could hardly be called a gentlewoman.' That was too much for Winefrid Wigmore. Before all present she reacted with a remark on the Nuntius' own origins. Mary Ward was noble by birth but that he, on the other hand, had bought his title. She added, moreover, that she knew his family and friends in Italy well.[40]

Fr Ducket describes the scene accurately enough, one feels. He was not an eye-witness, but Winefrid herself gave an account of it. It should not be given more importance than it deserves. Two fiery characters were on a collision course. Even if Carafa's remark about Mary Ward's background was hardly diplomatic, and out of place before her members, Winefrid Wigmore would have done better to have kept silence. It would possibly have been more effective. But she did not, and turned the Nuntius completely against her by her justified but unwise retort. After the following interrogations of the Englishwomen, the Nuntius told Fr Stafford that he would like above all things to tear their veils from their heads with his own hands, and throw the Visitor into prison.[41]

Fr Ducket concluded his account with the exclamation: 'O tempora! O mores!'

A letter of thanks from the Congregatio de Propaganda Fide was already on its way to Nuntius Pierluigi Carafa[42] when he wrote his incensed version of the affair in Liège to Cardinal Ludovisi[43] and Ingoli[44]. It has been shown how the Institute in Trier and Cologne had been affected; here it is Carafa's attitude to the community in Liège that is highlighted.

Although the Nuntius had just emerged from a disconcerting

confrontation with Winefrid Wigmore and the interviews with the other members — unpleasant hours of exasperation for Pierluigi Carafa — his letters do not convey much that is new. Only a brief glance will therefore be spared for the contents of his letter to Cardinal Ludovisi: after Mary Ward's representative had been able to succeed with her phantasies (chimere) in Trier and Cologne, she had come to Liège under pretext of negotiating with the creditors, to whom the women owed 40,000 scudi. It seems as though Carafa had been affronted most of all by the fact that Winefrid Wigmore had not presented herself before him, the Nuntius. Four members had left the house on Mont St Martin,[45] four others, among them two old Englishwomen[46] had remained behind with the Visitor. The Englishwomen had been allowed to continue living together in Cologne and in Liège, as they could not have survived otherwise individually because of their enormous debts. After which follows a description, in Carafa's letter, of how the Visitor had persuaded the four Englishwomen to stay (le ha scandalosamente sedotte). The Nuntius closed his letter with a request for instructions. The matter was by no means over. But he had not yet been able to take the women to court, as some of them had been in contact with a person ill with the plague. Perhaps it was one of the members of the Institute herself who was sick of this terrible epidemic. During those years, the community suffered much loss by death.

It seems strange that Nuntius Carafa should have reproached Winefrid Wigmore for not having requested an audience with him. It has been seen how carefully she entered on her mission. She did not even admit to the members on Mont St Martin, during the first weeks of her visit, that she was the Visitor. Should she have done so to the Nuntius, whom she did not know, and in whom she saw an enemy of the Institute, or at least, suspected him to be such? The alleged debt of 40,000 scudi seems extraordinarily high. Perhaps there was a confusion here with the rate of exchange, and it should be taken as 40,000 guilders.It has already been said that in 1621 the Englishwomen owed 20,000 guilders ; in that year there were about 50 people living together in community.[47] After the financial collapse of their house, many members of the Institute left. In the spring of 1630 there were still eleven Englishwomen in the Liège community.[48] If we take an average of 15 people between the nine years 1621 and 1630, who each needed 200 guilders per annum for their upkeep, the sum total is 27,000 guilders, provided that no single dowry had been paid out, and the Englishwomen had received nothing for their educational work. With the mortgage on the house in rue Pierreuse and the farms in the Condroz, that would have come to a total of 47,000 guilders. But that is still no way like 40,000 scudi or 100,000 guilders. Nor must it be forgotten that with the seizure of their goods, the debt of 20,000 guilders had been discharged to a large extent.

Some important points have been taken from Carafa's letter of 27th September, 1630 to Secretary Ingoli, phrased in highly indignant language, but containing on the whole the same matter as his letter to Cardinal Ludovisi. In a postscript Carafa added that the Visitor had declared that the Institute had the right to exist, as the Englishwomen were not undertaking any missionary work, as reported to the Pope, and that therefore the Pope had been incorrectly informed.[49]

Towards the end of his letter the Nuntius made three suggestions to Secretary Ingoli as to what to do with these women:

1.   The Pope should publish a Bull against these 'loglio' — poisonous plants. It should be anticipated here, that in the Decree of Suppression the term 'Zizania', or weeds, was used.
2.   The General Superior should be imprisoned and punished severely.
3.   The houses in Vienna and Munich should be dissolved, as there was no point in closing the communities of the Institute in some cities while allowing them to flourish in others.

Almost two months later[50] Carafa repeated his suggestions: the women had to be treated with a strong hand. The best means would be a Papal Bull against their Institute. By that, support of their congregation by princes and — just listen — by the people flocking to them — would be brought to a stop. It surely need not be particularly emphasized that such suggestions did not fall on deaf ears.

Although Nuntius Carafa was by no means a champion of the Institute, as the violence of his expressions demonstrates, he left the final act of settlement against the Institute to Rome, as had his colleague in Vienna. True, he had interrogated the small group of women. But it was not simply danger of the plague that prevented him from holding a trial, not even the fact that he had not conducted a criminal proceeding for some length of time.[51] If one looks into the matter more closely, it can be seen that the real reason the Nuntius could not quell these women — and with them their Institute — was their absolute loyalty to their vows.

The Interrogation

Interrogation but no trial — questions to the five members of the Institute in Liège, to the Visitor Winefrid Wigmore and her companion Mary Wivel — the community and the vows, loyalty and obedience in the answers of those questioned — imprisonment of Winefrid Wigmore on 13th February, 1631

The interrogation of the few members of the Institute took place on different days in September, 1630. Nuntius Pierluigi Carafa presided personally, Fr Rector Stafford acting as his interpreter. If it were not for his letter to Fr General Vitelleschi, there would have been no eye-witness' account. To turn once again to Ingoli's Compendium from the end of 1630, which has already been mentioned. The original of this report of the interrogation may perhaps be among the documents of trials in the Holy Office, but this source of the Vatican Archives is not open to professional research.

With his opening sentences, Ingoli imparted the information that the trial was not only instructive but also well-conducted. In so doing, he aimed at laying the blame squarely on the shoulders of the Englishwomen, for the Compendium is almost exclusively directed towards the establishment of the Englishwomen's guilt. Ingoli actually uses the word 'trial' but it is more accurate to talk of interrogations; there was no proper trial.

To turn to the text:

Certain 'Jesuitesses' in Liège and the Visitor (Winefrid Wigmore) have dared to continue their congregation, prohibited since the Suppression of their Institute by Papal Decree. The former superior, Mary Copley, and the house-prefect, Elizabeth Hall, were the first to be questioned. They stated:

1. In this Institute of the Jesuitesses three vows were taken. In addition, by a contract (civil contract), they pledged themselves to remain in the congregation. They renewed their vows annually before the Blessed Sacrament.
2. The Visitor Winefrid Wigmore was sent by the General Superior and she produced evidence of this by an letter patent signed and sealed by the General Superior.
3. The Rules of the Institute correspond to those of the Society of Jesus, although these had been altered by the General Superior.

The third Jesuitess, Anne Morgan, was questioned on 17th September.[52] She stated:

1. She had been released from the Institute by the Visitor, dispensed from her obligations to the vows, and released from the civil contract.
2. Concerning the authority of the General Superior, granted to the Visitor, Ingoli makes no new mention.
3. She is inclined to obey, as the Institute will be suppressed. The dispensation from her vows was to be effected by the Visitor. The General Superior is allowing each one to leave who fears excommunication and does not wish to remain in the congregation for that reason.
4. According to the Visitor, even after the Suppression, particular obedience towards the General Superior (civil contract) has not been dissolved.

5.   The Visitor has commanded the Englishwomen present to stay in the congregation, as the Pope did not intend to hinder anyone (non intende impedir) from remaining in a state (stato) freely chosen.
6.   After the Suppression they follow the usual order of the day except that they go to a public church. For the last twelve days they have rung the bell for prayer, for examen, for mealtimes and for school.[53]

The fourth Jesuitess, Catherine Smith, had not left the house on Mont St Martin, and did not wish to submit. She stated:

1.   She had taken the vows and the promise of obedience (civil contract) before the Suppression of the Institute had been announced. It is her view that the Suppression cannot dispense her either from her vows or her promise of obedience, as she desires to follow them. The Suppression is concerned with external matters, and not with what is essential to their state. She is also of the opinion that the Pope does not wish to dispense her from the vows against her will (non voglia abrogar). She had pledged these before God and her General Superior. She continues to be bound to the General Superior, as she is still alive and has not been deposed.
2.   Concerning the open letter of the Visitor, and keeping the order of the day, the General Superior and the Visitor should answer those questions.

The fifth Jesuitess, Bridget Heyde, stated:

1.   She too feels in conscience bound to keep her vows and does not believe that the Pope would wish to force her (voglia sforzar) to act against her conscience. She believes, on the contrary, that she would offend God if she did not live according to her vows after the suppression of the congregation. She also thinks that her congregation had been approved and that the relevant documents about it are in the hands of the superiors.
2.   Nothing was entered concerning the Visitor's powers or the continuation of the daily programme after the suppression, or the sounding of the house-bell.
3.   She knows of no other form of life to which she could commit herself with a good conscience, except that which she now follows.

If one considers that of the eleven members who on 30th April, 1630 heard the Decree of the Congregatio de Propaganda Fide for the suppression of their Institute, only five could be questioned[54] and that out of those five only two remained loyal to Mary Ward's Institute, then it was a meagre harvest, for the Nuntius too. But before turning our attention to the interrogation of the Visitor and her companion, it would be advisable to ask how these five women from the Liège house really stood in regard to their obedience towards the Pope, as that was the burning issue. In Fr Ducket's letter already quoted, Mary Copley and Elizabeth Hall are supposed to have left the house, partly from fear of the creditors and partly for reasons of conscience. Fear of their creditors is understandable, but not remorse of conscience. In Carafa's report[55] to Rome, he said that the Englishwomen had been compliant after the reading out of the Decree of Suppression, and submitted to the instructions. The interrogation of the two members was, then, purely a matter of information for the Nuntius. With regard to their attitude to the Visitor – and therefore to the General Superior – they were presumably not questioned. Ingoli, in his Compendium, does not give the least indication of any such, at least.

Anne Morgan's case was different. She left the Institute, not only under obedience, but also from fear of excommunication, therefore under pressure from the Decree, but with the approval of her General Superior. There is no mention of such a possibility in Mary Ward's letter of 9th April, 1630, or not at least in the version available. As to the Pope, Anne Morgan expressly stated that he did not intend to hinder anyone (non intende impedir) from remaining in a freely chosen way of life; in other words, to live according to the vows as the person concerned felt she was bound in conscience. Catherine Smith and Bridget Heyde were of the same opinion. There is no question of disobedience against papal authority here. Rather, the women were convinced that the Pope would not make such a demand of their conscience.

The Visitor and her companion were examined more rigorously. Mary Wivel answered as follows:

1. It was all the same to her what the Pope ordered. She had taken the three vows. She knew of the Suppression of the Institute. She had read the Decree.[56]
2. In the Decree, the Institute had indeed been suppressed, but the vows had not been dispensed. The essence of the Institute, however, lay in the vows and constitutions. She had never seen the latter.
3. She desired to continue in the way of life of the Institute. She too stated that the Pope would not wish to deprive them of the freedom (non crede que il Papa la voglia sforzar) of living in obedience to their General Superior. He knew neither their vocation nor the character of the Institute. He would certainly not bar the way to their souls' salvation.

The most detailed examination was, of course, reserved for the Visitor. Winefrid Wigmore was interrogated twice, under oath to speak the truth. According to the points given here by Ingoli, Winefrid Wigmore stated:

1. She did not have religious status by reason of her vows, nor was she to be regarded as a lay person.[57] She had taken her vows before God and also bound herself to her General Superior. She had, moreover, promised her that she would do nothing that might lead to the suppression of the Institute.[58]

2. The Councils and the Popes did not wish to forbid any new Orders. Nor did she believe that they would act against the Holy Spirit (che vogliano urtar lo Spirito Santo). The Holy Spirit can indeed, however, inspire a pious person to begin a new Order.

3. According to the opinion of the General Superior, the Institute was not ill-conceived; neither the Pope nor the Cardinals were sufficiently informed about it. She had no intention of reproaching them with any lack of consideration, but ascribed everything to divine providence. The vows were not dispensed. The Pope would not force them to act against their conscience (non voglia obligarla).

4. She had been sent to the members of the Institute in order to make the intentions of the General Superior clear, to tell them to remain true to God in what they thought was pleasing to Him. The General Superior did not intend to keep the members in the Institute. The call for that came from God.

5. The Pope did not wish to dispense people from the vows against their will. Loyalty to God, to whom they are in duty bound, would not be diminished by the suppression of the Institute. That is why she thinks that she is bound above all to the vows. Certainly, they owe more obedience to the Pope than to the General Superior, but the members of the Institute are not bound to follow orders from prelates which are directed against the instructions of their General Superior. In such a case the member ought to stand her ground, and prefer to accept suffering, than act against the will of the General Superior.

6. The house bell had been rung, and the order of the day reintroduced, in accordance with the orders of the General Superior. The same had been done in Trier and Cologne.

7. As to enclosure, Winefrid Wigmore answered that Orders were of divine origin. It was the General Superior who should be asked about the Institute, as it was not for her, Winefrid Wigmore, to give explanations on that matter.

8. She had received the order to visit the communities both verbally and in writing, in June (1630) in Munich, from the General Superior.

9. Winefrid was asked several times, under obedience, to relinquish her authority. She did not do so because she thought that she would offend God and create difficulties for the General Superior. When she was reminded that she had sworn to

tell the truth, she answered adroitly that she had indeed taken an oath to speak the truth, but not to answer every question. In other words, Winefrid Wigmore declined to comment on this point.

10. After she had been granted a limited time to relinquish the letter which she had brought with her, she explained that she had burnt it two or three days before, precisely for the reason given, and not because she thought the papers were wrong (ingiusta).
11. She had not wished to answer the question if she were a Visitor.
12. The question, what she would do after the Suppression of the Institute, would be answered by the General Superior. But it would be something that was permitted to any christian, as for example, the ringing of a bell...

Two facts must be assumed if one hopes to form as impartial a judgement as possible of this enquiry.

1. These women were not theologically educated. The members of the Institute were of course interested in the subject, but none of them could claim the thorough theological training of a priest, let alone that of the often highly-educated Jesuits. They did not even have the basic essentials for this, such as a thorough knowledge of Latin and Philosophy.
2. Added to which, they did not have at their disposal a summary of the Church Laws then in current use. The official codification of Canon Law was issued in 1917 only, with the Codex Juris Canonici (CIC).

We have already seen the essential differences between the opinions of Lessius and Suarez. They were not the only scholars with a personal view about this new style of Institute. One only has to think of Fr Burton, and that anonymous Jesuit who wrote the 'Pium Institutum' of 1625. There were, too, the well-intentioned authors of the various plans for the Institute but also, unfortunately, adversaries in clerical circles. There was much that was twisted and distorted and betrayed, simply to pillory these women's way of life and condemn it. This was certainly true of the really vituperative accounts from England, which were hawked about by successive English agents in Rome.

One would have to search for a long time before being able to establish any disobedience in the statements and therefore in the religious attitude of these women towards the Pope. It may well be that they were not able to phrase their opinions correctly, but there is no refusal of a papal command in their answers.

The Pope could, of course, suppress the Englishwomen's religious congregation. All members of Orders − and the Englishwomen were striving to be recognized as such — are subject to the Pope in virtue of their vow of obedience.[59] He is the juridical Head of the whole Church. That is why Winefrid Wigmore's answer is correct, when she said she would have to obey the Pope rather than the General Superior. Could the Pope dissolve the vows of the members? First of all, it would be wise to ask if Urban VIII did so. Not at all. There was no question of his doing so in the Decree of Suppression for the house in Liège. Catherine Smith had stated quite correctly that the Suppression was concerned with matters that were external and not essential.

Nuntius Carafa was not making a casual enquiry when he asked Ingoli on 28th December, 1629[60] and again on 19th February, 1630[61] for faculties to dispense the Englishwomen from their vows. This had been after he had received his instructions, and long before this interrogation. He had never received an answer. Quite apart from that, each individual concerned — not only those Englishwomen under interrogation — must of necessity face the question: how do I stand in conscience in relation to the vows? In a striving for christian perfection, these had been freely taken before God.[62] The Pope can dissolve the vows, he can even do so against the will of the individual concerned, always only insofar as these vows are a duty towards the Church. He is not able to annul the interior commitment between the person who makes the vow and God.

The members of the Institute took private vows as members of a congregation not (yet) approved by the Church. The Pope cannot suppress the freedom of conscience of an individual and, moreover, one striving for christian perfection. This is the heart of the problem. That is why the answers are utterly astonishing. The Pope did not intend to hinder any one from living in a freely-chosen state (Anne Morgan); he did not wish to dissolve the vows against the will of the person concerned (Catherine Smith); he did not want to force anyone to act contrary to their conscience in a commitment which they had undertaken (Bridget Heyde); he did not wish to bar the way to salvation of their souls (Mary Wivel).

It is clearer still in the opinion of the Visitor, which ends with the words: loyalty to God, to which the members are committed, will not be destroyed by the suppression of the Institute. By this she meant dedication by vow, and to the Institute as a community. The Englishwomen answered according to the view of the moral theologian Lessius, and they did so with the best of intentions.

Like the IHS emblem over the door of their chapel in St Omer[63] and the long black dress in imitation of the Jesuit talar,[64] their re-introduction of the order of the day, proclaimed by the public ringing of a bell was, however, unwise. Not only that, it was not permitted, as exterior signs were expressly forbidden by the Decree. Winefrid Wigmore did not believe that the Decree had come from the Pope, but she could have acted more prudently and more in accordance with Mary Ward's mind by not making her opinion quite so pointed, considering the gravity of the situation.

Apart from the differences between the members of the Institute and the Nuntius, hardly anything more is known about the rest of the community from the interrogation of the members. The poverty of the few women who remained will have stayed the same, for on 25th October 1630,[65] they received the modest sum of two patakons from the Chapter of St Martin. Nuntius Carafa did not relax his vigilance. His task was not yet complete; the Institute was still in existence. This was why he drew Ingoli's attention to Suarez' destructive suggestions, and advised him to obtain a copy of the treatise.[66]

After the Congregatio de Propaganda Fide had informed Nuntius Carafa of their decision on 2nd December[67] to imprison the Visitor Winefrid Wigmore, the way forward was clear.

On 14th February, 1631,[68] Mary Wivel and the other members told the Chapter of St Martin that on the previous evening – therefore on 13th February – Nuntius Carafa and the Bishop's official, Rosin Serau, had taken Winefrid Wigmore out of their house into the enclosure of the Collegiate Church, and placed her in detention. Some days later,[69] in a special session of the Chapter, a message from Carafa was read out in which he made known that by imprisoning Winefrid Wigmore, he had performed an official act within the enclosure of the Collegiate Church at the command of the Holy See.

Meanwhile, the decisive blow had fallen.

Notes

1. Admittedly, Andreas Nicoletti, a biographer of Pope Urban VIII, wrote that immediately after learning of the Roman decree, the Englishwomen had sent an express message to Mary Ward in Munich, but he refrains from saying from which house and at what time this message began its long journey to Munich. The Englishwomen would certainly not have had the money for a special messenger, who would have had to be paid. Nicoletti, Della Vita di Papa Urbano Ottavo et Istorra del suo Pontificato, BV Rom. lat. 4731, p.1656.
2. Chambers E II. p.285; D II, p.237; Grisar, Institut. p.437.
3. Mary Ward to Winefrid Wigmore, May–June 1628, Letter Nr.47, Inst. Arch. Munich. At one time Winefrid Wigmore brewed a drink which may have been wine, or beer. The process does not seem to have been entirely successful and this had consequences for the poor victims at table. That, at least, is implied by her reference to God's providence in Mary Ward's letter from Prague.
4. Fr George Ducket to Fr Michael Freeman, 8th September 1630. AGR Brussels, Arch. Jésuitiques, Prov. Gallo-Belg, Carton 32a.
5. APF Rome, SOCG Lettere di Spagna etc. 1630, 98, f.268rv.
6. ibid.
7. Of 27th September 1630. ibid. ff.261r–262v, 269r, 274v and regest.
8. " ... perchè non fanno missione, come era stato supposto à Sua Santità, la quale era stat mal informata ... " ibid.
9. ibid. f.267rv.

10. " ... e mentre si stava operando per far obbedire a quelle vergine al decreto ... le hà imbevute d'opinione scandalose ... onde impressionate di queste chimere hanno risposto al Suffraganeo ... di non poter risolvere cos'alcuna senza licenza della loro Generalessa ... "

11. Nuntius Carafa to Cardinal Ludovisi, 3rd May 1630. APF Rome, SOCG Lettere di Spagna etc. 1630, 98, ff.237rv, 244v, and on 24th May, ibid. ff.248r and 249v.

12. The Elector of Cologne to Nuntius Carafa, 22nd May 1630. ibid. ff.252r, 256v.

13. AGR Brussels, Archives Jésuitiques, Prov. Gallo-Belg. Carton 32a. Fr George Ducket SJ (ca 1590–1669) from Santon, Yorkshire, became a convert under the influence of his uncle Fr Richard Holtby SJ, studied first in Saint-Omer and then from 1612 in Rome, where he was ordained. In 1617 he entered the Society of Jesus, worked as professor in Saint Omer from 1622–28, and from 1629–33 in Liège. Later he held several posts, returned to England in 1652 (Northampton, Wales) and died there on 30th October 1669. Foley, II, p.437; III, p.17, 62–64; IV p.337, 403–405.

14. See p.231, note 20 and p.234.

15. ARSI Rome, Anglia 33/I, ff.169rv and 181rv. In his answer of 26th October 1630 Fr Vitelleschi expressed his disappointment at the attitude of the Englishwomen in Liège. ARSI, Rome, Amnglia 1/II, f.321v.

16. APF Rome, SOCG 98, f.267rv. resp. ff.261r–262v, 269r, 274v.

17. ibid. ff.278rv, 287v.

18. APF Rome, SOCG 205, ff.443v–445v, 446v, resp. ff.445v–446r.

19. Della Vita di Papa Urbano Octavo et Istoria del suo Pontificato scritta da Andrea Nicoletti, Canonico di S.Lorenzo in Damaso, BV Rome, Bar. lat. 4731, p.1641–59.

20. On 26th April, 1630. Stonyhurst Archives, Anglia, Anglia A IV 81 is silent.

21. " ... and to pay theyre debthes for what shall they beg!"

22. "God grant we feele not some part of the storme (when) they dissolve, I must confesse I have a horrour of itt ... "

23. See p.513.

24. See p.524 ff.

25. On 8th June 1630.

26. Fr Ducket to Fr Freeman, see above, note 4.

27. "It ever hath bene a hurlyburly amongst the English Gentlewomen."

28. Mary Ward knew. Vita E, f.40r.

29. See p.515 ff.

30. " ... trifled the tyme away in treating with creditours, which she hath awaked in such stat that they will hardly fall a sleepe without some satisfaction." Fr Stafford loc.cit., wrote Winefrid Wigmore had been a month in Liège, without revealing her mission; Nuntius Carafa also mentioned this space of time.

31. This is exaggerated. The sources mention repairs.

32. "Mistris Copley and Mistris Hall ther rectrice and minister, full of suspicions, cast ther matters so, that uppon any suddaine tempest they might have in naufragio tabulam."

33. " ... partly allso with the burden of conscience wher with I had charged them not to renew any vowes ... "

34. "I had a scruple in conscience, how I could proceed Mistris Winefrid in matter of conscience ... "

35. See p.424.

36. "I resolved at her first arrivall that if she wold abstaine from exacting vowes and quietly comply with what the decrees and Nuntio hath obliges them unto, that I would allso dissemble ... "

37. See p.146.
38. " ... how they behaved themselves to the Nuntio, when and at what words they made him reverence etc ... "
39. " ... the Nuntio had sayd that Mary Ward was scarse nor no gentle-woman ... "
40. " ... that he was a basse companion or fellow, she being more noble then himself as being nobly borne, whereas the Nuntio had bought his nobility and that she knew well his frinds and family in Italy."
41. " ... che mi disse di voler levarle le vela con le sue proprie mani, e metter'in prigione la visitatrice ... "
42. Of 20th September, 1630. APF Rome, Lettere volgari 1630, 10, ff.113v – 114r.
43. Of 27th September, 1630. APF Rome, SOCG 98, f.267rv.
44. ibid. ff.261r – 262v, 269r, 274v with the same date.
45. The Provincial, Anne Buskells, the Superior Mary Copley, the Procurator Elizabeth Hall and probably Anne Gage also.
46. Bridget Heyde, Catherine Smith, Mary Wivel the Visitor's companion, and an unnamed companion.
47. See p.365.
48. On 3rd April 1630, at the Suppression, see p.365.
49. " ... dice il decreto di Nostro Signore ester sorrettitio perchè in quello si fa mentione, che dette vergini pretendessero instituire missioni con predicar l'evangelo, il che asserisce esser lontano dal loro Instituto."
50. On 15th November 1630. " ... la bolla sarà il total rimedio, perchè li prencipi e potentati per la pubblicazione di essa rimarranno di proteggerle e i popli si asterranno di frequentar le case loro." APF Rome, SOCG 98, ff.278rv, 287v. With these words an authorised opponent of the Institute revealed the popularity of the Englishwomen among the people.
51. Grisar, Institut. p.701.
52. The date is taken from the statement that the house-bell had been rung for twelve days. (6 – 17th September).
53. From this answer it appears that the Englishwomen were still teaching and looking after children, after they had left their house in rue Pierreuse. It is not known if these were English girls.
54. Probably most of them, for fear of threatened ecclesiastical penalties, sought and found accommodation elsewhere. These were: Anne Buskells, Anne Gage (?), Elizabeth Tapne, Helen Pick, Frances Fuller and Frances Lametz.
55. Carafa to Cardinal Ludovisi, 3rd May 1630. APF Rome, SOCG Lettere di Spagna etc. 1630, 98, ff.237rv, 244v.
56. Probably only in Liège.
57. Namely as "faeminae ecclesiasticae" in a nascent Order.
58. In the Civil Contract.
59. Today can. 590, para. 1 CIC. Cf. Bruno Primetschofer, Ordensrecht, Freiburg/Br.(3) 1988, p.35.
60. APF Rome, SOCG Lettere di Spagna etc. 1630, 98, ff.214rv, 223rv.
61. ibid. ff.218r – 219v.
62. Today can. 1191 para. 1 CIC. Cf. Primetschofer, op.cit. p.175. Today's legal positions refer, as to contents, to earlier legal documents. Rudolf v. Scherer Handbuch des Kirchenrechts Bd. II, Graz, 1898, p.708ff.
63. See p.251.
64. See p.166.
65. AE Liège, Collégiale Saint-Martin 60, f.75v and 61, f.9r.
66. Carafa to Secretary Ingoli, 22nd November 1630. APF Rome, SOCG Lettere di Spagna etc. 1630, 98, ff.279r, 286v.
67. Congregatio de Propaganda Fide to Carafa, 2nd December, 1630. APF

Rome, Lettere volgari 1630, 10, f.132v. Ingoli entered the date as 21 November, but in that Session no decision was taken about the Englishwomen.
68.   AE Liège, Collégiale Saint-Martin, 60, f.83v; 61, f.15v.
69.   On 19th February, 1631, ibid. f.84r, resp. 16r.

XXIX

THE SUPPRESSION OF
THE INSTITUTE

Negotiations in Rome

Influence of Carafa's letters on discussions — Ingoli's evidence — decision of Congregatio de Propaganda Fide, 1630

Just as the letters of the two Nuntios in Vienna, Carlo Carafa and Giovanni Battista Pallotto, had been decisive for further measures of the Congregatio de Propaganda Fide against the Institute in 1628,[1] so too were the reports of the Cologne Nuntius, Pierluigi Carafa in 1630. Carafa's reports of 24th May and 7th June, 1630 described his problems with such effect that the Congregatio de Propaganda Fide, which met on 9th July on the Quirinal under the presidency of the Pope, decided afresh to suppress the Jesuitesses in the Archdiocese of Cologne. In almost each one of the subsequent sessions of the Congregation some item on the agenda was connected with the Englishwomen and their Institute. Matters were coming to a head.

In the session held in Cardinal Capponi's palace on 5th August, Cardinal Bentivoglio spoke from Nuntius Lagonissa's reports, upon which the Cardinals decided on the suppression of the English Jesuitesses in Flanders. That concerned their one and only house in Belgium, St Omer. The accounts of Carafa, Nuntius of Cologne, sent to Cardinal Ludovisi and to Secretary Ingoli on 19th and 26th July, were also dealt with in the 9th September session, although no decision was taken resulting from these. Once again, shortly before his death, Cardinal Klesl of Vienna sent Rome an account of the Englishwomen in his episcopal city. The session of the Congregation of 1st October was once again occupied with the total suppression of the Institute in Vienna. Bishop Klesl's death, however, and Pallotto's transfer resulted in different connections within the Imperial city, and the Congregation limited itself simply to informing Vienna that the Jesuitesses had not received confirmation from the Curia, and were to be suppressed in Vienna also.

Then Rome received the reports from the Nuntius of Cologne dated 27th September, 1630, sent to Cardinal Ludovisi and Secretary Ingoli, with Carafa's official account of the interrogation of the members of the Institute in Liège.[2] These alarming pieces of information, and Rome's awareness of the special position of the Institute in Munich and Vienna, brought about the Cardinal's emphatic stand in the session of the Congregation on 22nd November, 1630, with its grave consequences for Mary Ward and her Institute. The Cardinals met on the Quirinal under the presidency of the Pope. They decided to transfer the matter to the Holy Office. This, known until 1908 as 'Congregatio Romanae et universalis Inquisitionis', had been re-organised in 1542 by Pope Paul III; it was the papal authority for the teaching of faith and morals for the Roman Catholic Church, and had great juridic power.

The Congregatio de Propaganda Fide and its Secretary, Ingoli, did not even have to use their own initiative, for the way to the final annihilation of Mary Ward's Institute had already been sketched out for them by Nuntius Pierluigi Carafa: the Institute of the English Jesuitesses should be suppressed as a community by a Papal Bull, and the General Superior, Mary Ward, imprisoned. The houses in Munich and Vienna — those in the lands of secular princes, were to be destroyed at last. Carafa's final suggestion was by far the most damaging, as it entailed taking those sweeping measures which the Curia had so far avoided. For although there was no longer any threat of trouble for the Papal States over the possession of Mantua,[3] the houses of the Institute in Munich and Vienna were and remained foundations of Catholic overlords, Maximilian I of Bavaria and Ferdinand II of Austria.

To deal somewhat more comprehensively with the evidence produced by Ingoli for the consideration of Congregatio de Propaganda Fide on 22nd November, 1630:[4] although Ingoli, as already noted, did not deviate much from Carafa's suggestions, his testimony offered some items which justify closer attention. The undated document was written and corrected by the Secretary personally. There are further corrections added by a second hand.[5] The penalties are given first:

The imprisonment of the General Superior, the Visitor and her companion, by Nuntius Carafa. (From this it seems Ingoli thought that both Mary Ward and Winefrid Wigmore were in Liège.)

All writings, and Mary Ward's seal, were to be confiscated and the trial should proceed on the following evidence:

1. Non-observance of the Pope's orders and those of the two Congregations, namely Congregatio de Propaganda Fide and the Holy Office.
2. The spreading of erroneous or misleading doctrines, contrary to the teaching of the Church.[6]

3. The founding of a congregation without enclosure, against the current statutes of Canon Law.
4. Unlawful use of religious authority.
5. Enticing girls to enter the congregation by falsely declaring that their Institute had been approved by the Pope; inducing five members of the Institute (in Liège) to disobedience towards the Pope and the two Congregations mentioned above; false interpretation of papal and curial orders by re-establishing the suppressed Institute.

Because of these accusations, both women were to be tried by Nuntius Carafa in the manner usual with the Inquisition. If necessary, the visitations conducted by Winefrid Wigmore in Trier and Cologne could also be drawn on. After the trial was over, an order should be given to bring the women to Rome so that they should be imprisoned immediately.

From this it can be seen that Ingoli had originally intended the trial to be continued by the Nuntius, and the sentencing – the imprisonment of Mary Ward and Winefrid Wigmore – to be effected in Rome. At all events, Ingoli thought that the Institute would be more easily suppressed by these measures – rimedii!

As well as Nuntius Carafa, Monsignor Fagnano[7] the canonist, had suggested issuing a papal bull which, after publication, should be sent to the three Nuntios in Vienna, Cologne and Brussels with the aim of further distribution to the rulers, so that the secular as well as the religious princes might recognize the Pope's order and, if necessary, set their powers in motion – brazzo secolare – against these women. The Curia took the official line here, too, and their Nuntios had the doubtful pleasure of promoting the Decree precisely where there was no desire to suppress the Institute. Those who had to endure the suffering, the members of the Institute and their General Superior Mary Ward, were *not* informed of the Pope's decision against them.

By the Bull, it continued, the Bishops and Archbishops could be obliged to act under penalty of interdict or, respectively, confiscation of goods, and could threaten those who offered help to the Englishwomen.

A few words on some individual items:

1. By disobedience towards the Pope and the Congregations, Ingoli meant in particular the behaviour in Cologne of the Visitor Winefrid Wigmore, who had worked under orders from the General Superior.Here it must be remembered that Mary Ward and Winefrid Wigmore did not believe in a papal decree, but suspected intrigues on the part of their adversaries. That has already been pointed out.
2. Ingoli's assertion that the head of the Institute had spread erroneous or misleading doctrines could only refer to certain of the

Visitor's statements, such as Mary Ward's assumption that the Pope had not been sufficiently informed; to her sending the Visitor, and to the continuation of the order of the day, which meant, practically, the re-establishment of the suppressed Institute. Ingoli started from the view-point that Mary Ward knew about the suppression of her Institute. In any case, she had to obey a decree which had been conveyed by a Nuntius, whether she recognized its authenticity as a papal mandate or not.

3. To this item it must be remarked that the foundations of the Institute houses had been effected with the agreement of the Bishops. When founding the houses in Munich and Vienna the women were under the rule of the secular princes.

4. One might ask here, what did Ingoli mean by religious authority? Mary Ward and Winefrid Wigmore too, exercised one form of authority only, a potestas dominitiva. This they had in common with other communities.

5. As to what concerns this point, the Englishwomen had certainly not pretended to have obtained approbation. But they knew of the enlarged statement of the 'Laudatio' only[8] and not its original draft, which had been formulated in Rome in 1616, and which certainly did not contain any 'Laudatio'. It must be emphasized above all that there is no question of heresy here. If Mary Ward had wittingly and willingly acted against the Pope's command, one might at the most have spoken of disobedience, but never of heresy.

It certainly seems odd, too, that the interrogation conducted by Nuntius Carafa of Cologne was apparently not competent (for it had to be continued) to declare both the General Superior and her Visitor guilty a priori.

At the session of the Congregatio de Propaganda Fide of 22nd November, 1630, ten cardinals were present: Borgia, Ubaldini, Bentivoglio, Ludovisi, Antonio Barberini, Caetani, Zacchia, Pamphili, Francesco Barberini and Trivulzio, as well as Tornielli and the assessor of the Holy Office.

In item 35 of the agenda of the Session, there is a brief note: after Cardinal Trivulzio's speech about the letters and the interrogation of the Englishwomen conducted by Nuntius Carafa, the Pope gave the order to send these papers to the Holy Office.

Even if Urban VIII showed benevolence afterwards to Mary Ward, there can be no other interpretation of those words: 'Sanctissimus mandavit literas praedictas et processum ad Sanctam Officium transmitti.'

Mary Ward's letter to Pope Urban VIII

28th November, 1630

The enclosure which has not survived – last appeal to the Pope – divine commission to found the Institute

A great deal is known about Winefrid Wigmore, the Visitor, during this time of tension, but unfortunately not very much about the General Superior, Mary Ward. It is not even certain when she returned from Vienna to Munich. It was most likely *before* the 28th November, 1630, as that was when she wrote to Urban VIII from Bavaria. It may, of course, have been written earlier in Munich, where some of the first members of the Institute were still living.

The two oldest biographies[9] talk of a letter which Mary Ward wrote to some unnamed prelate or cardinal. The original has not survived but there is little reason to doubt the information, as Mary Ward's letter to the Pope of 28th November, 1630 mentioned in them has come down to us. The writing of the accompanying letter should therefore be placed in the second half of November, 1630. Whatever the case, Mary Ward wrote to some highly-placed prelate that she had come to the conclusion that a private congregation of the Holy Office had held consultations concerning the 'suppression of our manner of live', in practical terms therefore, of the Institute. If this piece of information is to be credited, then it must be remembered that it was only in the 132nd Session of the Congregatio de Propaganda Fide of 22nd November, 1630 that the decision was taken to send the incriminating papers about the Visitor's proceedings in Liège to the Holy Office. It must be assumed, therefore, that there had been rumours circulating earlier about the measures to be taken by the Curia against the Institute, and that these had reached Mary Ward. There is no sign of how she received this depressing information. Perhaps she was told by those members who had stayed on in Rome; perhaps the Jesuits knew of it, or someone close to the Elector's court in Munich. Mary Ward apparently even knew details. The suppression was intended to cause a sensation, and Mary Ward herself to be arrested as a heretic. But, as has been pointed out in the letter which has been lost, if the Pope considered it better that she, Mary Ward, should retire, he only had to let his will be known, and she would obey.

A memorial to the Pope was enclosed in the letter. This was undoubtedly the letter dated 28th November, 1630, for Mary Ward asked the recipient of the accompanying letter to make sure that her letter reached the Pope, otherwise she would have to look for other possibilities. From the urgency of her request, it is clear that it was a matter of great importance to her that this piece of writing should reach the Pope. It is the shortest of all the letters Mary Ward ever

addressed to a Pope. It is not a request, nor a petition in the strict
sense of the word. It is not even a recapitulation of the history of her
Institute, so familiar from her many letters to Popes or potentates.
In few and simple words she writes, by way of introduction, that the
spoken and physical obstacles put in the way of the Englishwomen
in western Europe had caused her to place the following facts before
the Holy Father for his consideration. She names four of the most
significant years of her life. These carry far more weight than any
long-winded request or explanation: thirty years have passed since
she knew of her vocation to follow the Lord more closely as a religious.[10] It was only later, twenty-five years ago, that she was able to
leave her country to follow this call.[11] For ten years she had been in
agonising uncertainty about the form this religious life should take[12]
and she had spent twenty-five years living in the way God had commanded.[13] Then comes the incontrovertible declaration: she had not
come to this way of life through any human suggestion but at His
word, Who can neither deceive nor be deceived.[14] It was from Him
that she had received enlightenment, and the love of this state, and
the clarity and interior conviction of the need for her Institute.[15]
God had invited her, with love, to found this Institute, and given
her the strength to endure many vicissitudes. He had given her
the assurance that this Institute would last until the end of the
world.[16]

These are almost the identical words she used in her account of
the vision of the 'Just Soul' to Fr Lee.[17] Fifteen years of spiritual
experience, but also of the bitterest deprivation and disappointment,
separated the two accounts. However, she continued in her letter to
the Pope, she did not wish to give the impression in this short explanation, that she preferred her revelation about her Institute to the
Church's decision. Still less (would she) give preference to her own
certainty over against an order from the Pope.[18] It was simply that,
in her great distress, she wished to show why she had felt obliged to
act in this manner. But if the Pope were to command it, she would
desist.[19]

The last sentence could carry some weight for a self-willed character such as Urban VIII. Mary Ward wrote: 'May God in his mercy
not look upon my misery in this matter, but inspire Your Holiness
to do whatever will be to His greater glory in this regard.'[20]

It will never be known if this letter reached its destination, for all
that remains is a copy in Elizabeth Cotton's handwriting.[21] This in
no way detracts from its contents, as here − in contrast to the muti-
lated letter of 6th April, 1630 − there is an entire letter, complete
with date and the name of the person who wrote it. There is not
much to be added. The first sentence shows that Mary Ward was still
not clear about the decision of the Curia at the end of November.
The fact that she had recourse to the Pope cannot be explained in
any other way. She did so confidently. She turned with trust to

the Pope's fatherly insight and consideration, as her words 'vista e ponderation paterna' show. Mary Ward would have been an accomplished liar to have feigned such an attitude towards the Pope, one that was almost childlike. But her love of truth, and above all her closeness to God has been amply demonstrated, and this carries with it the conviction that, at the end of November 1630, she still believed in the legitimate existence of her Institute and also that the Pope had not yet made a final decision. She defended her Institute to the end, and indeed in the Ignatian sense of 'Instrumentum caritatis Dei.' This woman must indeed have embraced her Institute both as task and gift of grace with an enormous strength of love.

Yet, inspite of all the contradictions which the struggle for this precious charge had brought her, in spite of all her certainty of the Institute's value for the Church and her people, she submitted herself to the Pope. It was precisely in this attitude that Mary Ward showed herself a real 'Jesuitess.'

When considering all this, one must remember that for Urban VIII, who had in fact suppressed Mary Ward's Institute and had made his decision known through the Congregatio de Propaganda Fide's statement to the Nuntios, this letter − if he actually received it − must have looked like incorrigible rebellion.

It is true, it spoke of submission and obedience. But what could Urban VIII and his Congregation make of the unswerving conviction uttered in the same letter that this forbidden Institute had been inspired by one 'Who can neither deceive nor be deceived'? It was precisely against this conviction of Mary Ward's that war had been declared.

This time, the Pope made his answer unequivocally clear.

The Bull 'Pastoralis Romani Pontificis' of 13th January, 1631

The Pope's attitude towards the Institute − the decrees of canon law and traditional attitudes − suppression of the Institute − measures taken against its members

Urban VIII phrased the document concerning the Institute's Suppression in extraordinarily harsh language.[22] Not only were the contents devastating, so too were the words of the text, which begins with a general reason for the following decisions. As paterfamilias, the Pope was entrusted with the care of the Church, and one of his greatest responsibilities was to protect the Lord's vineyard from undesirable labourers. These wished to destroy the good seed by sowing weeds that would smother the plants.[23] The general tone of the document is set with the words like 'zizanio','loglio', pernicious growths which had to be eradicated from the Church.

Next come the legal grounds. The Lateran Council and the Council of Lyons had prohibited new religious Orders. The decrees of Pope John XXII and Clement V considered that new congregations were perishable twigs on the branches of the Church, and condemned them.[24] Point two states: Certain women, who call themselves 'Jesuitesses', have founded a congregation without papal approval both inside and outside Italy. Under the pretext (praetextu) of living a conventual life, they have adopted a certain form of dress after the example of others (that is, the Jesuits), have founded colleges and houses of formation under the direction of a woman superior, and placed their congregation under a woman as General Superior. She possesses great power; they even make the three vows to her. In order to be able to wander here and there as they wish (pro libitu divagari), they do not observe enclosure.[25] Under the excuse of working for the salvation of souls they undertake various tasks which are not suitable to their sex, or to their weak intellect, or their womanly modesty or, most of all, to their moral life as virgins. Not even a man familiar with Holy Scriptures, one well-tried in virtue, would attempt to undertake such tasks without great circumspection.[26]

One can see here how canonical decrees have been interwoven with traditional concepts of the frailty of women. It must be pointed out once more that the apostolic activity of the members of the Institute, especially in England, was sharply condemned, not for any substantial failings but simply because they were women, and therefore beings of inferior intellectual capacity.

The third point announces the measures taken by the Curia:

In order to remove this thorny undergrowth from the Church's soil in time, the Pope has charged the Nuntius of Lower Germany (Pierluigi Carafa) and certain local bishops, to warn these women seriously in the name of the Holy See.[27] However, in arrogant defiance they have not complied but, on the contrary, have not ceased to contradict the sound teaching of the Church.[28]

From this it can be seen that it was for reasons of dangers to come, and fear of scandal, not because of offences committed, that the Nuntius and the Bishops received the commission from the Holy See. It is as though not one single good word had reached the Pope about these women and their work for the salvation of souls. One begins to wonder if Urban VIII had really been impartially and well-informed when he issued this harsh decree.

Point IV announces the measures to be taken. The text of the Bull continues to use its original imagery: In order that such pernicious plants may not spread further and do damage to God's Church, the Pope wishes to show particular severity. These excrescences must be destroyed, root and branch.[29] According to the Council of Cardinals and the Decrees of the Councils, the Pope declares the congregation of the so-called Jesuitesses, their sect and their status, to be null and void since the beginning of their existence. Their Institute must be considered as suppressed by the Pope.[30] The following prohibitions were named:

a) Their vows must be considered as dissolved. That too was covered with the harsh phrase 'We do not wish these women to be bound in any way to keep their vows or be obliged by them.'[31] It must be repeated, the Pope can dissolve vows, even against the will of the person concerned. Consequently all obligations are eo ipso removed. However, whether the Pope can prohibit commitments entered into with God in foro conscientiae, is another matter.

b) The offices (de facto usurpatis), such as the Visitor, the Superior or the General Superior of the Institute (congregationis et sectae) are likewise to be considered as suppressed. Each individual member of the Institute is thereby released from her tie of obedience.[32] It is clear that this particular point was aimed at the Civil Contract. Obedience itself came under the three vows.

Point Five refers to external matters: in holy obedience and under the threat of excommunication,[33] not only the communities or houses of the Institute (collegia vel domus) are suppressed but the members must leave them. They are not to come together in them in the future, to discuss either religious or secular matters. The clothing of the Institute must be laid aside immediately and never worn again; still less may any younger women be induced to join them. They are not allowed to call themselves religious but may, however, either enter an Order already approved or live in the world under vows in obedience to a bishop, or marry. In the last case, they may ask for the return of their dowry.

The remaining points deal with the publication of the Bull. As was customary, it was to be 'ad valvas', nailed to the doors of certain buildings in Rome. This was at the Lateran Basilica, St Peter's, at the Curial pulpit, and at the Campo dei Fiori, the place of execution.

The same was to happen in the towns where the Institute had houses. Public proclamation was to be made within two months of the Bull's date of issue. The Bull was written in the Vatican on 13th January, 1631, and put up in the places appointed in Rome on 10th May, 1631 by Mathias Spada, a papal official. That was almost four months after publication. In Bavaria, Vienna and Belgium this happened in July and August 1631 respectively. However, before that, certain strong measures had already been taken.

Arrest

7th February, 1631

Mary Ward's arrest on 7th February, 1631 — her two hour conversation with the Holy Office's commissioner, Dean Jacob Golla of Our Lady's Church, Munich — Mary Ward taken to the Poor Clare Convent, 'am Anger'.

Secretary Ingoli's 'remedies' contained various but connected measures: the Institute was to be wiped out of existence by a papal bull; by the condemnation and imprisonment of the Visitor and General Superior, the two people most responsible were to be rendered harmless.

We know what happened to Winefrid Wigmore in Liège on 13th February, 1631. Matters were very different when Mary Ward was arrested in Munich on 7th February. Winefrid — even if unpleasantly — was confronted by Nuntius Carafa; she now knew for certain of the Decree of Suppression, even if she remained totally convinced that this was not of papal authorization. And Winefrid Wigmore was questioned. Nothing like that happened to Mary Ward. Neither in Rome, Vienna nor Munich had she received any conclusive information, though she may have suspected the worst.[34] The exhausted woman was, moreover, extremely ill, enduring successive attacks of gall stone. The details of the events that follow come from various but complementary sources. Mary Ward's secretary, Elizabeth Cotton, took every opportunity of recording all that happened into a letter. It is not possible to say definitely whether this was a sort of round letter for members of the different houses, as the Institute and its houses were under threat at the time.

The original of this letter, certainly in English, has been lost, and an Italian summary is all that remains.[35] But it should not be given more value than that written in Latin on 6th April, 1630 by Mary Ward. However, there are some differences. In the other sources there is nothing inconsistent with the events described here.[36] Further, it must be borne in mind that the account is purely informative, and written without apportioning any blame. In addition, the authoress had to reckon with eye-witnesses, however much these remained in the background. There is no knowing if the translation was made in Munich, though it is known that some members there taught Italian, so it is more than possible that the English letter was abridged in order to inform the Italian members who had been driven out of the houses in the Papal States and Naples, and had found refuge and employment in Munich. The account has no date but it must have been written soon after Mary Ward's arrest.

As to the contents: on 7th February, 1631, towards four o'clock in the afternoon,[37] Jakob Golla, Dean of Our Lady's Church in Munich, came with two canons to the Paradeiser House. There the Dean read out a letter addressed to him, which contained the order to take Mary Ward prisoner.[38] The accusations were heresy, schism, and rebellion against the Church.[39] The English Life says that the horrified woman, who detested such things as hell itself, crossed herself at such an incomprehensible charge.[40] It is an irony of fate that it was Mary Ward of all people who was accused of rejecting the Church, and of heresy. She and those closest to her had spent their entire lives in loyal service of the Church.

Mary Ward offered no resistance, but handed over to the commissioner the papers he demanded – probably her correspondence – and presented herself. The interview that followed lasted two hours. Mary Poyntz and Elizabeth Cotton were present, otherwise the latter could not have written in such detail. Besides, it was not usual for a woman to be alone with a man for any length of time. There are unlikely to have been language difficulties, as Dean Golla spoke Italian, a language which Mary Ward could have known fairly well. Even at this late stage, she tried to make clear to the Dean and his companions that it was a misunderstanding. Her Institute had never been forbidden, she declared.[41] She had always tried to learn of the Pope's decision in Rome.[42] Pope Urban VIII had spoken of the Institute with praise; it was only their freedom from enclosure that had prevented him from giving it his approval.[43] It was incredible to her, Mary Ward, that the order for her arrest and imprisonment had come from Rome. The person who had commissioned it (Cardinal Antonio Barberini) was a close relative of the Pope. In the course of the conversation, Mary Ward asked if the Institute were now destroyed, or simply not tolerated.[44] Golla did not know the answer to that. He merely said that he had received the order to imprison her some fourteen days before, but that he had not had the courage to carry it out.[45] He had, however, found a worthy place for her 'improvement' (riparatione) – the Poor Clare Convent on the 'Anger'. At which Mary Ward said cheerfully (con sembiante allegro)'Your Grace speaks of worthiness, and yet you call me a heretic and treat me as such. But no matter – I have no worth.'[46]

She was not permitted to take farewell of the other members,[47] though they did let her kneel and pray. A coach was ready at the door, as she was not allowed to go on foot. Only the superior (Mary Poyntz) and her secretary (Elizabeth Caotton) were present when she left the house. Whether Anne Turner, who shared Mary Ward's imprisonment as her nurse, went to this convent only later, we do not know.

The Prisoner in the Convent 'am Anger'

7th February — 14th April, 1631

Imprisonment — lemon-juice letters — the Convent — Mary Ward's cell — Anne Turner, nurse — Abbess Katharina Bernardine Gräffin — Dean Jakob Golla and his task — Mary Ward's concern for Winefrid Wigmore and the Institute — Elector Maximilian's 'attitude' in the lemon-juice letters — Mary Ward's serene confidence in God

Let us imagine the prisoner's situation — Mary Ward had celebrated her forty-sixth birthday on 23rd January, 1631. In those days a woman in her mid-forties would have numbered among the elderly, people's expectation of life being far shorter. She suffered from gall-stone and was constantly ill, especially after violent and agonising attacks.

She was now locked up in a small room. One can only imagine what that must have meant for a woman who had walked the length and breadth of Europe freely. It had certainly not been luxury travel. Her journeys had always been connected with the future of the Institute, and she had always demanded the utmost of her frail physique. In spite of all this, she had covered great distances in recent years, over open countryside. Mary Ward was no townswoman; she had grown up in the country and remained a lover of nature all her life. She loved the vastness of the landscapes and the majesty of the mountains, and yet the narrow confines of her cell may have seemed insignificant in comparison to the fear of what was to come. Mary Ward had been accused of heresy. She was a prisoner of the Inquisition, which had the right to impose torture and often exercised this right. For the most part, death by burning at the stake was the consequence of the Inquisition's legal decisions. All this makes one understand why the tone of her letters during these months was uncharacteristically sharp, and why her attempts to escape the uncertainty and crippling anxiety could be controversial.

She was forbidden to write or receive letters. But Mary Ward had had experience of the 'penal times' in her own country — a reign of terror for catholics. She knew and used the means to protect herself from her enemies, by using terms in her letters which are often difficult to understand though clear to the recipient, such as aliases, or secret writings, or even inks made from juices which were only visible after certain treatment. Innocent before God and her conscience, imprisoned unjustly for heresy and for resisting the Church, Mary Ward mostly wrote short letters to the members in the Paradeiser House, to the Superior Mary Poyntz or her secretary Elizabeth Cotton. These are the 'lemon-juice' letters, so often mentioned in her biographies, named from the juice in which they are written.[48] This 'ink' was visible only after the piece of paper had been warmed. The Englishwomen were allowed to bring their General Superior food and fresh clothing several times a week and they did not forget to include lemons, to provide the necessary writing material. She made use of the wrappings around the things sent her, and returned them to the Paradeiser House. She was in constant fear of this correspondence being discovered. The Englishwomen had to be extremely careful on their visits to the Poor Clare convent. An unconsidered word could arouse the suspicions of the nuns and their Abbess, and consequently cause discovery. In view of the strict measures of absolute isolation of prisoners of the Inquisition, this would have been very much to Mary Ward's disadvantage. It is surprising that she had a quill pen – perhaps she took it in with her.

The secret correspondence contains personal news of the prisoner's health and her surroundings and instructions, or rather attempts, to save the Institute. This alone proves that Mary Ward had been left uninformed up to the very end. The Bull of Suppression had not yet been published.

The Convent 'am Anger',[49] founded in the first quarter of the thirteenth century as a Franciscan monastery, and lived in since 1284 by the Poor Clares, was already an old building by 1631. It is an exaggeration to use the word 'dungeon' or 'incarceration.'[50] By 'dungeon' one generally means a prison of a certain type, such as the keep of the Tower of London, or the State Prisons in Venice, to name only two of the better known. The cell in the Poor Clare convent was nothing like these, but none the less the suffocating room was anything but fit for human habitation.

A week after her arrest, on 13th February,[51] Mary Ward described her cell to Elizabeth Cotton in clear terms: 'I am in a convent (probably Order) which I know and we (that is Mary Ward and Anne Turner) are locked in a small, pretty[52] chamber (stone) on the first floor. It lies over the vault where the dead saints lie. Our living place has been the habitation of someone incurably ill, and we have apparently replaced a dying person who was ill for three years and has coughed her lungs out here. Sometimes we freeze and sometimes we fry, and perform everything that we have to do. The two small windows are almost completely blocked up with boards, our door is bolted and double locked. It is opened when the two (sisters) who guard us, and the Abbess, our highest wardress, go in and out. We were brought here by the three people who accompanied us here, and by two Franciscans, who speak Italian.'

They kept a strict watch over her. Immediately after her imprisonment, beds were placed outside the door, so that four sisters could keep guard.[53]

The nurse Anne Turner was closest to her. It was unusually compliant of the Inquisition, or rather Dean Golla, to allow one of her own community to be with Mary Ward. One gathers from this something of the state of health of the sick woman. The presence of a member of her Institute brought much relief; they could talk together and must certainly have prayed a great deal together. Anne Turner was the Infirmarian and trained to a certain extent to be with sick people and relieve their sufferings, or at least to support them lovingly. There is, though, the fact that hours of agony and fear are sometimes more easily borne alone. As well as that, there was (for us) the unimaginably unhygienic state of the room. Mary Ward's simple description gives us to understand, discreetly, how the two women were dependent on one another and at one another's mercy. Both of them must have suffered. Mary Ward and Anne Turner were not only cut off from the outside world but from the Poor Clare community too. Yet there does seem to have been some contact.[54] 'These sisters are full of esteem, love, and are certainly very good', wrote Mary Ward in the letter of 13th February[55] to Elizabeth Cotton. Two days later[56] she said: 'These people are so good. I can never praise them enough.' Shortly before she was released[57] she said, 'The love and charity of everyone in the house is unbelievable; they pray steadfastly. I have certainly profited both in body and soul.'

Her relationship with the Abbess was a different matter. This seems to have been strained. One can understand that, for the latter had to carry out the task of the Inquisition as well in her everyday concerns. But Katharine Bernardine Gräffin must not be regarded as a wardress. She was in a difficult position. It was probably without any consultation that a former Poor Clare was billeted on her peaceful house, a heretic who, as head of an unrecognized congregation, had contravened the laws of the Church.[58] What could have been more obvious for the Abbess than to attempt to bring the misguided woman back to her point of departure (in this case) to the prayer and penance of the Franciscan life?[59] But she was soon convinced to the contrary by her prisoner. Whether Mary Ward cherished great respect for the Abbess from a human point of view is matter for surmise. Elizabeth Cotton, who must be regarded as the most important link between the Paradeiser House and the Convent, received an order from her General Superior to show friendliness to the Abbess, or attention by means of a small gift,[60] but there are contradictory statements as well. There can hardly have been much warmth of feeling between the two women. The dangers for both and the consequent distrust prevented any deep association.[61] The almost approving, curious reverence of the Abbess before the Englishwoman's exalted rank may have resulted in Mary Ward showing a certain reserve.[62] The prisoner regarded Katharine Bernardine Gräffin first and foremost, and not without reason, as Dean Golla's instrument, before whom she had to be constantly on her guard.

Mary Ward's fate had been decided by the ordinaries of the Inquisition. She had been arrested as a heretic, and was being treated as such. The official in Munich immmediately authorized by the Holy Office was Dean Jakob Golla, who had arrested Mary Ward on 7th February. He was responsible for her imprisonment; he gave instructions to the Abbess which were carried out down to the last painful detail. Jakob Golla was a north Italian, from the Val di Non (Nonsberg). He was President of the Elector's Council for Religious and as such possessed authority and power of penalty over the convents and churches of Bavaria. It does not need to be particularly emphasized that, as General Visitor, he was a strict exponent of reform in the Church. This is not meant as any reproach, but simply as a comment. He carried out the duties allotted him, even if he found them difficult. It is all to his credit that he waited fourteen days before executing the orders of the Inquisition to imprison Mary Ward. His way of proceeding, such as his two-hour conversation with her, and taking her away after sunset in order to protect the prisoner from the inquisitive glances of the people, and his words about the 'worthy' prison of the Convent, reveal his understanding of the situation for this deeply humiliated woman. Dean Golla knew that the Inquisition had other possibilities for imprisonment. It could well have been a dungeon. But Golla had his instructions from Rome, and with them a set method of dealing with prisoners. Confined between the four walls of her cell, and in fear of the future, Mary Ward certainly did not judge this man fairly. After weeks of restraint, she asked for permission to leave the room to get some fresh air outside. Although this would certainly have been possible within the walled convent garden, the Dean refused her request.[63] Her confiscated correspondence was in Golla's hands. Mary Ward asked anxiously in a letter to Elizabeth Cotton and Mary Poyntz,[64] 'Visit the Dean and ask him what I am to do, where my letters are, and whether I shall have them returned. Strive to obtain everything possible from him, whatever it may be; show him trust and kindness.' Mary Ward never had her letters returned by the Dean. This request was not granted, either.[65]

On 17th February,[66] she asked Elizabeth Cotton if there were not some letters from her 'partner', which had been written too openly about 'the figure' and 'our black adversaries'. Who this 'partner' was, who had reported too clearly about Nuntius Pierluigi Carafa and the adversaries of the Institute among the Jesuits in Liège,(as we assume) and could have been in trouble as a consequence, cannot be named with certainty. One is, however, led to suspect that thesè hints refer to Winefrid Wigmore. Mary Ward could not have known by the middle of the month that Winefrid had been imprisoned on 13th February in Liège and was in conditions certainly similar to her own (solitary confinement, complete seclusion from the world). The fact that she writes of this 'partner' in the masculine form is insignificant. Mary Poyntz was 'Pitter' Peter; Elizabeth Cotton, 'James'. The expression 'partner' could mean envoy here, hardly fellow prisoner, as Mary Ward did not yet know anything of Winefrid's imprisonment.

Mary Ward prepared the secret exchange of letters with members of the Institute in the Paradeiser House with great care. This was not out of disobedience or defiance. It was in the interests of her Institute and its members that she had recourse to this means of contact. On 14th February[67] she warned Elizabeth Cotton to be extremely cautious. Apparently some news from the Paradeiser House had not reached her. Even enquiries about the health of their General Superior by the Englishwomen could have aroused the suspicions of the Abbess.[68]

As is evident, the thoughts of the unfortunate prisoner often hovered between anxiety and uncertainty, fear and suspicion; but she never complained. On the contrary, she once wrote to Elizabeth Cotton[69] 'Entrust the matter to God. He is able to enlighten everyone and excuse them and turn all that they do to his honour and for the good of the work (Institute). I do not doubt but that he will do so.'

Elector Maximilian and his wife Elizabeth occupy a special place in the lemon-juice letters. The two oldest biographies react somewhat acidly to the Elector's silence during these events that were so painful for the Englishwomen. As already stated[70] some two years before, the Elector had drawn a clear and justifiable line between his personal goodwill towards the members of the Institute and the juridical sphere of the Pope, which embraced the Institute and its members as religious. It is more than probable that Mary Ward knew nothing of this point of view. She looked on the Elector's reserve both during and after her imprisonment from a subjective angle, and therefore certainly not correctly. That, at least, is the impression given at the beginning of her imprisonment when an unusual bitterness escapes from her pen. On 13th February,[71] 'The two great ones (Maximilian and Elizabeth) are not afraid that I could now be at the point of death, but that I may die before I can be taken out of their country. That is why the doctor has been sent – unless I deceive myself.'

Elizabeth Cotton received an order not to go to the Electress unless she had been invited to an audience by her.[72] Mary Ward may have received a soothing letter from the Paradeiser House, for the next day[73] she thought that Mary Poyntz might write 'very kindly', for it was better to know beforehand whether an audience would be welcomed, under the circumstances. But, rather pointedly, she adds 'If the Duke will have an answer about the exile (command to travel to Rome) you will hear it from him, I can guarantee you that.'

Some days later[74] she wrote 'The old friend (Maximilian) is an out and out politician. I do not say, no friend. On account of God's service and His matter, he must be met with caution and friend-liness.' The warning is significant.[75] 'Do not trust your old friend. He knew all about it earlier, I warrant. He is familiar with the Elec-tress (your besse). Never let the Electress know anything about our exchange of letters.' Elizabeth Cotton received the order[76] to inform the superior in Vienna, Margaret Genison. But she was to moderate her statements and, above all, not say anything detrimental about the Electress.

It was only towards the end of her imprisonment that Mary Ward seems to have found her way back to the Bavarian rulers. At least, that seems to be implied[77] by her instruction to the Eng-lishwomen, that these may request the Electress to make it possible for two Englishwomen to accompany her to Rome. It was similar to the request of the 11th or 12th April,[78] asking if the Electress might possibly place a sedan at her disposal for her return to the Paradeiser House. For Mary Ward, the most painful of the Inquisition's commands was certainly the refusal to allow her the sacraments and to attend Mass. She was treated as a heretic, as one banished from the Church, without a trial, and without being con-demned. What little she wrote about it spoke volumes.[79] Her trust in God remained serene – He lays no overwhelming burdens,[80] He can be relied upon.[81] Among the topics and orders that occupied her mind, there are sentences such as[82] 'Whether here or there, if God would have me die, I would not live. It is but to pay the rent a little before the day. To live and suffer for God, or die and go to Him, are both singular graces such as I do not merit. One of the two, as I trust in God's mercy, will fall to my happy lot.'

The prisoner and her Institute

Dean Jakob Golla and the prisoner – Mary Ward's last letter to the Pope – the safe-keeping of the Institute's seal – the prisoner's anxiety concerning the fate of her Institute, her fear of an enforced journey to Rome – the prisoner in danger of death – Dean Golla's written declaration presented to her before reception of the last sacraments – Mary Ward's alteration of the text – release from imprisonment

Mary Ward was always and everywhere occupied about her Institute. This can be measured by the 'divina impazienza' with which she strove to carry out God's command. Even the confines of her cell could not contain her dynamism. It is no longer possible to make exact research into her attempts to save something, up to the very end. There is insufficient documentation. It is not certain if all the lemon-juice letters have been preserved, for one thing; several of them seem to be incomplete, and others barely decipherable.

Moreover, Mary Ward had to destroy those addressed to her from the Paradeiser House immediately, because of the danger of discovery. On the other hand, the documents in the Holy Office on the matter are not available. One has to use such sources as are available to give as complete a presentation as possible, without being able to guarantee that every detail is correct.

Mary Ward, it will be remembered, wrote an urgent letter to the Pope on 28th November, 1630. And, as mentioned earlier[83] it was precisely this letter which galvanised the Roman Curia into taking decisive steps against this apparently incorrigible woman, and the Institute she planned. It may have reached Rome by the middle of December. As a result, Cardinal Antonio Barberini ordered Dean Golla to imprison Mary Ward.[84] The wording of this order and its date are unknown.

On 7th February, 1631, Golla said that he had received it some fourteen days previously. To be exact, that would have been on 24th January, 1631. The English Life[85] is sufficiently well informed to report that Mary Ward was confined to her bed for three weeks as a result of an attack of her illness, and got up on St Sebastian's Day – so on 20th January – in order not to obstruct her enemies in their plans any longer. It is not known when Dean Golla first made contact with Mary Ward, or with what degree of precision these fourteen days are to be taken. But it is hardly likely that the arrest and imprisonment were carried out without previous contact having been made.

It is certain that Mary Ward had outlined instructions to the superiors of the houses *in advance*, which she charged Elizabeth Cotton to write only in the event of her arrest. These instructions are not known to us either, although Mary Ward had to repeat them on Golla's orders shortly *after* her imprisonment. The reason for this is unknown. Perhaps it was distrust on the Dean's part, perhaps merely a precautionary measure in a matter of such importance to Mary Ward herself and even more for Golla. In the second letter required by the Dean, instructions were given as an enclosure, and one can deduce from the letters that have survived that Mary Ward now foresaw the inevitable suppression of her Institute.

In her conversation with Golla, which had lasted two hours, she still had not been able to believe that the same Pope who had spoken in praise of the Institute was now prepared to destroy it. In the final sentence of her letter she wrote consolingly to the members of the Institute: 'In a secular state, you may doubtless serve God much, and without molestation to yourself or others.'[86]

But on that first night of her imprisonment she made a difficult decision, that of writing once more to the Pope.[87] There are some final sentences of the draft of such a letter still existing.[88] It must have been written with the Dean's approval, as it was not a lemon juice letter. Both drafts were written in normal ink. The complete letter is not available. If it actually reached Rome, it must lie among the documents of the Holy Office.

In one of her first notes from prison,[89] Mary Ward regrets her imprisonment, less for her own person than for the reputation of the members of the Institute. On 14th February[90] she wrote to Elizabeth Cotton among her instructions to make friendly advances towards the Abbess: 'by that I have nothing else in mind than the honour of our Master and the best for our way of life.' This way of life remained clear to her; that is why she hesitated to join with the Ursulines.[91]

Mary Ward's seal caused her a world of trouble. It was inscribed 'Praeposita Principalis Matrum Anglarum' and, because of its similarity to that of the Father General of the Society of Jesus, it was a bone of contention for many Jesuits. In a letter to Elizabeth Cotton, who as secretary to the General of the Institute, had care of the seal, Mary Ward wrote that this should not be handed over to the Dean. That Elizabeth might say that it could not be found, and a house search should be accepted.[92] At first this order looks like an incentive to tell a lie, but one cannot suspect that of Mary Ward. Her love of the truth has been shown often enough. One may safely assume that those members of the Institute entrusted with its administration had probably discussed any such eventualities long before. Their experience in their own country was enough for that. The guarding of the seal, which was the Institute's sign of authentication, must have formed part of these discussions.

A sure pointer to this is Mary Ward's order to Elizabeth Cotton of 20th February. Mary Poyntz, it said, could use her own seal until *the Pope* forbade her everything (all). Only then was she to answer that a friend, whose name the superior was not to reveal, had asked for it, and that she had given it to him.[93] By the words 'to forbid everything', the suppression of the Institute must be understood. When Mary Ward wrote this, it had already taken place, but she was not aware of the Bull. So, nothing was official. Had she not written again to the Pope? She clung to Urban VIII to the very end, and to his goodwill towards her. It is not easy to understand why the instructions given to Elizabeth Cotton differ from those to the Superior of the Paradeiser House. The arrangement previously mentioned has to be read: good friends of the Institute were to be given the seal for safe-keeping in case Dean Golla were to confiscate it. The Englishwomen need not know where it was deposited. In this situation − so before they knew of the suppression of the Institute by the Pope, the members could act as they had been told, without coming into conflict with moral law. Why should they have to hand over the authentication of the congregation to Dean Golla, before they knew for certain that this congregation had in truth been forbidden by the Head of the Church?[94]

One does not know if the Dean did wish to confiscate the seal. In his testimonial (22nd November, 1630), Secretary Ingoli suggested confiscating the seal; in the papal Bull of Suppression there was a demand for the correspondence to be handed in but no mention was made of a seal.

A week after her imprisonment, Mary Ward put on paper for the first time her thoughts about her enforced journey to Rome.[95] In this letter she used the word 'to kill'. By this she certainly did not refer to the journey or its length, but the death sentence. Elizabeth Keyes, in Rome, was to request friends of the Institute in Rome to intercede with the Pope.[96] 'No,no,' comes the passionate cry, 'it is not the Franciscans, nor the clergy, but the Jerusalems, etc., but not what they want but what God will' (shall happen).[97] By 'Jerusalems' she may have meant those among the Jesuits who were hostile to the Institute.

In the dimness of her cell, her enemies appeared as omnipotent, able to put a stop to everything that was being done to effect her release.[98] She was no longer aware of the many friends who were certainly loyal. This distortion of reality was a result of the severe imprisonment and, certainly of her physical condition also. She was awaiting the expulsion of the Institute from Munich,[99] and considered whether the women could not withdraw to Cologne or Trier. When one remembers that there were some 40 people to be accommodated,[100] and that the Englishwomen in Cologne and Trier were very poor, we have some idea of the anxieties that were torturing Mary Ward.

It is not known when she received orders to travel to Rome — only that the fear of it caused her pain.[101] She wanted to have Elizabeth Cotton and Anne Turner as companions. The Englishwomen were to try to obtain this favour from the Electress.[102] Canon Ansloe, an Englishman living in Munich, was to be asked for the money.[103] This was probably the security or bail which had to be paid before she was allowed to leave Munich.[104] In the middle of March[105] her illness worsened. She had severe migraines and symptons of paralysis in her arm. The Poor Clares considered asking for a second nurse.[106]

During this time[107] the members in the Paradeiser House addressed a petition to the Cardinals of the Holy Office. Since 7th February, it said, their mother (nostra Madre) had been in prison without being granted an opportunity to defend herself. As she was accused of heresy, she was not allowed to receive the sacraments. She was suffering greatly. The doctors stated that she was in danger of death, and advised reception of the Last Sacraments. The Englishwomen requested help. By that they probably meant Mary Ward's release.

The remark on the back of this letter is extraordinary. The members of the Institute named themselves as 'from all the nations who live under the direction of Maria della Guardia'.[108] This is obvious proof that the Englishwomen still had no idea of how things really stood with regard to their Institute. If they had, they would certainly have protected themselves from referring to Mary Ward as their superior to the Cardinals of the Holy Office. Still less would they have asked for help. One cannot be sure that this letter reached Rome, for it exists as a copy only. Also, even under the best circumstances, the distance and the ponderous methods of the Roman Congregation have to be taken into account. That would involve several weeks' delay.

Dean Golla gave his approval for the reception of the Last Sacraments, on condition that the prisoner accused of heresy first signed a declaration. The English Life[109] has provided a summary of the text: 'if she had ever said or done anything contrary to the Faith or Holy Church, that she repented of it and regretted it.'

When the Abbess gave her this statement, Mary Ward asked if it had come from the Pope or the Congregation.[110] It can be seen from this what distrust Mary Ward had towards her enemies at the papal Curia – after ten years of defensive action! The text put before her could be misinterpreted. This was because of the small but significant word 'if'. This did not preclude an offence committed against the Faith, or the Pope. Mary Ward refused to sign. On 27th March, some of the members of the Institute were allowed to visit the prisoner.[111] It is assumed that on this occasion they brought with them an altered version of the declaration, which survives. It is barely credible that this very sick woman composed this carefully-weighed declaration, which was of such importance for her fate, without some aid. She was far too weak to have done so. Perhaps Dean Golla had a share in the matter, one does not know. The great importance of the piece of paper justifies its being given here in the essential points, word for word:[112]

'Never have I said or done anything, whether important or insignificant, against His Holiness... or the authority of the Holy Church... and I would not do the slightest thing for a thousand worlds, for a present or future good, that would not be consistent with the real duties of a loyal catholic and an obedient daughter of the Church. If, however, the work which was allowed and approved at first[113] by the Head of the Church and the Holy Congregation of the Cardinals and by which I, according to the measure of my poverty, strove to serve Holy Church, and was assiduous in doing so, should be judged by those authorised to give such a decision (after they had found out the true state of affairs) as contravening in any way at all the duties of a true christian in the obedience due to His Holiness and the Holy Church, then I am ready and will always, with God's grace, be ready to acknowledge my faults, to beg forgiveness for the offences and, except for the public disgrace which has already been done to me, would offer my poor and short life as atonement for the sins stated.'

Munich, 27th March, 1631. Maria della Guardia

It has only to be added that those words were signed by a dying woman, who thought that she was soon to appear before God's judgement seat.

On 28th March, she received communion of the sick and on lst April, she was anointed.[114] Slowly, Mary Ward recovered. This is shown by the small number of letters written during this time to the Englishwomen in the Paradeiser House.[115]

It is not known why she was released from prison in the first half of April, as the exchange of letters between the Dean and the Holy Office are not known. It is possible that her release was in connection with the publication of the Bull in Rome. This was nailed up on 10th May. Mary Ward could have left her prison *before*[116] Palm Sunday but the unbelievable happened. She refused to do so, voluntarily, and wished to spend the day – always a special one for her – with the Poor Clares.[117] It will be remembered that it was on Palm Sunday, 1609, then 12th April, that she had taken a vow of chastity.[118] Twenty-two years had passed since then. On Monday, 14th April, 1631, she left the Convent 'am Anger'.

But was she really free?

Notes

1. See p.454.
2. See p.546.
3. The war of succession in Mantua ended in the peace of Cherasco in favour of the French claim to northern Italy.
4. Grisar, Institut, p., 719 ff, thinks that Ingoli wrote his paper only after the decision of 22.November 1630.
5. APF Rome, SOCG vol. 205, ff.445v. 446r.
6. "delle propositioni ch'asseriscono erronee, temerario e male sonanti in fede." See in addition Grisar, Institut, p.723, Note 63.
7. Prosper Fagnano, the then renowned canonist whom Paul V had appointed Secretary to the Congregation of the Council, (died in Rome in 1678). He belonged to eleven Roman Congregations at once!
8. See page 181.
9. Vita E, f. E2 speaks of a highly-placed Prelate; Vita I, p.30, of a Cardinal.
10. 1600/1601.
11. 1606.
12. 1600–1609 (Gloria Vision)
13. After the Gloria Vision, which confirmed her apostolate in the world.
14. " ... non fu (comme l'istesso Dio m'è testimonio) ne in tutto ne in parte intrapeso per persuasione ò soggestione de huomo vivente, ò ch'ha mai visuto, ma totalmente et intieramente (per quanto il giudicio humano puo arrivare) ordinato e comendatomi per parole espresse da colui, che non vuole ingannare, ne può esser ingannato ... "
15. " ... chi anco dava lume d'intendere, e conoscere detto statto, affetto d'abracciare, et amarlo, chiara dimostratione dell'utilta d'esso, ampia espessione della gloria da ridonderne alla Maesta divinia ... "
16. " ... ch'esso Instituto saria istante nella chiesa di Dio insino alla fine dell mondo."
17. See p.170.

18. " ... niente meno che di preferire simili lumi illuminationi avanti l'autorità de santa chiesa ne mia sicurezza interna avanti il giudicio e determinatione del Sommo Pontefice ..."
19. " ... se Vostra Santità mi commandara di desistere da simili essercitii non mancarò d'ubidire."
20. "Dio per la sua misericordia non habbia sguardo alla mia miseria in quest'occasione ma inspiri Vostra Beatitudine di fare in esso quelche piu sarà alla divina gloria."
21. Letter Nr.55. Instit. Arch. Munich. A later copy is in Biblioteca Casanatense, Rome, MS.2426. Actorum in causa Virginum Anglicanarum. II, f.412r.
22. The printed Bull was incorporated into several works. The text here follows that of Jakob Leitner, Gesch.d. Eng.Fräulein und ihret Institut, Reqensburg, 1869, Beilage 14, p.761–767.
23. " ... sata dissipent, consita evellant, zizania inferant, et adulterinas in eo plantas superinducant."
24. " ... Joannis XXII. virorum et ... Clementis V ... salutaribus constitutionibus mulierum coetus auctoritate privata et de facto instituti, tamquam exitiosi palmites damnati et sublati fuissent."
25. " ... clausuraque legibus non adstrictae pro libitu divagari ..."
26. " ... ac specie salutis animarum promovendae, aliaque opera permulta sexus et ingenii imbecillitati et modestiae muliebri ac virginali praesertim pudori minime convenientia, et quae viri ... attentare et exercere consuevissent."
27. "Nos excrescentes in agro militantis ecclesiae vepres, mature evellere satagentes venerabili Fratri Aloysio ... et nonullis locorum ordinariis dedimus in mandatis ..."
28. "Verum quia illae Dei timore ac nostro et Sedis Apostolicae respectu posthabito in grave animarum suarum praejudicium et bonorum omnium offensionem arroganti contumacia paternis et salutaribus monitionibus nostris nedum non paruerunt, sed etiam indies similia, attentare ac multa sanae doctrinae adversantia proferre non erubescunt."
29. "Nos tantam temeritatem acriori censura coercendam et plantas istas ecclesiae Dei noxias ne ulterius se diffundant radicitus evellendas et exstirpandas esse decrevimus."
30. With the harshness generally reserved for heretics: "Et quia de facto processerunt, eadem auctoritate penitus et omnino supprimimus et extinguimus ... subjicimus et ab ecclesia Dei sacrosancte funditus tollimus, delemus et abrogamus, ac pro suppressis, extinctis, evulsis, deletis et abolitis ab omnibus Christi fidelibus haberi et reputari volumus et mandamus ..."
31. " ... nec mulieres et virgines hujusmodi ad votorum praefactorum observationem ullo modo teneri aut obligari volumus."
32. " ... quae voti seu cujuscumque alterius vinculi, promissionis, vel cujusvis causae praetestu ad aliquam obedientiam se obligatas putarent, ab ea et quocumque vinculo et promissione hujusmode etiam rata et jurata absolvimus et totaliter liberamus."
33. The "little" Excommunication implied exclusion from the sacraments, the "great" Excommunication contained also the prohibition of civil business, possibly with repercussions at state level.
34. Vita E, f.40v. writes that on 20th January Mary Ward, hardly recovered from her illness, went out in order to show her enemies that she was not afraid. With f.42v. the Vita reports that Mary Ward enquired on the morning of 7th February, in which part of the city the Poor Clare Convent was situated. See Vita I also, pp.30–31.
35. "Old Writings". Inst. Arch. Munich, with the heading: Cavato fuore d'un'lettera della Madre Secretaria.

36. Vita E, f.40r; Vita I, p.30, the outline of a petition to the Pope, Letter Nr.79, 81, Inst. Arch. Munich.
37. So too Vita E, f.40v.
38. Questa commissione fu un'lettera scritta al dicano dal Eminentissimo Cardinale di San Onofrio (Antonio Barberini, Secretary of the Holy Office: see Grisar, Institut, p.169) nel nome della Congregatione del San Ufficio." This charge to Golla could be among the documents in the Holy Office, as a draft or regest.
39. Letters from Mary Ward; Vita E, f.40v: hereticke, schismatike and rebell to the Holy Church.
40. "She blessed herself with horrour to hear that named which she had as much aversion from as hell itself." Vita E, f.40v.
41. " ... che non era stata mai proibita di seguitare questo Institut ..."
42. " ... in Roma haveva sempre solecitato di sapere la determinatione di Sua Santità."
43. " ... e tutto quello che lei haveva inteso da Sua Santità era stato in singolar lode della nostra Compagnia et che si fusse rinchiusa saria un punto d'oro, ma senza clausura non lo voleva confermare ..."
44. " ... domando a Dicano si Sua Santità non vole confermarlo, si perro voleva distruirlo ò non tolerarlo ..."
45. Vita E, f.42r, dramatises the scene: the dean's voice shook, his hands trembled, and both his companions had tears in their eyes.
46. Vita E, ibid., has Mary Ward saying "Suffering without sin is no burden."
47. According to Vita E, ibid., Mary Ward did not wish to bid farewell to the sisters, in order to avoid upsetting the community. Here too a small difference of opinion is reported: the Commissar wished to convey her to prison after dark. Mary Ward is supposed to have answered that this would be a slight to her innocence, and that she had always loved the light. We would like to point out here that her imprisonment took place between six and seven in the evening. In February it was already dark at that time.
48. All these letters, sometimes difficult to make out, are in Inst. Arch. Munich.
49. St Jakob am Anger. Anon. in "Deutsche Illustrierte Rundschau," Sonderdruck, Munich, October, 1926.
50. The documents and writings about Mary Ward use these terms, at all events.
51. Letter Nr.56 (1). Cf. also Vita E, f.43r.
52. This is intended ironically, of course.
53. ibid.
54. Vita E, f.43r speaks of an elderly, holy Poor Clare sister, who showed deep reverence for Mary Ward, cf. also Vita I, p.32.
55. See above, note 51.
56. On 15th February to the members. Letter Nr.56.(4)
57. After 1st April, to the members. Letter Nr.64.
58. Prelate Golla gave permission to break the convent's enclosure. Elizabeth Cotton to members of the Institute (8–9.February).
59. At first Mary Ward had a good relationship with the Abbess. She wrote: The Abbesse is full of my writings. She has bin in some hopes to have me hers. She tells me my first vow was St Clares order but I will understood nothing and give lesse to be understood." Letter Nr.56(1) of 13th February to Elizabeth Cotton. "first vow" is to be understood as first choice, as Mary Ward never took vows as a Poor Clare.
60. Letter Nr.56(4) of 15th February to the members.
61. "Be carefull what you say heer and neither heer, nor to any complaine of any etc." Letter Nr.56 (6) of 17th February to Elizabeth Cotton.

62. Instruction not to mention any possible nobility of background of the Institute's members. Letter Nr.56 (3) of 14th February to Elizabeth Cotton. The Abbess' anxiety mentioned in a letter to Mary Poyntz, of having committed a social blunder, caused Mary Ward to answer that the members of the Institute should have given up their rank and forgotton about it. Letter Nr.56 (11) of 20.February to Elizabeth Cotton.

63. Letter Nr.75 at the beginning of March to the members.

64. Letter Nr.56 (5) of 16th February.

65. Letter Nr.74 after 17th February to the members. "Margery (the abbess) seth, as things stand I cannot have my writings neither may they be delivered you."

66. Letter Nr.56 (7).

67. Letter Nr.56 (3)

68. Letter Nr.56 (10) of 19th February.

69. Letter Nr.56 (6) of 17th February.

70. Elector Maximilian I to Cardinal Francesco Barberini, 25th January, 1629. BV. Barb. lat. 6707, ff.67r – 68v. See also p.522 ff.

71. Letter Nr.56 (1) to Elizabeth Cotton.

72. ibid.

73. Letter Nr.56 (2) of 14th February.

74. Letter Nr.56 (7) of 17th February to Elizabeth Cotton.

75. Letter Nr.56 (8) of 18th February to Elizabeth Cotton and Mry Poyntz. It is not know what it was about.

76. Letter Nr.56 (11). 20th February.

77. Letter Nr.70 from the end of February, beginning of March.

78. Letter Nr.85.

79. "Masse and sacraments are not feasts for us to frequent." Letter Nr.56 (1) of 13th February to Elizabeth Cotton. cf. also Vita E, f.46r, and Vita I, p.32.

80. ibid.

81. Letter Nr.69, at the beginning of her imprisonment.

82. "But heer or ther, if God would have me dy I would not live. It is but to pay the rent a little before the day, and to live and suffer for God, or dy and goe to him are both singular graces and such as I merit not, and one of the two, I trust in the mercyes of God, will fall to my happy lot ..."

83. See p.563.

84. Final report from Nuntius Pierluigi Carafa, 1634, BV, Rome, Barb. lat. 2691, p.87.

85. Vita E, f.40v.

86. "In a secular estate, you may doubtless serve God much and without your oune or others molestation." Letter Nr.81 of (10th February). The date emerges from Vita E, f.45r: "Three days after we receaved a note from her of what we were to doe, and the memoriall to be presented His Holines in our names ..."

87. Vita E, ff.44rv.

88. Letter Nr.79 and 80 of 10th February.

89. Letter Nr.69 to the members in the Paradeiser House.

90. Letter Nr.56 (3).

91. Letter Nr.56 (8) of 18th February to Elizabeth Cotton and Mary Poyntz.

92. "The seale doe not give him, say you find it not and be sure you be at all times ready for a search." Letter Nr.56(7) (of 17th February).

93. "Let Mother Rectrice seale with her owne seale till the Pope forbid her all; then keep it safe and tell whosoever askes for it, that a friend whom she will not discover begged it of her, and she gave it the said friend etc." Letter Nr.56 (11). The Suppression of the Institute naturally enough included the

prohibition to use the Institute seal, but did not entail the seal's surrender. This was not demanded by the Bull of Suppression.

94.   To the words quoted in note 93 follows: "She shall know more what to say about this matters, ere they can come to question of thes affairs. Till they heere from Rome, they will say noe more or doe noe other. Let them rest in peace but we will prevent time and not be behind hand with them."

95.   "It is not haling me to Rome will kill me, I warrant them. Who knows what God hath ditermined by this accidents? Truly neither they nor I doe I desire to know or have other than His will." Letter Nr.56(4) of 15.February to the members. "For my being sent up to Rome if soe it happen, wilbe perchance for the best for us; but for the adverse part I see not what it can profit them, for if they intend to have my life, they can kill me with lesse noyse, for in thes parts they know we have noe friends etc." Letter Nr.56, 16th February to Elizabeth Cotton and Mary Poyntz.

96.   Letter Nr.56(5) as above, note 95 and Nr.72 from the second half of February to the members in the Paradeiser House.

97.   Letter Nr.56 (5).

98.   Letter Nr.56 (6) of 17th February.

99.   Letter Nr.66 from the end of February.

100.   Vita E, f.42r.

101.   As above, note 98.

102.   Letter Nr.70 from the end of February, beginning of March, to the members. And Vita E, f.46r.

103.   Letter Nr.57, probably the beginning of March. Dr Henry Ansloe (1561–1633) studied first in the English College, Rome and was ordained there. He completed his studies in Ingolstadt and was made Canon of Liebrauenkirche in Munich. A. Meyer, Die Domkirche zu Unserer Liebe Frau in Munchen, München 1686, p.194, 279, and 546.

104.   Mary Ward to Urban VIII, 10th April 1631, Letter Nr.86.

105.   Vita E, f.46rv.

106.   Mary Ward to the members, Letter Nr.65 second half of March, 1631.

107.   Letter Nr.83 of 27th March. They sent the Petition probably as an enclosure to a letter dated 28th March to Cardinal Pázmány. Letter Nr.87.

108.   "Per tutte quelle di qualsisia natione che vivano sotto il governo della Madre Maria della Guardia."

109.   " ... that if she had ever sayd or done any thing contrary to faith or holy Church, she repented her and was sorry of it." Vita E, ff.46v–47r.

110.   Letter Nr.64 after 1st April to the members.

111.   Elizabetha Cotton to Cardinal Pázmány on 28.March, Letter Nr.87. Before this date Mary Ward advised the members to insist on a conversation with him. Letter Nr.62.

112.   Letter Nr.82 of 27th March. Translation from M. Immolata Wetter, Mary Ward, "Grosse Gestalten des Glaubens, ed. by Fr Gerhard Eberts, Aschaffenburg, 1985, p.68.

113.   Namely by the "Laudatio" of 1616.

114.   Mary Ward to Urban VIII, Letter Nr.86 of (10th April); Vita E f.47v.

115.   Vita E, f.48rv, reports that she recovered quickly.

116.   see p.567.

117.   Mary Ward to Elizabeth Cotton, Letter Nr.85 of 11/12th April.

118.   AB/G p.24.

XXX

THE LAST YEARS IN ROME
1632–1637

Mary Ward's third journey to Rome

Conditions imposed by the Holy Office before the journey – Mary Ward's petition to the Pope – her stay in Bologna – help given by the Jesuits – Fr Vitelleschi's testimony – the three journeys compared

After the publication of the Bull, and Mary Ward's arrest in Munich, the Curia acted on the final piece of advice given them by the Cologne Nuntius, Pierluigi Carafa: the sentencing of the accused by the Holy Office in Rome. Where else could she have been judged? In Liège? Carafa was not really prepared to do that. The few members of the Institute there, not to mention Winefrid Wigmore, had caused him trouble enough. In Vienna? The new Nuntius, Ciriacco Rocci, had moved there only a short time before. He knew precious little about the Institute and, in any case, showed no desire to be involved in such an awkward affair. Mary Ward had been accused above all of heresy, and rebellion against the Church. For such offences, the tribunal of the Holy Office was the competent authority, and it was to this that the matter had been referred by the Congregatio de Propaganda Fide.

Hardly anything is known of Mary Ward's third and last journey to Rome. First, she had to get used to the idea of a new expedition south, as has been seen.[1]

The conditions imposed by the Holy Office were stringent.[2] The journey had to be at her own expense, and in the company of a deputy chosen by Dean Golla. The time of the journey was stipulated, too, as her arrival date in Rome had been determined. Also, the Institute in Munich had to produce bail, the amount of which was to be decided by Nuntius Carafa.

After her release from prison, Mary Ward wrote a petition to the Pope.[3] Sadly, this has survived in an incomplete form only. It was clearly a request for remission, or some sort of mitigation of the conditions. These probably could not have been complied with, as where could Mary Ward have obtained the travelling expenses for a deputy? The Englishwomen's journeys had been laborious undertakings, on foot, staying at very modest hostelries on the way. Hardly suitable accommodation for a deputy commissioner of the Holy Office. The time-limit set would have been another heavy burden on the woman, who was ill to begin with and had been further weakened by long imprisonment. It is assumed that the demands – which reveal the Holy Office's deep distrust of the Englishwoman – were lifted, apart from the bail.

Tradition does not say who accompanied her. Mary Poyntz and Elizabeth Cotton certainly did not, as the correspondence of the following months shows. The documentary material does not tell us when the group left Munich, but we know that they arrived late into the Autumn in Bologna, and were delayed there by the plague from at least 29th November until 20th December, 1631. Fr Vitelleschi thanked the Vice-Rector in Bologna with words that showed his feelings, for the help he had given to the women.[4] It is not known what this was. Fr Vitelleschi was convinced of the Englishwomen's integrity, or he would not have given them such support during this time of their deep humiliation. There is uncertainty, too, about their date of departure from the plague-infested area of Emilia province and continued journey to Rome. Most probably they arrived in the first months of 1632.

A comparison of Mary Ward's three journeys to Rome shows the fateful stages of her negotiations with the Curia. At the end of 1621, as a mature woman of 36, she set out for Rome from Liège with full confidence. She was given a kindly hearing by the Pope and Cardinals, but the weeks of waiting turned into years, and she achieved nothing. True, the houses in Italy were suppressed but she, personally, learnt nothing about the fate of her Institute. She travelled north.

After promising results in the middle of Europe, she returned south at the beginning of 1629, having been persuaded to do so by Pallotto, the Viennese Nuntius, who pulled the wool over her eyes. Her request for confirmation of her Institute was dismissed, but once again, she was not informed of this.

Two years later, at the end of 1631, she was ordered to Rome as prisoner of the Inquisition, for her third journey. Ten years of fruitless negotiations and heart-rending struggles lay behind her.

She may have been weak in body; spiritually, she was indefatigable and unbroken.

The audience with the Pope

Unreliable accounts of the Pope's words in the two oldest biographies

Soon after arriving in Rome, Mary Ward had an audience with Urban VIII. In contrast to her earlier conversations with Popes Gregory XV and Urban VIII, it is not from Mary Ward herself that we know the date or even the content of the discussions. The English and Italian Lives record some momentous sentences, but it is difficult to credit them.

The English Life writes[5]: 'When she said: 'Holy Father, I neither am, nor ever have been a heretic, His Holiness, interrupting, would not let her go on, saying: We believe it, we believe it, we need no other proof. We and all the Cardinals are not only satisfied, but edified at your proceedings; neither must you think it much to have been proved as you have been, for such have been the proceedings of other popes with other servants of God.'

If we are supposed to take the Pope at his word according to this text, he is saying that similar trials of other saintly people by his predecessors were justified. His choice of words in simply dismissing such suffering seems superficial, in face of the facts. Urban VIII had never taken Mary Ward's visions seriously, not even when she had written to him about them a short time before.[6] On the contrary, he had destroyed her Institute, burdened her with the poverty and disgrace of a nine-weeks' imprisonment, and caused untold suffering to her members. And now, she was not to take all these trials seriously? Counsel not easily absorbed by an English woman who had believed in the Pope's benevolence. No – a different judgement was passed here. Even if Urban VIII was sometimes unpredictable, such words cannot be attributed to him – unless he said them to the shattered woman AFTER she had been informed of the decision of the Holy Office. The Pope, after all, had always been kind.

Acquittal

Limited freedom – adversaries in England – deliberations of the Curia concerning 'Turkish matters' – Mary Ward outside Rome

On one anonymous day, whose date has not even been recorded, Mary Ward was acquitted of the charge of heresy. The English Agent in Rome, Peter Fitton, wrote on 17th April, 1632,[7] that she was negotiating with the Inquisition about reparation for the harm done to her reputation by the Bull condemning the Institute. This seems a rather peculiar way of referring to what had taken place. However that may be, by 17th April, 1632, Mary Ward must have been free. She could never have voiced such a demand as prisoner of the Inquisition. Once again, the question must be raised, was she really free?

It also seems odd that it was about nine months later, on 15th January, 1633[8] that she wrote her first letter to Mary Poyntz in Munich. True, war had broken out over the greater part of Germany. The Swedes were ravaging Bavaria, and in May, 1632, King Gustavus Adolphus took Munich.[9] But was that enough to explain Mary Ward's silence? It may well be that several letters have been lost − but what is to be made of a sentence like this:[10] 'How much I feel it, not knowing how things stand or how you really are.' Then, immediately, there follows the warning: 'Above all, safety must be assured. Be discreet in everything.' She was just as anxious about her correspondence now, as she had been in prison, and her letters are codified to such an extent as to be sometimes indecipherable. From 1633 there is a string of letters from her to Munich and one to Pressburg. They mostly contain personal pieces of news about her health, the weather, and other slight grievances. But certain sentences scattered among them give us clues to the activity being taken for her Institute by this indefatigable Englishwoman. Some letters from the equally indefatigable English enemies of her Institute bear witness to that. A letter from England[11] stated that Mary Ward had been lured to Rome full of hope for the confirmation of her Institute, but that 'los padres' had advised her to stop her fruitless and presumptuous work for conversion, and concentrate on the one aim of obtaining confirmation for her educational Institute for young girls. By that means they (namely, the Jesuits and Jesuitesses) between them could have a hold on both sexes. The sender of the letter thought this plan of the Jesuits constituted a threat to the Church and all other female orders in particular, which was just as dangerous as Mary Ward's plan to co-operate in the active apostolate was ridiculous. As shown already, there was no change in the opinion that the Institute's work in England was regarded as the greater danger.

In 1633[12] the English secular clergy indicated to Urban VIII that the English Jesuitesses, whom the Pope had suppressed, were still helping the Jesuits in England, and introducing them to catholic families. Against this backdrop, Mary Ward's words to Mary Poyntz[13] become clear. She writes: 'What you received with the last letter was presented last Wednesday, (12th January, 1633) it has already been dealt with by the Curia and discussed vigorously. In my next letter you shall know what is done and said. Pray for poor me.'

On 19th February,[14] she wrote 'Fillice (Mary Ward) will shortly see all that was, and whether something is to be done or not in the

Turkish matter, and she is determined not to lose such valuable time. God's service is dear to her. It is truly so good to serve Him, for when he sees someone occupied in his service, He acts powerfully, and will turn everything to good at the proper time for Fillice.' (Mary Ward)

By 'Turkish matters', the activities of the members in their own country is to be understood. There, like the Jesuits, according to the phrasing of the Formula Instituti, they worked among the Turks and people of other faiths (..sive nos ad Turcas sive ad quoscumque alios infideles... mittendos...) In October, 1635, Mary Poyntz wrote from Rome to Winefrid Bedingfield in Munich, that she was to accompany Mary Ward to Turkey, in other words, England.

During those last years in Rome, Mary Ward suffered severe pain. Fever and kidney trouble were her constant and merciless companions and almost every letter contains some complaint about the poor state of her health. Mary Poyntz, while still in Munich, was able to help her with some money, and in June 1633 she went to Fiuggi, formerly Anticoli, a good place for those with kidney complaints. On 27th June,[15] she returned to Rome. She was not allowed to visit San Casciano the following year.[16] The spa lay at a further distance from Rome, and at that time was under the Duchy of Tuscany. She was allowed to travel within the extent of the Papal States only. It was probably at the Pope's intervention some years later[17] that she was able to seek some relief for her pain, and accept the invitation of the Marquis of Monte, who allowed her to convalesce on his property in Piano Castagnano. But wherever she went, the watchful eye of the Inquisition was on her, and she was surrounded by spies.[18]

The new house in Rome

The Institute in Rome on sufferance – difficulties in purchasing a house – Mary Poyntz summoned to Rome – Mary Ward supported by the Pope – twenty-three members in their own house near Santa Maria Maggiore

One has to be cautious in using the word 'House', as this must not be taken to mean 'foundation' in the sense understood by canon law. The Institute as a congregation had been suppressed. It may cause surprise that Mary Ward had decided to acquire a house in Rome at all, and that in actual fact she did so.

The Pope's readiness to tolerate the women in his city, even if not as an Institute, may have contributed to this.[19] Mary Ward could count on the help of some members of the Barberini family[20] and, after all, the women had to live somewhere. Their great poverty and the fact that they were exiles mitigated the stiff measures demanded by the Bull of Suppression. Not long after her release, on 30th July, 1633[21] Mary Ward wrote to Mary Poyntz in Munich that she intended to buy a house. Mary Poyntz was to see if she could obtain any financial help in Bavaria from the Elector, and was to come to Rome herself. They would meet in Loreto. She added that she would not act in the matter without Mary Poyntz. The superior of the Paradeiser House was also to bid a discreet and cautious farewell to the rulers. From this it is plain that Mary Poyntz' absence from Munich was intended to be of some length. But matters in Rome did not move as quickly as Mary Ward would have liked. On 6th August[22] she reported, ill as she was and suffering from the unbearable heat of a Roman summer, that she had the guarantee of 300 crowns. That was not even half the sum needed. The Pope's permission to buy the house – and with that, permission for the members to live in it – had not yet arrived. By the middle of August[23] she was able to say that she had received 200 crowns. She had asked the Pope for an audience and for approval of the purchase. That did not come about so quickly, either. On 20th August[24] Urban VIII had still not given an answer, and Mary Ward asked Cardinal Antonio Barberini to be her advocate.[25] He, too, needed time.[26] Mary Ward's ideas of action were very different from those of the Roman authorities, as has been said repeatedly.

Mary Poyntz set off from Munich at some date unknown, and was already in Ferrara when Mary Ward had to write and tell her that she could not leave Rome because of matters concerning the purchase of the house, but that Mary Poyntz was to be on her guard, as the 'Jerusalems' were not to learn of her arrival.[27] This code name has been met before and must once again be a reference to the Jesuits who were opposed to the Institute. They probably dreaded a revival of the congregation, which was still active on the English mission.[28] Fr Vitelleschi was now apparently among their number, for towards the end of October[29] he wrote to Fr Contzen, who was living in Braunau at the time, that both he and Cardinal Barberini thought that the best solution would be for the women to enter an enclosed order.

Mary Poyntz had arrived in Rome *before* 29th October, and Mary Ward addressed her letters subsequently to Winefrid Bedingfield.[30] In a letter from Mary Poyntz to her, as her successor in Munich,[31] we learn that the women had to wait until the end of November before they could move into their new home. This house was certainly obtained with the Pope's knowledge and permission. The mere fact that Urban VIII ordered bread and wine to be sent to Mary Ward from the supplies of the papal larder from April 1633 to the beginning of November 1637[32] is more than sufficient proof of that. Moreover, the settlement of a fairly imposing community of Englishwomen in Rome would have been unthinkable without his approval. The house was situated opposite the Paul V's Lady Chapel, in the Basilica of Santa Maria Maggiore. On lst December, 1635[33] Winefrid Bedingfield wrote to the Elector of Bavaria that twenty-three members were living in Rome.

By her blameless life and tenacious negotiations with the Pope, Mary Ward had won a measure of toleration for the members as a community in Rome.

Before turning to the last part of her life, a final glance must be given to those other members of the suppressed Institute on the continent.

The fate of the houses

1631–1637

Little documentation about the few members in Perugia, Naples and St Omer – the members from Pressburg and Vienna converge on Munich – Cologne and Trier – distraint on the members in Liège; Winefrid Wigmore imprisoned there – the Paradeiser House in Munich – threat of suppression, support of the Elector – the Swedes in Munich – Mary Ward and Elector Maximilian I

In the following account, the houses must not be considered as foundations in the sense recognised by canon law, any more than the building lived in by the members who were tolerated in Rome. The Bull of Suppression was normative for these too. However, there were still some members living in the various former houses. As foreigners with no possessions, they would have found it difficult to make ends meet.

Perugia: after the suppression of the Institute in the Papal States, there were probably no members of the Institute living there.[34]

Naples: thanks to Fr General Vitelleschi's support,[35] the members stayed on, though after Winefrid Wigmore's return to Munich in 1627, the number of members declined greatly. We learn of the presence of some members from a letter written to England by the English Agent, Peter Fitton in Rome, which is dated 3rd July, 1632.[36]

St Omer: after the suppression, nothing more is known of Mary Ward's first foundation, though it is possible that some members lived on there too, privately.[37]

Pressburg: there were certainly still some members there in 1633, under the jurisdiction of the Viennese Nunciature. While still in prison, Mary Ward had told her secretary Elizabeth Cotton to recommend the former members of the Institute to Cardinal Pázmány and asked him to have Barbara Babthorpe sent to Munich.[38] The Cardinal must have complied with this speedily, as she was already superior there in the spring of 1632.[39]

Contacts had already been interrupted earlier, for Mary Ward later complained to Frances Brooksby of Pressburg that she had received only one letter in two years, and ordered her to travel to Munich where 'Ours are still living.'[40] From this it may be concluded that Frances Brooksby was the last of the small community who had worked for some time in Pressburg. As in Pressburg so too in Vienna, the Bull was proclaimed in August 1631. The episcopal consistory court held consultations as to whether the papal decree should be made public, that is on Church doors, or privately.[41] There were sixteen members living in the house 'Stoss am Himmel' at the time. These obeyed immediately and put aside the Institute's dress.[42] At the end of the year, the Emperor's financial office withheld payment of the Emperor's support[43] though Margaret Genison's petition obtained the continuation of the annual grant of 600 guilders; there is no further mention of the Empress' support of 400 guilders.[44] As far as is known, the tax for the house continued to be paid until 1631.[45]

From a report from the Bavarian treasury of 10th June, 1633[46] to the Elector, we assume that Veronika von Maxlrain belonged to the community of the Institute in Vienna at that time. Apparently most members of the former community moved out of Vienna in 1634 or 1635, for on 10th February on one of these years,[47] Mary Ward wrote to Winefrid Bedingfield in Munich that she was to receive the members from Vienna with kindness. In this letter she mentions Veronika von Maxlrain and someone referred to simply as Catherine. Whether other members stayed on in Vienna cannot be stated with certainty. On 6th January, 1638[48] Bishop Anton Wolfrath threatened his priests with excommunication if they continued to celebrate Mass in 'Stoss am Himmel'. Not one of the inhabitants wished to accept the decree, and so the diocesan messenger Johann Georg Kahr pushed the piece of writing as far as he could under the door.[49] It cannot be stated definitely that there were any members then, among those inhabitants. It is probable that they left the city soon after the death of their benefactor, Emperor Ferdinand II (15th February, 1637).

Cologne and Trier: these houses under the Cologne nunciature were small and remained impoverished. At the end of February 1631[50] when Mary Ward was anxious about the house in Munich, she wrote from prison to the Paradeiser House that they might perhaps move to Trier or Cologne. Her suggestion must be regarded as a sign of her desperation, for she added that she had no other suggestion – 'I know no remedy'.

Liège: remained, as before, the most unfortunate of all the houses of the Institute. Soon after Winefrid Wigmore's arrest on 7th

March, 1631[51] the Chapter of St Martin decided to forbid the members to ring their housebell. By Easter they were to leave their dwelling within the enclosure. That meant before 20th April. Matters did not have to go to such extremes, as the end was already in sight.

On 22nd April, the Chapter gave three whole patakons for the members who remained.[52] However, on the same day[53] the lawyer Jacques Nixon, at the order of the Bishop's official, carried off most of these wretched women's furniture, in lieu of their debts. This was not a question of enormous sums, such as had encumbered the Institute when they had accepted the farms in Condroz. The proceeds from their belongings would not have been sufficient. It was more likely to have been the demands of tradespeople who had supplied provisions or material for clothes without being paid that was the cause of this. The Chapter intervened, and advised an amicable settlement, admittedly under penalty of legal proceedings against the lawyer and his assistants for breach of enclosure. It was one among many points of view, for the next day[54] the Chapter approved Canon Egyd Beeckmann's demand to take possession of his house, in which the members were then living. And hardly fourteen days later, on 4th September,[55] the Chapter approved the making of an inventory, and the sale of the English-women's furnishings. The independent action of lawyer Nixon was rebutted, and Canon Beeckman received at least one part of the rent outstanding.

With this, the end of the second oldest house of the Institute was, to all intents and purposes, an accomplished fact. There is no mention in the records where the few women were living in 1639, when Mary Ward tried yet again to do something for them.

The records say nothing about the length of time Winefrid Wigmore had to stay in Liège after her imprisonment on 13th February, 1631.[56] From her strait little cell in the Convent 'am Anger', Mary Ward sent greetings to Winefrid Wigmore and her companion Mary Wivel through the members of Paradeiser House.[57] She was concerned about the Visitor's letters – certainly compromising – because, of course, her own correspondence had been confiscated by Dean Golla.[58] One of Mary Ward's letters towards the end of February, 1631[59] may have been about Winefrid Wigmore's fate, but it is an almost indecipherable lemon-juice letter, and the context cannot be made out clearly. A letter from Mary Wivel, dated 14th March, 1631[60] from Liège, reached Elizabeth Cotton in Munich and contained news which must have brought great joy to those living in the Paradeiser House. Mary Wivel had managed to get a letter from Mary Ward to the prisoner – certainly an order to obey the papal decree. As the Nuntius was not in Liège at the time, Winefrid Wigmore first of all gave her submission to her confessor. She was again allowed to receive the sacraments, and letters, and visitors. Mary Ward's instructions for Winefrid Wigmore to Elizabeth Cotton are only partly legible.[61] All that emerges are words of caution. Mary Ward must have been trying to secure her friend's final release for, soon after reaching Rome,[62] she succeeded, though history does not relate when Winefrid Wigmore was allowed to leave prison.

The fate of the Paradeiser House in Munich has deliberately been left to the end of this passage. It was from this first foundation on German soil that the 'Institutum Beatae Mariae Virginis' developed, as we now know it.

After the suppression of the Institute the Paradeiser House was in danger from two sources:

1.   From the Bull of Suppression, which forbade the members a communal life. Elector Maximilian I, who greatly favoured the Institute, must have come into conflict with his conscience. Was he justified, as a loyal prince of the Church, in continuing to support these women?

2.   From the political situation in Bavaria. In the second half of 1631, the troops of the King of Sweden, Gustavus Adolphus, pushed up to the Rhine and swept across Bavaria in the spring of 1630. In May, 1632 they took Munich. The hands of the Elector were tied, and not only from a religious point of view. The war cost him a great deal of money.

To turn next to the material state of the Paradeiser House. Apart from the Bull of Suppression, which was proclaimed in Munich only in August, 1631[63] the Elector ordered his treasury on 5th September[64] to pay the annual grant of 2,000 guilders. The women received 3,000 guilders at the end of the year[65] for one and a half years, but that marked the last grant from the amount of 2,000 guilders agreed on annually from 1627. This meant that the material situation of the members in Bavaria was very difficult, as rising prices forced them to make retrenchments. At the end of 1631,[66] Mary Poyntz sent a petition for additional support. She obtained a further 1,200 guilders for her community.[67] Then donations stopped. The Elector caused enquiries to be made at the beginning of May, 1633,[68] on the approval of the payment of 150 guilders, as to how many members were still living in Munich and what they were living on. The treasury paid the sum approved on 10th June,[69] and reported to the Elector that there were still seven women living in the Paradeiser House, four in their own Institute dress, and three in secular dress. For some time now they had survived on Veronika von Maxlrain's dowry, which consisted of 4,250 guilders and brought in an annual interest of 212 guilders, 30 kreuzer. They would have received this amount from the 1st September only, however. On 19th October,[70] the treasury paid them half of the 200 guilders granted them by the Elector on 10th September. Seven women, therefore, had to live on a total of 462 guilders 30 kreuzer, an amount which in those times of inflationary prices would have barely sufficed for two.

At the end of 1634[71] the members only received 100 guilders and the additional 50 guilders approved and paid in case of need. One can see how the community had diminished from the fact that the payment of 100 guilders at the end of 1635[72] was for two people. These were probably English members, and the financial authorities made the proviso that the German women who lived in the Paradeiser House must be supported by their relatives or obtain money by their own work and services. In 1636[73] the members received 100 guilders annually only. Until 1639 they remained without any donations from the Elector.

These sums are eloquent. But perhaps the dependence of the women on the goodwill and severely reduced means of the Elector were as hard for them as their own oppressive poverty. As well as that, there was the situation of the country as a whole. As said previously, Bavaria had become a battlefield since 1632. In addition to shortage of money and the threat of enemy troops, there was the presence of that constant companion of war in early centuries: the plague. In almost every one of Mary Ward's letters to Munich one hears her frantic anxiety about the health of the members in the Paradeiser House. She knew only too well that entire families could be wiped out by this fearsome epidemic.

The number of the members in the Paradeiser House varied. On September 11th, 1631,[74] the Elector's secretary, Aurelius Gigli, spoke of 26 foreigners, meaning members of the Institute. In Mary Poyntz' petition just mentioned at the end of the same year,[75] there is mention of 10 young foreigners. So 16 members may have left the house, perhaps the city and the country, too, in the course of the year.

And this number diminished. In the middle of 1633[76] the Elector's treasury mentioned seven members and finally, at the end of 1635[77] there were only two left in the Paradeiser House. That was rock bottom.

One might ask how Mary Ward stood personally towards the Elector. As an Englishwoman and a member of an upper echelon of society, she treated reigning princes and the authorities of the day with obedience and respect. Mary Ward never spent long in Munich. Some six months after the founding of the Paradeiser House (in January, 1627), she left the city and returned only briefly in 1628. She went to Rome in 1629. An attempt has been made to show that she went to Munich once more in the spring of 1630, when she remained in prison there from 7th February – 14th April in the Convent 'am Anger'. It is not surprising, therefore, that shortly before her imprisonment she had asked Mary Poyntz in what part of the city the Poor Clare Convent lay.[78]

At the end of 1631, she left the Paradeiser House on the order of the Inquisition, and travelled to Rome. She never saw Munich again. Then there is the fact that when she left Rome in November, 1626, she did not intend to found a house in Munich, but simply go there to obtain financial assistance for the house in Liège, which was under such financial threat. But Maximilian was a pragmatist, and he offered her the possibility of teaching Bavarian girls in Munich. She seized the opportunity, and her Institute soon achieved great success in the Bavarian capital. The Elector apparently took no action on her imprisonment. Mary Ward was offended by this, one has to admit, without justification. In her letter of 17th February, 1631[79] from prison to Elizabeth Cotton, she wrote that Maximilian I allowed himself to be influenced by reasons of state. She had probably not grasped the amount of pressure laid on this good prince. Could he, as a catholic prince, act against the Pope's decisions? It would have been possible, after the Suppression, for Maximilian of Bavaria to have considered expelling the members of the Institute from his lands. The last instalment had been paid from his endowment for their 'clothing, arrangements and actual departure.' But then — however offensive this may sound — the war came to the members' aid. Mary Poyntz' petition to the Elector of 29th December, 1631[80] concerned the fate of the ten foreigners among the members who, through 'guerra et altri molti impedimenti' had been prevented from leaving. The special addition of 1,200 guilders may therefore have been intended for their 'clothing, arrangements and actual departure.'[81]

However, the war drew closer and flight was soon no longer an option. Mary Ward had often encouraged Mary Poyntz in her letters from Rome — and, after her departure, Winefrid Bedingfield — to hold out,[82] and above all to keep open the contacts with the Elector and his wife. She took a warm interest in the fate of the princes' family, who had to leave Munich because of the war. But it was the safety of the Paradeiser House for her community which had first place in nearly all her many letters. If it could remain in their possession, then there would be a further foundation on the continent of Europe of the same community that was permitted in Rome. On 1st December, 1635[83] Winefrid Bedingfield submitted a suggestion to the Elector: to educate the two remaining members of the Institute as secular teachers for Bavarian girls. By so doing they, as true daughters of Mary Ward 'nostra signora e madre' could do good service for Bavaria. Maximilian I accepted this suggestion on condition that 'they keep the Papal Decree and all else, and should in no way act against it.'[84] The Elector was able to do this because the same community of Englishwomen had lived in a large house in Rome since 1633, and Mary Ward was even being supplied with provisions by the Pope. Mary Ward's tenacious struggle for toleration of her community also had its reward in Munich. It is not certain if

Mary Ward planned to visit Munich again.[85] It could well be that the Holy Office forbade such a journey. But it was not by pure chance that her plan to return to England now began to take on a more definite shape.

To end with a few sentences from Mary Poyntz' account, written shortly before the Swedes took Munich:

'We have great trust in God's mercy. We have suffered much from Catholics in this city and, if it pleases his Divine Majesty to complete our suffering with the crown of martyrdom, we are willing and ready to drown the earth of Munich with our blood.'[86]

Notes

1. See p.578.
2. Mary Ward to the Pope, 10 April 1631. Letter Nr.86, Inst. Arch. Munich.
3. As above, note 2.
4. " ... lodo la sua molta carità congionta con la sua prudenza in fare questa buon'opera dovuta alla virtù delle medesime Signore." ARSI Rome, Venetia 9/II, f.430v. The 29th November was mentioned in this letter. In his letter dated 20.December Fr Vitelleschi mentioned again the Vice-Rector's readiness to help. ibid. f.432r.
5. Vita E, f.50r. "When she said: 'Holy Father, I neither am, nor ever have been heretike', His Holynes, interrupting, would not let her goe on, said: We believe it, we believe it, we neede noe other proofe, we and the Cardinalls all, are not onely satisfyed, but edifyed, at your proceedings, neither must you thinke much to have beene proved as you have beene, for such have beene the proceedings of other popes with other servants of God.' Vita I gives the text piecemeal and somewhat differently: "Siamo non solamente sodisfatti, ma edificati delle sua obedienza, e sappiamo che esercitava santemente il suo Instituto, sin che habbiamo voluto altrimente, e quando prontamente aubbidi ci edifico."
6. Letter Nr.55 of 28th November, 1630, Inst. Arch. Munich.
7. WA London, vol. XXVI, Nr.57, p.167.
8. Letter Nr.89.
9. Interesting details in Mary Poyntz' letter of 14th April, 1632, of what had been experienced. BV Rome, Barb. lat. 7054, ff.124 – 125. Its place in this archive points to its having been intercepted.
10. On 15th January 1633. Letter Nr.89.
11. Of 9th April 1632. WA London, vol XXVI, Nr.52, pp.157 – 158.
12. APF Rome, vol.297, f.6v, and vol. 347, f.395v.
13. Letter Nr.89 of 15th January, 1633. " ... what you had by the last, was the least wednesday presented hath alre dy byn treated of in the Kings court (the Curia, note), has byn fervously folowed, and by my next you shall know what ys done and sayd. Pray for poor me."
14. Letter Nr.91.
15. Letter Nr.92 of 22nd June, to Mary Poyntz.
16. Vita E, f.50v. The Pope sent a Prelate to Mary Ward who was to bring her the message. "It was his will for some respects and reasons of state, she should not goe out of Rome." To Mary Ward's question, as to whether she was a prisoner, the Prelate answered that this was certainly not the case. "You are free, most free, neither is there any thing in you doubtfull." Vita I, p.34. However, it was the Pope's wish that she should not leave Rome!
17. Vita E, f.50r; Vita I, p.35.

18. Mary Ward knew that. Vita E, f.51v, ff. and Vita I, p.35ff, report it in detail.
19. Vita E, f.50r. To this, the Pope's words: "Where should they live, or where could they live so well?"
20. The Pope's sister-in-law, Donna Costanza, and perhaps too Donna Anna, nee Colonna, who had married the Pope's nephew, Taddeus Barberini.
21. Letter Nr.93.
22. Letter Nr.94.
23. Letter Nr.107.
24. Letter Nr.95.
25. On 24th August, BV Rome, Barb. lat. 8620, ff.58r, 63v.
26. Letter Nr.96 of 27th August, Nr.109 from the end of August and Nr.101 of 1st October. All in Inst. Arch. Munich.
27. Letter Nr.100 of 5th October to Mary Poyntz in Ferrara. ibid.
28. See in addition p.589 ff.
29. On 22nd October 1633. ARSI Rome, Germ. Sup. 6. p.599. Probably Cardinal Antonio Barberini was meant here.
30. Letter Nr.102 from 29th October, Inst. Arch. Munich.
31. Letter Nr.103 of 5th November, ibid.
32. BV Rome, Ruoli di Papa Urbano VIII, aggiustato li 2 aprile 1633 Nr.13.ff, 17v, 18v. The Pope had already supported the impoverished Englishwomen with alms.
33. StA Munich, Kl. lit. 434/10, ff.3r–4v.
34. On 23rd August 1625, the Curia approved the transfer of a member of the Institute into the Benedictine Abbey of St Catherine near Perugia. Cardinal Bandini to the Bishop of Perugia. AV Rome, Sacra Cong. Episc. et Regul. Registrum Regularium 34, f.280v.
35. Cf. To the letters of Fr Vitelleschi already known, further instructions. ARSI, Rome, Naples, 15/I, ff.157v, Nr.423; 158v–159r, Nr.433; 186v, Nr.628; 198r, Nr.60; 15/II, ff.202v–203r, Nr.91; 266rv, Nr.527.
36. WA London, vol.A 26, Nr.91, 251–252.
37. The departing Nuntius, Lagonissa, did not mention the Englishwomen in his last dispatch 1634. BV Rome, Barb. lat. 2677, ff.23v–24v.
38. Elizabeth Cotton to Cardinal Pázmány, 28.March, 1631. Letter Nr.37, Inst. Arch. Munich.
39. Mary Poyntz' report of 14th April 1632. BV Rome, Barb. lat. 7054, pp.124–125.
40. On 26th November 1633. Letter Nr.104, Inst. Arch. Munich.
41. On 28th July 1631. DA Vienna, Suppressed convents, Jesuitesses.
42. Nuntius Rocci to Cardinal Francesco Barberini, 16th August, 1631. AV Rome, Nunt. di. Germ. vol. 122. ff. 286r, 289v. Praise for Rocci for assisting in the suppression of the Institute: Cardinal Francesco Barberini to Nuntius Rocci, 6.September, 1631. BV Rome, Barb. lat. 6223, f.300v.
43. HA Vienna, NO. Herrschaftsakten, Nonnenkloster der Matres de Jesu, 1627, 1632. W.61/B32.
44. On 13.October resp. 20th November 1632. ibid.
45. Arch. d. Stadt u.d. Landes Wien, Steuerbucher, Anschlagbuech des viertls Scotorum 1631, f.22r, Nr.911. A gap from 1632 to 1635 in the tax books prevented research into continuation of taxation.
46. StA Munich, Kl.434/10, ff.25rv, 26v.
47. Letter Nr.112B. Illegible correction of the year, Inst. Arch. Munich.
48. DA Vienna, Suppressed convents, Jesuitesses.
49. ibid.
50. Letter Nr.66, Inst. Arch. Munich.
51. AE Liège, Collégiale Saint-Martin 60, f.86v, resp. 61, f.19r.
52. ibid. f.95v, resp. 26v.

53. ibid. f.95v, resp. 26v – 27r.
54. On 23rd August 1631. ibid. f.96r resp. 27r.
55. ibid. f.98v. resp. 29r.
56. See p.555.
57. Letter Nr.56(1) of 13th February, Letter Nr.56 (4) of 15.February and Letter Nr.56 (10) of 19th February 1631. Inst. Arch. Munich. At that time Mary Ward could not have known that Winefrid Wigmore had also been imprisoned.
58. Letter Nr.56(7) February, ibid.
59. Letter Nr.66 to the members, ibid.
60. Letter Nr.132 ibid.
61. Letter Nr.68. before 28th March 1631. ibid. " ... to be secritt in all, all, all ... "
62. The English agent in Rome, Peter Fitton, wrote in his letter already mentioned dated 17th April 1622: "Mrs Ward is dealing in the Congregation of the Inguisition ... to get one of hers sett free, who is shut up in a monasterye in Leidg ... "
63. Nuntius Rocci from Vienna to Cardinal Antonio Barberini, 16th August 1631. AV Rome, Nunt. di. Germ. vol. 122, ff.286r, 289v.
64. StA Munich, Kl. lit. 434/10, ff.18rv. 19v.
65. ibid. HZR 1631, f.299v.
66. On 29th December 1635, ibid. Kl. lit. 434/10, ff.20r – 21v.
67. ibid. HZR 1631, f.300.
68. On 5th May 1633. ibid. Kl. lit. 434/10, ff.23r, 24v.
69. ibid. f.25rv, 26v.
70. Elector's approval, ibid. ff.27r, 28v. Express of 12th October, ff.31r, 32v. Treasury's approval. f.30rv.
71. Elector's intruction of 27th October 1634 for 50 Taler for provisions and 50 Taler cash. ibid. ff.33r, 34v. Payment on 8th November of 100 guilders for provisions and 50 guilders after a further inquiry. ibid. f.35rv.
72. Winefrid Bedingfield's thanks to the Elector in November 1635 for granting 200 guilders. ibid. ff.3rv, 4rv. Order of the Treasury on 3rd November for 100 guilders, ibid. f.38r and of 50 guilders, ibid. f.36r, 37v.
73. On 12th August, ibid. f.38r.
74. Gigli to the Elector's agent in Rome, Francesco Crivelli. Sta. Munich, Secret State Archives, Black Box, 7414, ff.422r – 423r.
75. On 29th December 1631. StA Munich, Kl. lit. 434/10, ff.20r – 21v.
76. On 10th June 1633. Treasury to Maximilian. ibid ff. 25rv, 26v.
77. Decision of the treasury, 3.November 1635. ibid. f.38r.
78. Vita E, f.42rv.
79. Letter Nr.56 (7), Inst. Arch. Munich.
80. As above, note 66.
81. StA Munich, HZR 1631, Bd.81, f.300.
82. On 15th January 1633 or thereabouts she ordered Mary Poyntz to remain in Munich until spring, so that the house should not be lost. Letter Nr.89. Inst. Arch. Munich.
83. StA Munich, Kl. lit. 434/10, ff.3 – 4v.
84. ibid. f.5rv.
85. Letter Nr.88. December 1632. Inst. Arch. Munich could indicate that.
86. On 14th April 1632. BV Rom. Barb. lat. 7054, ff.124 – 125.

XXXI

ENGLAND

The Journey

Cardinal Francesco Barberini's recommendation for Mary Ward's stay in Spa – travelling companions and route – unsuccessful negotiations with the Elector of Cologne – recommendation from Cardinal Francesco Barberini for Mary Ward to the Queen of England – Mary Ward's departure for England

Mary Ward began thinking of a journey to England soon after her release from prison.[1] Mary Poyntz, who had arrived in Rome in October 1633, was to accompany her.[2] But time dragged on, probably in negotiations about permission for the members to live in Rome and Munich and probably, too, because of the Curia's reluctance for her to leave the Papal States.[3] In any case, Mary Ward would not have been in sufficiently good health to have undertaken such a long and strenuous journey. She had not been able to leave her room[4] from 2nd–13th March, 1637, and had spent a little time in Nettuno for some fresh air. It was only in September, despite objections raised by the members in their concern for her, that she was able to leave Rome.

Except for the two oldest biographies which give several details, we have hardly any historical evidence about this last and agonising journey across Europe made by the very sick woman. We do not even know who was in the group travelling with her. It is from the recommendation of Archbishop Ascanio Piccolomini of Sienna to his brother, the Imperial Fieldmarshal, Ottavio Piccolomini,[5] that we know she had two companions and four servants. The companions, it emerges from other sources, were Mary Poyntz and Winefrid Wigmore. Anne Turner must also have been one of them. The names of the servants were not given. This time Mary Ward took few introductions with her: one for the Nuntius of Savoy in Turin, Fausto Caffarello[6] and one for the Nuntius in Paris, Giorgio Bolognetti.[7] These were issued by no less a personage than Cardinal Francesco Barberini, the most powerful of the Pope's nephews. Mary Ward therefore left Rome with valid passes and the express permission of the Pope.[8] A surprising fact is the destination, which was given as Spa. The Italian resorts could no longer help the sick woman, she had to resort to Spa, far off in the west of Europe. It would be well to remember this fact.

On 10th September, 1637, the group of travellers left Rome. Mary Ward was still so weak and in such pain that she had to be carried in a litter. To give a brief account of her state of health: during the first stretch of her journey, Mary Ward suffered severely from fever; travelling had to be interrupted for ten days in Siena. As stated, Archbishop Ascanio Piccolomini helped the travellers with recommendations to his brother Ottavio[9] in the dangerous war zone surrounding Siena. In Florence[10] she was once again forced to rest. They were the guests of the Earl of Northumberland for twelve days. In Bologna they were received by Senator Cesare Bianchetti, a friend of Mary Ward's, who was touchingly concerned about her. In the Duchy of Milan, about which both Spain and Savoy were in conflict, they had to make their way in a coach, in peril from the soldiery. This time, too, Mary Ward visited St Charles Borromeo's tomb in Milan. In the Vercelli region, the governor placed a coach at her disposal. They reached Turin on 2nd November[11] and remained there a week.[12] Although Nuntius Caffarelli invited them to stay longer, they set off on their journey in one of the coaches offered them. On 11th November, they reached the most difficult part of the journey, the crossing of the Alps. The storm was so fearful that four people died in the snow and ice. Their guide lost his way, and the travellers were saved by following the tracks of a dog. Mary Ward must have been carried in a litter across these pathless mountain ranges; she would never have survived the journey otherwise. It was only in Lyons that they allowed themselves a day of rest and then struck out for Paris. They were probably able to make use of horses here for the longer stretches, for the Italian Vita[13] supplies the information that they had been eight hours in the saddle on a rainy day, without eating anything or taking any refreshment. History does not relate why Mary Ward and her companions took this very divergent route. Perhaps it had to do with travelling money from England, which they expected to receive there. But the money had not arrived, and they had to turn to the Benedictines for help.[14] They received £50, which they repaid later. But it was not only money that was lacking. As so often before, after a long and strenuous journey, Mary Ward collapsed physically. The wintry coldness plagued her, and she suffered from kidney trouble. They remained in Paris until after 20th May, 1638.[15] Nothing is known of this stay, not even where they found accommodation, or what they lived on. Under very trying conditions,[16] sometimes using the waterways along the Meuse, they reached Charleville, Dinant and Charleroi (?)[17] and finally, at the end of May 1638, Liège.

What must have passed through Mary Ward's mind when she once again saw this city, so catastrophic for her Institute, after an

absence of seventeen years? The once flourishing community, which
had offered so much promise, was no longer there. The members
had had to leave their house in 1631 on the orders of the Chapter of
St Martin. Some few were allowed to have accommodation within
the enclosure of the Collegiate church until the spring of 1632. The
Chapter of St Martin had granted them 6 patakons as a donation
on 26th March, 1632.[18] Two members died in that same year,[19]
another in 1635.[20] There are no indications if these were still living
in the enclosure, but they did belong to the parish of St Remacle
en Mont.

Mary Ward certainly visited the graves of these unfortunate sisters
who had been provided with a burial place in the tiny cemetery of
St Remacle. It may have occurred to her then that the town of
Liège was the burial place of her Institute. Telling us more than
volumes of speculation, the English Life reports tersely that Mary
Ward withdrew for a short time to the old Benedictine Abbey of
Stavelot, (Stablo) to find peace and seclusion.

What had Mary Ward hoped to find in Liège? One cannot accept
the reason given, that she had come for the waters at Spa. Her
business-like activities disprove that. While still in Rome[21] she had
learnt how difficult matters were in Liège. That has already been
seen from various sources. It is rather to be assumed that she tried
to obtain something for the few members in Liège from Bishop
Ferdinand von Wittelsbach — such as permission for a small community, as had been allowed both in Rome and Munich. Such
efforts can be read into the few remaining sentences of an undated
letter from Mary Poyntz to Barbara Babthorpe in Munich.[22] In it
there is mention of negotiations with the Bishop who, as Elector of
Cologne, lived on the Rhine ('to be asked of ours at Leeg'). Whether
Barbara Babthorpe was summoned to Liège on this account is not
certain.[23] She was probably to try to effect it through mediating
with the sister of the Elector of Bavaria, Maximilian I. This was the
Pfalzgräfin Magdalena von der Pfalz-Neuburg. Mary Ward wrote
on the back of the letter[24] some sentences to Barbara Babthorpe,
but this merely dealt with an expected sum of money.

For the time being, Mary Ward remained in Liège.[25] When she
was able to take the waters in Spa, she was so attacked by a woman
suffering from cancer, that the cure did not have much effect. A
further stay in Spa could not help her. Her illness would have needed
other remedies, but medicine at that time knew nothing of them. On
24th September, 1638, Mary Ward received a recommendation from
Cardinal Francesco Barberini to Queen Henrietta Maria of England.
The Cardinal had issued the letter on 28th August.[26] The timing
of its delivery from Rome to Liège shows that the letter had been
sent there directly. So the Cardinal knew that Mary Ward would
be staying there. Immediately, one wonders why Mary Ward was
not handed this letter on her departure from Rome. At that time

she had been given only two letters for the Nuntius of Turin, and in Paris she received one for the journey to Spa. Only now, when she was far from her enemies in Rome, did she receive a recommendation, and that to the Queen of England. The letter is full of praise for Mary Ward: 'Before the devoted and highly-esteemed lady with her companions (ch'oltre le altre cognosciute qualità sue per la gran pietà) return to Rome, she would like to take the opportunity of seeing her country once more.'

Are we supposed to believe that the Pope's nephew would take the trouble to write to a queen, because some women wanted to see their own country again? It is not likely.

From this carefully phased recommendation it is more than likely that the Pope and his nephew knew of Mary Ward's plans for her institute in England, and, moreover, supported them.

Mary Ward thanked the Pope and the Cardinal.[27] As far as her health was concerned, she was not fit to travel to England. The cold time of year restrained her from doing so, but immediately after her business was settled (quello che vi hò da fare) in England, she would return to Rome. Mary Ward took herself first to Cologne and Bonn, to conduct some business there. She was successful and left Liège in December, 1638. But she only got as far as Antwerp before her illness and affairs in Liège prevented her from continuing her journey ('a business much importing God almighty's service'). Back in Liège, she learnt that her efforts had been in vain. Her enemies would no longer suffer any community of the members in Liège.[28]

We hold firmly to this, that neither the Pope nor Cardinal Barberini had frustrated this endeavour of hers but, on the contrary, had opened doors for her. It was far more likely to have been her adversaries, though it does not emerge clearly from the sources whether these were the Jesuits or the church authorities in Liège. Cardinal Barberini did not relax his vigilance over the resourceful Englishwoman either, as he asked the Nuntius of Cologne for information of the Jesuitesses' stay in his area. He received an unsatisfactory answer. Nuntius Martino Alfieri[29] had been in Cologne since 1634. He had done his best to effect a reconciliation between the Bishop and the city of Liège in 1636, but his attempts came to nothing, and the rebellion lasted into 1638. At that time Alfieri must have left Liège. Before he returned to Rome he went back there to take farewell of the clergy. It is hardly likely that he became closely acquainted with the few members of the Institute at that time. Rather, his answer to Cardinal Barberini contains confused information about Jesuitesses in Cologne. Of those in Liège he knew only enough to report that these lived as a community in a house, under the guidance of the Jesuits.[30] They did not wear Institute dress, nor did they do anything forbidden by the Pope. This was only partially true, for it is known that there were only a few members living in Liège, who hardly constituted a community in the generally accepted sense of the word, and who hardly received any direction worth mention from the Jesuits.

In January 1639, Mary Poyntz was in Cologne and Bonn,[31] certainly in order to have further consultations with the Elector, for which a further journey to Munich seems to have been suggested. Nothing came of it. In the second half of May, Mary Ward and her companions started on their journey to England. She had not achieved her aim in Liège.

England

1639–1645

Arrival in London – King and Parliament – papal envoys-extraordinary George Con and Carlo Rossetti – Queen Henrietta Maria – Mary Ward in London: activities and plans – her correspondence with the Pope and Cardinal Francesco Barberini

On 20th May, 1639, Mary Ward trod on English soil[32] for the first time for more than twenty years. Memories must have flooded back: of her youth, of the growth of her vocation and her hard struggle for recognition of her Institute, whose work was so closely bound into the history of her country. But much had changed in England and in herself, too. She was now an aging, delicate woman of fifty-four, matured by many disappointments and personal attacks, by self-abnegation and a whole-hearted commitment to the Institute, but above all by prayer and union with God.

Her prolonged stay abroad had sharpened and at the same time shadowed her awareness of the changes in her homeland. She would have noticed many of these, though possibly not read them correctly, as she had not shared the experiences that had brought them about. Mary Ward had left England soon after the Gunpowder Plot when the populace, whether Anglican, Lutheran or Puritan, stood solidly behind the King when it came to taking action against 'Papists'. Things were different now, politically, with Parliament. Under Elizabeth I, Parliament had been malleable. The Queen held a sumptuous court but managed a thrify national budget. Politically extremely adroit, she had an infallible sense of how to guide the country in an apparently sure-footed direction during its confrontation with the floundering might of Spain.

Her successor James I, on the other hand, was extravagant and surrounded by flatterers. He swerved from previous foreign policy by making peace with Spain, and even allowing his son to seek the hand of the Infanta Maria Anna. This roused the ill-will of his people. Towards the end of his life, James I came into conflict with Parliament. He regarded the rights of the House as a royal privilege, not as based on the freedom of his subjects. When these finally protested, he dissolved Parliament. It was first and foremost a matter of principle, which the king was unable to settle before his death.

His son and heir Charles I was rejected as a suitor in Spain, and shortly afterwards married Henrietta Maria of France. A pre-condition of the marriage contract of this future Queen of England was that she should be free to practice her catholicism. On his succession, Charles I inherited the outspoken opposition of Parliament, as well as the religious opposition of his people, who had to look on while their king drew closer to the 'Papists', under his wife's influence. Queen Henrietta Maria was not only a practising catholic but a protector of those who had remained loyal to the Roman Church. Soon, Mass was not only offered in the Catholic Embassy chapels but also in several houses in England. With regard to religion, England was no longer a unity, but those places of 'papistical gatherings' were regarded as undesirable alien elements in the capital. Things came to a head between Charles I and his Parliament at the beginning of his reign. The members of Parliament demanded first and foremost the implementation of the old recusant laws, and this, after a concession about taxes for a limited time, led again to the dissolution of the session. Charles I reigned as his father had done until his death, without a Parliament, from 1629. In the long term, this was a dangerous position for the king of a country which could boast the oldest Parliament in Europe. As regards Church policy, the king favoured the Anglicans. Many of his opponents were Puritans, and followers of democratic principles. The king's attempt to enforce his absolute ecclesial sovereignty on Scotland also met with bitter opposition. These difficulties, and the king's struggle with Parliament in London led eventually to Civil War.

When Mary Ward entered London, the Scottish priest George Con was the Pope's special envoy to the Queen. The king was friendly towards him and liked to talk with him, without wishing to draw any nearer to Rome.

Mary Ward praised the envoy. She reported to Rome[33] that everyone recognized his zeal and he was even praised by the Huguenots (delli Hegenotti) and highly esteemed. It does not need to be emphasized that this was her own subjective opinion. On 9th September, 1639 George Con left England. His successor, Carlo Rossetti, had already arrived in London on 28th August. Soon after his arrival[34] he paid Mary Ward a visit and gave her a letter from Cardinal Barberini. She had been recommended in Rome by Donna Costanza. The new envoy's stay in England was of short duration. Attacks on his life, and fear of arson forced him to seek refuge in the Queen's Palace. He left England at her request. The Pope transferred him to Cologne in 1651. Mary Ward worked with both envoys for the catholics[35] but she refused to become involved in their affairs.[36]

It is not really possible to learn of the Queen's attitude to Mary Ward. In his letter of lst July, 1639[37] to Cardinal Barberini, Con wrote that Mary Ward wished to have an audience with the Queen. She would be granted admission, though the Queen did not lay much value on her visit. A fresh introduction from Cardinal Barberini was acknowledged by Henrietta Maria, but only in courtly terms.[38]

Mary Ward kept in touch with the papal Curia. A few weeks after her arrival,[39] she wrote to Cardinal Barberini that she had come to London ill, but that the Queen had received the Cardinal's recommendation positively. She did not wish to write to him about the war and the brief peace (between Charles I and Scotland). The Cardinal would have better informants. The postal service was bad and dangerous. It was on 20th August, 1639[40] only, that Cardinal Barberini answered Mary Ward's first letter from England; this she received on a visit to the new envoy-extraordinary Rossetti in the second half of September. As far as one can see, Mary Ward wrote again to the Cardinal in February, 1640.[41] It was to be her last letter to Francesco Barberini.

Again, one would like to ask 'What did Mary Ward want in England? Even if homesickness is not excluded — and she never lost it — it must not be assumed that private reasons influenced her to return. Mary Ward lived God's commission to her, her Institute. Cardinal Barberini's recommendation to the Queen precludes secondary reasons, surely. It is unknown where she stayed in London, though it was probably in a house close to the French Embassy, or in Somerset House, the Queen's wedding gift.[42] Such a place would have offered the opportunity of Mass and communication with those catholics living in London. The English Life says: she received priests who could carry out their dangerous tasks only secretly and in disguise. She was also asked to receive distinguished young girls in her house, but she granted admission to children without means, too. So, despite all the danger, she possessed a large 'family'.[43] Mary Ward wrote to the members in Rome[44] that she would like to establish an elementary school. She added, however, that she thought it would never happen without a miracle for, apart from the ungrateful nature of the people, this plan could only be effected with prayer and personal zeal. But in her enthusiasm she gave the name of members in Rome who could be used in such an enterprise: Kate (Catherine Dawson?), who had to perfect her knowledge of Latin and Italian, Elizabeth (Babthorpe?) and one known only as Clare. A chapel was to be set up in the house, the beauty of which would put their calumniators and mockers to silence. For that, those members coming to London could bring the necessary vestments and books of devotion needed, as these were unobtainable in England. This shows that although she had been flatly rejected in Liège, she was once again trying to establish her Institute. That this attempt of hers was approved by the Pope can be seen from the secrecy about the real destination of her journey, which Urban VIII and his nephew did not reveal when she was leaving Rome.

Mary Ward did not intend to stay long in England. On 29th July, 1639[45] George Con told Cardinal Barberini that she was returning to Rome, for England no longer pleased her. This should not be accepted uncritically – it probably meant that Mary Ward did not have too much confidence in the discretion of those about her. She had many enemies in England, and not only among those who did not share her religious faith.[46] Barely a year later[47] the Queen wrote to the Cardinal of Mary Ward's longing for Rome, but that she was ill and could not leave England. Also, her work was needed by many people in London. The real reason Mary Ward wanted to leave England can be learnt from her own letters. She was still not well, she wrote to Cardinal Barberini on 14th February, 1640.[48] This was why she had not returned to Rome – 'mio centro' – the previous autumn, but that she would do so in the coming year, whether she was ill or not.

On the same day[49] she wrote to the Pope that she knew she would rather be close to him than here in her own country among her own relations (probably the members of the Institute). In Rome, she hoped she would one day receive a favour from the Pope which had been withheld from her until now. She continued, diffidently, that she did not wish to abuse the Pope' goodness, and make a request of which he could not approve. She asked forgiveness for her boldness.

By this hoped-for favour she undoubtedly referred to confirmation for her Institute, tolerated once more in Rome, Munich and England. Once again she hints, with these words, to an Institute whose 'matter and manner' she could not and would not be allowed to alter.

The End

1642 – 1645

Departure from London – travel to York – Hutton Rudby – Mount Grace – Civil Ward in north England – Heworth – York – the last days – death

The conflict between King and Parliament intensified. At the beginning of 1642 the capital turned against the King and placed armed guards round Parliament as a protection. Charles I left London for the North, to raise troops against the rebels (January, 1642). England was thus split into two camps — in the north, the nobles and anglicans stood by the King, in the south the citizens and puritans supported Parliament. Some months later the members of the Institute also left the capital, which had become unsafe. On 30th April, 1642[50] Mary Ward wrote her last letter to the community in Rome; it was addressed to Elizabeth Keyes. Constant house-searches, she said, had thrown everything into confusion. They were to leave London the next day (lst May, 1642). The archpriest and other fathers were with them at table. The priests came to her in droves. And then 'I am ill, but this is my worst day.'[51] Deep sadness lies in these hastily scribbled words. Urban VIII cannot be blamed for the fact that her wish to establish a new centre for her Institute in London remained unfulfilled. This was caused by the events in her own country, for England was just then tottering on the brink of an abyss.

There is no record of their journey. In three coaches and guarded by four men,[52] the women set out for the north, towards Ripon. The whole of England had become dangerous on account of the armies and skirmishes. The names of those who travelled with her are not recorded, though it emerges that Mary Poyntz and Winefrid Wigmore also went north. Perhaps Catherine Smith too, and Frances Bedingfield. Anne Turner would certainly have been there. Little is known, too, of those who stayed on in London, how many they were, or if some of them were active and scattered about the country.

It was a long journey, and it can be assumed that the small group often had to take cover. They must also have had to change their route. A long time was spent in the neighbourhood of Mary Ward's home, at Newby and Ripley castle[53] where old acquaintances still remembered her as a young girl and spoke of her father with great affection.

It was only after four and a half months, on 14th September, 1642, that they reached Hutton Rudby[54] where Mary Ward was able to rent an old house. Situated among the Cleveland hills, it offered the relative security of a retired spot. The house had belonged to the Carthusians of Mount Grace before the dissolution of the monasteries, and during these times it was in the possession of the Ingleby family. Mary Ward immediately arranged a room as a chapel where the Blessed Sacrament could be kept. The journey had taken its toll of Mary Ward. In October some of the members went on pilgrimage to the ruined chapel of Mount Grace.[55] The sick woman recovered and made a pilgrimage herself to this neighbouring shrine. Even the peace of their isolated house was destroyed[56] when Cromwell's soldiers approached, but the women came to no harm by some miracle. One of the soldiers even brought back twenty shillings which he had been given. From the 18th January, 1643, Mary Ward introduced a form of general prayer, placing her house under the protection of the nine choirs of angels. All her life she showed great confidence in the angels.

The remoteness of the house had one great disadvantage – Mary Ward could get neither post nor news from the members in London, let alone from Rome. Because of this, and probably for reasons of greater security, at the beginning of 1643 they moved to Heworth, at that time a village just outside York. The house belonged to the Thwing family.[57] Mass was offered daily in Mary Ward's room, for she was concealing two priests in her house. There were often three or five priests who met there. As long as her health permitted, Mary Ward received those who were oppressed or grieving, and offered them consolation. Her stay in Heworth was not as undisturbed as it had been in Hutton Rudby.

For the sake of the context, it is necessary to give a brief overview of the situation in England. At first, Charls I's position had not been unfavourable. His troops won at Worcester, and the Battle of Edgehill was indecisive. Even an attack on London was successful, but the King was not able to take the capital. He had to withdraw to Oxford. It was only when the Scots allied themselves to Parliament that his hopes of victory became doubtful. The King's troops now found themselves confronted by the rebels in the south, and the invading Scots in the north. The Battle of Marston Moor near York on 2nd July, 1644 sealed the fate of the north, as Cromwell gained the victory over the Cavaliers. The siege of York, which was taken by Cromwell on 11th July, 1644 was experienced by the members of the Institute who were living inside its protective walls.[58] Only one who has shared the horrors of a bombardment can know what dangers and terrors faced the people of York, among them, members of the Institute. Their rapid departure from Heworth had left their well-appointed house open to the beseiging soldiers. After the surrender of the city, when they returned to Heworth, they found that the house had been plundered and was without doors or windows. Four hundred soldiers, some wounded among them, had been quartered there. In the devastated garden the survivors had hastily buried their dead comrades. There was a threat of the plague, for the city did not even have three wells of water.

Since 26th July it had no longer been possible for the women to have a priest. Even letters from the south no longer reached the sealed-off north. The front lay in between.

Mary Ward celebrated Christmas with great devotion, and for the last time in her life received communion. The priest declined to give her extreme unction, ignorant of the real state of her health. At that time, and in that situation, she was drawing close to death. Her last days and her actual death are best described in

Mary Poyntz' loving words.[59] Its details cannot be replaced by a summary.

'On the 20th January, 1645[60] at eleven o'clock or thereabouts, our dearest mother departed this toilsome life at the age of sixty years and eight days. Truly, that I live to write it to you is through no strength of my own. She began to lose strength on All Saint's Day; towards Christmas complained of great pain. She grew feebler and was unable to find relief or rest, and seemed to long for that sweet repose which I am sure, through God's mercy, she is now enjoying. It was out of love for Ours, whom she loved above everything except God's will, that she was willing to do everything both by prayer and medicines, to prolong life. I do not think my pen could begin to express the least part of that love, which truly all the pens in the world can never do.

'On 28th December, she took to her bed and I perceived that her kidneys were swollen like a great roll. The whole of the lower part of her body was swollen. She was not able to move her legs without help, nor to put on a piece of clothing, which was never the case with her, even in the worst illnesses. Winefrid Wigmore came home only on 13th January. What was lacking then,[61] added to her sufferings, as you will hear when we meet. There was a great change in her condition on 15th; she was in dead agony. I asked her often where the pain was. She answered 'from head to foot'. She had pitifully sore eyes and her throat was greatly swollen, but we saw that after her death only. Yet her sweet, serene look never changed. Her expression remained half serious, half in jest. Ned said 'If you die, we will take pack and away to the heathen.' She answered, 'If I thought so, it would break my heart'.[62] On other occasions she gave us to understand how much it would express her children's love to take her death well, and show our love by continuing our way of life. She promised to pray for us to the Lord. Winefrid begged her to ask God for her own life. She made a sign she would. She had difficulty in speaking. Again Winefrid asked if she had done it. She answered: 'Yes, entirely, and most resignedly.' We now think that she had a greater knowledge of her death than her tender love for us permitted her to show, so as not to made us sad.

On 19th, in order not to make it a burden for us, she said: 'the chief business is neglected, to wit, a silver pin' (a priest). We agreed, although with heart breaking, and the next morning it was concluded that one should be sent for, and they are dear things and not to be had easily. That was a bitter night, sometimes she was as it were out of herself with pain and agony, but whenever she spoke showed perfect memory and understanding. About seven o'clock she desired us all to be present. Winefrid said we were all there. She replied with great feeling, 'I would you all were!' Then she said, 'I had resolved to speak of other things than I am now able. I refrained, not to make you sad, as also not to send for the priest in time.' She said that was the greatest thing she had offended God in, and through God's mercy it was the only thing that now troubled her. She wanted us to ask pardon for her, and that we should pardon her. Then she commended, with greatest feeling, the practice of God's vocation in us, that it be constant, efficacious and affectionate. She said 'God will assist and help you, where or through whom, is no matter. And when God shall enable me to be in place, I will serve you.' Then, with greatest love embracing each, seemed to mind us no more, but with eyes and hands gave signs of sweet, interior acts. She gave us to understand that she felt great heat, but would take no refreshment except water. She never sighed, groaned, nor rattled, nor sweated, never turned her eye nor writhed her mouth, only inclined her head.'

From Monday to Wednesday, her body was laid out as was the custom. The swellings diminished twenty-four hours after her death. The veins in her temples, hands, arms and feet were a lovely blue, as if they had been painted. Her lips were slightly red, as during her life-time. Except for the coldness, there was no sign of death.

Her coffin could not be lined for several reasons, but it was of good wood.

She was laid to rest in English earth, in the cemetery of the small church of Osbaldwick near Heworth. On her tombstone unskilled hands had chiselled the inscripion:

> To love the poor,
> persevere in the same,
> live die and rise with them
> was all the aim of
> Mary Ward
> who lived 60 years and eight days
> and died on 20th January, 1645 *

*old style — new style 30th January.

Only a few of her powerful benefactors survived Mary Ward. Thomas Sackville — a questionable friend at best — died in 1646; Bishop Ferdinand of Liège, 1650 and Emperor Maximilian I of Bavaria in 1651.

The number of her enemies was greater: in 1649 Francesco Ingoli died; the three Nuntios, who had done so much damage to her Institute, died one after another: Pallotto in 1651, Lagonissa in 1653 and Pierluigi Carafa in 1655. Her bitterest enemy in Belgium, Fr Henry Silisdon SJ, died in 1659.

And yet, out of the ruins there sprang life. In 1635, the two remaining members in Munich received the Elector's permission to teach as seculars in the Paradeiser House, and he supported them, often financially. From this nucleus there developed, in the course of almost 400 years, an Institute that was approved in 1877 by Pius IX, and which now extends over four continents. Teaching and education was, almost exclusively, the work of the Institute in Europe. It is only since the Second Vatican Council that the 'matter and manner' with which Mary Ward was entrusted in 1611 has been gradually realized.

Notes

1.   See p.589.
2.   Mary Poyntz to Winefrid Bedingfield, October 1635, Letter Nr. 123(a).
3.   Vita E, f.56rv, stresses the Pope's anxiety for Mary Ward's health. Other sources place justifiable doubt on this interpretation.
4.   Vita E, f.55rf.
5.   Of 28th August, 1637. Copy in StA Munich, Kl. lit. 432/1–3, f.29v.
6.   Of 9th September 1637, ibid. f.29r.
7.   ibid.
8.   Vita E, f.57r; Vita I, p.38.
9.   See above, note 5.
10. Vita E, f.57vff; Vita I, p.38ff.
11. Vita E, f.59r, gives 3rd November as day of departure from Turin, Nuntius Carafa on 9.November. Caffarelli to Cardinal Francesco Barberini, 9.November 1637. AV Rome, Nunz.di Savoia, vol. 58 ff.741r, 742v.
12. Vita E, f.58r ff; Vita I, p.39, more briefly.
13. Vita I, p.39.
14. Report from Fr Aemilian OSB, Douay Abbey, England, Council Book, 17th December, 1637.
15. Vita E, f.59r; Vita I p.39.
16. Vita E, f.59v ff; Vita I, p.40.
17. Vita E, f.59v, names a certain Charlemont, which is unknown in Belgium. Perhaps Charleroi was meant, which is further west than the route taken.
18. AE Liège, Collégiale Saint-Martin, 60, f.103r; 61, f.38r.
19. ibid. Registres Parroissiaux Liège, Église Saint-Remacle en Mont, Décès 234, f.91v. Before 22nd August.
20. ibid. f.92r.
21. Letter Nr.97 of 10th September 1633 to Mary Poyntz in Munich. Inst. Arch. Munich.
22. Letter Nr.127 (a) is undated but belongs to this time. Inst. Arch. Munich.
23. The words: "If you can stay till you have further advise it will be best" could suggest this.
24. Letter Nr.127 (b). Inst. Arch. Munich.
25. The reason given by Vita E, f.60v, that the season was not favourable for a cure, is not acceptable. Mary Ward arrived in Liège in May.
26. Copy in Inst. Arch. Munich.
27. On 19th November 1638 in Liège. BV Rome, Barb. lat 8626, ff.59r, 62v, resp. 60rv, 61v.
28. " ... but in her absence there was found who employed themselves to putt all backe." Vita E, f.62r.
29. As successor to Pierluigi Carafa in Cologne. Alfieri was recalled and died in 1641 near Naples. Hier. Cath. IV. p.171 and 210.
30. cf. the correspondence between Cardinal Francesco Barberini and Nuntius Alfieri. BV Rome, Barb. lat. 6761, ff.141r, 153v; 166r, 173v; 195r, 203v; 206r–207v; Barb. lat. 6762, ff.102r, 103v; 161r–163v; 164v, and AV Rom. Arch. Segreto di Stato, Colonia 19, ff.19v; 10rv; 15v–16r; 16r–17v; 30rv; 32v–35v.
31. Mary Ward to Mary Poyntz in Bonn, 4th February, 1639. Letter Nr.129, Inst. Arch. Munich.

32. Vita E, f.63 (a); Vita I, p.42.
33. On 28th June 1639, Copy in PRO London, General Series 92 (5) Barberini.
34. Rossetti to Cardinal Barberini, 23rd September 1639, PRO London, Roman Transcripts 31/9/18, pp.19–21.
35. Mary Ward to Cardinal Barberini, as above note 32, and to the Institute members in Rome, (1639). Letter Nr.130, Inst. Arch. Munich.
36. George Con to Cardinal Barberini, 29th July 1639. AV Rome, Nunt. d'Inghilterra, vol.7, ff.271v–272r.
37. BV Rome, Barb. lat. 8644, f.304v.
38. (June) 1640. BV Rome, Barb. lat. 8615, ff.145r–146v.
39. As above, note 33.
40. BV Rome, Barb. lat. 8620, f.65r.
41. On 14th February, 1640. ibid. ff.67r–68v.
42. Chambers E II, p.458; D II, p.382–383.
43. Vita E, f.64r.
44. (1639) Letter Nr.130, Inst. Arch. Munich. " ... that we may have coman scools in the great citty of London, which will neiver be without miracle but all els wilbe to little purpose the ungratfull nature of thes people considered ..."
45. As above, note 36. "La buona Signora brama d'essere in Roma, non riuscendo l'Inghilterra à suo gusto ..."
46. George Con to Cardinal Barberini, as above, note 37. and Vita E f.63r.
47. As above, note 38. "Elle a grand désir de retourner à Rome ..."
48. As above, note 41. " ... qual'indispositione m'ha anche impedito di mettermi quest'autunno in viaggio verso Roma mio centro ..."
49. BV Rom. Barb. lat. 8620, ff.66rv, 69v.
50. Letter Nr.131, Inst. Arch. Munich.
51. "I am il but this ys my worst day."
52. Vita E, f.64v.
53. Vita E, f.2r.
54. Vita E, f.65r.
55. ibid. The altar was dedicated to Our Lady, mother of Grace. The chapel was restored many years later.
56. Vita E, f.66rv.
57. The owner was married to a sister of Sir Thomas Gascoigne. He was therefore remotely related to Mary Ward. Chambers E II, p.483; D II, p.403.
58. The following events have been taken from the English Vita, ff.68r ff.
59. 24th January, old style. Probably addressed to the members in London. Copy in Inst. Arch. Munich. The events are also described somewhat differently in Vita E, f.71v ff., in Vita I, p.46 ff and also in all the biographies. We have decoded the text.
60. Old style, according to the new calendar on 30.January.
61. Winefrid Wigmore had gone south under dangerous conditions in order to gain news or fetch letters for the members. She returned to Heworth without them.
62. Mary Ward understood these remarks as an evasion of difficulties.

APPENDIX

Formula Instituti Societas Iesu (1550)

The text was taken from the 'Constitutiones Societatis Iesu', Rome 1937, p.XXIII-XXXIII. Differences on account of sex have been shown by italic script. Variations in the Englishwomen's 'Institutum' (BV Fondo Capponi 47,ff.56v-62r) are entered as footnotes.

Quicumque in Societate nostra, quam Iesu nomine *insigniri*[a] cupimus, vult sub crucis vexillo Deo militare, et soli Domino ac Ecclesiae Ipsius sponsae, sub Romano Pontifice, Christi in terris Vicario, servire, post sollemne perpetuae castitatis, paupertatis et oboedientiae votum, proponat sibi in animo se partem esse Societatis, ad hoc potissimum institutae ut ad fidei defensionem et propagationem, et profectum animarum in vita et doctrina christiana,

iuvando, ut ab haeresi et mala vita ad fidem et pietatem ac praecipuam quandam obedientiam erga Sedem Apostolicam reducantur, colligendo et disponendo populum

per ad

publicas praedicationes, lectiones et aliud quodcumque verbi Dei ministerium ac Spiritualia Exercita, *puerorum*[b] ac rudium in christianismo institutionem,

docendo Catechismum et reverendum usum rerum sacrarum ac dando illis eam educationem in scholis et convictoriis, quae videbitur maxime idonea ad commune bonum Ecclesiae et ipsarum particulare sive in saeculo vitam degere, sive in religione elegerint, atque demum ad spiritualem consolationem

a) *designari*   b) *puellarum*

615

Christi fidelium, in Confessionibus audiendis ac ceteris Sacramentis administrandis, spiritualem consolationem praecipue intendat;

Christi fidelium adducendo et disponendo tales ad confessionem et alia sacramenta, et procurando praedicatores Patresque spirituales in villas mitti et loca incultiora, tum exquirendo perditae vitae mulieres, illasque praeparando ad recipiendum gratiam per sacramenta, ut doctores, praedicatores, et viri apostolici Ecclesiae Dei plus otii habere possint, ut rebus maioribus et magis universalibus attendant,

et nihilominus ad dissidentium reconciliationem et eorum qui in carceribus vel in hospitalibus inveniuntur, piam subventionem et ministerium, ac reliqua caritatis opera, prout ad Dei gloriam et commune bonum expedire visum erit, exsequenda, gratis omnino et nullo, pro suo in praedictis omnibus labore, stipendio accepto, se utilem exhibeat; curetque primo Deum, deinde huius sui Instituti rationem, quae via quaedam est ad Illum, quoad vixerit, ante oculos habere, et finem hunc sibi a Deo propositum totis viribus assequi, un*us*quisque tamen secundum gratiam sibi a Spiritu Sancto subministratam et vocationis suae proprium gradum. Ideoque, ne *quis* forte zelo utatur, sed non secundum scientiam, proprii cuiusque gradus iudicium, et officiorum discretio ac distributio tota sit in manu Praeposit*i* Generalis seu Praelat*i* per nos quocumque tempore eligend*i*, vel e*o*rum qu*os* ips*e* sibi ea cum auctoritate substituerit, ut congruus order servetur, in omni bene instituta communitate necessarius; qu*i* quidem Praeposit*us*, de consilio consoci*o*rum, Constitutiones ad constructionem huius propositi nobis finis conducentes condendi,[c] maiori suffragiorum parte semper statuendi ius habente, et quae dubia esse poterunt in nostro Instituto, hac Formula comprehenso, declarandi auctoritatem habeat. Consilium vero necessario convocandum ad condendas vel immutandas Constitutiones, et alia graviora, ut alienare vel dissolvere Domos ac Collegia semel erecta, intellegatur esse maior pars totius Professae Societatis (iuxta Constitutionum nostrarum declarationem) quae sine magno incommodo potest a Praeposit*o* Generali convocari. In aliis, quae non ita magni momenti sunt, *i*dem Praeposit*us* adiut*us*, quatenus ips*e* opportunum iudicabit, fratrum[d] s*u*orum concilio, per seips*um* ordinandi et iubendi, quae ad Dei gloriam et commune bonum pertinere in Domino videbuntur, ius totum habeat, prout in Constitutionibus eisd*em* explicabitur. Qu*i*cumque autem in hac Societate professionem emiserint, non solum in primis professionis

c) *fundandi*   d) *sororum*

suae foribus intellegant, sed, quoad vixerint, memores sint, Societatem hanc universam et singulos, qu*i* in ea profitentur, sub Sanctissimi Domini nostri Pauli Papae III[e] et aliorum Romanorum Pontificum successorum eius fideli oboedientia, Deo militare. Et quamvis Evangelio doceamu*r*, et fide orthodoxa cognoscamus, ac firmiter teneamus omnes Christi fideles Romano Pontifici, tamquam Capiti ac Iesu Christi Vicario, subesse; ob devotionem tamen maiorem ad oboedientiam Sedis Apostolicae, et maiorem voluntatum nostrarum abnegationem, et certiorem Sancti Spiritus directionem, summopere conducere iudicavimus, singul*o*s nos, et qu*i*cumque eandem in posterum professionem emiserint, ultra illud commune trium votorum vinculum, spaeciali ad hoc voto adstringi, ut quidquid modernus et alii Romani Pontifices, pro tempore exsistentes, iusserint ad profectum animarum et fidei propagationem pertinens, et ad quascumque provincias nos mittere voluerint, sine ulla tergiversatione aut excusatione illico, quantum in nobis fuerit,[f] sive nos ad Turcos, sive ad quoscumque alios infideles, etiam in partibus quas Indias vocant, sive ad quoscumque haereticos, schismaticos, seu etiam ad quosvis fideles mittend*o*s censuerint, exsequi teneamur.

Et quia tum ratio tum experientia docet, eas communitates uberiores a Deo Creatore ac Domino nostro benedictiones accipere et universali bono catholico fructuosiores fieri, quae immediate a sola Sede Apostolica tantum pendentes, a Deo ipso proprius pendent, et certiori affluentiorique ratione gratiosae ipsius influentiae radios hauriunt; idcirco a nobis humillime exoptatur, ut tota operis huius hierarchia omnino a Sanctissima tantum Sede pendeat et non ab alia et inde in suam supremam Superiorem pro reliquo corpore lumen et motum omnem accipiat, minime dubitans, quin Deus loquatur in sancto suo et per eum ad maiorem suum honorem et gloriam illam sit gubernaturus; quemadmodum hactenus iam per tot annus fecit, sine ulla

e) *quinti.* f) *added: et predens ipsius charitas expedire iudicabit*

perticulari ab ordinariis
dependentia per specialem
superintendentiam aut curam.

Quamobrem qu*i* ad nos accessur*i* sunt, antequam huic oneri umeros supponant, diu multumque meditentur an tantum pecuniae spiritualis in bonis habeant ut turrim hanc iuxta consilium Dominicum possint consummare; hoc est, an Spiritus Sanctus, qui ill*o*s impellit, tantum illis gratiae polliceatur ut huius vocationis pondus, Illo adiuvante, se latur*o*s sperent; et postquam, Domino inspirante, huic Iesu Christi militiae nomen dederint, die noctuque succincti lumbos, et ad tam grandis debiti solutionem prompt*i* esse debebunt. Ne qua autem possit esse inter nos missionum aut provinciarum huiusmodi ambitio vel detrectatio, intellegant singul*i*, sibi, per se vel alium, de huiusmodi missionibus quidquam cum Romano Pontifice non esse curandum, sed omnem hanc curam Deo, et ipsi Pontifici, tamquam Eius Vicario, et Societatis Praeposit*o* dimittendam; cui quidem Praeposit*o* sicut ceteris, nihil de su*i*, ipsius missione in alterutram partem, nisi de Societatis[g)] consilio, cum dicto Pontifice curandum erit. Voveant etiam singuli se in omnibus, quae ad Regulae huius nostrae observationem faciunt, Societatis[h)] Praeposit*o* (qu*i* ad hoc munus, quam fieri possit idon*eus*, ad plura vota, prout in Constitutionibus declarabitur, eligetur) oboedientes fore. Ill*e* autem omnem eam auctoritatem et potestatem habeat supra Societatem,[i)] quae ad bonam eiusdem Societatis administrationem, correctionem et gubernationem utilis erit. Iubeat autem ea quae ad constructionem proposit sibi a Deo et a Societate[j)] finis cognoverit esse opportuna; et in praelatione sua benignitatis ac mansuetudinis caritatisque Christi, Petri Paulique formulae semper sit memor; et tam ips*e* quam Consilium praedictum ad normam hanc assidue spectent. Singul*i* vero subdit*o*rum, tum propter ingentes ordinis utilitates, tum propter numquam satis laudatum humilitatis assiduum exercitium, non solum Praeposit*o*, in omnibus ad Institutum Societatis[k)] perti-nentibus, parere semper teneantur; sed in ill*o* Christum veluti praesentem agnoscant, et, quantum decet, venerentur.

Cum autem expert*i* fuerimus iucundiorem, puriorem et ad proximi aedificationem aptiorem esse vitam, ab omni avaritiae contagione quam remotissimam et evangelicae paupertati quam simillimam; cumque sciamus Dominum nostrum Iesum Christum servis suis, regnum Dei solum inquirentibus, necessaria ad victum et vestitutum esse subministraturum, sic voveant singul*i* et univers*i* perpetuam paupertatem ut non sulum privatim, sed neque etiam communiter possint Profess*i*, vel ulla e*o*rum Domus aut ecclesia, ad aliquos proventus, reditus, possessiones, sed neque ad ulla bona stabilia,

---

g) huius Societatis   h) g)   i) *hanc Societatem*   j) *ab hac Societate*   k) *as* g)

praeter ea, quae opportuna erunt ad usum proprium et habitationem, retinenda, ius aliquod civile acquirere, rebus sibi ex caritate donatis ad necessarium vitae usum content*i*.

Quia tamen Domus, quas Dominus dederit, ad operandum in vinea Ipsius, et non ad scholastica studia exercenda destinandae erunt; cum valde opportunum fore alioqui videatur ut ex iuvenibus, ad pietatem propensis et ad litterarum studia tractanda idoneis, operari*i* eidem vineae Domini parentur, qu*i* Societatis nostrae, etiam Professae, velut quoddam seminarium exsistant, possit Professa[l] Societas, ad studiorum commoditatem, Scholarium habere Collegia, ubicumque ad ea construenda et dotanda ex devotione aliqui movebuntur; quae simul atque constructa et dotata fuerint (non tamen ex bonis quorum collatio ad Sedem Apostolicam pertinet), ex nunc Auctoritate Apostolica erigi supplicamus seu pro erectis haberi; quae Collegia possint habere reditus, census seu possessiones, usibus et necessitatibus Studentium applicandas, retenta penes Praeposit*um* vel Societatem omnimoda gubernatione seu superintendentia super dicta Collegia et praedict*os* Studentes, quoad Rect*orum* seu Gubernat*orum*, ac Studentium electionem, ac e*orum*dem admissionem, emissionem, receptionem, exclusionem, statutorum ordinationem, et circa Studentium instructionem, eruditionem, aedificationem ac correctionem, victus vestitutsque et aliarum rerum necessariarum eis ministrandarum modum, atque aliam omnimodam gubernationem, regimen ac curam, ut neque Studentes dictis bonis abuti, neque Societas[m] Professa in proprios usus convertere possit, sed Studentium necessitati subvenire. Qu*i* quidem Studentes, ingenii et morum indole, tales esse debebunt ut merito speretur, post absoluta studia, ad Societatis[n] functiones idone*os* fore, et sic demum, post cognitum in spiritu et litteris e*orum* profectum, et post sufficientem probationem, in Societatem nostram admitti possint.

Socii autem omnes cum Presbyteri esse debeant,	*Et omnwa Sociae, quae ad ulteriorem gradum admittuntur quam ad res temporales expendiendas,*

ad dicendem officium secundum communem Ecclesiae ritum, sed privatim, et non communiter vel in choro, teneantur; et in *i*is, quae ad victim et vestitum et cetera exteriora pertinent,

honestorum Sacerdotum	honest*arum* *matronarum*

communem et approbatum usum sequantur, ut quod inde, pro cuiusque necessitate vel spiritualis profectus desiderio, subtractum fuerit, ex devotione et non ex obligatione, rationabile obsequium corporis Deo, prout expediet, offeratur.

Haec sunt, quae sub praefati Domini nostri Pauli et Sedis Apostolicae beneplacito, de nostra professione typo quodam explicare potuimus; quod nunc fecimus, ut summatim informaremus turn illos qui nos de

---

l) *haec Peofessa*   m) *haec Societas*   n) as g)

nostro vitae Instituto interrogant, tum etiam posteros nostros, si quos, Deo volente, imitatores umquam habebimus huis viae. Quam cum multas magnasque habere annexas difficultates fuerimus experti, opportunum iudicavimus etiam statuere ne quis ad professionem in hac Societate emittendam nisi duiturnis et diligentissimis probationibus (prout in Constitionibus declarabitur), eius vita et doctrina explorata fuerit, recipiatur; quia revera hoc Institutum omnino humiles et prudentes in Christo, et in christianae vitae puritate ac litteris conspicuos exigit. Immo et *ii* qui in Coadiutores, tam in spiritualibus quam in corporalibus, et in Scholares admittentur, quorum utrique, post sufficientes probationes et tempus in Constitutionibus expressum, vota sua ad devotionem et meritum maius, non quidem sollemnia (praeter aliquos, qui de licentia Praepositi Generalis, propter ipsorum devotionem et personarum qualitatem, tria vota huiusmodi sollemnia facere poterunt), sed quibus teneantur quamdiu Praepositus Generalis in Societate[o] eos retinendos esse censuerit, emittere debeant (prout in Constituitionibus latius explicabitur), non nisi diligenter examinati et idonei reperti ad eundem finem Societatis,[p] admittantur ad hanc Iesu Christi militiam: qui tenuibus coeptis nostris favere dignetur ad gloriam Dei Patris.

Cui soli sit semper decus et honor in saecula. Amen.

o) as j)   p) as g)

ABBREVIATIONS

AB	Autobiographical sketches: Mary Ward
ADB	Allgemeine Deutsche Biographie
AE	Archives de l'Etat de Liège
AG	Archivo General
AGR	Archives Générales du Royaume de Belgique
AM	Archives Municipales
APF	Archivio della S.Congregazione de Propaganda Fide
AStW	Archiv der Stadt und des Landes Wien
AV	Archivio Segreto Vaticano
ARSI	Archivium Romanum Societatis Jesu
BNB	Biographie Nationale de Belgique
BCasR	Biblioteca Casanatense, Roma
BU	University Library
BV	Biblioteca Apostolica Vaticana
Chambers D	Chambers, German edition, see writings
Chambers E	Chambers, English edition, see writings
CRS	Catholic Record Society
DA	Diocesan Archives,
DNB	Dictionary of National Biography
EPCI	English Poor Clares
HA	Hofkammerarchiv, Vienna
Hier.Cath.	Hierarchia Catholica
HMC	Historical Manuscripts Commission
HZR	Hofzahlamtsrechnungen
LThK	Lexikon for Theology and Church
LR	Liber Ruber
MOL	Magyar Országos Levéltár (Hungarian State Archives)
PB	Parchment Book
PEA	Papiers d'État et de l'Audience
PL	Painted Life
PRO	Public Record Office
SLAL	Sheepscar Library, Leeds
SOCG	Scritture riferite nella Congregazioni Generali
SP	State Papers
StA	Staatsarchiv, Oberbayern
StB	Staatsbibliotek,
Surt.Soc.	Publications of the Surtees Society

UYBI	University of York, Borthwick Institute
Vita E	Oldest English biography of Mary Ward
Vita I	Oldest Italian biography of Mary Ward
VP	Various Papers, records by Mary Ward
WA	Westminster Archives
YATA (RS)	Yorkshire Archeological and Topographical Association, Record Series

UNPUBLISHED SOURCES

BELGIUM

Brussels
Archives Générales du Royaume de Belgique
Papiers d'État et de l'Audience vol. 456, 458, 459, 460, 462, 467,1894², 1944², 1944 ³,1946³, 1947 ¹, 2062
Archives Jésuitiques, Province Gallo-Belgique, Karton 31, 32, 32a; Province Flandro-Belgique vol.1079 to 1112, Res Missionis Anglicanae 1085–1096

Liège
Archives de l'État
Cathédrale Saint-Lambert, A.Sécrétariat. Registres aux conclusions capitulaires 22 (130) 1621 – 1622, 23 (131) 1622-1624, 24 (1624-1625), 26 (1626-1628)
Collégiale Saint-Martin 56,57,58,59,60; 84 Clausulae extractae ex libro testamentorum B concernentes legata pia facta ecclesiae collegiatae sancti Martini Leodiensis ab anno 1510 usque ad annum 1594 (Clauses extraites du livreaux testaments 1510-1759)
Registres Parroisiaux. Liège, Église Saint-Remacle-en-Mont Décès 234
Couvents, Jésuites Anglais 1, Registre concernant les Pères Jésuites Anglais Conseil Privé, Dépêches 18,113 (Inventaire Conseil Privé, Dépêches 1612-1792)
Chambres des Finances des Princes-Évêques de Liège, Chambre des Comptes 83 ⁸²,1651-1660
Spécification de ce que Son Altesse Sérénissime a donné à ceux, qui ont eu des biens enclavez dans les fortifications de la Citadelle de Liège depuis l'an 1650 Officialitè de Liège: Rendages proclamatoires Nr.17 (1615-1621) Parchemins des Eschevins de Liège Nr.1578
Recès du Conseil de la Cité de Liège 7
Notaires, Ruffin, J.
University Library
Ms.Delvaulx Annexe T.III.

GERMANY

Altoetting
Institute archives
Ms 1 Tobias Lohner, Gottseeliges Leben und frütreffliche Tugendten
Donna Maria della Guardia, Hochlöblichen Stüffterin der Engell-
ändischen Gesellschaft,1689.

Augsburg
Institute archives
Painted Life (fifty oil paintings with inscriptions, 17th — 18th
centuries)

Cologne
Historical archives of Cologne
Ratsprotokoll 67,76

Munich
Institute archives Munich-Nymphenburg
Mary Ward's letters
Various Papers
Early writings
Mary Ward's autobiographical sketches A — H
Liber Ruber
Parchment Book
Barbara Ward, Coppied out of three several papers
Calendar of members
French death register
Handwritten drafts
Vincenzo Pagetti, Breve Racconto della vita di Donna Maria della
Guardia, 1662.
Marcus Fridl's archive list, 1733
Documents concerning the diocesan process towards the canoni-
sation of Mary Ward, volume II.
Archives of the Archiepiscopal metropolitan chapter (Bishop's
archives):
The English Ladies A 258 III
State Secret Archives (Geheimes Staatsarchiv):
Black Box 7413,7414
State Archives for Upper Bavaria:
Kl.Lit.432 I-III,434/10,
Hofzahlamtsrechnungen 1627,1631
Bavarian State Library:
Cgm 5393,5399, Clm 1971 (Domenico Bissel, Vita Venerabilis
Virginis ac Matris Mariae Warth Anglae Fundatricis Societatis
Virginum Anglarum dictarum, 1674)

ENGLAND

Alnwick
Syon House
Mss from years 1584-1595, X.II.6, Box 7, 8, 11, 12, 14

Ascot
Institute Archives
A Brief Relation of the holy Life and happy Deathy of our dearest
Mother of blessed memory Mistress Mary Ward (Vita E)

Darlington
St Clare's Abbey
Ms 1, Gravelines Chronicles 1686 -1737
Annals of the English Poor Clares of Gravelines and of their foun-
dations in Ireland and at Aire, Dunkirk and Rouen
Douai Abbey (England)
Council Book
Hatfield House
Cecil Papers 113/26

Hull
University Library
DHO 8/37

Leeds
Sheepscar Library Archives
Archdeaconcry of Richmond, Register of Wills 1503 – 1546, RP
4; Ingleby Records Nr.364,994,1078; Newton Wallis Deeds (Bland)
DB 35/27

London
The British Library
Add.Ms.5506; Add.Ms 5847
Public Record Office
Chancery Series 2, vol.39
Chancery Rolls, Duchy Lancaster I/96
Patent Rolls 4th Pars 20 Elizabeth (1578)
Membrane 31 C 66 1167
General Series 92 [5] Barberini
SP 14/154, 14/216, 16, 31/9/121A, 77/9. 77/10, 77/11, 77/12.
77/14, 99/24, 99/25, 188 Domestical Series James I.
Roman Transcripts Borghese T.448
Westminster Archives
Ms vol.16,17,19,23,A 15, A26, B25, B47
Northampton
Lamport Hall Archives
J.C.3501

Ripon
Parish Archives
Parish Register SS Peter and Wilfrid I
Stonyhurst
Stonyhurst College
F.Chr.Grene SJ Collectanea M
Cod.A-I-40
Anglia vol.IV, vol.VII

York
University of York, The Borthwick Institute of Historical Research
Prob.Reg.vol.4, Wills; vol.15/I, 15/III
Act Book Holderness (DAB) 1575-1582; 1588-1596
York Diocesan Records, Archiepiscopal Visitation Book 1586/CB,
1590-1591/CB 1
High Commission Act Book 1599-1603

FRANCE

Paris
Bibliothèque Nationale
Ms lat 5175 I

Saint – Omer
Municipal Archives
Correspondence du Magistrat 38, 39A
Registre aux Déliberations du Magistrat 8
Box CCXXXIX Fille Anglaises 16,17,18
Ms 806 Annales Bertiniana ca. 1545-1655 by Gérard d'Haméricourt,
Abbé de Saint Bertin
Ms 808 Recueil Historique par Jean Hendricq, Bourgeois de Saint-
Omer T.I-III
Ms1358 Annales de la Ville de Saint Omer sous les Évêques de Saint
Omer T II by Ch.F.Deneuville

Valenciennes
Bibliothèque Publique de la Ville
Ms 75/171

ITALY

Milan
Biblioteca Ambrosiana
G.222 Inf.

Mantua
Archivio dei Marchesi Guidi di Bagno
Registro di Lettere volgari della Nunciatura di Fiandra T.V.

Perugia
Arlchivio dell'Abbazia S.Pietro, Congr.Cass.
SS (PD 42)
Biblioteca Augusta di Perugia
Ms.450 (G.39)

Rome
Archives of the Generalate, Institute of the Blessed Virgin Mary:
Outlines of various documents which were destroyed in World War II.
Archivio della Sacra Congregatione di Propaganda Fide:
Acta vol.3, 6, 7
I Anglia 347
Lettere latine vol.9
Lettere volgari vol.7,8,10
Scritture riferite nelle Congregazione Generali (SOCG)
vol.57,69,70,71,72,98,102,131,132,205,297,347
Istruzioni diverse degli anni 1623 -1628
Lettere d'Italia 3
Archivio Segreto Vaticano:
Misc.Arm.III,vol. 34,37
Nunziatura di Colonia vol.12,19
Nunziatura di Fiandra vol.20
Nunziatura di Germania vol.116,122
Nunziatura d'Inghilterra vol.7
Nunziatura di Savoia vol.58
Arch Borghese III, vol.12 ab
Fondo Borghese III, 88 E-F
Epistolae ad Principes T.43
S.Cong.Epp et Regul.Lettere G – O 1625
Reg.Regul.vol.34
S.Cong.Visit.ad Limina, Audomarensis
Arch.della S.Cong.del Concilio Positiones 223, Liber X Literarum
Archivum Romanum Societatis Jesu:
Anglia vol.1/I,1/II,13,31/II,32/II,33/I,37
Austria 3/II,4/I
Flandro-Belg.vol.1/II,9,10,51
Gallo-Belg.Vol.1/I,1/II.24,27,40
Germ.Super vol.4,5,6
Germ.Vol. 111,113
Italia Vol.72
Neap.vol.14/I,15/I,15/II,16,73
Necr.Belg.27

Rhen. Infer.vol.6
. Rom.vol.14/II,18/II,19
Sicula vol.9/I
Venetia vol.9/II
EPP NN vol.2.136
EPP Gen.1625-1628
Fondo Gesuitico vol.1435
Congr.vol.57
Catalogus Anglia 1610,1621 – 1649
Archivio di Stato:
Arch.della Famiglia Santacroce B 21 [63]
Archivio del Vicariato:
Arch.Generale del Vicariato San Lorenzo in Damaso Status animarum 1623-1624
Morti I (1591-1643)
Notari, Silvestro Spada anno 1625
Biblioteca Apostolica Vaticana:
Fondo Capponi vol.47
Ruoli di Papa Urbano VIII Barb. lat. vol.2677, 2691, 2818, 4371, 6202, 6223, 6706, 6707, 6717, 6728, 6761, 6762, 6812, 6945, 6953, 6956, 6957, 7054, 7061, 8615, 8620, 8626, 8644
Biblioteca Casatanense:
Ms 2426
Archivio della Curia Generalizia dei PP.Carmelitani Scalzi:
Ms 106v

Veroli
Biblioteca Giovardiana:
Ms.42.3.11, 42.3.12, 42.3.13
Breve Relazione della santa vita e felice morte della Signora Donna Maria della Guardia, nostra Signora e Madre (Vita I)

AUSTRIA

Innsbruck
Landesregierungsarchiv für Tirol
Hofregistratur V/1 1629

Vienna
Diocesan Archives:
Suppressed convents, Jesuitesses
Archiv der Stadt und des Landes Wien:
Grundbuch 1/13 (Stadt-Gew-hrbuch K)
Steuerbücher 1625,1627,1631
Hofkammerarchiv

N.O.Herrschaftsakten, Nonnenkloster der Matres de Jesu 1627–
1631 W 61/B 32, 61/C42
Hoffinanz Ungarn 135 rot

SWITZERLAND

Bern
Staatsarchiv des Kantons Bern:
Fürstbischöflich-Baselsches Archiv Abt.A 113'Ursulinae Bruntruti'

SPAIN

Simancas
Archivo General
E 906

TSCHECHOSLOVAKIA

Pressburg (Bratislavia)
Stadtarchiv:
Protocullum Actionum 1622-1633

HUNGARY

Budapest
Magyar Országos Levéltár (Hungarian State Archives):
E 21 Benignae Resolutiones
E 150 Acta Eccl.irregistrata Fasz.30
E 151 Acta Eccl.Ordinum et Monialium Posoniensium Fasz.14
E 152 Acta Irregistrata Collegii Posoniensis
Memorabilia Collegii Posoniensis 1622-1656
Historia Collegii Posoniensis 1622-1635

University Library:
Collectio Prayana V

PRINTED SOURCES AND OTHER WRITINGS

Abad, Camilo Maria,SJ., Una misionera espaçola en la Inglaterra del siglo XVII, Doña Luisa de Carvajal y Mendoza 1566-1614, Comillas 1966.

Allgemeine Deutsche Biographie Bd.VI.

Baildon W.Paley, Baildon and the Baildons, Vol.I,s.l.1912.

Baker, NN.(ed.), Acts of the Privy Council of England May 1613 – December 1614, London 1921; 1615 -1616, London 1925.

Barozzo Nicolo e Berchet Guglielmo (ed.) Relazioni degli Stati Europei lette al Senato dagli Ambasciatori Veneti nel secolo XVII, Serie IV, Inghilterra I, Venezia 1863.

Becdelièvre-Hamal, Antoine de, Biographie Liégeoise Tom.I, Liège 1836.

Belvederi, Raffaele, Guido Bentivoglio Diplomatico Bd.II, Parte II, Rovigo 1947.

Berlière, Dom Ursmer, Monasticon belge, Bd. II, Province de Liège, Liège 1928.

Biaudet, Henri, Les nonciatures apostoliques permanentes jusqu'en 1648, Helsinki 1910.

Biographie Nationale de Belgique, Tom.I, VII,XIII ,XVIII,XXIII.

Bled, O., Les Jésuites Anglais à Saint Omer, Saint Omer 1890.

ibid., Les Évêques de Saint-Omer depuis la chute de Thérouanne 1553-1619, Saint-Omer 1898.

Body, Albin (ed.), Extraits des lettres du chevalier Dudley Carleton = Bull de l'Inst.Archéol.Liégeois Bd.XXVII, Liège 1898.

Bragard, René, Vues anciennes d'églises Liégeoises d'après un manuscrit de 1584-1586 = Bull.et chron. de la Société Royale, Le vieux Liège, Bd.VIII (1971-1975), Liège 1976.

Brassine, Joseph, Les Jésuites anglais de Liège et leur orfevrerie = Bull.de la Société d'Art e d'Hist.du Diocese de Liège, Bd.XXXIII, Liège 1947.

Burton, E.H. and Williams, T.L. (ed.) The Douay College Diaries 1598-1654 I = CRS Vol.X, London 1911.

Calthrop, M.M.(ed.), Recusant Roll Nr.I, Michaelmas 1592 – 1593,Exchequer Lord Treasurer's Remembrancer Pipe Office Series = CRS Vol.XVIII, London 1916.

Caraman, Philip, SJ.(ed.) John Gerard, the autobiography of an Elizabethan, London, 1951. German translation: John Gerard, Meine Geheime Mission als Jesuit, Luzern 1954.

Carleton, Dudley (ed.), The letter to and from Dudley Carleton, London [3] 1780.

Chambers, Mary Catharine Elizabeth (ed. Henry James Coleridge,SJ), The Life of Mary Ward (1585-1645) 2 vols., London,1882-1885. German translation: Leben der Maria Ward, 2 Bde., Regensburg 1888.

Clay, Charles (ed.), Yorkshire Deeds VII = YATA RS Vol.83, Leeds, 1932.

Daris, Joseph, Histoire du Diocèse et de la Principauté de Liège, 1877.

Delattre, Pierre, SJ., Les Etablissements des Jésuites en France depuis quatre siècles, Tom.II.Enghien-Wetteren 1953.

Delrée, Pierre, Nandrin et Fraineux sous l'Ancien Régime, Notes historiques = Bull.de L'Inst.Archéolog.Liégeois Tom.LXXI, Liège 1956.

Deschamps de Pas, L., Recherches historiques sur les Etablissements Hospitaliers de la ville de Saint-Omer depuis leur origine jusqu'à leur réunion sous une seule et meme administration en l'an V (1797) = Société des Antiquaires de la Morinie, Saint-Omer 1877.

ibid., Histoire de la ville de Saint-Omer depuis son origine jusqu'en 1870, Arras 1880.

Dessart, Henri, La Visite du Diocèse de Liège par le Nonce Antoine Albergati (1613-1614) = Bull de la Commission Royale d'Histoire Tom.114, Bruxelles 1949.

The Dictionary of National Biography, Vol.III,VI,VIII,IX,XV,XVII,XIX,XXI, London,1917.

Doyle, J.E., The Official Baronage of England, 3 vols, London 1886.

Duhr, Bernhard,SJ., Geschichte der Jesuiten in den Ländern deutscher Zunge, 3 Bde., Freiburg/Br., bzw.Munchen/Regensburg, 1907-1928.

Durst, Paul, Intended Treason, London 1970.

Elesban de Guilhermy, P.,SJ., Ménologie de la Compagnie de Jésus, Assistance de Germanie 2. Serie Partie I, Paris 1899.

Feet of Fines of the Tudor Period I;, = YATA RS Vol.II, Leeds 1887; Vol.IV, Leeds 1890.

Foley, Henry, SJ., Records of the English Province of the Society of Jesus, 7 vols., London 1875-1883.

Fowler, Joseph Thomas (ed.), Acts of the Chapter of the Collegiate Church of SS Peter and Wilfrid, Ripon 1452-1506 = Surtees Soc.Vol.64/1874/ II, Durham, 1875.

ibid., Memorials of the Church of SS Peter and Wilrid, Ripon III, = Surtees Soc. Vol.81 1886/I Durham 1888.

Fridl,Marcus, Englische Tugend-Schul,2 Bde., Augsburg 1732.

Gillow, Joseph, A literary and biographical history or bibliographical dictionary of English Catholics from the breach with Rome in 1534 to the present day 5 vols., London 1885-1902.

Gnockaert, L., Giovanni-Francesco Guidi di Bagno, Nuntius te Brussel 1621 n-1627. Enige aspecten van zijn opdracht en van zijn persoonlijkheid = Bibl.de l'Inst.histor.Belge de Rome, Bd.VII, Bruxelles/Rome 1956.

Gobert, Theódore, Liège à travers les âges, Bd.II, Bruxelles ² 1975, Bd.VIII, Bruxelles ² 1977.

Green, M.A.Everett (ed.), Calendar of State Papers, Domestic Series of the Reign of James I 1611-1618, London 1858.

Grisar, Joseph, Das Urteil des Lessius, Suarez und anderer über den neuen Ordenstyp der Mary Ward = Gregorianum Bd.XXXVIII, Roma, 1957.

ibid., Die ersten Anklagen in Rom gegen das Institut Maria Wards 1622 = Misc. Historiae Pontificae Bd.XXII, Roma, 1959.

ibid., Ein schwieriger Rechtsfall zwischen den Englischen Fräulein und den englischen Jesuiten in Luttich 1618-1630 = Archivum Historicum Societatis Jesu Bd.XXIX Roma,1960.

ibid., Mary Wards Institut vor Romischen Kongregationen 1616-1630 = Misc.Historiae Pontificiae Bd.XXVII, Roma, 1966.

Guilday, Peter. The English catholic refugees on the continent 1558-1795 vol.I, London 1914.

Hamilton, A., OSB.(ed.), The Chronicle of the English Augustinian Canonesses of the Lateran at St Monica's in Louvain, (Now at St Augustine's Priory, Newton Abbot, Devon), Vol.l.London, 1904.

Hansotte, George, Règlements et privilèges des XXXII metiers de la cité de Liège,

Fasc.Ia.Les fèvres, Liège 1950.

Haust, Jean, Dictionaire Liégeois, Liège 1933.

Helin, Etienne, La démographie de Liège aux XVIIe et XVIIIe siécles = Acadàmie Royale de Belgique, classe des lettres et des sciences morales et politiques, Mémoires Tom.LVI,fasc.4. Bruxelles 1963.

Herckenrode, Jacques Salomon, Nobiliaire des Pays-Bas et du Comté de Bourgogne etc., Tom.II, Gand 1865.

M.Hereswitha OSSep., De vrouwenkloosters van het hl.Graf in het prinsbisdom Luik vanaf hun ontstaan tot aan de Fransche Revolutie 1480-1798, Leuven 1941.

Hierarchia Catholica Bd.IV, (P.Gauchat), Reprint Munchen 1935.

Hinds, Allan B.(ed.) Calendar of State Papers and Manuscripts, relating to English Affairs, existing in the Archives and Collections of Venice, vol.XVII (1621-1623), vol.XVIII (1623-1625), 1911-1912.

Historical Manuscripts Commission vol.XIII, London 1893,vol.XVII, London 1938.

Hunnybun W.M.. and Gillow J.(ed.), Registers of the English Poor Clares at Gravelines, including those who founded filiations at Aire, Dunkirk and Rouen 1608 − 1837 = CRS vol.XIV,Misc.IX, London 1914.

Jadin, Louis, Procès d'Information pour la nomination des Évéques et Abbés des Pays-Bas, de Liège et de Franche-Comté d'après les Archives de la Congrégation Consistoriale = Bull.de l'Inst.histor.Belge de Rome Tom.VIII, Rome/Bruxelles 1928.

ibid., Relations des Pays-Bas, de Liège et de Franche-Comteé avec le Saint-Siège (1566-1779) = Bibl.de l'Inst.hist.Belge de Rome Tom.IV,Rome/Bruxelles 1952.

Jougla de Morenas, H.Grand Armorial de France, vol.VI, Paris 1949.

Kelly, W. (ed.), Annales Collegii I (Liber Ruber ven.Collegii Anglorum de Urbe) = CRS vol.XXXVII, London 1940; vol.XI, London 1943.

Kenny, A. (ed.), The Responsa Scholarum of the English College Rome I 1598−1621 = CRS vol.LIV, London 1962; II avol.LV, London 1963.

Khamm, Corbinian, OSB, Relatio de origine et propagatione Instituti Mariae noncupati Virginum Anglarum, Monachii 1717.

Koch, Ludwig SJ, Jesuiten-Lexikon. Die Gesellschaft Jesu einst und jetzt.Paderborn, 1934.

Leitner, Jakob Geschichte der Englischen Fräulein und ihres Instituts seit ihrer Grundung bis auf unsere Zeit, Regensburg 1869.

Lejeune, Jean, La Principauté de Liège, Liège 1949.

Lexikon fur Theologie und Kirche, Vol. I, IX, X.

Meester, Bernard de (ed.) Correspondence du Nonce Giovanni-Francesco Guidi di Bagno 1621−1627, vol. I, 1621−1624 = Analecta Vaticano-Belgica 2e.serie, Nonciature de Flandre V, Bruxelles/Rome 1938.

Meyer, Arnold Oskar, England und die Katholische Kirche unter Elisabeth und der Stuart = Bibl.d.kgl.Preu. Histor.Inst.in Rom, vol. VI, Rome 1911.

Michelant, H., Voyage de Pierre Bergeron ès Ardennes, Liège et Pays-Bas en 1619 = Publ.de la Société des Bibliophiles Liégeois, Liège 1875.

Morey, J. La vénérable Anne de Xainctonge, fondatrice de la Compagnie de Sainte Ursule de Bourgogne vol.I, Paris/Besancon 1892.

Morris, John SJ., The Condition of Catholis under James I, London (2) 1872.

ibid., as above, The Life of Father John Gerard of the Society of Jesus, London (3) 1881.

ibid., Morris, as above, The troubles of our Catholic Forefathers, related by themselves, Third series, London 1877.

Northcote Parkinson, C., Gunpowder, Treason and Plot, London 1976.

Pas, Justin de, Vieilles rues-Mém. de la Société des Antiquaires de la Morinie, Vol. xxx, Saint-Omer 1911.

Pas, as above, Table de concordance entres les noms des rues actuels et les anciens noms = Mem. del la Société des Antiquares de la Morinie, vol. xxxi, Saint-Omer 1913.

Pas, as above, A travers le vieux Saint-Omer, Saint-Omer, 1914.

Pastor, Ludwig v., Geschichte der Päpste Bd.XIII/I, Freiburg/Br. 1928.

Phillips, Charles J. History of the Sckville family vol. I.

Pollen, John H. SJ. (ed.), The Note Book of John Southcote from 1623–1637 = CRS Series 1, Misc.I. London 1905.

ibid., Tower Bills, 1595–1681 with Gatehouse Certificates 1592–1603, – CRS IV, London 1907; CRS III, London 1960.

ibid., as above, The English Catholics in the Reign of Queen Elizabeth, London 1920.

Poncelet, Alfred,SJ., Histoire de la Compagnie de Jésus dans anciens Pays-Bas = Académie Royale de Belgique, classe des lettres et des sciences morales et politiques, Mémoires Tom.XXI/2, Bruxelles 1926.

ibid., Nécrologe des Jésuites de la Province Gallo-Belge, Wetteren 1931.

Poncelet, Ed., Les bons métiers de la cité de Liège = Bull.de l'Inst.Archéolog.Liégeois Tom.XXVIII, Liège 1899.

ibid., Inventaire analytique des chartes de la collégiale de Sainte-Croix à Liège, Bruxelles 1922.

Raine, James (ed.) Testamenta Eboracensia, A Selection of wills from the Registry at York II = Surtees Soc. vol.XXX/1, Durham, 1855; IV, Surtees Soc.vol.LIII/1868/2,Durham 1869.

Reinhard, Wolfgang, Nuntius Antonio Albergati, Nuntiaturberichte aus Deutschland Bd.V/1

Ricciotti, Giuseppe (ed.), Giacinto Gigl, Diario Romano 1608 -1670, Rome 1958.

Schrevel, A.de, Jacques Blaes ou Blaseus = Annales de la Société d'émulation de Bruges, Bruges 1933.

Smith, L.Pearsall (ed.) The Life and Letters of Sir Henry Wotton, vol.I and II, Oxford 1907.

Sommervogel, C.,SJ., de Backer A, SJ., Bibliothèque de la Compagnie de Jésus, Tom;.I-XII, Bruxelles/Paris 1890-1960.

Spink, Henry Hawkes, The Gunpowder Plot and Lord Mounteagle's letter, London 1902.

Statues of the Realm,vol.IV (ed.,)E.T.Tomline, London

Theux de Montjardin, J.de, Le Chapitre de Saint-Lambert de Liège, Tom.III Bruxelles 1871.

Trevelyan, George Macauley, English Social History. A Survey of Six Centuries, Chaucer to Queen Victoria, London [4] 1947.

Unterberg, Joannes v., Kurtzer Begriff des wunderbarlichen Lebens der Ehrwürdigen und Hoch-Gebohrnen Frauen Frauen Maria von Ward, Stiffterin dess mehr als vor hundert Jahren angefangenen und unter denen von Pabst Clemente XI gutgeheissenen und bestätigten Regeln aufgerichteten edlen Instituts Mariae, ins gemein unter den Namen der Englischen Fräulein genannt. Augsburg 1735.

Veith,F.A., Bibliotheca Augustana, complectens notitias varias de vita et scriptis eruditorum quos Augusta Vindelica orbi litterato vel dedit vel aluit, Bd.II/Augusta Vindelicorum 1786.

Walbran, J.R. (ed.), Memorials of the Abbey of St Mary of Fountains Vol.II/1 = Surtees Soc.vol.LXVII/1876/II Durham 1878.

Wetter, M.Immolata IBMV, Mary Ward = Grosse Gestalten des Glaubens, edit.P.Gerhard Eberts, Aschaffenburg.1985.

Williamson, Hugh Ross, The Gunpowder Plot, London 1948/50.

INDEX OF PERSONS

MARY WARD'S NAME is not given, nor are those of people mentioned in genealogies.